D1570907

Public Pulpits

Public Pulpits

*Methodists and Mainline Churches
in the Moral Argument of Public Life*

STEVEN M. TIPTON

THE UNIVERSITY OF CHICAGO PRESS   CHICAGO AND LONDON

WITHDRAWN

McConnell Library Radford University

STEVEN M. TIPTON teaches sociology and religion at Emory University and its
Candler School of Theology. He is author of *Habits of the Heart* and *The Good Society*.

The University of Chicago Press, Chicago 60637
The University of Chicago Press, Ltd., London
© 2007 by The University of Chicago   ·
All rights reserved. Published 2007
Printed in the United States of America
16 15 14 13 12 11 10 09 08 07   1 2 3 4 5

ISBN-13: 978-0-226-80474-3 (cloth)
ISBN-10: 0-226-80474-7 (cloth)

CIP data to come

⊗ The paper used in this publication meets the minimum requirements of the American
National Standard for Information Sciences—Permanence of Paper for Printed Library
Materials, ANSI Z39.48-1992.

FOR KRISTIN AND EVAN

Contents

Preface

In a nationally televised debate among candidates for the 2000 Republican presidential nomination, each was asked which political philosopher or thinker he most identified with and why. John Locke, replied Steve Forbes, because he set the stage for the American Revolution. The Founding Fathers, said Alan Keyes, because they conceived a constitutional government that has preserved our liberty for over two hundred years. "Jesus Christ," answered George W. Bush, "because he changed my heart." Prompted that viewers would like to know more about how Jesus changed his heart, Mr. Bush testified, "Well, if they don't know, it's gonna be hard to explain. When you turn your heart and your life over to Christ, when you accept Christ as a Savior, it changes your heart and changes your life, and that's what happened to me." In so answering, the president-to-be reassured many Americans of his faithful and trustworthy character, alarmed others by his testimony of heartfelt religious conversion offered in place of judicious political philosophy, and left still more surprised and wondering how his born-again Christian faith would square with the rule of law and the role of reason-giving in American public life as well as the separation of church and state.

President Bush's reelection victory in 2004 offered vivid, if uncertain, answers to such concerns with all the power of history itself to defy prediction and overdetermine events. "Moral values" mattered most to 22 percent of all voters surveyed in nationwide Edison/Mitofsky exit polls, and four out of five of these voted for Mr. Bush, reported the *New York Times* on November 4. Since pollsters left these values unparsed into specific issues, some observers inferred that banning gay marriage, abortion, and embryonic stem-cell research led the values list, and culturally conservative evangelical and Catholic "values voters" decided the election. Others

stressed, on the contrary, that one in five polled voters ranked the economy and jobs as their top concern, and one in six focused on the trio of
health care, taxes, and education. Terrorism mattered most to another
one-fifth, and Iraq to another one-sixth. By a margin of 6–8 percentage
points, most Americans believed that the war in Iraq was going badly and
had not improved the long-term security of the United States, but that
we were nonetheless right to go to war there. Why so? By a margin of
13 points, most Americans believed that the war in Iraq was "part of the
war on terrorism." In this light, it seemed that a slim but decisive majority of American voters judged that this was a just war that must be waged
and won, however messy and mismanaged it might be; that it came before
widespread concerns over economic security and fairness; and that Mr.
Bush was a more trustworthy and reliable commander in chief to face this
overriding military task and moral challenge.

Campaign advisers and religious leaders linked to conservative evangelicals and traditionalist Catholics claimed credit for carrying President
Bush across the finish line in battleground states such as Ohio and Florida,
and they celebrated an inaugural "Values Victory Dinner." Some Democratic leaders called for their party to get religion, moderate its stance
on abortion and gay rights, and get into mainline churches as effectively
as their opponents had mobilized conservative communities of faith with
targeted moral appeals. People should indeed vote their conscience and
their values, urged mainline religious leaders, but they should vote all
their values, including economic justice, care for the sick and poor, and
concern for a just or unjust war waged in Iraq. Issues of personal piety
such as abortion do not encompass the whole content of moral values,
they stressed, and the churches need to work hard to reclaim the real
breadth and depth of faithful moral insight in the shared understanding
and action of all Americans.

Such campaign testimonies and election results dramatize differences
in conviction and expression among more or less faithful Americans of
every kind, particularly between white Protestants who describe themselves as conservative evangelicals and those who identify with mainline
or liberal churches. They do not tell the whole story of faith in public, to
be sure, or fix its unfolding. Two years after the 2004 election, mounting casualties and costs in U.S. lives and dollars had brought no promise
of peace in Iraq or stability in the Middle East. Support for continuing
the Iraq war had ebbed to well below half of all Americans in national
polls, along with belief that the United States was winning the war on ter-

ror, even though Americans remained divided along partisan lines over whether the decision to invade Iraq was right or wrong. By mid-2007, fewer than one in four Americans thought things were going well for the United States in Iraq, and only one in three thought the United States did the right thing in invading. Economic expansion still showed scant signs of trickling down to working families, as health-care costs and energy prices soared and federal deficits deepened. This stalled proposals to privatize Social Security and cast greater doubt on policies to cut taxes for those at the top and shrink the social safety net for those below. The devastation of Hurricane Katrina, particularly for those left behind to face the flood on their own, laid bare the life-and-death necessity of a government willing and able enough to protect all its citizens and provide for them across the lines of color and class. The image of President Bush flying over a flooded New Orleans and looking down on the suffering city from a window of Air Force One, as he passed by, came to cloud the Good Samaritan vow of his compassionate conservatism.

Concerns to end the war in Iraq, undo partisan gridlock and corruption in Washington, and seek economic security and fair public provision for Americans across the middle class led political independents and moderates to enlarge the center of the midterm electorate in 2006. They voted 2 to 1 against Republicans, and removed them from leadership of Congress after twelve years. White evangelical Protestants turned out and held firm for the Republican Party. But mainline-church leaders claimed credit, through resurgent organizing and activism, for helping to awaken the moral commitment of citizens across party lines to move beyond the limits of wedge issues such as abortion and gay marriage in order to vote for the common good of the country.

The contested meaning of moral values in public also dramatizes deeper questions that Americans face as faithful citizens. How do religious and political institutions think through us and shape the ways we think about ourselves and our society? How do these institutions we inhabit and remake by what we do and say come to shift in turn our practical modes of moral experience and judgment? How do they reshape the ways we make moral sense—in principle and practice, story and metaphor, prayer and law—of good character, community, and the good of government? These questions lie at the root of continuing conversations I joined for over a decade in the Capitol Hill offices of the mainline churches, their colleagues and their critics inside the Beltway and beyond; in the corridors of Congress and the corridors of church conferences across the country; and at meetings of the Christian Coalition and its mainline-church contender, the Interfaith Alliance.

Behind the conversations spurred by these questions lies the social backdrop of increased interpenetration between an expanded state, with more explicitly moral and morally arguable public responsibilities, and more diversified religious institutions engaged in more politicized moral advocacy. The past generation has witnessed the explosion of hundreds of new nondenominational religious organizations devoted to governmental and public affairs on the U.S. national scene. The proliferation of these politically oriented "parachurch" groups has far outpaced the growth of denominational churches themselves. But their sum is topped in turn by the multiplication of thousands of nonreligious national political associations, from Common Cause to the Heritage Foundation, from MoveOn. org to Progress for America. Although formally free of political parties, they commonly couple public-interest advocacy, policy research, and civic education with political lobbying and ideological advertising, increasingly backed by direct electoral mobilization and organizing.

These institutional changes have crowded the American polity and made it more densely organized. They have framed a more nationally integrated yet more contested and multivocal argument about how we ought to live together and govern ourselves. This argument embraces issues such as going to war in Iraq and doing good at home through faith-based initiatives, as chapter 1 charts its back-and-forth course through voices raised from the mainline churches in critical give-and-take with other religious and civic leaders and with the administration of President George W. Bush. As conceived in chapter 2, such argument features diverse public theologies. They contest the meaning of civil religion in America even as they draw the coherence of their disagreement over its construal from deeper continuities of cultural conflict in our morally ambiguous polity. We are a liberal democracy that is also a civic republic, according to contrasting moral traditions in American culture, which shed light on faith in public and the good of government from very different angles.

How do conflicting religious visions of a good society in turn come to be voiced and enacted by national religious bodies organized as denominational offices or freestanding voluntary associations, moral educators or ideological lobbies? How do these bodies relate to one another, to an expanded regulatory and welfare state, to realigned political parties, and to proliferating parachurch and political advocacy groups? Part 1 of this study takes on these more specific questions through concretely detailed case studies that combine ethical, ideological, and institutional analysis of in-depth interviews, social-teaching documents, and comparative organizational histories. Chapters 3 and 4 explore the "prophetic witness" of the national denominational leadership of the United Methodist Church in behalf of peace and justice, particularly through its General Board of Church and Society. Preaching against it comes the crusade for "scriptural renewal" led by the Good News movement, an evangelical caucus group officially organized outside the Methodist denomination yet dedicated to transforming from within its structure and spirit alike. Chapters 5 and 6 show how the Institute on Religion and Democracy (IRD) formed the ideologically charged compound of a fluent religious lobby and a potent political-action committee to catalyze an alliance of evangelical renewal groups and neoconservative political forces to combat the mainline churches. It continues to fight them in culture wars shaped by the IRD's own remarkable origins in Cold War infighting waged among radical labor factions and Students for a Democratic Society, the AFL-CIO, and both major political parties.

Part 2 of this study expands its focus to take in the spectrum of mainline Protestant churches engaged in national public advocacy. Chapter 7 explores their struggles to work out a balance between "witnessing" and "winning" in Washington, through efforts to bring together the faithful in their pews from different wings of American cultural politics and to weave together the strands of Christian social teaching across different forms of ecclesiology in their denominations. To grasp the continuing challenge of the churches' long campaign to unify their multi-issue moral advocacy and education with political mobilization and community organizing, chapter 8 traces their collaboration in the rise and fall of Interfaith Impact for Justice and Peace, and their determined yet frustrating campaign for health-care reform. Chapter 9 exposes the dynamics of cooperation and clashing between the mainline churches and the National Council of Churches (NCC) in working to gain political efficacy without losing their moral integrity in the glow of access to the Clinton White House. Chapter 10 unfolds the NCC's backing of the Interfaith Alliance to resist the "radical religious right" and counterpunch the Christian Coalition in particular in the 1990s. It then shows how the NCC, under new leadership, has sought to remake the religious center within a changing ecology of key issues, White House policies, and shifting relations among parachurch groups, political parties, and election campaigns since 2000.

The course of this inquiry over parts 1 and 2 runs through two concentric circles of religious advocacy and controversy in Washington and in the mainstream of American religion. It reaches deep into the denominational arena of United Methodism, and it stretches across the range of public institutions that frame our cultural conversation over how we should live together and govern ourselves. This course of inquiry connects crucial points in order to map the movement and place of religion in the moral argument of American public life. It shades in the living languages, logics of argument, and modes of moral discourse that flesh out the social shape of faith in public and give it voice. It probes the problems of politicizing how religious institutions think in relation to the growing dimensions of moral depth and religious resonance within public life itself. It seeks to show how the religious visions of a good society that Americans share actually inform their disagreement over the good of government and underlie their divisions and disappointments over the democratic prospect in practice. It weighs the promise of religious efforts to enlarge civic conscience and cast clearer light on the commonweal for Americans wrestling with their faith in God, and their hope in the future, amid diverging fortunes and diminished dreams of middle-class progress for all of a people of plenty. It listens to the prayers they offer for an interdependent world grown smaller at the start of the twenty-first century, touched by terror, and left less safe and sure.

This work concludes by reflecting on how the mainline Protestant churches can practice their moral advocacy and teaching more fully in accord with their self-understanding as a truly conciliar and catholic public church. In a denominational society such as ours, can the churches become the Church? Can they better seek to serve all of the members of bodies of faith and the body politic? Can they help us engage one another in public argument over how we should govern ourselves, even as we embrace one another in mutual care and shared responsibility for the commonweal? That is a prospect worthy of thought as well as prayer.

*　　*　　*

To those whose voices fill this book I am indebted most directly. I am grateful for their insight and experience, their conviction and generosity of spirit, shared in hours of interviews, days of conversation, and weeks of conferences and committee meetings, over years of fieldwork. Arthur B. Keys, Jr., and Jay Lintner introduced me to the churches in Washington with unstinting hospitality, good counsel, and keen dialogue. A host of others likewise welcomed me into their offices, agencies, task forces, advocacy organizations, and renewal groups: Thom White Wolf Fassett, Elenora Giddings Ivory, Kay S. Dowhower, Gretchen Eick, Ruth Flower, Pat Conover, Jim McDaniel, Theodore H. Erickson, Audrey Chapman, Richard Penn Kemble, Kent Hill, Diane Knippers, Edmund W. Robb, Jr., James V. Heidinger II, David Saperstein, Lynne Landsberg, Robert W. Tiller, Carol Franklin, Curtis Ramsey-Lucas, Faith Evans, Belle Miller McMaster, Philip R. Newell, Walter Owensby, Sally Timmel, Melva Jimerson, Meg A. Riley, Richard A. Nugent, James M. Dunn, George McLain, Leon Howell, Tim McDonald, and Paul T. Stallsworth.

Joan Brown Campbell, Arthur M. Pennybacker, and Mary A. Cooper of the National Council of Churches broadened the scope of this inquiry and filled out its institutional interplay. So did J. Bryan Hehir and John Carr of the U.S. Catholic Conference, Nancy Sylvester of Network, and Herbert Valentine, Philip Wogaman, Weldon Gaddy, Ken Brooker Langston, and David Key of the Interfaith Alliance. At the United Methodist General Board of Church and Society and its environs, I learned much from Herman Will, Robert McClean, Jim Winkler, Jan Love, Jane Hull Harvey, Jaydee Hanson, George Ogle, Maria Paz Artaza-Regan, Hillary Shelton, Mark Harrison, Philip Amerson, Tex Sample, Steven C. Mott, Kim Jefferson, James and Philip Lawson, Donna T. Morton-Stout, Anna Rhee, Wesley Yamaka, and Bishops Joseph H. Yeakel, Melvin G. Talbert, Earl G. Hunt, Jr., C. Dale White, Leontine T. C. Kelly, William W. Dew, Jr., Bruce P. Blake, and Kenneth Lee Carder. At the Institute on Religion and Democracy, I was tutored by David Jessup, Alan F. H. Wisdom, Lawrence Adams, Greg Jones, and Mark Tooley; at Good News by Helen Rhea Stumbo and John Stumbo; and at Interfaith Impact by Martin McLaughlin, Paul Kittlaus, Joe Hacala, elmira nazombe, and James M. Bell.

Robert N. Bellah, Ann Swidler, Richard Madsen, and William M. Sullivan read almost all of this book, in more than one draft. It is immeasurably better because of the wisdom and criticism they offered as abiding colleagues, teachers, and friends. For the light of his work and example I thank Robert Bellah. I have profited from the research of John Green and Robert Wuthnow on American religion in public, and from their thoughtful answers to my queries about parachurch groups, religious voting patterns, and statistical portraits of denominations. I am also indebted to uncounted interlocutors at scholarly meetings and conferences where I have presented parts of this work, and to its two unnamed reviewers for the University of Chicago Press, where I have enjoyed the remarkable editorial care and good company of Douglas Mitchell, Tim McGovern, and Nancy Trotic.

At Emory University and its Candler School of Theology, my debts are both intellectual and institutional. Russell E. Richey, Brooks Holifield, Thomas Frank, and Theodore Runyon made straight my pilgrim's path through the landscape of United Methodism. Jon Gunnemann, Robert Franklin, Timothy Jackson, Nancy Eiesland, Elizabeth Bounds, and the community of my Candler colleagues helped sharpen the book's social and ethical analysis. With unfailing care, Sandra Tucker transcribed scores of interviews, and Matthew Bersagel Braley prepared the index and bibliography. Deans James L. Waits, Kevin LaGree, Russell Richey, and Jan Love gave me the encouragement and time needed to pursue this project, which was ably abetted by Rebecca Chopp, Gail O'Day, Carl Holladay, and Charles Foster and aided by a grant from the Earl Brewer Research Fund, along with a grant from Emory University's Faculty Research Fund. For their staunch support I am also indebted to Dean Robert A. Paul of Emory College, Graduate Dean Lisa Tedesco, and Virginia Shadron and Rosemary Hynes of Emory's Graduate School of Arts and Sciences, which contributed to the publication of this book.

Craig Dykstra and Jean Knoerle at the Lilly Endowment invited me to undertake this project and enabled me to do it with the invigorating, attentive support essential to conceiving its framework and carrying out its fieldwork. Emory's Center for the Study of Law and Religion, led by John Witte and sponsored by a grant from The Pew Charitable Trusts, likewise enabled me to complete the project's writing and subvened its publication. For the Center's visionary leadership and collegial company, I am also grateful to Frank Alexander, Don Browning, Eliza Ellison, and all its fellows and staff, and especially to Martin Marty for the graceful gift of his expert guidance in revising the manuscript.

First and last, Evan and Kristin deserve my heartfelt gratitude for living with this work, and living through it, as it spanned my son's coming of age and coincided with my wife's long labor on the social history of Lagos, *Slavery and the Birth of an African City*. For their patient, forgiving, and enduring love I give thanks, world without end.

Introduction

CHAPTER ONE

Faith in Public

Going to War in Iraq and Doing Good at Home

What is the role of religion in American public life? Prophetic witness, voice of conscience, social activist and reformer, moral advocate and interlocutor? Or is it Good Samaritan, helping hand, loving heart and saving grace, community volunteer and charitable donor? The answers are many and diverse, some linked and others at odds, all woven through the history of American ideals and actions, movements, and institutions. Recurring efforts to ask and answer this question in principle reach back to the beginnings of our society. They have multiplied in recent decades, as religious differences have resurged in our electoral politics and religious institutions have grown more politicized in themselves. This inquiry draws on such efforts to pin down our principles of religion in public. But it concentrates on tracing out this question in the practice of the mainline Protestant churches—Methodist, Presbyterian, Lutheran, and United Church of Christ—and their offices in Washington, D.C., over the past generation. It looks at what these churches have done, together with their allies and adversaries, in seeking to serve as "the public church." It asks how they have flourished or failed, and it weighs the reasons why.

The practical efforts of particular religious communities to live out and embody their faith in public inform the public rhetoric of religion and influence the moral argument of public life, just as religious communities in turn draw on these evolving and contested ideals to inspire their action and justify their practices. Thus the religious rhetoric of President George W. Bush—especially as it carried into policy debates and political struggles over his administration's "faith-based initiative" before September 11, 2001, and afterward as it called Americans to prayer and to arms—offers an apt point of entry into the ongoing argument about religion's public

presence and purpose, in instructive counterpoint to the self-understanding
of the mainline Protestant churches in their efforts to embody the public
church. For every answer to the question of religion's public role carries
with it a distinctive vision of good government interacting with communities of faith within the polity of a democratic republic. However conflicted
or unsettled, this is a drama that attests in practice to the moral integrity
of our society as a whole, even as church and state remain separate char-
acters as institutions each governed by their own members.

Witnessing and Winning: War on Iraq

"Jesus changed your heart. Now let him change your mind." So began an
open letter to President George W. Bush in December 2002 beseeching
him to turn back from the brink of war on Iraq. "Your war would violate
the teachings of Jesus Christ. It would violate the tenets, prayers and en-
treaties of your own United Methodist Church bishops. It would ignore
the pleas of hundreds of Jewish, Muslim and Christian leaders," declared
the letter, made public in full-page national newspaper advertisements
and signed by "Religious Leaders for Sensible Priorities," chaired by Rev.
Robert Edgar, General Secretary of the National Council of Churches
(NCC), and joined by prominent United Methodist officials among many
mainline Protestant, Catholic, Jewish, and Muslim clergy.[1]

We should stop the rush to war against Iraq, argued these religious
leaders, because it would betray the just-war principles rooted in Christian tradition and violate the United Nations Charter by launching "an
unprovoked, pre-emptive attack on a nation which is not threatening
the United States," however cruelly Saddam Hussein tyrannized his own
people. It would bring death and destruction to cities filled with innocent civilians and take the lives of too many young Americans. "And its
huge cost will be gouged out of the already unmet needs of the poor,
the underfed and the under-educated in our own country." It is "incon-
ceivable that Jesus Christ, our Lord and Savior and the Prince of Peace,
would support this proposed attack," judged the letter, quoting James E.
Winkler, the general secretary of the United Methodist Church's General
Board of Church and Society. He and other leaders of United Methodism—Mr. Bush's own denomination—had sought private hearings with
the president and were denied, reported the letter. It urged him, "You've
proclaimed the crucial role of your faith in your life, and you've said that

people of faith are often 'our nation's voice of conscience.' Listen to our voices now."

The president refused to listen, it seemed, as the White House failed to acknowledge or respond to this and other calls from a wide range of mainline religious leaders opposed to the war. They gathered three thousand of the faithful in the National Cathedral in Washington on Martin Luther King Day, January 20, 2003, to pray for peace, then walk by the White House in a candlelight procession. Fifty religious leaders affiliated with the NCC, including many Methodist bishops, sent an unanswered letter to the president on January 30, then followed up in February with an advertisement in *Roll Call*, the Capitol Hill newsletter, asking "Would President Bush meet with them if they brought along Jesus and Moses?"[2]

Opposition to war on Iraq was widespread among U.S. Christian leaders, spanning Roman Catholics and Greek, Syrian, and Coptic Orthodox churches as well as mainline Protestants, including the United Methodist Church, the Presbyterian Church (USA), the Evangelical Lutheran Church in America, the American Baptist Church, the Christian Church (Disciples of Christ), and the United Church of Christ. Some Muslim and Buddhist groups spoke out against it. Jewish groups were split, with most Reform and Conservative organizations opposed to a preemptive strike without UN authorization and some Orthodox groups favoring it. Some leaders of conservative evangelical and Pentecostal churches and independent ministries supported such a preemptive attack on Iraq. So did Richard Land, the high-profile president of the Ethics and Religious Liberty Commission of the Southern Baptist Convention, who declared it a just war.

"A strong faith-based revolt against war on Iraq is coming together in the first weeks of December," promised the open letter from the NCC's Robert Edgar. Later that month, he led a delegation of church leaders to Iraq to meet with Muslim and Christian groups, reporting that they affirmed the NCC's proclamation that the United States could "win without war": "You have won; you have disarmed us and humiliated us. You have inspectors in our country. Why do you now want to kill us? Can't you take yes for an answer?" To roll back what Edgar termed the tide of "war, destruction, suffering, and horror that the President and the Pentagon are urging as a misguided 'solution' to the 'threat' from Iraq," the NCC and related religious groups sent delegations of top Methodist, Presbyterian, Episcopal, and American Baptist leaders to Europe to meet with British prime minister Tony Blair, Chancellor Gerhard Schroeder of Germany, Pope John Paul II and leading French, Russian, and Italian officials. Blair did not move away from his position that war against Saddam Hussein was justified in order to prevent weapons of mass destruction from falling into the hands of terrorists. But he "engaged deeply in the moral and theological issues at stake" during an hour-long meeting, reported Rev. Jim Wallis, head of the progressive evangelical Sojourners movement and a member of the delegation.[3]

"We have been warmly received in every country—except our own," announced Edgar. "We have repeatedly asked to meet with President Bush, a fellow man of faith, and a committed United Methodist. We have been rebuffed or ignored." Wallis observed of the president, "I hope he hasn't walled himself off. I haven't heard a moral language or a faith language from him in relation to this momentous decision." The only antiwar religious leader received by Bush, in a private meeting on March 5, was Cardinal Pio Laghi, a Bush family friend and former papal nuncio sent as an emissary by Pope John Paul II with his prayer "to search for the ways of a stable peace, the noblest of endeavors."[4]

In a news conference the next day, Mr. Bush made clear that war was imminent and the United States would wage it alone, if need be, without UN support. Since Iraq had failed to disarm fully and unconditionally, as required by UN Security Council Resolution 1441, and it continued to possess weapons of terror and to provide funding, training, and safe haven to terrorists "who would willingly use weapons of mass destruction against America and other peace-loving countries," argued Bush, "Saddam Hussein and his weapons are a direct threat to this country, to our people, and to all free people. If the world fails to confront the threat posed by the Iraqi regime, refusing to use force, even as a last resort, free nations would assume immense and unacceptable risks."[5] The United States would disarm Iraq by force, vowed Bush, rather than risk a reprise of 9/11 raised to the power of mass destruction. "The attacks of September the 11th, 2001, showed what the enemies of America did with four airplanes. We will not wait to see what terrorists or terrorist states could do with weapons of mass destruction. We are determined to confront threats wherever they arise. I will not leave the American people at the mercy of the Iraqi dictator and his weapons."

Asked why protesters opposed war on Iraq, Mr. Bush recognized that "there are people who don't like war." He shared their feelings, he said, but stood ready to carry out his biblical oath as president to defend the Constitution and protect the American people in the wake of the September 11 attacks: "My job is to protect America, and that is exactly what I'm going to do." Asked how his faith guided him in a nation at odds over war, Bush replied that diplomacy had failed to disarm Saddam in a dangerous world full of new threats all Americans must face. "I know they remember the tragedy of September the 11th, but I hope they understand the lesson of September the 11th," he said. "The lesson is, is that we're vulnerable to attack, wherever it may occur, and we must take threats which gather overseas very seriously. . . . In the case of Iraq, it is now time for him to disarm. For the sake of peace, if we have to use our troops, we will."

Religious faith, continued President Bush, sustained him through the power of prayer, both his own daily prayers and those of others offered for him:

> My faith sustains me because I pray daily. I pray for guidance and wisdom and strength. If we were to commit our troops—if we were to commit our troops—I would pray for their safety, and I would pray for the safety of innocent Iraqi lives as well. One thing that's really great about our country . . . is that there are thousands of people who pray for me that I'll never see and be able to thank. But it is a humbling experience to think that people I will never have met have lifted me and my family up in prayer. And for that I'm grateful. . . . It's been a comforting feeling to know that is true. I pray for peace . . . I pray for peace.

Against the moral authority of Methodist bishops and critical church leaders, President Bush appealed to the faithful moral guidance of his own personal prayers, the comforting support of the prayers of countless other Americans, and, by implication, the moral sovereignty of individual conscience within a Protestant priesthood of all believers, at the root of a democracy of all citizens with equal rights to hold their own moral convictions.

Against Christian just-war teachings that require proper authority to declare war only as a last resort to defend against imminent armed threats with the clear promise of proportionality in protecting against even greater harm, Mr. Bush held the contrary view, summed up by Press Secretary Ari Fleischer: "The President thinks the most immoral act of all would be if Saddam Hussein were to somehow transfer his weapons to terrorists who could use them against us. So the President does view the use of force as a matter of legality, as a matter of morality and as a matter of protecting the American people." White House political advisers meanwhile expressed concern that a meeting with antiwar religious leaders would turn into a circus-like news conference. They reportedly insisted that even Cardinal Laghi could not speak to reporters in the area on the White House grounds where visitors to the Oval Office regularly hold news conferences.[6]

Unable to meet with the president or change his mind on war against Iraq, mainline church leaders joined together with the NCC in efforts to reach the public at large as well as the faithful in their pews by preaching and teaching, holding prayer services and organizing vigils in living rooms, churches, and cities around the country. The Friends Committee on National Legislation, for one, created and distributed a hundred thousand blue and white "War Is Not the Answer" bumper stickers and posters that were carried in marches and put up on front lawns nationwide. The NCC sponsored national television and newspaper advertisements and targeted them strategically, reported its head, Robert Edgar, a former Democratic member of Congress as well as a United Methodist minister: "We bought ads featuring United Methodist Bishop Melvin Talbert, that ran only on Fox News and CNN in New York and Washington when newsrooms are watching. We then saw the ads spread, as news, all over the country."[7]

Church leaders also worked with nonreligious partners in the United States and overseas—for example, antiwar advocacy groups such as MoveOn.org and Win Without War—to organize massive peace rallies. These culminated in what was likely the largest one-day public protest in history, as some ten million people marched in the streets of six hundred cities around the world on February 15, 2003. A record-high crowd estimated at a million people, for example, turned out in London to oppose the war. In San Francisco, two hundred thousand joined ministers, imams, and rabbis—along with social activists, actors, and musicians—to protest the war, urged on by the poet Lawrence Ferlinghetti exhorting, "Now is the time for you to speak / O silent majority" before "America turns the attack on its Twin Towers / Into the beginning of the Third World War / The war with the Third World."[8] By way of reply, the president afterward observed that he never listened to focus groups.

In a brief, one-page address to the nation delivered from the Oval Office late on the night of March 19, 2003, President Bush declared war "to disarm Iraq, to free its people and to defend the world from grave danger."[9] With respect for Iraq's civilization, citizens, and religious faiths, he said, and with prayers for the safe return of American troops, "our nation enters this conflict reluctantly—yet, our purpose is sure. The people of the United States and our friends and allies will not live at the mercy of an outlaw regime that threatens the peace with weapons of mass murder. We will meet that threat now," with our troops, "so that we do not have to meet it later with armies of fire fighters and police and doctors on the streets of our cities." Promised the president, "We will defend our freedom. We will bring freedom to others and we will prevail. May God bless our country and all who defend her."

A White House report sent to Congress on the same day set out the Bush administration's rationale for war in terms that carefully detailed the president's legal grounds to declare war. These rested on congressional authorization in 2002 for President Bush to use military force against Iraq (Public Law 107-243, preceded by Public Law 102-1) in light of the Clinton-era congressional resolution to support efforts to remove Saddam Hussein's regime from power (Public Law 105-338). This congressional authorization under the U.S. Constitution to use force to protect the security of the American people, argued the administration, was consistent with the 1991 UN Security Council Resolution 678, which permitted the United States to use military force to enforce the no-fly zones over Iraq imposed as conditions for a cease-fire to end the first Gulf War. It also enabled the United States to enforce Security Council Resolution 1441 of November 2002, which declared Iraq in material breach of its disarmament obligations and afforded it one final opportunity to comply. Since Iraq had failed to comply, argued the administration, the United States was entitled to enforce Resolution 1441 under Chapter VII of the UN Charter and to exercise its inherent right of self-defense, recognized in Article 51 of the charter, notwithstanding the Security Council's refusal to pass a second resolution explicitly authorizing war on Iraq.

The moral grounds for war, reiterated in brief by the White House report to Congress, continued to follow from the necessity of war to "adequately protect the national security of the United States against the continuing threat posed by Iraq"—the threat that it was developing weapons of mass destruction to attack the United States directly and abet terrorists in doing likewise.[10]

As the war progressed over the following month, President Bush continued to justify it as a means to ending the clear and imminent danger Iraq posed to America and the world. But the administration's emphasis grew stronger on the tyrannical evil Saddam Hussein's regime inflicted upon its own people. As the war wound down, the president emphasized the God-given gift of freedom brought to Iraq by American hands: "As people throughout Iraq celebrate the arrival of freedom, America celebrates with them. We know that freedom is the gift of God to all mankind, and we rejoice when others can share it," Bush said in his radio address of

April 12.[11] Throughout the course of his administration and the 2004 elec-
tion campaign, the president continued to stress this justification for the
Iraq war in terms of his conviction that everybody wants to be free, and
God wants them to be free. "Freedom is not America's gift to the world,"
he repeated in his stump speech for reelection. "Freedom is Almighty
God's gift to each man and woman in this world."[12]

This rhetorical emphasis culminated in President Bush's 2005 inaugural address. It justified America's forceful defense of freedom around
the world today—particularly, though implicitly, by the use of arms in
Iraq—as fulfilling the providential flow of history in the direction "set by
liberty and the Author of Liberty."[13] That divine author, said Bush, echoing Thomas Jefferson's "Laws of Nature and of Nature's God" yet linking
humans to heaven through the imago Dei, created America's founding
faith in freedom: "From the day of our founding, we have proclaimed that
every man and woman on this earth has rights, and dignity, and matchless
value, because they bear the image of the Maker of Heaven and earth."

That divine author also guarantees freedom's eventual triumph for
all humankind, testified Bush, and inspires our complete confidence in
our cause as its carrier, not because "history runs on the wheels of inevi-
tability. It is human choices that move events. Not because we consider
ourselves a chosen nation. God moves and chooses as He wills. We have
confidence because freedom is the permanent hope of mankind, the hunger in dark places, the longing of the soul." Because we have chosen to do
God's will in advancing the cause of freedom, given by God to fulfill the
human soul, we are an almost-chosen nation that can be confident in following our leaders along this course with God and history on our side.

Our ultimate goal is "ending tyranny in our world," President Bush
proclaimed in 2005, echoing but not repeating the post-9/11 promise of his
resolve to "rid the world of evil." Likewise echoed but not explicitly asserted in the 2005 inaugural is the power of this promise, reiterated in the
global defense of freedom, to justify U.S. claims to "preemptive actions to
counter a sufficient threat to our national security," as the 2002 National
Security Strategy declares, "even if uncertainty remains as to the time
and place of the enemy's attack"; and to justify the U.S. commitment to
maintaining military forces "strong enough to dissuade potential adversaries from pursuing a military build-up in hopes of surpassing, or equaling, the power of the United States." Thus, remaining the world's sole
superpower, reasoned the president in 2002, enables the United States to
seek "to create a balance of power that favors human freedom: conditions

in which all nations and all societies can choose for themselves the rewards and challenges of political and economic liberty." Accordingly, the 2005 inaugural reaffirms the president's introduction to the 2002 National Security Strategy, which concludes that the twentieth century's great struggles between liberty and totalitarianism have ended in victory for "a single sustainable model for national success: freedom, democracy, and free enterprise." This victory, Bush declared in 2002, fulfills the eternal and universal truth of freedom as "the non-negotiable demand of human dignity; the birthright of every person in every civilization," in singular terms that the United States now embodies.[14]

From self-sacrifice to serve a needy neighbor, as the president had urged in his inaugural address of 2001, Bush turned in 2005 to extol the sterner tasks soldiers serve by fighting for freedom. His earlier insistence that our public interest depends on private character shifted from self-giving to self-discipline: "Self-government relies, in the end, on the governing of the self. That edifice of character is built in families, supported by communities with standards and sustained in our national life by the truths of Sinai, the Sermon on the Mount, the word of the Koran and the varied faiths of our people." Rooted in religious faith, timeless and true moral ideals build moral character and advance democratic progress in America and around the world. "History has an ebb and flow of justice, but history also has a visible direction, set by liberty and the Author of Liberty." In its King James cadences, Enlightenment echoes of faith in service to society, and martial music rehearsed from FDR and JFK, the 2005 inaugural address called all Americans to march in a moral crusade for the cause of freedom given by God to set the course of history.

Prophetic Victory and Defeat

Announcing the end of major combat in Iraq from the deck of the aircraft carrier *Abraham Lincoln*, where he landed wearing a fighter pilot's flight suit, President Bush declared on May 1, 2003, "In this battle we have fought for the cause of liberty, and for the peace of the world." He assured the troops, "Because of you, our nation is more secure. Because of you, the tyrant has fallen, and Iraq is free."[15] The United States would help rebuild Iraq as a democracy, promised the president, and would stand with its new leaders "as they establish a government of, by, and for the Iraqi people." The battle of Iraq was part of a larger war, marking "one victory in a war on terror that began on September the 11, 2001—and still goes on," warned the president. "By seeking to turn our cities into killing fields, terrorists and their allies believed that they could destroy this nation's resolve, and force our retreat from the world. They have failed."

America's mission would continue, vowed President Bush. "The war on terror is not over; yet it is not endless. We do not know the day of final victory, but we have seen the turning of the tide." Free nations would press on to victory. Those bearing arms in this campaign, he concluded, had taken up "the highest calling of history": to carry the message of hope conveyed in "the words of the Prophet Isaiah, 'To the captives, "come out"—and to those in darkness, "be free."'" Thank you for serving our country and our cause. May God bless you all, and may God continue to bless America."

On the contrary, argued Jim Winkler, general secretary of the United Methodist General Board of Church and Society, the invasion of Iraq was wrong, unjust, and un-Christian. Writing soon after President Bush's declaration of Iraq's prophetic emancipation, and summing up a stance shared by mainline church leaders in Washington, Winkler countered:

> The invasion of Iraq is wrong. It is unjust, unnecessary and too uncertain. I write those words with the full confidence that Jesus Christ would assert the same.
>
> The invasion is unjust by the historic Roman Catholic "just war" standards. It is illegal under international law and it is a disastrous first step for the President's new doctrine of preemptive war enshrined in the National Security Strategy. In the past, the United States went to war when attacked, when neighbors or allies were attacked, or with the support of the international community. None of those conditions pertain in this instance.
>
> The invasion was unnecessary. Iraq did not represent an imminent threat to the United States. The weapons inspectors should have been given more time. Saddam Hussein is indeed ruthless. There are lots of ruthless leaders around the world. I dream of the day when the world united will insist that together we will not countenance brutal dictatorships, torture, arbitrary arrests, genocide, and tyranny and will pledge to free peoples everywhere from such rule. So far, that has not happened. The U.S. did not invade Iraq to free its people from Saddam Hussein, but to avenge the terrible events of September 11. Yet there is no evidence that Saddam Hussein had anything to do with the attacks on the World Trade Center and the Pentagon.
>
> The invasion is uncertain in its aftermath. The people of Iraq do not want a U.S. Army General as their new dictator, viceroy, or proconsul. It seems our leaders never paused to consider the notion Iraqis could be both anti-Saddam and

anti-American. We can understand how they would be anti-Saddam, but anti-American? Why? We're the good guys, right? Not everyone sees it that way.

Governance of Iraq must be turned over to the United Nations as soon as possible. Even if the United States had the willingness to spend a significant portion of its treasure to rebuild Iraq and to station tens of thousands of troops throughout that country for years to come, . . . it would prove to be an even greater provocation to the Muslim world than our current maintenance of thousands of our military personnel in the region.

How could this have happened? While September 11 was the excuse, these plans have been in the works for many years. The idea, however, that the United States can remake the Middle East into a pro-Western, democratic zone through a military invasion is a fantasy.[16]

Truth is often the first casualty of war, added a veteran of the mainline churches in Washington in criticism of the Bush administration in mid-2003. But in the case of Iraq, "the President asked Americans to trust him and take a great leap of faith over the facts of cause and effect. We had to trust that Saddam actually had the weapons and military power to pose a clear and present danger to our shores, and [that] he had the ties to terrorists to back them in attacking us."[17] According to polls in early 2003, noted this critic, many Americans believed Saddam Hussein was actually behind the attacks of 9/11, though most also had misgivings about the United States' launching a preemptive attack on Iraq without UN authorization. "We're still waiting for hard evidence of Saddam's ties to al Qaeda, and his stockpiles of weapons of mass destruction. Without that evidence, can we really decide this war was just, or hope it will turn the tide against terrorism?" In the absence of such evidence, these questions continued to be contested no less crucially through the long course of the Iraq war, as an occupation beset by an insurgency, brutalized by torture, and torn by sectarian violence. This dispute ran through the 2004 presidential election and beyond, underscoring its significance as a referendum on support for the war in Iraq as part of the war on terror.[18]

If American leaders take 9/11 as a first strike that allows us to wage a global war on terror wherever we see fit to strike back to prevent another possible attack, continued this mainline-church critic of invading Iraq, then "the war on terror could turn out to be endless." We weaken the UN and divide its key members, whom we need to help police, aid, and reconstruct Iraq and Afghanistan. "We set a bad example for other stronger nations to attack weaker ones they label terrorists. We speed up nuclear proliferation in places like Iran instead of stopping it in Pakistan and North Korea," he warned; weaker countries seek nuclear arms more intently in order to forestall likelier preemptive attacks, in a vicious cycle of armed conflict that has quickened around the world since the Cold War with a growing potential to turn nuclear.

"The war on Iraq may be over," this critic concluded in mid-2003, "but there's a lot of fallout from it the churches need to work on in the pews and in Washington." If the consequences of war on Iraq remain dangerously daunting overseas and its costs imperil social-welfare spending and economic justice at home, as many mainline church leaders deeply believe, they are both hopeful and wary in thinking about how the churches should respond.

Through the united leadership of its member communions, backed by individual donors and foundations, the National Council of Churches accomplished much on the U.S. road to war against Iraq, judged Robert Edgar. In so doing, he said, the council "found its prophetic voice." Jim Wallis concurred: "There's never been such unity among the churches in the country, even during Vietnam."[19] Other national church leaders were more ambivalent in their private evaluations. "It's the best of times and the worst of times," concluded one in 2003, explaining that

> the NCC under Bob Edgar has really stepped up and drawn church leaders together like it is supposed to do but hasn't done, in fact, since the civil rights era. People in the pews are really with us on this across political lines. They have real misgivings about attacking Iraq on our own instead of working with the UN to disarm it. We partnered with lots of nonchurch activist and peace groups at home and overseas to organize against the war. . . .
>
> And you can still ask, honestly, what difference has it made? Why haven't we made more of a difference? Sure, it's partly the fault of Congress for giving Bush a blank check for war last fall. It's the Democrats' fault for not finding the political courage to really resist the administration. Maybe it's the fault of the American people for not caring enough, or the UN and our allies for not fighting hard enough to stop Bush from going to war. But it's our fault, too.
>
> We know prophetic witnessing is not the same thing as winning politically. We know we have to keep on working to witness to the gospel truth of loving God and neighbor, again and again, even when we lose the political fight. But we also need to ask ourselves why we seem to have so little influence for good, even when we have the most going for us on an issue like this. We need to figure out what we need to do differently in order to do better.[20]

One response to such questions in the mainline churches about the relationship of prophetic witnessing, political winning, and persuasive public
influence came in late 2003 with the formation of the Clergy Leadership
Network, an activist political advocacy organization on Capitol Hill aimed
at countering the Christian right and mobilizing voters against Bush administration policies.

Backed by the NCC, the Clergy Leadership Network would be the first
national liberal religious group focused on electoral politics and political
organizing, not only moral advocacy on issues, according to its founders,
many of them church leaders active in opposing the war in Iraq. They included Rev. Joan Brown Campbell, former general secretary of the NCC,
and Rev. William Sloane Coffin, a leader in the movements for civil rights
and against the Vietnam War. "Clergy have to be careful not to rush in
with solutions to big problems, but when they see gross injustice they
have an obligation not to be silent," said Coffin. "The arrogance and self-
righteousness of the present administration are very dangerous. And
silence by members of the clergy, in the face of such arrogance, is tanta-
mount to betrayal of the Gospel or the Torah or the Koran."[21]

Economic injustice and joblessness, health care and civil liberties, foreign policy, and war and peace figured centrally in the Clergy Leadership
Network's list of issues, with faith as "the lens through which public life is
viewed and consequently engaged," attested its guidelines.[22] A year later,
according to one of its members, the network was "alive and not entirely
well"—present on the floor of the Democratic National Convention, for
example, but still seeking to find its political footing and traction to mobilize electoral support without losing its moral balance. "They don't have
a clue," tartly observed one veteran church leader in Washington.[23] By
the beginning of 2005, the group had been reorganized as the Clergy and
Laity Network, with a new nonprofit tax status more tightly restricting
its electoral involvement and a new focus on "grass-roots social impact
organizing."[24]

"God bless, and good luck," noted a more sympathetic church leader
about this effort, adding, "It comes out of the difficult, vexed history of
the churches in Washington for years now, not just Iraq," and not just the
age-old problem of distinguishing what to render to God and Caesar and
how best to do it.[25] What underlies the strengths and limits of the mainline
churches in seeking to act as the Church in American public life today?
What should they understand and do differently to diagnose their faults
and revive their faith in public? These questions lead to others within a

wider web of inquiry into the work of the mainline Protestant churches in
Washington over the past generation.

Faith in Compassion and Justice

Everything changed in American public life after September 11, 2001,
yet much remained the same. The shifting shape of religion in the rhetoric
of President George W. Bush before and after that terrible day, coherent in outline yet distinct in substance and shading, reflects the powerful
yet ambiguous moral dynamic of our polity today when it comes to religion's presence and purpose.[26] In contrast to the more austere, Calvinistic presidential rhetoric forged under pressure to meet the crisis of
September 11, harking back to Franklin Roosevelt's wartime speeches
and rehearsed in the 2005 inaugural address, the larger record of Bush's
moral rhetoric tells a more distinctive story about the limited good of government and the personal nature of faith in public. It depicts a vision of
compassionate citizens volunteering to heal and help others help themselves, inspired by a benevolent evangelical faith and aided by religious
communities as charitable providers of social services. It ignores the prophetic self-understanding of the mainline Protestant churches as conscientious moral witnesses, critics, and advocates of governmental policy
and action to make the world more peaceful and our society more just as
well as compassionate.

    In its fifteen-minute course, Bush's carefully honed and conciliatory
inaugural address in January 2001 was marked by a dozen religious references. The speech was most revealing in its masterly efforts to modulate
civil-religious discourse and turn it in the political direction of a "compassionate conservatism." It resonated with revivalist ideals drawn from evangelical Protestant faith, on the one hand, and free-market entrepreneurial
beliefs on the other. It joined them in a functionalist and therapeutic view
of religion serving to solve social problems by making individuals better.
Grasping the conceptual coherence of this vision, its ecclesiological implications, and its complex relationship to the realities of policymaking and
politics—for example, in the case of the Bush administration's faith-based
initiative—sharpens our rhetorical point of departure for thinking about
the moral stance and institutional place of religion in American public
life today. Seeing how and why the mainline Protestant churches came
to criticize this vision helps guide our line of inquiry into efforts by these

churches to live out their faith on Capitol Hill and around the world over the past three decades.

The grandest American ideal is an unfolding promise, Mr. Bush begins in his 2001 inaugural address, "that everyone belongs, that everyone deserves a chance, that no insignificant person was ever born. Americans are called to enact this promise in our lives and in our laws."[27] At moral odds with this national calling, Bush makes clear, are social conditions he will not allow to persist: "While many of our citizens prosper, others doubt the promise—even the justice—of our own country. The ambitions of some Americans are limited by failing schools, and hidden prejudice and the circumstances of their birth. And sometimes our differences run so deep, it seems we share a continent, but not a country." Bush makes a solemn pledge to "build a single nation of justice and opportunity. I know this is in our reach, because we are guided by a power larger than ourselves, who creates us equal in his image. And we are confident in principles that unite and lead us onward." So guided by providence and principle, Bush proclaims "a new commitment to live out our nation's promise through civility, courage, compassion and character." Among these virtues, he gives the greatest emphasis and elaboration to compassion, in the following key passage:

America at its best is compassionate.

In the quiet of American conscience, we know that deep, persistent poverty is unworthy of our nation's promise. And whatever our views of its cause, we can agree that children at risk are not at fault. Abandonment and abuse are not acts of God, they are failures of love. And the proliferation of prisons, however necessary, is no substitute for hope and order in our souls.

Where there is suffering, there is duty. Americans in need are not strangers, they are citizens; not problems, but priorities; and all of us are diminished when any are hopeless.

Government has great responsibilities, for public safety and public health, for civil rights and common schools. Yet compassion is the work of a nation, not just a government. And some needs and hurts are so deep they will only respond to a mentor's touch or a pastor's prayer. Church and charity, synagogue and mosque, lend our communities their humanity and they will have an honored place in our plans and in our laws.

Many in our country do not know the pain of poverty. But we can listen to those who do. And I can pledge our nation to a goal: When we see that wounded traveler on the road to Jericho, we will not pass to the other side.

America at its best is a place where personal responsibility is valued and expected. . . . Our public interest depends on private character, on civic duty and family bonds and basic fairness, on uncounted, unhonored acts of decency which give direction to our freedom.

Sometimes in life we are called to do great things. But as a saint of our times has said, every day we are called to do small things with great love. The most important tasks of a democracy are done by everyone.

Here the virtue of compassion that marks America at its best is held up as a moral inspiration and duty to respond to persistent poverty, proliferating imprisonment, and Americans in need. Compassion is both paired with justice and placed before it in practical importance.

In the political debate and moral argument of American public life, deep and persistent poverty may point to injustice, injury, and exploitation. It raises questions of cause and culpability that in turn guide efforts to seek greater justice in the law, public policy, and the arrangement of social institutions. In "the quiet of American conscience," by implicit contrast, poverty is, first of all, something unworthy of our nation's promise that everyone belongs and deserves a chance. They deserve not only opportunity but justice in the nation Bush pledges to work to build. That justice is presumably participatory and distributive as well as retributive and commutative. It requires, for example, honest work at a living wage for all who can labor and thereby support themselves, provide for their children, and contribute to the commonweal.

Compassion, to be sure, acknowledges disagreement over the causes of poverty and the necessity of proliferating prisons. But it stresses instead the innocence of children at risk, abandoned and abused from "failures of love." It announces a moral duty to respond to suffering, acknowledges the great responsibilities of government, and notes the need for civic duty and "basic fairness" to sustain the public interest. But it emphasizes the duty of individual citizens to respond to those in need, to listen to those who feel the pain of poverty, and to answer their hurt and suffering with a healing touch or a pastoral prayer.

Government is responsible for public safety and public health, civil rights and common schools. "Yet compassion is the work of a nation, not just a government," significantly enough, and Bush pledges the nation to being a biblical Good Samaritan to its wounded citizens, who are not strangers but by implication our biblical neighbors. He acknowledges governmental responsibility and honors the example of voluntary communities of faith. But what he stresses is personal responsibility as a call to conscience, a demand for sacrifice, and a promised path to personal fulfillment through finding that "children and community are the commitments that set us free." Civic duty, family bonds, and basic fairness all underpin "our public interest." But, first and last, it depends on "private character," and on the "uncounted, unhonored acts of decency" that individuals freely choose to do every day of their own accord, in a voluntarist echo of Mother Theresa's maxim that "every day we are called to do small things with great love." Such acts are the stuff of sainthood become the spirit of democracy.

By this account, generous and decent individuals acting as responsible citizens are inspired by "beliefs beyond ourselves" to seek a common good by coming together in voluntary action and association to serve the nation, beginning with their neighbors. Thus they build up "communities of service and a nation of character," in contrast to good citizens conceived more as members of a republic, engaged in public deliberation and debate over issues of common concern in conciliar, contentious assemblies that extend from town hall meetings to Capitol Hill. In President Bush's account, neither classical republican ideals nor bureaucratic government programs can challenge the neighborly, voluntarist, and personally compassionate spirit of citizenship he celebrates, and no wrong can stand against it. Poised at the functional intersection of evangelical Protestant faith and free-market belief, Bush testifies to each person's compassionate feeling for others serving to inspire Good Samaritan aid to them without constraining the sovereignty of individual conscience and choice, or the liberty of individual rights and entrepreneurial action.

Conspicuous by its absence from this moral vision of faithful individuals freely serving one another out of love is the Calvinist emphasis in the Reformed tradition of American Protestantism on lawful social justice and covenantal virtue in accord with divine sovereignty and natural law. Absent, too, are its counterparts in the naturally lawful and virtuous corporatism of Catholic social teachings, and the biblical covenant and holiness of Jewish law. Also missing is the conciliar character of the synagogue or church, whether presbyterian or episcopal in its polity, whose members compose a public assembly of their own to deliberate and debate common questions and likewise take part in the moral argument of the polity at large as exemplary advocates and interlocutors. Struck by the moral rhetoric and models that President Bush's 2001 inaugural address emphasized and by all it omitted, many mainline church leaders stressed the importance of what his administration would go on to do or leave undone in carrying out the responsibilities of government and leading the nation along the exemplary path of the Good Samaritan.

For and Against a Faith-Based Initiative

Within days of his inauguration, President George W. Bush signed two executive orders to support "faith-based programs and community groups" that perform social services. The first created a new White House Office of Faith-Based and Community Initiatives to oversee "fair and supportive" government cooperation with all such groups. The second created a network of offices in five government agencies—the Departments of Justice, Housing and Urban Development (HUD), Health and Human Services (HHS), Labor, and Education—to clear away "bureaucratic barriers" in the path of private groups seeking government support but wary of government regulation, for example, to check explicitly religious preaching and proselytizing by faith-based groups to the needy recipients of their social services.[28]

Much of the immediate controversy surrounding this initiative focused on the danger of its violating the separation of church and state, with the risk of religious meddling in publicly funded social-welfare efforts and the threat of political interference in matters religious, including the prospect of government's unfairly favoring some religious groups over others or funding their preferential hiring of the faithful.[29] In April of 2001, more than 850 members of the clergy signed a petition backed by the Baptist Joint Committee, the American Jewish Committee, and the United Church of Christ opposing the Bush plan in order to "keep government out of the churches, temples, synagogues and mosques." The plan's provisions, they charged, would "entangle religion and government in an unprecedented and perilous way."[30]

Unexpected criticism of the Bush initiative came from some culturally conservative evangelical Christian leaders, such as Pat Robertson. He had backed Bush's election and earlier promoted the idea of expanding government support for evangelical charities, arguing that government discriminated against them by favoring secular groups and mainline religious agencies such as Catholic Charities.[31] Subsequently, evangelicals' concerns over their equal access to public funding swung Robertson and others against the Bush plan, once the administration decided that "indivisibly conversion-centered" programs predicated on religious conversion as their central mission and method would be eligible for government support only through individual vouchers, not direct grants. No direct funding would go to programs to overcome drug addiction by urging the addict to "accept Jesus Christ as Lord and Savior," for example, in contrast to religious groups that rehabilitate housing and confine their faithful good works to hammering and plumbing.[32]

As political battle lines hardened in the debate, labor unions joined with educational, civil rights, and liberal religious groups in the Coalition Against Religious Discrimination to oppose the Bush plan's effort to "pit religious, non-profit and public agencies against each other and put government in the business of picking and choosing among religions."[33] On the other side, three dozen conservative advocacy groups closed religious and political ranks in the Coalition for Compassion to back the Bush plan in order to "change the last 30 years of religion being kicked out of the public square," according to Gary L. Bauer, a former Reagan aide and Republican presidential candidate at the helm of American Values.[34]

In the debate, a gap emerged along the lines of race and social class. Many urban black ministers proved much more willing than their suburban white counterparts to seek government aid, regulatory strings and all, to meet the challenge of greater social needs, given fewer resources of their own.[35] These racial divisions underscored the complex political dynamics of the Bush initiative. Administration officials defended it as an "antipoverty" effort and admonished white evangelical churches to heed and join with their brethren in urban African American and Latino churches more dedicated to community service.[36] Rev. Eugene F. Rivers, an African American activist pastor allied with the administration on the initiative, argued for its vital promise to facilitate new leadership in the black community "and/or some opening to the Republican Party," since "most black politicians and other elites are not accountable to a poor black base, and have been willing to let the Democrats have black votes essentially for free."[37] Countered Rev. Timothy McDonald, an activist black pastor lobbying members of Congress against the Bush initiative, "It's a hoax and a lie that doesn't add a single dime of new money to help poor communities. It pits black churches against one another and community groups to fight over the crumbs, while Bush gives millions of dollars in tax cuts to the rich. It's a political payback to the Christian Right for helping elect Bush, and a ploy to bribe black churches into the Republican party without doing a thing to help the black community."[38]

Religious, civic, and civil rights groups lined up on both sides of the faith-based legislation debated in the House in 2001, along with religious lobbies, moral advocacy groups, labor unions, and professional guilds. Three out of four Americans liked the general idea of giving public funds to religious groups to provide social services, according to opinion polls in 2001. But just as many held specific reservations about how any such program would work in practice and which groups should receive support.[39] Against this background of popular dissension, crosscutting interests and contrary moral ideals combined with commitments to diverse constituencies to mix and match political bedfellows among religious groups.

Endorsing the faith-based House bill were politically conservative white evangelical groups led by Gary Bauer and the National Association of Evangelicals, with Pat Robertson vigorously dissenting. They were joined by the Southern Christian Leadership Conference and by the U.S. Catholic Conference and Habitat for Humanity International. Opposing the measure were the National Association for the Advancement of Colored People, the American Association of University Women, the American Civil Liberties Union, and most labor unions, as well as the United Church of Christ and most Jewish denominations and organizations.[40]

After the House bill passed, albeit with scant funding approved by the House Republican leadership under Representative Tom DeLay (R-Tex.), the fate of faith-based legislation in the Senate appeared uncertain in 2001. So it remained thereafter through a series of complex legislative maneuvers in Congress, bold executive orders, and hopeful public announcements by the Bush White House. By mid-2002, the veteran legislative director of the United Church of Christ office on Capitol Hill, Pat Conover, concluded that the "charitable choice agenda has been marginalized," in good part by the progressive advocacy efforts of the mainline churches.[41] By then, the White House was lobbying Congress less confidently in favor of charitable choice. But President Bush continued to advocate with no less conviction for his faith-based initiative over the course of his administration and the 2004 campaign, pledging that it would be a top priority of his second term.

After hoping that Congress would pass a law to "end the unfair discrimination against faith-based charities by the federal government," Bush explained in late 2004, "I got tired of waiting. I got tired of the process debate. See, I'm focused on results, I want there to be positive results. I want lives to be saved, as best as possible. The process bogged down."[42] So the president issued an executive order in late 2002 "mandating equal treatment for faith-based charities in the federal grant-making process," and another order in mid-2004 adding faith-based offices at the Departments of Commerce and Veterans Affairs and at the Small Business Administration, to join offices added in 2003 at the Department of Agriculture and the U.S. Agency for International Development. By the 2004 election campaign, the White House could take credit for making discretionary grants of a billion dollars to faith-based programs in 2003.[43] After failing to win the votes in Congress needed to fund the initiative, the Bush administration, charged its sharp critics at Americans United for Separation of Church and State, seemed to be trying to "hijack every dollar [it] can and move it into faith-based ministries."[44]

In fact, judged policy analysts of the Roundtable on Religion and Social Welfare Policy, "in the absence of new legislative authority, the President has aggressively advanced the Faith-Based Initiative through executive orders, rule changes, managerial realignment in federal agencies, and other innovative uses of the prerogatives of his office."[45] Nonetheless, they concluded in late 2004, the federal funding streams most accessible to faith-based organizations "tend to be small and have shown little real growth in recent years," largely due to the effects of the 2001 recession, increased competition for social-service dollars from the Temporary Assistance to Needy Family (TANF) block grant, and the vigorous growth of Medicaid and related health-care programs that are relatively inaccessible to faith-based organizations.[46] In May 2004, a three-year tally of grants to faith-based and community organizations by HHS, HUD, and the Departments of Labor, Justice, and Education totaled $14.4 billion, awarded in 140 federal non-formula competitive grants, with only 8 percent ($1.17 billion) going to faith-based organizations.[47]

Government can hand out money, said President Bush in behalf of these efforts as he championed compassionate conservatism on the campaign trail at the Knights of Columbus Convention in August of 2004, but government can never "put love in a person's heart, or a sense of purpose in a person's life," as when "a loving soul puts their arm around [you] and says, what can I do to help you; how can I help in your life; what can I do to make your life better. Many are called by God to do so, and government must stand on the side of these millions of acts of mercy and kindness that take place on a daily basis."[48]

Beware of "false prophets which come to you in sheep's clothing," warned Senator John Kerry (D-Mass.) at the National Baptist Convention a month later. "For four years, George W. Bush may have talked about compassion, but he's walked right by," charged the Democratic presidential nominee to members of the nation's largest black Baptist denomination, comparing Bush to the priest and Levite who passed by the man robbed and beaten on the road to Jericho in the biblical tale of the Good Samaritan, often invoked by the president. "The president who turns away from African-American needs across the school districts and the communities of our country, who scorns economic justice and affirmative action, who traffics in the politics of division, and then claims he is a friend of black America, cannot conceal his identity no matter what clothes he wears," contended Kerry in indicting his opponent for unjust actions and policies at odds with ideals of compassionate aid to the needy.[49]

The Work of Nations and the Calling of Citizens: Faith First?

In the welter of debate to weigh the political impact of the faith-based initiative, detail its operation in practice, and predict which religious groups it would benefit or plague with problems, relatively little attention was paid to the initiative's overarching meaning and its underlying principles. In announcing it, President Bush echoed his inaugural address by stressing that "compassion is the work of a nation, not just a government."[50] Government and religious communities differ, yet they share in key moral responsibilities, Bush explained. "Government has important responsibilities for public health or public order and civil rights. And government will never be replaced by charities and community groups. Yet when we see social needs in America, my administration will look first to faith-based programs and community groups, which have proven their power to save and change lives."

This striking priority given to religious and community charities over governmental responsibility for meeting "social needs in America" draws its moral force and institutional plausibility from positing social needs in the personal terms of lives that need to be saved and hearts changed by the power of religious faith and charitable love of neighbor, in order to overcome "problems like addiction and abandonment and gang violence, domestic violence, mental illness and homelessness," for example. These personal terms contrast with the structural terms of political-economic problems such as adequate work, wages, health care, and affordable housing to sustain families on the lower rungs of the social ladder. These problems put the onus instead on governmental legislation, policy, and social spending to change the ways institutions shape human behavior within them.

President Bush's looking first to religious and community charities also relies on a functionalist logic of improving society by saving it one soul at a time through forms of "social entrepreneurship" that combine faith-based programs and nonreligious community programs into an ideal of social agency seen as uniquely innovative and effective. Thus Bush welcomed working with a "fantastic team" of "social entrepreneurs all across America who have heard the universal call to love a neighbor like they'd like to be loved themselves, who exist and work hard, not out of love of money, but out of the love of their fellow human beings."[51] Faithful social entrepreneurs, "blessed by a servant's heart," work no less hard out of universal love of neighbor in the voluntary sphere of religious charities and community civic efforts than do economic entrepreneurs out of love of money in the commercial sphere of the market. By supporting such faithful social entrepreneurs, government gives priority to religious charities and community volunteers to meet social needs beyond the irreplaceable but minimal legal responsibilities of government for public health, public order, and civil rights.

This ideal of social entrepreneurship, at once faith-based and market-based, joins together revivalist religion and libertarian political belief to make religious institutions largely indistinguishable from community social agencies, except by the faithful motives of individuals involved in them. Where does this leave religious institutions per se? They provide faithful volunteers for charitable and civic programs, and they benefit from public funding to become stronger providers in themselves of social services with a peculiar power to save and change lives. Policy analysts critical of the Bush plan highlighted just how partial, arguable, and inconclusive is evidence in support of the relative success of faith-based social services, compared to nonreligious service providers, in their efforts to rehabilitate drug addicts, train the jobless, and teach the illiterate to read.[52]

But this debate threw little light on just how profoundly Bush's view in favor of religious communities as social-service providers ignored the public role of religious institutions as conscientious moral witnesses, critics, and advocates of governmental policy and action in public life, including government's responsibility to make American society more just as well as more compassionate. The continuing commitment of the mainline churches to defining this public role over the past generation has been no less striking than their difficulty in enacting it successfully. This contest between contrary ideals of faith in public and the good of government marks a matter of moral conflict and quandary, not simply a conflict of political interests and ideologies.

Some mainline churches, such as the United Methodist Church— Bush's own church and the largest mainline Protestant denomination— adopted no official denominational position in the legislative struggle over the administration's faith-based initiative. But they took a definite stand in the moral argument over it, and they shed revealing light on the contrary ideals of good government and faithful churches that this argument involved.[53] In 2001 the Methodists released a detailed, thirty-page report, *Community Ministries and Government Funding*, which sums up arguments for and against charitable choice, including its threat to "mute the prophetic voices of churches (including criticism of government)." It pointedly observes, "No new money is allocated by the initiatives for social services and community programs and, to date, no new funding channels or mechanisms have been set up." President Bush, the report allows, "said he was 'leveling the playing field,' expanding the range of providers and giving faith groups a fairer chance in the competitive process of obtaining government grants and contracts through existing programs." But it also cites critics' charges that Bush was "dumping" governmental social programs onto the shoulders of religious and community groups, along with the administration's counterclaim that it was instead diversifying social-service delivery systems by allowing funds to go to whichever organizations get the best results.[54]

The Methodist report ties Bush's plan for faith-based initiatives to "a bipartisan movement toward a 'market-driven' approach to social service legislation: that is, what do consumers (the poor in this case) require and how does a free market, perhaps using public money, meet the need?" It links this approach to the legacy of "welfare reform" in 1996 and its ongoing influence on political thinking about the churches' role in overcoming poverty. U.S. poverty rates of 12 percent, including 23.6 percent for African Americans and 22.5 percent for Hispanics in 1999, persisted through the booming prosperity and welfare-to-work policy changes of the late 1990s, notes the 2001 report. The 1996 welfare reform law, entitled the Personal Responsibility and Work Opportunity Reconciliation Act, assumes that "personal irresponsibility and lack of initiative are among the major causes of poverty. The answer in this scenario is 'workfare' and the building of a sense of responsibility and self-sufficiency," states the Methodist report. But the broader array of poverty's actual causes and outcomes, the report argues, demands "changes in the [political-economic] system and in relationships between the powerful and the powerless" to reduce poverty. This broader view accords with United Methodist efforts to foster economic empowerment and meaningful job development within poorer communities, the report concludes, and with the basic Social Principles of the United Methodist Church: "Increasing technology, when accompanied by exploitative economic practices, impoverishes many people and makes poverty self-perpetuating. Therefore, we do not hold poor people morally responsible for their economic state."[55] Poverty, in this view, stems from political-economic relationships and practices, and democratic government bears the responsibility to change them for the sake of social justice and the common good of the people.

Compassion and Justice in the Balance

Government can promote compassion, but only citizens can achieve it, President Bush proclaimed in contrast to the Methodist view, in a remarkable commencement address at the University of Notre Dame. It was devoted to advocating a faith-based response to problems of poverty in America and delivered in late May of 2001, shortly before Bush signed his administration's first key tax cut into law. Lyndon Johnson's War on Poverty had noble intentions and some enduring successes, Bush began, since it gave poor families basic health care and disadvantaged children a "head start" in life. Yet it also had unwanted and unintended consequences: "The welfare entitlement became an enemy of personal effort and responsibility, turning many recipients into dependents. The War on Poverty also turned too many citizens into bystanders, convinced that compassion had become the work of government alone."[56]

In 1996, Congress confronted welfare dependency, said the president, and resolved it by limiting benefits to five years and requiring welfare recipients to work. "Instead of a way of life, welfare became an offer of temporary help—not an entitlement, but a transition. Thanks in large part to this change, welfare rolls have been cut in half. Work and self-respect have been returned to many lives." With welfare dependency resolved, Bush declared, our work is only half done, and we must now confront the second problem: "to revive the spirit of citizenship—to marshal the compassion of our people to meet the continuing needs of our nation." Welfare as we knew it has ended, said Bush, but poverty has not.

If we leave the poor to their own fate, Bush admonished, "America is condemned to permanent social division, becoming a nation of caste and class, divided by fences and gates and guards." Instead, we must be committed to compassion to "build our country's unity by extending our country's blessings" for practical and moral reasons alike, to strengthen our nation and to follow biblical teachings. "Jewish prophets and Catholic teaching both speak of God's special concern for the poor. This is perhaps the most radical teaching of faith—that the value of life is not contingent on wealth or strength or skill. That value is a reflection of God's image."

Yet the key reason Bush offered for a commitment to compassion, in contrast to justice, is not spelled out in the biblical terms of Jewish law or Christian neighbor-love. Instead, it lies deep in the American grain as he defined it: "Aspiration is the essence of our country. We believe in social mobility, not social Darwinism. We are the country of the second chance, where failure is never final. And that dream has sometimes been deferred. It must never be abandoned." Compassionate aid holds out hope for a second chance to those who have failed to make their way in America. It enables them to act on their aspirations to make the most of equal opportunities open to all.

The president dismissed "the stale debate between big government and indifferent government" in favor of a government "active enough to fund services for the poor—and humble enough to let good people in local communities provide those services." Out of the goodness of their own hearts, individual citizens, in this view, must respond to problems of poverty by acting to "serve a neighbor in need." Such is the overarching moral challenge and exhortation that Bush eloquently justified in fivefold fashion at the conclusion of his Notre Dame address:

> I leave you with this challenge: serve a neighbor in need. Because a life of service is a life of significance. Because materialism ultimately is boring, and consumerism can build a prison of wants. Because a person who is not responsible for others is a person who is truly alone. Because there are few better ways to express our love for America than to care for other Americans. And because the same God who endows us with individual rights also calls us to social obligations.

Such explicit moral justification for compassionate service by each faithful citizen to a neighbor in need offered a striking contrast, many mainline-church leaders observed, to Bush's oblique justification of key government policies in pursuit of justice, especially in favor of tax cuts at the expense of greater funding to provide for social welfare, health care, housing, schooling, and jobs.

"Why favor tax cuts for the wealthy instead of providing for the poor and taking better care of everyone in the middle?" asked one liberal church leader by way of rejoinder.[57] "We never heard much more from Mr. Bush than 'Basic justice means no one should pay more than one-third of what they earn in taxes,' and 'It's the people's money, not the government's.' That's not enough to go on. How much money belongs to whom is a question of justice in itself," countered this critic. "Our government is responsible to and for all the people to spend a fair proportion of our money justly and wisely, first of all, to meet the basic needs of people for food, shelter, health care, education, and good work at decent wages, and to protect their human rights to those goods. Taxes should be higher or lower depending on how we're doing in meeting these needs and assuring these rights."

If a few persons at the top are paying too high a proportion of our taxes, proposed this mainline-church critic of the Bush tax cuts, "maybe we should cut down on our ballooning economic inequality" by increasing wages, housing, and health care for the many working poor at the bottom of our society, instead of cutting taxes for the few very rich at the top:

> We need to talk that out and try out different alternatives, instead of just asserting what's basically just or what belongs to the people instead of the government. Which people are suffering or benefiting unjustly? Do we care so much and provide for our own so well that we leave many of our neighbors and fellow citizens to fend for themselves with whatever charity we spare? We need to face these questions when we debate tax cuts and deductions, not just charitable contributions and public housing. And we need to get the staggering burden of campaign finance out of our politics so we can have that debate open to all, not just the few with the biggest voices backed by the biggest wallets.

Reflecting on Bush's speech at Notre Dame, a church leader in Washington noted, "If you take it at face value as an expression of moral conviction, not political strategy, it's enough to make you weep over our big-hearted and selfish sincerity in celebrating charitable crumbs for the poor, a tax-break banquet for the very rich, and pious excuses for everyone else about feeling compassion for the needy while letting ourselves and our government go AWOL from pursuing justice for the least of these. If you don't take it at face value," he said, shaking his head, "it's stupefying, even infuriating, to see religious motives manipulated to serve an unjust, unfaithful kind of politics that bows down to the powerful and presses the powerless down in the name of compassion."[58]

Speak Truth to Power: Help for the Needy and the Deserving

By mid-2003, mainline-church leaders had raised their voices in greater unity against the Bush administration's faith-based initiatives, with stronger orchestration provided by the National Council of Churches. They could no longer remain silent, they explained, after several years of economic recession, the combined impact of federal and state cuts in social-welfare spending, billions to pay for war in Iraq and Afghanistan in the wake of 9/11, and a $350 billion tax cut targeted to wealthy households, with scant relief for the working poor. Backed by the NCC and convened by the progressive evangelical Jim Wallis in the name of a "call to renewal," more than a score of denominational leaders joined the NCC's Robert Edgar in addressing a Pentecost letter to President Bush. The letter charged, "The poor are suffering because of a weakening economy. The poor are suffering because of resources being diverted to war and homeland security. And the poor are suffering because of a lack of attention in national public policy."[59]

The tax cut offers "virtually no help for those at the bottom of the economic ladder, while those at the top reap windfalls," contended these church leaders, and the resulting spending cuts in health care, education, and social services fall most heavily on the poor. Without serious changes in the policies of the Bush administration, the poor would suffer even more, these church leaders warned, and communities of faith committed to their aid would feel even more overwhelmed and betrayed. "The lack of a consistent, coherent, and integrated domestic policy that benefits low-income people makes our continued support for your faith-based initiative increasingly untenable," they concluded. It's time to talk, they urged, in a plea that went unanswered.

By the end of summer 2003, key religious supporters of Mr. Bush were saying publicly that they felt betrayed by his abandonment of compassionate-conservative promises he had made as a candidate to lead faith-based efforts to fight poverty. "After three years, he's failed the test," judged Jim Wallis.[60] Again and again, critics charged, the president, in eloquent speeches that made headlines, called for millions or even billions of dollars for social-welfare initiatives to underwrite faith-based charities, along with No Child Left Behind education reform, AIDS relief, tax credits for low-income families with children, drug-treatment programs, and the like. Then he failed to follow through and push hard to support these programs on Capitol Hill. Instead, he backed off in the face of opposition from his conservative Republican allies, led by the House majority leader, Representative Tom DeLay of Texas. Compassionate conservatism, by this account, consistently turned out to be politically calculated conservatism.

Inside and outside the mainline churches, critics of faith-based initiatives increasingly framed them as part of a larger failure of social policy and political will by government, reaching beyond any one administration or political party, to act justly and responsibly to engage problems of persistent poverty and deepening economic inequality, especially among the working poor.[61] One of four Americans at work in 2002 earned less than the $8.84 per hour needed to keep a family of four above the official poverty line, critics stressed. Nearly one in three working families with children under twelve—many with two parents working low-wage jobs and earning incomes well over the poverty line—faced at least one acute hardship over the course of a year, such as going without food, being evicted, or failing to receive needed medical care, according to a 2001 study by the Economic Policy Institute. Without higher wages or a stronger social safety net, work alone could not ensure a decent standard of living for many families on the lower half of the income ladder in American society. Charity alone could not make up the shortfall.[62]

In 2001, direct government spending on traditional social programs made up a smaller percentage of the U.S. national economy than at any other time since the 1960s, with federal taxes at their lowest level since the 1950s, these critics noted; meanwhile, one in six American children were living in poverty, roughly the same proportion as in 1979 and well above the rest of the industrialized world.[63] But if we count public provision for all Americans, not just the poor, the United States actually committed some 24.5 percent of its gross domestic product to social spending, indirect as well as direct, comparable to Sweden at 27 percent, Britain at 26 percent, and the Netherlands at 25 percent. In the distribution of its benefits, however, U.S. social spending is skewed sharply upward. It includes indirect "tax expenditures" of $700–800 billion annually, provided by a "hidden welfare state" in the form of income tax credits and deductions as "upside-down subsidies."[64] These tax breaks go disproportionately to the well-off, for example, for spending and saving more on home-mortgage interest, employer-sponsored health insurance, pension plans, and higher education.

The United States is remarkable among industrialized nations for its paucity of public housing, for example. But its public provision for private housing in the form of mortgage-interest deductions alone approaches $100 billion annually, three times HUD's yearly budget, with most of these deductions going to the 8 percent of homeowners with expanded incomes of over $100,000 per year.[65] We help the neediest. But we give more help to those seen as the most deserving in terms of what they earn, spend, and save. Indeed, as fiscal conservatives protested, after 9/11 the federal government unleashed deficit spending to pay the spiraling costs not only of war but of middle-class entitlements, particularly Medicare, by writing checks against our children's future while cutting taxes.[66] Praise for small government in principle could not justify the practice of running a big government on low taxes, nor balance its books without piling up debt.

Americans remain deeply divided over what to think about the good of government and what to do about these matters, particularly when it comes to voting and paying taxes or wages, however united we stand on the power of prayer and the value of volunteer work. Both mainline-church supporters and critics of faith-based initiatives were left at last to face up to the challenge Jim Wallis defined in his initial diagnosis of the real danger posed to public faith by government backing for religious delivery of social services: "Those in power often prefer the service programs of religious groups to their prophetic voice for social justice," he noted. "But in the biblical tradition of prophets like Isaiah, the religious community is called to speak truth to power." To answer the question of how religious groups can safeguard their prophetic voice as they partner with government, Wallis quoted President Bush quoting Martin Luther King, Jr., who said, "The church must be reminded that it is not the master or the servant of the state, but rather the conscience of the state."[67] In practice, added Wallis, that means evaluating all of an administration's policies, not just those it puts forth for charitable care of the poor. "Will people of faith challenge excessive tax cuts and budget priorities that benefit the wealthy and deprive us of resources to fight poverty?" asked Wallis. "Will we insist on health care for the 10 million children with no coverage? Will we advocate for poor working families who need livable incomes and affordable housing?"

During the administration of George W. Bush, mainline-church leaders in Washington were asking their members these questions, and asking themselves how they could put into effective prophetic action their prayerfully affirmative answers to such questions. They were also asking themselves, not for the first time, how and why the mainline churches had reached this demanding juncture in American public life over the past few decades of persistent efforts and spotty results in their struggle to bring peace, fight poverty, and spread social justice in America. In the chapters that follow, we will pursue this inquiry.

CHAPTER TWO

Civic Republic and Liberal Democracy

Religion in an Ambiguous Polity

What is the place of religion in a free, self-governing society such as ours? Different answers to this question emerged in the previous chapter. Mainline Protestant ideals of the public church lift up its voice as a prophetic witness and conscientious advocate in the moral argument of public life, seeking to guide law and policy to serve justice and fulfill the common good. The religious rhetoric of President George W. Bush, by contrast, calls faithful individuals to volunteer as Good Samaritans and social entrepreneurs to help their neighbors face-to-face and so help change America, one heart and one soul at a time.[1] What stymies univocal efforts to answer this question in the United States today is not simply the conflicting play of political interests and ideologies. It is an argument between contrary ideals of faith in public and the good of government, as the preceding chapter shows. This contest of moral meaning and practice unfolds within the peculiar yet essential ambiguity of the American polity, both as a cultural constellation of shared meanings and a social order of institutionally structured relationships and practical activities. This ambiguity in turn frames the contest's bifocal flow and logic of argument. Given this premise, we can begin to grasp, if not resolve, the paradox of religion's situation in our public life and its constitutional expression.

Civic Freedom, Liberal Freedom

Freedom of religion means more than one thing in America, since it is construed within the context of more than one moral tradition in our culture. This becomes clear if we distinguish the meaning of freedom within the context of the biblical and republican moral traditions in our culture from its meaning in the traditions of utilitarian and expressive individualism.[2] In short, freedom in the biblical sense means freedom from sin, especially the selfish bias of "original sin," which delimits love to one's own kind, whether kin, class, race, or nation. It means freedom to do God's will and love all of God's children, accepting responsibility for them and to them. I am my brother's keeper, and my sister's, and they are mine. True moral freedom to do "that only which is good, just and honest," in John Winthrop's words, is defined by reference to a biblical covenant between humankind and God.[3] It consists of reciprocal duties and constitutive virtues based on divine command, first of all, to love God, and then to love one's neighbor as oneself. It is a covenant, too, to seek God. To this end, it makes of life a pilgrimage—not a free pass to go wherever one wishes, but a venturing forth guided by God, a journey like that of the people of Israel to the Promised Land.

Freedom in the classical republican sense, as conveyed by Plato's myth of the cave, for example, means freedom from ignorance and the biased understanding that chains each person in solitary shadows. The truth shall make persons free to live together in accord with the lawful moral order that informs nature and imbues human wisdom. Thus the "Laws of Nature and of Nature's God" entitle a people to be independent, Jefferson writes in the opening paragraphs of the Declaration of Independence, and all persons "are endowed by their Creator with certain inalienable rights." So freedom of religion, speech, and opinion, conceived as elements of the natural rights of humankind, aim at ensuring that true believers, including Bible believers, cannot impose their views on others through arbitrary state action and censorship and thereby foreclose the enlightening moral argument of public life.[4] The practical realization of freedom and its essential defense lie in an educated society of political equals responsibly taking part in this argument at the center of republican self-government.

In its utilitarian sense, by contrast, freedom means the individual's freedom from restraint exerted by another individual's will or by undemocratic social authority or hierarchy. Individual rights and due process of law reflect the nature of essentially self-defining, self-interested individuals and their social equality, rather than the dictates of Nature's God or God's covenant. Expressive freedom is, similarly, the individual's freedom to express oneself against the constraints of social conventions and others' expectations. It is the freedom to feel strongly and deeply, to be here now, in touch with the moment and open to all kinds of experience and people, and to explore the social and cosmic identities that make the self the very source of all existence.

These distinctive forms of traditional cultural construal accord with what we might simply term "civic freedom" in the positive sense of our freedom as a people to govern ourselves together, and "liberal freedom" in the negative sense of our freedom as individuals from others' interference.[5] Note how this distinction underlies a bifocal construal of religious freedom as the Constitution defines it. The First Amendment states, "Congress shall make no law respecting an establishment of religion, or prohibiting the free exercise thereof." The amendment's first clause prohibits a religious establishment or state church. The second clause protects the free exercise of religion. Seen from the traditional standpoint of civic freedom as defining the Constitution's final ends, the free exercise of religion is the controlling idea, which non-establishment serves. The establishment of any particular confessional religion or church is prohibited because it would infringe on the free exercise and positive institutionalization of religion generally in what was already a confessionally diverse nation two centuries ago.

Such infringement would not simply coerce some citizens to support a confession not their own.[6] It would exclude these citizens from full political membership and public participation on the basis of religious differences. Further, the act of disestablishing and deconfessionalizing religion in public does not simply serve to protect churches from state interference, and the state from wars of religion. It enables all citizens to conceive the common purposes of their lives together in relation to God's purposes and nature's laws, in the terms of the Declaration of Independence. In this universal light, it allows them to judge these common purposes, argue over them coherently, and live them out more or less persuasively. Thus religion lies at the moral center of public life, even as the institutional bodies of church and state remain distinct, each governed by its own members.

If the free exercise of religion is conceived primarily in terms of "liberal freedom," by contrast, the logic of the two clauses is inverted. Disestablishment controls the free exercise of religion and subsumes it into the concept of "the separation of church and state," a phrase without constitutional standing but with great intuitive power in this second cultural context. Religious freedom then commonly comes to be construed as the individual's right to worship any God one pleases or none at all, and religion becomes a private matter of no inherent concern to political society. Disestablishment and deconfessionalization imply privatization, and, by confusion with principles of religious toleration, they justify efforts to bracket religion outside of public life.[7]

These difficulties of constitutional interpretation stem from something more than cultural conflict disembodied from institutions, or confusion between two conceptions of freedom as a cardinal political virtue. They reflect a fundamental American ambiguity: Are we a republic in recognizable relation to classical or Calvinist republics, and dependent for our integrity upon a sense of civic virtue and the mores of republican citizenship? Or are we a liberal constitutional state, governed through the coordination of individuals' conflicting interests and equal rights? The American answer is, in sum, that we have sought to be both—to enjoy civic and liberal freedoms alike, to retain the moral integrity and binding public spirit of a republic in the political structure of a liberal constitutional state, with its stress on voluntarism and personal sovereignty.[8] In so doing, we have lived with profound tensions. Overriding concern for self-interest is the very definition of the corruption of republican virtue, which must check free choice even as it guides free conscience through a sense of mutual responsibility and duty.[9] Yet from the beginning, American society has been a mixture of republican and liberal political ideals and arrangements, not a pure type of either one.

We are both a religiously resonant republic that depends on the participation of public-spirited citizens for its shared self-government, and a liberal constitutional state that pledges to protect the individual rights of self-interested citizens who pursue wealth and knowledge through free markets for economic and intellectual exchange.[10] The liberal tradition of public philosophy in America conceives persons as independent selves, "unencumbered" by moral or civic ties they have not chosen.[11] Freedom consists in the very capacity of such persons to choose their own values and ends. The rival republican tradition conceives freedom as the fruit of sharing in self-government whose public-spirited character is cultivated by these very practices of deliberating together over common goods and sharing responsibility for the destiny of the political community.

Each tradition poses key questions of public life within a distinctive logic of moral argument. How can citizens become capable of self-government? asks the republican, who then seeks the social conditions and political arrangements needed to promote the civic virtue that self-government requires and the liberty it breeds. The liberal first asks how government should treat its citizens, then seeks the principles and procedures of justice needed to treat persons fairly and equally as they pursue their own ends and interests. Fair procedures take priority over particular moral ends posed as public goods. Individual rights function as moral trump cards, played to ensure the state's neutrality among competing conceptions of the good life, in order to respect persons as selves free to choose their own ends.

With this underlying ambiguity in mind, consider the unambiguous context in which philosophical liberalism characteristically sees religious groups, mainly as a divisive problem for modern democratic states, since these groups feature controversial conceptions of the common good, institutional strategies for realizing them, and conflicting ethics for evaluating them, which are all irresolvable in a morally pluralistic society.[12] Can we instead reach rational agreement on moral rules in the form of contractual principles of justice as fairness, principles that can be justified without favoring any one of the conceptions of good that divide Americans? Such justification itself turns out to presuppose a particular conception of the person as prior to, rather than constituted by, her moral commitments, as the legal scholar Michael Perry objects in criticizing the Kantian contractarian ethic of John Rawls.[13] Instead, as Perry concludes, "one's participation in politics and law is and must be based on one's most basic convictions about human good."[14] Such convictions are essential to constitute persons and to ground political deliberation and choice. In fact, such convictions do not only ground our public participation; they arise from it. They are defined and learned in terms of the multiple moral traditions within our culture. They are learned through our practical experience within the multiple spheres of social life to which these moral traditions ring true—our experience in families, schools, and religious communities, for example, as well as politics and law.

Thus democratic politics itself requires the moral commitments and practices of the varied moral communities that together make up our pluralistic culture and link the normative spirit of politics and religion, even as the institutional bodies of church and state remain distinct. Seen as an overlapping consensus, these commitments support rather than subvert democratic politics.[15] But part of the fundamental bias of modern liberal philosophical and sociological theorists of religion and politics—and their communitarian critics—is their common reliance on oversimplified consensus models of culture and community to grasp the nature of moral unity within social diversity.

On the contrary, what holds us together as a polity and a people is not some comprehensive cultural agreement conceived as a value consensus, or as a value-free arrangement of rules and rights to coordinate our disparate interests and ideals across seamless subcultural communities. Rather, we are held together by the coherence of our moral disagreement and argument within an ongoing cultural conversation that embraces multiple moral traditions, languages, and practices in the interrelation of their social settings.[16] Through this process come into being the "semi-covenants," the "conditional absolutes," and the situationally shared and varied "ought-to's," as the historian Martin Marty calls them, which critically rework and balance our social order across institutional spheres.[17] This argument does not go on among a collection of moral communities, each of which is organically fused together around shared values and myths that it socializes into its members. The moral argument of public life goes on within each one of us and among us all, because all of us share a common culture woven of contrasting moral traditions that themselves embody continuities of conflict over how we ought to live together. And all of us lead lives that span the different social institutions and practices through which these traditions ring more or less true to our experience, including a polity that is at once a religiously resonant republic and a liberal constitutional democracy.

Civil Religion and Public Theology

In addition to being a divisive problem in American society, then, religion has also been part of its mediative answer to problems posed by philosophical liberalism itself, in its moral and political tension with our republicanism. Religion mediates this tension by, first, establishing a "superstructural" locus of moral sovereignty above the sovereignty of the state and the people.[18] The Declaration of Independence points to the sovereignty of God over the collective political society itself when it refers in its opening paragraph to "the Laws of Nature and of Nature's God," which stand above the laws of men and women and judge those laws. Notwithstanding the subtle eighteenth-century relation of biblical to natural religion, the self-evident truths that "all men are created equal" and that "they are endowed by their Creator with certain inalienable Rights" reveal a distinctly though not entirely biblical God who creates individual human beings and actively endows them with rights that no government can abrogate or originate by its own legislative act. Nor can it even recognize such rights by its own constitutive social contract unless this contract is also a covenant in accord with the natural and ultimate order of existence.

Solemn public reference to a God who stands above the nation and whose ends are moral standards by which to judge the nation's conduct and justify its existence becomes a permanent feature of American political life ever after. But these religious and civic ideals are only thinly if securely institutionalized within American government, without explicit legal support or sanction in the Constitution or the liberal side of our cultural heritage that it expresses. It follows, argues Robert Bellah, that the religious needs of a genuine republic would hardly be met by the formal and marginal civil religion that has been institutionalized in the American republic: "The religious superstructure of the American republic has been provided only partially by the civil religion. It has been provided mainly by the religious community entirely outside any formal political structures." To refer to this symbolization of the ultimate order that frames the civic virtues and values of a republic, states Bellah, "we can speak of public theology, as Martin Marty has called it, in distinction to civil religion. The civil millennialism of the revolutionary period was such a public theology and we have never lacked one since."[19]

From the beginnings of the American nation, the diversity and range of its public theology have been significant morally as well as analytically, Bellah reflects, since "most of what is good and most of what is bad in our history is rooted in our public theology." Every movement to make America more fully realize its professed values has grown out of some form of public theology, from the abolitionists to the Social Gospel and the early Socialist Party to the civil rights movement under Martin Luther King, Jr., and the farmworkers' movement under César Chávez. But so has every expansionist war and every form of oppression of racial minorities and immigrant groups.[20] The pluralism of peoples that public theology engages in the larger context of American public culture can be distinguished from "the public church" as a specifically Christian polity, people, and witness, according to Marty.[21] In his usage, drawn from Benjamin Franklin on education instead of Jean-Jacques Rousseau on civil religion, such a church is a partial Christian embodiment within a public religion that overarches, rather than displaces, the many particularities of traditional faiths and their continuing contributions to public virtue and the commonweal.[22]

American Christianity counterposes diverse forms of public theology in this account, beginning with the Constantinian ethos of Catholic colonies and the Calvinist covenant of Puritan New England. It includes the anti-theocratic, critical theology of the dissenting Roger Williams; and the transcendent backdrop to civil affairs lit by religious affections in Jonathan Edwards. It embraces the immanence of the holy republic arising from redemption and liberal legislation, as envisioned by Horace Bushnell and revised by the Social Gospel. Varieties of public theology have multiplied in twentieth-century America with the cultural disestablishment of Anglo-Protestantism amid broader recognition of Roman Catholic and Jewish social teaching, exemplified by the Catholic bishops' pastorals on peace in 1983 and on the economy in 1986 and by the development of "Jewish social ethics."[23] The distinctive social witness of the African American churches has emerged nationally. Religious pluralism has grown to take in communities of Muslims, Buddhists, Hindus, and other faiths. Academic communities have nurtured liberationist, feminist, black womanist, ecological, and related theologies among religious leaders and encouraged them to tackle the task of constructing a public theology within wider communities of faith.[24]

From the beginning, public theologies have coexisted with various forms of public philosophy in America, grounded in traditions of civic republicanism, Lockean democracy, natural law, and constitutionalism. These philosophies reach from the Enlightenment faith in "the laws of nature" held by such deist founders as Jefferson and Franklin, through ideals advanced by Walter Lippmann and John Courtney Murray of a *consensus juris* capable of sustaining civil debate over public goods. They extend to current debates over the public sphere, multiculturalism, and the politics of recognition.[25] In Marty's view of their diversity, public theologies enter into a rich repertory of diverse national narratives and rites, conversationally commingled across group boundaries, to "re-story" and restore the bodies politic of the American republic into an "association of associations" through cohesive sentiments and symbols. These sentiments stem less from veneration of the Constitution than from family reunions, civic volunteering, and Labor Day weekend baseball games. Their mutuality of affection owes more to Jonathan Edwards and the Scottish Enlightenment than to the solidary sentiments of Rousseau or Emile Durkheim.

The "infrastructural" role of religion in the American republic likewise combines civil religion and public theology, according to Robert Bellah.[26] While the liberal state is constitutionally incapable of inculcating civic virtue in its independent citizens, federalism permitted the nation to foster schools of republican virtue in the institutions of state and local government, in the public schools, and most of all in religious congregations and denominational bodies. In addition to teaching republican values, religious communities nurtured the mores of their self-governing members through offering them practical lessons in public participation. Because it contributed so centrally to the creation of American citizens and the moral order of the life they shared, Tocqueville concluded that religion should be considered as "the first of their political institutions."[27]

Current research confirms that religious communities continue to provide a cradle for democratic citizenship and civic aptitude, one that is of particular importance for Americans who are otherwise institutionally disadvantaged or excluded.[28] Those most active in religious institutions, notably churchgoing African Americans and lower-middle-class white evangelicals, offer striking exceptions to the rule of class-bound declines in political participation in American society since the 1970s, with greater falloffs found the further down the social ladder one goes. With the sole exception of labor unions, now shrunk to one-third of the share of the U.S. workforce that they held fifty years ago, religious institutions provide the single most democratic counterweight to the cumulative process that favors those with more education, income, occupational clout, and connections when they take part in public life.

Recent studies of public theology within specific religious institutions, such as the National Baptist Convention and its Women's Convention, shift focus from the religious dimension of the public realm in the society as a whole to the public dimension of religious denominations and congregations.[29] Studies of the African American church in particular as a "church with the soul of a nation," in contrast to civil-religious visions of the "nation with the soul of a church," tend to close the distance between civil religion and "church religion" and expand the institutional range of public theology.[30] They also point up the value of theoretical efforts to pluralize the public sphere, understood as a society-wide realm of rational critical communication surrounding the state, in which citizens settle social questions on the merits of reason-giving argument. These efforts yield a picture of multiple publics, sometimes overlapping subsidiaries or concentrically nested circles, but often oppositional alternatives to the public at large, and to larger publics possessed of power to make decisions for the society as a whole. These "counterpublics" hold special significance for those barred by racial caste, class, or gender from full standing in the public at large—or the church at large—and betrayed by ostensibly universal representation of the meaning of such membership.[31]

Public theology, then, has always unfolded as an argument and a con-versation within communities of faith as well as among them, and in their relations to public dialogue in the polity. Compare the Social Gospel and the Gospel of Wealth, for example, or the movements to abolish slavery and alcohol, or outlaw abortion and nuclear arms.[32] Specific social issues and religious traditions describe dimensions of diversity and change in the history of public theology in America, marking shifts in its relationship to political ideology on one side and church religion on the other. So, too, do the institutional forms and settings of public theology, particularly those situated in between communities of faith and the national community.

Public Theology and Political Ideology

Since 1960 there has been an explosion of hundreds of nondenomina-tional religious organizations devoted to governmental and public affairs on the U.S. national scene. This includes the Christian Coalition and Fo-cus on the Family on the "religious right," for example, and the Interfaith Alliance and the Clergy Leadership Network along the religious main-line. The proliferation of these politically oriented "parachurch groups," as they have come to be called, has far outpaced the growth of denomi-national churches themselves.[33] But this proliferation is dwarfed in turn by the concurrent mushrooming of thousands of nonreligious national political associations, from Common Cause to the Heritage Foundation, from MoveOn.org to Progress for America. They stand formally free of political parties. Yet they often couple public-interest advocacy, policy research, and civic education on social issues with political lobbying and ideological advertising. Functioning as "paraparty groups," they have become increasingly involved in direct electoral mobilization, advertis-ing, and organizing, dramatized by the rise of the "527 committees" that raised a record $550 million in soft-money donations from corporations, labor unions, and special interests to back election campaigns in 2004.[34]

The recent rise of such freestanding political associations, religious and nonreligious alike, coincides with state-centered changes in the American polity and responds to them. As social rights and collective goods multi-ply and diversify in the name of justice and progress, government expands its regulatory reach, policies, and spending in efforts to provide more of its citizens better education, health care, public safety, economic oppor-tunity, and the like. Other institutions in turn grow more formally and specifically organized to promote or check government action in accord with the causes that different social groups and cultural communities uphold and the interests they advance. This increased interpenetration with an expanded state through a more crowded polity changes how other institutions work, and how they think and communicate. Not only commerce, defense contracting, and agribusiness but churches, schools, and families grow more legalized and politicized. The polity itself builds up a more nationally integrated yet more contested and multivocal argument about how we ought to live together.[35]

The mainline churches face new challenges in the altered institutional landscape they now inhabit. In this denser, more diversified polity, more political players contest more issues before an expanded state in a national debate among more independent voters, interest groups, and moral constituencies less ordered by party loyalties or platforms. These conditions place an even higher premium on the churches' efforts to act as the Church in enlarging public conscience and casting clearer light on the commonweal. They offer the churches new partners in doing so. But they also increase the dangers, in such ecumenical efforts, of flattening out the confessional and theological integrity of particular churches into the moral Esperanto of legal procedures, "rights talk," and the axiomatic individualism of client-citizens and market actors pursuing their own interests, ideal and material alike.[36] These ways of thinking center on the modern administrative state, and they yoke together the political partisans and ideologies that compete for the state's regulatory favor and welfare benefits.

Historically, the Christian churches have been tugged back and forth between churchly ideals of conciliar dialogue and teaching, on the one hand, and the prophetic action of witness communities on the other. In the United States today, they are also torn between two institutional models of religion in public: the public church and the religious lobby.[37] The first is a model of broad social teaching, focused policy research, and charitable service. It is typically situated in and around the offices of the major denominations and extends to related agencies such as the Church World Service arm of the National Council of Churches and para-denominational organizations such as Bread for the World. The second is a model of grassroots mobilization and political organizing. It is located less often today in broadly based social movements—for example, to defend or oppose abortion rights in the latter-day image of the abolitionist or temperance movements—than in freestanding, membership-based advocacy groups focused on hot-button issues and dependent on direct-mail fund-raising from individual contributors and grants from nonchurch sponsors specifi-cally concerned with these issues.[38] In between these two models, national church leaders actually commingle the practices of social teaching and preaching to the faithful in their pews with advocacy and lobbying di-rected at Congress and the White House. Particularly when government proves unresponsive to their moral advocacy, church leaders weigh the need for mass mobilization, grassroots organizing, and "building a move-ment" within or beyond their denominations.

Compared to major religious denominations, most parachurch organi-zations engaged in public moral advocacy and political lobbying possess notably narrower, more homogeneous social profiles by education, age, occupation, and income and by the partisan political affiliation and issue-specific opinions of their members. Sociological evidence indicates that the members of such politically oriented religious special-purpose groups tend to divide into two contrasting social clusters.[39] Typically older, less educated cultural "conservatives" fill the ranks of groups that fight abor-tion and pornography and champion creationism, school prayer, and fam-ily values. Typically younger, more educated cultural "liberals" belong to groups dedicated to nuclear disarmament, racial and gender equality, environmental protection, and economic justice.

Armed with such evidence, some observers warn against the social-class divisions and "culture wars" they see parachurch groups declaring.[40] Little hard evidence has emerged of more polarized or ideologized social opin-ions among Americans generally, or among religious liberals and conser-vatives in particular, with the significant exception of attitudes on abortion and differences between those who identify strongly with the Republican or Democratic Party.[41] Within religious institutions, however, major de-nominations and some congregations show "caucus-church" signs of grow-ing more politicized, if not polarized, along the lines of identity politics.[42] In media wars waged by direct-mail and e-mail campaigns, fax blitzes, and televised sound bites, religious lobbies turn public theology in the direction of political ideology insofar as they bypass the unifying demands of con-gregational religious practice and teaching, in strategic efforts to manage public opinion, mobilize partisan constituencies, and play interest-group politics with public officials. Political campaigns and parties in turn have grown more adept at turning these parachurch and caucus-church dynam-ics to their own electoral ends.

To balance the view that Americans now face a dangerous dichotomiz-ing of civil religion into "separate and competing moral galax[ies]" or an uncivil war between orthodox and progressive believers with worldviews that are "worlds apart,"[43] it is worth weighing the notion that we are in the midst of a fertile if painful broadening of public theology's contested ambit among a larger, more educated and urbanized middle class. Into this nonetheless coherent argument over how we ought to order our lives together have come culturally conservative Protestants, Catholics, Jews, and religious "others" in sufficient numbers and with sufficient eloquence as well as clout to make their voices heard.

If Americans are willing to keep listening to one another and trying to persuade one another by example and by critical, conciliar dialogue alike, then this broadening of public theology promises to enrich the moral argument of our public life as a whole. In a sense, it has already done so, particularly for those problems—such as abortion, gender and the family, peace and the poor—that have no neat solutions within the one-dimensional moral universe of individual interests, rights, and entitlements crowned by the national interest. For the contrary ideologies of free-market capitalism and welfare-state liberalism at the core of American party politics today are equally mortgaged to individualist axioms that leave citizens blinded to their interdependence and unmoved by their need to share responsibility for the commonweal, which public theologies persist in proclaiming.

Free-market capitalism begins with self-interested individuals whose personal preferences and free choices are best served by markets.[44] Market dynamics in turn are determined by immutable laws of human nature and rationality. This admixture of market determinism with absolute freedom of individual choice excuses the indifference of citizens toward exercising freedom of conscience to make good institutional choices in shaping the social order, since "the market decides," and private charity can take up whatever social slack remains.[45] Welfare liberalism no less paradoxically conceives politics to be the instrument of human desire, aimed at satisfactions that individuals need not share, if indeed they can. It turns on promises to deliver the material prerequisites of these individual satisfactions in the form of social services, benefits, and security to needful persons who qualify as its clients by virtue of their claims to individual rights and entitlements. Insofar as it fails to maximize the happiness of all its client-citizens, the liberal welfare state is always illegitimate. To the extent it succeeds, the liberal state and its interest-group politics both wither away into administrative agencies and their individual beneficiaries, each now free to leave behind the instrumental world of politics for the intrinsically fulfilling privacy of home and business, prayer and play. For welfare liberalism, as Michael Walzer observes, "happiness begins and ends at home."[46]

Public theologies proclaim their distinctive themes of human interdependence and shared responsibility for the commonweal within an ongoing cultural conversation that embraces multiple moral traditions and languages inseparable from the social practices and institutional settings that embody them.[47] So we often disagree, and understand one another when we do. Even as philosophical liberals and their communitarian critics debate the role of religion in forging or fragmenting political consensus, the moral argument of public life continues comprehensibly within each one of us and among us all.[48] In its course, diverse and often contrary public theologies contest the construal of civil-religious ideals, even as these ideals underlie and order the differing moral judgments that public theologies make on specific issues such as slavery or poverty, alcohol or abortion. This kind of reciprocal contesting and justification, syntactical ordering and axiomatic reshaping, sheds light on a living, moving picture of civil religion. It depicts no single template or fixed foundation for the moral order and authority of American society, however fragmented or divided. Instead, it unfolds a "dimension of depth" reaching through the multiple moral traditions and institutional arrangements that at once frame the many-layered, multivocal moral argument of public life and revise the object of this argument in an ongoing evaluation of how Americans govern their lives together.[49]

In this light, it is more apt to ask how civil-religious ideals have shifted shape and reframed the point of both new cultural conflicts and common assumptions in American public life than to ask whether civil religion in some fixed form has survived or indeed ever really existed. Such deeply rooted, dialectically developed ideals of civil religion run through recent efforts to chart epochal transformations in the hopeful ends of "the real American dream," as Andrew Delbanco terms it. This dream extends from divine deliverance in biblical terms in colonial New England through sacralized citizenship in a Union deified by the Enlightenment to the latter-day transcendence of a recreational self set free in the spiritual marketplace of a consumer culture.[50]

The dialectical continuity of civil-religious ideals likewise resounds through the definition of the sovereignty of individual conscience in grounding an equal right to religious freedom as a kind of common denominator spanning republican and Lockean liberal public philosophies, as the sociologist Phillip Hammond proposes, to provide the keystone of a constitutional faith "behind" the Constitution.[51] The philosopher Richard Rorty has recently reworked civil-religious ideals in an exhortation from the political left to re-embrace the participatory political good of "achieving our country," in the pragmatic terms of Deweyan notions of social justice and progress that are explicitly secularized into a this-worldly version of millennial hope.[52] The jurist John Noonan has reappropriated civil-religious ideals in calls to renew the Madisonian "lustre of our country," permeated by a faithful sense of its heritage of religious free exercise as an American invention.[53]

In this moral argument of public life, in sum, we are held together by the coherence of our disagreement, because all of us share a common culture woven of moral traditions that themselves embody continuities of conflict over how we ought to live. And all of us lead lives that span the different social institutions and patterns of practical experience to which moral traditions and public theologies ring true—more or less arguably true—including a polity that is at once a religiously resonant republic and a liberal constitutional democracy.

Inequality and the Good of Government

Americans have always wanted to do better and become better. They have sought to get ahead and make something of themselves by hard work and self-discipline in an open society, and to make their society itself a freer and fairer place. At the same time, the milk of human kindness has nursed Americans fed on freedom, and washed their wounds of anger and loss at the unequal fortunes they find in a land of equal opportunity. In both respects, communities of faith have played a central part in shaping our character as a people and ordering the public institutions we inhabit. Since the 1990s, amid clashing calls to "renew America" and combat our "crisis of values," Americans have continued to look to religious beliefs and institutions for answers to what ails us.[54] What is that? It is a quandary that has taken moral form in our politics of social difference and inequality over the past decade in a now-familiar question: why do those who work hard and play by the rules fail to find the rewards they deserve? This moral quandary amounts to an anthropodicy that spans the broad middle class, the citizens whose votes and interests make up most of our electorate. It also touches the prayers and troubles the consciences of the faithful who fill most of the pews in mainline churches.

With democratic ideals declared triumphant after a half century of the Cold War, Americans in the 1990s found themselves deeply divided over the meaning and prospect of their own democracy in practice. What good is government, they wondered, if it is unable to fix the things that have somehow gone wrong with our society in the experience of many "middle Americans"?[55] They felt the fabric of their lives and communities loosening around them, not only when they thought of health care, decent schooling, or deepening divides of income and opportunity as social problems, but when they worried about the future of their own wages and jobs, their families and children. Many of these doubts and fears arose from threats to the expanding prosperity, social security, and public provision most Americans have enjoyed since World War II. Between 1947 and 1973, the middle class doubled in size and in real household income, as income grew more quickly at the bottom than at the top of society. Since then, income has grown more quickly at the top than at the bottom, and it has sagged in the middle. This has made our prosperity less equally shared than it was a generation ago. It has left our rates of poverty about the same and increased extreme poverty, even though real per capita income grew by two-thirds from 1973 to 2000.[56]

Political events and economic changes have combined since 2001 to create a huge partisan gulf between Americans in their perceptions of the national economy, not just their ideological stands in favor of activist government or free markets. In looking at the same economic landscape over the past five years, observes a 2006 study by the Pew Research Center, Americans see different pictures. "Most Republicans see a rosy picture; Democrats and, increasingly independents, take a darker view of the economy generally, and, particularly, of the economy's most salient signal—jobs."[57] Why so? Partisan political ideologies matter, but so does personal experience, especially the diverging experience of average earners and those in the top tiers of the economy when they look at the labor market and their personal finances.

The U.S. economy grew at a respectable 3.5 percent inflation-adjusted rate in 2005, inflation and interest rates remained moderate, worker productivity rose 16.6 percent from 2000 to 2005, and the official unemployment rate stayed below 5 percent. Yet only a third of Americans judged the economy as good (30 percent) or excellent (4 percent) early in 2006, compared to 71 percent early in 2000. This included two of three Republicans but only one in four Democrats earning over $75,000; and one in two Republicans but only one in six Democrats earning less than $50,000.

Only those in the top tenth of the income pile have drawn extra income from recent productivity growth—gains in the value of hourly output per worker. Indeed, many American workers below the top have been harmed by the cost-cutting, layoffs, and slow hiring used to achieve the explosion of productivity growth in 2001–5, note the Pew analysts by way of explanation, while soaring health-care, energy, and college-tuition costs have cut into middle-income budgets.[58]

Average family income has continued to rise, but mostly as a statistical result of extra income gained at the very top. Just over half of the nation's income went to the top fifth of earners, but inflation outpaced raises for workers even at the ninetieth percentile—those making $80,000 per year— while the top 1 percent of earners received 11.2 percent of all wage income in 2004, up from 8.7 percent ten years earlier and less than 6 percent thirty years earlier. In 2005 the top 1 percent of Americans received 21.3 percent of all "total income"—including business profits, market income, and capital gains as well as wages—up by one-seventh, to an average of $1.1 million each, from 19.8 percent in 2004 and more than double their share in 1980. This marked their largest share since 1928 and almost equaled the income of the bottom 150 million Americans. Total incomes soared by about a fifth from 2004 for the top tenth of 1 percent—to an average 2005 income of $5.6 million, and to $25.7 million for the top one-hundredth of 1 percent—while dropping $172 on average for those in the bottom 90 percent. Politically conservative analysts attributed the widening income gap to quickening technological change and bottlenecks in education. Liberals stressed public policies that allowed cutbacks in fringe benefits to workers and sliced government services such as health care and school spending, in tandem with regressive federal taxes that have taken a constant share of earnings from Americans in the middle over the past four decades while halving the tax bite on those at the top, with tax cuts averaging $150,000 per year for earners making over $1 million annually.[59] Ebbing real wages in a "golden era of profitability" driven by a rising tide of productivity made headlines and heated up midterm election campaigns in 2006.[60] But for a far longer time, mainline-church advocates for social and economic justice have been troubled by what they see as a growing political unwillingness to respond with openhanded, evenhanded care to deeper divisions and hardships in the U.S. economy.

The social progress that spread across the American middle class in the postwar era has slowed and narrowed since the 1970s, with divisive downward effects that have persisted—especially for the less well-educated and well-employed—through the economic growth of the 1990s, the 2001 recession, and its slow, spotty job recovery.[61] Between 1960 and 2003, the proportion of Americans working in managerial, professional, and technical jobs rose from 22 to 34 percent, while those laboring in manufacturing, construction, mining, and other blue-collar jobs that require less education but pay well enough to support a family dropped from 44 to 23 percent. In the last thirty years, workers without a high school diploma suffered an 18.5 percent drop in real wages, while those with a college degree enjoyed a rise of 15.9 percent.[62] Today the average college graduate earns $45,400 per year, while the high school dropout earns an average of $18,900 and the high school graduate earns $25,900.[63] As this earnings gap has widened, it has grown harder to cross than a generation ago, with only half of low-wage families advancing into the middle class in the 1990s and only a quarter of the prime-age working poor emerging from poverty.[64]

The longest period of uninterrupted economic growth in U.S. history began late in 1991, quickened in 1995, and entered into its tenth straight year in mid-2000 before beginning to slip into recession. The value of the goods and services that the nation produced climbed more than 36 percent over the 1990s. Overall, this rate of growth was comparable to those in the 1970s and 1980s, albeit well off the pace of nearly 53 percent set during the 1960s.[65] But economic growth in the 1990s did not benefit people with modest incomes as it did in the 1960s, when median family income rose 40 percent, compared to 3.9 percent from 1990 to 1998.[66] In the 1960s a rising tide did, in fact, lift all boats. Since then, wages and salaries have risen slightly throughout the workforce, but except for the top quintile (20 percent) of earners, they have failed to climb back to levels reached in 1972–73, once adjusted for inflation.[67] "Virtually all of the past decade's economic growth has gone to the upper 5 percent of families," reported the economist Richard Freeman in 1999.[68]

The 2001 recession began by erasing many high-paying jobs and cutting investment returns and assets among the affluent.[69] But it went on to take its heaviest toll on working families of more modest means. By late 2005, employment in U.S. manufacturing had fallen by 17 percent since 2001, as manufacturers shed some three million jobs. Lower-paying service industries accounted for almost all of the 2.2 million new jobs created in 2004 and the 1.3 million added through mid-2005. These increases brought the nation to 133.8 million nonfarm payroll jobs, slightly more than the 132.4 million it had in early 2001, and lowered the official unemployment rate to 5.0 percent. Meanwhile, however, the population climbed by ten million people, sending 1.8 million new workers into the labor force each year and swelling the ranks of the "hidden jobless" to 9.4 million, in addition to the 7.5 million officially unemployed.[70]

Income inequality continued to widen as spotty job recovery and flat hourly wages concentrated on the lower rungs of the economic ladder, among blue-collar manufacturing and service workers, despite faster productivity growth, increased exports, higher corporate earnings and profits, and lower inflation. Median family income fell 5.9 percent from 1999 to 2005, with pay falling further for both rural and urban households—which were already below the national average—than for suburban households. In 2004 the median pay of full-time male workers fell more than 2 percent, and for women it fell 1 percent.[71] In the first three quarters of 2005, median weekly wages earned by African Americans fell by 5 percent, to $523, adjusted for inflation, led by the sharp loss of high-paying, unionized jobs in manufacturing. Median weekly wages for whites as a group dropped less than 1 percent, to $677.[72] The enormous wealth gap between white households and black and Hispanic families opened even wider with the 2001 recession. Nearly one in three African American families and one in four Hispanic families were in debt or had no net assets in 2002, compared with one in nine white families. White households had a median net worth of $88,000, eleven times that of Hispanic households and more than fourteen times that of African American households, although these earned two-thirds as much as white households. In all three cases, moreover, the top one-fifth of households owned more than four-fifths of the wealth.[73]

One in eight Americans lived in poverty in 2005, according to Census Bureau figures, as thirty-seven million earned less than $19,971 for a family of four. This proportion was comparable to that of a generation ago, after poverty rates dropped from more than one in five Americans in 1960 to one in nine between 1993 and 2000. But by 2005, the average person living in poverty had fallen $3,236 below the poverty line, the greatest shortfall ever recorded. Those living in "extreme poverty," earning less than half the amount of the poverty line, had jumped to a record-high 43 percent of all poor people. The poor included more than one in five U.S. Hispanics and nearly one in four African Americans, compared to one in twelve non-Hispanic whites, although whites made up 44 percent of all Americans in poverty.[74] The poor also included one in six children under the age of eighteen, one in five under the age of five, and more than one in three Hispanic children and African American children.[75]

Poverty grew more concentrated among women, children, and people of color between 1980 and 2000. From 1970 on, the population in high-poverty metropolitan neighborhoods—ghettos, barrios, and white slums—nearly doubled to eight million people in the course of middle-class flight, commercial decay, and "New Federalist" cuts in federal contributions to big-city budgets, from 18 percent in 1980 to 6.4 percent in 1990, according to William Julius Wilson.[76] With black ghettos accounting for almost half of all high-poverty areas, and five of six white Americans living in areas with few or no African American neighbors, the divide between increasingly job-rich suburbs and inner cities became in many respects a racial divide. Likewise color-coded was the divide between those in and outside of prison, with almost one in ten African American men aged twenty-five to twenty-nine incarcerated in 2000, compared to one in a hundred of their white counterparts and one in thirty of their Hispanic counterparts. With a tenfold jump since 1980, the total number of Americans in prison hit a record high of two million (one-quarter of them drug violators), equal to some 3 percent of the male workforce and close to Russia's mark as the country with the world's highest rate of imprisonment.[77]

Set against historic highs for home ownership, employment, and income reached by the expanding African American middle class by 2000, these trends draw a picture of two black Americas: one taking advantage of economic growth and bright-collar opportunities in the tightening labor market of the 1990s, and the other still excluded and deprived, notwithstanding gains between 1996 and 2000 in employment, minimum wages, and school enrollment among young black men.[78] This picture of two black Americas divided by education and earnings is especially striking for African American women. Less educated single mothers stayed stuck in poverty, while the numbers of black women earning bachelor's degrees jumped 77 percent from 1977 to 1997 (versus 30 percent for African American men) and 39 percent for master's degrees (versus 8 percent for African American men).[79]

In 2000, women earned an average of 75 cents for every $1 men were paid, up from 60 cents in 1980 and rising to 80 cents in 2004, with the drop in earnings by men due to the loss of high-paying managerial and manufacturing jobs hit hard by the recession. African American women earned an average of 64 cents for every $1 men were paid, and Hispanic women earned 55 cents. Single women headed one-quarter of all families with minor children, and 60 percent of all poor families with children. Children in families headed by a single mother, including six of every ten

African American families, were five times likelier to be poor than children in homes headed by a married couple. More than half of all women with young children were working in 2000, twice as many as in 1980. But poverty in these households rose to 28 percent in 2003, from 26.5 percent in 2002. Families with just one earner slipped toward the bottom of the household-income ladder, as more spouses went to work for longer hours to make ends meet. Single parents with children—women in nine of ten cases—also tended to face the least stable employment, at the lowest hourly wages.[80]

In sum, we are becoming a "two-tiered society," as Robert Reich puts it.[81] In the top tier, well-educated professionals, managers, and technical specialists solve problems in analytical and symbolic terms for a growing global market. They enjoy high access to health care, educational opportunities, and secure retirement income. In the bottom tier, poorly educated men and women without such access provide personal services in retail business, restaurants, hospitals, transportation, custodial and security work, child care, and elderly care. A generation ago, those who finished college earned 23 percent more than those who did not start it. Today, they earn 45 percent more.[82]

As the economy has grown and shifted its structure, inequality has widened. At the dawn of the twenty-first century, the United States has the most unequal distribution of income among all industrialized nations, with the greatest rate of increase in the degree of inequality. The poorer members of American society have been losing ground over the past generation, even as America as a whole and on the average has grown richer than ever, and richer than any other nation in the world, today or in history. Children in the lowest-income quintile of American families, for example, are now poorer than the children in fifteen other advanced countries, while the top quintile of American children are richer than the top quintile in those same countries.[83] The United States spends a much larger share of its economic output on health care than any other industrialized country—15 percent of its gross domestic product versus less than 12 percent for runners-up Switzerland and Germany. Yet the United States leaves one-sixth of its citizens not covered by health insurance, some 46.6 million in 2005. This includes one in nine whites, one in five African Americans, one in three Hispanics, and one in two of those living in poverty and working full-time. The United States ranks last among developed countries in rates of infant mortality and equal access to medical care, in a two-tiered system of "rationing by income classes" created by a peculiarly American exercise in the political economy of sharing, usually debated in terms of market competition versus government regulation.[84]

Growing inequality in earnings and household income is linked to different rates of productivity growth and levels of skill bias driven by changes in technology, immigration, global markets, and increased foreign trade and debt. But it also reflects weakening of the nation's "equalizing institutions," as the economist Frank Levy calls them in referring to "the quality of education, the welfare state, unions, international trade regulations, and the other political structures that blunt the most extreme market outcomes and try to insure that most people benefit from economic growth."[85] In the case of unions, for example, only 12.5 percent of all workers were unionized in 2004—7.9 percent of private-sector workers, down by half since 1983, and 36.4 percent of public-sector employees—compared to 35 percent of the nation's workforce in the 1950s and 20 percent in 1980.[86] Precisely because we cannot legislate rates of productivity growth or levels of skill bias, equalizing institutions are crucially important to the moral balancing of their social consequences.

Economic causes and effects certainly play a complex part in this story of deepening inequality and persistent poverty in the midst of prosperity only a few enjoy, as many work to make the economy grow. But it is nonetheless important to understand it as a moral drama with unsettling civic implications for how we identify and answer questions of what's fair, who deserves what, and who is responsible for making things right at what cost. This is especially true as poverty grows more concentrated by race and gender, and, moreover, as poverty grows more prevalent among those who work hard at wages too low to support their families.[87] A family earning the minimum wage is "literally earning thousands of dollars under the poverty line," noted the director of the nation's largest domestic hunger-relief organization in 2000. "You can get off welfare, work hard, play by the rules and still not be able to feed your family."[88]

Rising inequality and falling or flat incomes for most workers, not just the poor, threaten American ideals and practices of shared citizenship.[89] As our society grows more segregated by income into different towns, modes of transportation, and places of work and play, our social experience diverges further, not only our interests. Both bear on the differing consequences, for the better-off at the top and the worse-off below, of public decisions about taxes, trade, immigration, and social insurance to protect our health, welfare, and retirement. Our common reservoir of intuition and sensibility about the practical meaning of institutions such as schools, job markets, and law enforcement shrinks and shallows. So does our reservoir of trust and shared norms to deal with our differences. Democracy thrives only if it sees to the universal distribution of hope as well as rights, and gives to all its citizens a representative voice as well as a fair slice of the economic pie.[90]

Recent declines in public participation and civic engagement go hand in hand with our diverging fortunes and the shifting vistas of our enlarged or diminished dreams.[91] As taxes on the wealthy have been cut, along with provision for the poor and programs for the pinched middle class, those losing ground have disproportionately withdrawn from political participation, while those gaining ground at the top have also gained political influence and voice through their increased participation in single-issue politics and advocacy as well as their increased campaign contributions.[92] As government continues to pull back from entitlement programs such as subsidized housing for the working poor and aid to families with dependent children, the private nonprofit sector has been left to pick up the slack. "It's not that we're not a compassionate nation," notes Betty Breene, president of the United Way of America. "It's that we like to believe everyone is like us and lives in the same milieu." In these circumstances, adds Fred Grandy, president of Goodwill Industries International, "you'd think the only people we have to serve in this country are the middle class, with all this talk about tax credits or whatever. There's an attitude that given full employment and a strong economy in most sectors, we've solved the problem of the have-nots. We haven't."[93]

Prolonged declines in earning for most Americans and rising inequality in the midst of sustained job growth and economic expansion are unprecedented in U.S. economic history.[94] What can and should be done about it? The Clinton administration increased the earned income tax credit, proposed national health insurance, and increased job programs, all to little avail. The 1996 welfare reform joined with decades of rising immigration to help put downward pressure on wages among the working poor by increasing the market supply of less skilled workers. Raising the minimum wage in 1996 from $4.25 to $5.15 an hour aided workers at the very bottom of the wage scale, with little apparent loss of employment. But this minimum hourly wage remained well below a living wage and offered scant support to declining living standards among the lower middle class. Eroded by inflation, $5.15 per hour was worth only 33 percent of the average American wage in 2003, its lowest level since 1949, leaving a full-time worker more than $4,000 short of the poverty line for a family of three and more than $1,000 short for a family of two.[95]

Further cuts in income taxes could help wage earners in working families below the median income, but only if the cuts were properly targeted and deep enough to make a difference. Increased capital investment, sustained economic expansion, and job growth are valuable, but inadequate by themselves to shape a long-term solution to the problems many Americans face of declining incomes and rising inequality even in the midst of job growth and economic expansion, as the late 1990s made clear. Despite that boom, we have not solved the underlying challenge of generating jobs or increasing productivity to yield an adequate living wage for less skilled workers. Americans are working longer hours than western Europeans and the Japanese, but with no better results in terms of wages rising along with hourly output per person. Supply-and-demand market forces have likewise generated no solution to these problems. The American labor force has increased its schooling and improved its job skills over the past two decades. The real starting pay of college graduates has dipped over the past few years, but the long-term increase in real wages for college graduates has not narrowed income inequality to pre-1980 levels, as Richard Freeman notes, and the lower supply of "baby bust" workers on the job market has not yielded them higher wages.[96]

To address these problems, policy analysts have placed on the table numerous strategies of economic and social reform.[97] These include (1) increased public investment in children in the form of universal child care and health care, paid family leave for working parents, and income support when needed, to ensure more "starting gate" equality for children; (2) asset and income transfers, featuring greater earned income tax credits and reversal of recent declines in taxes paid by corporations and wealthy investors, in order to support public education, for example; (3) public provision to all citizens of social benefits—for example, universal health care and retirement benefits—as a "social wage" subject to steeply progressive taxation; (4) more effective measures against discrimination in the labor market by gender, race, and ethnicity; (5) strengthening and expanding unions as citizen organizations committed to improving the state of low-wage workers in particular; and (6) rebuilding the material and social infrastructure of central cities, to provide the basis for thriving urban businesses that can help provide the social wage all citizens merit.

If there is today no lack of policy ideas to debate and test, notably lacking is the political will to try them out and weigh the consequences.[98] More deeply, there is a softness of moral conviction about the need to wrestle with these challenges, and a wariness of moral commitment in meeting them if it turns out to require changing the arrangement of our institutions and the way we lead our own lives. As the baby-boom generation reaches retirement over the next twenty years, for example, the bigger burden on Medicare and Social Security promises to press harder on public decisions over taxes and social spending earmarked for the poor. As the realities of the business cycle, deeper deficits for foreign trade and borrowing, and rising costs for energy and housing intersect with hopes for a resurging "new economy" boom, better-off Americans may be compelled to look again at the welfare benefits, public housing, and food stamp programs cut back over the past three decades. We may have to think again about public provision in light of keener competition for survival in the low-wage labor market between the working poor and the jobless poor among the millions obliged to leave welfare for work.[99]

Partisan polarization over "tax-and-spend big government" versus "free-market prosperity" peaked in the mid-1990s. It stretched from the Republican Revolution of the 1994 midterm elections and the government shutdowns of 1995 through President Clinton's reelection in 1996 to the political drama of a centrist standoff at the polls in 1998, a president outlasting impeachment, and a House Speaker resigning from office.[100] The Balanced Budget Act of 1997 and booming economic growth in 1996–2000 combined to curb popular concern and policy debates over shoring up budget deficits and turn them instead to questions of how best to spend budget surpluses. In dueling over the details of central social-welfare and economic issues—later displaced by 9/11 and its aftermath in the war on terror and the war in Iraq—the Republican and Democratic presidential campaigns in 2000 highlighted a convergent "rush to the center." So did their mutually borrowed and blurred versions of centrist rhetoric attuned to the moderate, middle-class majority of the electorate. These were mostly middle-income white suburbanites, and they wanted Social Security, Medicare, and targeted programs to help their families thrive in the new economy without added spending that would yield bigger government or higher taxes. Muted were Republican calls to shrink the size and power of big government by cutting off its revenues, much as New Democrats had earlier forsworn tax-and-spend profligacy in favor of deficit reduction and welfare reform.

In his acceptance speech to the 2000 Republican National Convention, for example, George W. Bush pledged to support programs such as Head

Start and pay for prescription drugs under Medicare. At the same time, he reaffirmed Republican orthodoxy in promising to cut income taxes, abolish inheritance taxes, increase defense funding, and promote free-market solutions to remake Social Security and expand private health-insurance coverage.[101] Democratic presidential candidate Al Gore, conversely, appealed to moderate swing voters with vows to sustain budget surpluses and low interest rates with policies of fiscal responsibility, while he made more-populist promises to Democratic liberals and the economically excluded. He promised to make sure that "our prosperity enriches not just the few but all working families" by fighting for them with targeted tax cuts of $500 billion over the next decade, instead of $1.3 trillion in deeper cuts to advantage the affluent. He offered more funds for public schools and Social Security instead of private-school vouchers and personal investment accounts. He vowed to extend Medicaid to more of the working poor instead of providing tax breaks to help them buy private health insurance. Many voters marked differences along party lines on such issues, as well as abortion, gun control, and the environment. But they credited neither the Democratic White House nor the Republican Congress for the economic growth of the 1990s, which seemed driven more by technological progress, globalization, and economic forces beyond political control.[102]

Religious Faith and Moral Argument in Public

In an era of continuing prosperity, deepening inequality, and persisting poverty, two aspects of our religious life have come to the fore. Most obvious is the spirit of charity, compassion, and neighbor-love with which communities of faith have responded to care for the neediest, particularly where public aid has ebbed. Many mainline churches have multiplied their effort by four to six times what it was two decades ago, relying on public sources for some 30 percent of their funding yet contributing plenty of money, time, and helping hands of their own.[103] Less obvious but no less profound in its religious dimensions is the peculiar moral spirit Americans bring to the struggle to understand why some prosper and others suffer social and economic trials, and how we ought to face up to the problems both real-life dramas pose. For all of our supposed value conflicts and social differences, Americans have been remarkably alike in holding themselves individually responsible for their worldly success or misfortune.

More than 70 percent of Americans believe that people can get out of
poverty on their own, while 60 percent of Europeans think the poor are
trapped there, although the poor are equally mobile in both places. Most
Americans think those who remain poor deserve to be poor, since they
are too weak-willed or just too lazy to pull themselves out of poverty,
while most Europeans believe luck explains why people are rich.[104]

Other industrialized nations have undergone much the same sort of
global economic jolts as the United States at the end of the twentieth century, but none of them show comparable gaps between the best-off and
worst-off. Though many of them accept more joblessness and slower economic growth than we do, they also pay higher taxes and tolerate far less
poverty, neither stigmatizing the jobless nor excluding them from other
forms of social participation. Indeed, European governments define poverty in terms of income inequality and seek to eliminate it by decreasing
such inequality. The United States defines a "poverty line" in terms of the
cost of a good diet adjusted against the consumer price index and seeks to
end poverty by raising people above this line.[105]

When faced with worldly failure, why do Americans commonly find so
much fault with themselves and so little with the world? The distinctive
cultural values that lead us to do so have roots in "ascetic Protestantism"
and in secular strains of individualism that are formative in our history and
still influential in our shared self-understanding. We value independence,
self- reliance, and autonomy as intrinsic virtues, not merely as means to
win success or invite romance in a competitive society. We commonly
think of society as a free association of individuals who account for themselves and look after their own interests, thereby advancing the prosperity
of all in a fair and thriving marketplace, while in private life enjoying a
circle of freely chosen friends and family.

At once utilitarian and self-expressive, these convictions yield a kind
of "first moral language," in which Americans tend to think about their
lives in ways that can inspire great individual effort and achievement yet
leave us blind to our essential interdependence and unmoved by our need
to share responsibility for the commonweal.[106] In the name of defending individual liberty against arbitrary state authority, these convictions
also anchor the restricted jurisdiction and decentralized arrangement of
American political institutions—city, county, state, and federal. This arrangement makes it difficult to reduce poverty by sharing wealth across a
diverse society, especially across racial lines linked to residential segregation by economic class.[107]

By contrast, the chief social role of America's Jewish and Christian communities can be seen in this light as embodying biblical visions of life in their everyday practices and relationships as well as voicing them in public.[108] Contrary to models of social exchange and contract embodied by the market and the welfare state, religious congregations characteristically call for forms of covenantal fellowship and self-giving communion, comparable to the political friendship and mutual recognition among citizens that a classical republic extols. Especially in times of social crisis and renewal, religious communities in America have joined biblical and civic ideals in distinctive fashion to stress the common moral aims and responsibilities of our lives together as citizens. Yet these efforts fix no civil-religious consensus in cultural concrete. They draw no moral blueprint for public discourse. Instead, they inform the moral argument of public life that many voices unfold within and across traditions, understood as continuities of conflict over how we ought to live.

Thus this argument includes religious voices raised to give traditionally strong reasons to hedge against public participation in the larger society. God helps those who help themselves, after all, and God saves souls from a sinful world. Involvement in the body politic pales before the ideal body of a church whose members will care for one another in separated-out communities of the saved. Similarly, antifederalist strands of our republicanism, like Jefferson's "small republic" of yeoman farmers, inspire aversion to a society centered around big cities, big business, and big government alike. So it is that we can learn much but not everything we need to know about conflicting religious visions of a good society by conceiving them as ideological calls to arms in culture wars waged by Weberian class-carriers on opposing sides, or as dysfunctional divisions in a civil-religious consensus that threaten to break the Durkheimian template of social authority. We need a more layered, multivocal account of cultural pluralism, and a more dialectical, interactive analysis of moral disagreement in public. Only in this way can we explore alternative lines of interpretation to the strategically streamlined path of legitimation used to survey the familiar functionalist relationship of religion to political authority.

Increasingly diverse communities of faith have found their voices in a more democratized argument of public life within a more densely organized, decentered, and contested polity populated by a more sizable, educated, and religiously representative middle class. In the coherence of its conflicts, this cultural conversation bears the singular imprint of state-centered changes in our polity. The state has extended more rights to its citizens generally, and increasingly diversified social rights to more differentiated status-occupants, for example, women, children, homeowners, minorities, professionals, and the elderly.[109] Expanded rights more powerfully require reciprocal responsibilities and obligations to respect them. An enlarged, diversified demand for public moral justification finds expression in expanding claims to rights and entitlements, and counterclaims against them. It echoes in calls for broader civic membership and participation. But it also helps make public participation more competitive and unequal, pushing the less resourceful and advantaged to the edge of the polity. It spurs broader recognition of the public consequences of apparently private actions and decisions. But it also creates more occasions for disappointment at public failure to remedy the harm of these consequences.

The effective meaning of all claims to human rights rests, however implicitly, on deeper ideals of human nature and a good society that ground justice in telic visions of the dignity and goodness of persons and the social relations that bind them. In America, these ideals are inextricably rooted in the moral syntax of religious and civic traditions that mainline churches have long cultivated. So the modern state's expansion and diversification of rights have made greater demands on the polity for moral coherence in its efforts to argue out the public good and realize it in policy. Yet these same processes of expansion and diversification have posed sharper difficulties for defining the public good by simple reference to congruent interest calculation among similarly aligned social classes or broad moral consensus among similarly situated subcultural communities. New forms of religion in public have arisen and clashed in response to these state-centered changes.

Tensions between public-church and religious-lobby models of religion in public have gained force from the confluence between changing patterns of religious and political participation in recent decades. Lower and less solid participation in mainline churches since the 1960s, notably by educated young adults, has weakened the web of denominational loyalties and confessional commitments in mainline Protestantism in the last generation.[110] Meanwhile, more educated and elite Americans have led the way in withdrawing from the kinds of civic associations and political organizations that have long built bridges between more and less privileged citizens, and between national leaders and local groups. They have moved away from face-to-face membership in veterans' and fraternal groups, community clubs and women's associations, charitable and reform societies such as the PTA (Parent-Teacher Association), Elks, and American Legion. They have moved toward mailing-list membership in single-issue political associations and advocacy groups such as the AARP (American Association of Retired Persons) and ACLU (American Civil Liberties Union), and participation in socially narrowed professional guilds and special-interest groups.

Broader voluntary associations have flourished in tandem with electoral democracy and pervasive domestic activity by the federal government in American history, the sociologist Theda Skocpol argues, by uniting citizens for shared public purposes across local communities, states, and the nation as a whole. The chief problem in our civic life today, she judges, is "the weakening of such encompassing national associations and a breakdown of two-way relationships between leaders and actual groups of citizens."[111] This "missing middle" is conspicuous in its absence from the recent rise of national advocacy groups devoted to single issues and narrow constituencies, along with the proliferation of headquarters for professional guilds and trade associations, think tanks, and lobbies in the expanding "imperial capital" of Washington, D.C. Sharp, class-bound declines in almost every form of civic voluntarism show up in the broad surveys and interviews analyzed by Sidney Verba and his colleagues in *Voice and Equality*. Meaningful democratic participation, they conclude, requires that the voices of citizens in politics be "clear, loud, and equal: clear so that public officials know what citizens want and need, loud so that officials have an incentive to pay attention to what they hear; and equal so that the democratic ideal of equal responsiveness to the preferences and interests of all is not violated." Their analysis of voluntary activity in American politics suggests that "the public's voice is often loud, sometimes clear, but rarely equal."[112]

Although the worldly means and ends of politics cannot come first or last for communities of faith that recognize that "our kingdom is not of this world," religious institutions can and do exert a vital counterinfluence to such skewed declines in public participation and membership in American society. For all their voluntarist fluidity, membership and attendance in the mainline churches have stabilized over the past decade, after declining by about one-sixth from their baby-boom highs in the 1950s.[113] These churches continue to "play an unusual role in the American participatory system," as Verba and his colleagues observe, "by providing opportunities for the development of civic skills to those who would otherwise be resource-poor." American society is exceptional in "how often

Americans go to church—with the result that the mobilizing function often performed elsewhere by unions and labor or social democratic parties is more likely to be performed by religious institutions."[114] Communities of faith nurture democratic citizenship by serving as schools of civic virtue, not only civic skills. This is of particular importance for those who are otherwise left disadvantaged, excluded, or unschooled as citizens.[115]

Religious communities are among the least class-divided communities of moral discourse, reflection, and inspiration in American society. They are almost alone in reminding Americans of the moral implications of the greater inequalities that divide them from two-thirds of humankind around the world. In comparison to the major political parties or the biggest religious lobbies, that holds true for the mainline churches despite the greater individual voluntarism of religious affiliation and despite the increased internal polarization of denominational memberships along class and cultural lines of liberal-versus-conservative opinion drawn by age and education in particular. In contrast to their declining participation in other forms of civic voluntarism, more Americans from the lower-middle and middle-middle classes continue to fill church pews, notably in the large, "moderate" Protestant denominations such as the United Methodist Church and in the Catholic Church. That may make these churches more morally divided or equivocal on some issues, but in the longer run it makes their moral struggles all the more significant for the society as a whole.

Perhaps especially for the mainline churches in an era of recession for labor unions, the political Left, and the civil rights movement, comparative case studies of the churches' efforts to be faithful in their public voice and action can prove valuable if they reveal how the churches' moral visions and institutional arrangements animate the social appeals and political impact of their preaching from public pulpits and their incarnation of the public church. This is what the following four chapters seek to do by exploring the national denominational leadership of the United Methodist Church, especially its General Board of Church and Society, in its conflicted relations with a set of evangelical and neoconservative parachurch organizations—the Good News movement and the Institute on Religion and Democracy—linked to both major political parties and allied with causes that span the American Enterprise Institute and the AFL-CIO.

This politicized "caucus-church" conflict feeds on predictable social and ideological divisions. Yet it also springs from profound ecclesiological differences vital to American Methodism, for example, in its counterpointing of perfectionist piety and evangelistic voluntarism to the progressive concerns of social Christianity for the liberation and flourishing of all God's children across the lines of race, gender, class, and nationality. Within a denser, more diversified polity in response to an expanded state and realigned political parties, this argument over love and justice unfolds in a social landscape all of us inhabit. Whether we are Methodist, Protestant, or Christian, all of us have a real stake in its course and outcome.

PART I

Contesting Church and Society

CHAPTER THREE

United Methodism in Crisis

Prophetic Witness through the Board of Church and Society

On Capitol Hill, set so close to the U.S. Supreme Court that its gleaming white marble sides seem within reach from the windows, stands the United Methodist Building, the last nongovernmental edifice left facing directly onto the Capitol. Dedicated in 1924 by the Board of Temperance, Prohibition, and Public Morals of the Methodist Episcopal Church (North), the building today houses the Washington offices of the United Church of Christ, the Presbyterian Church (USA), the National Council of Churches, and a score of other religious agencies and advocacy groups, earning it the nickname "the God Box." The building's prime tenant and landlord is the United Methodist General Board of Church and Society (GBCS), established there to represent and give voice to "the religious conscience of America," in the words of one of its most influential leaders.[1] From this vantage point, the Methodist Church stands "visibly and symbolically poised on Capitol Hill to call the power-brokers to accountability" and witness to the world as a people of faith called to love, justice, and freedom.[2]

One of four general international program boards of the United Methodist Church, the General Board of Church and Society is officially charged to "relate the gospel of Jesus Christ to the members of the Church and to the persons and structures of the communities and world in which they live. It shall seek to bring the whole of human life, activities, possessions, use of resources, and community and world relationships into conformity with the will of God. It shall show the members of the Church and the society that the reconciliation that God effected through Christ involves personal, social and civic righteousness." To carry out this charge, the board is directed by the United Methodist Church to project plans and programs that challenge its members to work for righteousness through their own local churches, through ecumenical channels, and through society at large. It aims to analyze the issues that confront persons, communities, nations, and the world and to respond to them along "Christian lines of action that assist humankind to move toward a world where peace and justice are achieved."[3]

For decades, however, vigorous critics of the board have protested its public advocacy as politically partisan and radically left-wing and have rebuked its theology as heretical, even apostate. They have campaigned to cut its funding and staff and have petitioned the church's governing General Conference to eliminate the board altogether. Why has this praiseworthy and profound mission of gospel witness and biblical righteousness been so fiercely contested for so long in the United Methodist Church, and within the Board of Church and Society itself? Answers vary, from inside and outside the church alike. They include the view of social observers who see Methodists rehearsing disagreements between cultural conservatives and liberals in the larger society over issues that range from poverty and abortion to Iraq and Palestine. In response to such views, one former GBCS staffer comments, "Why should Methodists be so different from other Americans? We're far and away the largest mainline Protestant denomination, we're more diverse than any of the others, and we're more representative of the whole country. That said, since when has it been easy to love your neighbor as yourself, and agree on how to do that and with whom, when it really counts?"[4]

Indeed, the United Methodist Church, with some 8.3 million members on its rolls, is more than twice the size of any other mainline Protestant denomination—Presbyterian, Lutheran, or United Church of Christ. It makes up the third-largest Christian denomination in the United States, after Roman Catholics and Southern Baptists. Add in some six million self-identified Methodists not enrolled in local churches, and United Methodists make up roughly two-fifths of all mainline Protestants, one-sixth of all white American Protestants, and one-twelfth of all churched Americans.[5]

The membership of the United Methodist Church proves more representative of American society than other mainline churches in its internal divisions as well as in its overall distribution of social traits, religious beliefs, and political views. It numbers comparable pluralities of Republicans and Democrats, for example, in the revealing statistical portrait drawn by John C. Green and James L. Guth.[6] Forty-two percent of all

United Methodist laity are Republicans, and 45 percent are Democrats. This total includes self-identified Methodists who do not belong formally to any congregation, although they were typically raised in the church and occasionally take part in worship services. Such alumni make up six of ten "nominal" Methodists, those least likely to attend worship weekly (only 6 percent of them do), tithe (8 percent), or consider religion "very important" (7 percent). Relatively young, better-educated and well-employed suburbanites, these nominal Methodists are also likelier to be Democrats (53 percent) than Republicans (34 percent). Conversely, Republicans outnumber Democrats (48 to 39 percent) among "traditionalist" Methodists, a second group that Green and Guth distinguish by religious commitment and belief. They are the likeliest to worship weekly (66 percent), tithe (34 percent), belong to a congregation (81 percent), testify to being "born again" (62 percent), and believe in the Bible as the "inerrant" Word of God (100 percent) and in Jesus as "the only way to salvation" (81 percent). In between stand theologically more liberal or "moderate" Methodists by such measures. Their partisan loyalties tilt more modestly toward the Democratic than the Republican Party (47 to 40 percent). They are almost as likely as traditionalists to worship weekly (58 percent), tithe (26 percent), and belong to a congregation (68 percent), though fewer consider religion "very important" (34 percent, compared to 67 percent for traditionalists) or believe in biblical inerrancy (75 percent).[7]

By education, work, and metropolitan residence, moderate Methodists look more like nominal Methodists than like traditionalists, with almost as many (54 to 57 percent) pursuing professional and managerial occupations, compared to only 36 percent of traditionalists. Two-thirds of traditionalists are blue-collar workers and housewives. Seven of ten traditionalists are women, compared to two of three moderates and one of two nominal Methodists. Traditionalists are the most likely to fit the overall profile of United Methodists as "disproportionately older, white, middle- and lower-middle class, female residents of the Midwest and South," as Green and Guth summarize it.[8] Concentrated in the Midwest and middle South and overwhelmingly (94 percent) white European Americans, United Methodists nonetheless make up a "middle-class heartland church."[9] It spans the regions, states, and rural-urban boundaries that typically divide American voters and cultural constituencies, and it reaches across related differences in education, social class, and generation. Methodists straddle the Mason-Dixon Line and its new "red state, blue state" political permutations. They are also remarkable for their rural and small-town roots. Two-thirds of United Methodist churches remain in such social settings, many of them dwindling in size and aging in membership, although nearly two-thirds of the denomination's members now attend relatively large churches in metropolitan suburbs and cities, many of them marked by upward mobility from more modest middle-class origins a generation ago.[10]

Religious divisions among United Methodists run parallel to their social differences, particularly education, but they are not reducible to them. Methodists overall hold "modestly conservative" political views, usually close to those of the country as a whole, report Green and Guth.[11] They stand between other mainline Protestants on one side and evangelicals on the other, with traditionalists leaning to the right and nominal Methodists to the left. Methodists in the pews split almost evenly on abortion and gay rights. Fifty-one percent of all laity are pro-choice and favor gay rights. This includes three of four nominal Methodists on abortion and two of three on gay rights, with six of ten traditionalists opposed on both issues and 47–48 percent of moderates in favor. However, whether moved mainly by warmhearted Wesleyan compassion, Social Gospel concern, or the firsthand experience of less affluent women who make up their majority, more traditionalists (51 percent) favor government aid to minorities than do nominal (45 percent) or moderate (42 percent) Methodists. Sixty-four percent of traditionalists likewise support welfare spending to help the needy, compared to 54 percent of moderates and 42 percent of nominal Methodists. Most traditionalists (54 percent) side with majorities of moderates (58 percent) and nominal Methodists (68 percent) in favor of environmental protection. On these issues, all Methodists side more with other mainline Protestants than with evangelicals. But they stand with all white Protestants in opposing income equalization, and with evangelicals in resisting a greater role for government in health care. Despite the emphasis by Methodist leaders on peacemaking, disarmament, aid to developing nations, and international cooperation through the United Nations, lay Methodists resemble other white Protestants and the country as a whole in backing a "top" U.S. military and a strong foreign policy, though they are more critical than evangelicals of high defense spending (47 to 33 percent) and armed geopolitics to secure oil overseas (48 to 37 percent).[12]

Almost exactly one-third of all lay United Methodists are theological "moderates" and liberals. Traditionalists are slightly greater in number, and nominal Methodists are slightly fewer.[13] This diversity carries over among United Methodist clergy and lay activists, confirm Green and Guth, but here social differences narrow, and religious divisions grow greater and more intense. Forty-four percent of the denomination's twenty-five thousand active clergy are Republicans, and 43 percent are Democrats. But seven of ten traditionalist clergy are Republicans, and only one in six is Democratic. Six of ten moderate clergy are Democrats, and only one in four is a Republican. Methodist laity overall prove two times likelier to identify themselves as "conservative" in their general political outlook than do the clergy, but traditionalist and moderate clergy are divided more dramatically and consistently on almost every issue. On abortion, for example, three of four moderate clergy are pro-choice, but only one in seven traditionalists agree. Four of five moderate clergy support gay rights, but only one in three traditionalists agree. More polarized, politically mobilized, and theologically at odds, Methodist clergy disagree in ways that are more constrained and cumulative across issues than the laity. Methodist pastors generally see themselves as more liberal than the laity in their pews on race issues, first of all, then environmental protection, defense spending, and gay rights. Traditionalist pastors see fewer and smaller such differences. But moderate pastors see themselves as much more liberal than their congregations on gay rights, first of all, then defense spending, affirmative action, the environment, women's rights, free enterprise, and foreign policy issues. Most moderate pastors feel encouragement from denominational leaders toward social witness and political involvement, while most traditionalists report feeling discouragement instead.[14]

Predominantly conventional liberals combine with their quiescent colleagues toward the middle of the spectrum to make up some 45 percent of all United Methodist clergy, while their conservative counterparts make up 37 percent, according to a nuanced typological analysis by James Guth, John Green, and their co-authors.[15] The remaining fifth are politically "hyperactive" pastors at either end of the Methodist clergy spectrum. Two-thirds of them are "New Breed" activists. They typically majored in humanities and social sciences in the most selective colleges, studied liberal and liberationist theologies in university-related divinity schools, and plunged into the political controversies of the 1960s and early 1970s. One-third are "Christian Right" activists, who came of age in the evangelical resurgence and the Reagan Revolution of the 1980s. Upwardly mobile and more educated than their conservative colleagues, they come from less prestigious schools and less affluent, cosmopolitan social backgrounds than do their New Breed elders. "Although theological, ideological, and political measures differentiate these groups, only a few demographic or personal traits make much difference, primarily educational experience," concludes this apt analysis of these six types of United Methodist clergy.[16] The continuity of their contrary theological and political ideals can only be grasped in the drama of the United Methodist Church struggling to live out the Christian gospel in history and embody it in American society. As the historian Martin Marty sums up, "The fissure within Methodism goes back almost to its beginnings: soul-savers vs. world-changers."[17]

Thus the moral challenge of universal neighbor-love and the political pointedness of theological debate in and around the Board of Church and Society prove equally daunting and confusing, explains the board's general secretary, James E. Winkler, because the gospel asks us to live out our love in a culture that sees religion and politics as separate social realms:

> As Christians, we say we love the children, the sick, and the elderly. Our bishops have led a church-wide initiative for eight years focused on both children and poverty, yet church leaders have suggested to me that it would be better if the United Methodist Church refrained from advocating for specific public policies. We should just lift up principles, they say, and leave the details to politicians. I tell you that no politician would ever declare themselves "against children," but they regularly introduce legislation before the U.S. Congress that is neglectful of children at best, and downright injurious to children at worst! We cannot declare we love children and then silently allow our lawmakers to ignore their needs. How is love made manifest if we say we love children but won't see to it that they have housing, safe homes, excellent education, nutritious food, and health care? Our love of children is made manifest in our struggle against tobacco marketing to children, internet gambling, and child pornography.[18]

The church's public advocacy for laws and policies that aid children, and against those that harm them, proves controversial precisely because it is effective at home and around the world, argues Winkler. The same holds true for other issues as well, he vouches. The United Methodist Church helped move U.S. policy to stand against war in the Congo, for example. The board's outspoken opposition to the U.S. invasion of Iraq helped save the lives of many Arab Christians there, in danger of being persecuted as agents of a Western crusade, by enabling Muslims to separate the actions of the U.S. government from the faith of American Christians.

In contrast to Methodists who want their denomination to win disciples for Christ but avoid meddling in politics on Capitol Hill, or who urge their congregation to ring doorbells to evangelize their neighbors but refuse to open the door to the church basement to shelter the homeless, says Winkler, "when Jesus was presented with a coin bearing Caesar's likeness and he proclaimed that what is Caesar's should be rendered to Caesar, his listeners understood. The Romans thought Caesar was a god, but the Jews knew that everything belonged to the one true God, Yahweh." Given God's sovereignty over the whole of creation and human community, Winkler testifies, "those who don't want the Church to interfere with the status quo know that if the ways of Jesus were lived out in our laws, our economics, and our political system, it would turn the world upside down."

The challenge of Christian neighbor-love and the pointedness of theological debate surrounding the Methodist Board of Church and Society are sharpened by the board's organizational ordering and history within a larger institution, community, and tradition of faith. The GBCS is charged to carry out a remarkably broad array of missions of moral and social inquiry, advocacy, education, planning, and programming that extend nationwide from Capitol Hill to local church pews and back again. Members elected to the board are large in number and representative of social and theological differences within the church at large, although Methodists disagree about just how fully and fairly representative the board's membership is. The full-time staff members of the GBCS serve both as an executive agency to implement the board's policies and as a body of legislative aides to serve the board in its role as a legislative committee. They help it deliberate, draft, and offer proposals to the denomination's General Conference every four years, for a final vote by a thousand delegates evenly divided between clergy and laity, and genuinely divided by their theological convictions.

Theology, Polity, and History

Methodist theology and history have grown out of each other, in their coherence and conflicts, from Methodism's very beginning as an eighteenth-century revival movement in the Church of England.[19] It aimed to "reform the nation, particularly the Church, and to spread scriptural holiness over the land," in the words of its founder, John Wesley, an Oxford-educated Anglican clergyman whose heart was "strangely warmed" at a prayer meeting in Aldersgate Street, London, in 1738.[20] Methodism emphasized faith in God's grace, offered to all and equal to every human need. It fostered a morally rigorous ideal of "Christianity in earnest," embodied in practical disciplines of devotional piety, evangelical preaching, and communal discipleship in flexibly organized yet strictly governed "societies" and "classes" led by lay preachers. Methodists gathered weekly to nurture and sustain one another by shared study and prayer, testimony, and admonition.

Devout, diligent, and democratically oriented, Methodism flourished in post-revolutionary America, becoming an independent church in 1784. Fired by frontier revivalism, it surged in size to become the nation's largest denomination, with more than a million members in 1844 and nearly five million in 1890. Methodists continued to stress free will, infant baptism, and informal worship, in contrast to Presbyterians, Baptists, and Episcopalians, respectively. At the same time, over the nineteenth century Methodism led the denominations of English origin (Episcopal, Presbyterian, Congregationalist, and Baptist) in forging a "common-core Protestantism" around revivalism, perfectionist piety, and moral reform. Tied to popular ideals of democratic progress and America's manifest destiny, this Protestant consensus grounded a cultural quasi-establishment of churches that included four of five American Protestants and more than half of all churched Americans by 1890. "Methodism girdles the globe," wrote Jacob Riis, the journalist and social reformer. "It does definitely more than that. It lies close to the heart of mankind."[21]

From the beginning of the twentieth century, a history of social benevolence, coupled with the waning force of Wesleyan doctrinal discipline, made Methodism fertile ground for modernist theologies and a Social Gospel calling for sweeping social reform to bring closer the Kingdom of God. Since the 1960s, many Methodist leaders have grown receptive to liberationist, feminist, and black theologies. More recently, the denomination has experienced a resurgence of evangelical piety and a reaffirmation of concern with Wesleyan thought and classical Reformation theology, in efforts to renew its distinctive doctrinal heritage as "truly catholic, truly evangelical, and truly reformed." Since 1968, restructuring of the denomination's formal organization has required greater inclusiveness of its boards and agencies. It currently calls for a ratio of one-third clergy, one-third laymen, and one-third laywomen in most church bodies, with "racial and ethnic persons" (i.e., nonwhites) making up at least 30 percent of the members.[22] This has yielded representation of racial-ethnic minorities in United Methodist church government at levels much higher than their 6 percent of the denomination's general membership. It has also made for resentment against "special interests," and "special-interest theologies," on the part of some, though not all, of the "silent majority" of white middle-class Methodists.

In its official statement "Our Theological Task" in 1972, the denomination stressed the need for "theological pluralism" and a pluralist church "inclusive" enough to embrace liberationists and feminists along with spirit-filled evangelicals and liberals. This would enable the church to reappraise and apply the gospel in a new age of ecological and nuclear peril that was nonetheless filled with high hopes for justice, peace, dignity, and community, with a full share in the goods and goodness of life for all persons. While the effort to "substitute new creeds for old has a long history of partisanship and schism," wrote Albert Outler and the other authors of the 1972 statement, the catholic spirit of Wesleyan tradition and contemporary ecumenism provides a constructive alternative to confessional strife. Enacted in the mutually dependent interplay of Scripture with tradition, experience, and reason, they promised, responsible theological reflection would chart an inclusive, tolerant middle course between doctrinal dogmatism and indifferentism. Open to local church initiative and attentive to the common heritage of Methodists, such reflection and practical experiment would enable them to join with all Christians in ecumenical encounters across the boundaries of Christian unity and extend interfaith exploration. Thus they will realize the truth that "we are given to one another on this fragile small planet, to work out with God the salvation, health, healing and peace he intends for all his people."[23]

Since 1972, ongoing debates and declarations in United Methodism have sought by turns to reverse, redefine, or anchor this spirit of pluralism in terms of more traditional Wesleyan doctrines, practices, and structures of church polity. Church centrists, meanwhile, seek to embrace evangelical emphases on personal salvation through the spirit of Christ's love for every human being, while heeding the call to social sanctification to make the world a better place and bring it closer to the Kingdom of God. "Conservative evangelicals" represented by the Good News movement affirm the Wesleyan belief that the living core of Christian faith is "revealed in Scripture, illumined by tradition, vivified in personal experience, and confirmed by reason." But they stress the primacy of Scripture in grounding Christian orthodoxy. To underscore this point, they hold up the church's 1988 revision of its official statement "Our Theological Task": "Scripture is primary, revealing the Word of God 'so far as it is necessary for our salvation.' Therefore, our theological task, in both its critical and constructive aspects, focuses on disciplined study of the Bible. . . . In that task Scripture, as the constitutive witness to the wellsprings of our faith, occupies a place of primary authority among these theological resources."[24]

Methodists are a "connectional people," linked together by sharing a common tradition of faith, a constitutional polity, a common mission, and a common ethos that marks their distinctive way of doing things, according to the *Book of Discipline*.[25] The local churches of United Methodism, along with its boards and other agencies, are officially regarded as part of a single whole, long known as "the connection." Its ministers are bound by the same ordination vows across the connection. When persons join a United Methodist congregation, they are also becoming members of the connection. The property of every local church is held in trust for the connection. The basic unit in the connectional system is the *charge conference*, composed of church-council members of one or more local churches under the charge of a single pastor. Each charge conference sends its ministers and selected lay representatives to one of sixty-two diocese-sized annual conferences, seen as the fundamental bodies of the church, presided over by a bishop, and defined as the locus of membership of Methodist clergy. Annual conferences in turn select voting delegates to a quadrennial General Conference to legislate for the entire church.[26]

United Methodism separates authority over the church as a whole into three branches and bodies. It invests the General Conference with "full legislative power over all matters distinctively connectional." At the same time, United Methodism charges the Council of Bishops with "general oversight and promotion of the temporal and spiritual interests of the entire Church," as set forth in the *Book of Discipline*.[27] It authorizes a Judicial Council of non-episcopal clergy and laity to "determine the constitutionality of any act of the General Conference," upon appeal of one-fifth of the members of General Conference or a majority of the Council of Bishops, and to review all decisions of church law made by bishops in presiding over their respective annual conferences.[28] "The church created a system that in some ways parallels that of the U.S. government when it came to America," explains United Methodism 101, an online introduction to the church. "The church has a General Conference, its legislative branch; a Council of Bishops, somewhat like an executive branch; and a nine member Judicial Council, the judicial branch."[29]

But the church diverges from this model by establishing no chief executive comparable to the U.S. presidency. It features no continuing system of courts leading up to a supreme court. It elects no legislative congress based on proportional representation of the church as a whole. Half clergy and half lay, delegates to General Conference equally represent twenty-five thousand active clergy and more than eight million laity. United Methodism authorizes no executive agency to act when General Conference—lasting only eleven days every four years—is not in session, or to carry out initiatives or programs that General Conference has not authorized and charged to such agencies. "Deliberately, The United Methodist Church has no single central office, no archbishop, no pope," notes United Methodism 101, by counter-Catholic and Anglican reference to the priesthood of all believers and the democracy of all citizens. "This reflects the representative nature of the church's organization—which also provides a system of checks and balances."[30] It also provides moral ideals and institutional space to argue contrary views and organize counter-caucuses, within and beyond the General Conference, on the lawful authority and representative integrity of national denominational bodies such as the Board of Church and Society in relation to United Methodism's bishops, conferences, and local congregations. This argument reflects the several branches of United Methodist polity and their balance of powers. But it also enacts the ongoing struggle of United Methodists to realize the difficult yet essential truth that "this is a covenant community, not a democratic government," as Methodist scholar Thomas Frank puts it.[31]

"Multi-leveled, global in scope and local in thrust," connectionalism is an essential feature of Methodist tradition, practice, and identity.[32] Yet division has helped shape American Methodism from its very beginning, in fact, as a reform movement within the Church of England that eventually separated from it, then from Anglicans in North America, and from British Wesleyanism. Internal differences among Methodists also go back to the beginning and stretch through the nineteenth century, as the historian Russell Richey makes clear.[33] The creation of African American "Methodist Episcopal" churches in protest against racial subordination in the church left American Methodism divided along racial lines. Methodists split between North and South in 1844, etching regional fault lines over slavery that reverberate today through such issues as abortion and homosexuality. From the 1860s on, the fervent piety of the holiness movement fueled schismatic splits along social-class lines, parting a people once brought together by enterprising circuit riders and disciplined in class meetings. It separated out "primitive" Methodists loyal to spirit-filled camp meetings, shouting preachers, and anxious benches in side-street preaching houses from those more at home in genteel Sunday services and Sunday schools in uptown Gothic cathedrals. Here, more educated,

stationed clergy took over pastoral roles once stirred up by class leaders
and lay preachers and settled them down within an increasingly nationalized, centralized church structure of corporate boards and agencies, authorized in 1872.[34]

Like the Pentecostal movement to follow, holiness associations and
conventions gradually took form as separate denominations, such as the
Holiness Church and the Church of the Nazarene. This left Methodism
freer to consolidate its historic connectionalism into the forms of a national denomination. Freestanding voluntary societies for missionaries,
tracts, and the like became accountable to the General Conference of
the Methodist Church in the North and South alike in the 1870s, when
the conferences began to elect the officers of these societies. The union
of northern and southern Methodism in 1939 to create a more national
church further consolidated national boards into stronger bureaucracies empowered to select their own professional staff. Ironically, argues
Richey, it also unraveled much of the church's surrounding connectional
fabric by draining authority and elective power into jurisdictional conferences, making Methodist bishops regional instead of general superintendents, bloating General Conference, and regionalizing seminaries and
teaching agencies.[35]

From the Methodist restructuring of 1939, then, instead of the 1968 reforms, stem many of the protests against unrepresentative denominational
bureaucracies that critics of the General Board of Church and Society
have voiced over the past generation as part of a larger cultural quest for
new forms of decentralized community, cooperation, and congregational
self-governance. From the gradual development, over a century, of more
urban, middle-class "main street church" congregations on a more Calvinist model likewise stem controversies between the settled realities of
congregational life in local churches that hark back to Anglican parishes,
however paradoxically, and the dynamic ideals of an evangelical revival
movement dedicated to reforming church and nation alike in the spirit of
scriptural holiness.[36]

Social Principles and Practice

Set within this layered landscape of conditions for contesting the nature
and role of the Christian church in society, the moral coherence and theological integrity of key conflicts within United Methodism shine through

the institutional order and history of its Board of Church and Society. The board's primary practical responsibility is to implement the United Methodist Church's broad Social Principles and specific policy statements on social concerns. These principles are set out in twenty pages of the *Book of Discipline*, and the policy positions are detailed in the seven-hundred-plus pages of the current *Book of Resolutions*. Both are legislated by the church's quadrennial General Conference by votes of its thousand clergy and lay delegates. So the Board of Church and Society, states the *Book of Discipline*, is to provide "forthright witness and action on issues of human well-being, justice, peace, and the integrity of creation that call Christians to respond as forgiven people for whom Christ died." It is to analyze "long-range social trends and their underlying ethical values," explore "systemic strategies for social change and alternative futures," and "speak its convictions, interpretations, and concerns to the Church and to the world."[37]

Accordingly, the board's representatives and staff testify before Congress on issues such as reforming health care, welfare, and campaign financing. They meet with members of Congress, their staffers, and administration officials, and they write to them to advocate the church's principles and positions. The GBCS long published a bimonthly newsletter, *Christian Social Action*, now folded into an e-newsletter as part of the Web site the board maintains.[38] By e-mail, fax, and mail, the GBCS puts out periodic "legislative alerts" to inform church members on current social issues and pending bills and to urge them to write or call their government representatives. GBCS staff members travel the country to teach and train Methodist clergy and lay leaders in regional conferences and local congregations. Not least important, in the four years between meetings of the General Conference, the GBCS staff spends months researching and revising the draft resolutions and related statements of policy and principle that the board members will spend weeks deliberating before deciding to bring them before the General Conference—some eighty of them in 2000 and seventy in 2004—for legislative passage, to become part of the *Book of Resolutions* and the *Book of Discipline*.

Nowhere in its broad mandate is the GBCS specifically directed to lobby Congress or the administration. Nowhere is it told to mobilize Methodists as voters, political-party members, or contributors to influence legislators directly on given issues. No member of the staff is registered as a lobbyist. Whether its public advocacy and moral witness amount to political lobbying, or where they come close to it, remains a question debated by GBCS board members and staffers themselves, along with the board's allies and critics in the church and beyond. In light of its broad mandate, the board's thirty-plus full-time program and support staff (two dozen of them working on Capitol Hill and the rest at the Church Center for the United Nations in New York City) and its annual budget of some $5 million may seem modest. But they dwarf those of other mainline Protestant denominational offices in Washington, which often have no more than a few staffers and budgets well under half a million dollars. The sixty-three members of the GBCS (reduced from ninety-two in 1996) normally meet twice each year to determine policy and set program directions in six work areas gathered into three ministries: Peace with Justice and Environmental Justice in the Ministry of God's Creation; Human Welfare and Drug and Alcohol issues in the Ministry of God's Human Community; and Congregational Life and Communications in the Ministry of Resourcing Congregational Life.[39]

The General Board of Church and Society incorporates and succeeds by law more than a dozen related boards, departments, and church offices. These include the General Boards of Temperance, World Peace, and Social and Economic Relations, which merged in 1960 to create the GBCS's predecessor, the General Board of Christian Social Concerns.[40] These denominational agencies stretch back a century, to powerful movements for moral rigor and social reform bred by the intersection of revivalist piety and Calvinist activism within the cultural establishment of Anglo-Protestantism. Religious voluntary societies carried strands of this Social Gospel into the burgeoning offices of national denominations, and into Progressive-era social movements, too. These ideals of social justice, equal rights, and a morally healthy community informed American government on its path to the New Deal, and in turn the twentieth-century American state transformed the meaning of these ideals for its citizens today.

Methodism played a signal role in institutionalizing the Social Gospel. In 1908 the Methodist Episcopal Church (North) made the Federation for Social Service an official church agency and adopted as a church its very liberal Social Creed:

> The Methodist Episcopal Church stands—
> For equal rights and complete justice for all men in all stations in life.
> For the principles of conciliation and arbitration in industrial dissensions.
> For the protection of the worker from dangerous machinery, occupational diseases, injuries and mortality.

For the abolition of child labor.

For such regulation of the conditions of labor for women as shall safeguard the physical and moral health of the community.

For the suppression of the "sweating system."

For the gradual and reasonable reduction of the hours of labor to the lowest practical point, with work for all; and for that degree of leisure for all which is the condition of the highest human life.

For a release from employment one day in seven.

For a living wage in every industry.

For the highest wage that each industry can afford, and for the most equitable division of the products of industry that can ultimately be devised.

For the recognition of the Golden Rule and the mind of Christ as the supreme law of society and the sure remedy for all social ills.[41]

At its first meeting the same year, the Federal Council of Churches incorporated this creed into its bold assertion of "the rights and objectives of the laboring man"—including a number of issues not yet on many denominational agendas, as Martin Marty notes.[42]

In 1912 the Federal Council of Churches adopted a revised and even more sweeping Social Creed. It remained the chief ecumenical Protestant statement of social teaching until 1932, when each Protestant denomination took responsibility for revising the creed according to its own tenets and social concerns. Although Methodists did not make the Social Creed an official part of their *Book of Discipline* until 1972, in many respects and through many revisions it still stands as the founding charter of the GBCS and its predecessors. It proclaims the Social Gospel in its criticism of self-interest in American culture and institutions. It offers Christ-like love of neighbor and Golden Rule cooperation to order society, cure its ills, and inspire full justice and equal rights for all, concretely enacted in fair labor practices, living wages, shared wealth, and social reconciliation.

Though chastened by the Christian realism of Reinhold Niebuhr toward the sinfulness of society and its constraining structures of power, the original Social Creed informs the Social Principles that the Board of Church and Society is charged to implement. Elaborated after the 1968 merger of the Methodist Church and the Evangelical United Brethren (EUB) and first written into the United Methodist *Book of Discipline* in 1972, this statement of principles expresses the prophetic spirit of a realist Social Gospel. It frames specific policies, programs, and resolutions of the United Methodist Church under the rubrics of the Natural

World, the Nurturing Community, the Social Community, the Economic Community, the Political Community, and the World Community.[43] These principles are invoked in the prayerful themes of the current version of "Our Social Creed," which the United Methodist Church recommends for frequent use in Sunday worship:

> We believe in God, Creator of the world; and in Jesus Christ, the Redeemer of creation. We believe in the Holy Spirit, through whom we acknowledge God's gifts, and we repent of our sin in misusing these gifts to idolatrous ends.
>
> We affirm the natural world as God's handiwork and dedicate ourselves to its preservation, enhancement, and faithful use by humankind.
>
> We joyfully receive for ourselves and others the blessings of community, sexuality, marriage, and the family.
>
> We commit ourselves to the rights of men, women, children, youth, young adults, the aging, and people with disabilities; to improvement of the quality of life; and to the rights and dignity of racial, ethnic, and religious minorities.
>
> We believe in the right and duty of persons to work for the glory of God and the good of themselves and others and in the protection of their welfare in so doing; in the rights to property as a trust from God, collective bargaining, and responsible consumption; and in the elimination of economic and social distress.
>
> We dedicate ourselves to peace throughout the world, to the rule of justice and law among nations, and to individual freedom for all people of the world.
>
> We believe in the present and final triumph of God's Word in human affairs and gladly accept our commission to manifest the life of the gospel in the world. Amen.[44]

The moral mandate of the GBCS is inseparable from its history as an organization. This is particularly evident in the manifold aims of its present mission, which are rooted in the Boards of Temperance, World Peace, and Social and Economic Relations before they merged in 1960 to form the trunk of the GBCS. The General Board of Temperance dates back to 1888, when the Methodist Episcopal Church formed a permanent committee on temperance and prohibition. It led Methodists to Capitol Hill to pursue legislative action in tandem with programs of education and rehabilitation. Its last head, Caradine R. Hooton, served from 1960 to 1963 as the first general secretary of the merged General Board of Christian Social Concerns. He secured the abiding concern of the GBCS for the family and personal problems of addiction (gambling, pornography, drugs, and alcohol).

"We were moving from three boards into one," recalls Herman Will, who helped lead the board across five decades.[45] "Temperance had been fading as an issue for a long time and branching out into a larger framework of social welfare and health. But temperance was really the issue that sharpened the political teeth of the Methodist Church in this century" and built the Methodist Building on Capitol Hill. The church, says Will, "was very active in the Anti-Saloon League, which endorsed candidates for office—not just parties, but candidates—by whether they voted wet or dry, in a single-issue litmus test, like abortion today." Temperance pioneered the kind of political activism and moral advocacy in Washington that the mainline Protestant churches later brought to issues of war, peace, civil rights, and economic justice. Sometimes they did so to charges of "politicization," Will smiles, from religious conservatives whose current concerns for pro-family values, conscientious character, and hardworking self-discipline hark back to the temperance movement. On the other hand, he notes, apparently liberal pro-labor movements for economic justice among the mainline churches actually stem from "heartfelt Christian concern for the suffering of children and women" working long hours in unsafe conditions for wages too low to live on. Such concern springs from the neighbor-love of evangelical Protestantism in the industrializing cities of late-nineteenth-century America. Its benevolence was tempered by faithful attention to the just laws needed for a good commonwealth in the Reformed tradition, and prodded by Social Christianity on the model of Walter Rauschenbusch.[46]

The General Board of World Peace began in the wake of World War I, waged as a "war to end all wars" that killed millions. The board arose in answer to the call of the 1924 Methodist General Conference for a "great crusade for a war-free world," inspired by the faith that war was not inevitable and that its continuance would bring about "the suicide of civilization." Given this charter, the Board of World Peace staunchly supported the United Nations after World War II as essential to achieving world peace. It criticized belligerent American foreign policy during the Cold War, urged nuclear disarmament, and took up issues of poverty and overpopulation around the world as barriers to peace.

The Board of Social and Economic Relations was launched in 1952 under H. Dudley Ward, to address social and economic problems set out by the Social Creed with a specific mandate to tackle issues of aging, race, faith and war, and church-state relations. When the General Board of Christian Social Concerns began in 1960, Ward continued at the helm of what was now called the Department for Social and Economic Justice, as an assistant secretary. Herman Will, who succeeded Daniel Taylor as head of World Peace, likewise continued to guide that department, quickening the pace of its legislative action and ecumenical cooperation when it moved from Chicago into the Methodist Building on Capitol Hill. "I got a lot of that legislative action from the Quakers, especially their National Council for the Prevention of War," Will recalls. "Lobbying, peace action, mobilizing letters, testifying before Congress. Good work!"

In 1963 Ward became the general secretary of the General Board of Christian Social Concerns, and he remained the head of the GBCS until 1976. Under his confident, outspoken leadership and organizational acumen, the GBCS pressed forward on every front. Ward was particularly concerned with issues of race tied to economic and social justice. Some see the civil rights era as a golden-age high point in the board's history, before it turned to meet the controversial challenge of opposing the Vietnam War and then entered the choppier crosscurrents of cultural politics in the Reagan era amid the rising tide of Methodism's "evangelical renaissance." Upon Ward's retirement, George Outen was elected general secretary, the first African American to hold such a position of leadership in the United Methodist Church. Four years later, Outen died suddenly of a heart attack at the age of 49. He was succeeded in 1980 by Haviland Houston, the first woman to serve as the board's general secretary; and in 1988 by Thom White Wolf Fassett, the first Native American.

Saluted for staying the course of the board during "the most difficult and dark political upheavals and disquieting blows sustained by this very visible Gospel witness," Thom Fassett retired in 2000.[47] His tenure approached that of Dudley Ward in length and impact, and it ushered James Winkler into office in 2001 as general secretary of the board. Through the views and voices of its last two leaders in particular, there emerges a picture of the board over the past two decades remarkable for both the difficulties it has faced and the determination it has shown.

Prophetic Witness and Scriptural Holiness

What is it about the ministry and calling of the Board of Church and Society that makes its mission as disquieting and controversial as it is inspiring and compelling? It serves to deepen the faith of Christians by connecting their personal faith with social action, writes Jim Winkler, the board's general secretary. "Sometimes we Christians think our main task is to be nice all the time and to avoid offending anyone. But disagreement need not be disrespect." The board is not "the paid court prophet of any government." By contrast, "we are speaking God's word in difficult times and the truth can be disquieting." Echoing William Sloane Coffin, Winkler distinguishes between Christian charity and justice: "Had I but one wish for the Christian churches of America, I think it would be that they come to see the difference between charity and justice. Charity is a matter of personal attributes, justice a matter of public policy. Charity seeks to alleviate the effects of injustice, justice seeks to eliminate the causes of it. Charity in no way affects the status quo, while justice leads inevitably to political confrontation." "And that's the sticking point, isn't it?" Winkler concludes. "Political confrontation. That's where most Christians head for the hills."[48]

Through such sticking points and moral predicaments, the United Methodist General Board of Church and Society, its friends and critics alike agree, consistently charted its course through the 1990s by a distinctive vision of the public church. Through the board, declares Rev. Thom White Wolf Fassett, its general secretary over this period, "the church calls the secular powerbrokers to accountability when the decision-making processes threaten the viability of our mother, the earth, or the animal nations or diminish the health and welfare of women, children and men." Through the GBCS, the church speaks out when "actions endanger our continuing existence as human beings in the face of questionable social systems—which do not empower people of all nations and races, which yet enslave women by closing them out of political, economic and social orders, which continue to lengthen the hateful shadows of racism, and which thwart the forces of justice that could bring lasting peace."[49]

Emphatically clear in this view are the explicitly Wesleyan heritage that the church's calling embodies for Methodism, and the sort of politics it rules out: "We are not interested in trying to recover a sentimental, secure or nationalistic past," writes Fassett. "We are, in fact, the historical expression of Wesley's answer to Jesus' challenge to faith and discipleship." As Wesley was called to spread scriptural holiness, "we are compelled to affirm this calling, bonding ourselves together as people of faith demonstrating a visible corporate response to Christ, thereby unleashing unheard-of power to change society as a means of proclaiming the salvation of Jesus," Fassett promises. "We are not called to be politicians of any secular brand. We are called to love, justice and freedom. We are called to be born again—more precisely—to be born from above."

By failing to clarify the power and purpose of scriptural holiness in the social ministry of the United Methodist Church, warns Fassett, its leaders have allowed others to misappropriate the meaning of such holiness and turn it to secular, partisan, and nationalistic ends in a church grown "overweight" and unprepared for prophecy. "Ultimately, at judgment, the questions will not be whether we have balanced our books or organized our communities, placed our own special issue passions at the top of the agenda or more narrowly defined our differences," Fassett concludes. "Instead, the question will be, '. . . have you loved my children—all of them?'"

Posed in terms of loving all of God's children instead of only our own kin, and following Christ instead of playing politics, questions of the church's public vision and conduct mark striking spiritual choices. Yet they also point up difficult institutional predicaments. Fassett develops both in setting out a "starter list" of social issues the Methodist Church must face at the threshold of the twenty-first century.[50] At this point, the future of the United Methodist Church itself lies in the balance, as he sees it. Pressing global and national social issues—"Creation, Violence, Racism, Sexism, the City, Abortion, Alcohol and other Drugs"—come together to compel Christians to examine their conscience and their church's moral integrity. In weighing environmental issues under the rubric of God's Creation, for example, Fassett draws on the Bible and common sense to warn, "If we despoil the organism that gives us life, we die!" Nonetheless, we "keep selling our mother for a few pieces of silver," and too often the churches look the other way. The abuse of alcohol and other drugs is "a scourge upon the face of the earth," insists Fassett. "For openers," he urges, "let's outlaw the most prevalent, easily obtained, legal and widely used drug in The United Methodist Church—alcohol!"

The churches decry the societal, sexual, and media violence surrounding us, Fassett observes, yet they do little directly to fight back against its blinding power to obscure our actual understanding of forgiveness and redemption. "As we look at the current divisiveness in the church," he advises, "we must come to terms with our own institutional violence so we can more effectively ameliorate the world's violence." On issues of protecting the environment, fighting drug addiction, and restricting pornography and media violence, significantly enough, Methodist laity and clergy agree across liberal-conservative divisions. On all these issues, though, clergy press ahead and laity lag behind in taking stronger stands. When it comes to violence among nations, however, both clergy and laity

prove polarized and part ways on cutting defense spending and demilita-
rizing U.S. foreign policy.[51]

Racism and sexism pervade the arrangement of our institutions, including the churches, yet remain largely unseen, Fassett charges. Now coming to light, for example, is environmental racism—the dumping of toxic
wastes near populations and communities made up mainly of racial and
ethnic minorities. Modest gains among women in Congress and in statehouses serve justice, but they should extend to equal representation of
women in every arena of social life, including Methodist pastors, bishops,
and district superintendents. Racial bloodletting in America's inner cities reminds the church of its part in abandoning the city during the white
flight of the previous decades, and the moral necessity of reclaiming the
inner city as "God's place for ministry" if the racial wounds of American
civilization are to be healed. Methodist clergy and laity alike are deeply,
if subtly, divided on racial issues, more obviously polarized on women's
rights, and most explosively split on abortion, with clergy more tightly
clustered into camps than laity on all three matters.[52]

In 1972, less than a year before the Supreme Court decided *Roe v.
Wade*, the Methodist General Conference revised the church's Social
Principles to "support the removal of abortion from the criminal code,"
explaining, "Our belief in the sanctity of unborn human life makes us
reluctant to approve abortion. But we are equally bound to respect the
sacredness of the life and well-being of the mother, for whom devastating damage may result from an unacceptable pregnancy. In continuity
with past Christian teaching, we recognize tragic conflicts of life with life
that may justify abortion."[53] In 1988 the church added, "We cannot affirm
abortion as an acceptable means of birth control, and we unconditionally
reject it as a means of gender selection." It noted that governmental "laws
and regulations do not provide all the guidance required by the informed
Christian conscience" to decide such matters in the light of prayerful consideration and pastoral counsel.[54] In 2000 the church banned "partial-birth
abortion," except when the mother's physical life is in danger or there are
"severe fetal anomalies incompatible with life."[55]

The Methodist Church, then, is "pro-life," affirms Thom Fassett, even
as it claims the right for women to make their own decisions about abortion in the light of their own conscience. Yet some "pro-choice religious
folks are in denial," he charges, about the terrible, tragic waste of human
life abortion poses.[56] Some anti-abortion crusaders, meanwhile, use "dis-
information" to impugn the integrity of the church's teaching on abortion.

Methodists need to study and discuss this teaching with one another instead of polemicizing it in attacks on one another.

In surveying its own house, urges Fassett, the United Methodist Church must question its privatizing drift away from traditionally Wesleyan forms of education, discipleship, polity, and evangelism. "How in the world," he demands, "can children pass through our Christian education programs without knowing the love of Jesus Christ and understanding how that love graces everything they do, touch, think?"[57] The drift of local churches to de facto congregational autonomy can only be reversed if Methodists today revive the spirit of genuine Wesleyan values and the genuinely connectional structure of the church as a conciliar and covenantal body. Methodism's Council of Bishops should "come off the islands and out of the rural countryside to meet in cities where we say we have failed in witnessing God to a troubled world."[58]

The most immediate proof of the failure of Methodist bishops, pastors, and laypeople to reclaim the denomination's evangelical Wesleyan witness and truly embody Christ's Church, Fassett claims, is to be found in the 20 percent loss of members the denomination has suffered over the past generation, especially among youth and young adults. At least two-thirds of those raised in United Methodist churches have quit by the time they finish high school, according to varied denominational estimates, and more have left by the end of college. Less than half have returned after marriage and parenthood, led back by their little children but too often remaining only "nominal" Methodists, little involved in local churches.[59] Some critics charge that "we are losing members because of our Christian social witness. Nonsense!" counters Fassett. "We are losing members because our Christian social witness has become something of an add-on often unrecognizable as a Wesleyan paradigm in youth confirmation or adult membership classes." The church must learn all over again how to minister to its own younger members and make strong disciples of them if it is to address the world's suffering sacrificially, with a methodical discipline that honors the living spirit of its historic mission.[60]

Face the Nation, Face the Church

Six months after taking office as general secretary for the General Board of Church and Society in 2001, Jim Winkler reported a new, positive atmosphere in gatherings of United Methodist leaders, marked by efforts to "provide and model more open and responsive leadership to our Church" and "avoid old, unnecessary turf battles." He also reported the critical diagnosis that a colleague, the new general secretary of the General Council on Ministries, delivered to the United Methodist Council of Bishops:

> First, he noted, there is lack of trust for those in power and a belief that those in positions of authority do not respect the needs and views of others. Second, there is no central person or group at the top of the church structure. Third, many important decisions are driven by money, not mission. Fourth, there is a desire for our church to be truly global. Failing that, let's stop pretending and admit that the U.S. is the home office of a denomination that has branches in other countries. Fifth, we have made a god of inclusivity. Finally, there is a sense, an expectation, that something big is about to happen.

These symptoms must be addressed, Winkler urged, and Methodists must find new meaning and purpose in Christian discipleship in a better future. "Our church is not closing in on itself. We are not dwelling in negativity. There's too much to be done for that to occupy our time and energy," he judged.[61] With an eye to the board's past and future, a veteran church leader in Washington notes, "Jim's a healer and a collaborator; he knows how to get out front and take a strong stand, like he did against the war in Iraq—go in with the NCC, and bring others along, without making enemies when you don't need to. That's not to say it'll all be sweetness and light in the board from now on. They've been arguing for good reasons about things that matter. That's been going on for some time, and it will keep going on."[62]

A veteran member of the GBCS staff who served across generations of the board's recent history sees arguments over its stance and aims resolving into two contrary visions of what it should be and do. Looking to the board's social-activist engagement on civil rights, peace in Vietnam, and antipoverty struggles from the inner-city ghetto to the rural farmlands organized by the United Farm Workers (UFW), George Ogle sees the board as embodying a biblically "prophetic" church. It stands in public on Capitol Hill, across the country, and around the world, "at the intersection between justice and injustice." It responds, first of all, to "the people who are being treated unjustly in our society."[63] Thus the board embodies the church itself in serving Methodists in local churches and their fellow citizens by enabling them to "see justice and injustice actually conflicting in our society." It inspires the faithful to act as members of the church in its entirety to make a difference in these conflicts and make society more Christ-like.

On the other hand, says Ogle, a more "localist" ideal of the board stresses its primary responsibility to communicate with local Methodist churches and represent their concerns faithfully, not only teaching people in the pews but heeding them as well. This second ideal conceives "the local churches as the Body of Christ, who have established certain denominational agencies in order to help them carry on their business. Therefore, the board is not itself the church, but merely a service agency for local churches. It should reflect the standards of right and wrong and carry out the standards of justice that come from the local churches."

Of course, "that's an ass-backwards way of looking at it," this veteran GBCS activist charges, since "the United Methodist Church has established the board to be as much a part of the church in worshipping, preaching, and practicing the gospel as any other part, not as an organizational appendage" of local congregations in all of their cultural-political differences and social homogeneity. Nonetheless, Ogle observes, political infighting and organizational strife in the denomination since 1980 have led to "bloodletting and housecleaning" in the GBCS. This has left it by turns more wary and conflicted, more centralized and socially diverse, more ecumenically reticent yet still outspoken on key issues, and still subject to continuing criticism and controversy within the United Methodist Church at large.

The board's vocal support of the UFW boycott of table grapes during the 1980s triggered a backlash among grape growers and their friends in California Methodist churches, recalls Ogle by way of example. " 'My church has betrayed me in my time of need,' one of them protested at a board meeting," he says. "She lambasted me for being a knee-jerk liberal and a political flunky. Later I got called onto the carpet and told I was giving too much time to this issue, I had a lot of other things to do, and they wanted to see that reflected in my work schedule. Then, after three years of infighting over the issue, the General Board voted officially at the 1988 General Conference to boycott table grapes in California." After 1980, comments Herman Will, "there was a break in the board's program, and cuts in budget and staff. It was such a bad break that my ecumenical friends in Washington complained, 'We don't see anything more of the Methodists. Where are they?'" Where indeed, ponders Will, concluding, "We have to face the nation and the world, and we have to face the church. We have to do both, and we're still struggling to work that out."[64]

The board's critics fault it on both fronts. In the church, they charge, it stands too isolated and aloof from all but the most activist Methodist congregations, pastors, conferences, denominational leaders, and constituencies, such as the General Board of Global Ministries, its Women's Division, and the Methodist Federation for Social Action. In Washington, other critics add, the board is often "too radical to be political" in reliably joining more practical collaborators in persuasive moral advocacy and legislative lobbying on Capitol Hill and at the White House. The board's defenders, on the other hand, salute it for fully heeding the gospel's radical call to love our neighbor and bring society closer to the Kingdom of God. They see it holding true to the tradition of Wesley working to reform the nation as well as the church, and following faithfully in the footsteps of "Christ transforming culture," instead of compromising with it or surrendering to it.[65]

Consensus, Control, Conversion

Asked to diagnose the virtues and problems of the mainline churches in their social witness and action midway through his twelve years as general secretary of the GBCS, Thom Fassett distinguishes between internal conflicts in the church over organizational "control" and the meaning of "consensus" held up by the United Methodist Church and set out in its *Book of Discipline*:

> Consensus is a radically different concept from agreement. It resembles the process of coming to consensus that the six nations of the Iroquois originated and still practice to this day, in what is probably the oldest surviving democracy in the world. They do not necessarily agree on everything, but they establish parameters within which all people can live consistent with their moral principles.
>
> We have yet to capture that understanding for ourselves. What stands in our way are the extraordinary needs for control that drive us. They drive our theologies, our social perspectives, our organizational behavior. They drive our relationships with each other and create competitive urges among church leaders in what is fiefdom-building, after all, not kingdom-building.
>
> The church often provides the last great bastion of control and power for those who have given up the contest for worldly power. Now they are struggling over being controller of the keys to the church kitchen![66]

They are also struggling over denominational power and funding, acknowledges Fassett. "We're empowering forms of control and giving
them broader institutional representation. We're funding them more than
we're funding the agenda of social conscience and the critical ministries
that are going begging today. We are doing programming by beginning
with our pocketbooks rather than starting with the moral imperatives of
ministry and backing into the dollar."

True consensus, explains Fassett, is more akin to the way "we understand the world in which Jesus lived, and the environment of the Essene
community. It is much more tribal and spatial." Control, dominance, and
competition rely more on a linear concept of spirituality. "You nail experience to a certain time and place: the event, the date, how many people
were there. Nail everything to linear planes, and it's much easier for us
to manage it." Yet the linear trajectory of spiritual progress, moving onward and upward like the plotted line of ideal church growth, economic
production, or polled political opinion, fears Fassett, obscures the God-
given spiritual reality of human beings. It has also confused the church
about its inherently public mission. "There is an almost Hellenistic separation of spiritual power and worldly issues," he says. "If the church addresses issues like speaking out against going to war in the Gulf, then we
are traversing territory alien to the Christian experience. We are going
up against the president and opinion polls that show an overwhelming
majority of the American people supported going to war [in the Persian
Gulf in 1991]."

This dualistic conception of the life of the spirit set apart from public
life calls for conversion, argues Fassett. "Go back to John Wesley standing in the town square preaching, and you find true conversion. You find
a witness for demonstrating public righteousness. You find you cannot
have faith without works. You cannot have works without faith." In this
account of the public church, an evangelical emphasis on profound personal conversion joins a Reformed stress on the sovereignty of God over
all of creation and social life, and the stance of a church militant against
the world of partisan political powers and principalities. Fassett comments accordingly on reports that some church advocates, in the course
of lobbying members of Congress against authorizing the Gulf War, justified shifts from their own Christian pacifist or "just-peace" convictions
to narrower just-war arguments for the sake of political persuasion: "We
need to understand the nature of conversion. We are called to be Christians. We are not called to be Hellenists separating the psyche from the

soma. We aren't called to be Americans. We're not called to be patriots. One reason I am not currently a practicing Republican, Democrat, or member of any party is because as a Christian, I don't believe I personally can walk both sides of the street." Fassett pauses for emphasis. "We Christians are a different kind of party. We do not understand the nature of our conversion if we do not understand that we separate ourselves from political powers."

For the unconverted, paradoxically, this biblical sense of divine sovereignty over all social life and human responsibility for its moral ordering appears to violate conventional construals of a "wall of separation" between church and state by leading the church to meddle in politics. Acknowledges Fassett, "Once people accuse us here of acting politically as an arm of the church, however, there's nothing we do that can be cited that is not political, because there is nothing in life that we do that is not associated with some question of Christian understanding or conviction." So to a Hellenist who is also a registered Republican or Democrat, says Fassett, "that sounds like everything we do is political, and therefore our faith witness is political, because it witnesses with a certain bias that calls for certain [legislative or policy] outcomes that agree with one party's position and disagree with another's. Actually, our witness does not necessarily call for any specific outcome. It calls for us to live our faith, and witness to society by the parameters of our faith."

This view differs radically from the construal of the legal separation of church and state, as institutions each governed by their own members, to mean the moral separation of religious faith from government, family, education, and economic and public life as discrete social spheres each with their own moral ends, rules, and norms of relationship and activity. That perverts the biblical integrity of divine sovereignty over creation. It privatizes and imprisons the universal love of neighbor at the heart of the Christian gospel. "The Christian message as I understand it and try to live it is one in which we become liberators of systems and principalities and powers," testifies Fassett. "Liberators to the degree that the people will order them justly, and these principalities and powers and institutions will serve us to become a truly human sort of people. In the language of the six nations of the Iroquois there is a word called the *homahoay*, which means 'the real people.'"

For Christians today to realize their integrity as God's people, declares Fassett, "the best thing that we could do in poverty or wealth is to declare the sovereignty of God and the ongoing power of the Spirit in our lives to guide our decisions: the way we walk and talk, the way we build our houses, the way we order our governments, the way we develop our sewer systems and dispose of toxic wastes, the way we exploit or sustain natural resources, the way we elect officials and hold them accountable for the quality of their leadership." Do we govern ourselves justly? Do we produce and consume and compete justly? "Or is what we have here in this hemisphere something more like a magical corporate empire?" Fassett asks, with a critical eye to the way Americans live their daily lives and order their society.

A truly Christian church made up of a priesthood of all believers should exemplify democratic self-government for all peoples, in this view. Christians should not think of the church as a separate world of prayer and love violated by social witness or moral advocacy in public. Instead, this exemplary model of the church implies the need for striking changes in the structure of the United Methodist Church as it actually exists today. Begin, Fassett urges, by merging the Board of Church and Society with the Board of Discipleship, charged with overseeing religious education and formation in local churches. "Bring them all together, slowly merge them, and get us out there in every local church working with people to sharpen their understanding of what witness is today and how connected historically it is to the practice of our faith. Wherever we have personally been able to do this, it has brought about an incredible conversion of understanding."

For example, Fassett reports, "we can cut through the misleading imagery of [the Board of] Church and Society as a national and international agency of the denomination tying the hands of the local church," as many GBCS critics charge, because it takes so much money for spending on social welfare, peace, and justice that it soaks up an outsized percentage of what congregations have to give the denomination in levied "apportionments." If only they had those monies to keep, local church members protest, think of all the good they could do at home. They question how the denomination's social activism can be more important than fixing their own church roof or helping the needy nearby. "Once you talk that out," says Fassett, "then you move to the evangelical dynamics of our ministry, and how the local church can relate to them, take part in them, and use them. We really do stand in the same place. If you establish a food pantry, say, and it's the first time you have done anything like that, it may feel like a tremendously radical political act for a local church to take. In fact, it is a radically Christian act to follow Christ and feed the hungry."

What stands in the way of such epiphanic changes of heart and under-standing, even when local churches set up food pantries, says Fassett, is not so much the internal differentiation of agencies in the structure of the Methodist denomination. It is its failure to engage and educate its own lo-cal pastors. "We're moving toward a congregationalism where pastors are taking what it means to be a New Testament Christian, not only a United Methodist, and they're using it for their own personal purposes," Fassett contends. "They are narrowly defining the local church as an expression of their own personal faith and capitulating to others there who want a very privatistic faith." If such Methodist pastors are not "reborn from above" and their churches reinspired with an active spirit of social witness, fears Fassett, then "the ordained ministry as we know it today is going to be radically changed and perhaps eliminated, because this is going to become a lay movement." The diaconal ministry now growing in United Method-ism is an intriguing alternative, in Fassett's view, to an overspecialized yet undereducated professional clergy, more committed to advancing their careers and balancing their budgets than to answering the gospel's call to feed the poor and shelter people sleeping on the streets. It is inspired "remnant groups" of laypeople in local churches throughout Methodism, declares Fassett, who represent the church's best hope for the future as the prophethood of all believers, despite being misunderstood and barely accepted in many local congregations.

Through the prism of war in Iraq, Jim Winkler reflects on related ques-tions about the practical ties that bind Christian faith, Wesleyan holiness, and American democracy. The war was wrong, unjust, unnecessary, and un-Christian, he argued forcefully and publicly as it approached and un-folded. How could it have happened? "While September 11 was the ex-cuse," he answers, "these plans have been in the works for many years. The idea, however, that the United States can remake the Middle East into a pro-Western, democratic zone through a military invasion is a fan-tasy."[67] Civic and moral apathy in the face of an administration intent on acting out that fantasy plays a central role in what happened, and it stands as a challenge and a reproach to truly Christian churches in America:

> The U.S. is a democracy. Members of Congress, while heavily influenced by vested interests, still must be elected by ordinary citizens. There's really no excuse for the apathy that plagues this nation. Our churches should be active centers of education, reflection, and action. John Wesley asserted the aim of the Methodist movement is to reform the church, reform the nation, and spread

scriptural holiness across the land. That's true disciple-making. If pastors are not preaching and teaching with a Bible in one hand and a newspaper in the other, they're not doing their job and should be held accountable. We have a lot of accountability-holding to be done.[68]

Why have Methodist pastors in particular fallen short of their calling to incarnate the Christian church in public? Winkler answers:

The Cult of the Majority is a powerful force in The United Methodist Church today. It is closely allied to the Cult of Church Growth. A great many clergy have succumbed to or enthusiastically embraced these cults. Their basic suppositions are that the majority must be pleased, the majority is right because they are the majority, controversy must be avoided, bigger is better, services and programs must be provided to attract the largest possible audience.

The strength of these cults is not surprising in a democratic culture. As citizens, we vote people in and we can vote people out. . . . Yet too many clergy have abdicated their prophetic responsibilities. Too many of our lay people see Christianity as a form of comfort food. In a day when people cross denominational lines with ease, unhappy parishioners do not feel loyalty to denominations or even congregations.[69]

In Romans 13 Paul counseled, "Let every person be subject to the governing authorities. For there is no authority except from God, and those that exist have been instituted by God." By contrast, argues Winkler, "Jesus did not set out to please the government" or merely encourage moral improvement by asking, "Can't we all get along?" Instead, he and his disciples "set out to change the world by challenging the status quo. . . . He was out to change lives and communities. He fundamentally threatened the ruling order. It is the same difference between churches today that function as social clubs and those that change the communities around them," Winkler judges. "The latter see hunger, homelessness, racism, violence, crime, decay and confront and change reality. That's the business of the gospel."

Reviving the Church, Transforming the Culture

A half century ago, H. Richard Niebuhr summarized the dialogue between Christ and culture in the Christian conscience and community in terms so vividly clear that three generations of mainline Protestant ministers can rehearse them with ease. "Christ against culture" counterposes the church to "the world" in either-or terms that echo through monastic orders and sectarian movements the call of the early church to "come out from among them and be separate." "Christ with culture" upholds the life and teachings of Christ as the culmination of human culture and civilization, stressing the congruence of religious with political institutions, whether they be capitalist or socialist democracies in our time. "Christ above culture" both synthesizes and transcends the opposition of the first two types, instead entering into culture from above—much like Thomist faith perfecting reason—with gifts that can fulfill human aspiration and society but that neither stem from them nor contribute to them directly. "Christ in polarity and tension with culture" synthesizes opposition between the two with the inescapable authority of each without accommodation, as does Luther in positing two kingdoms in which Christians must live by faith and the hope of a justification that lies beyond history. Finally, "Christ transforming culture" offers an active, conversionist solution, rooted in Augustine and sharpened by Calvin, to the opposition between Christ and a culture that transmits the sinfulness of human nature yet permits Christ to work through us to turn humans to God.[70]

The conversionist possibility of Christ transforming culture runs like a soteriological red thread through much of what the United Methodist Board of Church and Society stresses today in its social teaching, spanning conventional dividing lines between religious "liberals" and "conservative evangelicals" in contemporary American Protestantism. Yet this conversionist stance is tempered by the strong emphasis board leaders place on just how demanding such transformation turns out to be in light of the deep opposition between the Christian gospel of neighbor-love and the sincere self-concern and blindered social outlook that seem to them so deeply ingrained in contemporary American culture and political institutions.

"Everywhere I go, I challenge people to become full-time Christians," sums up Thom Fassett. "That means some strange imperatives suddenly emerge about new ways of living and developing the church as a community as one lives out this faith journey with brothers and sisters. That means that our world is not the materialistic, capitalistic Western phenomenon that we see around us every day." Many Methodists today find it hard to heed this challenge, despite its deep roots in Wesleyanism, or perhaps because of them. "I always look at how people learn what it means to be a

United Methodist," explains Fassett. "I don't meet that many Wesleyans. That's a distinctive problem for us, because over 50 percent of the United Methodist Church's membership were not raised Methodist. When I go around talking about how we live full-time Christian lives, I have pastors that don't understand what that's about," and they cannot teach their people what it means to live as Methodists in the Wesleyan tradition. As long as this default goes on, says Fassett, "we'll continue to collapse as a moral force in society."[71]

How does such weakness of will express itself, and from what sources does it stem? In commenting on the 1996 legislation aimed at ending AFDC welfare, Bishop Melvin Talbert, then president of the General Board of Church and Society and also of the National Council of Churches, emphasized how compassionate and big-hearted Americans can be in their face-to-face personal relationships while remaining unaware of institutional injustice. "If there was a hungry child next to us and we had a loaf of bread," he said, "I can't believe we wouldn't share it."[72] The best thing we could do to reorder our society, he urged, would be to bring more and less needy people together to live near one another instead of segregating them by social class and race. In light of this gap between Americans' big hearts and the institutional matrix of human suffering and sin, Fassett weighs the church's potential to remake community in a divided society: "The church is the place for the reconstruction of community. We can be the integrative chemistry to take on the issues of desegregation, in a natural, not a forced, manner; not according to law, but according to practice. But that means we are going to have to look at some rather radical lifestyle shifts to figure out how you live a full-time Christian life in the context of this new community."[73]

What holds Americans back from such self-scrutiny and conversion? Why does the prospect of such a cure seem as intolerable as what ails us? "We're so enamored with this Western materialistic experience," replies Fassett, "that we're not sure if we could extricate ourselves from these lifestyles. We are tenants in this big, comfortable house. If we stepped out of it, we would no longer have the support structure of the economy and all those perks that help us do our job. The fact is, we're chained to them. They're not enablers at all. They're really preventing us from doing the work Christians are called to do."

To revive the Christian church, insists Fassett, "We need to purge the false gods and clean out the pantheon." The church can be revived, he warns, only if it is willing to give up its powerful idols; and "if it means that we lose 50 percent of the membership in the United Methodist Church to be the moral witness that we need to be, then so be it. We have to do that." To counter the accommodation of Christ to a culture as imperial in its syncretism as the pantheon's, Fassett proposes returning our attention to the church's own self-understanding and discipleship in terms marked off from the conventional vision of social institutions aimed at "meeting the needs" of their individual members and representing their interests, instead of transforming them by God's grace.

"I think the vast majority of the middle ground [members of the mainline churches] have been on the wrong end of giving," says Fassett. The government and the church, too, are "out of favor with them, because they feel as if these institutions have been takers. So they're saying, 'I'm not going to be used like that anymore. I want something out of this. I want something in return.' I think the churches have been takers in a way," agrees Fassett, insofar as they have failed to help their people engage in learning to practice their faith and express it in the world. "That's missiology of the highest order, and we have failed at it to the extent that the vast middle ground of people in our pews are takers, too. They know how to get into the church, they know how to use the church, they know how to cooperate in it. But they don't know how to get out of the church and give to the world," he charges. "That's the major problem that we have to deal with."

To exemplify how this larger vision of Christ and culture informs the stance of the Methodist Board of Church and Society in its work in Washington, Fassett cites the board's strong stand in behalf of health care as a universal right of all peoples, and its vigorous advocacy on this front in the United Nations, in Congress, and in the churches. Accordingly, the Methodist board refused to follow the National Council of Churches and sign on to a 1997 initiative mounted by the Children's Defense Fund (CDF) and backed by the Clinton White House and Democratic Party leaders as a last-ditch compromise effort to extend existing forms of Medicare coverage to the children of working parents near the poverty line, while leaving others uncovered.

Defending health care as a universal right, and all humankind as members of one body and one creation, the board objected strongly to the CDF initiative's implicit justification of health-care coverage for the innocent children of more deserving, harder-working Americans while the putatively less deserving remained excluded. "We don't have time to fool around with that kind of stuff," Fassett remarks, dismissing political pragmatism calibrated in light of polling that shows most Americans think health care is a right yet most favor cuts in welfare spending on the poor.[74] "We're saying health care is a human right. This is going to be very discomforting to the vast majority of the middle ground, because they are piecemealing it" in terms of those more or less deserving of health care, just as opinion polls report and pragmatic politicians preach. "We're just saying it doesn't matter, friends. Medical care is a human right! Food is a human right! Shelter is a human right!" Fassett proclaims.

Such proclamation and institutional commitment to democratic self-government around the world flesh out the meaning of a church universal made in the early Christian image of a community of goods, bound together in one body by all-forgiving neighbor-love. It rises above procedural ideals of democracy centered around fair play and representation among competing interest groups contending over issues and agreeing on individual rights and liberties, epitomized by the right to vote. "Democratic values are something worth talking about in the light of Christian tenets," allows Fassett. "But we're not doing that, because democratic values are now misunderstood to mean whatever congressional action and policies most of us support" as members of a self-interested, middle-class majority of the U.S. electorate, and to rule out whatever we are unwilling to pay for when it comes to providing health care, welfare, or housing to the needy at our expense. First and finally for Christians, however, comes the question of what it means to follow Christ as members of his church. Concludes Fassett, "We define Jesus by who we become as a community, what we believe as individuals, and how we shape the world around us. That's the answer to the question, and we're failing the exam."

After September 11, 2001, it was often said that the world was a different place and everything changed that day, wrote Jim Winkler a year after the attacks. "Little, if anything has changed," he argued instead.[75] With the Afghan war just concluded and the march to war in Iraq already begun, he noted, "wars continue and have even escalated." So has public spending on arms instead of on the poor: "Vast sums of money and resources have been poured into the war machine while Congress and the Administration quibble over scraps for needy families." When Methodist bishops appealed to U.S. senators in mid-2002 for more aid to the poor, he reported, they were met with polite indifference. "The rich are getting richer and the poor poorer. Nothing different there. Government reports indicate inner-city poverty in Washington, D.C., is higher than it was more than 30 years ago. Hunger is on the rise. Huge tax cuts for the rich have been enacted. The Middle East remains a mess. Ruinous Israeli and United States policies toward the area exacerbate tensions and create new terrorists and suicide bombers. Compromise is considered to be unthinkable surrender."

When it comes to the moral authority of government in relation to God, concludes Winkler, "God is not the God only of our country. 'We must obey God rather than any human authority.' (Acts 5:29) God is infinitely greater than we are." As with the Israelites' straying from God's word, meeting calamity, then seeking God's forgiveness and being granted it, "our hope and trust must be in God," Winkler testifies to the faithful as members of the Methodist Church and the American people who are, first and finally, members of the People of God and the Body of Christ. "Our hope is in the resurrection of Jesus, not in the resurrection of the World Trade Center." Christians must begin anew, as in the renewal of Advent, and pledge themselves to a truly just and peaceful future.

Amen, affirm activist Methodist pastors and people in the pews who are committed as faithful citizens to living out this prophetic message of justice and peace. No, counter Good News critics of such admonition and advocacy by the Methodist Board of Church and Society in Christ's name. Socialism and sociology are no substitutes for the gospel truth that alone saves souls and renews the church. Many more Methodists, meanwhile, stand somewhere in the middle. They are likelier to feel ambivalent than indifferent, and likelier to be ill-informed than utterly ignorant, when it comes to heeding calls to join in actively sharing—or opposing—the work of the board as the mission of all the members of the United Methodist Church as the People of God and the Body of Christ.[76]

CHAPTER FOUR

United Methodism in Crisis

Scriptural Renewal through the Good News Movement

After years of strong, steady sailing under the magisterial hand of General Secretary H. Dudley Ward, the United Methodist General Board of Church and Society by most accounts tacked leftward in the late 1960s and the 1970s, in response to the growing force of social movements to end the Vietnam War, achieve full racial and economic justice, liberate colonized peoples, and protect the environment. At the same time, it retained its historically central commitments to the causes of defending labor, ending poverty, and upholding civil rights. It continued to campaign for world peace and nuclear disarmament advanced by international cooperation through the United Nations.

In the late 1970s, questions about charting a course for the GBCS through this wider agenda of causes and issues rose with the current of greater representation for women, people of color, and ethnic minorities at the national level of the United Methodist denomination, and with stiffer headwinds of dissent over social activism from "conservative evangelical" Methodists. Shortly before his untimely death in 1980, the board's general secretary, George Outen, dismissed many of its longtime staff members. "The revolution came, and greater inclusiveness brought in women and minorities," recalls one non-Methodist church leader in Washington. "Out went the older white males who had been in there for so long. They were great people, but the new wave decided there's no way out of rebuilding the staff, it's time for a new day. So Outen fired them all with two weeks' notice, just before Christmas. He had in his head a design for rebuilding, but then he died of a heart attack. It took them a long time to recover from that and rebuild."[1] After an interregnum and holding action that reportedly lasted well into the 1980s, the board began mapping its present course under General Secretary Thom White Wolf Fassett, elected in 1988.

Some analysts of this denominational sea change and its long, con- flicted aftermath have cast it as a case of "culture wars" waged between typically younger, more educated cultural liberals and typically older, less educated conservatives in a denomination with a membership remarkable for representing both sides more evenly than do other mainline Protes- tant churches or white evangelical denominations. Subtler social profiles of United Methodism's membership lend some credence to such views but complicate them, too, as we saw in chapter 3. Moreover, Method- ists responsible for leading the church and familiar with its conflicts from within underscore the theological integrity of the debates that surround its social concerns and policies, and they highlight the ecclesiological im- plications of the issues at stake. They acknowledge the theological plural- ism and mobilized caucus groups of the denomination today. But many emphasize the importance of transformative social sanctification no less than the evangelically warmed heart of revivalist piety in the Wesleyan heritage that underlies the theological pluralism and caucus-church inter- est groups of the denomination today. Others stress the genuinely bibli- cal grounding that liberationist, feminist, and black theologies share with more evangelical Methodists, and their common concern for the church as a connectional body bound in communion and conversation by an all- reconciling love of God and neighbor.[2]

Awakening Methodism's Un-Silent Minority

The Good News movement in the United Methodist Church likewise dis- sents on fundamentally theological grounds. It indicts denominational leaders for betraying the church's heritage of Wesleyan piety, prac- tice, and doctrine so profoundly that it has led the church's social wit- ness and action far astray from its evangelistic roots. It has left Christian orthodoxy to be kept alive in the United Methodist Church by those who have composed its "silent minority" for far too long, left voiceless in its higher councils, overlooked or misunderstood by its majority, and often abhorred by its officials. So argued the pastor and journalist Charles W. Keysor with such eloquent force—in "Methodism's Silent Minority," published in 1966 in the *New Christian Advocate*, the denomination's leading general periodical—that his "voice for orthodoxy" in Methodism inspired and chartered the Good News movement that he came to head.[3]

"There lurks in many a Methodist mind a deep intolerance toward the silent minority who are orthodox," wrote Keysor, as if its members were "*ipso facto*, narrow-minded, naive, contentious, and potentially schismatic." Yet that familiar stereotype contains only a shadow of truth. "Intellectual honesty—let alone Christian charity—demands more objectivity than the church now accords to its silent minority." In fact, "we who are orthodox believe that the Christian faith is comprehensively declared in Holy Scripture and is succinctly summarized in the Apostles Creed," centered around "five fundamentals":

(1) **Inspiration of Scripture**. Orthodoxy believes with a passion that the whole Bible is God's eternal, unfailing truth. . . . Everything in the Scriptures has sacred significance. A thing is not true because it happens to be included in the Bible; we believe it is in the Bible because the thing itself is true. . . . Historic orthodoxy regards inspiration of Scripture as a dynamic, continuing activity of the Holy Spirit [in the authorship, canonical translation, and illumination of God's intended meaning for each faithful reader of Scripture today].

(2) **The virgin birth of Christ**. We believe that our Lord was, literally "conceived by the Holy Spirit, born of the virgin Mary." This must be true, or it would not have been written and transmitted in Holy Scripture. . . . Christ is not subject to known limitations of "natural law." He is, in fact, the source of "natural law." Order and unity and coherence for the entire cosmos center in Christ.

(3) **The substitutionary atonement of Christ**. . . . Somehow Christ on the Cross paid the price of transgression which a righteous and holy God properly requires. . . . Our Lord "for a world of lost sinners was slain."

(4) **The physical Resurrection of Christ**. We think that Christianity is a hoax unless Christ rose bodily from the grave—as the Scriptures report.

(5) **The return of Christ**. . . . Jesus Christ will return physically to "judge the (living) and the dead." . . . We are to let our Christian light shine in a dark world. Our calling is to be redeeming the time for the days are evil. . . . We live in the eschatological twilight zone, between promise and fulfillment.

"How many orthodox believers are there among the people called Methodist?" asked Keysor. More than Methodists may think, he answered, judging from the ten thousand local churches using nondenominational Christian-education material based on orthodox theology, and from the numerous defenders of "good old gospel songs" threatened by revision of the Methodist Hymnal.

What is orthodoxy's future within the Methodist Church? Persecution, perhaps, answered Keysor, in the name of stamping out the last vestiges of fundamentalism within Methodism, as a national denominational official declared, he reported. Or the more likely prospect of a "continuing eclipse of orthodox influence within the seminary-trained Methodist ministry." Concluded Keysor:

> Orthodoxy seems destined to remain as Methodism's silent minority. Here lies the challenge: We who are orthodox must become the **un**-silent minority! Orthodoxy must shed its "poor cousin" inferiority complex and enter forthrightly into the current theological debate. We who are orthodox must boldly declare our understanding of Christian truth, as God has given these convictions to us. We must speak in love and with prophetic fearlessness, and we must be prepared to suffer because we are a minority.
>
> But regardless of the consequences we must be heard in Nashville, in Evanston, and on Riverside Drive. Most of all, we must be heard in thousands of pulpits, for the people called Methodist will not cease to hunger for the good news of Jesus Christ, incarnate, crucified, risen and coming again.
>
> We must not speak as right-wing fanatics, intending to subvert the "establishment" and remake it in our own orthodox image. Instead, we must speak to our Christian brothers as Christian brothers, trusting that God will direct and prosper our witness to the truth as we see it in Christ Jesus our Lord.

Available, affable, arcane, and argumentative, Keysor went on to found and edit *Good News* magazine, incorporated in 1967 as "a Forum for Scriptural Christianity within the Methodist Church," with an activist board of twelve resourceful members, later multiplied to forty. It became the catalyst and then linchpin of a national movement given birth by the first Convocation of United Methodists for Evangelical Christianity, held in Dallas, Texas, in 1970. There, some sixteen hundred faithful heard "a literal battle cry for 'Scriptural renewal' within the denomination," reported John Lovelace of the *Christian Advocate*. The movement seemed to him "predominantly white, southern and male-oriented," an *aginner* movement that mixed "emotional, pietistic religion and conservative political acumen" into a cause rooted in "a tunnel-vision interpretation of Wesleyanism."[4]

But even critics of the Good News movement were obliged to recognize its growing power, generated by linking annual national convocations to

a spreading grassroots network of "renewal groups" for evangelical advocacy and support that extended to more than two-thirds of United Methodist annual conferences by the 1990s. As a movement built to reform
United Methodism from within, Good News reflected Keysor's diagnosis
of its institutional ills as well as its theological errors. "After World War
II, the zeal of the original social gospel hardened into liberal institutionalism," he wrote. "Its exponents had become old men as resistant to change
as had been their traditionalist opponents of the previous generation."
After forty years of struggle, theological liberals had triumphed in American Methodism by 1920, but professional church bureaucrats were the real
winners of power and influence in the church over the twentieth century,
contended Keysor. This led to the "formation of power blocs within the
church. The earliest of these were the Boards of Social Concern, Missions,
and Education." Then, in the late 1960s, "so-called caucuses emerged to
complete and make visible the politicizing of Methodism." This politicization threatened to eclipse "Wesleyan passion for meeting human needs,"
said Keysor, with a towering organizational superstructure and "a quietly
deepening emphasis on conformity to denominational thinking, in spite of
much-advertised 'pluralism.'"[5]

This politicization became by turns theological, generational, and coun-
tercultural, Keysor judged, with the 1968 General Conference in Dallas
serving as a portent of things to come.[6] There he sat watching the debate
over whether to abolish the Methodist Church's historic standard prohibiting the use of tobacco and alcohol by ordained clergy. Sitting nearby in the
observer galleries were a group of noisy young men who cheered the voices
of change and jeered the defenders of tradition. "They seemed to have
drifted up out of the counter-culture," recalled Keysor. "Their appearance,
their open disdain for the church, and their language all reflected the then-
prevalent hippie protest mentality." Amazed to discover that they were
students from the local Methodist seminary, Keysor was no less amazed to
find a majority of General Conference delegates voting in favor of the very
changes they cheered. This was "letting the world set the agenda," Keysor
decided, "a kind of an ecclesiastical hedonism that can be seen today in
'liberationism,' ideological heir to New Leftism of the late 1960s."

Yet another image stayed with Keysor from the 1968 General Conference: a large, angry-looking man in clerical dress pacing to and fro in
the entrance to the hall carrying a sign that read, "Prepare to Meet Thy
Change!" A dozen years later, Keysor reflected on the deeper meaning of
such protest and its progress in the United Methodist Church:

God, it seemed had been superceded! The Transcendent One had been set aside in favor of an ongoing process of societal evolution—and revolution. This protestor's angry attitude, and the deeper meaning of his placard, all exemplified a powerful undercurrent flowing in this historic General Conference. The influence of Herbert Marcuse, Harvey Cox, Saul Alinsky, et al., sowed at Dallas in 1968, produced a bitter harvest of secularism. This would dominate the General Conferences of 1970 in St. Louis, 1972 in Atlanta, 1976 in Portland, and 1980 in Indianapolis.

By 1976, New Leftism had undergone a quiet evolution. Given a bath, a haircut, a briefcase, a desk in denominational headquarters, and a plentiful supply of church dollars, radical secularism became highly institutionalized within the UM Church. Instead of being angry protestors seated in the galleries of General Conference, by 1976 the institutionalized New Left dominated not only General Conference but also the episcopacy, annual conference power structures, and our denominational boards and agencies.

Theological liberalism had gained "full domination of official Methodism" by the 1920s, by this account, and New Left liberationism had followed its lead a half century later. Over these decades, as Keysor saw it, evangelical conservatives had been increasingly excluded and eventually disenfranchised as second-class citizens in the Methodist Church:

Conservatives have been excluded increasingly from our denominational seminaries, our colleges, our publications, our curriculum, our church programs, our church agencies, and our episcopacy. Beyond filling the pews and writing checks to finance the liberal establishment, conservatives seem to have little place. . . .

Forthright evangelicals became scarcer in larger pulpits and district superintendencies as well as national boards and agencies of the church. Regarding institutional conformity as a prime virtue, the church institution often rewards subservience with advancement. . . .

So it was that by 1969, Methodist evangelicals had existed for decades as second class citizens, riding in the rear of the denomination bus. The irony was that once Methodism had been totally evangelical! But this fabric of orthodoxy had been torn to shreds. Starting to knit it back together has been an important work for Good News.

In pursuing this work and pushing against the consensual weight of the ecumenical liberalism prevailing in the church, reported Keysor, Good

News grew more aware of "a dominant UM power-elite." It gained "deeper knowledge of the labyrinthian ecclesiastical power complex which determines and controls denominational politics touching every local church."

Good News mobilized to combat this threat. From the pages of its magazine sprang a stream of ten petitions and four resolutions, carried by Good News board members into the legislative proceedings of the 1972 Methodist General Conference. In response to adoption of a resolution accepting abortion and an official denominational statement of faith affirming theological pluralism at the 1972 conference, Good News redoubled its advocacy and lobbying efforts at subsequent Methodist General Conferences in "the struggle against doctrinal compromise." Good News began organizing in Methodist annual conferences to elect evangelical and traditional delegates to vote in General Conferences. It channeled petitions and published position papers on a widening range of issues for the sake of "calling the church back to doctrinal fidelity"—for example, to combat unacceptable new God-language, radical feminist theology, and "goddess worship." It urged the United Methodist Church to act to strengthen the family, reverse acceptance of abortion, and resist affirmations of homosexuality. It pushed for church reforms to change "designated-giving" funding in order to curb the power of denominational boards and their staffs, to assert the fiscal freedom of local congregations, and to strengthen the authority of bishops.

In 1976, for example, Good News sent a team of twenty-five lobbyists and observers to General Conference. They helped to reject efforts to remove from the church's official Social Principles a key stricture against homosexuality stating that "we do not condone the practice of homosexuality and consider this practice incompatible with Christian teaching."[7] Good News sent a team of sixty-five to the 1980 General Conference, underwritten with a budget of more than $60,000 and lifted up by a prayer chain of more than fifty thousand United Methodists. This team was backed by seventeen published position papers, fourteen thousand petition packets mailed in advance to Methodists in the pews, and letters sent to all General Conference delegates arguing in behalf of Good News' stands on the issues. Good News supported a successful initiative by layman David Jessup, an AFL-CIO labor organizer active in founding the Institute on Religion and Democracy in 1981, to investigate funding grants to allegedly left-wing or radical political groups by Methodist boards, notably Church and Society and Global Ministries. It demanded that they report and be held accountable for all grants given to organizations, individuals, coalitions, and programs not formally part of the church.

In 1974 Good News authorized a Theology and Doctrine Task Force to prepare a statement of "Scriptural Christianity" faithful to Methodist tradition. It pressed protests against theological pluralism in terms that eventually helped to shape a new official statement citing "the primacy of Scripture" to guide theology in the United Methodist Church, accepted by the church's General Conference in 1988. From its early years, Good News attacked denominational church-school literature as dismally devoid of biblical theology and salvific faith in the "spiritual new birth" offered by Christ's atonement. In 1975 Good News published its first edition of *We Believe*, a confirmation series for junior high youth, then an adult edition, followed by the evangelical and Wesleyan *Bristol Bible Curriculum*. Also in 1975, it championed a blistering attack on liberal Methodist seminaries by the spirit-filled and outspoken Methodist evangelist Ed Robb, Jr., demanding their return to Wesleyan doctrine and evangelism. To this end, Good News backed the formation of A Foundation for Theological Education (AFTE) to train and place evangelical scholars in Methodist seminaries and colleges. Then it began publishing an evangelical newsletter for seminarians, *Catalyst*, which AFTE went on to underwrite.

In the mid-1970s, Good News helped spark and direct criticism of United Methodist world missions as distracted by social-political concerns and disinterested in saving souls and planting new churches. It organized the Evangelical Missions Council as a counterweight to the General Board of Global Ministries in 1974. In 1983 it formed a "supplemental" mission-sending agency, the Mission Society for United Methodists. It has since raised millions of dollars directly from Methodists through "Faith Promise Support for second-mile missions," to send hundreds of missionaries into more than a score of foreign fields. Good News joined in the founding of the Institute on Religion and Democracy, with Ed Robb as president, to counter what it saw as the leftist politics and social activism of the GBCS and related mainline Protestant church offices active in Washington and allied with the National Council of Churches.

Organizing Methodism's Evangelical Majority

Looking back over this record of accomplishment to Chuck Keysor's seminal view of Methodism's "silent minority" as a kind of ingathered remnant, evangelist Ed Robb recalls, "Oh, it seemed to me that every time somebody quit the church, Chuck would rejoice. And it would break my heart. So he had a different concept than I did for that."[8] Despondent over prospects for Methodist renewal in the wake of the 1980 General Conference, Keysor left Good News and the Methodist Church in 1981 to become a member and minister in the Swedish Evangelical Covenant Church. At the time, recalls Robb, "they asked me to be the executive at Good News," but "I knew I could not do it, and I recommended Jim Heidinger for the job." If Good News lost its most eloquent theological voice when Keysor left, as some of its friends regret and many of its critics insist, it gained organizational focus and political resilience.

"Chuck really felt that the church was not going to change, could not be reformed," recalls James V. Heidinger II.[9] "We spent [more than] $50,000 at the 1980 General Conference in Indianapolis and saw virtually nothing happen. We left feeling we'd been hit by a truck." Deeply distressed, weakened by cancer surgery, and wounded by "fifteen years of guerilla warfare, scars, [and] bruises" as a target for the anti-evangelical animus of Methodist leaders, Heidinger explains, Keysor departed at a moment that became an ecclesiological turning point for Good News:

> Chuck looked at Good News as a remnant. As a small ingathered remnant we can be prophetic, but we'll never be dominant. But many of us have felt that Good News, rather than representing an extreme, represents the broad middle, and we feel like if we can pull the group together, that we're expressing their concerns.
>
> So when I became editor and executive secretary, we knew we had bad press and a bit of a reputation for being abrasive, hard-hitting, too prophetic, not pastoral enough. The board said—and I love Chuck and Chuck had the ingredients necessary to start a movement—but the board said, "It's time for us to fire fewer broadsides across the bow, and be more pastoral, and to nurture the evangelical community and to try to deal with this perception that we're only negative. What are you for?"
>
> That's, frankly, how we got into publishing. We wanted to provide material to nurture the evangelical constituency, and we found there was a need, there was an interest in that stuff, and people had confidence and that went well.
>
> Now, after ten or eleven years of being very pastoral [into the 1990s], we are beginning to say we want to penetrate and be a leaven in the system. We want evangelicals to get off the sidelines, stop throwing stones, and get into the fray at every level of the church. And in doing so, I'm convinced that I have been a healthier evangelical, and others are healthier when they have a group to which

they can belong, that at Annual Conference sessions they can meet with, plan, and be part of the process.

I've come to discover what some people say about a democracy—that we're really a government of the groups, by the groups, and for the groups. And that's true of [church] bureaucracies; you've got to find a group to play into. In isolation you're little good, and many evangelicals who tried to work in their local church in isolation would often get discouraged, bitter, alienated. Isolated, they didn't have the support they needed.

Taking this centrist, gradualist tack checked the separatist and schismatic impulses of some early supporters of Good News. It found in a 1970 poll of its members that 77 percent of them wanted "stricter standards" of membership in the United Methodist Church, and 40 percent favored some form of trial membership, or at least evidence of genuine conversion required for full membership. "My guess is that when 77 percent of the people want stricter standards," judges Heidinger, "that's a cry of people who see the church abandoning nearly any standard, or becoming fuzzy in simply what it means to be a part of the church and a follower of Jesus Christ." The vigor of Good News in stressing the loyalty of its opposition within the United Methodist Church kept would-be defectors within the Methodist fold. One in seven of those polled in 1970 said they thought about leaving the Methodist Church and might well have left were it not for Good News. "We hear that all the time," noted Heidinger in the 1990s, "and I spend a good chunk of time urging people to stay in. People look to us with a nearly messianic hope about the church one day being different."

Ed Robb backed Good News from the outset as "a loyal opposition in the church," theologically grounded, boldly evangelistic, and organized for the long run. "You don't turn a battleship around on a dime, and you don't turn around a great denomination like this all at once. If we can just keep patient and stay in there and keep working, we're making real progress."[10] So many good things have come forth, Robb attests, from renewing Methodism's evangelistic heritage and contending against its this-worldly corruption by theological liberalism. For many denominational leaders in the Methodist Church, "the evangelist is kind of a fifth wheel that they tolerate and marginalize," says Robb. "And they're absolutely astonished that the church without evangelism is going by the boards!" The reason that evangelism is dismissed and denied credibility in American Methodism today, argues Robb, stems from its century-long infection by theological liberalism. "When we no longer have a gospel for the salvation of souls, which would make for their eternal destiny, then we have to try to repair this world. Try to make this world your heaven, and when you do that you only succeed in making it your hell. Without a personal gospel, the Social Gospel became the dominant expression of our faith. That's basically the problem."

For Robb, the fallout from this profound theological and soteriological error is both institutional and personal. Now, he says, liberal theological degrees make ministers think they're "experts in statesmanship and economic and military affairs, and sometimes I think we make ourselves look very foolish" in the eyes of a world that sees liberal Methodist ministers speaking out on "every conceivable issue on which they have no expertise whatsoever," and no constituents either. Methodist bishops abdicated their religious authority to worldly experts and turned denominational operations over to bureaucrats, until "now bureaucrats control the church" and its budget. "If this money were going to feed the hungry or to evangelize, I'd say great," Robb avows. "But bureaucrats' salaries I'm not so excited about, and neither are most United Methodists. The Board of Global Ministries has lost its budgetary credibility, and certainly the Board of Church and Society never had very much," charges Robb, in support of a "tax rebellion" backed by Good News since 1980. It would cut the budgets of these boards, demand greater accountability of their leaders, and allow local churches to decide how much they will give the national denomination by making their levied "apportionments" voluntary instead of required. Thus local churches could "decide whether or not to support financially the ministries of the connection, based upon that congregation's perceived value of the services rendered," its advocates explain. They would rebel against paying a levy imposed on them in the single World Service Fund block that contains support for national boards with annual-conference benevolences.[11]

Struggling against a Two-Tier Church

As a movement for "scriptural renewal within the church," Jim Heidinger emphasizes, Good News focuses first on theological concerns, in light of its officially stated purpose: "To affirm United Methodism's commitment to Jesus Christ as Savior and Lord, to the historic Christian faith, the Wesleyan doctrinal standards and the Holy Scriptures as authoritative for faith and life under the guidance of the Holy Spirit."[12] But this theological concern, argues Heidinger no less pointedly than Ed Robb, must lead to specific institutional changes to renew and unify what has become "a two-tier church." As a congregational community of worship and ministry, the local Methodist church "deals with the real basic existential issues of the human heart, where people are living together, pastors are ministering to them, counseling them through hurts, deaths, marital difficulties." Scripturally literate and faithful, most Methodists in the pews of local churches are very traditional, affirms Heidinger. "Maybe 70 percent are self-identified conservatives," he estimates, laying claim to the roughly 64 percent of surveyed United Methodists who identify themselves as some kind of religious, cultural, or political "conservative," including three of four traditionalists and 57–58 percent of nominal and moderate Methodists.[13]

Most of the bureaucrats heading the national boards and agencies of the Methodist denomination, by contrast, are liberals who represent "the professional class," argues Heidinger. Why this yawning chasm between the two groups? People who move up into positions of leadership in the denominational bureaucracy, he answers, are those who have failed to find local church ministry fulfilling or rewarding. "I think the conservative pastor, the evangelical, if you will, loves local church ministry, sees its fruit, sees lives change, sees the church grow. I think the graduate of the typical liberal seminary who has bought into much of liberal theology realizes in the first few years that doesn't play in Peoria." Those who fail to get "the fulfillment and the strokes" as pastors of local churches, says Heidinger, before long begin looking to move to "where the action is" in the church as an institution wielding public power to make an impact on society.[14] This chasm between the two tiers of the Methodist Church violates the integrity of orthodox scriptural Christianity, Heidinger charges, and it violates the principles of democratic representation in America and its corollary of no taxation without representation. "There are the people in the pews that are paying the money, and the people at the board and agency level that often are taking the church in a different direction. I liken it to a hijacking," says Heidinger (prior to 9/11), "where just a few people get into the cockpit of a large jet and take it to a destination that hundreds of passengers do not want to go." What is to be done in response? Regain control of the denomination through representative, democratic means, by enabling "evangelicals to get involved more on the district, conference, and national levels" of its leadership, answers Heidinger. By way of example, he points to the growing number of Good News board members serving as delegates to the church's governing General Conference and its jurisdictional conferences.

But mobilizing through such political processes to place more scripturally orthodox and evangelical Methodists at the helm of the United Methodist Church requires in turn a deeper diagnosis of what ails the Church theologically, Heidinger argues. It also requires the will to act on this critical diagnosis with organizational patience, denominational loyalty, and Christian love in the midst of ongoing disagreement and the heat of arduous debate. "We believe we're dealing with a theological struggle that runs deep," says Heidinger, epitomized by ideals of theological pluralism that encourage Methodists to "embrace any expression of heterodoxy, but when one becomes evangelical, that is the brand that seems to be unacceptable." Liberals' tolerance of everything except the intolerance they impute to orthodox evangelical Christianity must be understood, by this account, in terms of cultural conflict and change rooted in theology and reaching across generations. It began a century ago, peaked in the 1960s and 1970s, and is now giving way to an evangelical renaissance. Social Gospel reformers a century ago began to move the church away from the importance of individual conversion and commitment to Christ, argues Heidinger. This led to "belittling" of Christian formation through congregational worship and Bible study. Instead, it favored social redemption brought about by government. That became the model that liberals used to reform the church itself.

In the guise of concern for social ministry, liberal political ideology, in this view, distracted the church in the 1960s from prayerful evangelism. The pluralism of liberal theology relativized doctrinal orthodoxy as universities captured the spirit of Methodist seminaries. "We went after the approval of the university," explains Heidinger. "We wanted to prove to them that we could be as academically sound as the university was. In doing that, we seemed to have lost our commitment to our guiding foundational theology, so that even to question whether a seminary is faithful to the doctrinal standards is assumed to be violating academic freedom." From conflicts in theology stemmed conflicting kinds of Christian practice and motivation. "The evangelical Christian is convinced that it's his experience with Christ that motivates his good works. It's the love of Christ that constrains me," Heidinger says, referring to Paul (2 Cor. 5:14–20). On the contrary, liberals stress "so much laying on us the guilt trip of woe. 'Look how bad the world is! Don't you feel bad? So go do something about it. Get out there and get involved!' Well, if I don't have the motivation of Christ's Word compelling me," Heidinger warns, "I'll burn out in three weeks, three months. And that's the genius of Wesley: faith working through love," instead of "the liberal agenda that used to be identified with the McGovern-Kennedy wing of the Democratic Party," putting its faith in political activism and government programs.

Despite the mounting efforts to reform the United Methodist denomination's national boards and agencies by choosing their leaders through democratic elections from the church's annual conferences, says Heidinger, "the people that move to the top, to be elected from annual conferences, seem to be people who resonate with the boards. There's a great deal of ingrown homogeneity and lack of diversity, so that the boards tend to perpetuate themselves. I don't think we know how to change the character of those boards. How do you break into a Board of Church and Society? How does an evangelical? Would he even want to be part of that group, frankly?" asks Heidinger. The answer to this problem lies in larger structural and attitudinal changes in the denomination, he proposes. Quickened by generational turnover in step with the spreading evangelical renaissance, these changes must be driven by grass-roots organizing in the pews and inspired by prayer to sustain the struggle for the soul of the United Methodist Church. In the 1980s, for example, Methodist General Conferences passed stricter legislation on abortion at the urging of Good News, notes Heidinger, banning its use for birth control or gender selection. But the Board of Church and Society, he adds, "has done nothing to implement that. They continue as if it's business as usual. They keep co-sponsoring abortion-rights marches and policies in cooperation with abortion-rights groups" beyond the denomination, such as the Religious Coalition for Abortion Rights (RCAR). Indeed, the board sheltered RCAR as a tenant in the United Methodist Building, despite strong pressure from Good News and its allies against abortion (and bomb threats from unnamed foes), until RCAR finally decided in 1994 to move to larger offices in downtown Washington under a new name, the Religious Coalition for Reproductive Choice.[15]

Like the Board of Global Ministries in its entrenched resistance to reviving missionary work to save souls and plant churches, judges Heidinger, such conduct reflects a dangerously deluded self-identification by the denomination's national boards and agencies with the church universal. "We think they have become, for all practical purposes, nearly autonomous," he says. "Almost an entity unto themselves: 'We understand what's best. You keep your cards and letters coming in, trust us. We're not going to change our liberationist themes, but continue your support, and if you don't, you're not a team player.' "[16] After twenty-two meetings over eleven years with leaders of the Board of Global Ministries held at Good News' expense, recounts Heidinger, "pleading with them that the day of the missionary was not over, that they ought to be concerned with establishing churches, reaching the lost," the board dismissed Good News' concerns and obliged it to launch an alternative mission-sending agency, the Mission Society for United Methodists. "It's as if they see themselves not as the servant of the church," says Heidinger of the board, "but as a group to whom the church is beholden."

Because the denomination's national boards and agencies have "usurped what used to be the bishops' role, and that's overseeing the spiritual and temporal work of the church," charges Heidinger, Methodism faces a spiritual crisis. It includes the long-running constitutional controversy surrounding the oversight role of the General Council on Ministries usurped from the bishops.[17] But the crisis extends far beyond this, to the church's need to "let the bishops be the bishops" and act accordingly, as general superintendents of the church as a whole, to hold its national boards and agencies fully accountable to the church as a whole. Likewise, let the pastors of local churches preach and minister freely to their congregants in order to "let the church be the church," Heidinger pleads, instead of being overwhelmed by the bureaucratic weight and budgetary demands of boards and agencies with all their programs, staffs, and media spending. As Good News builds its own widening web of organizations and communications into a network offering a grassroots alternative to an unresponsive denominational bureaucracy, says Heidinger, "I find myself wondering, is the day coming in the mainline churches, not just Methodism, when we'll realize that what we have is an aging bureaucracy held together by intimidation and no popular support that will crumble" as quickly as the totalitarian Soviet bloc came undone during the Velvet Revolution? A millennial hope? Such church renewal is already well begun and growing in strength, Heidinger testifies, grounded in the "genuine heartfelt conviction of people who are praying, tithing, witnessing, living out their faith."

Return to Classical Christianity

The 2000 General Conference may have been a turning point for scriptural renewal of the United Methodist Church, proclaimed James Heidinger in the wake of the conference.[18] All the apprehension and media exposure of its long-anticipated debate over homosexuality climaxed in the arrest of two activist Methodist bishops and twenty-seven fellow demonstrators on the conference floor during the proceedings. But conference delegates voted against liberalizing United Methodist standards on homosexuality. By majorities ranging from 65 to 74 percent, they defended and retained the church's 1972 language that "we do not condone the practice of homosexuality and consider this practice incompatible with Christian teaching." They upheld its 1996 ban on same-sex unions, stating, "Ceremonies that celebrate homosexual unions shall not be conducted by our ministers and shall not be conducted in our churches."[19] Against the claim of Bishop Melvin Talbert for the authority of the Northern California Annual Conference to permit such ceremonies to be performed there, the Methodist Judicial Council ruled that the annual conference is not "a more basic and fundamental covenant" than the church's *Book of Discipline*. Moreover, noted Heidinger, "it appears that framing the matter almost entirely as a 'rights' issue, rather than as a long-standing moral issue about a behavior, is a last-ditch effort to shore up a sagging and unpersuasive movement," which failed in its efforts to tie "gay rights" to the nation's noble civil rights movement. Significantly, three evangelicals won election to the supreme court of the church—its nine-member Judicial Council—in 2000, Heidinger pointed out. Furthermore, changes in delegate representation brought more voting delegates to General Conference from the church's more evangelical Southeastern and South Central jurisdictions and fewer from its Northeastern, North Central, and Western jurisdictions.[20] The 2000 General Conference also voted to oppose partial-birth abortion and support voluntary prayer in public schools. It passed a statement reaffirming Jesus as "Son of God, the Savior of the world, and Lord of all," reported *Good News*, although it rejected a resolution to eliminate the General Board of Church and Society.[21] While cautious about "victory language" or any sense of triumph over the 2000 General Conference, Heidinger did invoke the analogy of Gettysburg that was spelled out by an evangelical reporter on the scene, depicting Methodist liberals who "failed repeatedly in assaults on key conservative positions[,] . . . then limped home to tend to their wounds and ponder what to do next."[22]

Reporting from these ranks in the pages of *Christian Social Action*, published by the Board of Church and Society, Rev. Harry C. Kiely, an activist arrested in the "Soulforce" demonstration against anti-gay bias, observed that two-thirds of the General Conference delegates "seemed

bent on silencing gay and lesbian persons."[23] Yet the gay/lesbian community and its many supporters spoke out boldly on the issue that had been
haunting United Methodism for decades, wrote Kiely—namely, homosexuality and discrimination against gay and lesbian persons, who were
seen as second-class citizens in the Kingdom of God and made unwel-
come in the Methodist Church. "This is the surface issue—but underneath
is something deeper, namely who will determine the future direction of
and control of the character of the UMC. The Cleveland Conference was
the latest and most dramatic installment of a long-brewing power struggle within the denomination," Kiely claimed. A movement led by Good
News, he charged, "has exploited cultural homophobia for years as the
wedge issue in a divide-and-conquer strategy for undermining the UMC's
Wesleyan social witness."

This strategy was at work in legislative committees debating the issues, said Kiely, in sessions filled by an atmosphere of "ruthless power-
maneuvering. Scripture was used as a battering ram rather than as a
doorway to mutual understanding," in meetings "more akin to a floor
fight at a political convention than a gathering of the faithful seeking guidance of the Holy Spirit." At one point, he observed, a GBCS staff person
assigned as a consultant on issues of abortion to the Faith and Order Legislative Committee was invited to speak by a sympathetic delegate who
so moved. Before the chair could act on this motion, another delegate
stood up, pointed to the staffer, and said, "We don't need to hear from
Church and Society because we know what she would say. She believes
in abortion." Another delegate immediately jumped up and added, "And
we know why they want abortions—they need the body parts." There
were audible gasps, reported Kiely, but no apologies forthcoming, and the
committee voted not to allow the GBCS staffer to speak.

The 2000 General Conference was nonetheless striking in its more
cordial and respectful mood as well as its more orthodox theological understanding, judged Jim Heidinger. Perhaps that was because "thousands
of persons were plugged into what was happening and were praying for
God's blessing on the gathering," in prayer vigils in hundreds of local
churches nationwide and on-site, the latter led by several hundred "prayer
delegates" organized by Good News. "I believe we are seeing across the
church a crescendo calling for a return to the *sensus fidelium*, the consensus of the faithful—that is to the central doctrines of classical Christianity, we have too long ignored," Heidinger declared. "The church is
tired of our doctrinal trendiness, which has made us open and susceptible

to nearly every theological aberration coming down the road. It is the doctrines of classical Christianity which United Methodist pastors attest they have studied, embraced, and will faithfully preach. It must be so once again. This General Conference said that in a number of new and fresh ways."[24]

Looking back at the 2000 General Conference soon after it ended, James M. Wall of the *Christian Century* concluded, "The United Methodist Church has made a sharp turn to the political and theological right, and it appears that it will continue to move in that direction." Good News and its allies not only prevailed in battles over the status of gays in the denomination, thought Wall, but they also seemed to turn the tide of the larger struggle to govern the church. "The liberal dominance in United Methodism, the denomination that helped end the war in Vietnam and bring a halt to racial segregation in the church, has ended. The Good News movement, the United Methodist wing of the Institute on Religion and Democracy, and many of its bishops and tall-steeple pastors have taken over the church's governing body. That means in the long run that it will also take over the national and regional institutions."[25] That remains to be seen, countered a liberal Methodist leader shortly before the church's 2004 General Conference. The two sides may be stalemated on high-profile issues such as gays and abortion, he argued, but the tide has not yet turned in the institutional struggle to control the general boards and councils that administer the national denomination and decide its budgets. "They're still coming, and we're still holding them off. If that changes, everyone will know it. There's that much at stake."[26]

The Specter of Schism

At the 2004 General Conference in Pittsburgh, scriptural orthodoxy sustained its momentum in United Methodism from General Conference 2000, according to James Heidinger, moving the church away from "libertarian sexual ethics" and toward "strengthening biblical values."[27] Delegates affirmed the prohibition against ordaining and appointing "self-avowed practicing homosexuals" to the ministry by a 73 percent vote. They defeated a motion to allow gay marriages by an 83 percent vote and made performing such unions a "chargeable offense" under the *Book of Discipline*. By a 77 percent majority, they voted to "support laws in civil society that define marriage as the union of one man and one woman," making United Methodism the first and only mainline church to take this stand. The Judicial Council, moreover, ruled the prohibition against ordaining or appointing avowed homosexuals to be a "declaration of the church," with the binding power of church law, not only a moral and social principle. It affirmed that the practice of homosexuality is "a chargeable offense" under the 2000 *Discipline* of the church.[28] More broadly, noted Heidinger, the delegates' vote to extend more-proportional representation by region to the denomination's national boards and agencies, including the GBCS, would make them more accountable to "the growing, more traditional Southeastern, South Central, and Central Conferences" and would weaken the sway of voting board members from conferences in the more liberal Western, Northeastern, and North Central jurisdictions.[29] So would the continuing growth of the church in Africa, Asia, and Latin America, whose delegates now cast one in five votes in General Conference.

Despite these victories, confessed the president of Good News, "many of us returned home feeling anything but victorious" from Pittsburgh, after yet another General Conference turned into a two-week battle over homosexuality. "We recall a shattered communion chalice that was broken by a pro-gay activist after delegates voted to retain our stand on homosexuality," reported Heidinger, and "we endured the 35-minute protest orchestrated by Soulforce, a gay-rights organization, which had unhindered access to the floor of General Conference." There hundreds of Methodists came to kneel or stand in prayer, drawn from caucuses such as the Reconciling Ministries Network, the Parents Reconciling Network, and the Methodist Federation for Social Action. With the support of more than twenty-five Methodist bishops who stood in solidarity with the protesters, they placed a rainbow-colored candle on the altar of the conference and poured water into a baptismal font on the stage to signify that "we are of one faith and baptized by one God." In so doing, said Heidinger, they left many evangelicals with "a sinking feeling in the pits of our stomachs" at the drama of sacred worship profaned into political theatre.[30]

Against this backdrop, stressed Heidinger, the 2004 General Conference "will be remembered as the one at which the subject of amicable separation was placed on the table for United Methodists to discuss. We must listen prayerfully to discern what the spirit is saying to the church about this. But continued defiance of the *Book of Discipline* and repeated declarations by 'progressives' (and for that matter the entire Western

Jurisdiction) that they plan to ignore the church's standard, leave us asking if there is not a better way forward."[31] During the 2004 General Conference, Heidinger and two Good News colleagues had brought a draft resolution for amicable separation, together with talking points supporting it, to the second session of a dialogue on homosexuality between evangelical and progressive caucus leaders, initiated by two General Conference delegates elected as members of the General Board of Church and Society, who were seeking to bridge their opposing standpoints.[32] On one side, the dialogue included three other evangelical leaders—William Hinson, Maxie Dunnam, and Patricia Miller of the Confessing Movement. On the other, it included gay-inclusion leaders from Affirmation and the Methodist Federation for Social Action. The two sides were brought together by Rev. Bruce Robbins, former general secretary of the United Methodist General Commission on Christian Unity and Interreligious Concerns.

On the opening night of the dialogue, a dozen leaders of the gay/lesbian coalition joined the six evangelicals in "holy conferencing" to exchange views on the church's long conflict over homosexuality in heartfelt, if uncompromising, fashion, mediated by Tom Porter of JustPeace, an agency for conflict resolution in church settings. The morning after, on the heels of a General Conference vote to stiffen the church's stand against homosexuality, only two progressive leaders showed up, frustration flowed on both sides, and dialogue halted. Convinced that any separation proposal to General Conference would have to come from both sides of the evangelical-liberal rift, the evangelical leaders "left the proposal with those at the meeting without having discussed it," reported Heidinger. "We suggested they share it with those not present and possibly get back with us if interested" in joining together to present such a proposal for separation to the General Conference. Instead, said Heidinger, "someone made copies of it and gave it to the press."[33] CNN, the Associated Press, and the *New York Times* made the draft resolution public to the church and to the world. This led to confusion of the unsigned resolution with a poignant, widely published speech made two days later by Rev. William Hinson to a Good News briefing breakfast covered by the press.

"I believe the time has come when we must begin to explore an amicable and just separation that will free both sides from our cycle of pain and conflict," urged Hinson. "Such a just separation will protect the property rights of churches and the pension rights of clergy. It will also free us to reclaim our high calling to fulfill our mission in the world. Therefore, let us, like Paul and Barnabas, agree to go our separate ways."[34]

Hinson, president of the evangelical Confessing Movement and former pastor of the denomination's largest single congregation, had felt sadness sweep over his soul after the late-night meeting held earlier that week to discuss homosexuality in the church with liberal leaders, when he became "fully persuaded we cannot bridge the gap separating us." Why not? "Our friends in the Western Jurisdiction have left us. Our covenant is in shreds," mourned Hinson, and "our friends who have broken our covenant feel that they themselves are broken."

Hinson described the pain and frustration felt by both sides across this divide. He also emphasized how profound and essential were the differences between evangelicals and liberals in conceiving the church in relation to the Word of God and the culture of an increasingly godless society:

> Because the votes of this Conference have largely gone against them, they feel disenfranchised, they feel we are committing spiritual violence against them, and have told us clearly that we are not truth tellers. In addition they are seeking autonomy from the larger body. They garnered more than 300 votes in an attempt to do things their way with regard to ordination [of homosexuals] in the Western Jurisdiction. Let's set them and ourselves free to pursue our highest aspirations. . . .
>
> There is a great gulf fixed between those of us who are centered on Scripture and our friends who are of another persuasion. Repeatedly they have spoken of the need to get our church in step with our culture. We, on the other hand, have no desire to be the chaplain to an increasingly godless society. Rather, our desire is to be faithful to the Word of God. . . .
>
> If you are being led by a spirit to do something that is contrary to the Word of God, you must test the spirit, because it is clearly not the Spirit of God. The Holy Spirit will never contradict Himself. The Holy Spirit always fulfills Scripture, never contradicts it.
>
> For many, truth is still evolving. They sincerely believe that the world has the wisdom we need and we should relativize the Bible so as to bring our thoughts into harmony with whatever the current worldly wisdom suggests. We on the other hand believe that Jesus Christ is the same yesterday, today, and forever.

Hinson's speech met with both enthusiasm and disdain across the spectrum of conference delegates. "John Wesley said schism is a sin," responded Rev. Troy Plummer, executive director of the Reconciling Ministries Network, which is committed to gay inclusion.[35] "We will remain here in the United Methodist church today, tomorrow, and however long it takes to have a fully inclusive church," Plummer vowed.[36] "It is not only a foolish idea, it is really a very hurtful and destructive idea," said retired bishop Dale White of a schism that could be neither amicable nor just.[37]

The separation resolution that had been drafted by Good News called for a Task Force on Amicable Separation, which would work out a process of separation and present it to a special session of the General Conference in 2006. The resolution provided for congregations to keep their own property and for clergy to keep their pensions, as the two sides went their own ways toward separate denominations. A coalition of evangelical leaders met after Hinson's speech to consider bringing this resolution to the 2004 General Conference, reported Jim Heidinger, but they were not of one mind and decided not to move forward.[38] Talk of schism so consumed the conference, however, that a resolution on church unity was brought to the floor for a vote by a group of delegates from each jurisdiction. It read: "As United Methodists we remain in covenant with one another, even in the midst of our disagreement, and reaffirm our commitment to work together for our common mission of making disciples of Jesus Christ throughout the world."[39] The resolution was affirmed by an overwhelming 96 percent of the delegates, after which they rose to sing prayerfully "Blest Be the Tie That Binds."

Good News affirms the goal of unity in the church, Heidinger agreed afterward. "However, it should be very clear that the unity resolution passed at General Conference was little more than window dressing," he warned. "Despite the unity resolution, we are not a united church."[40] The Good News board accordingly resolved that unity "can only be attained when we share common commitments to our United Methodist doctrinal standards" as the church's covenantal bedrock. Therefore, Good News called on all of the church's annual and jurisdictional conferences to "act in accordance with church law and doctrine" not to perform gay unions and not to ordain or appoint self-avowed practicing homosexuals as ministers. "We will uphold the unity of the United Methodist Church as long as our common covenant is upheld by the actions of the church," pledged the board of Good News. If it is not, they vowed, they would "recognize the splintering of that unity." They warned, "Failure to uphold our doctrines and *Discipline* is what could further threaten the already fragile unity of our beloved church."[41]

Other conservative Methodist leaders announced their intention to carry their proposal for schism to congregations around the country. "Our statement is galloping across the earth and percolating in the hearts of our people," declared Hinson of the Confessing Movement at a breakfast meeting of several hundred supporters at the close of General Conference. Then, nine conservative leaders committed to mobilizing disaffected Methodist congregations and pastors to the cause of separation were called to the podium and given a blessing with the laying on of hands.[42] By contrast, declared church leaders opposed to schism, the vast majority of General Conference delegates, who voted 869 to 41 for church unity, represented the "Methodist middle" who would never give in to dividing the church. "We have a diverse group of delegates who overwhelmingly affirmed our unitedness," reported Rev. John Schol, who brought the unity resolution to the convention floor. "There might be a small fringe group that wants to divide us."[43]

Only about 1,400 of 36,000 United Methodist churches in the United States belong to the Confessing Movement, for example, and only 194 belong to the Reconciling Ministries Network. However prophetic or spirit-filled in their self-understanding as salt of the earth and leaven of the church, activist clergy and laity on both sides can also be seen as countervailing camps mobilized in a caucus church. They can be seen, too, as elites located on the small statistical tails of a bell curve of laity, or a two-humped curve of clergy, with a "moderate conservative" mixture of the not-so-political faithful in the middle.[44] "What about the rest of us, the middle who want to stay together as a family and learn how to live together?" asked Rev. Alice Rogers, a North Georgia delegate. "There's another group in our denomination—faithful United Methodists not identified with any cause," added a Mississippi delegate, Rev. Bill McAlilly. "More often than not we are silent, and perhaps that is our sin [as we] let other voices speak."[45] Trying to divide the United Methodist Church over homosexuality could backfire against conservative caucus groups, noted their critics, since many Methodists may disagree over homosexuality, but the centrist majority rejects such disagreement as a good and sufficient reason to separate the church into two denominations.[46]

Although efforts to create a schism in the United Methodist Church were soundly rejected, Methodists "will be hearing a lot about a schism these next four years from the same folks who relentlessly attack our denomination both from within and without," predicted James Winkler of the Board of Church and Society. "They have a strategy to turn back the clock in this country and around the world. Diversity and difference [are] anathema to those who want conformity or banishment. But the United Methodist Church is diverse in every way—theologically, racially, ethnically, ideologically, and geographically." As a consequence, reported Winkler, delegates of the 2004 General Conference adopted the vast majority of the board's fifty resolutions, thirteen proposed changes to the Social Principles, and four proposed changes to the *Discipline*. They handily dismissed three petitions to eliminate or defund the board or to check its social witness by turning it back into a Board of Temperance.[47]

Instead, General Conference approved new language in the *Discipline* directing the Board of Church and Society to aid "other general agencies as they work as advocates with the U.S. Congress." At the board's urging, the General Conference strengthened the church's stand against the death penalty and sharpened its call for global trade agreements that "enforce labor rights and human rights as well as environmental standards."[48] A new resolution on terrorism warns against unilateral and preemptive military and political policies that undermine the international cooperation essential to prevent further terrorist attacks. Stronger language also calls for cuts in U.S. military spending in order to fund education, housing, health care, and employment. It points out that African Americans, Hispanics, and Native Americans suffer disproportionately from joblessness, poor housing, cutbacks in education, and lack of health care.

A few days after the General Conference, where it had failed to reach the floor for a vote, a resolution was passed by the Council of Bishops against the continued warfare by the United States and coalition forces in Iraq. It emphasized that the cycle of violence there had led to the "denigration of human dignity and gross violations of human rights of Iraqi prisoners of war." The bishops called on the U.S. government to request that the United Nations become involved in the transition process to a new Iraqi government, and it urged that a multinational development plan be started to rebuild Iraq and other nations in the Middle East.[49]

On these social issues and moral mandates, the Board of Church and Society would continue to work closely with annual conferences and local churches to help United Methodists "join mercy and justice," promised Jim Winkler. "And with God's help, we will continue to speak truth to power."[50]

Coherence and Conflict in a Caucus Church

Without denying the fierce conflict within General Conference as the governing body of United Methodism, there is, suggest some critics of Good

News, nonetheless good cause for hope about the prospects of the church as a whole. It stems from the underlying coherence of Christianity in the Methodist tradition that is evident in the vitality of grassroots activity on various fronts of the Methodist Church, irreducible to the false dichotomy Good News proclaims between heterodox theological liberals and orthodox evangelical conservatives.

So argues Philip Amerson, a longtime Methodist seminary president, educator, pastor, and activist member of the Board of Church and Society.[51] Among self-styled progressives in local churches around the country and on the board, too, says Amerson, there is "an openness to healing services, new spirituality, prayerful witness and worship." It converges with new concern for social justice among evangelicals, and their new willingness to discuss controversial issues such as abortion across conventional cultural and political dividing lines. Rather than adopting the quasi-Calvinist stance of Good News to fix on declarations of doctrinal "fundamentals," the structures of Methodist polity, and its checks on local churches, Amerson sees Methodists getting "more in touch with who we have been, in the best of the revivalist tradition." Here, in fact, "you had folks riding across the prairie preaching, 'Come to Jesus, and by the way come to the abolition meeting next week.' Or 'Come to Jesus, and let's work on getting these damn saloons closed.'"

The heart of Social Christianity is truly evangelical in this view, and Methodism betrays its own heritage by becoming rigidly concerned with fundamentalistic creedalism, biblical inerrancy, and end-times eschatology. "How can you preach about the sanctified life and not also be saying it's possible to be engaged in holy living on earth, and be working toward the reign of God's kingdom on earth?" Amerson asks. Methodists need to recall not only Wesley's born-again experience at Aldersgate, he urges, but Wesley's work in Bristol, Newcastle, and London. There, as in the Foundry, Wesley and his followers "administered the church, held class meetings, and prayed. But they also founded orphanages and schools, cared for the sick, fed the hungry, visited prisoners, and did all those things Luke tells us true Christians do."

In this Christian spirit, argues Amerson, reflecting on efforts backed by Good News in the 1990s to curb the worldliness of the General Board of Global Ministries by removing its offices from New York City to the Midwest, "the problem isn't that we need to get the mission board out of New York. It's that we need to get the mission board into New York!" Ignoring that need, and the underlying evangelical spirit of social Christianity, leaves Good News headed in the wrong direction. "My father was on the original board of Good News, and early on I would go to their convocations," Amerson recalls. "I got increasingly uncomfortable with it. So let's say you take over the United Methodist Church, I used to ask them; what have you got? 'Well, we think we can do better with the structures,' they would say. Maybe they could, but what have you got without the Spirit?"

What else is missing from the "scriptural renewal" that Good News champions within United Methodism? The integrity of Scripture itself, counters the veteran GBCS leader Herman Will. "What are they going to do with Amos? Are they going to write him out of the Bible?"[52] Concern for justice that is both loving and lawful goes to the root of biblical faith, he argues, and it rises above American ideals of free-market rights for individuals to pursue their own happiness while giving back only a bit to the neediest. "We can't be content with charity any longer," he says, because by itself it's condescending and unjust. "It's rewarding the people who have taken more than their share for turning back not even that, but only a portion of that share."

American Christians can no longer be content to evangelize a world that our society exploits economically and that our nation dominates by its military might and political power. "You and I never intended it, but every day of our lives, we are riding on the backs of the poor and the third world, every day," emphasizes Will. "If they were paid our minimum wage, what would we have to pay to buy the goods they make, and what would happen to our purchasing power and our standard of living?" Our privileged way of life and powerful ascendency as a nation actually amount to an idolatrous kind of false sovereignty, argues Will. "As Christians, we believe that God is sovereign and that all nations live under the judgment of God, and by the love and mercy of God. So there is really no such thing as true sovereignty for nations, and what we must do as best we can—imperfectly, to be sure—is to create in the actual reality of political structures the truth of a world sovereignty under God, who looks upon all the nations alike."

This argument goes on within and around the Methodist Board of Church and Society precisely because it is a moral and theological conflict, attests activist bishop Dale White, not an ideological struggle between political left and right. "I want to try to be faithful to the biblical mandate, as far as I can see, and I stand in the Wesleyan heritage, so I try to understand the differences between myself and a good many people from the Good News environment," he says.[53] They claim to be Wesleyans, but "if you challenge them in terms of their real effectiveness in social analysis and social witness and action to organize for social change and make a difference in the world, they immediately say, 'Well, look at all the money we're giving to all these good causes,' and divert the argument back to localized relief." It is a response innocent of prophetic social criticism and involvement beyond simply passing good resolutions and expressing good intentions. "The difference between my mentality and theirs is, I'd guess I'd have to say"—White pauses for emphasis—"I've been radicalized," by the suffering he has seen firsthand in Mozambique, throughout Africa and the Middle East, and among America's poor in the midst of plenty. "Our current situation is intolerable for most of the human family, if you take the whole flow of Scripture seriously, including shalom and biblical righteousness."

In response, urges White, Methodist bishops, boards, pastors, and people in the pews must come together, as they did in standing against apartheid in South Africa and in joining the initiative White led "in defense of creation" against the threat of nuclear winter. Thus Methodists can help develop "global institutions to mobilize the common will and resources of humanity" to care for the whole human family. They can work to contain outlaw nations and secure peace, share work and wealth, balance population growth, and empower a true forum among nations. In doing so, warns White, faithful Methodists must be prepared to "run afoul of countervailing theological perspectives that seek to individualize and localize" such prophetic work for peace and justice and return Methodism to "the last century by reinstating the ole boy network" and discrediting the church's new feminist and liberationist leaders. They must likewise be prepared to resist related efforts to "systematically marginalize" the Board of Church and Society by stripping it of resources and assigning it to "the ritual task of resolution-drafting with the expectation that the resolutions will sound good, but no one will do anything about them."

To the extent that cultural politics and social differences figure in this theological feuding, adds Bishop William Dew, Methodism needs to open its eyes to the plurality and diversity of its own changing congregations in a world changing around them, and recognize the gospel truth that the church must bring alive in this world.[54] From the first year he was appointed as a pastor in California, Dew recalls, he found socially mixed congregations that were not in the least creedally homogenized. Yet they were nonetheless ready and willing to come together in "a culture that had dropped its props" under religious orthodoxy long before the present moment so decried by orthodox alarmists. "Let them come to the West Coast," he laughs, before he makes the serious point that today Methodists everywhere, particularly those raised in the church who have left it, are better educated but no less faithful at heart. They are truly hungry "to discover who they are as a child of God with a new sense of freedom from the malaise of personal success and failure by experiencing God's grace in their life." The Methodist Church must respond with a truly nurturing spirit that is at odds with both American ideals of getting ahead and "neo-Fundamentalist saving stations," where strivers can stop in and fill up spiritually before getting right out on the road again on the drive to success and security.

Such evangelism escapes the usual boundary lines dividing conservative evangelicals from progressive theological liberals and liberationists, adds George McLain, head of the Methodist Federation for Social Action (MFSA), long seen as embodying the latter pole among Methodists. Recalling the moral urgency and vigor of the civil rights movement he experienced as a young activist in Alabama in the 1960s, McLain testifies that "we could go to rallies in churches, then march on City Hall, you know, Bible in one hand and newspaper in the other, and say, 'This is the way it's supposed to be. The church is at the forefront of the struggle.' But we were building on an enormous amount of work and suffering and struggle that had been going on since slavery, and a lot of that came from the black church, not the churches as a whole. When we moved back into the mainstream of the white churches in everyday life, it almost never lives up to that."[55]

Nonetheless, McLain avers, "out of the civil rights movement and the Vietnam antiwar movement comes the feminist movement, then the gay/ lesbian movement, and a set of new issues that are the ones bedeviling the churches now." Still in the process of theological gestation, these issues strike deep at the most intimate relationships of people in the pews and their most powerful images of God. They have already exploded politically into controversies over abortion, gay marriage, and gay ordination. Given MFSA's founding to seek economic justice for labor and its continuing commitment to racial and social justice, allows McLain, "it's hard for a group like ours to let gay/lesbian issues become the litmus test for social witness. We continue to fight for workers' rights and relate these to racism, environmentalism, and justice for working women and workers in the third world," in step with similar reframing of such issues in the Board of Church and Society. The board's growing concern for reaching and teaching Methodists in local churches should complement and support its public advocacy in Washington, urges McLain, "if it nurtures a constituency in the churches, more like the United Methodist Women's Division, so the legislative action grows out of a larger living movement in the church, not just coalitions in Washington." Turning toward Methodists in the pews to nurture social witness in the congregational practice of their faith, believes McLain, can also deepen the experiential roots and communal embodiment of this witness, in contrast to its intellectual and political rationalization on every side:

> Whether it's the fundamentalists or the theological liberals, we have all been very rationalistic preachers of the Enlightenment. Good News is very rationally religious in stereotyping what your experience of sin and salvation is going to be. And some of us are waking up to the limitations of our theological upbringing, at Union Seminary or wherever in the 1960s, to discover more of the luminous sense of life in faithful communion with God. That becomes experiential. Our religion is not just ethical.

Instead of the secularized "institutionalism" epitomized by political infighting over control of denominational bureaucracies and budgets, concludes McLain, "we need to nurture the Spirit in order to live out our analysis of a world where there's a hell of a lot of entrenched resistance to justice and peace. At the cutting edge of that effort is how to unite the spiritual sense of our connectedness in dependence on God to the equally inner call to become prophetically involved. That comes out of personal struggle, but it's communal. It isn't just my own, it isn't just in my head."

Good News and its adversaries in the United Methodist Church continue to cross rhetorical swords and clash in their campaigns to renew or transform the church. "The church is under assault by Good News, the IRD [Institute on Religion and Democracy], the Confessing Movement, and the Mission Society," charged James Lawson, a longtime church activist for racial and social justice in a much-quoted speech to the MFSA during the 2000 General Conference. "They are not interested in serving Jesus Christ. They are interested in the management and control of the United Methodist Church" and in "preserving white supremacy and male domination," said Lawson. "They are not voices of God but voices of white privilege, greed, capitalism, racism[,] . . . and American domination of the rest of the world."[56] So much for inclusivism, riposted James Heidinger. "This kind of vicious verbiage represents the last gasps of a fading, dying liberalism."[57]

However painful and troubling these conflicts over theology, authority, policy, and programs may be, they are also a measure of the integrity of the United Methodist Church along dimensions that are both spiritual and political, contends Lawson. "I'm not against the political process in the church, no, because I think the political process is exactly the way in which God makes decisions in the world."[58] Full political participation and fair representation in the Methodist Church are vital for the sake of its theological insight and moral decision-making. This holds true, Lawson explains, for General Conference, annual conferences, and the Board of Church and Society alike. It holds true in, for example, enabling the church to grasp the moral unity of civil rights with abortion and homosexuality as expressions of Christian love of neighbor, human hospitality, and social inclusion. "At one time, the General Conference was 85 percent white males," Lawson recalls, "and they were completely in charge. Women largely kept quiet and were invisible. There were very few people of color anywhere to be seen, and those who were there were acquiescent. That world has changed," he proclaims, both in the Methodist Church and the larger society. Abortion and homosexuality are linked to racial justice within their common embrace by true "human hospitality, community, and love, especially from the perspective of African Americans and Native Americans in the history of this country," stresses Lawson, "where it's a question of whether or not we are human. Or whether we are not acceptable, we are not to be treated with hospitality as a part of the human family, because we have defects."

Pious pleas and political strategizing to return the United Methodist Church to so-called orthodoxy, argues Lawson, reflect "a lot of fear and insecurity in a world full of ambiguity, even in our own families and communities, where being a pastor is far more challenging and perplexing, where our moral authority is being questioned on every hand, and where some folks are trying to put it all back into the bottle." Instead, the United Methodist Church needs to keep struggling not to turn its back on the surrounding society and not to turn back to resegregating itself. "We should love our land like Jeremiah and Jesus," Lawson sums up, "and embrace our church as a church for the whole gospel and the whole community of the human family."

In the caucus churches of mainline Protestantism today, "almost every cause and group has a voice now," observes the Methodist theologian Theodore Runyon, and almost every view is represented by an interest group. Like many responsibly reformist church leaders, Runyon is dismayed by "orthodox reaction or rigidity that has set in to close off new possibilities for dialogue and rapprochement between the church and the modern world." But he also criticizes the debilitating effects of "a pluralism that has no center, in which there is no clear, common commitment to what unites us as a body." From this standpoint, two related prospects seem most likely to unfold. "Institutionally we seem to be moving toward more of a confederation within our denomination and across the Protestant churches generally," thinks Runyon. "Different groups with their own identities will sit down together in mutual recognition. They'll dialogue and cooperate as closely as they can, without denying the differences that continue to separate them. We'll continue to pay careful attention to democratic representation for different groups, especially minorities. We'll keep relying on constitutional sorts of rights to protect them from the tyranny of the majority." At the same time, thinks Runyon, "losing our easy association as mainly male, middle-aged members of the WASP middle class presents itself as an opportunity to rediscover what holds us together as a church that's not defined or limited by a dominant class or race. It can lead us back to our own denominational roots" in Methodist practice, teaching, and polity, reworked in graceful response to the present historical moment. It can nurture congregational community without severing the connection. It can decentralize the denomination without fracturing it into voting blocs or splitting it in schism. Runyon sees hope for this prospect. In Methodism a generation ago, he recalls, "you couldn't get anyone to talk about Wesley. He'd been done in by theologians as diverse as Karl Barth and Dietrich Bonhoeffer as just a pietist sentimentalist who began and ended with the warmed heart." Today there is much greater recognition that "Wesley understood that salvation and human destiny require the transformation of persons to overcome the effects of original sin, almost on the model of the Eastern Fathers; and that salvation requires social sanctification as well, in order to return us to the purposes for which we were created."[59]

The Covenant of a Conciliar Church

Ecclesiology underlies political and cultural conflicts among Methodists over decisive moral issues and their theological interpretation. Indeed, ecclesiology may be a vexing part of the problem, say some church leaders, since Methodism lacks a well-defined and unified ecclesiology to draw it together. Wesley took Anglican ecclesiology for granted, even as Methodism transformed church polity, explains Bishop Bruce Blake of Texas, and Methodists today continue to argue over multiple models of the church that pull it in different directions. "We're a fellowship of believers, we're a communion of saints, we're the people of God. Go to ten local churches, or ten denominational board meetings, and you will find a range of ecclesiologies from high-church to low that stretches from Anglicans to Quakers."[60]

A crisis of spiritual and moral authority lies at the heart of Methodism's ecclesiological confusion, Bishop Blake contends. "Authority comes from God through Jesus to the individual, then to the community and back to the individual. The authority of the community is key in the book of Acts," he emphasizes. Christians are subject to each other's authority within a priesthood of all believers that enables and inspires them to be "priests to and for each other." In terms of their heartfelt intentions and powerful resources, Methodists have "absolutely the best organization to deliver God's mission in the world," Blake believes. But "you cannot have well-defined authority in the church without a well-defined ecclesiology, and that's where we slip on the banana peel." To recover its balance and authority, specifies Bishop Blake, the United Methodist Church must begin its renewal through bishops working with pastors in annual conferences and people in the pews of local churches. "Renewal can only come where a person's membership is, and there are three places for membership in the United Methodist Church: the local church, the annual conference for pastors, and the Council of Bishops. That's the genius of connection," and the essential starting point for church renewal that is "going to happen in little pieces" and achieve critical mass conference by conference, foresees Blake. "Anyone who wastes their time trying to turn around the whole denomination is going to become very, very frustrated," he attests from firsthand experience.

Methodism's multifocal ecclesiology can, however, serve to clarify conflicts over the denomination's mission and meaning as the Christian church, even if it cannot resolve them. So proposes Bishop Joseph Yeakel, president of the Board of Church and Society from 1993 to 1996. In his opening address to the board, Bishop Yeakel began by professing, "The very heart and core of what we're about is that we truly are the church when we gather as the General Board of Church and Society."[61] Because its members were not sent to represent the annual conferences that elected them but to practice "how to be church," their self-understanding must begin with the biblical foundation of covenant. Voluntarily "shackled

and fettered to Christ" and to one another in Christ, members of a covenanted church seek to live out "a gracious and grace-filled relationship
as an agreement entered into prayerfully before God on a basis of mutual
understanding and trust, faith in others in response to faithfulness and
love received." Unlike a conventional contract, bargain, or pledge, which
can be broken by an individual, the covenant of the church is marked by
a sacramental kind of mutuality. It "twines together" its members and
enables them to "go on in affection," with a love that expects nothing in
return, including invulnerability, and demands nothing at all.

Within this covenant arises the essentially conciliar nature of the
church, Yeakel states. It precedes and makes possible the connectional
organization of Methodism: "We're a connectional church because we're
first a conciliar church." As such, "we count if we counsel together, in
council, to know what God would have us do. We're not a creedalist, confessional church, although we have creeds and confessions, and they are
helps to us in our lives of worship together. But we're not a church that
says, 'This is exactly what we believe in,' or 'You can test our followers
against such creedal or confessional statements.' We're a conciliar church
in saying simply that God has not spoken the last word in that sense, and
that the Word of God is best understood in the councils of the church.
When we counsel together, the counsel of God is with us."

So it is that the conciliarity of the Methodist Church grounds its character and structure as a "connectional, itinerant and episcopal church."
As opposed to the congregationalism of a denomination in which each local church calls its own ministers, Methodist bishops appoint members of
an itinerant clergy to local congregations. Members of one or more congregations under the charge of a given pastor meet and make decisions
in "charge conferences" within the church's "basic body" of diocese-sized
annual conferences and their districts. Bishops appoint district superintendents from the ranks of the ordained elders in an annual conference,
and the district superintendents authorize and preside over charge conferences. Connectionalism in the United Methodist tradition, explains its
Book of Discipline, is "not merely a linking of one charge conference to
another. It is rather a vital web of interactive relationships."[62] Within this
web, the General Board of Church and Society constitutes "the ongoing expression of our conciliarity," as Bishop Yeakel puts it, between the
quadrennial meetings of the church's General Conference.[63] The heavy
responsibility of the board for counseling together and "listening to what
God is saying to us in council" offers a striking counterexample to the con-

ventional activities of bureaucratic agencies and offices focused on "collecting our agendas to see how we can work things through." It marks the board off from assemblies of representatives elected to voice the views of their constituents and vote their interests. The Social Principles and Social Creed of the United Methodist Church, set out in its *Book of Discipline*, express the conciliar integrity of the church's General Conference and make up the normative law of the church, Yeakel stressed to the members of the GBCS. As individuals, each of them "has the right to your opinion on any subject, and especially on any subject that's contained within the normative law of the church," he allows. "But as ordained and consecrated persons in the life of the church, before you give your opinion, you have a commitment to teach what the church has said with integrity. Then give your opinion." It is, then, as a conciliar embodiment and teaching office of the church—not a legislative lobby, political-action committee, or freestanding moral advocacy group—that the Methodist Board of Church and Society should take up its mandate to facilitate church programs of social action and education, speak truth to the powers that be, and witness prophetically in the public square.

The challenges the board faces in carrying out its mandate do not arise simply from worldly resistance to its mission, though that inheres in its charge to transform social principles into the reality of social institutions. The board is "entrusted with all of the controversial stuff the church faces," explains Yeakel after his address.[64] "At times we've led well. When you really study our Social Principles, it's not too bad a statement. When you come to making them real and tangible in the world, that's a whole other story." It is a story in which conflict inheres not so much between political liberals and conservatives, or between liberal Protestants and conservative evangelicals, but between the beloved community the church seeks to instantiate and the existing institutions it seeks to transform. Christians, too, inhabit these institutions, and bring to the church the contrary social models and moral habits these institutions breed.

So when the church institutionalizes a prophetic ministry, Bishop Yeakel reflects, it should expect conflict as well as controversy to center there. It should expect to become a focal point of misunderstanding about the distinctive nature of the church itself in precisely those ways that it does not resemble a modern bureaucracy, marketplace, or political arena:

> Wesley formed the church in a conciliar mode. The annual meetings of the preachers in a city grew into conferences, and gradually into the whole series of

charge conferences, annual conferences, and the quadrennial General Conference the United Methodist Church has today.

The basic questions the preachers started with in their meetings were, "Who are we, gathered as Christ's Church? What does God want with us? How are we going to discern what God would have, and how are we going to respond?" Then they started going around and around the table.

One of the problems you have when you get to be the size we are, and you live in the world we live in, is that you start to move away from discernment and conciliarity into a legislative mode, and then you're in a win-lose setting. You come into the plenary, you vote yes or no, and you win or lose.

This win-lose setting bears on a thousand delegates voting on hundreds of resolutions over eleven days every four years at the church's General Conference. Some three thousand resolutions and petitions were submitted to General Conference in 2000, for example, consolidated from more than ten thousand, submitted by twelve thousand groups and individuals. The win-lose setting also bears on members of the Board of Church and Society who are tempted to see themselves as political representatives of the conferences that elected them, notes Yeakel, and thereby mandated to set the board right by trying to control its staff of "church bureaucrats" in their employ, or trying to serve as adjunct staff and would-be religious professionals in their own right.

Drawing on his experience of responding to civil litigation on behalf of the United Methodist Church, Bishop Yeakel observes, "The church is no longer safe just because it's a church." It's not above the law or beyond the courts, of course. But more profoundly, what this means is that "we cannot safely suppose our own people understand what the church is," living as they do in a free country with free associations. Here, at almost every turn, "we can litigate or we can leave," says Yeakel, since everyone has a right to hold their own opinion, litigate their claims, and vote with their feet. De facto drift toward a more associational model of the church shows up, Yeakel notes, in the guise of greater congregational autonomy in local Methodist churches to call their own pastors, rather than have bishops appoint, or "deploy," the ministers that each annual conference sends him or her. "Constitutionally, bishops have the right and duty to deploy," he explains, "and constitutionally, the local churches have the responsibility to accept the pastors we deploy." The General Conference has added "consultation" to this relationship, which it defines as sharing information and advice, but not negotiation. "Local churches today almost never hear

that it's not negotiation," says Yeakel, "because everybody else is nego-
tiating these things, and everybody thinks they ought to have the power
to negotiate. So when push comes to shove around changing pastors, I
can see the day coming when we will not have an itinerant system in the
Methodist Church. We'll have a call system, because there will be no other
way" out of a rising sea of controversy with local churches, and a growing
impasse Methodist bishops face in making appointments.

The authority of a connectional and episcopal church comes to seem
more like the arbitrary exercise of autocratic power as local churches see
themselves in more associational terms. Individuals and families voluntarily choose to join, stay in, or leave a local church. Their views and votes
should likewise count first in democratically choosing their own pastors
and priorities, which are funded by their own financial contributions to
pay the church bills. "We're running against the tide on this," reports
Yeakel, "and the thing is that the clergy are also joining in the tide. We
have what I call 'yes-but itinerancy.' 'Yes, I'll go,' newly appointed pastors tell me, 'but my wife has a good lawyer's job here . . . Yes, I'll go, but
my kids are in a good school . . . Yes, I'll go, but I can't be any farther than
thirty minutes from here.' " When careers come first in dual-professional
families, it is particularly hard to accommodate these circumstantial restrictions, notes Yeakel, but it's still not easy in the case of dual-clergy
couples with more of a shared sense of being called to ministry.

After decades of striving and investing to attain an educated clergy,
the United Methodist Church is now struggling with the difficulty of placing and paying for them in a dual-career world that combines more equal
opportunities for women, higher expectations and costs of middle-class
life, and more pinched resources for mainline denominations. "There was
a day when fully 20 cents of every dollar put in the plate escaped the local church, and 5 cents reached the general boards and agencies of the
national denomination. Probably only 16–17 cents escape now, and only
2–3 cents get beyond the annual conferences to the national level," Yeakel
reports. "This year, only three of the seventy regular annual conferences
paid their full apportionment for World Service," which funds the boards
and agencies of the national denomination. "So the folks here are being
constantly shrunk, and I don't see that turning around," Yeakel worries.
"That scares me." But shifts away from denominational activism toward
congregational localism are driven by more than pinched dollars. The
pressures exerted by the working demands of dual-earner families may
make more impact at the level of the denomination than in local churches,

Yeakel suspects, reinforced by much more denominational switching and looser loyalties in a "maximum-mobility society" driven by the demands of middle-class education and careers.[65]

What Methodists must hope and work for through all these changes, counsels Yeakel, is that the church now be "freer to be the church" in the vigor and diversity of its expression in local congregations. What should concern Methodists most is the capacity and willingness of the church to educate its members, form them as disciples of Christ, and bind them together in the body of the church. "Personally, I am not so worried about the future of the institutional church as I was for a while," says Yeakel. "If I worry about anything, it's about the lack of educational work in the church. You can't go and talk to a congregation today and presume that everybody knows about Noah's ark and the rainbow. You've got to tell the whole story." In the face of such experience, he finds scant reassurance from "Gallup polls that tell us the baby-boomer generation is more religious than ever; they're just not so committed to religious institutions."[66]

The denomination must acknowledge the responsibility it shares for helping to create its present predicament. During the postwar heyday of mainline denominational growth, Yeakel says,

> we made church members. We didn't make disciples. Everything was going one way—up—except for professions of faith. They started down in 1958, about the same time the bumper crop of baby-boom kids became confirmands, while our membership kept going up until 1963–64.
>
> We were so good at making members, and so many of them were coming in and bringing in so much money, that we didn't ask the other questions about who we are as the church, and what God wants with us. We didn't rein in our own entrepreneurs and hold them accountable. Now we're on the downside of that. We're having to account for it.

From this accounting, what should the Methodist Church learn in order to renew the vision and work of its General Board of Church and Society? Go back to the beginning of Methodists' covenantal commitment to a conciliar church, Yeakel answers. Recognize the responsibility of its ministers to teach the good counsel of this church in its integrity, before giving their own opinions. Recognize the great trust this lays upon both the ministers and people of the church, and then undertake to form them as disciples capable of bearing it together.

Finally, Yeakel concludes, the Methodist Church needs to recognize the theological integrity of its historically distinctive social concerns. This includes the evangelical heritage of its concern with how persons live their everyday lives and how they nurture or harm those closest to them. "Let's really take seriously the traditional issues of alcohol and drugs," he urges. "Treat it with integrity, and it's like you're a pastor holding hands with your parishioners," and thereby renewing Methodism's historic union of social sanctification with personal piety and conversion. Without weakening its commitment to social justice or world peace, the church can critically remake its vision of the kingdom in terms less indebted to the welfare-state or free-market ideals rehearsed by political campaigns. In 1998 the United Methodist Church celebrated the seventy-fifth anniversary of the Methodist Building on Capitol Hill. "There are people alive who remember giving pennies to build it. It was built with alcohol money," Yeakel says gently. "That is still out there. It's part of our heritage." After having come through Prohibition as well as the Depression and the New Deal, the Great Society and the Reagan Revolution, he prays, "we need to ask what that kind of issue means at the end of the twentieth century instead of the nineteenth. We need to make sure we're not the Pharaoh, who does not know Joseph."

To Name Sin and Proclaim Grace:
Connectional Revival and Reform

The primary paths toward realizing a vision of God's reign on earth as it is in heaven, Jim Winkler affirms, lie in "the intertwining ministries of evangelism, justice and mercy," within the connectionalism that is the great strength peculiar to the Methodist Church.[67] Relationships are healed, Christian discipleship takes on new meaning, and "true happiness comes only when we receive God's love and begin to love God and others" in return.[68] But justice calls Christians beyond personal acts of charity into the public realm of prophetic witness and action, where political confrontation inevitably follows. There they must be willing to witness with little prospect of winning politically, on the model of the Christian pacifist A. J. Muste, standing in front of the White House night after night with a candle during the Vietnam War and responding to an incredulous reporter wondering whether he really thought this would change the country's policy: "Oh, I don't do this to change the country. I do this so the country won't change me." Christians must be willing to accept that the "primary task of the church is to be a community of resistance." Imagine what could be done in the areas of health care, the environment, education, hunger and poverty, and the fight against AIDS, urges Winkler, "if we were to resist the lie that safety and security lie in military spending? It seems to me this is exactly what we United Methodists mean when we say that the purpose of the church is to make disciples of Jesus Christ."[69]

If we are to be transformed into the likeness of Christ as persons, we must repent our sins. As American citizens today, we must likewise renounce all weapons of mass destruction and doctrines of preemptive military action, Winkler argues, and accept moral responsibility for the fact that U.S. military spending now exceeds that of all the other nations on earth by taking to heart what President Dwight Eisenhower said fifty years ago: "Every gun that is made, every warship launched, every rocket fired, signifies in the final sense a theft from those who hunger and are not fed, those who are cold and are not clothed. This world in arms is not spending money alone, it is spending the sweat of its laborers, the genius of its scientists, the hopes of its children." What would Jesus do? "There is absolutely zero evidence to suggest that Jesus would condone war," Winkler answers, since Jesus lived under military occupation by Rome's client rulers who terrorized the Jewish populace to pacify them. Yet Jesus accepted neither violent nor passive resistance to such aggression. "On the contrary, he showed us a third way—that of active nonviolent resistance to evil and injustice," Winkler says. This is the way, also taken by Martin Luther King, Jr., to stand up to the powers that be and stand against the violence of the state by following the true Prince of Peace.[70]

Loving our neighbor and acting justly both lead the Christian church to name sin and proclaim grace in public. "We know there's enough food to feed everybody, but right now there is insufficient will to accomplish this achievable goal," Winkler wrote during the 2002 congressional debate over inheritance taxes, even as "the wealthiest one percent of our nation stands to reap half a trillion dollars of their own if the estate tax cut is passed! That's a sin."[71] Ending hunger will require reordering our national and global priorities as Americans, judges Winkler, and it will mean facing up to our responsibilities as Christians in light of Paul's counsel to the Ephesians (6:12): "For our struggle is not against enemies of blood and flesh, but against the rulers, against the authorities, against the cosmic powers of this present darkness, against the spiritual forces of evil in the heavenly places." Environmental degradation, pandemic poverty, and a world awash with weapons are the true "axis of evil" we face—not Iran, Iraq, and North Korea. Resisting these evils continues the work of Christ's disciples, Winkler promises, and it fulfills Wesley's aim for the Methodist movement to "reform the church, reform the nation, and spread scriptural holiness across the land."[72]

At present, charge its critics, the Methodist General Board of Church and Society betrays Wesley's vision for the church and epitomizes the larger failure of general agency connectionalism in Methodism today.[73] It stands for what is worst in the church: a bureaucratic elite advocating liberationist theology and left-liberal politics at odds with Methodists in the pews of local churches, unwilling to heed them, and unable to embrace them in the prayerful spirit of orthodox Christian belief and congregational practice. Critics on the right such as Good News have indicted the GBCS, demanded its radical reform, and backed the Institute on Religion and Democracy as a freestanding advocacy group to counter it (as chapters 5 and 6 will detail), much like the Mission Society for United Methodists serves as a kind of government-in-exile to oppose the General Board of Global Ministries.

At the same time, some Methodist bishops, as well as radical reformers, have championed new norms of decentralized, local-church initiatives to revitalize congregations and parish ministry in the face of declining denominational membership and contributions: "The local church truly is the church through whose ministries the reign of God must be made known if we expect that reign to be known anywhere," proclaims the Council of Bishops in *Vital Congregations, Faithful Disciples: Vision for the Church*.[74] On the other hand, warns Russell Richey, denominational self-incrimination for abandoning local churches in order to bear the burdens of national agencies runs the risk of "slighting the translocal, collective, and connectional revivalism of quarterly conference, camp meeting, conference, a moving people, and an itinerant ministry" that have shaped the soul of American Methodism.[75]

Instead of further corroding connectional confidence in their national boards and agencies and subverting the connectional grammar of their history by disconnected congregational initiatives, urges Richey, United Methodists need to revive the Methodist movement by new experiments in connection itself. They need to recognize the vibrant promise of their proliferating national caucuses, however diverse and conflicted, to reconnect Methodism beyond the boundaries of local churches.[76] They need to shape smaller and more collegial yet no less inclusive boards, and to strengthen the historic connectional capacities of General Conference and the bishops as truly itinerating general superintendents. They need to link local experiments in disciplined holiness, and reach out to the larger society through more innovative media and Sunday-schooling ventures. Set within this larger context and seen at its best, controversy over the Methodist Board of Church and Society rises above the schematic oppositions of local church versus denominational bureaucracy, or cultural liberals versus conservatives. It promises to help renew the connectional identity of Methodism as a dynamic movement dedicated to both evangelistic revival and social reform, equally in tension with denominational bureaucracy and congregational establishment.

John Wesley conceived a movement to reform the Church of England and the nation by spiritual revival and social action alike. This movement engaged the church and the nation by acting as an *ecclesiola*, or exemplary "small church," not as a sect standing apart from both established church and nation. For precisely this reason, urges Jim Winkler, Methodists, as members of the third-largest church in the denominational society of America today, should be the first to look beyond their own pews to grasp "how important our denomination is in the life of this nation, indeed in the world." Instead, he writes, "we spend a lot of time lamenting our numerical decline—as if John Wesley had the slightest intention of creating a prosperous denomination ever-increasing in numbers—while we miss the good news of the prophetic and merciful ministries in which we are engaged." Winkler concludes with a vow and a challenge:

> The third largest church is ours, and we stand ready to work ecumenically and through interfaith partnerships. We participate in social and economic justice coalitions and are part of the struggle for environmental justice, for peace, and for the rights of women and racial and ethnic minorities. People depend on The United Methodist Church. Praise God. We have much work to do. Even in the midst of an economic downturn we are in the grip of "prosperity theology." Here's a statistic for you: $40 billion a year—about 10 percent of U.S. military spending—would provide universal access to healthcare, food, clean water, and sanitation for all who go without worldwide. It is a sin that healing such pain stands within our grasp, and yet there is absolutely no political will in Washington, D.C. to make that happen.
>
> The question is whether the church has the moral will to demand the economic values of the New Testament. Do we?[77]

This vow and challenge from the United Methodist General Board of Church and Society sound particularly welcome to leaders of the other mainline Protestant church offices in Washington, for reasons explored in part 2 of this book. In their ears, too, this final question rings true and troubling. For leaders of the Institute on Religion and Democracy, this vow is all the more troubling, as the next two chapters reveal, because the politics of peace and justice in the mainline churches rings false to the gospel truth and the American Creed alike.

CHAPTER FIVE

Faith and Freedom

The Institute on Religion and Democracy

The Institute on Religion and Democracy began with a bang. It issued from a report fired across the bow of the United Methodist Church in 1980, aimed at challenging the "peace-and-justice" course set by leaders of the Methodist General Board of Church and Society and the General Board of Global Ministries. "Most Methodist church-goers would react with disbelief, even anger," the report began, "to be told that a significant portion of their weekly offerings were being siphoned off to groups supporting the Palestine Liberation Organization, the governments of Cuba and Vietnam, and the pro-Soviet totalitarian movements of Latin America, Asia and Africa, and several violence-prone fringe groups in this country."[1]

So charged the report's author, David Jessup, a new member of the United Methodist Church in a large suburban congregation outside Washington, D.C., and a longtime labor organizer then working for the AFL-CIO Committee on Political Education (COPE). Jessup became concerned about the political orientation of the United Methodist Church when he and his wife began attending Methodist services after moving to the Washington area in the mid-1970s. A veteran of the Peace Corps in Peru and of the civil rights and farmworkers' movements in California, Jessup was interested in becoming involved in church-related projects such as refugee assistance. "When my children brought home Sunday school appeals for wheat shipments to the government of Vietnam, and the controversy over Methodist support for the Patriotic Front in Zimbabwe became public, I was troubled," he reported, "but not persuaded that these projects represented anything more than minor aberrations from a more consistent tradition of Methodist support for democratic values."[2]

After several months of asking church officials where they sent church funds and researching their recipients at home and abroad, Jessup concluded that funds were going to "the totalitarian left," as opposed to "the democratic left" represented by "Christian social-democratic parties, free trade unions and democratic governments" such as those of Venezuela, Costa Rica, and Colombia. Jessup also found evidence of related ideological biases in Methodist Church agencies. "Judging from their financial contributions, statements, and actions," he concluded, "several agencies of the Methodist church seem to be favoring the totalitarian option."

A decade later, David Jessup looked back on the peculiar political geography he found in the mainline churches, earnestly describing it in deliberate yet dramatic terms. "My kids brought home a little leaflet from Sunday school. That launched a chain of events. I started reading church publications, then writing to some of the church agencies to ask them who they were giving money to. Some of them made the mistake, they later decided, of answering me. I was flabbergasted when I read their lists of grantees, because I knew who many of these organizations were." Jessup knew them from "being a student in political movements on campus in Boulder and Berkeley, where we had every conceivable left-wing group, and from working with the AFL-CIO on political education and campaigns with COPE. So I knew who was on the left and the right, and I was thunderstruck. These were not just grants to liberal organizations. These were grants, materials, seminars, devoted to bolstering the likes of Fidel Castro."[3] Seen in the light of Jessup's experience as a political activist and union organizer, grants that Methodist Church agencies presented as aid to the cause of peace and justice turned out to be aiding America's enemies on the totalitarian, socialist, and radical political left.

Jessup's report, entitled *Preliminary Inquiry regarding Financial Contributions to Outside Political Groups by Boards and Agencies of the United Methodist Church, 1977–1979* (April 7, 1980), asked Methodists to weigh the facts and figures detailed in its twenty-six single-spaced pages and seventy-eight footnotes. It then invited them to support Jessup's petition to the 1980 Methodist General Conference for a churchwide Committee on Accountability. With full access to church files and staff, this committee would establish the facts and test the justification for such political activities. It would make sure that misguided denominational bureaucrats and leaders were not betraying the church's membership and the gospel by funding totalitarian governments, socialist movements, and left-wing political groups. After issuing his report a few weeks before the

1980 General Conference met, Jessup circulated copies to conference delegates and actively organized support for his petition. It did not pass, but
the General Conference did move to make records of receipts and expenditures of boards and agencies available to annual conferences and local
church administrative boards upon request.

Viewed narrowly, the Jessup Report, as it came to be called, did no
more than ask United Methodist leaders to keep their long-standing
promise—reaffirmed in publications such as the Methodist "white paper"
of October 1980 titled "The Use of Money in Mission"—to see that "all
expenditures are open to scrutiny and are available on request to any individual or congregation."[4] But the Jessup Report triggered a chain of
events that reached far beyond a modest reaffirmation of Methodism's
long-standing commitment to making public the details of its denominational donations. Seen more broadly, the report is remarkable for the
larger questions it raises about the mainline churches' moral vision and
political commitments.

Jessup allows in the report that a full inquiry may turn up plausible
explanations for the pattern of political contributions he describes. But
he suspects it may also turn up several million dollars' worth of in-kind
services beyond the $442,000 in twenty-one direct grants that he found.
Jessup credits the Methodist bureaucracy with doing much good, with its
hundreds of staff and $200 million in annual regional and national bud-
gets, and he urges Methodists to continue supporting it. But "Methodists should also continue to scrutinize it," he urges, "lest their generosity
be transformed into the financial underpinning of a political movement
that might, in the end, destroy it altogether." Left-wing politicization of
the United Methodist Church may divide and conquer the church from
within, Jessup warns, or allow it to be led further astray from without,
notably by greater political biases in the National Council of Churches.
"Based on occasional stories in the press," he concludes, "it is easy to
speculate that an analysis of the political orientation of NCC programs,
one bureaucratic step removed from our own Church, will reveal an even
more flagrant misuse of funds that may link together churchgoers of many
denominations as victims of an enormous political swindle."[5]

These broader charges stirred a controversy that brought into being
the Institute on Religion and Democracy (IRD). The institute has in turn
deepened that controversy and cast its political and theological terms
in new light. For all its development and changes since its founding in
1981, the IRD, in the eyes of its leaders and supporters, has continued to

question with good reason the political bent of mainline-church programs and funding and to criticize the social witness of the national staff and appointed leaders of these denominations. It has continued to ask whether their views are representative of their denominations' larger membership, whether denominational discussion of policy-related advocacy and programs is open to the full range of theological conviction and moral commitment held by people in the churches' pews, and whether it is consonant with their traditional creeds and confessions of faith. "No" on every count, the IRD has continued to answer emphatically and argue vigorously.

For church leaders critical of the IRD, the institute embodies instead an essentially political movement rooted in the neoconservative ideology of the Reagan era and aimed at undercutting the churches' prophetic witness in public and their faithful social teaching in the pews. It misrepresents this witness and teaching as left-wing politics in traitorous service to a socialism equally at odds with the gospel truth and the American Creed of a free people and a free market. Thus, for example, James Wall of the *Christian Century* credits the IRD with a key role in using gay/lesbian wedge issues to polarize and take over the 2000 General Conference of United Methodism: "It is important to remember that the IRD came into being in the early 1980s with support from, and as part of, the conservative movement that elected Ronald Reagan president. Why this happened, and how long this trend will prevail, is a more complicated matter. But this much is clear: what started in the age of Reagan is now a reality in United Methodist power circles."[6]

For a quarter century, in this view, the IRD has persisted in declaring and waging "culture wars" along the polemical lines of the Cold War. It flies the benign banner of orthodox evangelical "church renewal" as a flag of convenience. Yet it actually serves the propaganda interests of a clique of neoconservative ideologues, hawkish political partisans, and right-wing foundations epitomized by Richard Mellon Scaife. The IRD and its allies "indulge in character assassination and seek to drive the church apart by the use of wedge issues, calculated to cause dissension and division." They aim to discredit and muffle the social witness of the mainline churches, especially Methodism, and to gain control of their governance, as cultural-political conservatives did in the case of the Southern Baptist Convention. So charge Methodist bishop Dale White and others who sponsored a 2003 "wake-up call" to alert church members to the great risk rising against the church's life and witness and to move them to fight back.[7]

While attention has been paid to relations between parachurch groups and the established denominations, relatively little notice has gone to their complex interrelations within a broader network of voluntary political associations, religious and nonreligious alike. They interact within the larger context of more polarized yet nonetheless overlapping political parties, an expanded state, and a more formally organized, densely crowded, and morally contested polity. Looking closely at the Institute on Religion and Democracy allows us to map such interrelations, particularly the IRD's dynamic relations with the United Methodist Church, the Democratic Party and its neoconservative critics, the AFL-CIO and organized labor, and the political-cultural left since the 1960s.

This inquiry allows us to see how the expansion of government's moral concern and regulatory reach into a wider range of American social institutions—families, schools, and work—has in turn drawn churches and communities of faith more intricately and controversially into public life. It allows us to hear the ways in which religious faith in our society now converses with other forms of cultural meaning and social arrangement, and how it argues with them in public. We can listen to how this conversation unfolds in American society as it is today—not only divided into a dozen major denominations and hundreds of smaller communities of faith, but multiplied by thousands of religious and nonreligious lobbies, moral advocacy groups, and voluntary political associations. Together, they span and blur old boundary lines between church and state. They enrich and complicate the multivocal public argument that mixes politics and faith in the course of democratic self-government.

Challenging the Churches on Peace and Justice

The Jessup Report linked United Methodist boards and agencies to more than a hundred questionable political organizations. These ranged from the "Castroite" Chile Legislative Center and the "Hanoi Hawk" Friendshipment agency for Vietnamese reconstruction to the "Moscow run front group, the World Peace Council," and the pro-PLO Palestine Solidarity Committee. They included the National Conference of Black Lawyers, "the legal support arm of the black revolution" and courtroom defenders of the Black Panther Party. Jessup's report questioned a score of Methodist grants in detail. For example, Methodists took the lead in million-dollar "wheat shipments to the government of Vietnam" sponsored by the

National Council of Churches, charged Jessup, and thus helped the Communist regime to control its own people and free government resources to sustain soldiers in neighboring countries. The Cuba Resource Center received some $17,000 from two United Methodist agencies in 1977–79, Jessup specified, while promoting the virtues of Cuban society as "a virtual paradise for workers and women," celebrating it as a Soviet-backed symbol of revolutionary hope and courage in the third world and lobbying for diplomatic recognition of Cuba and against the U.S. trade embargo.[8]

The Cuba Resource Center was founded by missionaries and endorsed by the Cuban Council of Churches and the Methodist Church in Cuba, replied the head of the United Methodist Committee on Relief (UMCOR), Rev. J. Harry Haines. "The Jessups of this world would like to have us turn our back on the suffering church in Cuba," he charged in turn. "The man has tunnel vision."[9] Haines represented the United Methodist Church on a fifteen-member committee of the National Council of Churches, led by Dr. Paul McCleary, a Methodist churchman at the helm of Church World Service, the NCC's arm for global disaster relief. The committee raised $5 million for humanitarian aid to postwar Vietnam, with Methodists giving as much as $2 million to the cause. This paid for a 1978 shipment of 230 tons of wheat, sent in response to severe food shortages from successive crop failures in 1977–78. It was used to make noodles and bread to supplement the diets of schoolchildren and hospital patients.

These Methodist funds raised by the NCC "went to the purchase of relief and medical supplies to minister to the people in Vietnam," who had suffered from decades of war, and "to help rebuild a devastated area where the human needs were great," reported Herman Will of the United Methodist Board of Church and Society in mid-1980. "I think there is no problem with justifying this need in terms of humanitarianism," he concluded. Of aid to the Cuba Resource Center and related groups, Will noted that these grants primarily supported "research and publication materials from a perspective critical of United States foreign policy and with sympathy and understanding of the revolution taking place in Latin America. One could disagree with the points of view expressed, but the money has not been used to the best of my knowledge in any support of guerilla, military or similar revolutionary activities," Will testified.[10] No firm allegations of fact made by the Jessup Report undercut Will's conclusions, in the eyes of Methodist leaders. "When the church commits itself to identification with the poor and the oppressed," explained Bishop Roy C. Nichols, president of the Council of Bishops, in a public letter officially responding to Jessup's report, "we may sometimes become involved with people whose blend of Marxist interpretation and Christian theology may be different from our own. Furthermore, with millions of professing Christians in the Marxist orbit in other parts of the world, contemporary Christians must risk association with those labeled 'sinners' in order to convince and convert."[11]

Many Methodist leaders saw something besides theological misunderstanding at work in the Jessup Report. To them, at least some of the allegations made by the report and amplified by its successors seemed at best wrongheaded, irresponsible untruths, and at worst malicious lies. The report not only leveled charges against the African National Congress as being backed and influenced by the Soviet Union, for example, but also raised suspicions of leftist bias on the part of the anti-apartheid South African Council of Churches under Bishop Desmond Tutu and the South African Christian Council Refugee Program. "The report contains factual inaccuracies," Rev. Peggy Billings of the Board of Global Ministries said of Jessup's report. "His conclusions are matters of opinion, not of substance. The only 'revelation' in the Jessup report is Mr. Jessup's own ideological persuasion. I'm sure it will be of aid and comfort to those who for years have made careers out of attacking the church for its commitment to justice and advocacy for poor and dispossessed people, and for its commitment to be at work in the real world for which Christ suffered and died."[12] The United Methodist Church welcomed critical engagement in legitimate controversy and moral debate over the gospel truth of "the alleviation of injustice and suffering, the recognition of new nations, the ending of all forms of colonialism, and the rights of all races and both sexes to equality and, thus, full humanity," affirmed the denomination's official reply to Jessup. But instead of dealing responsibly with controversy, it charged, Jessup's report demonstrated the tactics of "today's right wing extremism" in its antidemocratic assault on the church's accountable decision-making, in its assigning moral guilt by political association, and in its Communist-coded innuendo and inference.[13]

In 1980, Jessup's original report anticipated countercharges of "witch-hunting and McCarthyism." It denied any intention to stifle the civil liberties of church staff members or delimit the political activity of church boards and agencies. In the report, Jessup testifies, "I, for one, hope that at least some official church effort will be expended on questions of human rights, democratic freedoms, and economic and social betterment, over and above the more fundamental church mission of religious persuasion." He calls for a continuing debate over what the church's commitment to such rights, freedoms, and betterment means in practice. He also calls for the church itself to be accountable along the lines of trade-union democracy:

> The fundamental question posed concerns the direction of political activity, and whether the membership has any say in determining that direction at the all-important level of staff and funding decisions. In other words, it is a question of accountability. It is the same question that was faced by the labor movement of the 1930's, when many trade unionists had to reach an internal decision over the question of whether their organizations would represent their own aspirations or those of the defenders of the Hitler-Stalin pact.[14]

As this striking parallel between the mainline churches in the 1980s and the trade unions in the 1930s suggests, the IRD has offered insight into the question of the churches' moral and political accountability informed by the distinctive institutional outlook of its own leaders. It is an outlook bred by their experience not only in the churches but in ideological and organizational struggles in the AFL-CIO and the labor movement, infighting in the Democratic Party between Cold War hawks and anti–Vietnam War doves, and the conflicting visions of student activist movements since the 1960s.

In the year leading up to the IRD's founding in the spring of 1981 and stretching through its first few years of existence, the gist of the Jessup Report and the story of its origins became central themes in public controversy over politics in the mainline churches. They were rehearsed in meetings, pamphlets, and two widely reprinted articles in *Reader's Digest*. The first article, in August 1982, challenged the World Council of Churches (WCC) as to who it represented: "Karl Marx or Jesus Christ?" The second asked mainline Protestants in January 1983, "Do You Know Where Your Church Offerings Go?" and warned in a subtitled reply, "You better find out because they may be supporting revolution rather than religion." Within fifteen months in 1981–83, the *New York Times* published a series of articles featuring the IRD quite credibly, with such headlines as "New Church Group Assails Support of Left."[15]

Most dramatically, the television news program *60 Minutes*, in a January 1983 segment titled "The Gospel according to Whom?" attacked the World Council of Churches, the National Council of Churches, and their mainline allies for their ties to third-world liberation groups such as the anti-apartheid African National Congress, asking if these churches were funding revolutionary armed insurgents. "What worries me most—indeed outrages me most—is when the church starts telling lies, when we start just sheer telling lies," testified Rev. Richard John Neuhaus to *60 Minutes* correspondent Morley Safer and forty million American viewers. He continued:

> And when we start telling lies about countries where people are being imprisoned and tortured and slaughtered, as in Indochina, for example, after the American withdrawal. And we paint a rosy picture of this, and pretend it isn't happening. And then, the height of hypocrisy is to pretend that in painting a rosy picture of the suffering of the poor, and in making excuses for those who oppress the poor, that one is speaking on behalf of the poor.
>
> So we have religious leaders who go to countries which are massively oppressive, in which Christians are in jail, are being tortured, have been killed by the thousands, and they go to those countries and our religious dignitaries consort with the persecutors of the Church of Christ. This is evil. This is wrong. This discredits the Church as social witness, it undermines any elementary notion of justice. We have to turn this around.

Where is this evil rooted in the churches? "There's certainly many in the churches," declared Neuhaus, "who will quite frankly say that they are committed to the global revolution, of which they believe the antithesis is the United States and United States influence in the world." Faithful Americans are concerned and aroused, specified Ed Robb—who was also interviewed in the segment—"about the radical leftwing views of the National Council of Churches, and also the views expressed by the bureaucracies of the mainline denominations," namely, their "pattern of support of totalitarian, leftist regimes across the country, across the world, and apology for this type oppression."[16]

For supporters of the IRD, these well-documented indictments made dramatically clear what had gone wrong in the mainline churches. For the IRD's critics in the churches, by contrast, the Jessup Report's unproven innuendo and smears, their high-volume amplification in the media, and their author's political perspective demonstrated a new strategic angle and ideological intensity of partisan political bias. This was an offensive advanced by neoconservative hawks marching in step with Reaganism, to retool and sharpen slanderous right-wing attacks on the churches' faithful efforts to work for justice and peace during the 1980s. The IRD maliciously misconstrued their humanitarian aid to feed hungry Vietnamese in a country left ravaged by war, to teach Nicaraguan peasants to read, and to help Bishop Desmond Tutu's South African Council of Churches work against apartheid. It remade Christian charity and moral advocacy by the churches into the image of benighted backing for revolutionary politics in a global game of Cold War chess played out between the United States and the USSR around the third world.[17]

Fighting Politically against Politicized Churches

After David Jessup began to do some firsthand investigating, he grew even more troubled by the extremist political ideas and loyalties he found Methodist leaders spreading with "these incredible mass-education projects" and their "cadres" that echoed the political left and exceeded the efforts of the AFL-CIO in scale.[18] The failure of Methodist leaders to reform the national denomination belied its claims to represent an internal democracy, Jessup decided, and betrayed its vow to steer the church's social witness by a theological compass. Their harsh political treatment of theological dissenters and spiritual-renewal groups such as Good News pointed to the need for a different kind of organization to combat them. "Once I saw what was going on," says Jessup, "I decided these churches were already heavily politicized, and they needed to be fought politically, too."[19]

To this end, Jessup conferred with Richard Penn Kemble, a close colleague of his in the AFL-CIO, a leader of the pro-labor, anticommunist Social Democrats, USA, and a friend and fellow activist since they attended the University of Colorado together in the early 1960s. Kemble, the architect of the Coalition for a Democratic Majority and its longtime executive director, was a veteran political organizer and strategist with great organizational drive, rhetorical verve, and combative zeal. He was dedicated to recentering the Democratic Party along lines defended by Senator Henry "Scoop" Jackson and Senator Daniel Patrick Moynihan—on whose staff he worked in the late 1970s—against the New Left tangent drawn by George McGovern's failed 1972 presidential bid.

Penn Kemble and David Jessup's shared diagnosis of what was wrong in the mainline churches set the political and strategic thrust that gave birth to the Institute on Religion and Democracy. It powered a theological matrix mixed from evangelical Methodist, Lutheran, and Catholic elements, represented respectively by Ed Robb, Richard Neuhaus and Peter Berger, and Michael Novak. But the IRD began, stresses Kemble, with a striking recognition of how thoroughly the mainline churches were politically corrupted, and the practical political response this demanded. "We were naive in the beginning," Kemble recalls. "We found what they were doing in the churches so blatant and shocking that we thought that just exposing it, as David did with the Methodists, would right the ship and swing it around. The bishops and grandees of all the church councils would wake up and straighten things out."[20]

Trying to grasp the reasons for this failure of church leaders to repent and reform taught Kemble and Jessup an ironic lesson, since their naïveté turned out to be political as well as theological. "I'm no theologian," Kemble readily acknowledged. "Like me, David had been all involved in social action. I never really discussed religion much with him in the years I had known him. I had no reason to think he was not religious, but it wasn't a big thing in his life." Kemble was no less shocked than Jessup to find the United Methodist Church supporting third world revolutionaries: "Methodists! We know about Methodists. They're all those Rotarians who sing hymns!" Why did Jessup and Kemble meet with such resistance from the apparently responsible church leaders of such faithful folks? "They realized things had gone so far," answered Kemble, "the left had so permeated the churches that if the story got out, it would cover everyone with mud. These denominations rest on pretty conservative local congregations. The bishops didn't want their local church parishioners and deacons to hear this. The denominational leaders were tacit collaborators with the left-wing bureaucrats who tried to discredit us as political kooks and extremists trying to destroy the faith. The high church officials, the high priests and notables, the scribes and pharisees, just stood by and gave their blessing to this."

From this frustrating experience Kemble concluded, "You have to have a body of conviction that enables you to arouse a kind of moral spirit and indignation in other people in order to get them to take part in your strategy. If you just have a brilliant strategy, you're not going to get anywhere." Kemble learned this lesson for wrestling with politicized churches from his experience in ideologically charged party politics. Commenting on changes in denominational rules of representation in the 1970s that mandated increased memberships of minorities and women on Methodist boards and agencies, Kemble remarks,

> I went through that in the Democratic Party. When I was director of the Coalition for a Democratic Majority, we fought the McGovern Rules. The regular

pols used to say to us, "Don't worry, we can get *our* blacks and women. We can handle them." They didn't understand what was happening. It's not simply a mechanical process of selecting delegates. You are accepting their vision of the world and what is wrong with it, and how to make it right.

Therefore, even though you have *your* blacks and women, they are gonna win. Because you're accepting their terms. So Jesse Jackson can get up in 1984 [at the Democratic National Convention] and give this rhapsodic speech about how he suffered and therefore, "Elect me president." And that has standing in the Democratic Party! Hey, a lot of people suffered, and that doesn't make you a candidate for president.

Political strategies and organizational tactics require compelling moral visions and reasons to inspire and justify people in working to realize them. "This is very important," Kemble stresses. "The people who began IRD who had been through the left—Jessup, Novak, Neuhaus, me—believed that you could not turn back what was happening in the church world unless you had a moral-religious vision. You could not do it just by nattering about procedures. We used the procedure argument to show how they were doing it, but you also had to show why." Countering leftist politics in the churches required coupling moral ideas—in theological terms that Jessup and Kemble could not articulate by themselves—with political organizing of a kind that most theologians could not conceive, let alone manage to execute. This necessity led to the invention of the IRD's alliance between religious thinkers and political organizers.

Furthermore, Kemble points out, on the political side alone, the IRD's origins are remarkable for joining neoconservative thinkers and Social Democrat Party organizers. Building labor unions and reforming denominations alike call for organizing to go along with teaching, he notes. In United Methodism, for example, reformers must elect delegates to conferences and members to boards, such as the Board of Church and Society, in order to draft and pass resolutions. They must win the appointment of general secretaries and staffers to boards and agencies in order to enact principles in programs. Paying attention to the requirements of organizing efforts and building movements in order to change institutions, emphasizes Kemble, marks a crucial "difference between our Social Democrat tradition of the left and the neoconservatives":

They have a great faith that all you have to do is write an article in a magazine someplace. I call it "the article-beam weapon": you write it and the problem

is vaporized. Anybody who is smart will see the light, and the rest of them are
hopeless. But because of our involvement in the labor movement and the political work we have done, we have a movement orientation: truth and action
are not separate things. "Ideas have consequences." That's a slogan of the Ethics and Public Policy Center. Well, I know a bunch of people I grew up around
politically who have had wonderful ideas and very little consequence in the last
ten years. If you are going to make any impact, you have to organize.

From these political and theological ingredients, the IRD created a pattern its supporters found clearheaded, groundbreaking, and equal to the
crisis at hand in the mainline churches. The IRD's critics in the mainline
churches found this pattern to be an irreligious carryover from faction-
alized, wedge-and-splinter infighting in the Democratic Party, political-
action committees, labor unions, and radical politics. For them, it robed
in religious rhetoric the animus of ideologically driven neoconservative
think tanks, lobbies, and political-action groups on the model of Kemble's
own Coalition for a Democratic Majority. It lined its pockets with funds
from Cold War hawks, small-government libertarians, and big-business financial interests smarting from churchly critiques of American militarism,
imperialism, and unfettered capitalism in the Reagan era.

In April of 1981, the Institute on Religion and Democracy was formally
founded and legally incorporated. Penn Kemble served as its de facto executive director, CEO, and president, although the IRD would have no
official executive director or president until Kent R. Hill took over from
Kemble in 1986 and took on these titles. The IRD's founders included
Jessup and Kemble; Richard Neuhaus, a prolific Lutheran pastor and
church critic; Michael Novak, a Catholic theologian, political commenta-
tor, and scholar at the American Enterprise Institute; and Edmund Robb,
Jr., an inspiring Methodist evangelist and key leader of the Good News
movement, who chaired its board of directors from 1976 to 1978. Robb
also chaired the IRD's board of advisors from its inception until 1993,
when he turned over its reins to Helen Rhea Stumbo, first vice-chair of
the IRD, United Methodist evangelical reformer, chair of the Good News
board a decade after Robb, and heir to the Blue Bird bus fortune.

Kemble recruited a small staff for the IRD of veterans remarkable for
their experience in political, labor, and student activist groups, including
Frontlash and Students for a Democratic Society (SDS). Recruits also
came from Good News and *Challenge*, the magazine of the Ed Robb
Evangelistic Association, edited by his son, Edmund "James" Robb III,

before he joined the IRD's Washington office and became its administrative coordinator. Kemble secured $200,000 in start-up funding for the IRD, mainly from conservative foundations, with $65,000 coming from the Smith Richardson Foundation of North Carolina, dedicated to "promoting and achieving a better understanding of the American economy and society" and a sponsor of the American Enterprise Institute and supply-side economic policies.[21]

Rev. Ed Robb remembers first meeting David Jessup: "Virginia Shell from Good News came up to me at the 1980 Methodist General Conference and said she had someone I should meet, because he was fighting for accountability against the left-wing bureaucrats in the church, who were after him, and he didn't really know how to find the evangelical Methodists who would support him or how to talk with them. I met David and liked him. There was something there, and we decided to build on it. The IRD was what we built."[22] Given the IRD's genesis in the throes of David Jessup's struggle against Methodist church leaders, Kemble in turn underscores just how importantly Robb figured in its founding, with his unquestionable commitment to scriptural orthodoxy, spiritual revival, and personal piety in the Methodist tradition as the basis for reforming the United Methodist Church.

Buffeted by the angry reaction to their attacks from United Methodist Church leaders, later joined by leaders of the other mainline churches and the NCC, Jessup and Kemble were all too vulnerable to being dismissed as outside political agitators with an effectively partisan agenda thinly disguised as church reform. "That's where the alliance with the evangelicals saved us," Kemble recalls. "My church credentials were nonexistent. David Jessup was an active Methodist, but he also had these political and labor associations. We were able to bring in people with both evangelical and Catholic credentials. Ed Robb was really heroic. He had everything to lose. I could go and get a job in a Senate campaign or something. Ed Robb had put his whole life into the Methodist Church. He had some hope that they might make him a bishop. He is a deeply faithful Methodist."[23]

Thinking back to the IRD's organizational birth, Kemble remembers, "We couldn't get anybody else. Richard Neuhaus was very nervous at the time, because he was working for this Council on Religion and International Affairs. That was a mushy group, and he was uncomfortable there. Michael Novak was supportive of us, but this wasn't his battle. He was studying the economic thought of the Catholic Church. I had known Michael from the Democratic Party, and Neuhaus from New York. David

[Jessup] reached out to Ed Robb." Why? "We could see that with just a few evangelical Methodists who could be cast as coming from outside the mainstream culture, we could turn back the charges against us as political agitators," replies Kemble. "Ed Robb happens to be from the mainstream. His father was a union organizer. He's a sophisticated, sensible man. But he's also a real East Texas evangelical," Kemble smiles. "When he starts to preach and his hair hangs down, mainline-church types look at each other and smirk. But put him together with Novak and Neuhaus, get the Ethics and Public Policy Center into the game, and the IRD can no longer be dismissed as political outsiders who have nothing to do with the churches." Politics makes strange bedfellows, as the IRD confirms to its critics in the churches, while its defenders see it as an honorable marriage, sophisticated yet sensible, of down-to-earth strategy and high ideals, made in the heaven of a compelling, if complex, cultural politics.

Christianity and Democracy

In the fall of 1981, the IRD issued a formal statement, "Christianity and Democracy," to set out its "philosophical and theological purpose."[24] The statement was drafted by Richard John Neuhaus, an eloquent, activist Lutheran minister who later converted to Catholicism, was ordained as a priest by New York's Archbishop O'Connor, and established his own Institute on Religion and Public Life. The statement extends "an invitation to Christian leadership in this country to consider the Christian stake and the Christian warrant for democratic government." It begins by proclaiming, "Jesus Christ is Lord. This is the first and final assertion Christians make about all of reality, including politics," so "every earthly sovereignty is subordinate to the sovereignty of Jesus Christ." Because "the church is pledged to the Kingdom proclaimed by Jesus, it must maintain a critical distance from all the kingdoms of the world, whether actual or proposed." The IRD statement continues:

> The first political task of the Church is to be the Church. That is, Christians must proclaim and demonstrate the Gospel to all people, embracing them in a sustaining community of faith and discipline under the Lordship of Christ. In obedience to this biblical mandate, Christians give urgent priority to all who are in need, especially the poor, the oppressed, the despised and the marginal. The Church is called to be a community of diversity, including people of every race,

nation, class, and political viewpoint. As a universal community, the Church witnesses to the limits of the national and ideological loyalties that divide mankind. Communal allegiance to Christ and his Kingdom is the indispensable check upon the pretensions of the modern state. Because Christ is Lord, Caesar is not Lord. . . .

    While our first allegiance is to the community of faith and its mission in the world, Christians do not withdraw from participation in other communities. To the contrary, we are called to be leaven and light in movements of cultural, political and economic change. . . . Among Christians today, as in times past, there are significant disagreements . . . on how best to advance freedom, justice and peace in the world. . . . Within our several churches disagreement about the meaning of social justice should not merely be tolerated; it should be cherished. . . . An open church welcomes dissent . . . makes decisions in the light of day . . . has leaders who are not afraid but eager to engage in the fullest consultation with all its members . . . addresses social issues not so much to advance a particular position as to inform and empower people to make their own decisions responsibly . . . understands that the church speaks most effectively when the people who are the church do the speaking, and the leaders speak most believably when they speak with the informed consent of those whom they would lead. . . . In these ways, an open church becomes a zone of truth-telling in a world of mendacity.[25]

These opening paragraphs of the IRD statement are remarkable for their theological depth and ecclesiological breadth. Christian faith is wed to no particular political agenda or order, yet Christians are to care first for the needy and engage in public life through taking part in an "open church." This church is marked by a diversity of views and peoples equally active in transparent debate and democratic decision-making. This conception of the public church clearly seems to transcend any partisan political program and to defy any characterization of the IRD as "baptizing Reaganism," as Peter Steinfels puts it. Yet that is precisely the upshot of its overall logic of argument, according to Steinfels's close analysis of the statement as it moves from these encompassing premises to narrowly partisan conclusions through five exclusionary steps.[26] A keen critic of New Left radicalism and liberation theology as well as neoconservatism, Steinfels was executive editor of the Catholic religion-and-politics journal, *Commonweal*, and an institutional outsider to the combat between the IRD and the mainline Protestant churches, with a sharp eye for its maneuvering.

    First, Steinfels points out, the IRD statement moves directly to set ideals of an open church against the idolatry of totalitarian politics. "In this century of Hitler and Stalin and their lesser imitators the most urgent truth to be told about secular politics is the threat of totalitarianism," writes Neuhaus.[27] For totalitarianism declares only one sovereignty, in denial of the Christian dualism of powers, societies, and laws between spiritual and temporal, divine and human. With every other, less urgent political truth dismissed from consideration, observes Steinfels, the statement takes a second step to insist that totalitarianism assumes only one dangerous form in the present. "Totalitarianism takes either leftist or rightist forms," Neuhaus specifies. "Today, however, the only global ideology that is committed to the monistic denial of freedom is Marxist-Leninist."[28]

Next, in a third step, the IRD statement offers "the Democratic alternative" to the idolatrous political monism of the totalitarian impulse. As such, says Steinfels, democracy comes to be defined in terms of one overriding characteristic instead of a panorama of political possibility debated since antiquity.[29] "Democratic government is limited government. It is limited in the claims it makes and in the power it seeks to exercise," stresses Neuhaus. Democracy distinguishes between state and society, making clear that "the state is not the whole of society. . . . Other institutions—notably the family, the Church, educational, economic and cultural enterprises are at least equally important actors in the society," with their own peculiar forms of sovereignty that the state must respect. As the opposite of political monism, then, democratic governance is "pluralistic governance," open for many institutional and individual actors to take part in, and open to many alternative visions of the future. Democracy is likewise based on a morality of respect and fairness for all, the rule of law, and the rights of free individuals and institutions, especially religion. Most importantly, as Neuhaus defines it, "democratic government does not seek to control or restrict the sphere of religion."[30] Thus democracy is defined contra totalitarianism in terms of "limiting the state rather than empowering the citizen," notes Steinfels, or embodying the civic community through full public participation, fair public provision, or reciprocally shared responsibility for the commonweal.[31]

In a fourth step, following naturally from this definition, the autonomy of economic life, according to the IRD statement, comes in for protection from the state by analogy to freedom of religion. "As democratic government does not seek to absorb the sphere of religion, so it does seek to respect the autonomy of cultural and economic life." Notwithstanding debates about the achievements and problems of capitalism, argues Neuhaus, a primary concern to preserve and strengthen democracy tends to justify "the personal and institutional ownership and control of property—always as stewards of God to whom the whole creation belongs." For as a matter of historical fact, Neuhaus contends, "democratic governance exists only where the free market plays a large part in a society's economy." Likewise, experience in America and the world "suggests that when a market economy is open to the participation of all, it works to the benefit of all, and especially of the poor," by focusing "on the production of wealth rather than on the consolidation and redistribution of existing goods," while the command economies of totalitarian regimes impoverish all but their political elites.[32]

Fifth and finally, the IRD statement declares that "the United States of America is the primary bearer of the democratic possibility in the world today. The Soviet Union is the primary bearer of the totalitarian alternative." Between the two, in "our dangerously divided world, choices must be made." For ideals "do not make their way in history except they be carried by persons and institutions," though they fall short of the ideals to which they witness, just as the church itself is the imperfect bearer of the gospel.[33]

By these steps, the leaders and members of the Christian church are obliged to choose between capitalist democracy and the political monism of totalitarianism, which denies the sovereignty of Jesus Christ. Totalitarianism is embodied in Marxism-Leninism and the Soviet Union. Democracy is defined by limited government, the rule of constitutional law, and the priority of individual legal rights. The United States of America is its primary bearer in the world today. Capitalism and a free-market economy are vital conditions of democracy, and both may indeed be necessary, if not sufficient, conditions of its survival. Stripped to the skeleton of its essential points, says Steinfels, this argument undeniably defines "the guiding principles of the Reagan Administration's approach to international affairs."[34]

But why must Christians first be obliged to choose only "*the* most urgent political truth, and to choose it for the whole world and the whole century," asks Steinfels, while dismissing all others in conceiving the nature of democracy and the social witness of the church? There is, for example, the urgency of seeking to end starvation and torture, or to curb nuclear arms, racism, or structural joblessness. Why must threats of right-wing tyranny and dictatorship, whether distinguished as authoritarian instead of totalitarian in neoconservative usage, be eliminated from consideration to concentrate solely on the threat of Marxism-Leninism? Why must democracy be defined solely in terms of limited government, to the exclusion of educating and empowering citizens to participate equally and fully in self-government, and nurturing social and economic equality? Why ignore the problems capitalism has historically posed for social justice and moral integrity in democracies? Finally, why choose two single nations, the United States and the USSR, to be the "primary bearers" of democracy and totalitarianism, instead of choosing broader international groupings, wider social movements, or a continuum of cases?[35]

At every step of this either-or argument, "vast and complex realities are pared down to a single element," concludes Steinfels. The world's political problems are reduced "to the threat of totalitarianism; the threat of totalitarianism to Marxist-Leninism; the definition of democracy to limited government; the role of capitalism to its autonomy from the state; the multiplicity of actual political forces to the two superpowers alone. 'Christianity and Democracy' can reach its destination only because its choices are relentlessly guided by the same worldview that guides the [Reagan] Administration" to defend the free world of democratic capitalism against the evil empire of Soviet communism via a U.S. government expansive on national security, limited on social welfare, and loose on economic regulation.[36]

What is made emphatically clear in the final pages of "Christianity and Democracy," though left unspecified by event or agent, is the failure of social witness in the mainline churches to grasp the true meaning of democracy or to respond with more than selective compassion to human suffering in today's world. In a section titled "Democracy and the Witness of the Churches," Neuhaus charges that "arguments for oppression are pervasive in our several churches, in some churches more than others. Those who advance such arguments become, whatever their intent may be, apologists for oppression. These arguments are voiced at various levels of episcopal, administrative, journalistic and academic leadership," notably by those "professionally involved in shaping the social witness of the churches."[37]

"Christianity and Democracy" closes by reaffirming that the IRD is taking a moral stance, not a partisan political position, on the churches' social witness. "The debate is not between liberal and conservatives, between left and right. The debate is between those who do believe and those who do not believe that there is a necessary linkage between Christian faith and human freedom."[38] Yet this brands the IRD's critics as heretics, Steinfels protests, and it miscasts the real nature of the moral debate over the church's social witness and its voice in the moral argument of American public life. For that is a debate over moral goods, dangers, and duties knotted in dilemmas that sometimes permit no unequivocal answers and spur profound disagreement among faithful Christians and church leaders of comparably good will.[39]

Christians and citizens debate, for example, whether they should indefinitely back unjust authoritarian regimes in South Vietnam or El Salvador, or aid their opponents, where religious or democratic loyalties remain contested and unclear. They debate how and how far they should carry their concerns for democracy at home, says Steinfels, beyond delimiting the state and defending the civil rights of individuals. How should they move to strengthen the family, or make the economy more just in its outcomes and more equal in its opportunities? How should they enable full public participation by citizens left disadvantaged by scant social, economic, and educational resources? The IRD's statement gives no clue, Steinfels points out. Instead, it tables compelling questions of national self-determination essential in today's revolutionary world order, and it disqualifies appeals to principles of self-determination used to justify criticism of U.S. intervention abroad. It begs the empirical question of whether a democratic middle way actually lies between the "totalitarian" forces of the left and the "authoritarian" forces of the right in specific cases such as Vietnam, Angola, and El Salvador. Begging this question effectively silences critics of U.S. foreign policy in such cases, who protest that faint hopes for eventual democratic reform do not justify indefinitely prolonged military, economic, and political support for authoritarian dictatorships.[40]

Careful examination of "Christianity and Democracy" uncovers nothing to contradict suspicions raised by the IRD's founding and funding in the minds of mainline church leaders, concludes Steinfels—namely, that "it was a conservative-neoconservative alliance intended to advance a distinct political agenda while claiming only a broad Christian concern."[41] Accepted or rejected, this conclusion still leaves us with questions about the origins and implications of the IRD and its admixture of moral ideals and social arrangements, which now span three decades since the IRD issued "Christianity and Democracy."

Defending the American Creed against New Left Churches

The IRD's "manifesto," as it came to be called, offered a rationale, at once theological, cultural, and political, for mainline American Protestants of good faith to support the IRD's efforts to counter and correct the "apologies for oppression" in their churches' public witness. In contrast to the Jessup Report, with its stress on the facts of church grants and funding to allegedly pro-Soviet, totalitarian, and left-wing political groups, the IRD manifesto offers a sweeping proclamation of its allegiance to the lordship of Christ and the sovereignty of God, whose kingdom is not of this or that political regime or partisan program.

But the IRD's political origins shed no less valuable light on its moral aims and self-understanding. Describing the values at the taproot of the political commitments he shares with David Jessup, Penn Kemble thinks back: "David and I were both seized by the challenge communism posed to our American values, to human rights and democracy. The Social Gospel and American religion generally had a big impact on this 'American Creed,' as Gunnar Myrdal calls it. David and I were true believers in it. We were also very middle-class, middle-American young people of the Kennedy generation, with feelings of great confusion and bewilderment over Sputnik, Nixon being spit on in Venezuela, the Berlin Wall, and Castro."[42]

In Kemble's view, the links are causally clear and compelling that reach from the IRD to Jessup's and his own early labor-union socialism, anticommunist activism, and commitments to the Democratic and Social Democrat parties:

It was not just a coincidence that we got involved in starting the IRD, given our political and AFL-CIO labor backgrounds and our coming out of the student Young Left movements of the sixties and seventies, although we had a very clear-cut anticommunist position. We were associated with the old Norman Thomas Socialists. My father had been an organizer for Thomas in the Pennsylvania mining area where I grew up. We met some people in college, at the University of Colorado, who had been in the CIO and the radical movements of the thirties, including our favorite professor, who taught the Russian Revolution, communism, the debates between Lenin, Trotsky, . . .

The first political thing we actually did on campus in Colorado was a series of debates against Fair Play for Cuba, a left-wing group of academics and scientists. We were in a group of Democratic Socialists, many of whom had broken with the Communists in the 1940s or after the Hungarian Revolution, so they knew what Castro was up to. We supported the Kennedy blockade, given the threat of the Soviet system Castro was trying to export to Latin America. He was the creature of Moscow, we knew that. But we also knew everybody hated

Batista, and our record in Latin America had hardly been spotless in backing these oligarchs and gangsters, although the Peace Corps was out there dealing with poverty.

There was a real debate, and we got swept up in it. We were defenders of the American Creed, but we also became Democratic Socialists. People who had broken with the Communists but were still on the left were the only ones who understood what communism was about and why it should be opposed without going off into the mindless panic of Birchers or Goldwater types. A lot of liberals fell into the trap of accepting abuse of freedom of the press or religion in these societies because they seemed to promote equality and provide medical care for all. We were saying, "Wait a minute, do you have any idea what it's like living in these countries, just enduring everyday life?"

A lot of people on the right saw communism getting support from the masses as if it were an excess of democracy instead of its antithesis. We were defending a centrist democratic outlook. We fell in with the Norman Thomas people, Sidney Hook, and eventually people who went on to become neoconservatives, like Norman Podhoretz, Irving Kristol, and the crowd around *Encounter* magazine, *Dissent* magazine.

Here the ties between the mainline churches and the IRD's Social Democrat political origins reach from the history of Social Gospel influences on American socialism in the Progressive era to the religion-like intensity of anticommunist belief in a Kennedyesque "American Creed" during the Cold War. These ties bind the two sides in conflict over many of the same social issues, notably civil rights. "Our Social Democratic groups were deeply involved in civil rights before the big churches," claims Kemble. "We got involved through socialist labor—A. Philip Randolph, Bayard Rustin—when the only churches involved there were the small witness churches, the Quakers. I quit graduate school to work on the March on Washington," testifies Kemble. "I was standing right there when MLK made his 'I Have a Dream' speech. Actually," he laughs, "I was there working for the *New York Times*!"

In Kemble's account, the penetration of the mainline churches by New Left political ideology follows from the civil rights era, seen as a telling example of the churches' moral confusion and timidity, not their courage. The civil rights movement was led by the African American community itself, including the black churches, and it was backed by socialist labor, argues Kemble. "Finally, the big churches were shamed into becoming part of the civil rights movement, after the rough stuff was over, in

the legislative period when the momentum was ours and the movement
had captured the moral high ground. There were a lot of people in the
churches who really lost their moral bearings in that experience." The
civil rights movement actually embarrassed the mainline churches, asserts
Kemble. "It didn't embarrass us. We were on the right side. We always felt
a certain disdain for them. Like Michael Novak or Richard Neuhaus, I had
this strange sensation of watching church people who had been on our right
moving to our left. When I was a Young Socialist, they were telling me I
was just turning people off and throwing away my future, picketing for civil
rights on campus in 1961."[43] Ten years later, "with Vietnam, they're with
the radicals on the left, surging with moral self-confidence. It deepened
the humiliation of the church moderates and conservatives." The institutional life of the mainline churches could not withstand this raging movement of the New Left through the whole of its organizational leadership,
says Kemble, and it became both thoroughly politicized and polarized.

On the domestic side, observes Kemble, the influence of political ideas
from the New Left meant "sneering at mere charity and good works as
Lady Bountiful, taking food out of the mouths of the poor and money
out of their pockets with one hand and building hospitals with the other.
The accused were humiliated, and their response to their accusers was,
'Oh, join our board, and tell us how to do better.'" In foreign affairs, it
meant that "missionary work was seen almost as collaboration with the
CIA. We became cultural imperialists, threatening and bribing people to
act like Americans. We were out there trying to get these people to act
like Americans, clean up their act, clean up their drinking water, learn English, join the Presbyterian Church and the new American empire. So the
moderates and conservatives in the mainline churches were just ravaged."
Only in the evangelical churches did a traditional Christian outlook hold
firm, notes Kemble, and "the mainliners dismissed them, of course, as
kooks caught in the backwash of the Scopes trial."

The New Left's penetration of the mainline Protestant churches in the
late 1970s and early 1980s and its corruption of their social witness and
action set the stage for the IRD, concludes Kemble, since "we were a
group of people who knew a great deal about the left and how to combat
them. Carter's defeat in 1980 brought a lot more people from the left
into the churches, into parallel political work with the religious auxiliaries
of the Democratic Party," which were radicalized in the 1970s. "These
people didn't really become churchmen and women. They forged new
political networks that relied on church funding, church moral capital,

institutional supports like the Methodist Building on Capitol Hill." They turned the organizational infrastructure of the mainline churches into "a support system for the New Left politics that couldn't win an election." In the churches, though, they routed the opposition. "Internal democracy in the church world failed because by then the moderates and conservatives had collapsed," says Kemble. Interlopers from the New Left "didn't rise to the top on their own," he explains. "It was more a loss of faith in the broader church world that sought them out and pushed them forward in an act of repentance." Getting this message out to the public of left-wing politicization and antidemocratic corruption in the mainline churches became the IRD's first mission.

Thrust, Counterthrust: Guilt by Political Association?

In the months after David Jessup carried his report to the 1980 United Methodist General Conference, its gist led to highly critical and controversial exposure of the mainline churches and the National Council of Churches in the national media. It ranged from the reports on *60 Minutes* and in *Reader's Digest*, *Time* magazine, and the *New York Times* to a seminal public-television documentary hosted by Ben Wattenberg and entitled "Protestants Protest," featuring Ed Robb and produced by Penn Kemble.[44] Concern over the IRD's media campaign reverberated among leaders of the NCC and the mainline churches under attack. They weighed how to respond to the falsehood they found not only in the IRD's charges but in its self-presentation as a centrist organization for religious reform, equally distant from the Moral Majority on the religious right and the NCC on the left. This falsehood was epitomized by Rev. Richard Neuhaus, in clerical garb, telling forty million viewers of *60 Minutes* that church leaders in the NCC and World Council of Churches were guilty of "the height of hypocrisy" for "telling lies" that betrayed the trust of the faithful.[45] In October 1981, shortly after the IRD's official founding in April of that year and just before it issued its official statement "Christianity and Democracy," it was met with an investigative report that marked a counterattack mounted by mainline church leaders in terms comparable to those of the Jessup Report.

A Report on the Institute on Religion and Democracy was written by Eric Hochstein with the aid of Ronald O'Rourke. Educated at Oberlin, Hochstein had served as a congressional aide to House Democrats and

Senator Carl Levin (D-Mich.). O'Rourke, with a graduate degree in international studies from Johns Hopkins, had worked as a congressional intern and political journalist. Their report was commissioned for $6,000 by the General Board of Church and Society and the General Board of Global Ministries of the United Methodist Church, acting through the church's Joint Panel on International Affairs, and by the Board for Homeland Ministries of the United Church of Christ. Its self-described purpose was "solely to provide an introductory body of information on the IRD and its supporters," not to "judge the merits of the policy views and goals of the IRD or to suggest any course of action to be taken in response" to the IRD's activities.[46]

In the account of the Hochstein-O'Rourke Report, as it came to be called, the IRD was "formed to investigate and oppose certain social action programs of the mainline Protestant churches, specifically those involving the funding of leftist groups in the developing world, as well as support reform measures inside the churches establishing bodies to monitor and in part determine future disbursements of social action funds." The IRD is identified as one of three advocacy groups—along with the tax-exempt Foundation for Democratic Education and the Citizens' Committee for Freedom in the Americas—"under the rubric" of the Coalition for a Democratic Majority (CDM). CDM was formed in late 1972 by Penn Kemble, Ben Wattenberg, Jeane Kirkpatrick, Elliott Abrams, Michael Novak, and other neoconservative members of the Humphrey-Muskie-Jackson wing of the Democratic Party to combat the McGovernite "New Left" that had led the party to defeat in the 1972 elections.[47]

The IRD, according to Hochstein and O'Rourke, "presents itself as a fully independent organization, but is actually an autonomous 'special project' of the Coalition for a Democratic Majority," linked mainly through Penn Kemble as CDM's executive director.[48] This claim of CDM linkage was fiercely contested by the IRD, with Penn Kemble in November of 1981 denying having had any connection to CDM for more than two years.[49] "Fundraising material developed by the IRD requests that contributions to the Institute be made payable to a joint account with the Foundation [for Democratic Education] and states that the IRD is a special project of it," Hochstein and O'Rourke also pointed out. Penn Kemble was then president of the Foundation for Democratic Education (FDE), and this specific claim of CDM linkage through the foundation went unargued, as the IRD was legally a project of the FDE until November 1982, when the IRD received tax-free status of its own.[50]

In the same fund-raising brochure, the IRD describes itself as "an inter-denominational association of clergy and laity, representing a diversity of theological viewpoints, working to revitalize our religious institutions by reaffirming the link between Christianity and democratic values." The FDE was itself incorporated with no listed religious purpose, insisted critics of the IRD, who saw it as an essentially political creation funded through a tax-exempt funnel. Moreover, the IRD, along with the foundation, was first housed in the suite of offices that belonged to the Coalition for a Democratic Majority. The CDM, in turn, began with seed money from the AFL-CIO's Committee on Political Education, where David Jessup worked before and after the IRD was formed.

The Coalition for a Democratic Majority provides a "base for neo-conservative political thinkers and office holders," reported Hochstein and O'Rourke, with strong connections to the Reagan administration through UN Ambassador Jeane Kirkpatrick and Elliott Abrams, Assistant Secretary of State for International Organization Affairs (later for Human Rights, then for Inter-American Affairs). The coalition is tied to conservative think tanks such as the American Enterprise Institute via Michael Novak, Richard Neuhaus, and Peter Berger; and to the Committee for the Free World (CFW), whose members included twelve members of the IRD's original board of directors and board of advisors. These links run chiefly through Penn Kemble, whom Hochstein and O'Rourke identify as the IRD's executive director in fact if not in official name. They also identify Kemble, along with David Jessup and IRD founding board members Paul Seabury and Mary Temple, as a leader of the Social Democrats, USA (SD/USA), "a relatively small, pro-labor and anti-Soviet organization with links to the AFL-CIO, the Democratic Party and CDM." Through these ties, Hochstein and O'Rourke say, SD/USA exerts outsized influence behind the political scenes, especially to fight communism in the developing world, notably in Latin America, for example, by CDM backing for the Contra war in Nicaragua.[51]

The Hochstein-O'Rourke Report goes on to trace connections among a wider web of IRD neoconservatives, Ernest Lefever's Ethics and Public Policy Center (EPPC), the American Enterprise Institute, and the Smith Richardson Foundation, a key contributor of one-third of the IRD's first-year budget of $200,000. On the evangelical side, the report singles out Ed Robb, a leader of the Methodist renewal group Good News and head of the Ed Robb Evangelistic Association: "Robb has strongly criticized the UMC leadership for years regarding Methodist social action

programs in the Third World. The Institute virtually embodies Robb's
goal of reforming the methods by which UMC social action funds are
collected and distributed." The IRD's founding board, report Hochstein
and O'Rourke, "is in essence a composite of two groups—the SD/USA
members and their associates, and the Good News leaders."[52] They are
linked by the Social Democrats' opposition to Soviet-style state socialism,
because it restricts political freedoms and independent labor movements;
and the evangelicals' anger at how Marxist revolutionary doctrines have
sapped the missionary fervor of Methodists and other mainline Protestant
churches misled by liberation theology.

In thirty dense pages backed by seventy footnotes and several appen-
dixes, the Hochstein-O'Rourke Report maps in detail the IRD's genesis,
activities, and agenda. It pays particular attention to tracing the ties interlocking the IRD to anticommunist evangelicals on one side, and on
the other to (a) the Coalition for a Democratic Majority and the anticommunist, anti-McGovernite wing of the Democratic Party; (b) the supply-
side, laissez-faire, and big-business economic conservatives of the American Enterprise Institute and their funders at the Scaife, Olin, and Smith
Richardson foundations; and (c) the anticommunist, free-labor aims that
tie the Social Democrats, USA, with the AFL-CIO through its Committee
on Political Education (COPE) and its American Institute for Free Labor
Development (AIFLD), in which Penn Kemble and David Jessup were
deeply involved. Co-sponsored by the AFL-CIO and the U.S. Agency for
International Development, AIFLD repeatedly denied alleged links to
the CIA via USAID, report Hochstein and O'Rourke, allegations dating
back to 1969 and explored in hearings of the Senate Foreign Relations
Committee under J. William Fulbright.[53]

In fact, Hochstein and O'Rourke point out, David Jessup had joined the
United Methodist Church on January 6, 1980, only three months before
he issued his report on April 7, 1980, on the eve of the United Methodist
General Conference. But Jessup had joined COPE in 1976, helping to distribute labor money to political candidates and working through AIFLD
to back anticommunist organizations in the third world that were locked
in political struggles against precisely those groups he was indicting the
churches for aiding in the name of peace, justice, and Christian charity.
Prior to 1980, neither Jessup nor his wife had been members of the United
Methodist Church or more than fringe members of the suburban congregation where they attended services, note Hochstein and O'Rourke. But
in May of 1979, Jessup had begun seeking information from the United

Methodist Board of Church and Society and the Women's Division about their funding, sponsorship, and coalitions. This information found its way into a pointed, polished, heavily footnoted report that echoed earlier charges of left-wing politicization made by Good News against "Marxist Methodists" and by SD/USA hawks against "trendier-than-thou" liberationist Episcopalians. Jessup's report was circulated to a well-organized network of some one hundred General Conference delegates within days of its publication just before the conference opened. If this wasn't conclusive evidence of a preset strategy between neoconservative political activists and evangelical Methodist protesters, claim Hochstein and O'Rourke, the personal and professional connections among them certainly lent suspicion to this possibility.[54]

The IRD's anticommunist, free-labor aims reach back through a thick web of political activism and organizing, report Hochstein and O'Rourke, to the early days of Penn Kemble and David Jessup in Students for a Democratic Society (SDS) and the Socialist Party under the influence of Professor Alex Garber, who taught them political theory at the University of Colorado at Boulder in 1959–63. Garber was a follower of Max Shachtman, a spellbinding Trotskyist who turned Socialist in 1956 and who held that the "only hope for socialism lay with the democratic capitalist countries, since workers there at least possessed rights such as free speech and association essential to their survival."[55] A founder of the SDS chapter at the University of Colorado at Boulder, Kemble, with Jessup's help, moved to break their local chapter away from the national SDS organization. They aligned it with a youth organization tied to the Socialist Party (the Young People's Socialist League), after the SDS National Executive Committee recognized members of an organization associated with the Communist Party in the United States (the Progressive Youth Organizing Committee).

After college, Kemble joined Tom Kahn, a well-placed Socialist ally in SDS and a Shachtman disciple, in working with Bayard Rustin in the civil rights movement, where Kemble was on staff at the Congress of Racial Equality (CORE) until 1965. Then he left to widen his involvement in free-labor, anti-Soviet political organizing against the New Left in the national labor movement and the Democratic Party. Leading the way was Kahn, whom Kemble admired as "an incandescent writer, organizational Houdini, and guiding spirit" and who had served as chief speechwriter for Senator Henry "Scoop" Jackson (D-Wash.) during his bid for the Democratic presidential nomination in 1972 as a cold warrior opposed to

George McGovern.[56] At the AFL-CIO from 1972 until his death in 1992, Kahn served as a top assistant to President George Meany. Kahn was a close associate of Lane Kirkland (Meany's successor, serving from 1979 to 1995) and a key leader of the AFL-CIO's Department of International Affairs in pressing its fight against communism around the world.

Penn Kemble and Tom Kahn also collaborated closely in creating the Coalition for a Democratic Majority in late 1972 and in splitting off the Social Democrats, USA, as a faction from the Socialist Party in order to support continuing U.S. involvement in Vietnam and strong backing for Israel. On both fronts, they were likewise fighting what they saw as the growing takeover of Socialist and Democratic Party organizations by the "New Politics" of a New Left elite cowed by Vietnam and soft on Soviet communism. After his return in 1969 from Peace Corps service in Peru, David Jessup became the chief West Coast political organizer for Frontlash, a youth organization sponsored by the AFL-CIO, with Kemble and Kahn on its board of directors. From Frontlash, in turn, Jessup recruited pro-labor, anti-Soviet minority members and women to the predominantly white male CDM to help represent its causes within Democratic Party decision-making bodies, where quotas for racial and gender representation had recently been instituted.[57]

For several years following its release, the Hochstein-O'Rourke Report figured prominently in the revelations and charges the IRD exchanged with the mainline churches in print media that ranged from the *New York Times* and *Time* to *Christian Century*, *Christianity Today*, and *Christianity and Crisis*, supplemented by television newscasts and documentary features. It shadowed public dialogues between IRD and National Council of Churches leaders, such as a 1982 debate hosted by the NCC and titled "The Relationship of Christianity and Democracy." There, Richard Neuhaus charged that the integrity of Christian witness was sorely violated by a pattern of leadership in the NCC and its dominant member churches that amounted to "first, a betrayal of the liberal tradition; second, an abandonment of the ecumenical task; third, and most solemnly, a compromise of the gospel of Christ."[58] Neuhaus decried the NCC's "condemning of the Reagan Administration and all its works and all its ways," and the council's contempt for Christian critics of its "obsession with the allegedly systemic and inherent injustices of America at home and abroad." The NCC's "perverse liberalism," said Neuhaus, debased the prophetic witness of social Christianity with "calls for a return to the failed policies of the past" and proclamation of "revolutionary

fantasies for the future." Countered Arie Brouwer, then head of the executive committee of the National Council of Churches, "By placing its
trust in political imperatives, The Institute on Religion and Democracy
demonstrates yet again that sometimes comic, sometimes tragic, faith of
extreme opponents condemned to recreate one another in their respective images."[59]

Hochstein and O'Rourke charted an area of ongoing controversy over
the IRD by highlighting its funding from foundations, notably Smith
Richardson and Scaife, dedicated as a group to backing right-wing political causes and branded in some cases by alleged ties to the CIA.[60] Between 1981 and 1982, the IRD's annual budget jumped from $200,000 to
more than $350,000, with Smith Richardson giving $81,000 and the Scaife
Family Charitable Trusts donating $200,000 in 1982. By early 1983, Scaife
had contributed $300,000, and Smith Richardson $146,000, to the IRD.
Together with $33,500 from the Olin, Earhart, Ingersoll, and Cullom
Davis foundations, this totaled $479,000 of the IRD's initial revenue of
$533,000. This meant that 89 percent of the IRD's funding was coming
from foundations on the political far right, which was widely reported
in the mainline religious press. So was a picture of the larger pattern of
funding that these foundations shared. They were backing the anticommunism and the military buildups of President Reagan's foreign policy
and supporting his domestic policies against progressive labor, social
welfare, and environmental protection. They were seeking to achieve
these ends through interlocking grants to the Heritage Foundation, the
American Enterprise Institute, the tax-exempt arm of the National Right
to Work Committee, Ernest Lefever's Ethics and Public Policy Center,
James Watt's anti-environmentalist Mountain States Legal Foundation,
and the like.[61]

To the IRD's critics, following the trail of its money shed light on
its contradictory identity as a group of self-described religious centrists
funded by the political right wing to attack religious liberals for consort-
ing with alleged extremists on the political left. To Penn Kemble, such
suspicions were themselves a projection of the religious left. "Why does
the Left always assume that in this kind of relationship with someone to
your right, he's manipulating you?" asked Kemble with exasperation in
1983. The IRD's funders, he affirmed, "are people who, whatever their
views on domestic issues, are very seriously anti-Communist. They agree
with what we're doing and what we're saying. We don't necessarily agree
with what they do."[62]

Infighting: Religion and Labor Team Up and Square Off

The Hochstein-O'Rourke Report reflected the doctrinal intricacy and organizational intensity of infighting in the labor movement since the 1960s. In late 1972, the Socialist Party split into three factions, each claiming the legacy of democratic socialism in the United States. Penn Kemble's right-wing Social Democrats, USA, were headed by Bayard Rustin and championed militantly anticommunist trade unionism. The Democratic Socialist Organizing Committee, led by the "Other American" liberal socialist Michael Harrington and including Congressman Ron Dellums (D-Calif.), later merged with the New America Movement and was renamed the Democratic Socialists of America (DSA). A relatively small and stagnant residual faction retained the Socialist Party name, while SD/USA went on to proclaim itself "the successor to the Socialist Party, USA, the party of Eugene Debs, Norman Thomas and Bayard Rustin."[63] Though the SD/USA and the DSA each numbered little more than a thousand in their core ranks, the two major factions waged an ideological war that continued to reverberate through the larger bodies of organized labor in the United States, with those on each side often impugning the other's motives. Jack Clark of the DSA and the Democratic Socialist Organizing Committee, who fought against Kemble in the old Socialist Party, declared in 1983 that his factional rival "came out of a Marxist tradition in which religion was actively sneered at and looked down upon. He's part of the crowd that always laughed at Norman Thomas for being a Protestant minister. I suspect this [the IRD] is just a cynical ploy on his part—he had realized that religion is just another lever to pull in his political machinations."[64]

Differences between the two factions were still playing themselves out in struggles among unions within the AFL-CIO in the 1980s, observed Robert McClean of the United Methodist Board of Church and Society, with the Cold War hawks of the pro-Vietnam, pro-Israel SD/USA strongly aligned with the top leadership of the AFL-CIO. "Teachers, ILGWU [garment workers], and 'headquarters' persons such as Lane Kirkland, Tom Kahn, and David Jessup are SD/USA leaders, while 'progressive' branches, such as the Auto Workers and the Machinists leadership, are primarily DSA."[65] For ideological reasons rooted in Trotskyist-Leninist debates in the labor movement of the 1920s, McClean notes ironically, the IRD was attacking the churches for marching with communists in the Cold War of the 1980s, while church leaders in fact marched with David Jessup and other union members in the May Day rally for labor in Washington in 1982. They were marching in support of the rights of labor that had been championed by the churches since their Social Creed of 1908 and nurtured by the Gospels' quest for biblical justice over eons.

Controversy between the IRD and the churches washed back into these internal conflicts within the labor movement when mainline-church leaders with ties to labor unions sought to win their repudiation of the IRD. These efforts culminated in 1984, when the executive council of the AFL-CIO's Industrial Union Department denounced the IRD for its attempts "to weaken the links between religion and labor" and its "effort to mask its neoconservative program by paying lip service to trade unionism," according to the department's vice president, Jack Sheinkman, secretary-treasurer of the Amalgamated Clothing and Textile Workers Union (ACTWU). Twelve of the AFL-CIO's international affiliates likewise condemned the IRD. The international executive board of the United Auto Workers, for example, denounced "the IRD's scurrilous attacks on churches and church leaders and its shameless pandering of 'intelligence' reports on church activities to anti-union corporations."[66] According to Philip R. Newell, Jr., Presbyterian economic-justice official and convener of the Religious Committee on Labor Relations to counter the IRD's labor leverage, "the committee will continue to expose the retrograde nature of the Institute," reported the *Christian Century*. The IRD's true purpose, charged Newell, is "to silence the churches' public witness through attacks designed to put religious organizations on the defensive and undermine their credibility through half-truths and innuendo." Moreover, he added, "the Institute is a small, self-accountable body that received 89% of its seed money from a group of conservative foundations, including the Scaife, Olin and Smith Richardson Foundations."[67]

Commenting on the counterattack the mainline churches mounted against the IRD in the early 1980s, Penn Kemble recalls, "Mainline-church people with union connections tried to get [AFL-CIO president Lane] Kirkland and then Sheinkman to muzzle us. It didn't work that well, because frankly, the union movement doesn't really hold church people in high regard. In any strike situation, which is what it comes down to, the local clergy always wind up weaseling their way into the hands of the bosses. I don't care how left-wing they are on Vietnam or anything else," Kemble explains. "When you start going after the local powers, everyone in the labor movement is accustomed to hearing from some local clergymen's committee that the strike should be called off and the two sides should sit down together in reconciliation. When they went in and tried to see Lane Kirkland, I think he was genuinely offended. He didn't agree with them, and the idea put him off. Other people in the labor movement were kind of amused," smiles Kemble, "that we had gotten these clergy politicos so hot and bothered they were trying to get us fired."[68]

Recalls David Jessup, more painfully, "People in the Methodist leadership were convinced I couldn't simply be a Methodist who cared about the church. They thought I had to be a political agent of some kind from the CIA or the Reagan administration, so they commissioned a study to expose me," says Jessup, referring to Hochstein and O'Rourke's charges that linked clandestine CIA funding to the AFL-CIO's Committee for Political Education through the American Institute for Free Labor Development in its efforts to organize overseas labor groups and land-reform programs against communism. "They called up my old college professor, and the minister at my church, who, I'm sorry to say, didn't have the decency to tell me what they were doing. They tried to get me fired from my job at the Committee for Political Education at the AFL-CIO," Jessup emphasizes. "They wrote letters and made calls for about a year in a campaign within the labor movement. I kept my job, but they were finally successful in getting a number of unions to issue a statement denouncing the IRD. They were playing political hardball. They went to trade unionists who had had their help in religion-labor coalitions like the Farah boycott. They applied pressure and called in their counters."[69]

Was this political payment in kind? Replies Jessup, "We have to acknowledge, too, that on our side we weren't just questioning their teachings. When they got hit with the *Reader's Digest* and *60 Minutes* pieces, those were heavy body blows we delivered. We were operating politically, too," because the churches were politicized past the point of reform by internal theological dissent and democratic debate. What of institutional alternatives for democratic debate, resolutions, and legislated changes within the churches, for example, the United Methodist General Conferences in which Jessup took part in 1980 and 1984? "I've been to a lot of big national conventions in labor and a few in the church," he answers. "The Methodist General Conference is no different. The leadership and staff try to wire the convention as much as possible. They do a pretty good job at that. There is not much room for making change." In 1980 the Methodist General Conference passed a resolution on accountability that required all the denomination's boards and agencies to publish all their grants, Jessup acknowledged. "But the problem is that these are just resolutions at conventions. Afterwards, it's up to the church bureaucrats to implement them. They didn't implement the human rights resolution we got passed in 1984. They may have paid lip service to it here and there, but they really just went about business as usual in terms of where they were spending their money and putting their energy."

Mainline-church leaders insisted at the time that they were not seeking to get David Jessup fired or censored. But they were asking the AFL-CIO to repudiate his extracurricular activities and make clear that it did not stand behind his charges against the churches. The church leaders had no basis for this demand, because the AFL-CIO had no official relationship to the IRD, objected AFL-CIO organizing director Alan Kistler, co-chair of the federation's Religion and Labor Conference. But members of the conference's board of directors nonetheless issued a statement decrying the IRD's "pernicious attack" and protesting to the AFL-CIO executive board against "the active participation by certain elements and individuals within organized labor, including staff of the AFL-CIO, in this assault on labor's traditional allies in the religious community." Other union officials privately told AFL-CIO president Lane Kirkland of their support for the churches' protests against the IRD, and they reportedly intervened to block Jessup's appointment as assistant director of COPE in 1982.[70]

Trade unionists who took the churches' side, including the Clothing Workers' Jack Sheinkman and the Machinists' president William Winpisinger, were members of labor's more liberal wing and were seen as supporters of the Democratic Socialists of America. They were aligned with church leaders in the Vietnam peace movement. They opposed the AFL-CIO's traditionally hawkish Cold War foreign policy, defended by Lane Kirkland and anchored by the Social Democrats, USA, on labor's more conservative wing. Sheinkman called the IRD "the Institute Against Religion and Democracy" for robing itself in a cloak of concern for labor while it actually "appeals to and works through members of religious organizations consistently opposed to church support of labor's efforts."[71]

Sheinkman wrote top AFL-CIO officials that IRD attacks on the churches were endangering their support of labor causes: "During labor law reform, right to work referenda, boycotts, Solidarity Day, and strikes, the labor movement asks, and in most cases, receives, the church's help. But when it comes to the church's agenda of disarmament and Third World political struggles, they are attacked by a not so covert front of the Social Democrats, U.S.A., read by the churches as AFL-CIO." That was neither fair nor wise, judged Sheinkman. When his Molder's Union was striking the Magic Chef Company and he appealed to national church leaders to write letters to the company in behalf of the union, he reported, "in all my years of dealing with church people on labor issues, from the farm workers and Farah right up through Hanes, this is the most anger I have encountered. For all basic purposes, I was turned down on support for the Molders by long-time allies in the United Church of Christ and the United Methodist Church."[72]

In August 1983, AFL-CIO president Lane Kirkland wrote to Claire Randall, then general secretary of the National Council of Churches, and stated that the federation would not interfere with David Jessup for criticizing the churches because he "conducts these activities entirely on his own time and at his own expense." Kirkland's spokesman charged church groups with "being pigheaded" in continuing to "make a big issue out of it."[73] What would critics of Jessup's IRD activities have the AFL-CIO do? demanded Kirkland in his unsolicited letter to the NCC, widely publicized by the IRD:

> Would they have us fire or muzzle him for exercising his rights as a member of the Methodist Church? Would they have us publicly denounce the IRD—that is, to take a position on the issues now being debated within the churches? Is it seriously proposed that the AFL-CIO should review the international funding activities of the NCC and pass judgment on them—or that we should investigate the political character of the IRD, which has neither requested nor received support from the AFL-CIO?[74]

These issues properly belong within the church community, Kirkland contended, just as labor issues belong within the AFL-CIO's own policy-making process, in which church groups should not intervene. Kirkland concluded by declaring, however, that "while the AFL-CIO and the NCC may have some differences on foreign policy issues," the AFL-CIO "will not be a party to outside assaults on America's churches." With backers of both sides well-placed in the AFL-CIO, the dispute between the IRD and the churches remained unsettled and simmered on.

Each side saw the other as breaking an earlier implicit agreement between the mainline churches and organized labor to avoid issues of foreign and military policy that had polarized the generally dovish churches and hawkish unions since the Vietnam era, when vigorous backing for the Vietnam War from national leaders of the AFL-CIO also produced bitter internal divisions with its liberal wing. By counterattacking the IRD through the unions, charged Penn Kemble, church leaders were trying to "muscle into" the labor movement's internal process of setting its agenda for foreign policy. "They're saying, 'You've got to agree with our position on international issues, or we won't work with you.' "[75] Countered a United Church of Christ official, "The subterranean issue is the control of the [AFL-CIO] foreign policy apparatus by a very right-wing, cold-war, anti-Communist group."[76]

Anticommunism in the American labor movement stretches from AFL founder Samuel Gompers through cold warrior George Meany, the AFL-CIO's first president. It inspired Lane Kirkland, a founding board member of the Committee on the Present Danger, a hawkish pro-defense group that included Ronald Reagan until his election to the presidency. With Penn Kemble and Tom Kahn serving as two of Kirkland's top aides, the Social Democrats certainly helped stiffen the AFL-CIO's hard-line foreign policy stance, while Kirkland's more diplomatic style helped salve the wounds of Vietnam-era infighting in the federation under the autocratic George Meany. But wider tensions on defense and foreign policy between the AFL-CIO's liberal and conservative wings surfaced early in the Reagan era.[77] Recognize "the special menace of Communist totalitarianism" and the danger of Nixon's "false and one-sided 'detente,' " the SD/USA urged the incoming Reagan administration, in order to overcome the illusion bred by Vietnam that "American power was its own worst enemy" and correct the growing U.S.-USSR military imbalance.[78]

To reverse the "retreat and humiliation" of Jimmy Carter's McGovernite "New Politics liberalism" on foreign policy, resolved the SD/USA national convention in 1980, the United States must rebuild its nuclear and conventional military power. It must strengthen its political will to deter, contain, and finally unravel the Soviet empire. The United States must fortify NATO to reverse Europe's drift toward neutralism and overcome the Warsaw Pact's growing lead in Euro-strategic weapons. To defend the Persian Gulf, "the United States will need a permanent military presence in the region itself," established in the Sinai, if possible, after the Israeli withdrawal under the Camp David accords. "A democratic and equitable Selective Service system should be instituted, as changing circumstances require, to meet America's manpower needs." The United States must check expansion by the Soviets and their proxy forces in Afghanistan, the Middle East, and throughout the third world, especially by backing anti-Castro freedom movements in Cuba and democratic land-reform programs in El Salvador. In the aftermath of the 1980 election, resolved the SD/USA, there is "an increasingly urgent need for an ideological re-alignment in American politics. The notion that 'guns and butter' cannot go together, whether adopted at the behest of the right or the left, is bound to have disastrous consequences." A labor-oriented domestic policy combined with a firm democratic foreign and defense policy is not only possible, urged the SD/USA, but also "necessary for the creation and maintenance of a viable political majority."[79]

By contrast, some of the AFL-CIO's largest unions, such as those representing autoworkers, machinists, food workers, and government employees, dissented in 1982 from the AFL-CIO executive council's call for defense spending increases of 5–7 percent beyond inflation, citing polls that showed 61 percent of union members behind them. They lobbied Congress against the MX missile, even as AFL-CIO headquarters reaffirmed its support for the controversial weapon.[80] Dissenting union groups also branded as a total failure the land-reform program in El Salvador, celebrated as the cornerstone of the AFL-CIO's anticommunist platform in the Caribbean cold war. The program was carried out by its American Institute for Free Labor Development, with millions of dollars in U.S. government funding via the U.S. Agency for International Development, and was boldly championed by the IRD in the early 1980s.[81]

Liberal labor officials tugged the federation's stance on El Salvador from unqualified support for U.S. backing of the military government there to measured criticism of its violent excesses. They protested Lane Kirkland's presence on President Reagan's policy commission on Central America. "It's clearly stacked in favor of Ronald Reagan," charged one, arguing that "shoring up Reagan's military policy at the same time that labor is working to unseat him just doesn't make a whole lot of sense."[82] Labor conservatives such as the SD/USA argued that the AFL-CIO could resist Reagan's antilabor domestic policies yet remain staunchly anticommunist in defending the president's foreign policy. Liberals in the federation dissented from its hawkish stance on foreign policy as being wrongheaded in itself, disastrous in its impact in helping to hike defense spending and slash social-welfare programs, and unwise in handcuffing AFL-CIO efforts to work against President Reagan's expected bid for re-election in 1984.

Seen from either angle, the unionized conflict between the churches and the IRD sheds light on the IRD's institutional backdrop. It situates the institute within a larger alliance of anticommunist cultural conservatives in the churches with like-minded SD/USA conservatives in the labor movement and hawkish, anticommunist political conservatives in both the Democratic and Republican parties during the Reagan administration. If the SD/USA hawks moved first to rally the religious right around Reaganite foreign policy, they did so in the midst of broader changes already under way in the de facto dynamics of church-labor relations since the 1960s, as Penn Kemble claimed in justifying the IRD as a response to New Left churches.

The postwar New Deal synthesis of strong industrial unions made up of working-class Democrats fighting for the free world, higher wages, and fuller public provision alike gave way to smaller unions and a larger middle class split by diverging fortunes in an increasingly white-collar and services economy, not only divided by Vietnam. Weakened unions in need of like-minded friends had begun forging closer ties to the peace-and-justice churches to fight plant closings, organize service workers, defend social-welfare spending, and lobby against the laissez-faire domestic policies of the Reagan White House.[83] So proclaimed the 1983 Labor Day message of John Sweeney, then president of the Service Employees International Union, who was elected AFL-CIO president in 1995 and went on to dissolve AIFLD and its anticommunist Caribbean campaigns:

> No more important vehicle for social change exists today than our churches and no more important alliance exists for the defense of the common people than a coalition of religion and labor. Through the six decades of the contemporary American labor movement, working people and their organizations have had no stauncher ally than religious groups.
>
> Just as business mounted new, sharp attacks on labor in the late seventies, so too are arch-conservative forces now training their well-financed guns on the churches. In particular, the major Protestant denominations are under scurrilous attack today, and the same money that funds right-to-work efforts is now financing smear campaigns aimed at silencing the witnesses to the laws of God.
>
> In the past 8 months charges have appeared in *Readers Digest, Time* magazine, and on "60 Minutes" that the major Protestant denominations are run by left-wing clerics who use Sunday collection money to buy guns for Third World revolutionaries and to produce anti-American propaganda at home.
>
> Just as the churches have often come to the defense of working people, when they organize, so is this the time when organized labor should cry out against these assaults and denounce the attackers as the agents of reaction that they are.[84]

On the political right and left alike, significantly, these opening rounds of combat between the IRD and its foes in the mainline churches were justified by reference to many of the same exemplary cases in order to underscore the churches' important voice and influence in the larger moral argument of American public life. In 1984 business, labor, and government leaders were invited to subscribe to a new IRD newsletter monitoring the churches' economic involvements. The newsletter was edited by Kerry Ptacek, a Presbyterian layman who was the IRD's research director and a former colleague of David Jessup in SDS and Frontlash, the AFL-CIO youth organization. "Decision-makers in business, labor and government are learning that the concerns of the Christian churches can have a power-ful influence on the climate of economic affairs, both in the United States and worldwide," the IRD's newsletter prospectus explained. "The signifi-cance of church-sponsored campaigns for disinvestment in South Africa, the [Nestlé] infant formula boycott, and the opposition to U.S. aid pro-grams in Central America has made that apparent to most."[85]

For related reasons, explained a researcher at the leftish Institute for the Study of Labor and Economic Crisis who analyzed the IRD's role in shap-ing "a new authoritarian populism" for the Reagan era, the neoconserva-tives intensified political attacks on the mainline churches in the 1980s. "One reason is that the churches have served as an effective rallying point for both social justice agitation at home and opposition to U.S.-backed repression abroad. Religiously based pacifist organizations were among the first vocal domestic opponents to the Vietnam War, and the churches have served as one of the few institutional bases for human rights demands for El Salvador, opposition to apartheid in South Africa, support for the Nestle boycott, and early support for the Nuclear Freeze initiative."[86]

Thus the IRD began by exchanging blows with mainline-church lead-ers, with both sides moving and jabbing in ways that each recognized in the other. They knew each other from long experience in a ring where religious conflict overlapped with political counterpunching and labor-movement infighting, particularly factional fighting waged with wedge is-sues by splinter groups. Should the churches have turned the other cheek instead? Of course, grants one of the ecclesial combatants years later, if they had it to do all over again. "They were slinging mud at us, we got mad, and we got down in the mud with them instead of rising above it all. I regret that now. But at the time they were defaming us, and we felt we needed to defend ourselves and stick up for the truth, too."[87] Third parties to the mudslinging also expressed regrets later on. Asked in 2002 if he regretted any show in the long history of *60 Minutes*, its creator and producer, Don Hewitt, answered yes: "We once took off on the National Council of Churches as being left-wing and radical and a lot of nonsense." After receiving congratulatory calls from right-wing political sources the morning after the show, Hewitt recalls, he reflected, "We must have done something wrong last night, and I think we probably did."[88]

Whether right or wrong, inspired by faith or driven by power, this mix of moral drama and religious witness with ideologically charged political combat and propagandistic mudslinging on prime-time television is worthy of note and cause for concern. It marked a striking escalation of continuing conflict and commingling, too, among denominational religious bodies and parachurch lobbies, freestanding political-action committees and decentered political parties, activist social movements and divided labor unions, big-business interests and private foundations. Did the IRD arise in an empty public square? Emptying of New Deal Democrats and Taft Republicans, along with many traditionally faithful voters too doubtful or disappointed to stay involved in public life, this polity was crowded nonetheless, and it was being transformed by the amplified voices and organizational agility of its innovative adversaries and their diverse allies.

CHAPTER SIX

From Cold War to Culture Wars

The Evolution of the IRD

In the first five years of its existence, the Institute on Religion and Democracy launched an influential investigation of Methodist "peace-and-
justice" grants and programs it found tilted to the political left. It allied
with Good News, the leading evangelical church-renewal group in the
United Methodist Church, to organize Methodists opposed to these policies. It expanded this criticism to the political stance and religious integrity
of the World Council of Churches, the National Council of Churches, and
other mainline churches such as the United Church of Christ and the Presbyterian Church (USA). The IRD won wide publicity for its attacks in
mass media such as *Reader's Digest* and *60 Minutes*, leading NCC leaders
in particular to respond to IRD charges in shared forums and the media.
It also led to an investigative counterattack mounted by mainline-church
officials, which the IRD weathered defiantly.

"Our early years were very feisty and combative," later recalled Diane
Knippers, a seven-year veteran of Good News who joined the IRD's staff
in 1982, became its president in 1993, and was named one of America's
twenty-five most influential evangelicals in 2005. "We actually believed we
were going to clean up the mess in the mainline churches pretty quickly.
Whatever naïveté we had about that had begun to fade by 1984–85." If
response to its *60 Minutes* and *Reader's Digest* exposés hadn't turned the
tide of battle, the IRD realized, it was clearly in for more of a long haul.
"So we had to do more than just take potshots at what we were against
in the mainline," judged Knippers. "We had to dig in and figure out what
we're for, beyond our manifesto, and work for that. As early as 1984, we
were asking what were the churches most ignoring in public policy, and
we felt it was religious liberty."[1]

The IRD organized its first religious-liberty conference in 1984, co-sponsored by the National Association of Evangelicals and the Jacques Maritain Center, a conservative Catholic research and advocacy group. "We wanted partners, we wanted to build alliances," Knippers stressed. A second such conference followed in 1985. By this time, the IRD had won the interested attention of the national political media and the allegiance of the Reagan White House as well, earning it the title of "official seminary of the Reagan administration" from mainline-church leaders.[2] Marking this recognition and allegiance, the IRD joined the Jacques Maritain Center and the like-minded Ethics and Public Policy Center to co-sponsor with the U.S. State Department the 1985 conference on religious liberty. President Ronald Reagan addressed this conference, and Assistant Secretary of State Elliott Abrams helped organize it to highlight religious repression in the Soviet bloc, Iran, and Nicaragua under the Sandinistas. "In our first phase, we concentrated on tracking what the mainline churches were doing wrong in supporting groups and governments that did not recognize religious liberty or human rights," explained Diane Knippers. "That led into our second phase of concentrating on more direct support for religious liberty around the world."[3]

Through the 1980s, the IRD focused on international issues. It championed U.S. policy in the Caribbean cold war, demanded alternatives to the African National Congress in South Africa, and cheered the decline and fall of the Soviet bloc as the dawn of a new era of democratic capitalism around the world. At its outset, the IRD emphasized the case of El Salvador. There it backed continuing U.S. aid to the current Christian Democratic government to bolster land reform and "protect innocent people from threats of violence and terrorism from both right and left," in line with the revised AFL-CIO position on the situation. It opposed the mainline churches in their support for "the campaign to legitimize the Democratic Revolutionary Front in El Salvador" as a popular guerrilla movement fighting against a right-wing military dictatorship seen as a de facto "thugocracy."[4] Later, the IRD turned to Nicaragua under the Sandinistas as a decisive case, where it saw the mainline U.S. churches such as the UCC and Methodists following the liberationist lead of the NCC and WCC: blinded by false visions of reconciling Marxism and Christianity, they were blessing and justifying a communist dictatorship guilty of violating human rights and repressing religious freedom. In 1984, demanded the IRD, "the time has come for the mainline churches to end their assistance to organizations that support or excuse the actions of the Sandinista dictatorship."[5]

In 1990, after the fall of the Berlin Wall and the USSR, the IRD championed the prospect of twin democratic and capitalist revolutions to transform North-South conflicts as well as East-West divisions. "Throughout the underdeveloped world, and particularly in Latin America, a capitalist revolution is unfolding, with ramifications as portentous as those of the democratic revolution," proclaimed a briefing paper released by the IRD's new Economic Studies Program. It called on U.S. churches to rethink their own socialistic, state-centered schemes of relief and development ministries, in a world where walls "erected against free markets and free trade in the name of socialist development" were being torn down.[6]

The Turn toward an Evangelizing Think Tank

In 1986 the IRD's board of directors appointed Dr. Kent R. Hill to succeed Penn Kemble as the IRD's top executive. Self-described as a genuinely ecumenical "moderate evangelical," Hill had earlier joined the IRD board as a professor teaching church history at a Nazarene college, Seattle Pacific University, and pursuing research on Christian churches in the Soviet Union and Eastern Europe, begun when he was a doctoral student in history at the University of Washington. What attracted him to the IRD, he explained, "as an evangelical Nazarene without any prior knowledge of the problems the IRD exposed, was studying religion in the Soviet Union and discovering the failure of the NCC and the mainline churches to handle that challenge." Slow at first to grasp why the churches were overlooking religious persecution under communism and siding with the Soviet state, Hill finally began to realize that "the problem was in the 'old-line' church world itself. The IRD was the only voice telling the truth about religious freedom and democracy. That belied what the churches were saying, and it fit perfectly with what I had been experiencing directly. Otherwise, I had nothing to gain by agreeing with IRD."[7] The IRD's first task, as Hill summed it up broadly in a 1986 public letter, is to call all Christians to be faithful to "those classical Christian traditions and doctrines which soar above denominational differences and contrast so markedly with the dominant secular ideologies of our time." Its second task, he specified, is to "call for more responsible discussion of foreign policy issues within the church world." For more than five years the IRD has done just that, confirmed Hill, as "we have sought to challenge church pronouncements, policies, and funding allocations which serve forces ultimately destructive of democracy, human rights, and social justice. Many who design such policies are consciously hostile to Western societies and endorse or are influenced by Marxist economic and social analysis."[8]

Hill reissued the IRD manifesto, "Christianity and Democracy," with an added preface of his own. It likewise struck a more ecclesiological chord in softer evangelical tones, followed by a sharper note to reassert the IRD's role in debating the churches on public policy. His preface began by stressing that "worship, evangelism, and discipleship are essential to the Church, as is the obligation of calling Christians to be instruments of healing in a suffering world," in light of the Two Great Commandments to love God and neighbor. "In its productive early years," wrote Hill, "the IRD emerged as a major and respected national voice in the effort to promote renewal and a more responsible religious involvement in the foreign policy debate." It remains "committed to renewal within the Church, including the promotion of a more balanced and tempered discussion of the foreign policy questions of our day."[9]

Asked in 1991 to trace the IRD's evolution during his tenure, Hill replied, "Ten years ago, the founders of the IRD were in a radically different place than we are today. I came on board in 1986 and inherited a situation where the battle lines were already drawn. The hatreds and bitterness were already ingrained. We had one person in particular in the IRD before I got here, a former SDSer, who left a trail of bitterness behind him. Those kinds of political converts can move closer to the truth but still be just as much trouble as before, because they're no more charitable," judged Hill. "Political trench warfare takes extraordinary spiritual grace to do right and not have it poison your life."[10] The IRD's strongly adversarial stance at the outset toward the mainline churches, Hill suggested, emerged less from its own political instincts than from the political antagonisms of its Cold War context during the Reagan years, and from the extreme politicization of the liberal churches to which it reacted.

Hill featured this mix in comparing his tenure as IRD director with Penn Kemble's term as its founding de facto executive: "One interesting thing about the IRD's evolution is that it didn't have an executive director for the first five years. I was the first one, and in 1991 the board changed the title to 'president.' That's because Penn was the one member of the group who didn't fit theologically," Hill reflected. "When I came on board, it could have been a moment of some tension, because this was really his organization, yet he always said he was never the person to direct it. His spiritual beliefs were not what the organization needed. The board always knew it, and he always knew it. In 1986 they felt like they found someone who could represent them." Hill accepts some credit for the marked difference many observers found in the IRD during its second five years, in contrast to its first five. "It's quite remarkable that an ecumenical organization made up of one-fourth Catholics and three-fourths old-line Protestants finally found a director from the evangelical world. I am genuinely ecumenical, or it wouldn't have worked. But I tease the Methodists on our board," Hill laughs: " 'You had to go to a Nazarene to find somebody who still believes what you do.' "

But the IRD's evolution has reasons that go well beyond its change in executives, as Hill readily recognized. For one thing, he said, "it's the natural aging of an organization that clearly wasn't going to go away" after surviving the "cheap shots" of the counterattack launched by the mainline churches. A second change stemmed from the easing of the conflict between the Sandinistas and the Contras in Nicaragua during the later 1980s. "That caused tremendous tension between us and the churches," noted Hill, particularly because Penn Kemble, David Jessup, and other IRD members so actively favored the Contra cause through public advocacy and political fund-raising by Kemble's Coalition for a Democratic Majority and related groups. These tensions were amplified by political struggles that reverberated from the Reagan White House through Congress to the Democratic Party and the AFL-CIO, and included allegations of illegal involvement in military, financial, and intelligence aid to the Contras. "I'm not sure it would have gotten out of hand like it did if I had been here," Hill reflected. "Some of it would have happened anyway. It wouldn't have mattered who told the truth; they would have been caricatured, and I would have been called an extremist if I had been here the first five years instead of coming in and being hailed as a moderate."

Summing up the IRD's situation in the early 1990s and its plans, Hill judged, "What I think is important about IRD is what we're for, not what we're against." Nonetheless, the IRD's chief accomplishment in its first decade in existence, said Hill, lies in its success as "the single agent most responsible for making the case intelligently to teach people in the media and the general public that the politics coming out of the NCC and the mainline-church world were not representative of the people in the churches, and they were certainly not 'middle of the road.' " Agree or not with their specifics, said Hill, "nobody today has the gall to call these politics 'mainline' or 'moderate.' The leadership will admit that these are 'liberal' positions, and that's where they stand. So there was a real reorientation in the media and the public mind about the churches," Hill stressed. "One, they were not really coming from the mainline 'middle.' And, two, there was a real split in the churches, with the great majority of the moderates in the middle taking what are in fact much more morally and theologically conservative views of social questions."

In Hill's view, the IRD succeeded chiefly in countering the mainline churches' claims in the eyes of the media and the general public, not in organizing the denominational faithful themselves to disavow and replace their leftist leaders. This view dovetails with the assessment of mainline-church leaders who see the IRD—and its politically conservative funders such as the Scaife foundation—as more interested in discrediting the mainline's moral authority in the larger public sphere than in reforming the churches themselves. "Yes, the IRD has become a lot less nasty and less ideologically predictable since Kent Hill came in," allowed Bob McClean, head of the Methodist Center at the United Nations during the 1980s and 1990s, "and maybe they have had their hearts warmed by his evangelical touch. But the fact remains that the IRD has never been a membership organization with a broad base in the churches. It's been a kind of political-action committee all along, set up to 'jam' the churches' public voice and question their authority to speak out on public questions," said McLean. "It's always been funded by big-business, conservative foundations outraged by our teaching on social justice and looking for someone to pose as the 'silent majority' in the churches and call us extremists. They could care less about the churches themselves. That's why their money keeps flowing, even though the IRD hasn't really made much headway inside the denominations."[11]

Hill saw the adversarial success of the IRD's first decade leading to a broader, more constructive agenda in its second decade, building on the ashes of communism's Cold War defeat: "The IRD wouldn't have come into being except for the outrage over the churches' witness in the political arena. Yet the IRD has continued to expand since the end of the Cold War by 12 percent or more the last four or five years, while other good organizations like Keston College have declined precipitously, because the public saw them limited to fighting Cold War battles over religious freedoms and persecution, refugees, and the like." By contrast, testified Hill, "there are five times as many funders now available to us, and it's because we've been able to argue that this is the day we have been waiting and working for. What we believe in is now possible to accomplish actively, namely, to do proactive work for democracy and religious freedom."[12]

Beginning in the late 1980s, under Hill's leadership, the IRD began to seek allies to sponsor a wide range of programs for evangelism, education, church-building, and the formation of church-state institutions in Russia and the former Soviet bloc. For example, with the aid of the Faith, Hope, and Love Foundation, headed by a Russian Orthodox lawyer, it arranged for the entry of independent Methodist missionaries backed by Good News into Russian prisons. There they evangelized, distributed religious literature, founded Methodist Societies, and donated funds to help indigent prisoners supplement their rations.[13] The message the IRD delivers through such programs, said Hill, is manifold in its moral meaning and main audience. What the naive Western audience needs to hear, first, is that "the defeat of communism does not begin to win the victory of human rights, religious freedom, and democracy. What it does is remove the major obstacle to making the effort to win those victories." Second, those in the post-Soviet East need to hear that "you cannot decide today that you believe in free markets and democracy, and immediately have what we have in the West."[14] Prosperity and peace, a middle-class majority, political stability across parties, and religious tolerance across confessions all take time and effort to achieve, by putting new ideals into practice and changing institutions to embody them.

But the foundation of the IRD's message, argues Hill, is neither democratic government nor free enterprise, American style. It is the Christian gospel of faith, hope, and love, and the salvation of souls: "When the Methodist Church decides to give hundreds of thousands of dollars to do humanitarian work to help in the Soviet Union and Eastern Europe, and they want to funnel it through the Orthodox Church or the Peace Fund, you know they're lost. The fact that they're doing that instead of dealing in any way with this incredible spiritual hunger and planting churches is proof that the gospel has died here, in our own churches." Counters a Methodist theologian who works on world missions, "Eastern Europe and Russia have their own churches, you know, with complicated bonds and differences among Orthodox, Catholics, Protestants, and Jews." That history offers some of the best possible reasons for the wisdom of the mainline churches' position on the indigenization of missions, explains Theodore Runyon: "You try to help other peoples build their own churches, renew them, reform them. We'll find that out if instead we try to go in there and aggressively evangelize and back the evangelicals, Pentecostals, or fundamentalist Protestants in planting churches most like our own. We'll stir up a religious hornet's nest like the ethnic and nationalist conflict we have already seen. We certainly won't be doing the work of Christ and the church universal."[15] In this debate, the IRD instead sees the prospects for its work in the wake of the Cold War as beginning and ending in the Christian gospel, in contrast to the politicized, secular thrust of social action in the mainline churches that continues to reveal their betrayal of the gospel.

Notwithstanding the urgency of this ongoing debate, the IRD's overarching goals, and its vigorous new initiatives, Kent Hill resigned its presidency in 1992 to become the president of Eastern Nazarene College. The following year, Diane Knippers became the IRD's new executive. Soon thereafter, Rev. Ed Robb resigned after more than a decade's loyal service as chairman of the IRD's board of directors, to be succeeded by Helen Rhea Stumbo, a longtime United Methodist leader of Good News and related evangelical renewal groups. Despite the new funding prospects the IRD announced after the end of the Cold War, its foundation support ebbed in the early 1990s, and its budgetary belt needed tightening. In reexamining its trajectory, the IRD surveyed its members and donors, who responded in favor of more attention devoted to "the 'culture war' going on in the United States" and "the general health of American churches," with less attention given to religious persecution and new democracies overseas.[16]

During the 1990s, the IRD's publications began to shift accordingly in both tone and topic—after having grown longer, deeper in detail, and denser in think-tank analysis under Hill, most notably in his own five-hundred-page tome on Christian churches in the USSR under glasnost, *The Soviet Union on the Brink*. During Hill's tenure, for example, the IRD published a detailed analysis of "the misuse of just-war thinking in the churches" during the Persian Gulf War, *Sowing Confusion among the Flock*. In *Reading the World: An Integrated Reference Guide to International Affairs*, the institute put forth an extended critique of "liberationist and sectarian radicals" in favor of a new consensus between "transformationalist and temporalist reformers," to back fresh American leadership of a post-Marxist world ordered by democratic capitalism. After 1992, IRD publications grew shorter, punchier, and more oriented to cultural issues and church-renewal audiences within the mainline denominations. They looked more like denominational newsletters, rather than think-tank white papers. The IRD's most notable book-length publication, significantly enough, was *Prophets and Politics* in 1995, a journalistic investigation of the Washington offices of the mainline churches, which "reveals that the liberal churches—whose policies and theological perspective represent the fewest of the country's churchgoers—have the most influence in Washington."[17]

Democratic Revolution as Cultural Reconstruction

The IRD's new emphasis was announced by Diane Knippers in an address at her installation as the IRD's new president in 1993. For all the progress of freedom made in Eastern Europe, Latin America, and Africa since the IRD's birth, she warned, "serious threats to democracy remain and are indeed growing. Not the least of these is the cultural situation of the United States. Democracy requires a virtuous citizenry, committed to the pursuit of the common good and defense of individual liberties." Yet contemporary American culture increasingly "celebrates immorality, violence, and license, and evidences increasing hostility toward vital religious faith."[18] The churches must help strengthen the foundations of freedom at home as well as abroad, urged Knippers, to meet threats to democracy that "arise from ethnic and religious hostilities, the lure of statism and anti-democratic authoritarianism, the weakness of non-political or 'mediating institutions,' and persistent poverty." Armed with this mandate, the IRD began to reorient itself.

The IRD changed partly in response to the spirit of the times and the exigencies of the moment, including budgetary pressures and its members' surveyed interests. But this reorientation arose, too, from ideals of the church and public culture long established in the IRD. In particular, Kent Hill emphasized cultural and spiritual renewal as the underlying answer to the problems of Marxism, seen as just one branch of a Western secularism whose self-centeredness and social determinism must be countered like "a spiritual AIDS" that infects American media and schools, marriages and families.[19] This gave distinctively evangelical religious content to the calls for cultural reconstruction that Penn Kemble issued in response to post–Cold War conflicts after the breakup of the Soviet Union and the electoral defeat of the Sandinistas in Nicaragua. In turn, Kemble's emphasis on cultural reconstruction closer to home helped guide the IRD away from concentrating its attention on seeking to build new democratic and religious institutions in Russia and the former Soviet bloc.

Asked to name the single most important change in the world bearing on the mainline churches and the IRD's progress since it began a decade

earlier, Kemble pointed to the 1990 victory of Violeta Chamorro over
the Sandinistas in Nicaragua. Their defeat, he said, exploded the mainline
churches' political faith in the coming of third-world revolution, its primary object of devotion since the Hungarian uprising discredited Soviet
state socialism in 1956. "On election night, when Daniel Ortega came out
in the Olaf Palme Center, the entire Western left was represented there—
and they all knew he lost. He couldn't hide it. He had to admit it."[20] At
that point, Kemble argued, the Sandinistas' justification of their state-
socialist government in populist terms blessed by liberation theology was
revealed as a fraudulent facsimile of democracy by the Nicaraguan people
themselves. The Sandinistas did not embody the democratic aspirations
of peasants so favored by liberationists' preferential option for the poor.
The campesinos were not, in fact, a noble Christian proletariat whose os-
tensible dictatorship would usher in a new Christendom.

The mainline Protestant churches erred by adopting an adversarial
posture toward America in the millennial expectation that "if we somehow changed the system, we would have the new Nicaraguan Man walking right up Pennsylvania Avenue," contended Kemble. "It's not going
to happen. What is going to happen is that people are always going to sin
or fail, and we need to have the House of Ruth pull up with the sandwich
wagon to feed them." The Catholics, he noted, "are much closer to that
truth when they reinterpret 'the preferential option for the poor' away
from revolutionary solidarity with the proletariat to compassion for the
poor." This is a job for those whose "faith is not a faith in the things of
this world," stressed Kemble. "You're not going to get aides in the House
of Representatives to do it. It's too discouraging," he explained, in terms
consonant with the rhetoric of a kinder, gentler America lit by a thousand points of voluntarist light during the presidency of George H. W.
Bush, and later warmed by the compassionate conservatism of President
George W. Bush.

At the same time, however, Kemble in 1992 foresaw in the new opportunities of a high-tech economy with an educated workforce a bright new
future for Social Democrats in the labor movement and the Democratic
Party. Together they could move to reconcile capitalism and economic
democracy, beyond the failure of supply-side economics on one side and
the constraints of socialistic welfare states on the other. "You can only
contend with the injustices of capitalism if you recognize what works
and is valid in it, and if you are proposing to change things that don't
work with things that are demonstrably better, not with the workers'

paradise," said Kemble. "Look at how capitalism at its best can do that, and how it can bring labor, managers, and investors together to do that," he urged, in terms that recall Michael Novak's neoconservative praise for democratic capitalism yet echo Bill Clinton's neoliberal prospect of booming economic productivity, driven by high technology, education, free trade, and capital movement within a globalized division of labor. "I look forward to a new mode of worker-manager relations as a way to create a more productive economy. That's our case," Kemble proclaimed. "If we want more democracy and equity in the workplace, we've got to show that this will not only be fairer to workers. It will create a stronger, more competitive economy. That's one of the things that really intrigue me. If the Democratic Party, the labor movement, the Social Democrats, are going to make their comeback," he predicted, "it will be by taking the productivity argument away from the laissez-faire crowd. That's our challenge."[21]

How have these historic changes reset the stage for the IRD after the Cold War? "The IRD is now in a situation where it has a great challenge and opportunity," answered Kemble, "if it can build on the foundation we laid in the struggle with the mainline churches. Marxism-Leninism is the creature of Western society, just like Solzhenitsyn says. The collapse of communism really begins with the collapse of its moral support in the West," and that is where it must end. "What the IRD needs to do now is not just tackle the job of political reconstruction in the East. I'm almost a little nervous about that focus," Kemble confessed, "because a great job of moral, spiritual, and civic reconstruction remains to be done here and in Europe." Since the fall of communism, he noted, "you can go over there to Eastern Europe and Russia, preach and start churches, and be welcomed with open arms. That's a temptation for evangelicals in particular, while the struggle here is so important."

Commenting for the IRD on the upcoming 1992 presidential elections, Kemble highlighted this theme: "The future course of American politics is not going to be set by who comes out ahead in November, but by a much more mysterious procedure in which our culture responds to the ending of the Cold War and the challenges of reconstruction at home," he promised. "We are now in the situation where a community of people with common values and ideas about what needs to be done can, by pulling together, exert enormous influence. The time is ripe for some kind of social movement." Such a movement, prescribed Kemble, "has to be built on the values that were broken down in the 1960s and its aftermath.

This is not the grasping and bitterness we see in some on the right, or the irresponsibility and enviousness that has spread through the left. This has to find ways [to] involve Americans in helping sustain the remarkable worldwide revolution for democracy." Kemble challenged the cultured despisers of this vision of democracy's new dawn, "Go ahead and sneer at such innocence. See where it gets you."[22]

Does this vision hold a place for the mainline churches? "They really have to search their souls," judged Kemble.[23] Otherwise, he observed, "I don't see what will become of them. They're like the Communist Party. They're true believers, while everybody else is increasingly distrustful and contemptuous of them," in a world that has left them behind. But instead of repenting their political sins, they persist in rehearsing them, Kemble concluded, like the defeated Sioux after Wounded Knee, at the end of the Indian wars, who "go off into this forsaken wilderness to do the Ghost Dance. They think somehow it will bring back their way of life, their ancestors, all their people killed in the bygone wars. It's so pathetic because it's so clearly hopeless. I look at the NCC and the mainline churches and I think, my God, they don't even understand what's happening in the world. They're just dancing the Ghost Dance on into oblivion," abandoned to the indigenous equivalent of the trash heap of history.

Early in 1992, Kemble reportedly negotiated with the Clinton campaign to organize on its behalf staunch anticommunists and foreign policy hawks in the Democratic Party and the labor movement, in return for a place in the Clinton administration. In December 1992, Clinton appointed Kemble to head the transition team overseeing the U.S. Information Agency (USIA), of which he was later named deputy director, then acting director. When the agency was merged into the State Department, Kemble served through the second Clinton administration as a senior State Department official.[24]

As Kemble took the helm of USIA, a critic on the political left, writing in *The Nation*, indicted him as a partisan infighter remarkable for his political "passion for sectarianism," and for his mastery of organizing and funding ideologically charged lobbies: "In the heyday of the contra cause, Kemble was a chief cheerleader," noted David Corn. "His Friends of the Democratic Center in Central America (a k a Prodemca) lobbied for military aid to the rebels while funneling National Endowment for Democracy funds to anti-Sandinista outfits in Nicaragua, including *La Prensa*. Some of Prodemca's dollars flowed from far-right foundations; others came from Carl (Spitz) Channell, the conservative fundraiser who schemed with Oliver North," reported Corn. "Kemble also ran another shop, the Institute for Religion and Democracy, which specialized in assailing liberal church groups." In light of this record, concluded Corn, "political payback aside, there is a compelling logic to handing the USIA to Kemble. Who better to run an ideologically loaded propaganda machine?"[25]

Thus point and counterpoint continued in exchanges over the IRD across religious and political boundaries. Church-state boundaries were blurred by a web of institutes, lobbies, political-action committees, and ideological "shops" officially standing free of churches, political parties, and government alike, but actually sitting bound together with all of them in intricate ways that reshape the moral argument of public life and remake the public space citizens share with people of faith.

From Cold War to Culture Wars

In the 1990s, the Institute on Religion and Democracy gradually shifted its focus on issues from the Cold War to culture wars. It sought to bridge these earlier and later rubrics as strongly as possible, and in their linkage to sustain its stance as a catalyst to reform the public witness of American churches. "We are sounding a warning against marrying the churches to a neo-pagan 'green theology'—just as earlier we warned them away from their dangerous romance with Marxism," wrote Diane Knippers in a 1993 membership letter. Instead of "looking for salvation in all the wrong places," the mainline churches should be committed to "spreading the gospel, building strong families, and equipping Christians to be salt and light in the world."[26] Now radical feminist theology, instead of liberation theology, poses the greatest threat to the churches from within. "Ten years ago, extremist forms of liberation theology and secular Marxist-Leninist ideology were the central errors of our churches' social and political witness," charged the IRD in 1995. "Today, our churches face a more insidious and dangerous threat—neo-pagan forms of feminist theology married to a radical feminist agenda in society." In response, the IRD pledges to continue "fighting in the forefront of this new battle for the heart and soul of our churches."[27]

While established as "an anti-communist, pro-religious liberty group," the IRD stayed in business after the fall of the Berlin Wall due to "the continuing oppression of tens of millions of Christians under communist dictatorships in China, Cuba, and North Korea," and the growing repression of Christians in Islamic nations as well as the increasing concerns of Christians in the United States "about religious freedom right here at home." So explained Diane Knippers, the articulate daughter of a Navy chaplain posted at Guantánamo Bay during the Cuban missile crisis, with sharp memories of growing up at the armed edge of Castro's Cuba.[28] The IRD remains an advocate for those who are persecuted for their faith around the world, but now it must look homeward, too. For here at home both religious freedom and the moral survival of American democracy hang in the balance, in the IRD's updated diagnosis, while the mainline churches abdicate their true social role: "Crime, entrenched poverty, a debased and exploitative popular culture, decaying cities, fragmented family life, abandoning of sexual morality—all are symptoms of the underlying moral confusion and the deterioration of civil society. It is not alarmist to ask—Will American democracy survive to benefit our children and grandchildren?" This question gives rise to the chief indictment the IRD levels against the mainline denominations: "Is your church abdicating its responsibility in society?" By this account, "we cannot hope to defend and support a free society without the vibrant and wise witness of the Church. But large portions of the American religious community have offered inadequate, irresponsible, or even destructive responses to these pressing social and political crises," charges the IRD. "Too many declining denominations seem captive to left-wing politics, socialism, radical feminism, and even neo-pagan forms of environmentalism. The Churches have abdicated their essential role in society."[29]

In response, the IRD offered itself as a catalyst "to strengthen the moral values that undergird democratic society." Central among these values, and first among the casualties of secular radicals engaged in culture wars, is the Christian truth that anchors "universal human rights" such as freedom of religion and speech. The IRD defends these human rights from being relativized and displaced by social rights put forward from the religious and political left, a charge leveled by the IRD manifesto in 1981 against moral relativists robed as fashionably faithful fellow travelers of communist revolution in the third world. So the IRD in 1995 vows to campaign both at home and abroad "to mobilize Christian advocacy on behalf of universal human rights—and against moral and cultural relativism that would dilute those rights."[30]

For example, to defend the universal rights of individuals and traditional family values alike from attack by the combined forces of radical feminism and socialist statism, the IRD fought the "profoundly disturbing" agenda of the Fourth World Conference on Women, sponsored by the United Nations in Beijing in late 1995. The draft of its Platform for Action calls for women to have "full and equal participation in all spheres of public and private life, including economic and political decision-making," noted Knippers in early 1995. The platform specifies that women are to make up 50 percent of the world's parliaments, economic institutions, and environmental programs to usher in greater peace and social development and a cleaner environment, while men and women are also to share child-rearing and domestic chores equally. "Government agencies, the media, and educational institutions are all supposed to help re-socialize men and women, boys and girls, about these new gender roles," reports Knippers. But the document "offers not one shred of evidence for this glowing picture of the future of planet earth," in which "more men changing diapers and more women in board rooms" are to bring about world peace, Knippers objected. In short, she charged, "the draft Platform for Action for the Beijing World Conference on Women represents the most arrogant, intrusive and comprehensive experiment in social engineering and restructuring society in human history—all on the baseless assumption that this will produce a just and peaceful world."[31]

Instead of traveling this statist "road to tyranny and oppression for men and women," Knippers pledges, the IRD will work for a world in which "women and men have the right to enter the workplace– or the right to be home-makers—without an international bureaucracy dictating those choices." It fights for individual rights and liberties, linked to traditional family values, against statist regulations and social engineering in the service of an arrogant radical feminism. What does this have to do with the mainline American churches in particular? In reply, Knippers observes that "many of our major denominations are sending delegations of women to the conference (held ironically in communist China) to support the radical agenda outlined in the Platform for Action. Many of our own church representatives will be a part of the attack on America, the undermining of the family, the promotion of abortion, and the undercutting of religion that will be a part of this United Nations women's conference."[32] The IRD won approval as an NGO (nongovernmental organization) delegation to the conference and sent its own team of women to Beijing to counter these inimical ideas and the church representatives backing them—including the National Council of Churches, the World Council of Churches, and in particular the United Methodist Women's Division, with its million members and multimillion-dollar resources.

   Thus the IRD lifted up religious faith and individual political liberties, united in America's heritage, in terms that mainline-church leaders
ignore and betray. It likewise linked secularist ideologies and statist policies at odds with religion, the family, and America's moral responsibility
in world affairs. Without the IRD, then, the "National and World Council
of Churches would still be portrayed in the media as the authentic voice
of Christians in the United States—even when they took positions church
members deplored. More church agencies would make secret grants to political causes—and more church meetings would be closed to the public—
just as they used to be before the IRD led the fight for open meetings
and full financial disclosure. Our church leaders would be even more
radical," warned Knippers. "And, you in the pews would know even less
about what was being said and done in your name. There would be far less
hope for the future of many of our denominations," concluded the IRD
president.[33]
   How should the churches change their public witness and social activism? They should "get out of partisan politics," urged Knippers. "They
should stop passing judgment on dozens and dozens of bills before Congress and taking sides on every political issue that hits the front page."
The mainline churches have, by this account, colluded with the expansion
of an overreaching regulatory state in America, not only with the liberal
wing of the Democratic Party. The mainline churches have thereby ignored the essential social message of the gospel. For it responds directly
to deeper questions "about our rights and responsibilities as individuals
under God, about how different people can live together in community,
about sin and forgiveness and reconciliation." Mainline-church leaders have too often perversely politicized the gospel or displaced it with
their own views, thereby violating the integrity of Christian conscience
among their own people in the pews. Instead, counseled Knippers, mainline leaders "should recognize and articulate the difference between the
Word that they have received of God and their own personal political
opinions. And they should always respect the Christian consciences of
church members."[34]
   By the mid-1990s, then, the Institute on Religion and Democracy had
at once changed and steadied itself. First, it had regained its organizational balance after its heady early successes in unsettling mainline-church
leaders and enjoying inside access to the Reagan White House and State
Department. Second, it had recovered from its decline in influence and
funding after the Reagan years and its uncertainty of aim after the Cold

War was won. In shifting from Cold War to culture wars, the IRD focused on issues of abortion, homosexuality, feminism, and family values pregnant with theological meaning, epitomized by the controversial efforts of mainline Protestant feminists to "re-imagine" the nature of biblical divinity and Christian liturgy, acted out with milk and honey in place of bread and wine. The IRD thereby took hold of hot-button issues that typically split theological liberals from evangelicals, and younger, more educated and urbane members of mainline churches from their older, less educated and less cosmopolitan counterparts. These issues served the IRD as organizing issues, especially in the biggest, broadest mainline denominations such as the United Methodists and the Presbyterians, with large liberal and evangelical wings. These include women highly committed to feminist and liberationist ideals and activism on one side; and, on the other, women no less committed to traditional works of charity, missions, and family life.

Reforming America's Churches

The IRD aimed to make a strategic shift away "from the media aspect" to become "a permanent presence within a variety of denominations" as early as 1984, according to staffers. But only a decade later did that shift hit full stride.[35] To advance its culture wars against its target of the mainline churches, the IRD revitalized its three denominational committees in the mid-1990s, including Presbyterians for Democracy and Religious Freedom and the Episcopal Committee on Religion and Freedom. This move proved most effective in the case of the United Methodist Committee for Faith and Freedom, which worked in conjunction with Good News and other evangelical renewal groups in Methodism. The IRD eventually renamed and refined all three denominational committees along similar lines: Presbyterian Action, Episcopal Action, and United Methodist Action, shortened to UMAction. To concentrate on reforming mainline denominations from within, the IRD cooperated more closely with Good News to expand and strengthen a network of denomination-specific church-renewal groups such as the Confessing Movement among United Methodists, founded in 1994–95, and its counterpart in the Presbyterian Church (USA), begun in 2001.[36]

Claiming some 600,000 individual members, 1,400 local churches, and 4,000 pastors, the Methodist Confessing Movement calls on Methodist bishops to reassert their traditional doctrinal teaching authority. It urges all Methodists to "repudiate teachings and practices that misuse principles of inclusiveness and tolerance to distort the doctrine and discipline of the church." To this end, it has issued a series of creedal declarations, for example, the "Confessing Church Declaration" of 1997. It has asked all Methodists to sign these declarations in order to affirm orthodox formulation of Methodist tradition in the light of Scripture, applied clearly enough to moral issues such as abortion and homosexuality to outlaw abortion except to save the life of a mother and to forbid the ordination of practicing homosexuals to the ministry.[37] In 1996 the IRD joined with Good News, the Confessing Movement, and a score of other conservative renewal groups in mainline denominations—for example, Presbyterian Layman, Episcopalians United, American Baptist Evangelicals, the Evangelical Lutheran Confessing Fellowship, and the Biblical Witness Fellowship in the United Church of Christ—to form the Association for Church Renewal, under the leadership of Good News president James V. Heidinger II. The association aimed to reach an estimated 2.4 million members of mainline churches to address and mobilize reform around their common concerns, including "moral relativism, marriage and family, human sexuality, neo-pagan worship, God-language, the free exercise of religion at home and abroad, the sanctity of life, and world mission and evangelism."[38]

In 1994 Mark Tooley, a lifelong Methodist, joined the IRD after serving eight years as a CIA reports officer. In 1996 he took the helm of UMAction to "reclaim our church from its captivity by remote church bureaucrats" and reverse its "decline into a small, self-absorbed sect of radical, secular political agitators." Indifferent to people in the pews and to Methodism's urgent need for evangelism and church growth, these bureaucrats support "dangerous, anti-democratic foreign governments," higher taxes and larger government, and "the homosexual agenda," Tooley charged. They oppose "nearly all U.S. defense programs" and voluntary, student-led school prayer. They lead church agencies that are "using collection plate money to promote a divisive, highly partisan political agenda," while "assailing central Christian beliefs, . . . ignoring the Bible on theological and moral issues, . . . [and] allowing our overseas missionary force to decline dramatically while missions dollars fund radical, secular organizations."[39]

Mild-mannered, sharp-tongued, and organizationally energetic, Mark Tooley worked to strengthen UMAction's network of allies, its sources of funding, and its polemical punch, often aimed at the United Methodist

General Board of Church and Society. In 1997 Tooley launched a broad media campaign to stymie the board's $4 million fund-raising efforts to renovate its headquarters building on Capitol Hill. The campaign made full use of direct-mail "UMAction Briefing" newsletters and public letters sent to national Methodist periodicals and regional newspapers, in addition to the media outlets of Good News, its allies, and the general media. Tooley argued that contributing to the ostensible cause of enhancing the social-justice witness of the Board of Church and Society would actually lend support to its "opposition to the death penalty, its hostility to welfare reform, its aid to Cuba's repressive communist regime, and its support for homosexual rights."[40]

In its opposition to tax cuts and its support for increased environmental regulation, added Tooley, the board, by its own class-conscious account, was at odds with upper-middle-class Methodists, allegedly focused on their own pocketbooks. In its defense of homosexual liberties, he pointed out, the board was linked to Affirmation and other caucus groups that advocate removing all United Methodist opposition to homosexual practices. There is "little that is specifically United Methodist about the Board's very secular political agenda," Tooley concludes.

> Not surprisingly, the Board's building, strategically located across the street from the Capitol and the Supreme Court, houses not only UM offices but a host of interlocking left-wing lobby groups. They will all benefit from a $4 million refurbishment of the UM Building.
>
> How many missionaries could $4 million fund? How many churches could be built with this money? How many hungry could be fed? "Enhancing" the image of secular political lobbies is hardly an urgent cause for our shrinking church in a world of increasing needs.[41]

This UMAction campaign hindered and slowed the ultimately successful fund-raising efforts of the Board of Church and Society to renovate its headquarters on Capitol Hill. It also outraged a great many United Methodists, according to the board's staffers, and it underscored the new turn taken by the IRD back to its roots in aggressive political infighting, and the new lengths to which it would go to obstruct United Methodist leaders. "Political propaganda is one thing, and political dirty tricks are another. This is more like sabotage," testified a senior staff member of the GBCS. "It's crossing the line from playing political hardball into doing real harm with real malice."[42]

In late 1999 the Good News board authorized "pursuit of dialogue with the General Board of Church and Society, possibly to be done jointly with the leadership of UMAction."[43] By the spring of 2000, however, at the United Methodist General Conference, Good News and UMAction were pursuing the elimination of the Board of Church and Society. Delegates voted against this resolution by a margin of 70 to 30 percent, but the IRD vowed to try again in 2004 with a much more intensively organized effort. In late 2001, Tooley sent out some three hundred thousand copies of the UMAction newsletter featuring a "Sample Resolution for Shutting Down the United Methodist Lobby Office in Washington, D.C." to United Methodists with directions to "consider submitting your resolution to your Annual conference, your local District's annual meeting, or simply send copies to your bishop and district superintendent."[44]

Why should the Methodist Board of Church and Society be shut down? For the following reasons, Tooley argued in his resolution:

·   Whereas the Board takes sides on dozens of political issues every year, using the name of our denomination to promote or oppose specific, controversial proposals before the U.S. Congress and the nation;

·   Whereas many of the board's positions are not based on the clear commands of Scripture, which should hold the highest authority among United Methodists; and

·   Whereas the Board repeatedly goes beyond what is authorized by the UM Social Principles and the resolutions of General Conference, injecting its own slanted political judgments.[45]

UMAction will seek to incite Methodists in annual conferences to offer resolutions that "inflame the church," warned Bishop Clifton Ives, president of the General Board of Church and Society, at a 2001 meeting of its members, since the IRD's "intent is not reconciliation but division." Instead, he urged, "do not allow a force from outside the church to separate you from brothers and sisters in your conference. Liberals and conservatives must stay together, must work together, must love and reach out to a hurting world together."[46]

The IRD set out the larger framework for its current priorities in 2000 in a $3.6 million funding proposal for the "Reforming America's Churches Project: 2001–2004." Concentrating on the United Methodist Church, the Presbyterian Church (USA), and the Episcopal Church, the project aimed to "redirect these churches away from their reflexive

alliance with the political left and back toward classical Christianity,"
according to its executive summary. "Conservatives have won surprising
victories on key theological and sexuality issues at recent church conventions. Now is the time to translate those victories into real influence
for conservatives within the permanent governing structures of these
churches, so they can help renew the wider culture of our nation," proposed the IRD. In this effort, the IRD promised to mobilize its alliances
with socially conservative Roman Catholics and evangelicals. It justified
the importance of this effort by underscoring the disproportionate moral
influence of these three churches in American public life beyond their
numbers: United Methodists number 8.3 million, Presbyterians 3.5 million, and Episcopalians 2.3 million, but "their respective memberships
include remarkably high numbers of leaders in politics, business, and
culture. For example, over one-third of the members of the U.S. Senate belong to these three denominations. These denominations include
a disproportionate number of higher income and educated Americans.
Every year they collect about $8 billion from their members" to enrich
the denominations themselves, over fifty thousand local churches, and
hundreds of affiliated colleges, universities, seminaries, academies, and
charities.[47]

The IRD lays out its strategy to reach these "flagship churches," influence their influential members, and reach beyond the churches to win
converts to its cause:

> We disseminate news releases to broadcast media, to every major newspaper
> religion writer in the country, to every major religious magazine, and to key
> columnists, for a total of over 1,000 media contacts. We place op-eds exposing
> the Religious Left on the editorial pages of major newspapers, in religious jour-
> nals, conservative publications and church renewal media. Our staff regularly
> speaks on radio talk shows and occasionally on television. IRD's quarterly
> *Faith and Freedom* journal is sent to over 12,000 supporters, church leaders
> and media contacts. Our denominational publications now reach 285,000
> households and we project growth to 560,000. The combined audiences of re-
> form publications in the Association for Church Renewal total nearly a million
> households.[48]

In efforts to influence the governing church conventions of the three denominations, promises the IRD proposal, it will target the 2004 United
Methodist General Conference, the 2003 Episcopal Assembly, and annual

Presbyterian meetings, concentrating on the Methodists as "America's third largest religious body, and the largest denomination under Religious Left control."[49]

To fight for control of church conventions governing national denominations, the IRD stresses, it will use grassroots organizing drives to initiate resolutions around key issues to mobilize supporters. It will likewise identify conservative candidates to run as delegates, back their election, train them to lead these conventions, and aid them as board members of key denominational agencies in exercising direct influence over the permanent staff of these agencies:

> We will annually prepare resolutions for local and regional church conventions in the three major denominations. These resolutions will call attention to egregious behavior by radical church leaders and will be important tools for grassroots organizing. They will also focus on positive, proactive initiatives that unite traditional religious believers and discredit the Religious Left. Working with other renewal organizations, we will identify electable conservative candidates for national church conventions. We will help train elected delegates to be effective at church conventions. We also will assist conservatives who serve on the boards of key church agencies so as to have direct influence over the permanent staff.[50]

How should the IRD's organizing efforts be evaluated? The IRD proposal sets out criteria that include an expanded audience for its own publications—UMAction Briefing went to 275,000 households in 2000 and 315,000 by 2002—and increased publication in both secular and religious media outlets of information originated by the IRD. But the real test of its success will be "passage of our resolutions in regional and national church bodies. Long-range results will be expressed through the election of conservatives and moderates to the boards of church agencies—a more indirect process, but one that is vitally important to long-term reform." To that end, the IRD proposed to use the Association for Church Renewal, its coalition of "conservative/evangelical renewal groups" in all the major mainline churches, in order to "synchronize strategies across denominational lines and to counter the influence of liberal ecumenical groups, such as the National and World Councils of Churches." Together with this coalition, the IRD began the Next Generation Project to fulfill its promise that the key to "the longer-range success of the church reform movement is recruiting a younger generation of reformers. The IRD has the experience, expertise, connections and vision to recruit and train young church members for this task."[51]

Takeover, Schism, Loyal Opposition?

How well the IRD fulfills its task and keeps its promise of "reforming America's churches" is not yet decided. Some of its most confident supporters anticipate steadily mounting progress toward taking over the United Methodist Church in particular and remaking its social witness on the model of conservatives who took control of the Southern Baptist Convention a decade ago. This overpowering scenario is likewise what some of the IRD's most alarmed adversaries fear. Other militants, such as the former chair of the IRD's board, Professor Thomas C. Oden of Drew University, foresee a more schismatic outcome, set out in his influential article "The Trust Clause Governing Use of Property in the United Methodist Church." They urge United Methodist renewal groups to prepare to use the "nuclear option" of challenging the church's trust clause in the U.S. courts in order to claim their rightful inheritance of all denominational property and corporate legitimacy, since they are the only Methodists true to the church's tradition and history of theological orthodoxy.[52]

At a Good News caucus meeting during the 2004 General Conference, Rev. William Hinson, president of the Confessing Movement, proposed that the denomination resolve its gridlock over homosexuality, social witness, theological diversity, and scriptural truth by splitting into two churches, with each side keeping its own congregational property and clergy pensions. "It is time for us to end this cycle of pain we are inflicting on each other," Hinson announced to church members and the media as a first step to proposing such a schism at the 2008 General Conference. "There is a great gulf fixed between those of us who are centered on Scripture and our friends who are of another persuasion" and are apparently willing "to be the chaplain to an increasingly godless society."[53]

Although it surprised and saddened many Methodists in the middle of a centrist church, the prospect of a divorce instead of a winner-take-all "nuclear" conflict or a conservative walkout was gaining ground among conservative caucuses in the church, declared Mark Tooley. Although Good News leaders left open the door of continuing church renewal within United Methodism instead of separating from it, during the 2004

General Conference Tooley announced a clear-cut strategy behind the proposal to split the denomination, as reported by the *New York Times*:

> Mark D. Tooley, who works at the Institute for Religion and Democracy and directs United Methodist Action, its program focused on Methodists, said in an interview that the proposal was intended not for the delegates here, who are "institutionalists" likely to defend church unity, but for church members and clergy around the country.
>
> The strategy, he said, is to float the idea so it would be embraced by church members around the country, both conservatives and liberals, who would come to see that separation is a practical solution. Four years from now, after the proposal has had time to be thoroughly digested, the actual dismantling of the church could begin to be put in motion when the church meets again for its next general conference, he said.
>
> Mr. Tooley said that conservatives had been hoping to engineer a divorce from liberals for years. He said that a large group of conservative caucuses in the church supported the idea, even though Dr. Hinson said in making his proposal that he was speaking only for himself.[54]

"They've been talking about it for years, but they're dreaming," counters a centrist Methodist leader. "If they try a walkout, they'll wake up to how few congregations go with them."[55] Such talk of schism nonetheless reflects both the growing security and the rising frustration of the church-renewal movement in United Methodism, and its growing sense of realism about the limited possibility of taking over the denomination as a whole, unlike the case of the Southern Baptist Convention. A likelier prospect may more closely resemble conservative efforts to form a rival network of parishes and dioceses in the Episcopal Church, USA, likewise split on issues of homosexuality by theological, cultural, and regional differences.

In the meantime, the IRD's programmatic priorities to gain control over governing church bodies are clear enough, charge its critics, and so are its commitments to funding them. In 2001 the IRD spent $358,667—46 percent of its total program expenditures—on "monitoring" the activities of the United Methodist Church, according to a 2002 analysis of IRD financial statements by Guidestar, a liberal watchdog of grants made by conservative foundations.[56] In 1999 the IRD spent $337,636 for the same purpose, reported Guidestar, more than six times what it spent on the "religious-liberty" program it declared in IRS documents to be its primary purpose. In 2002, foundations managed by Richard Mellon Scaife gave $225,000 to the IRD for its Reforming America's Churches Project, according to Media Transparency, another liberal watchdog group.[57]

Since its inception, the IRD has received almost $2 million from the Scaife foundations, its single biggest contributor among a dozen highly conservative foundations. It was given $485,000 from the John M. Olin Foundation "to counter the political influence of the Religious Left." It received $1.5 million from the Bradley Foundation, funded by a family tied to the John Birch Society, and more than $500,000 from the family of Howard Fieldstead Ahmanson, a champion of Christian Reconstructionism whose wife serves on the IRD board of directors. Between 1985 and 2002, reported Media Transparency in 2003, the IRD ranked in the top 3 percent—eighty-first among 2,609 recipients—of funding received from "ultraconservative" foundations that share an unusually aggressive, politically partisan pattern of funding at odds with prevailing norms of the philanthropic sector, according to the National Committee for Responsive Philanthropy.[58]

What implications should be drawn from such funding of the IRD? Replies Mark Tooley, "It should not be shocking that conservative groups receive their support from conservative individuals and conservative foundations" that are not extreme or outside the political mainstream, contrary to the allegations of their liberal critics.[59] What has the IRD done to merit such support over the course of its evolution? its critics persist in asking. It shifted its focus from the Cold War to culture wars, they answer, while carrying over its "faith and freedom" thematic focus on religious liberty as a model for individual rights, including rights to own property and capital freed from fair government regulation, taxation, and social spending. It has thereby held to the antistatist stance of Penn Kemble, David Jessup, and Lane Kirkland's AFL-CIO, not only their hawkish anticommunism—even as it appeals, however ironically, to antitax and laissez-faire business conservatives better known for their hawkish patriotism than their staunch support of organized labor. These include, for example, David M. Stanley, chairman of the steering committee of the IRD's UMAction. He is also chairman of Pearl Mutual Funds; longtime chair of the National Taxpayers Union, a pioneering antitax lobby; and co-founder of Iowans for Tax Relief and its Taxpayers United political-action committee. This PAC is officially nonpartisan in advancing the antitax cause but has contributed some 97 percent of its campaign funding to Republican legislative candidates.[60]

At the same time, note its critics, the IRD has indeed concentrated more of its organizational attention on fighting for control of the governing bodies of the mainline denominations, especially United Methodism, by intensifying its efforts to elect conservative delegates to their legislative assemblies and executive boards. It has pursued judicial trials and suits in the denominations against alleged violators of church statutes against gay ministers and gay marriages. It publicized opposition to the social witness of the mainline churches on peace-and-justice issues such as stopping the Iraq war and cutting military spending, defending welfare aid to the poor, and protecting the environment.

Thus the IRD backed Dr. Richard Land, president of the Southern Baptist Convention's Ethics and Religious Liberty Commission, in taking a strong stand in September 2002 in behalf of preemptive war against Iraq. "Saddam Hussein is developing at breakneck speed weapons of mass destruction he plans to use against America and her allies," he argued, and "there is a direct line from those who attacked the U.S. [on September 11] back to the nation of Iraq."[61] The IRD did not take sides by signing on to a public letter endorsing war on Iraq written by Land, the only official of a major Protestant denomination to call for war. Instead, the IRD counterpunched church leaders critical of invading Iraq, notably Jim Winkler, general secretary of the Methodist Board of Church and Society, and Robert Edgar, general secretary of the National Council of Churches. "These church officials cannot be relied upon to contribute intelligently to the war with Iraq," charged IRD president Diane Knippers, according to press reports, since "their vision of the world is largely divorced from historic Christian teachings about the use of force."[62]

This response was in keeping with the crucial distinction, explained Mark Tooley, between the IRD's criticizing church leaders for their political position on a given issue and the IRD's taking a contrary political position of its own on that issue: "I think that's a common misunderstanding, that when we critique or disagree with the political stances taken by the lobbying offices of the denominations or of their bishops or other church leaders, that we are endorsing a contrary position or encouraging a church to endorse a contrary position." Didn't the IRD derogate church leaders, such as Jim Winkler and Robert Edgar, who were speaking out against war on Iraq? "That's right," agreed Tooley. "But basically, we questioned whether the institutional church should permit its clergy, its agencies, in the name of the church, to be routinely used to endorse specific political policies."[63]

Shouldn't conscientious Christians speak out as citizens? "I don't think the specifics of politics are the vocations of bishops or clergy or full-time church employees," answered Tooley. "I think it's the calling or vocation of Christian lay people." Why so? "I would say Christianity understands human sinfulness and should be skeptical about all structures and powers, including government or any bureaucracy, which could include church structures."[64] A powerful sense of sin extends from political to religious institutional structures, argues Tooley, so the conscience of individual Christians should be left free and sovereign to weigh public issues, unswayed by the suspect authority of their churches, according to a moral logic that turns a populist evangelical voluntarism against a more Calvinistic commitment to the moral authority of the church and the law to guide Christian conscience.

Notwithstanding this pledge against taking policy-specific political stances of its own, commentary written for the IRD and posted on its Web site in May of 2003 announced that "the war in Iraq is coming to a victorious close" and attacked, among its critics, "the godless army of American mainstream Protestant leaders" who "worship at the altar of the United Nations" and give "aid and comfort" to America's enemies. Among them it singled out United Methodist GBCS secretary Jim Winkler, GBCS president Bishop Clifton Ives, and Bishop William Dew as harboring "hatred for President Bush and for America itself."[65] Mark Tooley castigated the United Methodist bishops en masse as "fatuous" and "pompous" for voting early in the administration of George W. Bush against its expenditure of tens of billions of dollars to restart the "Star Wars" missile-defense system (the Strategic Defense Initiative) in violation of the Anti-Ballistic Missile Treaty. Such statements from United Methodist bishops, charged Tooley, "are often inarticulate and sometimes downright nonsensical."[66] In 2005 the Council of Bishops issued a Statement of Conscience committing them to pray for the end of war in general and in particular "the immoral and unjust invasion and occupation of Iraq," after staying too silent in the face of the Bush administration's "rush toward military action based on misleading information." The IRD accused the bishops of "flogging the President" and insulting the "brave young men and women" serving in Iraq by echoing the "warmed-over 1960s utopianism" of flower children unwilling to grow up and face the real, sinful world infected by an evil comparable to Hitler's. "No doubt, if transported back in history," declared Tooley, "these bishops likewise would have impartially 'lamented' the 'continued warfare' between Allied and German forces in

Normandy in 1944, while blaming the plight of the millions of victims of fascist aggression on the United States."[67]

Early in 2000, the IRD joined with Good News and the Confessing Movement to establish the Coalition for United Methodist Accountability. Steered by three representatives from each founding group, with former law professor John Stumbo serving as its legal coordinator, the coalition assembled a team of attorneys and legal advisers to assist "local clergy and laity in responding to other clergy, district superintendents and bishops who are persistently neglecting church law. Responses have included the filing of charges against church leaders, where a conviction can mean a suspension or removal from the ordained ministry." By means of filing such charges and instigating church trials, the IRD aimed to combat "increasing disobedience to church doctrine and standards, neglect of due process and unfair administration on the part of some bishops and district superintendents."[68] As part of its 2001–4 project to reform America's churches, the IRD proposed to intensify its efforts to instigate church trials of liberal ministers and denominational leaders charged with violating church laws, notably the statutes and rules of the United Methodist *Book of Discipline*. "Over the next three years, we expect involvement in at least a dozen different cases around the country," the IRD predicted in 2001.[69] These cases turned out to include suits against Methodist ministers for allegedly performing gay-marriage rites, engaging openly in same-sex partnerships, and taking part in "neo-pagan" feminist rites.[70]

The IRD's record of results in judicial decisions from church trials, reviews, and judgments remains mixed. But it highlights the IRD's increased focus on pressing the struggle over church creeds and codes into the actual governance of mainline denominations, particularly United Methodism, and thereby mobilizing its supporters and encouraging its contributors. In 2000, three evangelicals gained election to the nine-member Judicial Council of the United Methodist Church, the denomination's supreme court. Changes in delegate representation promised to bring to General Conference in 2004 and beyond more delegates from the church's more conservative Southeastern and South Central jurisdictions and fewer from its more liberal regions in the north and west. In the light of these changes, and given the lightning rod of gay/lesbian church controversies and trials, the IRD and its allied church-renewal groups look forward to bright prospects in the longer run for both their judicial and legislative initiatives.

They point, for example, to the front-page trial of Rev. Karen Dammann, a United Methodist pastor in a Seattle suburb, for openly declaring

that she was "living in a partnered, convenanted, homosexual relationship," bound by lifetime vows taken in a sacred union ceremony with a
partner who had since given birth to a son the two women were raising together.[71] The acquittal of Rev. Dammann by a jury of her fellow ministers
in the relatively liberal Pacific Northwest region of the United Methodist
Church outraged Methodist traditionalists, encouraged reformers, and
energized both groups to resume their thirty-two-year struggle over homosexuality at the 2004 General Conference. There delegates defeated,
by a vote of 638 to 303, a proposal to allow local regions of the church to
decide whether to allow openly gay ministers. By a vote of 527 to 423,
delegates also rejected a resolution to soften the church's standing declaration that homosexuality is "incompatible with Christian teaching"
by adding to the *Book of Discipline* a sentence stating, "We recognize
that Christians disagree on the compatibility of homosexual practice with
Christian teaching."[72] At the same time, the Judicial Council decided it
lacked the authority to reconsider Dammann's case. But it restated the
church law that bishops may not appoint to the ministry anyone found
by a trial court to be a self-avowed practicing homosexual, leaving Rev.
Dammann likely to be barred from the annual reappointment that members of the Methodist clergy need to continue in ministry.

Noting the fruits of its labors in guiding Methodist governance, the
IRD reported that by a majority of 77 percent, the 2004 General Conference "endorsed language submitted by IRD/UMAction supporting
laws in civil society that define marriage as the union of one man and one
woman." By 88 percent, it endorsed another IRD/UMAction addition
to the United Methodist Social Principles, affirming "the importance of
both fathers and mothers for all children." But the IRD also warned that
liberal political statements were often adopted, with little discussion, for
inclusion in United Methodism's official *Book of Resolutions*. "Largely
introduced by the Board of Church and Society or liberal caucus groups,
these resolutions are ignored by most Methodists but nonetheless give
seeming legitimacy to Church and Society's political lobbying on Capitol
Hill."[73] Conversely, three petitions backed by the IRD and its allies at the
2004 General Conference in "attempts to defund and destroy Church and
Society were easily rejected," declared Jim Winkler, the GBCS general
secretary, in celebrating an outcome that the IRD left unreported.[74]

Widespread coverage of the Dammann trial and subsequent controversy over schism at the 2004 General Conference marked a measure
of success for the IRD in its drive to gain access and respectability in

prominent national media such as the *New York Times*, after a long eclipse since Penn Kemble's initial round of media access and influence during the Reagan years. Speaking to national media in behalf of the IRD as "a conservative group that watches mainline Protestant denominations in the United States," Mark Tooley attested, "A strong majority of members of the denomination would say that Karen Dammann has a right to her point of view, but if she can't with integrity uphold the church's teaching, then she should step aside." Tooley declared the Pacific Northwest region out of step with the rest of the Methodist church and saw its influence waning as the Western Jurisdiction loses church members and conference delegates. "I suspect that homosexuality will be a point of contention for at least the next two decades," Tooley judged. However, he concluded that "those of us on the traditional side are at least hopeful that in a demographic sense, the church is going in our direction."[75]

On the eve of the General Conference in the spring of 2004, the IRD circulated 315,000 copies of its UMAction newsletter.[76] It rehearsed the demographic shift from the West and Northeast regions of the United States to the American South and Africa as a providential dynamic "helping the church to be more faithful on moral and theological issues." It spotlighted a United Methodist pastor who officiated over possibly the first gay couple ever married in the sanctuary of a United Methodist church, as part of "the homosexual 'wedding' frenzy in San Francisco" two months earlier. It asked, "(1) Will church officials take effective action to stop this blatant violation of church law and of Christian Scriptural truth? (2) Will the 2004 General Conference strengthen the Discipline enforcement process to halt this defiance and anarchy within our church?"

The lead feature of this 2004 UMAction newsletter harked back to the IRD's beginnings in the 1980 Jessup Report. Headlined "UM Church Lobby Violates Trust and Donors' Restrictions," it challenged the GBCS by asking, Has the Board of Church and Society "wrongly spent on far-left political activism many millions of dollars that could lawfully be used only for work on alcohol problems? Is the BCS continuing its 38-year violation of its own Trust Agreement and its disrespect for Methodist donors who restricted their gifts for work on alcohol issues? Does this BCS violation threaten our church's integrity?" All three questions seem to demand an affirmative answer, if the evidence adduced by the article is to be believed. The board's 1965 Trust Agreement for the Methodist Building Endowment, argues the IRD, should restrict it to devoting a large share of its current budget and attention to temperance and alcohol problems instead of lobbying "actively for a whole array of liberal causes including abortion rights, socialized medicine, expanded welfare programs, and opposition to U.S. military programs." The IRD calls for a complete public accounting of the trust fund from 1965 to date, including its principal, income, appreciation, assets at fair market value, and allocation of each. It demands of the Board of Church and Society, "Will you start complying fully with the 1965 Trust Agreement and stop seeking ways to evade it?"[77] In such terms, sex and money continue to come together with law and theology across the boundaries of religion and politics in the IRD's quarter century of struggle over peace, justice, and scriptural renewal in the churches.

Between Churches and PACs:
Think Tanks, Lobbies, and Renewal Groups

The IRD's organizational ambiguity and its moral implications have been objects of curiosity and controversy from the institute's beginning, often expressed in questions of accountability. To whom is the IRD accountable? demand its critics. To no one, they reply, beyond its self-appointed directors and foundation donors as a freestanding political-action committee unaffiliated with any religious community, including the mainline churches it criticizes and claims to renew. To whom are the churches themselves accountable, demand the IRD's defenders in turn, if not to God and their own members? Yet the voices of both are ignored, replies the IRD, by unfaithful and unrepresentative governing cliques running left-wing political machines to dominate pastors and people in the pews, despite democratic procedures for denominational self-governance.

In 2006, for example, the IRD pointed out that rising NCC funding under Robert Edgar from "secular liberal foundations" surpassed support from its member communions in 2004–5. This made the NCC even less accountable to the faithful in the pews of mainline churches than when it relied on money from liberals at denominational headquarters, contended the IRD, and drove it deeper into the pockets of the partisan political left. Instead of faulting the IRD for its funding by conservative foundations, argued the IRD, the NCC should examine its own politically guilty conscience as a church body, in contrast to the IRD's integrity as a parachurch group:

The NCC is a church body, supposedly focused on achieving unity among all Christian churches and believers in the United States. Actions and alliances that pit the council against large portions of those churches and believers—the conservatives and the Republicans in particular—are deeply destructive to its purported ecumenical mission. The IRD, by contrast is a parachurch group devoted to advancing a particular set of convictions about democracy and Christian faith. Naturally, it draws most of its support from moderate and conservative Christians who share those convictions. . . .

In its lobbying, the NCC claims to speak for "the churches"—even though the churches are no longer the council's principal source of funding. By contrast, the IRD has never claimed to speak for anyone other than its own friends and supporters who share its convictions.[78]

The NCC takes invariably liberal positions in close step with its donor foundations, by this account, while the IRD rarely takes positions on specific legislation. The NCC has joined more closely with partisan allies to influence electoral politics in behalf of Democratic candidates by registering and "educating" voters, while the IRD has never endorsed any candidate for office or set up any voter-registration program.[79]

"In a democratic system, you have lobbying groups," explained Ed Robb in 1983. "We are lobbying, seeking to influence policy within the denomination. It's my firm conviction that the policies advocated by IRD have the support of the vast majority of church people in America."[80] If the IRD seems to be a representative church-renewal group or responsive religious lobby from one side, observe its critics, from another it propagandizes and mobilizes in the spitting image of a partisan PAC and front organization, still true to its hawkish neoconservative origins in both party politics and the labor movement.[81] So, for example, the IRD's critics in the mainline churches point to the report it released six weeks before the 2004 presidential election, "Human Rights Advocacy in the Mainline Protestant Churches (2000–2003): A Critical Analysis."[82] The IRD began, explained Diane Knippers in announcing the report, out of concern with "a serious imbalance and deficiency in the foreign policy advocacy of mainline churches," which was tilted toward pro-Soviet positions and largely silent regarding human rights abuses in the Soviet bloc. "Today we are here because we have discovered another serious imbalance—overwhelming criticism of Israel and the neglect of many other countries guilty of egregious human rights abuses."[83] The gist of the report was stunning, according to the IRD: "The results show that over one-third of all church criticism of human rights abuses were aimed at a single small nation: Israel. Slightly less than one-third were aimed at the United States, and the rest were distributed among twenty other nations. Only 19 percent of the church criticisms were aimed at nations deemed 'not free' in the 2004 Freedom House assessments."[84]

The IRD's report was "fatally flawed" by its ideological bias and its aim to "play partisan, secular politics with important matters of Christian faith and ministry," retorted Robert Edgar, the NCC's general secretary. As its barometer on human rights, the IRD used "another ideological conservative group, Freedom House," long a bastion of Penn Kemble's aggressive anticommunism. The IRD equated criticism of the Israeli government and its policies with anti-Semitism, charged Edgar, "blatantly planting seeds of suspicion that the mainline churches are anti-Semitic" while willfully ignoring NCC efforts to seek justice for all people in the Middle East.[85] The IRD, in turn, defended its data and its suspicions: "Our report shows that, during 2000–2003, the [NCC] council's resolutions and news releases criticized Israel 20 times, while not once criticizing the Palestinian Authority or any of Israel's immediate neighbors. . . . We simply ask, 'Given the excessive focus on Israel in these mainline human rights statements, the question must be faced: Could anti-Semitism of some sort be a factor?' "[86]

While this debate played out in public letters read on the Internet by core supporters of each group, the gist of the IRD report spread to a much wider circle of mass media, from the *Washington Post* to the Web site of Focus on the Family.[87] The controversy culminated in a nationally syndicated column by John Leo featured in *U.S. News & World Report* on October 18, 2004, two weeks before the presidential election. It began, "America's mainline Protestant churches are in trouble. One sign is shrinking membership. Another is turning their political policy-making over to fringe leftists whose deepest instinct is to blame America and pummel Israel whenever possible."[88] The IRD's "measured and devastating report" showed that "Israel was twice as likely to be hammered by the mainliners as all the unfree authoritarian nations put together," wrote Leo, proving that

> the rights work of the mainline churches is basically a one-sided expression of ideology—America is essentially viewed as a malignant force in the world, while Israel is seen as nothing more than a dangerous colonial implant of the West. The IRD report says the mainliners' "pervasive anti-Americanism is

demonstrated time and again in their public-policy advocacy, and one need not investigate far to find it." Later, the report says, "When U.S. policy cannot be blamed the mainline denominations seem less interested in speaking up for the victims."

Anti-Americanism is an old story in the mainline-church bureaucracies, Leo noted. The Presbyterian plan to divest from companies such as Caterpillar that do business with Israel in support of military action against Palestinians "seems to be an obvious effort to get an anti-Israel bandwagon rolling among the churches," he judged. It abets a movement in which "Israel is routinely equated with the apartheid regime in South Africa and, by implication, with the Nazi regime" in Germany. "Many Jews see the divestment movement as an instrument of anti-Semitism. Maybe it is," Leo concluded, "but the efforts of the woeful mainline churches are better seen as classic knee-jerk leftism, an expression of hardcore loathing for the United States and the West, with Israel as a stand-in for America. The mainline churches believe they still stand for high moral purpose in politics. They don't. They can no longer be taken seriously on politics or human rights."

Calling it a case of "journalistic malpractice," the NCC's Robert Edgar charged in turn that Leo's column "employs the smear tactics of McCarthy-era propaganda, and contributes to the abuse of religious belief as a tool of partisan politics."[89] The column claimed that 80 percent of the NCC's human rights resolutions in 2000–2003 were aimed at Israel, Edgar noted. Yet in fact, only five NCC statements about Israel were issued during that period, and several of those also criticized Palestinian leaders. Indeed, in the NCC's entire fifty-four-year history, only two policy statements have referred to Israel and Palestine, said Edgar, and fewer than forty of 650 resolutions have dealt with the Middle East, including war in Kuwait and Iraq.[90] A few weeks later, John Leo held up the decisive role of values voters in reelecting President Bush as an object lesson for Democrats and their moral allies to desist from suppressing almost "all dissent from elite opinion on social issues" as "a human-rights violation of some kind." Instead, he advised, "Democrats might want to tone down the contempt for evangelicals in particular and religious people in general that increasingly flows through their secular-dominated party. This is a very religious nation. If the Democrats aspire to become the majority party, why do they tolerate so much antireligious behavior and expression?"[91] Soon after the election, Robert Edgar acknowledged,

"The religious right has successfully gotten out there shaping personal piety issues—civil unions, abortion—as almost the total content of 'moral values.' And yet you can't read the Old Testament without knowing God was concerned about the environment, war and peace, poverty. God doesn't want 45 million Americans without health care." The mainline churches, he concluded, "need to work really hard at reclaiming some language" to reveal the true breadth and depth of moral values in Americans' shared understanding, experience, and action.[92]

The IRD describes itself as "a small organization at the hub of worldwide research and activity" that stretches from human rights activists, church leaders, and journalists around the world into the grass roots of mainline churches in the United States. Its Washington base and national reach give it a mix of religious, political, academic, and journalistic contacts and expertise needed to tie together religious debate and church controversy with advocating public policy, pursuing cultural politics, and influencing public opinion through the mass media. Unique among church-renewal groups for its focus on social questions and the ecumenical span of its vision and analysis, the IRD's activism in the churches marks it off from academic or political think tanks. "We don't merely research and write," notes a 1995 IRD membership letter. "We get directly involved at church conventions and conferences—drafting legislation, offering testimony, and training other activists. The IRD isn't just a think tank; we don't sit still enough for that!"[93]

The IRD's self-image as a courageous, if well-connected, David locked in feisty combat against the still-arrogant, if aging, Goliath of the mainline churches finds media confirmation that the IRD welcomes, for example, in rehearsing a 2005 article in the *New York Times* that stated, "Although the institute [IRD] has an annual budget of just less than $1 million and a staff of fewer than a dozen, liberals and conservatives alike say it is having an outsized effect on the dynamics of American politics by counteracting the liberal influence of the mainline Protestant churches."[94] The image of the IRD at the hub of a complex of right-wing religious and political lobbies figures significantly in the outlook of mainline-church leaders, and in their fund-raising appeals. Thus Robert Edgar appealed in a 2005 fund-raising letter for the NCC, "A sustained investment of $1,000,000 per year is needed to make us truly competitive with the Heritage/Cato/ Institute for Religion and Democracy complex that sustains and backs the right wing agenda."[95] This view figures, too, in the alarm that critics of the IRD continue to express in tracing the influence of its networks across

Washington and into Congress and the White House—for example, the "fair amount of under-the-radar influence" IRD director Richard John Neuhaus exerts with President George W. Bush, as a senior administration official confirmed to *Time* magazine in 2005, on such issues as abortion, stem-cell research, cloning, and the defense-of-marriage amendment. "Father Richard," the president explained to religious journalists at a meeting in May of 2004, "helps me articulate these things."[96]

In neoconservative religious and political circles, argues one critical mainline-church leader, the IRD fills a crucial niche in the middle: "Look at the IRD from the bottom up, and it's a think tank and an ideological clearinghouse for all sorts of reactionary dissenting groups in the mainline churches, like Good News in Methodism," points out Leon Howell. "It helps them out with the big picture and ties them into a bigger movement, since on their own they don't have all that much intellectual firepower or ideological sophistication." In return, these groups give the IRD the appearance of a popular constituency, or at least an audience in the churches, says Howell. "That gives the IRD's big ideas a semblance of popular clout and helps the IRD turn around and raise money from conservative foundations that don't care that much about religion but resent the liberal churches' sounding off about peace, poverty, and economic justice."[97]

Seen from the top down, says Howell, the IRD is "an organizing arm, a distribution outlet for retailing and implementing the big ideas that come out of the neoconservative intelligentsia and their think tanks: Neuhaus's Institute on Religion and Public Life, George Weigel's Ethics and Public Policy Center, Michael Novak at the American Enterprise Institute." This is "a wannabe-academic, baby-Brookings world of big thinkers who need somebody else to do their legwork," says Howell, "since they're too busy being scholars and policy experts. Besides, they're intellectuals. They're not ideologues, let alone organizers. So the IRD has helped their cause by being willing to go out there, particularly in the churches, and keep agitating and obstructing and nay-saying, just like Penn Kemble wanted them to do in the first place."[98]

The IRD has shifted tactics and organizing issues with the times, say its critics, but its strategic aims and the stance of its interlocking allies have held steady. So has its underlying ideology, no matter how contrary its high moral principles and partisan polemical practice. The continuity over the years of the IRD's board and staff reflects this steady aim, claim Leon Howell and other critics of the IRD. It spans three decades with a core of insiders tied to a spreading web of neoconservative political organizations and conservative evangelical church-renewal groups.[99] Yet it stands free of both churches and parties, and answers only to its own directors and funders. Consistent with the IRD's core of insiders yet well-connected within its web of both evangelical and neoconservative allies, according to this view, is the IRD's new president, Dr. James Tonkowich, who took the helm a year after Diane Knippers died of cancer in 2005. He was formerly managing editor of *BreakPoint*, published by Chuck Colson's Prison Fellowship and long a model of "how to communicate the ortho-dox Christian view of the world and apply it to hot-button public issues—a crucial task for the IRD as it engages social and political issues within the American Protestant churches," as the IRD board noted in announcing its choice.[100] Ordained in the Presbyterian Church in America and schooled at Gordon-Conwell seminary, Tonkowich resembled Kent Hill in coming from a non-mainline denomination and rehearsing in evangelical tones the IRD's mission to serve its members as "we work together for the restora-tion of Christ's church to the glory of Father, Son and Spirit."[101]

Mostly on the strength of its denominational activities and committees for "reforming America's churches," the IRD has increased its dues-paying members from a few hundred to a few thousand in the decade since 1993. In 2002–3, the IRD had thirty-five hundred or so individual donors (three thousand of them United Methodists), compared to two hundred in 1994, according to Mark Tooley. They provided half of the IRD's operating bud-get of $1 million per year, with one-third going to UMAction.[102] The IRD increased its revenue to $1,120,508 in 2001, at the start of its Reforming America's Churches Project, compared to $777,654 in 2000 and $818,380 in 1999. But by 2005, the IRD counted a staff of only nine, and a budget of barely $1 million.[103] These are modest numbers indeed, stress IRD crit-ics, for an organization seeking donors among millions of mainline-church members for a quarter century. Using interlocking mailing lists shared by conservative church-renewal groups, the IRD sent out its own quarterly publication, *Faith & Freedom*, to twelve thousand donors and others in 2000. Its *Episcopal Action* and *Presbyterian Action* went, without subscrip-tion, to a total of eight thousand people, although the IRD predicted a near doubling of those numbers by 2004, and UMAction expanded its much larger mailing list to 315,000 by 2002, without requiring subscrip-tion.[104] Such low numbers of IRD donors and de facto subscribers, its crit-ics insist, highlight its limited success in winning the loyalty of grassroots Methodists, let alone Presbyterians, Episcopalians, and others in mainline Protestantism.

These numbers cast doubt on the IRD's status as a membership organization, charge critics, and underscore its continued dependence on
the patronage of a few wealthy right-wing foundations such as the Scaife,
Ahmanson, and Bradley foundations. They make up a small circle of
"wealthy non-United Methodist backers whose social agendas are at
odds with the historical witness of the church."[105] Such foundations provided more than 80 percent of the IRD's income during its first decade,
Leon Howell calculates, and some $4.4 million from 1981 to 2001. Donors
and members provided as little as one-tenth and no more than one-third
of its annual revenues over much of that period, as the IRD's funding
fluctuated but did not grow steadily or significantly. It had revenues of
$477,589 in 1988, $629,932 in 1989, $704,609 in 1992 (with only 13 per-
cent, $92,000, coming from donors and members), $483,820 in 1993 (with
31 percent, $148,000, coming from donors and members), and roughly
$450,000 in 1994 (with 31 percent, $141,000, coming from donors and
members).[106]

In 1995 the IRD pledged to contact more than 100,000 concerned
Christians with its message of change needed in the churches. In 2001
it reported reaching some 300,000 households directly, with more than
500,000 projected by 2004, and nearly a million reached indirectly through
a wider network of conservative and evangelical church-renewal groups.
Thus proclaimed and promised, such media reach and reverberation raise
the IRD's voice well beyond its own membership and extend its influence
into the public at large. Over the past decade, the IRD has not rivaled its
initial media prominence under Penn Kemble on prime-time television
or in the pages of the *New York Times*. But stories and information it
originates appear regularly in *Christianity Today*, *Good News* magazine,
and its Presbyterian equivalent, *Presbyterian Layman*, sent free to 600,000
readers six times per year. They also appear regularly, if less frequently,
in secular media such as the *Washington Times* and *Insight* magazine and
in items syndicated by United Press International, all three of which are
owned by the Unification Church of Sun Myung Moon.[107]

IRD staff are regularly mentioned and quoted by religious and secular news outlets in the United States and around the world, announces
the IRD Web site, citing *Time* magazine, the *New York Times*, and the
Washington Post first among these outlets. However, in the list that follows for February–August of 2006, for example, there are no references
to *Time* and only three apiece to the *Times* and the *Post*, compared to
twelve for the *American Spectator* and nine for the *Weekly Standard*,

much smaller periodicals devoted to neoconservative political opinion.[108] Leading the way with twenty-four citations is *Frontpagemag.com*, self-identified as the online journal of news and commentary of the conservative, libertarian David Horowitz Freedom Center, whose eponymous head is "the Left's most brilliant and articulate nemesis." It receives sixty-five million hits per month, and it is linked to two thousand other Web sites, including "the largest publicly accessible database defining the chief groups and individuals of the Left and their organizational interlocks."[109] This linkage flags the IRD's political salience in no uncertain terms. It also suggests the cyber-metastasis of IRD opinion across an Internet and "blogosphere" that increasingly tie together parachurch and political lobbies, think tanks, and issues advocates with church agencies on the one hand and partisan political associations on the other. At work on the religious-political right and liberal left alike, this process paradoxically makes communications in the two camps look more alike in presentation, if more polarized in substance, and more unlike the conventional mass media long at the center of communications in the mainline churches and the public square.

However arguable in impact and uncertain in actual extent, it is this larger public voice and profile that justify the IRD's crucial support from ultraconservative private foundations, say its critics. This support ebbed well below $1 million annually in 1990–94, after Ronald Reagan left the White House and Kent Hill left the IRD, before rebounding to $1.3 million in 1995 with the high tide of Newt Gingrich's Republican Revolution. Then it dipped again below $1 million annually in the late 1990s before rallying after 2001, when George W. Bush won the White House.[110] Beyond the IRD's expanding efforts at intradenominational organizing or education, it continues to offer to the larger public a voice on moral and social issues that challenges how true, faithful, and representative are the social teachings of mainline-church leaders, the National Council of Churches, and the World Council of Churches. In doing so, the IRD makes clear that Christians can disagree in good conscience about what should be done on specific public issues contested in Congress, party politics, and the American polity at large. It also makes clear that Christians can likewise disagree on whether specific social issues such as reforming welfare, reducing auto emissions, restarting "Star Wars," raising defense spending, or cutting taxes are essentially moral and religious issues at all.

In such matters, the IRD charges, mainline-church leaders neither voice the moral consensus of their members nor exercise the moral authority of their tradition. Contending that mainline-church leaders misrepresent their own members, mistake the gospel truth about Christians' rights and responsibilities under God, and meddle in partisan politics carries significant implications for religion in the moral argument of American public life. For many in the pews and for the public at large, that is no less true if these contentions come to their attention through an organization such as the IRD. Yet it own genesis and history reveal the complex confluence of political struggles and moral debates in the mainline churches, the labor movement, the political left and neoconservative right, the Reagan White House, and both the Democratic and Republican parties. For many critics and supporters alike of the IRD, the currents of this interplay remain unclear in their implications for the framework of an expanded American state, a more crowded and contested American polity, and a richer but more unequal American economy. Yet it is here, clearly enough, that the voices of Protestant faith have diversified to question and clash with one another in search of renewal on the road from the Cold War through the culture wars.

Within a year of the IRD's beginnings, its critics in the mainline churches were convinced by its manifesto as well as the conditions of its founding and funding that "it was a conservative-neoconservative alliance intended to advance a distinct political agenda while claiming only a broad Christian concern," as Peter Steinfels judged in 1983. They were also struck by its singular intensity, and its contradictory ideals and institutional identity. The IRD is a "highly political and partisan organization [that] marches under the banner of church independence," observed Steinfels. It demands the accountability of church leaders to those in the pews and to the public at large. Yet it is itself responsible only to a small, self-selected executive committee and a handful of major funders from private foundations. It affirms in principle that the church should embrace diversity and disagreement in its social witness. Yet it makes sweeping, damaging charges of misconduct against church leaders that either indict or ignore their diversity. For all this, "the IRD has talent, money and a galvanizing sense of grievance," confirms Steinfels. Why? The IRD, he answers, is "obviously part of a larger movement in American politics and culture, the growth of a network of intellectual institutions that function to dampen outbreaks of fundamental social criticism."[111]

Behind the emergence of the IRD seen as part of a larger neoconservative movement in a war of ideas lies a theory of the "new class," familiar since the 1960s in terms elaborated by Irving Kristol, Peter Berger, and others.[112] It posits a new class and generation of educated "knowledge workers," disaffected from traditional American values by the adversary culture of the New Left and the 1960s counterculture. This new middle class threatens the traditional moral consensus of American society and its "old middle class" of businessmen, small-town professionals, white-collar office workers, and blue-collar handworkers. This challenge to the moral foundations of American democracy, its economic institutions, and its foreign policy needs to be challenged in turn, particularly with the strategic help of former leftist intellectuals and now-dissident members of the new class.

As a social theory based on the facts of education-specific and occupation-specific shifts in the moral outlooks of middle-class Americans today, this view is highly arguable, if not downright muddled.[113] But notions of class-bound cultural conflict do resound as rallying cries and tactics in a war of ideas between opposed intellectual elites and lobbying groups in search of resourceful allies and responsive constituencies in a larger public sphere. Here moral ideals engage government policy, influence electoral politics and parties, and intercede where the rule of law meets powerfully organized interests. The notion of culture wars within the middle class also outlines a social vision and ethic that have grown more intuitively appealing over the last generation, as most Americans have struggled to secure their place in an expanded middle class that has since grown more economically pinched, socially insecure, and morally confused. They wonder why those who "work hard and play by the rules," and sacrifice to serve their country, do not find themselves better rewarded in the present and more assured of enjoying the good life in the future. They worry about the future in a rich yet uncertain economy with deepening divides of income and employment between the more and less educated, and greater gaps in schooling between the more and less affluent.

The conviction that others have lost faith and betrayed freedom, slacked off at work and shirked their responsibilities at home, makes up one element in an uneasy anthropodicy of diverging fortunes and diminished dreams for middle-class Americans. That rationale in turn exerts real moral leverage to justify ethically knotted, politically explosive decisions over trimming public provision and shifting the distribution of politically balanced benefits in a public household strained by the rising costs of guns, butter, and oil—and the rising challenge posed by the world since 9/11 to its sole superpower. What of Medicare for the middle-class elderly, college aid for their offspring, living wages for the working poor, and aid to the jobless? What of tax exclusions for corporations and tax cuts for their shareholders to create jobs or reward investors? What of support for the troops of an all-volunteer army disproportionately drawn from those downscale on the job ladder, to assure them arms and numbers enough to carry out missions multiplied by the war against terror? We face such questions in an era of more rapid yet uneven economic growth, lower mobility, greater social interdependence and inequality, and more difficult debate in a more crowded polity. Here we wrestle with our moral differences and our common fate within a world of advancing divisions of global economic labor and spreading problems of shared political-military responsibility.

It is worth noting that the neoconservative movement extended its network of intellectual institutions into the mainline churches relatively late in its war of ideas, observed Peter Steinfels in 1983, and it is worth asking why it took so long to reach the mainline churches.[114] This reflects, he said, how distinctive the churches are, in fact, despite their overlap with political and academic institutions. It reveals how puzzling they are to the politically and academically bred intellectuals who led the neoconservative charge in other institutional theaters of the culture wars they declare. Significantly enough, their campaign reached the ambit of the churches in the form of freestanding parachurch advocacy groups, think tanks, and policy institutes built less on the pattern of traditional religious voluntary societies than the pattern of explicitly political organizations such as the American Enterprise Institute, funded by the same small, deep pool of private foundations with predominantly political and economic aims.[115]

It took a while, concluded Steinfels, for the neoconservative sponsors of this war of ideas to find their "*condottieri* in the field of religion," but the emergence of the IRD indicated that at last they did. Perhaps in the long run, Steinfels allowed, the IRD would prove to be something more or different than a strategic political alliance with a narrowly partisan, ideologically predictable agenda. That would require more candor about its own political viewpoint, more specific criticism of church programs and policies without assuming them to be apologies for oppression, and more attention to monitoring human rights violations coming from right-wing sources.[116] On each of these fronts, a quarter century later, the IRD's defenders can point to a lengthening record of accomplishment before reversing requests for such evidence from their critics in the mainline churches, who have meanwhile found little reason or evidence to change their minds about the contradictory character of the IRD.

Political animus or admiration aside, the institutional origins and trajectory of the IRD exemplify crucial changes in the institutional environment of American religion in public. Here churches and parachurch groups engage no less idealistic moral advocates beyond the religious sphere, and they struggle with interest-driven lobbies and ideological factions. These public actors share many organizational characteristics, and some cardinal virtues and vices, which blur conventional distinctions among political party, church, and state as they contest and complicate the moral argument of public life.

PART II

Witnessing versus Winning in Washington

CHAPTER SEVEN

Religious Lobbies and Public Churches

Ecclesiology Matters

Ecclesiology matters. It leads United Methodists to fight for the soul of their church, not only to struggle over abortion and gay ordination, social justice and world missions. It frames their fighting. They contest their connectional covenant through conflicting appeals to the apostolic authority of Scripture, to episcopal leadership, congregational community, General Conference rules and representation, and the catholic spirit of Christian love.[1] More broadly, ecclesiology marks off the mainline Protestant denominations from religious lobbies on the Christian right, but also from mainstream parachurch groups such as Bread for the World and nonreligious liberal advocacy groups such as the Children's Defense Fund, in ways explored later in this chapter.

No less crucially, ecclesiology distinguishes the mainline denominations from one another in how they think and act in public. It articulates their soteriological integrity as the Body of Christ into different sorts of social bodies, each with its own stance and history of growth, and each with its own moral map of the society surrounding it. So each stands peculiarly poised to act as "the church in the world," to answer the question of what we must do to be saved by its living example of Christ as sacramental redeemer or personal savior, ethical lawgiver or inner spiritual light.[2] These exemplary currents in the conversation of Christian tradition move the mainline churches to come together as a multivocal communion of communions that resists strategic demands to focus and enforce the faithful "witness" of their moral advocacy into univocal terms and ranks in order to "win" political victories by grassroots organizing and mobilization.

Together, the mainline churches embrace a recognizable public discourse of justice and love, probed below in contrast to conventional moral languages of individual interests, contractual rights, and procedural rules. But ecclesiology continues to diversify dialects and inflections in this discourse across the mainline churches. It continues to challenge the unity of their ecumenical advocacy as well as inspire it.

Maximalists, Minimalists, and Methodists

The churches in Washington can be divided into two parties, according to a distinction well traveled among their staffers. The "maximalist" party wants strong ecumenical cooperation among the churches to agree on priority issues, develop their own denominational constituencies behind these issues, and bring them to bear in concert in public advocacy and legislative lobbying, backed by grassroots organizing and voter mobilization. The "minimalist" party wants to stay closer to home in confessional and theological terms, turning first to witness to its own members and sticking more strictly to public moral advocacy as opposed to insider lobbying. It wants to pick its own priorities and pursue its own issues more freely, and hold onto its own social-action networks and mailing lists more tightly.

The Presbyterians and the United Church of Christ are often cited as typical of the maximalist party, the Episcopalians and Lutherans as more typical of the minimalists. "The Methodists are the swing party," points out one veteran of the churches in Washington. "They sit there in the middle. On some issues they move toward the maximal side, on others they move away. Some of them are clearly maximalists, some are minimalists. They are the biggest mainline denomination by far, with the biggest Washington office. They are a key to the success or frustration of much of what we try to do together." What frustrates the maximalists when the Methodists won't join in comes "partly from a lot of them being too radical to be political. They've really given up on our political process. They're ready to judge it, but not to take part in it."[3]

Does this critical diagnosis make sense? Is it fair? What are its underlying reasons, its key implications, and its practical consequences? Measures of success or frustration in the mainline churches in Washington, and reason-giving for both, vary critically among the denominations and within them as well. Debates over "witnessing versus winning," or "faithfulness versus effectiveness," define some of this variation. So does emphasizing public moral advocacy in contrast to insider lobbying on Capitol Hill or in the White House. Stressing teaching efforts invested in local churches likewise contrasts to organizing and mobilization efforts aimed at getting social action or political influence out of them, that is, getting their members out to vote, march, or write and call their members of Congress in behalf of their denomination's stand on this or that critical issue.

Deepening the distinction between faithful witnessing and winning at religious lobbying, Thom White Wolf Fassett compares the different relationship of faith and work in the "two cities" of the public churches and the Congress in light of his dozen years as general secretary of the United Methodist General Board of Church and Society. Many devout Methodists wish the church could simply stand above political machinations and focus on saving souls, he says, while many "so-called social activists in the United Methodist Church, it's my hunch, really believe in works. There's a faith foundation there, of course, but they don't want to be bothered by the principles of faith. They don't want to deal with the witness of faith, articulated in evangelical terms. They want to act," in response to human suffering and injustice. But, Fassett warns,

> what distinguishes us in the city on this side of the street [in the Methodist Building across from the Capitol] from those sitting on that side of the street [in the Congress] is that here the principles of faith come first and the action comes second. Over there, the action comes first, and only God knows the point where faith comes in second anywhere along the line.
>
> Now if people on this side of the street want to act that way, then they should go across the street. I don't want anyone in this organization who believes they should function the way they do across the street, because that's what separates us and who we are and what we are about. If we do not first and foremost, in everything we do and every way we express ourselves, help people understand that we are the incarnation of the Word, then we have no business being in front of anybody saying anything about joining a socially active church.[4]

From this standpoint, the calling of Christians to act faithfully in public is no different than the gospel call to love God and neighbor, and the calling of church leaders to public advocacy is no different than a calling to the pastorate.

The problem of "witnessing versus winning," as pondered in the Washington offices of the mainline churches and highlighted by academic analysts of their efforts, takes on emphatically either-or shape in this view of the church and the Congress as two cities on opposite sides of the street.[5] "I don't think we ever win," says Fassett bluntly. "I think we lose a lot, but we never win." How so? The answer rests partly with Augustinian differences between the City of God and the worldly city inherent in religious and political institutions, Fassett suggests, but it also rests with the particular nature of government in this place and time in history. "I don't think there's a winnable solution anywhere," he says in 1992, "because we're dealing with a corrupt system." He explains,

> So long as we deal with a corrupt system that does not value human beings; so long as you have an administration and Congress, let's say, for example, that eviscerate the social-service delivery system, that empty mental hospitals and place untold numbers of unwitting people on the streets; so long as you allow hunger and homelessness to persist in our central cities because funding for food and shelter is withheld—I could go on and on—there are no winnable solutions.
>
> We're talking about oppressive principalities and powers, for the most part. The only thing that can be said about the government of the United States is that it is not as oppressive as some of the other governments oppressing people in other parts of the world. But it still makes war. It invades a little island in the Caribbean [Grenada], it creates havoc in the invasion of Panama. It covers its tracks in its criminal activity [in the Iran-Contra affair]. It supplies the government of El Salvador with the wherewithal to commit mayhem and murder and brutalize its own people.
>
> There are very few people who understand this, and it is hard for me to explain it. I believe that the foreign policy of the United States of America, at least some of it, is driven by racist motives. That's hard to explain if people don't understand it.[6]

How can the churches tell such truths to people who know better, or who want to believe better but fear the worst, even if they don't know the facts? "You meet people where they live," replies Fassett. "You pick the side they're on as human beings. You walk over the political lines that divide them from you, and you live with them. You have to understand our human oneness first, the rudimentary similarities and basic needs all of us have, in order to gain their respect."

However eloquently an activist preacher speaks out against the powers that be, says Fassett, members of that congregation are not going to be moved unless that pastor does the work needed to develop their spiritual sensitivity and Christian conscience. "Only then will that pastor be able to stand in the pulpit and decry the outrageous behavior of a president of the United States; and though people do not share that perspective or support that pastor politically, because that pastor has not violated the integrity of the gospel witness, they will respect that." The necessity and difficulty of such prophetic witnessing, predicated on social sanctification taught by pastoral example, underscores the importance of questions concerning where and how this witnessing is to enter public life. It also counterpoints other answers these questions find across the mainline Protestant churches.

Some critics continue to label the mainline churches in Washington as "the Democratic Party at prayer," the last bastion of the cultural-political left, or a pale slice of Jesse Jackson's Rainbow Coalition. But leaders of the churches in Washington see key shifts in their stance over the last three decades, moving away from predictably partisan alliances with the liberal wing of the Democratic Party, organized labor, or the radical successors to the New Left and Black Power movements of the late 1960s and early 1970s. "By the mid-1970s, we made the switch and stopped polarizing faithfulness and political effectiveness," says Jay Lintner, Washington head of the Office for Church in Society of the United Church of Christ (UCC) through the 1990s. "We started trying to be faithful in effective ways. We started organizing more seriously in more places instead of relying so heavily on the San Francisco Bay Area, Boston, and Ann Arbor, where they love us. We started relating to central Pennsylvania and North Carolina, where they used to hate us. We began doing a lot more grassroots training there. Now the relationship between our office and those people is very close, although we have to step out ahead of our constituency occasionally"—for example, in backing gay rights in the military in 1993 or gay marriage in 2003—"even if that may alienate some of them, because it's the right thing to do, not because we need to do something for the Berkeley crowd."[7]

Social analysts of denominational differences among mainline Protestant public churches grant the real social diversity of the UCC and the Presbyterians, indeed even of the Unitarians and the Quakers. But they emphasize nonetheless the relative homogeneity these churches enjoy, in comparison to the Methodists, in terms of socioeconomic standing and education tied to more liberal cultural politics in support of their peace-and-justice social teaching—even if Presbyterians and Episcopalians remain split over homosexuality, and Quakers agree to disagree on abortion.[8]

Washington church leaders and activists, on the other hand, emphasize denominational differences in ecclesiological order and theological outlook that frame their view of given issues and their public response to them. In its connectional incorporation of public advocacy disciplined by denomination-wide doctrinal definition, with core concerns to nurture discipleship in the pews, the Methodist Board of Church and Society is unique among the Protestant agencies and church offices in Washington. So argues Jaydee Hanson, long head of the board's Department for Environmental Justice: "Our closest counterpart is the U.S. Catholic Conference, in terms of joining those responsibilities, so the board is not just looking at public-policy questions and asking ourselves, 'Where are the folks on the Hill on this? What can we get done this year on the Hill?' It's real easy to make the Hill your constituency, and measure your success by what you get done there."[9]

Such public-policy orientation leads in the main to "fairly incremental piecework to make legislation a little bit better, dotting the i's, crossing the t's," says Hanson. Methodists do less of that than some other church offices in Washington, notably those organized more like public-policy agencies or lobbies, concedes Hanson. But Methodism's ecclesiological integrity enables it to take crucial stands on key moral issues and "do big pieces with Congress," by appealing to both church members in the pews and Methodist members of Congress in terms true to the Wesleyan faith they share.

A century ago, Methodism made the most of its more marked preeminence among American Protestants and members of Congress with "a very clear, hierarchical understanding of who we were, what our mission was, and how we were to carry it out," says Hanson. "Since 1968, we have tried much more seriously to democratize the church at all levels. When you do that, you're bound to come out a whole lot messier" than would a more hierarchical, smaller, or socially homogeneous denomination, let alone a freestanding single-issue religious lobby with a self-selected membership. In comparison to such "a small cadre with a few good men ready to storm the Congress at a single point and turn it upside down," Hanson contends, Methodist democratization and tradition have combined to guide the church in its own distinctive and truly faithful course of advocacy.

For example, Methodists have led the way in combating drug use as a moral, medical, and criminal issue that exerts evil by corrupting personal

piety, discipline, and responsibility for the fabric of family life sustained
by steady work. "We are the only folks in the mainline-church community in Washington working intensively on drug issues," declares Hanson.
"Not just because temperance is part of our church history, but also because our people care desperately about it. It's a defining issue for the
working people and people of color who are our members, and who have
more say in our leadership today. Slightly over half of our Washington
staff are people of color," notes Hanson. "That's true of only one other
church office here, the Presbyterians. There are other very active church
offices in Washington that are almost entirely white." Outsiders "may see
us stymied or slowed down by our evangelical 'right wing,'" acknowledges
Hanson. "What they miss seeing is our integrity with the whole of the
Methodist Church," expressed by the General Conference in the Social
Principles and the resolutions that the GBCS is charged with implementing. "That's where our first responsibility lies," Hanson stresses. "We're
held to it by the way we are set up, by our board members and bishops,
with all their different views. Still, that's where the real influence we have
comes from. We speak for the church, not just for its Washington office
or a handful of its most liberal leaders." Like the UCC and its General
Synod, or the Presbyterian Church and its General Assembly, the Methodist Board of Church and Society is bound to follow the broad social
teachings and specific policies of the denomination as a whole, decided by
its General Conference.

But Methodist leaders typically see themselves as more thoroughly
and strongly bound than many of their counterparts in Washington to
follow this denominational course by their own constitution as a nationally elected board, representative of the church's entire membership and
specifically charged to carry out a much more comprehensively detailed
set of Social Principles and issue-specific resolutions. They see themselves
with less leeway than some other denominations offer their Washington
offices, which may appeal directly to a presiding bishop or denominational
head to pursue given issues according to the Washington staff's own lights
as leaders of a relatively autonomous church agency, unburdened by an
elected board of representatives. Methodist GBCS leaders are certainly
not free to set their moral compass by the convictions of a core circle of
particularly committed, self-selected members on the model of a parachurch group or a freestanding religious lobby.

By comparison, suggests one Methodist church leader in Washington,
"look at the Friends Committee on National Legislation [FCNL]. They're

pretty much on their own, free to go wherever their staff wants to take them and their own members want to follow."[10] Ruth Flower, a veteran staff member of the FCNL, pursues the comparison: "On the committee, we try to speak from the heart of the denomination. But we are not the denomination. We are a separate organization. If you want to belong, you sign up. You subscribe to our newsletter. We have meeting contacts in each Friends meeting. They're supposed to promote the committee, and some of them do."[11]

With a self-selected membership of its own, the FCNL can concentrate its efforts. "We know who's interested, and we're always trying to go further and bring them along. We invite them to tell us what issues and areas they're involved in, how active they want to be. We call them when an issue comes up or a bill is pending. We ask them to write or call" their members of Congress, and to become financial supporters of the committee itself. Given such focus and freedom of action with its own members, testifies Flower, "I'm forever grateful that we do not have the bureaucratic complications and the puzzles of the big mainline denominations." For example, she specifies,

> The Methodists are a branch of their central denomination. Their denomination is much more centralized than the Friends when it comes to how they get their budget, how much they have to clear through their church hierarchy, including every fund-raising letter they want to send out to their own members. They can't communicate with their own base without clearing it up above.
>
> You hear a lot from the other big denominations, not just the Methodists, about problems with internal disagreements among their own church people. They need to soft-pedal some positions here [in Washington], or let someone else go out front with a sign-on letter they can agree to in their Washington office but not have to fly by everyone in their own hierarchy.
>
> We have a denominational statement of faith we go by. But it's short, and it's pretty general. To a great extent, the big denominational offices tend to be hooked on faith statements that tie them down much more. We abide by ours, but we are freer, too.

Understood in an ecclesiological context, the organization of denominational offices, committees, and agencies devoted to moral judgment, teaching, and advocacy in public life remains permeated by distinctive forms of theological understanding. This holds true however culturally complex their self-understanding, however clearly their operations bear the rationalized imprint of bureaucratic structuring and high-tech communications, and however ambivalently they reject or mime the associational model of freestanding religious lobbies.[12]

In but Not of the World of Washington

In contrast to the "two cities" of Congress and the churches in Washington, serving to temper the promise of Christ transforming culture in the Wesleyan moral theology voiced by Thom Fassett of the Methodist Board of Church and Society, note the confluence of Calvinist activism with the thought of Teilhard de Chardin and social-democratic ideals in framing the theological outlook of the UCC's Jay Lintner on the mission of the church in Washington:

I really do see God active in the world. I see the world really becoming more and more conscious, or more and more intentional. In terms of history, I think we are at the point where the human species is facing more responsibility for the evolutionary process itself. The human mind is more engaged in the process of our evolution. We are deciding we want to go this way as opposed to that way.

That fundamental change at the human and social and planetary level means that the political process is essential. If you will, it makes Washington, D.C., as much or more than any place else, the place where the world is taking part in deciding how we evolve.[13]

Notwithstanding attempts since the Reagan era to shrink government and unshackle the free market, notes Lintner, government has continued to expand further into the economy, as corporate interests exert greater political influence in turn. That makes it essential for faithful citizens to engage in public balancing of the roles that markets and government should appropriately play, while they remain wary of the worldly dangers of such engagement.

There is enormous potential for abuse, for pride, enormous potential for idolatry in Washington as a place for global decision-making. Many Christians are fundamentally opposed to that, whatever Washington decides, because of its worldly pretension. It is the place where the devil is most likely to be located, not where God is making the planet more human, so it must be resisted.

The Anabaptist side of the church is most prone to saying, "Whatever it is, we're against it," and there are some nights I agree with them. That isn't theologically wrong, and in some ways it is helpful, but it's not the theological language we choose to speak in the UCC.

The moral and social activism of the Reformed Church tradition in American society must persist in engaging legal and civil institutions in the moral argument of public life, Lintner contends. It must also stay alert to the peril of humans' seeking to take self-centered charge of the evolutionary process, and to the danger of the United States' trying to take charge of global political decision-making for its own ends. "The danger is that the center overrides the periphery, and that the powers and principalities that are clearly in there come to hold sway." To defend against this danger, the churches need to help open up the processes of political decision-making more fully to the public, slow them down, and make them more transparent.

Such efforts certainly include democratic aims of bringing all citizens into civic deliberation. But they also extend to making governmental deliberation embrace its moral responsibility to and for all the peoples of the world and their global fate in the light of God's grace. Thus, warns Lintner, church leaders working in Washington and seeking to represent the church at the center of political decision-making have to be keenly aware of "the dangers for abuse within their own actions to the church and to the world."

Generally, I think people here recognize that. Not that we never cross over the line into playing politics, but that we continue to see that this is a deeply offending place, with all of its marble pillars and monuments to power. As soon as it quits offending you, you need to get out of here. You've got to be offended by this place if you're going to remain human, let alone remain the church.

This account is marked by more world-acceptance than its Methodist counterpart yet likewise balanced by wariness of the world's idolatry. Its predominantly activist and engaged ideals of a church that embodies Christ transforming culture nonetheless include themes and images of the church in but not of the world of the imperial city, criticizing its monuments to conquest and commerce as well as teaching in its temples to liberty, justice, and the spirit of the Republic.

Denominational differences in the stance of the mainline churches in Washington toward the political world resonate with classical ecclesiological distinctions among sects standing against "the world," churches steadily engaging the society for the sake of making it more Christian, and reformed churches actively seeking to shape the laws of government according to the Kingdom of God. "Some of the denominations in Washington tend to be much more on the witnessing side and don't really worry about being on the winning side. They don't lobby much or push to get things through Congress. Others do," distinguishes Gretchen Eick, an accomplished lobbyist on Capitol Hill for the UCC and ecumenical groups for more than a dozen years. "The Mennonites and the Brethren and the Quakers tend to take the harder-line positions, the more 'witnessing' positions, for example, on war and peace issues. The UCC and, to some extent, the Presbyterians tend to be the most pragmatic, and to be more on the lookout to do what it takes to get things through."[14] Such distinctions can cut across "maximalist-minimalist" party lines, not only run along them. They lie along a continuum, cautions Eick, with constant movement back and forth, depending on the issues and the principles involved—and sometimes depending, too, on the outcome of strong arguments within denominational staffs as well as among them.

"There are times when you come to the point of not being able to get a consensus to come together or stay together. People fall off," recalls Eick—for example, in the case of stopping U.S. aid to the Contras fighting against the Sandinista government elected in Nicaragua. "The Democratic House leadership, with whom we were working to oppose aid to the Contras, decided that there was no way to stop all the aid. So we should move to a fallback position of stopping the military aid that was most clearly illegal. We had really heated arguments over it in the churches, with people falling off every which way. But finally we decided we couldn't go with the fallback. I remember getting a call afterward from a congressman, David Bonior [D-Mich.], calling a lobby meeting to get us back on board on it. But we didn't get back on." However difficult the split decision the churches reached, it rested with the case, held in the balance between stopping weapons supplied to the Contras and permitting penicillin, opposing tyrants and destabilizing democratically elected governments, discerning just from unjust wars, seeking to save lives and to stand for peace with the Prince of Peace.

Pluralism and Difference in the Public Churches

In comparisons that leaders of church offices in Washington draw among themselves, theological and ecclesiological forms of self-understanding frame the meaning of their differences in policy, organization, and social composition. Yet these comparisons also make clear the common characteristics they share as public churches, in contrast to the religious lobbies and political-action groups they see crowding the polity around them. That includes the Protestant Principle of Christian faith. "We do not equate our way of life or our institutions with true faith," judges Bob Tiller of the American Baptist Church office in Washington.[15] "That means we have to be critical about ourselves and the institutions we're part of. It goes back to what Jesus said in the Sermon on the Mount: 'Best not to go around trying to pick the speck out of your brother's eye while you've got this log in your own eye.'"

Thus truly faithful Christians, in contrast to political zealots or operatives, have to be particularly critical of themselves and their government as being mutually responsible for the sinful institutional order in which they both take part. "The churches can claim the work they did on civil rights since the 1960s, on de-escalating the arms race, on cleaning up the environment and sharing sustainable resources," Tiller allows. "But we can't lose sight of our own finitude." "We're not necessarily on the wrong track just because we don't have a big bandwagon of political support behind us, especially when we're resisting the politics of self-interest. But we're not necessarily on the right track just because we think theologically we're being the 'remnant' of the true church. You have to be humble if you're being a righteous remnant. There's some tricky stuff there." Indeed there is, especially where advocacy meets the numbers of denominational budget tightening, and the polling of intradenominational differences in both political views and social attitudes.

Compared to the United Methodist Church, for example, the United Church of Christ enjoys a relatively small, homogeneous membership, with a relatively large proportion of politically liberal members of the educated upper middle class. "Sure, I'm grateful we're not paralyzed by right-wing internal politics," concedes the UCC's Jay Lintner. "But it's a mistake to see us as the left wing of the Democratic Party at prayer," and that mistake applies to the other churches in Washington as well.[16] Numbers matter in denominational accounting, but the church is a moral community irreducible to the model of an electorate as a sum of individuals aggregated into voting blocs by their political views and preferences. "We aren't driven by majority votes or Gallup polls," asserts Lintner, "and neither are the Presbyterians or the Methodists. This is how the political analysts totally miss the point, if they think the critical vehicle for the churches is the Gallup poll of the Presbyterians or a majority vote of all Methodists. We never view the church like that." In the case of the UCC, Lintner explains, the denomination numbers 1.6 million members:

> I'm very much aware of that, but I'm also aware that some of them are "Easter Christians" on the fringes of their local church and the denomination. They're the ones you've got into the church, you've baptized them, and you're trying to encourage them into more serious Christian growth. But they don't know as much about the social teaching and policy formation of the church, and they don't count as much when it comes to it.
>
> Most local churches have a 10 percent core of very active leadership, and a pool of maybe 30 to 60 percent from which the leadership is drawn. I'm much more interested in knowing where that 10 to 30 percent stands than I am in knowing where the 100 percent stands. We have to trust that their understanding translates into what our General Synod decides for us. We have to work as a body to earn that trust.

Reflecting on its scriptures, tenets, and traditions, arguing over them and revising them, church synods and assemblies are "representing" the church itself as a conciliar body by embodying and enacting it. They are not representing their members as individuals or interest groups.

Freestanding, subscriber-based religious lobbies, by contrast, are "representing whomever they can appeal to," argues Lintner, in light of their individual opinions and group interests. Their entrepreneurial leaders speak neither to nor for the churches, but to their individual members with issue-specific appeals. This distinction may be hardest to understand, for faithful individuals and enterprising religious lobbyists alike, in the case of denominations with more individualistic forms of polity, whether the Southern Baptist Convention or the Unitarian Universalist Association. For they bear the closest resemblance to the associational model of freestanding religious lobbies, in contrast to churches with more episcopal or presbyterian forms of polity.

In key respects, the rise of the religious right, exemplified by the Christian Coalition and Focus on the Family, has had a salutary effect on the mainline churches in Washington, Jay Lintner believes. "We have a covenant with the church and its people as a body to build our mandate to be here in Washington. We don't have that mandate automatically or without qualification. We have to keep building it as we go." The mainline churches have been building this mandate over decades, according to Lintner, while facing new demands since the 1960s to build moral consensus across a wider range of issues and across a wider, more representative range of active constituents among the members of their own denominations. "It was easier in the 1940s and '50s for the mainline churches in Washington to operate here as experts. They were doing great work in testifying on public housing or tenant farmers, say, but doing it largely out of sight of many of their members, sometimes maybe intentionally out of sight on some of the more daring things." Since the 1970s, when many mainline-church offices in Washington were rebuilt, they have grown more intentional in their recognition that "we're not here to do social action apart from the whole church," as Lintner puts it. "We're not going to be the prophets. We're going to be the organizers of the prophetic church."

Spurred by the religious right in this effort, mainline-church leaders have engaged a wider range of their own members. They have grown more mindful of their members' social diversity and moral differences on specific social issues, and so more open to taking up issues such as drug abuse and gambling, not only poverty and racial injustice. Broader, more careful efforts to discern the church's moral mandate in public life address a deeper problem that church leaders must tackle in order to fulfill their social mission, according to Lintner. It stems from the powerful American impulse to privatize religion. For the mainline churches, that problem increased with their postwar success, he says, "when you had suburban churches growing the fastest and Norman Vincent Peale talking the loudest about what religion can do for me, what I can get out of it. Religion is about meeting individual needs, not bringing individuals together to transform society."

The contrary truth of the church's calling to transform society has come to the fore since the 1960s, and it has revived the church's "serious lover's quarrel with the world," says Lintner. It also led to a predictable plunge in the worldly popularity of the mainline churches. Instead of passively falling victim to the conventional wisdom of church-growth strategists, Lintner advises, the church should "continue to build its body from the core, as you watch the last 40 percent of your membership heading out the door," in order to renew itself. "Let's quit worrying so much about conservative churches growing on the right, and start worrying more about losing our own members to the secular world on the left. How do we become the kind of healthy church that holds these people and attracts them?" Lintner asks. In counterpoint to the Wesleyan revival Thom Fassett calls for in the United Methodist Church, Lintner answers, "That kind of healthy church is one that's got conflict in it. It's a lively place, it's a zone of freedom for free discussion where lots of different points of view are encouraged, not just tolerated. That's one of our strengths. We should build on that strength, and help churches heal their own conflicts and confusion in learning how to quarrel with the world and finding out how to transform it."

In this light, the "pluralism" of churches such as the UCC offers a key to differences among denominations in their ecclesiological self-understanding and their public stances as prophetic witness, moral advocate, and social activist. "The UCC is intentionally pluralistic," says Jay Lintner. "We affirm it theologically and in all kinds of ways that more confessional churches don't. When I'm speaking to my constituency in the church, I don't assume we all have the same religious language system. I'm committed not to do that. We want more languages than one spoken. We want to be a multilingual religious community."

Instead of trying to appeal to people's conscience on an issue like abortion, assuming they all have the same conscientious intuition of its theological meaning in their own experience, states Lintner, "I'm much more interested in trying to figure out what their theology and language tell them about abortion. Then I might appeal to their conscience on their own terms."

> I do that all the time in Congress as well, in fact, when I go lobby people. I don't try and say, "Here is what God wants you to do," or "Here's the right thing to do." I kind of poke around trying to find out what this person's values are, what moves this person. You know, you sit there and you'll make eight arguments, and you think the first four are brilliant and can carry the day. But you notice they're not working at all. It's number five, six, seven, or eight that finally speaks their language. It hits their values, it touches their experience.

In this conscientious yet multilingual modality, moral persuasion and argument in the church and in the Congress look much more alike than different. This picture of pluralism differs from the imagery of two cities in worlds apart, moral languages divided by a wall of separation between the faithful and the secular, or two moral worldviews, one orthodox and the other progressive.

To enable such efforts of moral engagement and persuasion, significantly, the church as a community of mixed moral discourse and reflection turns out to be a much more vital school of mutually attentive civic participation than government itself, according to standard models of interest-group politics in America today, even if it avails little in the conventional calculus of lobbying. "Any political scientist or sociologist will tell you how decisions are made in Washington," says Lintner ruefully. "The number one consideration is, 'Will this help me get reelected?' The number two consideration is, 'Will this advance my standing amongst my party or my peers?' The third consideration is, 'Is this good policy?' So the church is more of an advocate than a lobby. Most lobbyists are, if you will, special-interest lobbyists. We are more like a general-interest lobby."

As a consequence, when it comes to combating special interests, says Lintner, "that makes us impotent in this place, because the Hill hears only special interests. It says, 'Show me what's in it for me, buddy, and maybe I can accommodate you.' Put up the money, the votes, the constituencies you can mobilize, and you get a hearing. When you say, 'What's in it for you is the good of all humanity,' they say, 'Right. Next!' " Because the church is committed to common goods in the form of general interests, good policy, and the issues themselves, Lintner concludes, "it's only directly involved in half the political process, because the whole process is both issue-oriented and electorally oriented."

The mainline churches may indict the electoral excesses of freestanding, politically connected religious lobbies and voting blocs such as Focus on the Family. They may be tempted to emulate such strategies of direct mobilization and campaign-style organizing. They may chafe at the tax-exempt status that excludes them from electoral politics and restricts their spending on issue politics to 20 percent of their total budget.[17] But the fact that the churches have so little electoral bite enforces their need to listen more closely and speak that much more persuasively in public. This vital necessity leads the churches back to their own councils to address the critical theological and moral tasks that await them there, and thence out again into the world of Washington and beyond.

Religious Lobbying: Oxymoron or Moral Dialogue?

In the spring of each year for the past quarter century, timed to coincide with cherry blossoms and mild, sunny weather in the nation's capital, the mainline-church offices in Washington have held a "National Briefing" for their most active, committed members and the leaders of their regional and local bodies. Midway through these annual meetings, church members

break up into small groups to visit the congressional offices of their senators and House representatives, in order to engage them persuasively on issues such as reforming health care, welfare, and campaign financing. They
urge raising the minimum wage, fighting AIDS in Africa, making peace in
Palestine, or withdrawing from Iraq. The churches give them instructions
on "how to advocate" that highlight the following points:

> Effective advocacy takes simple and clear preparation, as well as strategy on
> your part. . . . Review the legislator's voting record, the committees he or she
> serves on, and what issues he or she is the most involved in.
>
> Decide what action you want! State a clear definition of the issue based on
> the information you have gathered. Show how there is something very specific
> that the legislator's office should do on the issue. . . . Visit legislators even when
> they oppose your position. You may lessen the opposition's intensity.
>
> State your message briefly: explain your reasons for having this view (i.e.,
> "talking points"), and mention other constituents who share your view, including
> organizations. Ask for specific action and how they plan to vote. . . . Keep ask-
> ing until you get an answer. If they do not have a position, ask how they plan to
> decide. . . . Ask if they are hearing from people who disagree with your position.
> Who? What are their arguments? How much pressure are they putting on?
>
> If you disagree on facts, offer to look into them and follow up. Don't guess
> or fudge. . . . If you have contradictory sets of facts don't waste valuable time
> debating or trying to convince.
>
> Learn from the visit and decide what to do next. . . . How do you feel the
> legislator or staff person responded to the group? . . . What did you really learn
> about the legislator? Any insights into their "world view," political motiva-
> tions, feelings about your issue, constituents? . . .
>
> What, given all the above, should be the next step? Letters? Media? An-
> other visit?[18]

Such instructions are astute and valuable. But they only begin to tell the
layered, complex story of what it is that mainline religious lobbyists and
advocates actually do, and what it means.

Learning such strategic guidelines and how-to rules plays a part in becoming a good lobbyist, grants UCC lobbyist Gretchen Eick. So does "being extremely persuasive, so you can go into congressional offices, argue
them to the point of your position on an issue, give them all the data,
counter their arguments." But something more and deeper is involved in
this process, says Eick. "It's a dialogue about values and convictions that

makes you think about things in a new way. It reconnects you to what is happening" in mutually unexpected ways that sometimes make all the difference in opening up answers to legislative or policy questions that transcend predictable political interests, ideology, and strategy. At other times through such dialogue, says Eick, "you don't come out changing each other's mind about the issue. Maybe you even create some conflict with political realities and dynamics on the Hill when it comes to settling some issue. But you really encounter each other, and something really significant happens even if you don't know what will happen next."[19]

Mainline-church ideals of prophetic social witness have long upheld the virtues of conciliar conversation and moral dialogue in the public forum, while decrying absolutist admonition and preachy monologues. These ideals found new justifications and new challenges, too, when they entered a new era of more independent voters and a Congress of incumbents more responsive to their interests in an electorate with a middle-class majority eager for tax cuts but averse to shrinking public provision at their own expense.[20] Now, easy assumptions of liberal Democratic loyalty to the churches' pleas for justice for the poor were not so readily borne out as in the era of the Great Society or the New Deal. "I came here in 1981, right when Reagan came in," recalls Ruth Flower of the Friends Committee on National Legislation. "A lot was changing then, because he changed it."[21] In the 1970s, Quakers were concerned mainly about the Vietnam War and the draft, nuclear disarmament, and peace in the Cold War with the USSR. "Those were the things that always made everybody's heart beat faster in those days. We had someone on farm issues and civil rights, but we had to invent a whole new domestic economic-justice program, which became mine."

> I was very much on my own. I proceeded to go by subject matter, looking for other advocacy organizations and coalitions that were working on the same things I worked on. I had interviews with them, and I did the same thing on the Hill with staff people that worked on committees that seemed like they'd be naturals for my economic-justice issues. It turned out to be a great introduction, because I needed all those contacts for all the work I did later.

The best Capitol Hill advocates for the churches have learned, since the Reagan era, to talk to everyone on a congressional committee, reports Flower. "We don't stick to the Democrats, the liberals, or whatever. We really try to talk with everyone, even when we disagree."

Q: Even when you're not going to pick up a vote, or budge someone?

I don't know that. We don't focus on vote to vote to vote. Of course, we'll work like crazy on a big vote [to authorize the Gulf War or end AFDC (Aid to Families with Dependent Children) welfare in the 1990s, for example], but that's not the end of the ballgame for us. We invest time in helping people think. I feel more useful in an office where I think the person doesn't think like me. I want to understand why that is, and I want them to understand how I think.

I actually enjoy the discussions more when we disagree, because it's a live, open question, usually. As opposed to the ones where they at least nominally agree with you, but they'll try to tell you that you are so naive, you church people. "You think we can do everything, we can't do anything." You have to believe that isn't so.

You know it's up to them to decide how far they can go. But you can't be satisfied when they won't even engage with us on the importance of the issue itself. I've done this long enough that I know political reality as well as they do. But I also know that if you really care about something, you can be imaginative about it, talk tactics together, and march it forward a little. People in the churches can help you do that.

So I was taken aback when I came here that one would get lectured to by one's friends and told essentially to shut up. "I wish you guys knew what we have to deal with here on the Hill, and the reactionary people that don't agree with us," as if we hadn't talked to them, too. So we started thinking of what we do in terms of a ministry to people who are afraid to stick their necks out. We also started to think of it as a direct challenge to people where perhaps the commitment isn't really there.

Now we lobby them more the way we would lobby someone who doesn't agree with us. Lobby their sense of priorities, what's most important to them. Let them know about the people in their district that we know of who think that this is a critical issue. Encourage church people in their district to make it an immediate issue locally, and then bring in the media to report on it and raise its importance in the member's district. This was a turnabout of expectations in encouraging people to stick their necks out.

By these criteria, congressional lobbying efforts by the mainline churches to urge greater economic justice for the poor in the 1980s offer an example of the public church at its best.

This example is instructive for its mix of persuasive moral appeals made under the political circumstances of partisan stalemate in the midst

of spreading social need, appeals aided by interdenominational cooperation among the Washington church offices in Interfaith Action for
Economic Justice (detailed in the following chapter). As a key lobbyist in these efforts, Flower recalls how the churches responded to deep
cuts in the social-welfare budget made by the Reagan administration in
1981–82. They began an intensive emergency campaign in local churches,
under the banner "The Poor Have Suffered Enough," to keep poverty
and welfare programs in place.[22] Then, says Flower,

> along about 1983–84 we decided that this is not good enough. What we want
> is a sense of responsibility about poverty. So we worked through "the poverty
> agenda" and set some goals for ourselves. We got a statement signed by church
> leaders and started taking it around to offices on the Hill, eventually to more
> than two hundred of them.[23] For a few months we were doing that with no
> other agenda, really, than to elicit ideas: proposals that might be in someone's
> drawer that they hadn't ever brought out, thoughts of possible things that could
> happen sometime in the future, possible tactics in getting something through
> committee. We just wrote all these ideas down, I'd collect them, and we didn't
> really know what our next step would be.
>
> Then it took off. We almost couldn't keep up with it. I know we weren't
> the only ones behind it, and the timing was right. Every crazy committee, even
> Government Operations, began having hearings on poverty. They would say,
> "We agree with you on the problem, but there's nothing we can do." To answer
> them, we put out thousands of printed flyers with all these ideas we had come
> up with [for programs for infant feeding and health care, public housing, child
> care, job training, and job creation].
>
> We argued to members of Congress, "Think of the size of the problems in
> your own district beyond the means of any family or church or local commu-
> nity to solve. There's a need for societal responsibility to take this on. Why is it
> government's problem at all? Because in a democracy, if people cannot survive
> economically, how can we expect them to participate socially and be good citi-
> zens? Isn't this a country for all the people?

By contrast, many other antipoverty advocates and coalitions stuck to defending specific programs such as Head Start. They represented this or that
government-sponsored program and worked to keep it funded and functioning. For the churches, however, "it was more our responsibility to look
at the whole picture," says Flower, "and ask, What is our responsibility as
a faithful people in a democracy for the fate of the poor? Can we let them

be locked out of the economic system we have devised in this country?" Should the government raise interest rates and simply "let poor people fall out the bottom without stepping in to help them?" asks Flower. "Do we want to be that kind of people? Can we be faithful and allow that?"

How does theology enter into the formulation of such moral questions, if at all, and how does it affect the response of members of Congress to such questions? On issues of poverty, work, and welfare reform over the past three decades, replies Flower, mainline religious advocates have appealed to ideals of participatory justice set within communities that embody human interdependence, share responsibility for the commonweal, and enact the gospel ethic of neighbor-love.[24] But mainline advocates often begin with "the dignity of the individual. Honor that dignity!" she urges. "Give people a chance to go to work and be a part of this society as we designed it. It's not a question of handouts or benefits doled out because they're legal entitlements. We are told in the Gospel to love one another. We are called into community with one another. We're called to build our society in ways that let us live good lives in common. To be faithful, we have to give up being gray when it comes to work and raising children in our economy."

American society is not called by God to have this particular kind of economic policy or AFDC or Head Start program. But we are called to be accountable "not to punish innocent children, and to give their parents every chance to raise them well," argues Flower. "Raising children well is valuable work in itself. Going back and getting your high school certificate, going out and working hard all day, all year round, should be enough in itself to enable you to support a family of three or four on the minimum wage." Americans live in a country with a strong enough economy to do that, judges Flower, "without putting people with small children on a breadline for years. Other Western nations do that; there's nothing morally wrong with it. We should commit ourselves to do it, too, because that's what kind of country we are. We are that good, that decent."

To such moral pleas and persuasion, members of Congress and their staffs respond in mixed fashion, according to Flower. With few exceptions, they are averse to being preached at. Yet they are often unaware of their own moral premises, especially in urging that "moral values" be acknowledged and then set aside in the course of effective policymaking. She observes,

> On the Hill, members of Congress and their staffs really seem to resist having anything that smacks of theology mentioned to them. It's called, "Don't preach

to me." We will typically mention our doctrinal beliefs, and then set them aside. Lobbying against the Gulf War, for example, I'd say that the Friends are a peace church, but we're not going to argue over this.

About 80 percent of the time, their reaction is that we've all got our own personal values, but they don't ever come in here. This is a major denial, since so much of economic- and social-justice issues comes down to the combination of cultural and religious beliefs that go into what you really think about people. How changeable they are, how valuable they are, how much they are to blame for their own success or failure in the world.

It's the same kind of discussions we've had in the Washington churches on theologies of work. In Congress, they'll hotly deny it has anything to do with that. But there's that little gut reaction that tells you what they vote is based on what they were taught at their mama's knee. That is the thing that I like to engage and talk about, although they won't always talk about it so openly.

What sort of implicit theologies come to the fore in Congress on questions of economic and social justice? Explicitly religious creedal or confessional views are rare. Members of Congress now come from more diverse religious backgrounds, although they still come disproportionately from mainline Protestantism. But these are people who have been very successful in our society, Flower points out. "Mostly they have worked hard to succeed, and they have come to believe that they have succeeded because of their own intrinsic effort and merit, and their parents'. So don't blame the society that enabled them to succeed for the failures of others, who could have worked harder and been more responsible for themselves. Older people here are children of the Depression, and they'll tell you from experience that you can almost always overcome barriers by working hard."[25]

Members of Congress and their staffs, in sum, have not been systematically left out or deprived of success in our society. "So by and large, when they discover this kind of deprivation, or they have their noses rubbed in it because of where they sit now," observes Flower, "they tend to want to find good reasons why they are not to blame for it, and neither are we" as a people or a government. At the same time, members of Congress who stand in between governmental activists on the liberal left and laissez-faire or small-government conservatives on the right voice contrary views of what government can and should do in response to such social problems. "People say they want to find solutions," notes Flower. "But they think they can't really do anything"—for example, about flat wages and vanishing industrial jobs since the 1980s, or shrinking health-care coverage and deepening income inequality since the 1990s. Congress and the administration have responsible choices to make, counter mainline-church advocates, to care for those caught in the gaps of the economy and existing social-welfare programs, including the working poor and the uninsured. And they can make those choices without thereby unbalancing the federal budget, neglecting the nation's defense, or infringing the authority of the Federal Reserve Bank.

Rights Language, Public Provision, and Shared Responsibility

Mainline-church leaders in Washington often begin to describe the aims of their advocacy by distinguishing justice from charity, much like Methodism's Jim Winkler echoing William Sloane Coffin's wish that Christians in America would come to see charity as a personal virtue enacted to alleviate the effects of injustice, and justice as a matter of public policy exercised to eliminate the causes of injustice.[26] The churches need to emphasize that charity is vital, but it cannot do the work of justice, and Christians are called to do both. So argues Elenora Giddings Ivory, head of the Presbyterian Church (USA) office in Washington, elaborating the distinction into a trio of moral roles the churches must play in public.[27] "We need to be Good Samaritans, to save the suffering and nurse the needy. Pick them up and give them first aid and carry them where they need to go." But, she says, "we also need to be like the Prophet Amos to establish justice at the gates. Take on the king who's causing the problems and tell him what he should do for his people. Take on the priest in the temple who's twisting God's Word to defend what the king is doing." Finally, "we need to be like the good pastor and teacher who goes out and educates those who are unaware of what's going on and enables them to get involved in the work of charity and justice."

The church offices in Washington are particularly responsible for seeking to establish justice at the gates, stresses Ivory. To that end, rights are essential, especially for those denied their rights every day in a society divided by race, gender, and economic advantage. "The issues we deal with in this office continue to be civil rights, religious liberty, and the rights of all persons to get the housing, health care, schooling, and jobs they need to live like the children of God that they are." Talking to religious and civic groups around the country, says Ivory, she often finds agreement on these ideals, and debates over "where we should begin, how much the government should do, and whether we can pay for it." Usually left unspoken, she adds, is the appeal of a voluntary charity that "allows us to give up a little extra as long as we don't lose too much," and fear of a binding justice that demands too much sacrifice of an increasingly pinched middle class: "If you only have ten good jobs for twenty people, then you have people who once thought, 'Yes, everybody should have the right to a decent job' thinking now that they never realized that meant they may not have a good job themselves. So affirmative action and equal opportunity start getting scary."

Since the 1960s, the mainline churches in Washington have argued for social and economic justice in terms of the moral axiom that "basic human needs are human rights," explains the UCC's Jay Lintner. But the churches have done so in piecemeal, policy-specific fashion, he notes, by affirming this equation issue by issue—for example, regarding food stamps or universal health insurance. "Freedom from hunger is a human right. Health care is a human right. The right to work is a human right," the churches have proclaimed, says Lintner. "But nobody has ever talked comprehensively about it. We are incredibly thin on language to do this. When you try to get the church to talk about economic peace and justice in this way, people resist. They start saying, 'Don't go at it that way. It loses us votes.'" Americans find it so hard to accept the moral linkage between "basic" human needs and social rights, especially in theological terms, Lintner suggests, because ours is a society that finds it so difficult to "draw a line between needs and wants."[28] Everybody wants all kinds of things and more of everything, according to one current of American common sense, which skews the way we grasp our rights to life, liberty, and the pursuit of happiness.[29]

The so-called rights revolution of the 1970s was already floundering by mid-decade, observes one Washington church leader tartly, and so was the Democratic Party.

By then, a lot of people weren't doing so well economically, and the rights talk offered a target for the politics of resentment. Tell them that you're not doing so well because these other guys are taking what you've earned, as if they have a right to it. Nineteen-eighty was a brilliant campaign for the Republicans, and the Democrats responded beautifully to it. They all became Republicans. You could not tell them apart by the way they voted [in Congress], or the bills they put their names on. There were no alternative ideas.

Certainly politicians have to respond to that big, broad group in the middle who work hard and get in there and vote, this critic concedes. "But what happened then was that Washington responded to the top 1 percent or so, and left everybody else in the middle pretty much the same. 'A rising tide will lift all boats,' they said. It turned out to lift the biggest boats the most."[30]

Through the 1990s, by this account, campaign consultants and poll-takers advised politicians to be more like one party, the incumbency party, with Bill Clinton leading the way and George W. Bush as well as Al Gore and others following the path of triangulation. "There is a wide window for someone with a brain, a heart, and a program to talk about what we the people ought to be doing with the country," urges this critical church leader. "This is a democracy where we all have a right and a responsibility to participate, and that goes for the economy, too. We all have a right to be part of that circle and share in what goes around and comes around." On issues of economic justice and social inequality, what sort of arguments and modes of moral discourse have mainline religious lobbyists advanced since the 1980s in particular? Visions of the Great Society have long since faded, they acknowledge. The promise of expanding social rights and public provision has given way to ongoing wars of attrition over smaller government and tightened social spending in the wake of the Reagan Revolution. These lines of battle have persisted in conflicts over tax cuts and entitlement spending—especially on Medicare, Social Security, and AFDC-to-TANF welfare for needy families—through the rising tide of economic prosperity, employment, and inequality of the 1990s and into the jobless recovery from recession, lagging wages, and mounting deficits since 2000, as defense spending shot up and economic expansion failed to trickle down.

In a polity crowded with more players ready to trump each other's rights and contradict each other's claims to statistical truth, incontrovertible "rights talk" and statistical data by themselves rarely carry the day. Comments Ruth Flower,

I don't usually push the statistics that much, because I've become painfully aware that people with a lot more money than the churches [have] can come up with statistics that can bury mine. I can either spend my precious time with a member of Congress, fifteen minutes altogether sometimes, trying to undo their statistics and tell them why mine are better. Or I can talk about what makes them think about the problem the way they do.

I look a lot about what's going on in their own district. If a mill closed there, for example, I ask them about the people who lost those jobs. How many were they? These are not people that are lazy, are they? These are people that have been working hard their whole lives. They used to make how much an hour? Enough to pay their own bills and mortgage. Now they can't make their monthly payments. They can't sell their house and move somewhere else to find work, because nobody's buying.

Now what exactly do you expect this person to do? What would you do in this situation? Frankly, I try to imagine myself in that situation, and get the person I'm with to come and join me there, because it's really hard to think you wouldn't be asking for help of some sort, even if it's the first time in your life for that.

Sometimes we'll just leave a question out there, without assuming that all questions have to be answered at all times, that we have to have an answer in order to think seriously about the question. I wonder what this is going to mean in the long run, I might ask, all the mill closings and lost jobs? Have you had any thoughts about new economic development in your district, or new prospects for public investment to create new jobs?

Even though there's not a bill or program there to lobby on, I want to engage the person's mind and help them recognize that there's a big, long-term problem here. There's a lot to be done, and Congress has some role in it, so we can't just throw up our hands and say there's nothing we can do now. You have a moral responsibility to look out for your brother. You've got to put it out there, and not let them off the hook. Not let ourselves off the hook.[31]

Where do rights enter into such moral dialogue, if at all, and what do they mean? "On minimum survival, I'll talk about the rights everyone has not to be hungry or homeless and living on the sidewalk," answers Flower. "It matters to me that we recognize everyone's right to a fair trial, their right to vote, the civil rights of women and people of color, just like every one else."

Beyond that, though, I try not to get into claim-jumping contests over rights, where whoever disagrees with you claims their right is more important than your right. Or at least it's just as important, so they don't have to give up something in order to grant your right.

I talk instead about, What do we all want as a society? What kind of society do we want to be? Do you want to step over people on your way to work? In some other countries, it might make you proud of yourself or your work. But here it should make us ashamed, make us want to change things. That gets us into the value of things in the way we live, what the trade-offs are, what the balance should be. For example, how do you find a better balance between the liveliness and competitiveness of our society, and how fearful it is to lose out and barely be able to survive at the bottom?

Seen from these angles, religious lobbying on Capitol Hill does indeed turn on recognizable forms of moral advocacy and dialogical persuasion. Efforts to bring complex social problems such as joblessness down to human scale and immediacy invite moral intuition and imagination to flesh out the relevant social facts. They try to avoid being blunted by factual indeterminacy or bracketed by the mechanics of complex causal arguments over precisely how to solve problems such as industrial-plant closings in the 1980s, NAFTA (North American Free Trade Agreement) in the 1990s, or outsourcing jobs in today's global economy.

Rights language, by this account, remains crucial for expressing the fundamental nature of "minimum survival" within the moral logic of human need and mutual responsibility rooted in biblical ethics of neighbor-love. Rights language also remains crucial in the primary sense of legal and civil rights to life and liberty on the model of the Constitution's Bill of Rights, based on the dignity of every person and extending to every citizen. Beyond this, caution tempers conviction about rights language when it comes to arguing for social goods such as decent work at living wages, universal health care, and adequate public housing and provision for the poor.

The multiplication and diversification of "positive social rights" prove puzzling, if not threatening, for many Americans, at least when this shifting moral logic promises to oblige them to defer to others or pay to benefit them.[32] Rights claims to decent jobs, livable minimum wages, health-care coverage, welfare benefits, and affirmative-action admissions invite "claim-jumping" counterassertions of rights to private property, lower consumer prices and labor costs, and untaxed returns on capital at risk in free markets. Considerations of compensatory justice and Head Start aid to the disadvantaged meet counterarguments in behalf of meritocratic competition in hiring and college admissions, and emphasis on equal opportunity unfazed by vastly unequal outcomes along lines drawn by race, gender, ethnicity, or educational background.

Instead, this account puts positive emphasis on the moral goods a society shares as part of its way of life and institutional arrangements.

These are practical moral attributes and structured relationships that the citizens of a democratic society can discuss critically and judge with one another and with their elected representatives. We can evaluate the practical attributes and arrangement of our social institutions as virtuous or vicious, as enabling or hindering persons in their efforts to flourish together within these structured relationships. We can cultivate our moral character through taking part in these social practices, including the opportunities we find and the initiatives we take in a market economy. We can weigh alternative social arrangements and moral goods in terms of trade-offs and balances as well as rights in consonance or conflict.

Shared moral goods that characterize society as a whole can be made immediate, local, and personal. For example, justice and charity can inform questions of economic development and public provision that arise in the everyday experience of both members of Congress and ordinary citizens on their way to work, walking past panhandlers and homeless people sleeping on the sidewalks in 1990, or wondering why poor children cannot be well-fed and well-schooled in the midst of growing prosperity and low unemployment in the year 2000 or during the lagging recovery of good jobs and living wages after the 2001 recession.[33] Asked what justice means in her lobbying work on Capitol Hill, the UCC's Gretchen Eick replies,

Gandhi said whenever the world is too much with you, bring to mind the poorest, most powerless person you've ever seen. Hold that person in your mind. That will clarify your vision.

"Justice" is an abstraction, and you can have real trouble around here if you can't get beyond abstract thinking about justice. You have to make it personal. It is very personal. It's very much about the guy who comes up to my car as I'm parking behind Capitol Hill and asks me for money for food, and when I give him twenty dollars he starts to cry, and I think, "Why?"

It's about a young woman I know who is an unwed mother and who has the courage to decide she is raising her child together with her partner, and I'm a pro-choice advocate who's grateful they made the choice to let this child have life, and I'm wondering how are they going to take care of this child and make it in this society.

It's about all those people in Angola and Mozambique without any limbs, because we sent land mines there to tilt the fight in our favor between their governments and their guerrillas.[34]

Whether in the halls of Congress or the pews of local churches, justice must be brought down to the ground of such felt meaning, immediately embodied and experienced, in order to stir moral recognition to lead to legislative and political action.

In coming down to the ground of seeing and responding to human suffering and need, justice becomes reconnected to Christian love and to a sense of moral urgency quickened by moral indignation, and anger too, says Eick. That is because "we can't be sweet, kind Christians all the time," nor should we try to be, given the unfair cost of closing our eyes to the world around us, at once broken and blessed. Such moral reconnection cuts through the relativizing difficulty of the multiplication and division of meaning among different kinds of justice in a society like ours, affirms Jaydee Hanson of the GBCS, and opens up a Christ-centered love of neighbor: "That's the gospel truth, 'Whatever you do to the least of these, you do to me.' It doesn't say go out and try to get the greatest good for the greatest number, and let the rest take care of themselves. It doesn't say go out and make the most efficient economic decisions you can, or work even harder to get ahead."[35]

When ethics of earning and economic efficiency, social utility, and legal rights conflict or fall short, Christians face a special responsibility to live out their faith in Christ-like love. They must face the fact that they, too, share in these contrary moral myths. They live by them in some slices of their lives, and often hide behind them as well. To free ourselves from this confusion and shed the light of conscience on the political economy of sharing, Christians everywhere must elicit from one another and their fellow citizens the stories and visions of these competing moral myths of justice that can do without love. They must expose the partial truth of fair play to the gospel truth of neighbor-love.

At the heart of moral dialogues carried on in such terms lie common sense and shared conviction, to be sure, but moral difficulty and theological difference, too. For the sake of unifying the power of their moral appeals, if not their lobbying clout, church leaders in Washington rarely pursue theological lines of disagreement for their own sake. But neither can they ignore them on such crucial moral matters as the meaning of work, charity, and neighbor-love without vitiating their own self-understanding and persuasive authority on issues of economic justice and social welfare.

In collaboration among the mainline churches on issues of poverty, welfare, and workfare in the 1980s, recalls Ruth Flower, theological differences emerged that fueled a series of discussions and informed a joint statement on work:[36]

> Quakers share a view that human beings are essentially good and that there is in each person something that can be spoken to by the spirit. That tends to make us want to find ways to improve things socially as a natural sort of outgrowth of this human goodness.
>
> Well, in working together on welfare policy, we began bumping into different views in different places from different traditions, especially on the good old Protestant work ethic. Yes, work is good, but what do you do when people don't work? When does it come down to people who won't work? Are they really just lazy? Do you punish them for their sins, or threaten to punish them to make them work? What is sin, what is evil?
>
> The Presbyterians in particular pushed the essentially sinful nature of humans, which can be redeemed. So you have to discern the evil that social forces can do and try to restrain it, and do all you can to change those forces, besides trying to overcome the evil in individuals and change their lives. That's a very different approach from where Quakers begin theologically. It doesn't really send us at all, and we agreed to disagree on some of the theology.
>
> But we also agreed that whatever your theology, you don't threaten to starve people to make them work. You don't bribe them with welfare not to work. Being poor or out of work is not a punishment God visits upon us because of our sins, and we have no excuse for doing nothing about it.[37]

Thus do moral differences and difficulty run through the middle of mainline churches on issues beyond abortion and homosexuality, including questions of economic inequality and social justice.[38]

These differences also follow the currents of theological confusion and change within religious communities in terms irreducible to their members' politically predictable ideological loyalties or class-specific social attitudes and interests. "Most of the people who come to the UCC General Synod are liberal Democrats in their politics," the UCC's Jay Lintner acknowledges, "and our social statements certainly resemble Democratic Party platforms more than they do Republican ones."[39] UCC members fully support church stands on issues of civil rights and civil liberties in terms of freedom of conscience and the sacredness of every human being. They likewise support disarmament and nonintervention in foreign policy matters in terms of justice and peace for all peoples of the world. But they are not so strong or united in their support for food stamps and welfare for the poor.

What are the reasons for such weak support on this front, and what are its implications for the church's social teaching and action? Lintner compares the impact on the mainline churches and the Democratic Party of 1970s stagflation and the ebb of U.S. manufacturing jobs in the globalizing economy that Keynesian policies could no longer tame. He muses,

> It took away the Democrats' economic model and put them in a funny place. But it put us in a funnier place, because the Democratic Party still had its interest groups and constituencies. It could still say, "Give us this, because this is who we are. Give us the minimum wage, we're the union. Give us food stamps, we're the poor."
>
> That's not how the church functions. Yes, we have a theological commitment to the poor as "the least of these." But we're not so clear how we actually stand by that commitment when we don't have access to economic growth.
>
> Protestants had a paradigm of the free market and the work ethic that remained coherent for our people, even if our leadership abandoned it as long as a century ago. Now it's broken down, and we're having to face up to the consequences of still relying so heavily on Andrew Carnegie for our real economic theology. We've been saying we want the best of both the free market and the welfare state. But compared to the Catholics, who have always distrusted the market and affirmed the state, we have distrusted the state and affirmed the market.

Now mainline Protestants must rethink their economic theologies in more practically nuanced and more profoundly biblical terms, Lintner and others propose, if the official social teachings of their churches are to coalesce coherently with the deepest moral convictions of their people in the pews.[40] It remains to be seen how fully this task can be accomplished, however well begun, and how far its moral influence will reach in our time. For we are sustaining cyclical yet real economic growth that has yielded rich rewards for those at the top of the American social ladder, rising job insecurity and lagging wages for those in the sagging middle, and greater hardship for the bulging ranks of the working poor at the low end. Greater inequality in incomes and wealth has brought with it widening differences in our social experience and deepening divisions of our civic intuition of its meaning. This both permits and follows from the erosion of public services once thought essential—for example, in American public schools, transportation, health, and safety.[41]

Without a People, Visions Perish:
The Church and Community Organizing

For decades, mainline-church leaders in Washington have weighed the value of mobilizing church members to back their national advocacy efforts and their lobbying of Congress and the White House. They have debated when, where, and how to engage in such mobilizing, and how far to pursue it, on issues ranging from resisting Reagan in the Central American Contra war and opposing George H. W. Bush in the congressional vote to declare the 1991 Gulf War to protesting loudly against invading Iraq. They have organized around efforts to reform health care, welfare, campaign financing, and immigration laws and to move the World Trade Organization to check the injustices of globalization.[42] At the same time, grassroots organizing and social movements for reform stretch back through the churches' public witness for peace in Vietnam, nuclear disarmament, and civil rights to movements for temperance, suffrage, and the rights of labor a century ago.

Set within the context of an expanding state and a more diversified polity, concern with educating and mobilizing local church members to support national religious lobbying by denominations and parachurch groups seems to be a natural concomitant of the growth of such lobbying. It also seems to be a natural response to the challenging capacity of freestanding religious lobbies such as the Christian Coalition and Focus on the Family to flex their strength at the local level on Capitol Hill. "The Christian homeschooling groups shut down the Capitol switchboard for three days in support of school vouchers," marveled one mainline-church leader in Washington in 1997. "Just think if we could turn out fifty or a hundred thousand phone calls overnight on something like campaign finance reform."[43]

Moral values underlie the social intricacy of issues such as budget priorities for health care, welfare, or education. But moral advocacy alone often fails to make these values self-evident to all, to spark moral outrage, or to sustain resolve in their behalf. This leads national religious advocates toward community organizing and education. So, for example, the Friends Committee on National Legislation began community organizing and education in the early 1990s in order to back its congressional lobbying for the deepest possible cuts in post–Cold War military spending in the wake of the Gulf War. Patriotic fervor and economic concerns over lost jobs, military bases, and industries led the committee to look beyond Washington and initiate a campaign to "reinvest in our communities" with grassroots organizations in ten key states that were heavily dependent on defense spending. "We couldn't work on the budget numbers without looking at what military spending does in the communities and states where it's concentrated, and what other things people there can do instead," reported Ruth Flower. "This is the first time we've tried to get grassroots groups into our research and lobbying on an alternative budget. If it works out, we're toying with doing more grassroots organizing on an alternative budget for 1993."[44] This the FCNL did, in conjunction with the Center on Budget and Policy Priorities and with Democratic leaders in Congress and the White House in the first years of the Clinton administration.

Voiced from a more radical standpoint within Protestant ecclesiology and set within a longer history of the churches' role in popular social movements, calls for the mainline churches to commit themselves first to prophetic forms of community organizing have evoked sharp criticism against lobbying the state as a primary mission of the public church. "The strength of the church nationally doesn't lie in getting access to Capitol Hill or the White House," argues Philip R. Newell, Jr., a longtime Presbyterian activist, denominational leader, and onetime head of the Washington, D.C., Council of Churches.[45] "It lies in tens of thousands of local congregations, in every kind of neighborhood across this country. That is the 'access' that really matters for the church, to care for the souls and bodies of people in their daily lives and local communities. That's real ministry, and real democracy, too. Start with your own neighborhood, start knocking on doors and listening to the people who open the door," urges Newell. "That's what the church needs to learn to do, first of all, in order to help build accountability in our national politics and economy."

A generation ago, mainline Protestant church leaders were distracted from this genuinely prophetic mission in public life, Newell charges, by the heady experience of working in tandem with national government officials in behalf of the Great Society. "The access was seductive," he recalls. "Tennis in the morning with a Democratic senator. Scotch in the evening with the mayor. When the D.C. riots came in 1968, we got into the ready room, the command center underneath the municipal building. We talked Kleindienst, the attorney general, out of issuing live ammunition to the National Guard." In the generation since, says Newell, "we went from partnering with the Democratic White House and Congress in the Great Society days, and making deals with Bobby Kennedy later on, to learning harder lessons on the ground."

What sort of lessons engaged mainline-church leaders concerned with social justice and change after the high point of liberal-Democratic national politics in the 1960s? "We had to sort out the seduction from the substance," replies Newell, and move from influence politics through access to government, to working for the national church but working with people locally to serve the community. "We're not doing influence politics anymore, because we don't think making unholy alliances with the administration—no matter who it is—is really God's work." Instead, the primary mission field of the public church, by this account, lies in working with local congregations and communities. That insight springs not from denominational strategizing for a new political era, says Newell, but from theology in action. Particularly in the Reformed tradition, the heart of Christian spirituality is "a biblically based passion so to reform the community that all citizens can live in peace and harmony with each other," Newell emphasizes. Here, too, a peaceable society is one in which "different communities negotiate together for the turf they share." Together they define the institutions they have to be accountable to, by responding not only to one another but to the larger truth that "we are beckoned toward the future we believe God has in mind for all creatures."

From the standpoint of a church beckoned to witness actively in behalf of the Kingdom of God, says Newell, "I can't understand why church leaders try to turn themselves into Washington lobbyists and policy experts. We need to play our long suit. Our long suit is theology. It's interpreting the claims of justice inspired by faith, and professing our vision of the Kingdom of God." Professing such faith means practicing it, "not simply thinking about it while you're sitting in a Washington church office, putting out a newsletter, or having lunch with some congressman's legislative aide." Is such criticism the churchly equivalent of political organizers and social activists indicting policy analysts for seeking to understand the world instead of changing it for the better? No, counters Newell, for publicly professing biblical faith means praying together over social ills and moral dilemmas, talking them over and arguing over them as well as taking action. "There are critical times when we belong on the barricades," he testifies. "I marched in Greenwood, Mississippi, to end segregation. I marched on the Pentagon to end the war in Vietnam. But if that's all you do, you're just an activist, not a prophet or a faithful witness."

In contrast to the influence politics of insider lobbying or policy analysis, what can and should the churches do to profess their faith more truly in public? Answers Newell,

All the church can do is hold up Moses' brass snake! And as Moses lifted up the serpent in the wilderness, so must the Son of Man be lifted up, that whoever believes in him may have eternal life. That is the restoration of community! Lift up wholeness! That is all we can do.

So the church can and should stand up to the Pittston Coal Company and say, "If you continue to deprive retired miners of the benefits they need and they earned, you will have social unrest. If you continue to demand unjust givebacks on wages and pensions and workman's comp[ensation], you will destroy the community, and we will stand against you."

That's why we were against Pittston, Youngstown Steel, and Control Data, not because we are against big business or for big labor. Did Pittston have to make the cuts to make a profit and keep the company alive? What do they need to change to be good members of the community? How can we help them, because that's the side we're on."

Read the prophets. Read Amos, read Micah, read Hoseah. What they were doing was saying to the king what we should be saying now: "If you keep doing that, this is going to happen. You are going to get bit, burned, wounded by race, dismembered by favoring haves against have-nots. You are going to wind up in captivity—the bond market is going to own you! We were so driven by the bottom line and the next quarter that we didn't bother to invest in poor children, in decent ghetto schools, in real job training for welfare mothers and real jobs for the fathers of their children, and all the rest.

Everyone's making that case now, as a matter of prudence. The church doesn't have to. But as a matter of sin and salvation, it is ours to make, when our soul is still on the line even if we think our body is safe and secure.

This biblical promise of the Mosaic snake for the politically snakebit, and the redemptive Christ for souls sick with social sin, brings the transcendent good of salvation down to the ground of social justice in the form of the Kingdom of God. It is normative in history, if only realized fully in the life to come. This biblical imagery also resists redefinition of the church's working with government to deliver the kingdom come on earth in terms inspired by political ideologies, whether devoted to the Great Society administered by LBJ, a Reaganesque morning in America dawning on Main Street—lit by a thousand points of light and warmed by compassionate conservatism—or a Clintonesque bridge to the twenty-first century built on high-tech prosperity in a global economy. Instead of serving as an ally of political agents or a justifier of political programs, the church must be a proclaimer of salvation and wholeness of spirit that infuses the moral coherence of political community.

The Mutuality of National Advocacy and Community Organizing

To meet such prophetic arguments in behalf of community organizing as opposed to insider lobbying, mainline-church leaders committed to national advocacy and religious lobbying emphasize the mutuality of the two kinds of efforts pursued by the churches in practice, however polarized they may seem in principle. "We're doing what we do on Capitol Hill not only for the sake of national advocacy, but for education in the churches," attests Jay Lintner as head of the UCC's Washington office.[46] "People in the pews grow and learn when they have to make a decision, when they have to decide to come down on an issue like the Gulf War or gays in the military, and take a position on it." So denominational leaders are well justified in their ongoing efforts to move their congregations to decide to support this policy or oppose that bill, instead of asking them only to understand this or that issue. The mainline churches certainly pursue education on social issues with their members, Lintner stresses. "But we keep saying there are moral decisions to be made here. What do you think? We keep wanting focus, so people can make a good decision and take action." In this effort, the UCC's Office for Church in Society relies on its Board for Homeland Ministries to offer theological and moral guidance to local churches as crucial communities of moral reflection and social action—in contrast to the shared responsibility of the Methodist Board of Church and Society with the Board of Discipleship, as stressed by Thom Fassett.

Nonetheless, argue denominational leaders active on Capitol Hill, calls to subordinate national religious advocacy to grassroots organizing in local churches mistakenly place in opposition these two mutually related activities, when both are morally necessary for the public church to pursue. In the name of local congregations and communities, such calls ignore the larger reality of the church itself. In the name of localism and political populism, they also ignore the larger reality of the political process and the penetration of the modern state into the ordering of the local communities, schools, workplaces, and families in which Americans live. Thinking back to his exposure as a seminarian to Martin Luther King, Jr., organizing the South and to Saul Alinsky organizing neighborhoods in Chicago, Lintner sees the churches' turn toward Washington as heeding the practical question, "How do we organize the church for effective social transformation in the world?" Once that question is posed in the world of real communities and persons, with an eye to the root causes of social problems, not simply their symptoms, then "you can't avoid the political process," argues Lintner. "Grassroots organizing and nitty-gritty community issues remain important, but they're interrelated with the political process right up to the state and national level."

Once religious leaders seek to organize churches beyond the local level, moreover, their organizing task becomes intrinsically more political in itself. "Try to organize a hundred churches across a state, or thousands of churches across the country," proposes Lintner, "and you have to function more politically, even when you're deciding where to put your resources, how the trainings should go, where the money should go." Grassroots religious activism requires national planning and political engagement to make a difference in getting at the root causes of social ills such as poverty, violence, and disease. Local mobilization of church members proves no less vital in supporting national religious advocacy on politically controversial moral issues. In sum, testifies Lintner, "I operate in basic denial of 'we-they' opposition between the church in Washington and grassroots people in local churches. I see us in a systemic relationship with them. It's a covenant of the church, and it's a mandate we have to keep building as we go."

The church's covenant to preach and embody the gospel in public includes its mandate to justify its presence in Washington and its position on given issues. But it transcends this mandate, too. This covenant requires denominational leaders to elicit church members' views with continuing care in the process of teaching and forming them into the Body of Christ. For the church cannot and should not seek simply to "represent" its members' views in conventional political terms. So national church leaders worth their salt should "see the local all over the place, and you see how different the local is all over the place," says Lintner, referring to his experience of six months on the road of every year he spent as national coordinator of UCC peace activities before settling in Washington. "If national people pay attention, they should understand more locals than the locals do. They'll come to understand a lot of different local people, help them make sense of their profound differences, and help us all make sense of that, too."

UCC members in California and Massachusetts, for example, are much more emphatically "pro-choice" on abortion and opposed to the death penalty and prayer in public schools, compared to UCC members in Pennsylvania, who are likelier to be Reformed than Congregationalist in background. Their moral differences are not simply a function of liberal-conservative differences in cultural politics or greater secularity in the West, and their meaning is not self-evident from polling data. "You can assume everybody wants world peace and social justice, and freedom of conscience," Lintner concludes. "But you also assume there are different languages spoken with theological integrity in the church about how we're going to achieve peace and justice, and respect freedom of conscience. You have to try and listen for those different languages theologically running through all kinds of social differences." From its socially and ideologically diverse constituents, then, the church must continue to try to form disciples and members of one body through shared prayer and worship, teaching, and dialogue.

When wise church advocates in Washington join with conscientious pastors and people in the pews, together they can help make a better world, not just better public policy. So argues UCC lobbyist Gretchen Eick, for example, in the case of the churches' efforts in the 1980s to stop the planned production of a new generation of nerve-gas weapons with a "binary" design that promised to make them more mobile and more deadly than ever. "If you're going to lobby, you have to do your home-work and master the technical side," says Eick, and not just make abstract arguments in terms of moral principles and Bible truths:

> We went through the Army's technical material very carefully to get hold of the solid data. We showed where the fallacies of their argumentation actually distorted their own data. In binary form, the weapons are stabler and supposedly safer, so you can send them out to troops in the field, and they can use them with less chance of gassing themselves. That actually makes them more dangerous.
>
> The fact is that these weapons are as devastating to the civilian population as nuclear weapons. They're really cheap, and really appealing to terrorists. So once the U.S. put them into production, the Iraqs of the world would have a tremendous new weapon of choice to try to get hold of. Nixon, Carter, and Ford had all agreed these were weapons from the horror chamber that should never be produced again, so why should we get them out to the troops now?[47]

Eick got to know the head of the Army's Chemical Warfare Division, who opposed any production or deployment of binary weapons. She worked with him to master technical arguments over the issue. "I'd draft things for him. We'd help each other testifying and writing letters to the Hill," she recalls. She brought into the debate the profound opposition to deployment from the churches in Germany, where U.S. nerve-gas weapons were then stored at two bases. This enabled faithful Americans to stand in solidarity with those likeliest to suffer if the gas were used.

> Our big breakthrough on mobilization came when we decided to target the Defense Appropriations Subcommittee considering funding for the weapons. We went to the districts of the five members where UCC churches were strong, and called our local pastors there and said, "Your members have a closed meeting in two weeks to vote money to produce a whole new generation of nerve-gas weapons. No one is going to be there to watch what your representatives do. If this is something you care about, we can get you all the background information on it, and we'd really encourage you to be in touch with your representative."
>
> One black pastor in Queens was incredible. He got on the phone to his congressman, who was the chair of the subcommittee, and convinced him to oppose the funding. He called him up every day. Every day!
>
> We wound up getting all five of those members. We lost the subcommittee vote 6 to 5, but we got the five. That was a very critical moment of learning, to see where people could focus their energy around an issue and make a real difference.

The mainline churches continued to work on the issue on the Hill and in their grassroots organizing. They eventually helped to block production of the binary nerve-gas weapons and remove related weapons from storage overseas for deployment to the field.

The churches need to pursue two kinds of advocacy on social issues, concludes Gretchen Eick. One should be framed theologically and morally by the national denomination as a whole and carried out by church leaders in Washington. The other must be "organized from the bottom up" in local churches and communities across the country.

> It makes all kinds of sense to do both, because only a very small proportion of people in the church, and the population, are going to be involved in direct advocacy at the national level. We need grassroots support. Even more, we need to know what the problem is from the folks who are experiencing it, who

are jobless or homeless or dirt-poor in rural Alabama, or sick from toxic wastes dumped in their backyard in urban slums. We need to know what they feel and think. We have to respect their ability to come up with solutions themselves, not just overlay our analysis on their problems.

Moreover, mobilizing grassroots support from the pews of local congregations for the advocacy of public churches in Washington does not fulfill the highest value or full calling of bodies of faith in the body politic. "Our highest value is enabling people in congregations and communities to experience their God-given power and responsibility to shape the world in which they live, locally as well as nationally, and accept citizenship as a gift of God," Eick affirms. "If that empowerment is our primary goal, as opposed to changing this piece of environmental legislation or that housing policy, then we need to start with the injustices people are actually feeling. Where's the pinch in this community? What is standing in their way of coming together as a community and doing something about it?" asks Eick. That requires, she says, that "you dialogue with people, and stay with it when they come up with different priorities than yours, or real radical or conservative solutions you don't want to hear, because the denominations have a lot at stake in the policy positions they have worked through their national agencies."

Public policy can contribute to solving many problems of social injustice and suffering, but it can't do everything, and it can't be effective without the larger process of faithful civic participation. As a consequence, proposes Eick, "the churches must bring people to the table to dialogue about living in this world in a covenantal relationship with their neighbors. OK, you know I may disagree with you 180 degrees in my position on some issue, or even on how you and I look at the world. But if we spend some time really talking about it under the umbrella of the faith we share in the church, then we will begin to move in the spirit of feeling that you are my brother and I am your sister." Then, promises Eick, "we can become part of faithful answers to social needs by coming together in ways that respect our differences but aren't limited by Karl Marx or Milton Friedman. Capitalism isn't working, socialism isn't working. We can do better!" Beneath differences on political issues and ideologies lie a common faith and an animating sense of shared responsibility for the commonweal that church members can bring to life through sharing dialogue as well as worship. Indebted to Paulo Freire's work to "conscientize" members of local communities and churches in Latin America to work together to name and combat injustice, this approach has helped convert some mainline-church lobbyists from the assurance that they have all the answers, as Eick puts it. It inspired in them more willingness to "trust and respect people you disagree with that there's something of God in them and they have part of the answers you're seeking in your political work."[48]

Ecclesiology cuts more than one way in the dynamic relationship of local churches to national denominations in shaping different forms of public-church advocacy. The contrast between the UCC and the United Methodist Church makes this clear. "UCC polity is extremely autono- mous," Gretchen Eick observes. "Constitutionally, each local congrega- tion is autonomous, and so is each national church agency. No one person can speak for the church as a whole, no one can speak for a conference. The presiding officers of the denomination have no power over the agen- cies except by commission." For all the leeway for initiative in public- church advocacy that this congregationalist form of polity provides, it also poses challenges for unifying support for these initiatives among na- tional agencies and local churches within the denomination, and for col- laborating with other denominations and nonreligious moral advocates in Washington.

To meet these challenges in the UCC, says Eick, national boards and agencies reorganized in the 1970s. Then they used parallel structures in 1988 to set up a Peace and Justice Network deliberately based in regional church conferences to draw them into more collegial cooperation. "Now we want to see if this model can grow into a more inclusive, cross-sectoral approach to problem-solving around social-justice issues in study circles in local churches," notes Eick in 1991. "Agree to meet for an hour and a half one night a week for the next six weeks and look at U.S. policy, say, on the Caribbean or Africa. Start with Bible study, do some read- ing on UCC social teachings and policy positions, be willing to hear the other person." Invite professionals in business, government, and health care into these study circles, urges Eick, and let them meet with working families, single parents, and the jobless. "How do we get them talking about these problems, studying the Bible, and thinking together about what they really care about?" she asks. In answering such questions in the UCC, allows Eick, "no one from the national church is going to come out and tell everybody to focus on this or that issue for the next year."

Methodists, Episcopalians, Catholics, and other churches with a more connectional, episcopal, or corporatist polity have greater institutional authority and leverage to pursue such study and discussion for the benefit of the public church as a whole, says Eick. For example, she notes, "one of the greatest gifts of Methodism is the United Methodist Women's Division structure of Schools of Christian Missions. They have twenty-five thousand people every summer doing a study course in one of three different issue areas, spending a week to learn how to teach and discuss it with people in their local congregation and how to get them involved in it. With Congregationalists, you'd never get to do that!" Within such ecclesiological differences lie difficulties of coordination and disagreements of theological substance, to be sure. But they also point toward larger forms of moral coherence and conciliar action within a complex division of civic labor. Such conciliar coherence offers a sharp contrast to the spreading pattern of freestanding parachurch and public-interest groups organized as look-alike voluntary political associations defined by a single issue but moved by disparate ideals and interests.

Public Churches, Parachurches, and Public-Interest Groups

The growing prevalence of issue-specific coalitions that reach across church offices and parachurch groups to nonreligious moral advocacy groups—whether for gun control, health-care reform, or environmental protection—offers new challenges for the churches, as well as new opportunities. "You get this heady mixture of young interns, all sorts of religious people, and everybody else in town with a million different perspectives," reports one church leader. "It can be a zoo."[49] The sheer proliferation of issues and the breadth of some issue coalitions, add other church leaders, bolster a "lowest-common-denominator strategy." It aims at flattening out theological and ethical differences for the sake of heightening political unity and impact. Issue proliferation and the specialization of religious lobbyists to keep pace with a greater number of complex legislative issues, such as health-care reform or globalized trade policy, tug at the theological fluency and coherence of the church in Washington from several angles. "As you add more issues to your agenda, and you get more specialized policy people to handle them," notes veteran church lobbyist Jay Lintner, "they may be less tied into the whole denominational reason that brought church folks here in the first place," such as temperance for Methodists or pacifism for Quakers.[50]

Religious advocates on Capitol Hill today work through more complicated legislative issues. They cooperate more often with legislative aides in congressional committees and members' offices. They collaborate more closely with specialized lobbyists and policy analysts from public-interest groups such as the Center on Budget and Policy Priorities, the Sierra Club, or the Children's Defense Fund. As they do so, confesses Gretchen Eick, "you want to be recognized as competent. You don't want to appear foolish. That need may be the strongest pull of all I feel toward backing a 'credible' agenda instead of a prophetic agenda. When I feel we've been at our best in the church community, it's usually been when we've been meeting together very regularly, not bashing heads but very vigorously testing our sense of unity about what we're doing."[51]

Thus the challenge for the churches lies in doing more than one thing well: vigorously sustaining their own councils within and across denominations in order to define and guide their voices in public advocacy, persuasive engagement with government, and cooperation with parachurch and nonreligious public-interest groups.

The development of religious single-issue groups, particularly parachurch groups outside or in between official church bodies, narrows the institutional gap between religious and nonreligious public actors. Freestanding, member-based, single-issue religious groups more closely resemble their nonreligious counterparts than they resemble churches, political parties, or government itself. They are more prone to fuse absolute moral principle and particular legislative provisions. They are likelier to mobilize members to vote for or against candidates given their stands on single issues, and to rise or fall on their ability to win issue-specific fights.[52] In their evolution over the past few decades as moral advocates, lobbyists, and organizers, the mainline churches have indeed been influenced by the mobilizing and pressure-politics example of the religious right and the growth of single-issue parachurch groups. But no less significant has been the broader influence of single-issue, public-interest, and protest politics carried out by freestanding, member-based voluntary associations, from Common Cause through the Sierra Club and the National Organization for Women to MoveOn.org.

In distinguishing the peculiar nature and role of the churches as public moral advocates and lobbyists of government, religious leaders instructively compare them to parachurch advocates, such as Bread for the World, and to nonreligious yet morally focused public-interest groups, such as the Children's Defense Fund (CDF). One dimension of these comparisons underlines the less central concern of the churches for political effectiveness and their less direct use of political means to this end.

Another is the characteristically broader range and diverse nature of the issues on which the churches focus. Comparing the church offices in Washington to the Children's Defense Fund, for example, Jay Lintner observed in 1996,

> The political connection comes first for CDF. That was true even during the Reagan-Bush years, when they worked more with Congress. They have had a very clear, well-defined, limited agenda for a long time. Only since Clinton came in have they really tried to do much grassroots activity, or even work very publicly in Congress. They work their issues through the background with people who already recognize them. It's very often Marian Edelman's personal influence. They concentrate a lot on developing those personal connections. They sit in a different place than we do, so it makes a lot of sense for them to do that.[53]

Fortified by close, though eventually strained, political ties to the Clintons and by the loyalty of Health and Human Services secretary Donna Shalala, CDF grew in the 1990s to a staff of over one hundred. It was underwritten by a mushrooming membership, a lengthening list of contributors, and substantial grants from foundations. Its budget of $13 million in 1995, for example, topped the combined budget of all the Protestant church offices in Washington, financially strapped and understaffed as they are. But CDF's political intensity also derives from its relatively tight focus on children's issues, backed by a well-defined political constituency and strategy yet presented in terms of a broad, explicitly moral appeal.

Many mainline-church leaders appreciate both the unique strengths of the Children's Defense Fund and its usually complementary relationship to the churches. Reports Lintner, "CDF complements what we do, by and large. It also owes a lot to the church. If you listen to Marian [Edelman], you hear the daughter of a black Baptist preacher talking about being mentors and protectors to children, just like the elders and parents in her father's church."[54] In forms that recall the century-old roots of Progressive, feminist, and other political movements in the voluntary societies and "benevolent empire" of nineteenth-century evangelical Protestantism, contemporary public-interest advocacy groups and lobbies outside the churches borrow religious images and echo religious ideals. They do so in the very process of originating moral themes and visions of their own, for example, of the natural environment as an organic, spiritual whole.[55] CDF took the lead outside the churches in redefining the Great Society's more legalistic social rights and welfare-state entitlements as prayerful appeals to shared moral responsibility and compassionate concern for children in need of our help. Thus CDF offers up the English prayer that serves as its logo: "Dear Lord, be good to me. The sea is so wide and my boat is so small," colorfully crayoned in the hand of a five-year-old above her drawing of a tiny boat and child barely balanced in a boiling sea.[56]

But relations among the churches and parachurch groups such as CDF also include disagreement and give-and-take on specific policy positions. So indicates Jay Lintner, who differed with CDF's stands on whether to provide funds to upgrade church facilities in child-care legislation, and how best to design the bill for church-based, publicly funded day-care centers to avoid violating church-state separation:

> We campaigned to keep construction and rehab money for poor churches in the child-care legislation, because we knew a lot of inner-city churches would need it to fix their substandard facilities, or they wouldn't be able to get the child-care funding at all. CDF agreed that all facilities had to meet the same standards for good-quality care, but they didn't back us against the opposition, who refused to allocate public funds to rehabilitate church buildings on the grounds of church-state separation.
>
> We had to negotiate that on our own. We got it in, but not with any help from CDF. In fact, we had to fight with them on their insisting on high standards but not being willing to help the churches that needed it most to meet those standards. That wasn't a priority for them.
>
> On the bill to support church-based day-care centers for working parents, CDF backed the Catholics against the mainline Protestants and our attempt to structure a day-care bill that would meet the needs of people and of churches but not violate church-state [separation] in the ways that the Catholics, in our judgment, were willing to violate it.
>
> Did CDF do their own analysis of church-state relations? No, they purposefully went with the Catholics on a political basis. The Catholics are bigger, and they simply said they were going with the Catholics on this. To have those kind of decisions made on the basis of power choices is very painful.[57]

Here one can find mainline Protestant views of church-state relations no more justifiable than Catholic views, and CDF decisions on day-care legislation no less principled. Yet one can still recognize that nonreligious advocacy groups may well find church-state questions less familiarly nuanced, less profoundly important, and much less relevant to settling details of day-care legislation, for example, than do either Protestant or Catholic churches. Such differences in moral understanding and cultural construal make a real impact. Combined with the resources of intellectual acumen, political connections, and economic backing that are brought to public debate by advocacy groups such as CDF or the Sierra Club, these deeper differences alter the meaning and flow of the moral conversations that the public churches join, not only the legislative results they achieve.

Underlying differences between CDF and the churches reach into the distinctive ways they link moral advocacy, social teaching, and political action. "Protecting and caring for our children is a worthy theme for the churches to stress," affirms Lintner. "We're committed to doing that. And it's more. It's a love that epitomizes our relationship to God and our neighbors." He pauses, then adds,

> But politically, right now I have to say for CDF it's more a way of packaging stuff like food stamps, WIC [Women, Infants, and Children nutrition program], school breakfasts. . . . I am comfortable leaving it up to them to do that. We can and do support all those pieces of legislation on the Hill. We also try to educate our church members about what it means to love our children as God loves us.
>
> But for us it's more educational than concrete politics. It doesn't transfer across so directly. We don't receive the foundation support that gets funneled into winning concrete political fights. I don't have one hundred staff people like CDF to produce fact sheets and go out and put on the pressure when it gets down to a real fight on a bill. But it's not just that, at least I hope it's not.[58]

From this denominational viewpoint, the churches may have fewer funds and staffers. But they have more freedom in not having to use their moral teaching strategically in order to raise funds directly or lobby legislation successfully. This allows the churches to teach more freely, and in some respects more truly, than can nonreligious public-interest lobbies and parachurch groups devoted to issue-specific lobbying and backed by their supporters for this strategic purpose.

In short, the churches need to steer clear of conventional insider-lobbying and political-pressure tactics in their public advocacy. "We almost have a responsibility—we do have a responsibility—to stay on the outside and see the whole picture, and push the whole picture," stresses Ruth Flower of the Friends Committee on National Legislation. "We're often told by Marian's folks and other single-issue, public-interest groups that we're asking for too much on too many issues. So we become politically incredible. We're never going to get what we ask for. None of those are things we don't know!" she laughs. "But this is the place we need to be," she concludes.

> It's a place somebody needs to be, and almost nobody is besides us, because everybody knows you can't build a membership organization on this kind of issue base. It doesn't even add up to a "something for everybody" base like you see candidates trying to put together in a campaign. It's almost the opposite. It's something of the truth that runs counter to almost everybody's interests for the sake of what's actually good for all of us. Somebody needs to be out there holding up a placard for that.
>
> Usually that leaves plenty of room for CDF to press through and get childhood immunization. Or Marian will make sure the new child-care bill has a certain sort of licensing procedure she likes that maybe nobody else does. In practice, it usually comes out to us standing on two sides of the same street on most issues. But CDF is working more for a defined client or program. We're working more for a position or a vision of the whole.[59]

Self-selected political constituencies define key issues and positions more narrowly for groups like CDF, by this account. The churches follow out faithful positions on a range of issues that may cut across the predictable allegiances of such constituencies, and may sometimes divide church members along such lines. This wide-ranging commitment to the common good can undercut the churches' effectiveness as political lobbies compared to their potential if they concentrated on fewer key items in behalf of constituencies like those attracted to issue-specific, membership-based advocacy groups.

By virtue of self-selection and recruitment based on issue-specific appeals, freestanding advocacy groups tend to be more unified and tightly bounded in their moral views than are religious communities, and thus more narrowly clustered in their social backgrounds by class, education, and political loyalty.[60] "People don't join the Episcopal Church, or the Quakers even, because they like our position on health care," jokes Ruth Flower, "and we don't get to choose the folks in our church on that basis."[61] That makes the churches act and look quite different in their public advocacy than issue-specific, member-based groups, religious or not. Even if they wanted to, the mainline churches could not focus their attention on just a few issues. Neither could they mobilize large segments of their membership on the full range of the issues they do cover.

Indeed, as one sympathetic critic of the mainline churches puts it, "Their problem is they want to be too much like God. They want to have everything on their mind. But you can't do that and function effectively. You have to pick a few things, do your homework, get organized, stay organized, and keep plugging away on those few things."[62] Avers Flower, "I don't think the problem is really lack of knowledge or homework. On most of the issues I work on, my church colleagues are pretty well versed. They are writing for a broad policy-based community, not a group of true believers who already agree with them."[63] But when a church is able to take a strong stand on a controversial key issue, its voice can be all the more noteworthy coming from a less politically predictable source within a more socially diverse and less self-interested body.

Among parachurch groups, on the other hand, denominational leaders in Washington often single out Bread for the World for praise. Founded in 1974, this "Christian citizens' movement" has grown into a "nationwide faith-based citizens' movement against hunger," with 58,000 members, including 3,000 churches. It mobilizes some 250,000 constituent letters to Congress each year.[64] Church leaders admire the careful constancy and breadth of Bread for the World's education about problems of hunger and poverty. They respect its long reach down into local congregations and communities to build up and cultivate networks of members, and its practicality in organizing its members by congressional district in support of its highly focused congressional lobbying. Bread for the World, notes Flower, "will choose just a few issues a year and sometimes construct a vehicle like a hunger fast or resolution to give people that exercise of writing to Congress and having something happen. And they will choose or construct something that will happen, so that people will have a successful experience. And they will keep doing that over and over again."[65]

By contrast, reports Flower, the Children's Defense Fund "has been working for years to do what Bread does best, which is to line up the churches as allies for their agenda. But I don't have the sense they know how to do it nearly as well," despite growing efforts by CDF to work with the National Council of Churches both nationally and regionally. But, Flower points out,

> you can't really do it from the top down, through the NCC. To get information out to churches like Bread does, you have to do it like they do. You have to work very, very locally, organizing and talking to people one by one, in small groups.

Everybody keeps looking for one point person in Washington hooked into all the denominations to press one button, and the next Sunday everyone is preaching their message from a million pulpits. That just doesn't exist, and it's probably a very healthy thing it doesn't. We don't have a single authority at the top of a single network for all the churches.

We have a lot of folks who talk to a lot of folks and can get the word around. But it has to be by personal contact, talking it out in congregations and maybe agreeing to come in and do something together.[66]

Denominational structures can make a big difference in terms of access and information distributed to congregations. But they face limits in leading pastors to mobilize their congregants to act in concert, especially on issues that divide them or appeal to only a committed few. That is particularly true when mainline denominations are strapped for funds and fighting to stem losses in membership. Interfaith or interdenominational groups that depend on denominational contributions, as the case of Interfaith Impact for Justice and Peace makes clear in the following chapter, have been hit hard by these denominational constraints. And they are adamant in turn about the need for the denominations to strengthen their social witness if the churches are to inspire their members and deepen their ranks, instead of muffling their witness for fear of offending the fainthearted.

Issues Advocacy and Spiritual Vision

Discussions of organizational structure and strategy among religious leaders in Washington commonly begin and end with the issues themselves. And rightly so. For in evaluating both the political efficacy of national religious advocacy and the persuasiveness of its moral authority, the nature of the issues it addresses is crucial for both the priorities the churches choose and how they cooperate in doing so. So argues David Saperstein, longtime director of the Religious Action Center of the Union of American Hebrew Congregations.[67]

The religious community is most influential in public policy when we speak out on an issue no one else is speaking out on, and no one speaks out against us, for example, on environmental justice.

Or it happens when all of us agree this is a consensus issue we have to put our resources behind. On domestic and world hunger, we did that in the mid-1970s, when George Chauncey and the Presbyterians took the lead and began the churches' Taskforce on World Hunger and U.S. Food Policy. We really had an impact on that issue.[68]

When we all got behind the human rights provisions of the foreign aid legislation that [Congressman] Tom Harkin introduced in the late 1970s, we were instrumental in getting that through. On nuclear disarmament, too, we made a big difference.

Recognition of the distinctively moral character of a given social issue, and the genuine moral authority of religious communities to speak to it, can be spurred by persuasive argument, careful ethical justification, and inspiring revelation. But it cannot simply be assumed or commanded, Saperstein points out. It can rarely be induced in politicians by appeals to interest, since they are so overwhelmed by issues crosscut by conflicting interests and politically powerful, moneyed constituencies contesting them.

On health-care reform, for example, the Clinton White House and key members of Congress were constantly asking themselves, "Where are we with the doctors, insurers, big business, small business, the economists?" recalls Saperstein. "If you can't do everything, you try to do what will get you in the most trouble if you don't do it, so it's easy to slough off the religious communities. They don't have the money to give to PACs, to the Democratic Party, to Senate campaigns. They don't have their people sitting on the Democratic National Committee." Compare the mainline churches in such respects to the environmentalists, for example, equipped as they are with political-action committees, deep pockets, and electoral leverage. "They're single-issue, so they always work better," says Saperstein, because they have members and backers who will vote and work for or against a candidate based solely on what the group says about her or him. "We don't have voters like that, except maybe on one or two issues"—for example, with more conservative Catholics on abortion, or the Jewish community on Israel. But that is the exception, not the rule, for the mainline churches.

Given such comparisons to single-issue, public-interest groups, should public churches refrain from political horse-trading and pressure politics based on voter mobilization? Saperstein replies, "I'm not sure it always behooves us to separate the politics of moral principle from the politics of the possible here and now. Some issues affect us directly, and we need to decide how best to help define laws on those issues and get them passed, like the Religious Freedom Restoration Act, religious exemptions from the lobby-disclosure act, and the gay-rights bill. Somebody has to make decisions about those things." If no one in the churches is willing to compromise and negotiate on those issues, warns Saperstein, then "the political players are going to decide them on their own or with somebody else, and you end up being written off as a player in shaping your own fate. If you become a player and make compromises, then you can help shape your own fate." That is especially important on church-state questions, religious freedom, and related issues of faith, he points out, "since nobody else is as involved in them as we are. Then you have a vacuum and a real problem," if religious groups don't join the political fray on this front. "If religious groups want all or nothing, then fine, stick to your all, and you'll get nothing," Saperstein cautions. Or more purely political players will engage in horse-trading anyway, with less grasp of what is at stake morally and more inclination to make trade-offs simply in terms of interests, at the risk of "trading away the baby as if it were just more bathwater."

What of the churches as "players" on issues that do not directly concern religion but possess clearly moral dimensions? "Take the Violence against Women Act, and the question of what sort of civil rights ought to be in it," suggests Saperstein.

> We know in principle what we want. But if everything we want will come only at the expense of the bill failing to pass, what do we do? Let the bill go down by fighting those who want to compromise to get it passed?
>
> If you have the courage of your pure convictions and fight the compromisers, then you wind up implicated politically. You're a player then, too. The only other option you have is to set out the moral principles, then withdraw and sit out the political fray.

But moral principles and political negotiations over the specific provisions of legislation are often tied up with each other. On a technically complex issue such as health care, for example, the churches "can stand outside the mechanistic component of the debate about the most efficient, economical delivery systems," proposes Saperstein, "and say, 'These are the moral principles of inclusion and fairness it ought to have.' But we should be at the table where compromises are made and strategies are worked out when it comes to judging whether whatever system we get fulfills the moral minimum. We should do our best to see that doesn't get sold out."

Thus there is a place for these denominations to act as communities of moral witness, at times standing in sect-like fashion "against the world" of mundane politics. There is also a more church-like place for them to engage government in ongoing conversation and wrestle through its hard choices. The churches must argue these choices out together with the state's officials and elected representatives, with the public at large, and with the smaller publics, political parties, lobbies, and public-interest groups that crowd the American polity today. Indeed, what distinguishes the public church in its advocacy from other kinds of lobbying in the public interest transcends the dichotomy of "witnessing versus winning," however true it may be at times and however partial that truth later proves to be.

Even on Capitol Hill, affirms Gretchen Eick, "there's a kind of hunger for, How do we make sense out of this world and take care of it? When the religious community is at its best, it is able to meet that hunger in its lobbying like nobody else can. It can reach people when they're besieged by claims on their attention and loyalties, claims of different values and constituencies, when they're caught in the grip of their own interests and ways of seeing the world. It can create room for the Holy Spirit to move, and let people trust each other when they disagree politically."[69] The practical political consequences of such mutual moral transformation are not always predictable or evident, allows Eick, yet their larger value is unarguable.

However self-evident or problematic it may seem to consider how the churches should enter the public square and conduct themselves there faithfully and ethically, it is no less true that the political sphere enters into the churches in turn. It influences their ways of thinking and communicating, not only their ways of organizing and functioning. The following chapter shows how Interfaith Impact for Justice and Peace embodied the churches' highest moral ideals, and wrestled with their deepest political difficulties, in its pioneering efforts to unite the mainline Protestant denominations in moral advocacy in Washington and in grassroots community organizing across the nation on a full range of issues at the center of American public life.

CHAPTER EIGHT

The Challenge of Ecumenical Advocacy

Interfaith Impact for Justice and Peace

In 1990, Interfaith Impact for Justice and Peace represented the primary ecumenical public-policy coordinator and advocacy organization for thirty-six national religious agencies in the United States, including all of the mainline Protestant churches. It numbered local and regional affiliates in twenty-three states, and some ten thousand individual and congregational members on its rolls. Five years later, Interfaith Impact existed only in name. Its offices were closed and its staff dispersed. In its name, staff members of denominational offices in Washington continued to organize an annual national briefing on public issues for church leaders and activists. Members of the Interfaith board of directors and their denominations were raising funds to pay off Interfaith's remaining debts of more than $100,000, and were preparing to defend themselves against a million-dollar lawsuit for wrongful termination brought by Interfaith's former director. What happened?

The rise and fall of Interfaith Impact for Justice and Peace from 1975 to 1995 offers a telling example of the conflict between two models of the public church in mainline Protestantism within its wider institutional landscape in America today. One is a model of broad social teaching and focused policy research typically situated in and around the established offices of the mainline denominations. The other is a model of mass mobilization and political organizing, forged in the moral inspiration and outrage of sweeping social movements such as temperance and civil rights, but now often recast in freestanding, membership-based lobbying groups focused on hot-button issues.

For centuries, the Christian churches have been tugged back and forth between churchly ideals of conciliar dialogue and teaching on the one had, and the prophetic action of more sect-like witness communities on the other. But today the mainline churches and interdenominational bodies such as the National Council of Churches face new challenges and possibilities in a more diversified public square, crowded by a greater array of moral advocates, religious lobbies, and parachurch groups, along with realigned political parties and an expanded state. These conditions place an even higher premium on the churches' efforts to act as the Church in enlarging public conscience and casting clearer light on the commonweal. They offer the churches new partners in doing so. But they also increase the dangers in such ecumenical efforts of flattening out the theological and ethical integrity of particular churches into the moral Esperanto of "rights talk" and legal procedure. They threaten to plunge the churches deeper into the competitive play of political interests that are ideological as well as material.[1]

In response to their sense of a grave poverty crisis in American society unheeded by the Reagan administration in the early 1980s, mainline Protestant church leaders sponsored rapid expansion of the organization that became Interfaith Impact from a small research office on world hunger and U.S. food policy. It turned into a much broader cooperative forum and coordinating agency to support the full range of research, writing, testimony, and advocacy pursued by the mainline church offices in Washington. In this new role, the organization gradually grew more directive in selecting and stressing issues. It began shaping strategies across the churches for national publicity and activist organizing as well as Washington lobbying. It expanded its search for allies beyond the churches, among labor unions, public-interest advocates, and community-organizing groups. Strains widened between the original model of an interdenominational "community of religious communities" and a more aggressive, issue-driven, and freestanding membership organization dedicated to grassroots organizing and directly mobilizing constituents to back moral advocacy with political action. By 1991, these institutional strains came to a head. In their wake emerged a consolidated, more carefully cooperative interdenominational group, which struggled to renew itself during the Clinton years as it wound down to the end of its funding and active operations in 1995.

Denominational church offices, interdenominational groups such as Interfaith Impact and the National Council of Churches, and freestanding parachurch groups such as the Institute on Religion and Democracy are all, in fact, situated within a complicated network of relations with non-religious advocacy groups, political-action committees, and lobbies. They are tied in turn to activist elements in the major political parties and to organized labor, business interests, congressional offices, and the executive branch of government. The reciprocal exercise of political influence, quid pro quo exchanges on legislative support and mobilization, and access to funding run through these relationships. These developments pose even deeper moral and institutional challenges for the churches than they do for a polity beset by special interests and awash in soft money. They bear further inquiry, lit by the recognition that they are certainly not restricted to the religious right, however notable may be its recent prominence as a voting bloc and power broker in the Republican Party, underscored by the counterpunching launched against it by the Interfaith Alliance of mainline Protestants, Catholics, and Jews, traced in chapter 10. Such relationships also linked mainline-church offices, the Children's Defense Fund, and the Democratic National Committee during the Clinton administration, for example, charging discussion among NCC and church leaders over their unreconciled roles in the 1990s endgame of the legislative struggle for health-care reform, traced later in this chapter.

Genesis: To Feed the Hungry, to Engage the State

The origins and evolution of Interfaith Impact for Justice and Peace reveal in practical detail larger patterns of continuity and change in the institutional landscape and moral climate of American cultural politics since the 1960s. It is a story of morally urgent issues emerging, expanding, and shifting. It is a tale of denominations and their Washington offices growing and shrinking, pulling together and sometimes apart, enjoying access and coping with closed doors on Capitol Hill and Pennsylvania Avenue. It shows them making new allies outside the churches, and finding new adversaries in their own pews and offices.

The organizational taproot of Interfaith Impact begins at two points. On one side, it was inspired by the moral example of the civil rights movement and the urgency of faithful public responses to the crises of 1968 that linked race, poverty, and Vietnam. These crises were inflamed by the murder of Martin Luther King, Jr., and driven home by ensuing riots across the nation, including those that burned to within a few miles of Capitol Hill. The Washington Interreligious Staff Council (WISC) and its IMPACT network for political education and mobilization across the mainline Protestant churches began in 1968 "after the devastating death of the Rev. Martin Luther King," writes one of its founders, Mary Cooper of the NCC. "Religious advocates in Washington met, struggling with recent events, and tried to find better ways to work together. Out of that vision, IMPACT was specifically begun so that the religious agencies working in WISC could have a constituency education and action network through which to mobilize voter pressure on members of Congress."[2] Although it originally targeted only one hundred congressional districts, focusing on the appropriations process, IMPACT quickly expanded to all 435 districts in its growing efforts to end the Vietnam War and bolster funding for antipoverty programs.

On the other side of its mixed parentage, Interfaith Impact began in 1974 with a single issue, "the world food crisis."[3] Yet the complex character and global reach of that issue sprang from a network of institutional roots widespread through governments and nongovernmental organizations as well as the churches themselves. American media gave increasing attention to hunger and famine in third-world countries during the early 1970s, as the United Nations announced several years in advance the 1974 World Food Conference, which it convened in Rome in November of that year. This was the first such conference officially sponsored by the UN and attended by government delegations, 134 of which took part. The prospect of this "hunger summit" spurred wide discussion, planning, and organizational efforts within and beyond the mainline churches, much like those spurred by the ecological "Earth Summit" in Rio de Janeiro two decades later.

In 1973 nongovernmental organizations, including churches, formed an ad hoc committee, the World Hunger Action Coalition, to press for active U.S. government participation in the Rome conference to forge needed changes in U.S. food policy. Mainline religious groups in particular began to rethink their ethic of concern for world hunger and famine in more political-economic terms, defining it less as a call to charitable relief and more as a cause for international development and global justice. They concluded that "we are at a critical point in the historical process, in which God is at work, and which places before us the possibility of a global community in which the eternal values of the kingdom can find worldwide expression. . . . Our task as religious communities is to join hands with people everywhere—especially with the poor, the powerless, and the oppressed—in common struggle for the liberation of all."[4]

These trends took hold of existing "hunger ministries" and projects in the National Council of Churches, the World Council of Churches, and national denominations such as the Presbyterian Church (USA), whose hunger program was headed by Rev. George Chauncey. In July 1974, Chauncey called together his peers in other denominational offices in Washington to found the Washington Interreligious Staff Council Taskforce on World Hunger.[5] This was the forerunner of the Interreligious Taskforce on U.S. Food Policy, begun in 1975. It broadened its social scope and moral diagnosis to evolve into Interfaith Action for Economic Justice in 1982, and eventually into Interfaith Impact for Justice and Peace in 1991.

Stimulated by a new taste of joint advocacy and convinced that issues of hunger and food would spearhead a broad-based movement for global justice, denominational agencies engaged in backing the UN World Food Conference through the WISC Taskforce and the World Hunger Action Coalition soon began to plan for a permanent interreligious coalition to press for economic justice. In April 1975, twenty-six staff members of national religious agencies and church offices in Washington launched the Interreligious Taskforce on U.S. Food Policy, led by George Chauncey and backed chiefly by Presbyterian funding. "They thought of themselves as a new model of religious cooperation," observes Martin McLaughlin, a longtime member of the Taskforce, "neither a governing board nor an advocacy group, but a working team, which depended not on other staff, but on each other to do the work of the Taskforce."[6]

The Taskforce was not simply a coalition of existing denominations and related religious groups. Nor was it to become a membership organization for individuals, like Bread for the World, which Arthur Simon had founded a year earlier as a "Christian citizens' movement." Instead, the Taskforce's membership was made up of national religious organizations. Conceived as "a community of religious communities," the Taskforce depended chiefly on its denominational members for funding and on their paid staff members for its own workforce of volunteers. With the approval of their denominational office directors, these volunteers pledged to work together and in their own organizations for a responsible U.S. food policy by monitoring, reporting, and writing on assigned areas of its agenda. Each also pledged, "when and if he or she deems wise, [to] call upon his or her constituency to support the policies advocated by the Taskforce" and to help secure funding for it.[7]

The Taskforce grew quickly for three reasons, explains Jay Lintner of the United Church of Christ (UCC), a veteran church leader in Washington.

"First, hunger was a hot issue in the mid-seventies, and the churches were looking for a hot issue then," since civil rights had become law and their defense had turned to the courts. The War on Poverty had halted in the face of stagflation, and the peace movement had slowed since Nixon's pledge of "peace with honor" in Vietnam. Second, "there was money to fund the hunger issue. The denominations poured a lot of money into world hunger then, when there wasn't a lot to go around for most things." Third, there was "an open field for new interdenominational groups dealing with the new approach to hunger, because the churches and the NCC didn't already have competing agencies and offices on the ground there," with their own budgets and experts in place.[8]

The mainline Protestant churches had long maintained agencies for famine relief and charity in response to world hunger. But they had no such agencies to respond to economic injustice by tackling the political economy of hunger and the international economic order of trade and debt. To attack world hunger, church leaders now recognized, Americans must ask what should be done about U.S. foreign aid and trade, farm policy, agribusiness, and agricultural research. Because these questions appeared to be at once pressing and complicated, the idea of the Taskforce appealed to denominational leaders in order to do the homework and provide the expertise they needed to work out policy positions, testify before Congress, and help educate church members about the etiology of hunger. Nonetheless, it was an unprecedented step to form an interdenominational organization to engage in direct advocacy on such specific issues, and authorize it to speak in its own name rather than the names of its member denominations. The national office of IMPACT (known as National IMPACT), by contrast, was incorporated to serve the religious advocacy offices in Washington by producing background papers on major political issues, publishing a related newsletter, and mailing "alerts" urging its members to constituent action on key legislative decisions before Congress. But it could not speak in its own name to Congress or the public, take independent positions on policy, or develop its own legislative strategies.

From its beginnings, then, this new undertaking in direct advocacy was a "convulsive experience for the interfaith community," observed Martin McLaughlin, freighted with second thoughts on the part of many of its founders and backers. They remained concerned and unsure about its effects on the authority and integrity of the denominations, and on their less binding collegial, cooperative relationships within the Washington

Interreligious Staff Council and its national IMPACT network for education and voter mobilization.[9] "These questions continued to influence the Taskforce's activity throughout its sixteen years," noted McLaughlin in 1990, "and still swirl through the community, as the two-year effort to combine IMPACT and Interfaith Action attests."[10]

The Taskforce originally aimed to "work together to facilitate the witness of the American religious community for a responsible U.S. food policy," by seeking, first, to "clarify moral issues." It would "monitor U.S. government options, decisions, and activities; provide information and recommendation to co-workers, constituents, and policymakers in the Congress and the executive branch; coordinate the witness of the religious community on these issues; and issue statements in its own name." It would seek consensus in all its decisions and "refrain from recommending any public policy to which any member objected on principle." But it would otherwise establish policy positions by majority vote. Only the Taskforce's chair or the chair's designee would be authorized to speak in its name. Its member churches and national religious agencies in turn authorized the Taskforce to name them as "cooperating bodies." This served both to enable the Taskforce to broaden its scope, and to protect its denominational members from "identification with policy positions that might prove contentious or especially difficult for one or more of them."[11] This institutional arrangement joined with the moral vision of hunger as a symptom of a deeper social disorder, shared by key leaders of the mainline churches in Washington, to set the course later advanced by Interfaith Action for Economic Justice through the 1980s and by Interfaith Impact for Justice and Peace in the 1990s.

World Hunger and American Poverty

From its beginnings in 1975, the Interreligious Taskforce on U.S. Food Policy concentrated its analysis, advocacy, and education on U.S. food aid, economic aid, and development assistance to other nations. But, as Taskforce chair George Chauncey told the House in his first congressional testimony, "practically every federal policy affects the production and distribution of food." Its production depends on fuel, fertilizer, energy, and environmental-protection policies. Because poverty underlies hunger, food policy includes "policies affecting income distribution, monetary and fiscal polices, taxation, welfare, aid and trade agreements." Because the federal budget is limited, however large, "the level of military spending dramatically affects the availability of funds for global and domestic food assistance."[12]

The Taskforce espoused a holism that was moral as well as analytical. The religious community would witness for a responsible U.S. food policy, Chauncey promised the House, in the conviction that the world food crisis raised the question of justice, not simply charity, for America as a nation. Its challenge was "whether we shall respond to the claim of justice itself." For "there is something fundamentally unjust in the present distribution of the world's scarce resources." Indeed, he said, "equitable distribution, that is, fairly balancing and reconciling competing claims, is what justice, in its most elementary form, is all about. . . . People, as the World Food Conference declared, have a basic human right to eat. When people have a basic human right, and when we have the capacity to respond to that right," testified Chauncey, "we have a moral duty as an act of justice to do so."[13]

The new Taskforce quickly gained a reputation in congressional offices for "doing solid homework and presenting cogently, but not confrontationally, a well researched moral viewpoint on the issues," reported a well-placed observer.[14] First among those issues were international food aid and development assistance. These should be given directly to serve the human needs of hungry people, urged the Taskforce, not in government-to-government programs designed to serve U.S. strategic objectives in the Cold War, U.S. foreign policy aims, or the balance sheets of commerce and agribusiness.[15] The Taskforce also advocated building domestic grain reserves to back food aid through times of tight U.S. supply, and efforts to protect family farming in the United States. By 1978, it was also working on food stamp regulations in the United States, welfare reform legislation, and the implications of the federal budget for hungry people.

Two key conditions sparked the growth of the Taskforce during its first years. First, denominational funding proved robust. It began at $52,000 in 1975 and quadrupled by 1979, fed by "special offerings" most churches authorized for hunger, unlike many other good causes. Second, the political context changed. The Ford administration was sympathetic but not notably responsive to calls for greater global food aid. From 1977 on, however, the Carter administration responded boldly, and it courted the Taskforce. Leaders of the Taskforce took part in White House sessions on domestic food policy, and they worked closely with Carter's secretary of agriculture, Bob Bergland, and Nutrition Office director, Robert Greenstein.

They helped organize religious leaders to meet with Carter and lobby the House just before it voted to increase foreign aid, as the president had requested, and they received media credit for much of this success. Meanwhile, as rising domestic poverty in the late 1970s highlighted hunger issues, public advocacy groups, religious and nonreligious alike, expanded in numbers and strength. This offered the Taskforce greater possibilities for partnership in its efforts to engage these issues. For example, Robert Greenstein went from directing the Nutrition Office in the Carter administration to heading the Center on Budget and Policy Priorities, which became a crucial Taskforce ally in the 1980s.[16]

Near the end of its first five years, the Taskforce commissioned a study of its goals and achievements. Then the Presbyterian Church commissioned the Taskforce vice-chair, Paul Kittlaus, to evaluate joint efforts by the Washington offices of the mainline Protestant churches. Taken together, these reports describe a striking expansion of issues and activities beyond the Taskforce's original agenda, albeit in keeping with its overarching moral vision from the outset. They also marked a new nexus for the work of the churches in Washington that was at odds with the small-government outlook of the new administration of President Reagan. In its ten-point "Food Policy Agenda for 1980" and the decade to follow, the Taskforce urged reforming the International Monetary Fund to honor the "basic human needs" of debtor nations in IMF borrowing agreements. It pledged to shift U.S. bilateral aid to developing nations to speed their social-economic progress in feeding and providing for their peoples. The Taskforce backed the goal of strengthening reclamation laws to protect small farmers in the United States, and it helped to shape the Farm Act of 1981 accordingly. It advocated funding the food stamp program adequately in the face of rising costs, greater numbers of needy recipients, and sharper competition for the resources of the Agriculture Department. It supported congressional resolutions for the Agriculture Department to set up local programs to monitor nutrition nationwide and plan operational remedies to domestic hunger problems. It pledged the churches to protecting child-nutrition programs from Reagan administration budget cuts and defending the priority of "human needs" from contrary economic and strategic priorities in budgeting across the board.[17]

Over the 1980s, this daunting agenda would become a "litany of nonachievement," as one Taskforce member put it, in light of the federal government's going on to spend more on defense and less on social welfare in the Reagan years, heat up the Cold War, cut taxes, and enact the

Gramm-Rudman-Hollings bill to tighten budget competition in favor of those constituencies with the greatest political leverage. Yet in this very light, the Taskforce's expanded agenda was seen by its members "less as cause for despair than as the rationale for renewed determination to continue, and indeed, increase the effort."[18] The sweeping range of its national and global goals across the full reach of American government, coupled with its opposition to Reaganite policy priorities and parallel currents of public opinion, served to energize and enlarge the Taskforce rather than stymie it. Its change of name to Interfaith Action for Economic Justice in 1982 reflected decisions by mainline-church leaders in Washington to add domestic welfare and health programs to the Taskforce agenda. This change built on their shared experience that other WISC task forces on issues of economic justice could gain by allying themselves with efforts on hunger. They could benefit from the Taskforce's unique ability to speak in its own name. Without having to seek and get the agreement of each of their supporting denominational organizations, they could speak more quickly and effectively, in one voice, on a wider range of policy issues, even if they could not speak on behalf of particular churches. Moreover, they could more readily collaborate with nondenominational and nonreligious advocacy groups on key issues where the churches themselves were not of one mind. The proliferation of single-issue groups beyond the churches offered additional supporters and resources on behalf of specific positions they shared with Interfaith Action in the cause of economic justice.

These changes accorded with conclusions drawn by the Taskforce vice-chair, Paul Kittlaus, in his 1981 evaluation of the mainline-church offices in Washington. These offices, he recommended, should collaborate more closely to develop expertise on selected issues to match that of the government itself. They should devise an ongoing strategy to gain national media access for their positions. They should work the halls of Congress more intensively, in tandem with grassroots organizing and direct mobilization of churchgoing constituents to influence their congressional representatives and senators in their home districts and states. In the 1980s, this four-pronged plan was carried out most dramatically in a campaign entitled "The Poor Have Suffered Enough." It was conducted in collaboration with the new Center on Budget and Policy Priorities and coupled with the Churches' Committee for Voter Registration and Education, begun in 1983 to increase voting among low-income Americans in particular.[19]

This plan embodied a conviction spreading among religious leaders in Washington that issues of social and economic justice, domestic and global, were profoundly interconnected and were being only superficially addressed by routine legislative processes. So the churches should seek first to "help frame the debate" in faithful terms of justice, peace, and mutual care. They should not keep trying first to improve this or that existing legislative statute and lobby for it in order to provide small solutions to problems of economic injustice. In this light, there appeared a shift of emphasis from "statutes" to "issues" in the advocacy that the mainline churches pursued with members of Congress and their committee staffs, officials of the executive branch, and international aid and financial institutions based in Washington.

At the same time, in light of the chokehold exerted on social spending and programs by budget cuts and priorities during the Reagan era, Interfaith Action began to focus on the budget as a moral document. Together with the Center on Budget and Policy Priorities, it published *End Results: The Impact of Federal Policies Since 1980 on Low-Income Americans* in 1984, and a 1986 follow-up, *Hard Choices: Federal Budget Priorities in the Gramm-Rudman-Hollings Era*. Both highlighted the dangers to social welfare and economic justice, particularly for the poor, posed by mandates from Reagan to end deficit spending without raising taxes, cutting defense spending, or touching statutory entitlements such as Social Security that were earmarked mainly for the middle class.[20]

In the later 1980s, Interfaith Action for Economic Justice pursued a widening range of projects that lived up to its new name—including projects on U.S. food policy, foreign aid, security assistance, and third-world debt—in closer cooperation with similar religious or moral advocacy organizations overseas, along with U.S. analysts and activists outside the religious community. Together they founded the Debt Crisis Network, for example, to educate Americans in the pews on how a third-world debt total of $1.2 trillion fell most heavily on poor people who had nothing to say about accruing it and nothing to gain from austerity in repaying it. According to the network's *Putting People First*, "People of faith in the Jewish-Christian tradition are reminded that the covenant community was to resist the granting of special privilege in society to an elite group," including IMF bankers.[21]

Domestically, in 1986 Interfaith Action organized an ecumenical convocation to study and publicize the economic-justice documents and pastoral letters that mainline Protestant and Catholic churches issued in the mid-1980s, as economic inequality and poverty deepened in the United States. In 1987 it joined the National Council of Churches to sponsor a conference on welfare reform, and it undertook its own study of work and joblessness to map new directions for employment policy. Interfaith Action joined with state-level religious agencies, minority farm organizations, and the NCC to support legislative action to protect farm families, including minority farmers facing land loss. This effort began with the 1987 Agriculture Credit Act, aimed at saving the debt-burdened banks of the farm credit system. Experience gained in this legislative effort informed similar strategies adopted by the Financial Democracy Campaign and other nonreligious advocacy groups to influence congressional debate over the savings-and-loan bailout. These alliances between Interfaith Action and legislative advocates beyond the churches continued into the 1990 Farm Bill debate and culminated in the passage of key provisions of the Minority Farmers Rights Act.

In 1989–90, Interfaith Action actively supported the United Mine Workers of America (UMW) in their strike against the Pittston Coal Company after it cut off health-care and pension benefits promised to its workers. Answering a call for help to the national churches made by the Commission on Religion in Appalachia, Interfaith Action joined miners' marches, marshaled and released statements of support from three hundred religious leaders, and handled media coverage. It met with Labor Department officials, who eventually entered the dispute and helped settle it in early 1990. This marked the mainline churches' closest involvement with labor in decades. It led Interfaith Action to decide to add labor issues to its legislative agenda, including workers' rights and justice in the workplace.[22] This widening web of collaboration on such issues of economic justice arose from church leaders' long-standing conviction that these issues were religious as well as social. It arose, too, from growing recognition by nonreligious lobbies, not only organized labor, that these were moral matters on which the churches had something valuable to say and do.

Merging Two Models of the Public Church

In 1985, a decade after the organization began, the founder of Interfaith Action weighed its continuity and its changes. It remained, said George Chauncey, "an organization of the churches with work done by the churches," whose denominational staff members in Washington made up its volunteers. At the same time, its original twenty member agencies had nearly doubled. Scores of religious leaders met to conduct its business, hundreds of activists attended its public conferences, and its annual budget had multiplied sixfold, to $320,000. "Over the years," Chauncey observed, "the organization has become more institutionalized. We incorporated ourselves, our steering committee became a board of directors, and our advisory committee became our priority-establishing and budget-approving membership."[23] As the agenda, activities, and budget of Interfaith Action for Economic Justice grew in tandem, it hired more than a dozen staff members of its own and gradually enlarged the operational role of its executive director. By 1985, the first generation of Interfaith Action's leaders had departed. A new generation began its second decade, led by the Rev. Arthur B. Keys, Jr., of the United Church of Christ.[24] A resilient veteran of social-witness work in the churches, Keys championed a proactive outlook bred by his involvement in church-based community organizing and the labor movement, beginning with the United Mine Workers in his youth in western Pennsylvania and extending to the Churches' Committee for Voter Registration and Education. The committee helped register a half million new voters between 1983 and 1990, mostly from low-income and minority areas. It spawned local projects of education and public advocacy on issues such as public housing, welfare, and jobs. It also offered an activist example of cooperative mobilization between national religious advocates, local churches and ecumenical groups, and some of the nation's neediest citizens, especially among people of color and the urban poor. That example would come to the fore and prove controversial in subsequent discussions of how to reorganize ecumenical advocacy with greater grassroots support without recruiting "local cadres" as members of an activist organization distinct from the churches themselves.[25]

As Interfaith Action extended its reach and consolidated its growth from 1985 onward, the question of its relationship to National IMPACT called for clarification from the leaders of both organizations and the church offices in Washington. Two meetings for this purpose made little headway in 1986, and the question was tabled. But it did not go away. For one thing, it stemmed from Interfaith Action's growing concern to back its advocacy on issues with direct mobilization of religious groups and activists in the pews to influence government officials and members of Congress in Washington and in their districts. This put a premium on the functions of nationwide communication and education that IMPACT had long represented. Indeed, IMPACT sought to strengthen these functions in its own right during the late 1980s.[26]

Furthermore, overlapping work on issues and committee memberships multiplied meetings and assignments across the two organizations for many staff members of the church offices in Washington. Constituency groups outside Washington, especially ecumenical organizations involved in public-policy advocacy at the state, regional, and local levels, pushed for a more unified ecumenical advocacy organization on Capitol Hill to better coordinate their own work.[27] Finally, during the 1980s, declining contributions to the mainline Protestant denominations that funded both Interfaith Action and IMPACT put pressure on them to cooperate more efficiently in carrying out their overlapping functions. That message came through most clearly from the Presbyterians, who had long been the largest single financial contributor to Interfaith Action through the Presbyterian Hunger Program. These conditions converged by 1990 to create a mandate in the mainline churches for the two organizations to merge.[28]

Representatives of the boards of Interfaith Action for Economic Justice and National IMPACT met in late 1989 to weigh the feasibility of a merger. In the spring of 1990, a plenary meeting of more than sixty members of the two boards, joined by others in the religious advocacy community, adopted a mission statement to create a new organization by means of a merger. It declared,

> INTERFAITH IMPACT for Justice and Peace is an inter-religious organization of member denominations and faith groups, state Interfaith IMPACTs, local and regional affiliates, and people of faith which, responding to God's call, seeks to advance the cause of justice, peace and stewardship of creation in the public policy arena. It facilitates, advocates, and advances the public policy perspectives of its member religious groups and works in partnership with poor people, disenfranchised people, and all who are involved in the struggle for justice, peace and stewardship of creation.[29]

A new board of directors for Interfaith Impact met for the first time at the end of 1990. Its composition marked a key change from the governing structure of Interfaith Action for Economic Justice, with the merged organization adopting IMPACT's model of multiple forms of membership. Interfaith Impact pledged to become "a membership organization with individual and congregational memberships along with local, state, regional and national organizational memberships."[30] The board included representatives of national religious organizations and their local affiliates, along with congregations and community-based advocacy organizations such as the Peoria Citizens Committee for Economic Opportunity.

It included the state-level units of IMPACT and their regional affiliates such as ecumenical councils, and regional advocacy and social-justice organizations such as the Southwest Voter Registration/Education Project. It also included at-large members, notably Richard Trumka, who was then president of the United Mine Workers of America.

These changes in governing structure reflected the view held by many within the national religious advocacy community in Washington that its work there required the direct involvement of those people and community groups at the grass roots most affected by the national issues and policies under debate in Congress. To those who backed these changes, faced with the prospect of less funding from the mainline denominations, enlarging Interfaith Impact's board and membership also raised the possibility—however difficult it would prove to realize—of gaining support from new sources: nonreligious community groups, advocacy groups, and public-interest associations; foundations and unions; and congregations and individuals contributing outside denominational channels.

To those critical or unsure of such innovations, they threatened to weaken the capacity of Interfaith Action for Economic Justice to speak clearly and decisively in its own name, even if it could not speak in the name of its member denominations. Critics charged that such change risked, on the one hand, overstretching the collegial conversation of like-minded churches, synagogues, and religious agencies in order to take in more diverse groups beyond the religious community. On the other hand, it also threatened to narrow that conversation too strategically, in order to focus on fewer key issues at the intersection of a larger, less culturally coherent circle of political advocates with diverse moral visions and social interests. It risked making Interfaith's organization by turns too large and unwieldy, and shifting its center of gravity from the interconnected church offices in Washington to a larger coalition of advocacy groups. That enlarged coalition would likely be held together less by the web of their mutual linkage than by Interfaith's own executive leadership, connecting them like spokes from a hub by taking up their issues and advancing their causes.

A Membership Organization for National Advocacy and Grassroots Organizing

In behalf of the merger between Interfaith Action for Economic Justice and IMPACT, Interfaith Action's executive director since 1985, Arthur Keys, argued boldly for enlarging the membership and refocusing the direction of the new organization along lines already charted under his leadership of its predecessor, Interfaith Action. The purpose of a merger was "not primarily to build a stronger organization that served the national religious organizations," Keys stressed, but rather to "preach Good News to the Poor and work to improve the common good."[31] As such, the new organization followed on the basic commitment of Interfaith Action to articulate its vision of economic justice in more "candid and forthright" fashion than before and pursue its advocacy more directly to follow the biblical lead of the prophet Isaiah, that "people should build houses and live in them, plant vineyards and eat their fruit; they shall not build and another inhabit, they shall not plant and another eat."[32]

Through this merger, Interfaith Action could strengthen its grassroots network of advocates and activists to back its lobbying on Capitol Hill, Keys promised, and it could "broaden its funding base with individual congregational members and donors."[33] IMPACT, on the other hand, could extend its reach directly into lobbying on Capitol Hill and could gain stronger organizational and financial support among national religious agencies, particularly the national mission boards of the mainline Protestant churches.

More broadly, Keys foresaw the potential for a unified interfaith advocacy organization based in Washington to become a new nexus of cooperation and coordination among U.S. Protestant denominations and other religious bodies. Given the relocation of several Protestant denominational headquarters out of New York City, especially those of the United Church of Christ and the Presbyterian Church, thought Keys, "New York, and specifically the National Council of Churches, would no longer be the central place for interdenominational or interfaith cooperative work as it had been for decades. As a result, Washington became a more likely place for national and international religious meetings," such as those Interfaith had already held with third-world church groups through the World Council of Churches' Commission on the Churches' Participation in Development. "Washington became the primary place where persons worked together on a daily basis across confessional lines" within American Protestantism and beyond it, believed Keys, and Interfaith Impact should develop to better coordinate such work.[34]

Keys sought to structure a merger to resolve larger problems of focus, funding, and organization that he found besetting ecumenical advocacy during the late 1980s. In this period, under the pressure of declines in denominational membership and contributions, especially in "national mission giving" as opposed to offerings earmarked for local churches, dioceses, and districts, the mainline Protestant churches had struggled to hold the line of their financial support to Interfaith Action at roughly one-third of a million dollars annually. Their contributions made up some 94 percent of Interfaith Action's financial support in 1987–89, by Keys's analysis.[35] Meanwhile, the views of their church members showed relatively weak support for key issues on the agenda of Interfaith Action, such as increasing government spending to help the disadvantaged via programs such as food stamps. By contrast, its agenda enjoyed strong support from black Protestants and moderate support from Jews, the un-churched, and Roman Catholics. Interfaith Action's own surveys of local voter-registration groups, with whom it worked in mostly lower-income areas, showed strong support for its chief issues.

These findings showed the crucial need "to receive more support from Catholics, Jews, black Protestants, moderate Protestants, other religious people, and those of no religious affiliation who share our public policy goals," decided Keys. National ecumenical advocacy based in the liberal churches "needs to develop and evolve in a way that maintains the support of its friends even as it makes new friends." Keys pledged Interfaith Action to broaden its base of contributors in the liberal and moderate Protestant churches by better matching its program priorities to their social commitments—for example, to shelter the homeless and develop housing for them. New sources of funding should be sought among local church members, and "better ways [found] to obtain funds from local congregations, dioceses, and foundations where more and more of the mainline religious communities' mission monies reside—and from individuals." Interfaith Action should likewise "learn from poor people and others engaged in justice struggles." It should "forge closer links between our Capitol Hill advocacy and new voter registrants, low-income people on whose behalf we advocate, and our regional and local ecumenical partners."[36]

Accordingly, the boards of Interfaith Action and IMPACT voted in the fall of 1990 to develop "categories of membership and membership services which enable the broadest possible participation from individuals, congregations and religious organizations" in constituting Interfaith Impact. They vowed to "increase, substantially, the individual membership base by 1992"; and to cultivate "partnership relationships with people who are affected by the policies on which Interfaith Impact advocates."[37] These plans would strengthen Interfaith Impact to do the work of national religious advocacy, promised Keys, by freeing it to focus more aggressively on key issues and to join more readily with its closest issue-specific allies among nonreligious advocacy groups. Thus Interfaith Impact would develop its full potential as a no less ecumenical yet more freestanding, member-based advocacy group in its own right.[38]

A Community of Religious Communities

A countervailing view came from Jay Lintner, head of the UCC office in Washington and chair of a financial advisory committee to the Interfaith Impact board, which was charged with diagnosing the organization's need for new sources of financial support. Reflecting on the future of Interfaith Impact in mid-1991, after an interregnum marked by completion of the formal merger, delays in choosing a new executive director, and shortfalls in projected fund-raising, Lintner wondered "where Interfaith Impact went wrong." It was right to merge, he judged. It needed to resolve the competition between two overlapping organizations and the critical dysfunction of splitting the mainline churches' advocacy on Capitol Hill from their grassroots organizing in the field. But political pressures to merge, combined with institutional inertia in the face of the difficulty of the underlying problems involved, pushed church leaders in Washington to make "structural decisions without taking the time for real consensus on where we should be."[39] Hard decisions remained to be made by Interfaith Impact's board of directors, executive committee, and its incoming director, argued Lintner. They would have to begin by recognizing that Interfaith Impact not only had failed to raise new money in the new ways its planners projected, it had also failed to raise as much money in old ways.

Contributions to Interfaith Impact in 1991 from denominational offices and agencies equaled levels projected from 1990 funding. But membership fees from nondenominational national groups fell 30 percent below projections. Designated grants from foundations and denominations aimed at special projects such as voter registration collapsed by 70 percent. Caught in the throes of reorganization and staff turnover, Interfaith Impact sought to raise money in a number of new ways: from individual members, individual contributors, local congregations, local affiliates, and foundations, and via special events for individual and organizational contributors. By trying to raise funds in all these new ways at once, it failed to develop the organizational focus needed to carry out any one such strategy. "We sent mixed signals to our constituencies," observed Lintner, "so that they did not know whether they should try to get individuals to join or contribute, or try to promote congregational giving, affiliate memberships, or contribute to a special event, etcetera. The message we are sending out is fuzzy," he judged. "Are we an organization of denominations? Members? Contributors? Congregations? Affiliates? We have no focus." Interfaith Impact's lack of organizational focus, in this view, resulted in a lack of fund-raising focus and success.

Interfaith Impact lacked members as well as funds. IMPACT had been established in 1968 as a network to educate constituents in the churches on public issues and move them to act on key issues, in particular to mobilize voter pressure on members of Congress. As such, IMPACT was an organization composed chiefly of individuals, albeit of individuals largely affiliated with specific denominations and congregations. They numbered some 15,000 by 1980. But their numbers began slipping soon thereafter, to 10,000 after membership in state-level IMPACT affiliates was uncoupled from National IMPACT membership in 1985. They fell to 6,800 in early 1991 as renewal and recruiting efforts flagged, and to 2,200 a few months later, when rolls were scrubbed of those with fees unpaid for the past year. Whatever the reasons, judged Lintner, "the fact itself is overwhelming, and must lead to this conclusion: IMPACT is not working as a membership organization." Indeed, to work effectively, a nationwide education and mobilization network would require far more than 15,000 members, many Washington church leaders agreed. So, asked Lintner, "why not emphasize what Interfaith Impact really is: an organization of organizations, instead of continuing to confuse people into thinking it is an individual membership organization?"

This organizational ambiguity reached beyond the matter of membership to Interfaith Impact's staffing and operations, Lintner suggested in weighing the question of what went wrong: "Did Interfaith Impact move too far away from a coalitional style toward an organizational style that operated independent of the denominations, causing the loss of support of the DC denominational offices? Were hard choices ever made as to whether Interfaith Impact staff should have issues expertise and serve as Capitol Hill lobbyists, or instead be facilitators and field organizers?"

From this diagnosis followed a strong prescription of what should be done by Interfaith Impact as an organization of predominantly denominational organizations. It needs to "facilitate and organize the religious community, on the Hill, in the field, and in the media, for effective public

policy advocacy around peace-and-justice issues," urged Lintner. It needs
to "organize itself around the strengths and needs of its member denomina-
tional/faith groups. It should see itself enabling interfaith witness, not representing the interfaith community." Therefore, Interfaith Impact should
concentrate on "how to build on the strengths of existing denominational/
faith group offices. Right now Interfaith Impact is existing too independent of the Washington church offices," Lintner charged. "Particularly at
the grass-roots level, we need to figure out the best way to interrelate what
ecumenical organizing is done with denominational organizing."

For example, instead of a single mailing list of members, Interfaith Impact should build three lists, advised Lintner. First would be a "donors"
list of 100,000–200,000 people who share its goals and want to help advance them financially. Second would be a list of "organizational leaders," key activists with mailing lists and organizations of their own in
local churches, religious agencies, and denominational units such as the
United Methodist Women's Division. Third would be a list of "contacts"
in key congressional districts, where field organizing should concentrate
by "building up the big numbers for phone banking and direct action-
alert mailings"—some 25–100 people in each of 100–200 congressional
districts. By this logic, Interfaith Impact should raise funds from "donors"
and keep concerned church members informed through activist religious
"leaders" nationwide. It should concentrate its efforts at voter mobilization on "contacts" in crucial congressional swing districts, typically conservative Democratic and liberal Republican districts, via rapid-response
networks running through the denominations and related religious organizations in these areas. Interfaith Impact should facilitate these mailings
and telephone calls, not do them directly. It should have field organizers
to carry out this work, and facilitators on Capitol Hill to support the issue
experts already at work in the denominational community, instead of trying to duplicate or direct these denominational efforts.[40]

Interfaith Impact: Beginning to End

The formal terms of merger between IMPACT and Interfaith Action for
Economic Justice were settled by late 1990, when a single board of directors was formed and met for the first time. A year later, the immediate
question of Interfaith Impact's future was decided when a search committee drawn from its board named a new executive director from outside the

organization and the Washington religious community. In doing so, they passed over the executive directors of both Interfaith Action for Economic Justice and IMPACT before their merger. "It was a referendum on the immediate past," observed a board member.

> We voted "no" to a more aggressive, autonomous version of Interfaith Action organizing around its own issues and mobilizing its own members directly. Exactly what we voted "yes" to wasn't as clear, at least to some of us, although it was more going back to the denominations, and this being a coalition and forum to support the churches in Washington. It was also a decision to begin again, more modestly, and gradually find our way to what Interfaith should be by taking it one step at a time and seeing what arose.[41]

"Give us about five years," suggested Jay Lintner in light of Interfaith Impact's slashed budget and lingering wounds from infighting over the terms of its merger and the direction of its future course. "Interfaith Impact will be weaker for a while. It needs to make some hard decisions in order to become stronger and less divided than it has been. There are still factions pro and con left over from struggling to sort things out during the merger. That didn't so much create conflicts as give freer play to long-standing conflicts among staff members in the denominational offices about how to do our work."[42]

Meanwhile, Interfaith Impact itself had been distracted from its own functioning and fund-raising, which were critical in a period when overall funding was down and the denominations were not about to make up the difference without real changes. The Presbyterian, Methodist, and UCC church offices put together a financial bailout package for one year to stem the financial crisis. "Now Interfaith has to put its house in order and live within its means. It has to get some work done and show that it can serve the community of the churches and earn its keep in the future," stressed Lintner in 1992. "What that future should be, I think, is a community of religious communities, the denominations and related national religious agencies, working together to make government more just and faithful."[43]

By late 1991, Interfaith Impact's new director was in place. The search committee settled on James Bell, an ecumenical activist and church leader seasoned by long experience in Midwestern metropolitan areas and national networks of the National Council of Churches but new to the capital and its religious community. He faced a formidable challenge in taking over an organization convulsed by the process of merger and caught between an oversold program and an underfunded budget. It had promised much to many constituencies yet counted fewer resources to deliver on its promises in an era of tightening denominational support, compounded by its own distraction from raising funds and recruiting members. With a winnowed staff and fiscal transfusions from key denominations, Interfaith Impact weathered its first year or so of existence at the end of the administration of George H. W. Bush.

A year later, Jim Bell looked back over the biggest lessons he had learned since coming to Washington as a local church leader who had worked in regional and state networks through the NCC:[44]

> The image I had of the denominations, the NCC, the National Association of Evangelicals through to the World Council of Churches, was one of groups working cooperatively. I think the hardest lesson I've had to learn, the biggest disappointment to me, is the extent of the turf battles we fight here in Washington at the national level. It's much more intense than I ever saw at the state or local levels.

> Q: Because the stakes are so high, or the pie is so small?

> That was the first shock to me, how small the national religious community actually is in numbers, compared to the image of it being a massive thing you have in the local church. But then when you come to work in it, all of a sudden it's a very small community. Many of the people in Washington and New York have been in it a long time. They have long histories, they have long memories. They have a lot of things that get in the way of pulling together sometimes, particularly when it looks like there is turf they have to protect or give up.

> Q: For example?

> In the last month or so, we got in four new national members of Interfaith Impact—the Commission on Racial Justice of the UCC, the Graymoore Ecumenical Institute, the Episcopal Mission Board, and the Metropolitan Community Church. One old member said to me, "You realize that by bringing in these folks who don't have Washington-based offices, who are not involved in day-to-day lobbying and advocacy here, the danger is you're going to water down our political voice, because we now have to consult with people who aren't in the community."

Well, that says to me we're not willing to reach out, we're not willing to empower anyone who's not an insider, unless that means adjusting them to the established interpretation of power and its purposes. That spells death to the gospel.

Asked to spell out some of the predicaments and conditions of partisan
or exclusionary power politics in national religious advocacy, Bell turned
to the ties he saw between funding, denominational support, and moral
controversy:

Every single mainline denomination is hurting financially, even if they are not
losing members. That hurts us all the more. Church giving is actually up among
better-off Protestants, but more of the money is staying local. It's going into
local churches, charities, relief and community programs. That affects us dras-
tically at the national level, of course. It cuts what's available overall, and it
increases competition for funding inside the denominations, where the denominational offices in Washington are not the big players dividing up the national
church budget.

So in many cases, like the Presbyterians and Methodists again this year, the
churches in Washington have been getting a smaller share of a smaller denominational pie. It makes the denominations, especially the denominational offices
closest to us, less willing to fund ecumenical or interfaith groups like us when
they feel like they don't have enough for themselves.

Instead of pooling more-limited resources to get the most out of them
across the mainline churches, said Bell, "what you hear everybody saying
is, 'Sorry, but we've really got to survive, so we'll have to cut down on our
working together.' That can be really frustrating."

Tighter denominational funding in the early 1990s coincided with higher
expectations by denominational churches of ecumenical groups like Interfaith Impact in the face of hard moral choices on politically controversial
and divisive social issues, according to Bell. "The more controversial the
issue politically, the more a particular denomination is going to pass that
ball to the ecumenicals and interfaith groups like ourselves to push, so they
can distance themselves from the repercussions in the pews" on issues such
as abortion and gay rights, the Gulf War, and workfare. Observed Bell,

On the one hand, you've got your friends being the ones who are wagging their
fingers in public, saying, "Don't go too far, too fast. Don't make the churches

too political." But then at the table with us they're saying, "We really need to take a stronger position on this issue and move it forward." At the same time, they tell us they're cutting their contributions to our budget, because they have a tighter budget. They have other priorities, or people in the pews are complaining about political activism.

Many denominational leaders in Washington disagreed. Particular denominations can and do take stronger stands on given issues, they testified—for example, on abortion, school vouchers, and gay rights—than do many ecumenical and interdenominational groups, including the National Council of Churches, which are hamstrung by the contrary and offsetting views of their various members.

The linkage of declining membership, church giving, and social activism in the mainline churches has been debated in academic and church circles alike since the mid-1960s.[45] Like many leaders of mainline-church offices in Washington, Bell is left dissatisfied by academic analyses that attribute declines or divisions in mainline-church membership to broad demographic downturns and cultural cleavages along generational and educational lines. More adamantly he rejected analyses, like those favored by the Institute on Religion and Democracy and Good News, that the liberal churches are themselves to blame for losing their own members' loyalty and generous financial support by engaging in left-wing social activism and political lobbying instead of preaching the gospel and saving souls. Bell reversed that view:

> We're suffering because the church has refused to be prophetic and stand up for justice strongly enough. Therefore people don't see any reason to continue support of an institution that is basically just bogged down in its own bureaucracy. If we stand up and claim our prophetic ground, the people we would lose are the very people that are already causing us to lose money and members, and to lose our way, really. They're the ones that want us to do nothing in terms of social action, social justice. They are controlling the churches with their pocketbooks right now. We have to decide whether we are going to let them go on doing that.

Such criticism echoed that of many denominational leaders committed to prophetic activism on peace-and-justice issues and scarred by budgetary struggles with more conservative church leaders, who grew better organized during the 1980s.

Bell defended charitable giving by local churches but noted, "This goes back to the problem that historically the church has taught charity rather than justice. So you can raise lots of money for food banks or night shelters. You can't raise lots of money to change a system of social injustice that causes the need for so many food banks and shelters." At some point, said Bell, the church has to bear responsibility for that kind of teaching, because "we have taught people to feel good in their giving to charity, but not to worry too much about social justice. That's why missions are easy to raise money for," he explained. "It's saving the souls of people who are out of sight and out of mind. But we can't ignore how we contribute to their suffering by the ways our society works that are not so just."

Interfaith Impact and the NCC: Activism and Ecumenism at Odds?

Sympathetic observers in the Washington religious community of the Protestant churches gave good grades to Interfaith Impact in the early 1990s, as it struggled to survive and reinvent itself after the difficulties of its merger. They credited it with resuming its publications, pruning its staff, and reducing its deficits. Most denominational leaders in Washington were generous, if careful, in commending changes Interfaith Impact had made by 1993 and 1994. "Interfaith Impact is trying to rebuild and get healthy after a difficult transition," noted Thom White Wolf Fassett, general secretary of the Methodist Board of Church and Society, in 1994. "Starting up, the new organization still had a lot of shaky parts. Now we're beyond that point. We've got some funding from the Mott Foundation. We've made a denominational commitment to contribute to the organization's health." But significantly enough, Fassett pointed out, Interfaith Impact's destiny rested not only in the hands of its leaders and denominational backers, but also in the evolving role of the National Council of Churches in mediating the churches' relationship to one another, the government, and the public: "In the longer run, a lot of what happens with Interfaith Impact is going to be determined by where the NCC decides to go and what in the world it's going to do relative to the mainline denominations."[46]

Another veteran church leader in Washington, Kay Dowhower of the Evangelical Lutheran Church in America, expanded on themes that linked Interfaith Impact to the NCC as well as the denominations:

Interfaith Impact is in an in-between time. They want to expand their base of members, very appropriately. That complicates life for them, too, because each of the different pieces of that base has its own priorities, just like our denominations do, and most of them are in the same challenging time of tight resources. So then what you have done in expanding membership is bring in more complexity. Maybe it makes you broader and stronger once you find the common thread that pulls it all together. Maybe it makes it harder to find that thread of consistency in selecting issues and taking faithful stands on them. I think it's both-and.[47]

In any case, Interfaith Impact decided not to continue trying to be "a corral of experts on issues," noted Dowhower, even if it did not simply commit itself to the interdenominational alternative of helping to fill in the gaps in the denominations' work of mobilization, education, and advocacy.

What remained to be resolved for Interfaith Impact to move beyond its in-between transition state? Replied Dowhower in 1994,

It comes back to what I think is the core structural question for Interfaith Impact: "Are we a collaborative effort on behalf of mainstream faith groups, or are we a collaborative effort on behalf of our individual members? Are we a counterpart to the Christian Coalition or any of the other individual member–based organizations?"

Then we have to make our decisions, select our issues, do our advocacy and recruiting in a far different way than we do in the churches. You really have to market your issues and make your fund-raising pitch directly to your members. Interfaith Impact has tried to do that a little bit, enough to prove to some of us that it's pretty darn hard to pull off!

I think we have our greatest moral force as a community of faith groups, with all the credibility and inhibiting accountability to the authority of our different kinds of church governance and creeds that that brings.

The other question we need to keep asking about Interfaith Impact now is, "How is it going to differ from the National Council of Churches?" Yes, it differs because it's "interfaith" by definition. But we need to work out their cooperation, or at least the boundaries between them, and not be competing, not have them gobbling up the same resources.

I don't think we have the ability to turn Interfaith Impact into a mainly membership-based organization. I don't think we should try. To put that sort of operation in place, you need somebody to give you an umpteen-hundred-thousand-dollar grant to do something they want done that nobody else is doing. There may be a need for that in the larger political arena, for instance, for someone to step up and respond to the Christian Coalition. The mainline churches just won't get down in the political gutter enough to fight them. And maybe that's the way it should be.

The question of how Interfaith Impact differed from the National Council of Churches grew more salient with the start of the Clinton administration and its dramatic efforts to engage the mainline churches as a unified ally through the NCC and the denominational offices in Washington.

How knotty this question turned out to be is underscored at points where denominational diagnoses of Interfaith Impact intersected with lines of criticism drawn from the perspective of the NCC itself. From this standpoint, Interfaith Impact lacked clarity in defining its stance and direction in relation to the mainline churches in Washington and to the NCC, according to Mary Cooper of the council's Washington office: "There has never been clarity about what's primary and secondary for the organization. The merger between IMPACT and Interfaith Action for Economic Justice was a big mistake. All it did was erode the base of both organizations. In effect, IMPACT died and only part of Interfaith Action survived, and the churches never got clear about what to do as a result."[48] By this account, what went by the board was IMPACT's key capacity to help the churches educate and mobilize their members across denominational lines, and Interfaith Action's distinctive expertise to analyze hunger issues and lobby on behalf of them. What remained were unfocused aims to select key issues across the board and then direct the churches in lobbying and mobilizing efforts to back these issues.

In the early 1980s, Interfaith Action for Economic Justice was working well, its latter-day critics largely agreed. It offered denominational leaders and staffers in Washington a locus for collegially structured joint working groups to criticize and counter the Reagan administration's agenda on poverty, joblessness, welfare, education, and defense spending. It concentrated its lobbying efforts on Capitol Hill and its mobilizing efforts in the pews. Carried over from its initial focus on world hunger and agricultural policy, Interfaith Action's own policy portfolio remained narrow, linked as it was to staff expertise in that one area. Interfaith Action began running into trouble later on and disrupting the community of Washington church offices, Cooper contends, when it started trying to steer their policy positions and strategies across a broader range of issues. It was selective enough in its priorities to put it at odds with denominational groups with priorities of their own. Its implicit claim to speak for its member churches on these issues brought it into competition with the NCC.

Given its use of paid denominational staffers as "volunteer" legislative analysts and lobbyists of its own, Interfaith Action's increasing drive and range in seeking to shape policy initiatives and coordinate their execution among the mainline-church offices in Washington led to organizational problems, too, especially in the allocation of staff resources and the attribution of credit for their work. Argues Cooper,

> The only reason that the denominations fund either Interfaith Impact or the National Council of Churches is that these organizations help the churches get their job done. When it turns out that what's happening is that the denominational staff people are being co-opted to do the job of another organization, a job the churches haven't clearly agreed needs to be done in the first place, then the interdenominational organization ceases to be useful to them and they draw back.[49]

At issue is not simply giving credit where it's due, Cooper explains, but acknowledging the significance of the churches' public identities.

> When people on the Hill and people in the White House want to know where the Protestants are on something, they don't call Interfaith Impact. They call us, because they know the National Council of Churches. We've got fifty years of name recognition on the Hill. A Presbyterian member of Congress will call the Presbyterian office, an Episcopalian will call that office. But a generic Protestant or a Protestant who wants to know where the mainline churches are across communions will call the NCC.

During the 1980s, Interfaith Action for Economic Justice sought to expand its portfolio of issues. It aimed to define priorities among issues more urgently for the mainline churches and to pursue these priorities more aggressively in organizing and mobilization efforts. In so doing, it found itself at odds with the mainline churches in Washington and with the National Council of Churches.

Against the established grain of the Washington church offices' moral advocacy and congressional lobbying based on religious-ethical analysis of policy, there arose support among mainline activists for a stronger stance. It should, they felt, be based less on the role of the "political insider" and more on a model of grassroots community organizing indebted by turns to the labor, civil rights, and antiwar movements and to populist protest politics since the 1960s. These activists felt stymied by congressional gridlock and Reaganite resistance to the churches' advocacy and legislative initiatives in behalf of justice and peace—especially as this resistance stiffened into a crusade against activist government, a crusade marching under the banner of personal piety as well as free markets. In response, mainline-church activists sought mobilizing strategies to combat what they saw as the growing poverty, economic inequality, and Cold War militarism of the 1980s, with the Reagan administration's cuts in social spending, defense buildups, regressive tax cuts, and quadrupled deficits in the face of economic slowdown.

Explains one backer of this more activist tack, " 'Talk all you want, we don't care.' That was the message the Reagan people sent the churches. From Congress it was more, 'We care, but we don't have any money to do anything about it. Sorry.' "[50] Counters the UCC's Jay Lintner, a critic of this more activist tack,

> Grassroots efforts and mobilization are fine in themselves. They just don't mean you can give up talking to people in Congress. That made a world of difference during the 1980s. Things would have been much worse if we'd just written them off and tried to go the route of pressure and protest politics. Most church people here in Washington realize that. There was plenty of frustration at what we couldn't do. But remember, except for a few moments on big issues like starving children or going to war, you are not going to get the saints out marching all the time. The middle class in the big middle-class churches just isn't like that.[51]

Nonetheless, during the 1980s the churches grew more open to efforts to educate and mobilize moral constituencies around specific issues. They sought to apply pressure to members of Congress and to charge public opinion on issues such as opposition to the Nicaraguan civil war. They worked to inspire local church and community groups to "think globally and act locally" in response to the plight of the hungry, homeless, and jobless. Then the Clinton administration came in, and everything changed— or so it seemed at first.

Between 1992 and 1995, Interfaith Impact for Justice and Peace struggled to establish itself at the center of the religious community in Washington. Finally, it failed to do so. Meanwhile, the National Council of Churches took on a larger, more active role on the national political scene. It spoke out more loudly in the name of the mainline Protestant churches. It enjoyed remarkably ready access to the Clinton administration and close communication with it. Indeed, the mainline Protestant churches themselves reported striking changes in their relationship with the White House, government agencies, and the Democratic National Committee. This held true especially during the more "liberal" first half of Clinton's first term in office, from 1993 to the 1994 midterm elections, when Democrats still held a majority in both chambers of Congress.

These changes began with cooperation on issue-specific lobbying tactics and mobilization strategies to bolster food stamps or pass the Family and Medical Leave Act, for example. They continued at a quickening pace to create the promise of shaping broader social policy, given agreement on overarching conceptions of a more activist federal government. For all the qualifying conditions and paradoxes involved, the Clinton administration's start after the Reagan-Bush years shifted the mainline churches' public presence in favor of cooperative, if sometimes critical, lobbying, rather than the stance of oppositional organizing and mobilization that had served its resistance to the Reagan administration in particular. This shift helped draw to a close the ongoing efforts of Interfaith Impact to strike a new balance between advocacy in Washington and grassroots mobilization of people in the pews, and so to survive.

Epitaph: What Went Wrong, and Why?

At its creation by merger in 1990, Interfaith Impact for Justice and Peace was the primary ecumenical advocacy organization for thirty-six national religious agencies in the United States, including all of the mainline Protestant churches. Five years later, Interfaith Impact was gone. What went wrong? The answers go back to the beginning of Interfaith Impact, according to Arthur Keys. They lie in institutional strains evident in the process of merger and left unresolved by it. He explains,

> We had two different models of advocacy we tried to put together. They didn't fit, politically or organizationally. If Interfaith Action had been able to "buy out" IMPACT, we might have been able to make it work, but that wasn't possible.

Q: Why not?

Different institutional actors saw the world differently, through different lenses.[52]

Their differences in institutional needs, aims, and interests gave rise to contrasting pictures of what Interfaith Impact should be. On the one hand, some activists stressed the need for a large membership organization committed primarily to making ecumenical advocacy more effective, rather than loyally serving the denominations in Washington. This model of Interfaith Impact intended it to "gain national recognition as the most effective religious advocacy organization" among the mainline churches, as Keys conceived it, and to push otherwise equivocal "faith groups to state and implement [their commitments to peace and justice] 100 per cent."[53] This view was held by ecumenical activists at the local, regional, and state levels, as distinct from national leaders of the NCC. In particular, the independent chapters of IMPACT at the state level wanted a strong national advocacy organization to serve and represent them directly.

This view was shared by key religious leaders and activists in mission agencies and boards within the mainline denominations, who often wanted moral stands on key social issues represented more vigorously than did denominational leaders per se, especially those elected locally or at large. The latter were likelier to back broader compromise or less emphatic legislative stands on social issues that proved morally divisive or politically controversial among those in the pews. This was especially true in larger "moderate" denominations such as the United Methodists, with their members more widely dispersed across the broad middle class and across "liberal-conservative" boundaries in American cultural politics and left-right party lines between Democrats and Republicans.

Grassroots groups in local communities, particularly among the poor and minority groups such as those involved in the Churches' Committee for Voter Registration and Education, wanted a strong national religious organization to empower poor people to advocate for themselves, coordinate their efforts, and lobby in their behalf in Washington. Such desires were shared by staff members at denominational headquarters outside Washington, who often worked with such local community groups and church activists, for example, through the UCC Board for Homeland Ministries and the Office for Church in Society. "Interfaith Impact is useless," charged one such staffer in 1994, in urging the mainline churches to organize grassroots religious communities and mobilize them into strong moral constituencies.

> It's nothing but a letterhead organization. It has no grass roots, no constituency. When Interfaith Action and IMPACT finally merged, the numbers of

people who were members of IMPACT had fallen from 14,000 to 6,000. When they looked for those 6,000, they couldn't find them. All they had was a mailing list. There was no organization, no network of committed people and churches on the ground in real communities, working together on real issues.

It was just a paper factory that sent out newsletters to people. It didn't do anything for them or with them besides fill up their mailbox. It didn't ask them to do anything besides send in a check or send their congressman a postcard. It didn't build a network or coalition of people and move them to come together and become a public that lives out a real vision of the gospel.

Its potential was done in by mindlessness in the church, by people who think that "social witness" means getting people in the pews to write checks to their church offices and postcards to their congressman.[54]

Grassroots organizing demands a sustained effort on the ground in local churches and communities that concentrates on one or two key issues, emphasizes Kim Bobo, an accomplished religious organizer with long experience at Bread for the World. She was brought in to join a last-ditch effort to revive Interfaith Impact. "I walked into this big meeting of all the groups that belonged to Interfaith," she recalls. "On the walls were all their lists of all their issues, dozens of them. Dozens! Right there I knew it was a long shot."[55] Agreeing to organize behind just a few issues picked as priorities was hard enough to do for the mainline-church offices in Washington among themselves—more difficult than joining forces to tackle one urgent issue at a time, such as hunger (at the root of Interfaith Action itself) or health-care provision (at the root of the Interreligious Health Care Access Campaign). That challenge became all the more daunting as the membership of Interfaith Impact expanded beyond the mainline churches in Washington to include groups as diverse as the United Mine Workers, the Southwest Voter Registration/Education Project, and the gay/lesbian Metropolitan Community Church, each with their own priorities.

On the other hand, leaders and members of "church and society" denominational offices based in Washington tended to stress the need for a model of Interfaith Impact that maximized denominational visibility on Capitol Hill and in the field. That amounted to "a service department for the denominational faith groups," objected Arthur Keys. It conceived Interfaith as a "coalition of faith groups," as he termed it, helping them facilitate their common policy positions and lobbying strategies. Instead, he backed Interfaith's becoming a membership "organization" in its own right, acting as a catalyst for religious advocacy, with a strong voice, high name recognition, and issue experts of its own directly engaged in the political process.[56] Given this conflict between models of advocacy, ongoing controversy over several questions plagued Interfaith Impact from its original merger: Should it be a coalition or an organization in its own right? Should it speak in its own name? Should it have an issues staff of its own or simply support the issues expertise of its member groups? The merger created "an organization, but one that functioned often like a coalition," as Keys saw it. It could speak in its own name as an organization, but only when its members authorized its executive leaders to do so. It could not speak for the denominations per se, which retained their right to dissent from Interfaith's position on any given issue. Interfaith Impact retained current staff members with issues expertise. It sought to reconfigure them to better complement their denominational counterparts, until it eventually had to sacrifice them under the pressure of financial attrition.

One of these veteran staff members, elmira nazombe, reflected on Interfaith Impact's 1993 national briefing in the wake of budget and staff cuts:

We have lost so much staff and resources that we can't stay in touch with the issues by working on them ourselves in any detail or depth over time. The result is, we have lost touch with people on the Hill and around town who are working on them. That's the only way you earn respect and trust in this town. That's the only way you earn influence if you don't have the money to buy it.

Otherwise, you don't know who is doing what on an issue. That became painfully clear when we were trying to organize the 1993 briefing. We are out of touch. We don't know who to call, we're reduced to looking up phone numbers in the Congressional Directory. When we do call, they don't know us. They don't owe us, or have any real reason to do us a favor by giving us somebody important to come and talk.

We can't even do a good job for the church offices just by functioning at this level, especially on issues like welfare mothers, minorities, the poor, where the people in the denominational staffs are not really tight with groups like the National Welfare Rights Union. There are not that many poor people in these churches, for one thing. The denominational staffs mainly know their own members, not the outside groups that are more important nationally and politically.[57]

Compromise over keeping issue experts on the staff of Interfaith Impact reflected, on the one hand, criticism of Interfaith's own issue experts as repeating or infringing on the work of denominational staffers in Washington. On the other hand were pledges of continuing support for Interfaith from member groups and funders outside Washington, who insisted on keeping its established staff members at work on key issues they backed.

By helping to produce and distribute publications, schedule lobbying appointments, staff phone trees, and the like, Interfaith Impact on the model of a coalition facilitated lobbying, mobilizing, and issues analysis led by the Washington offices of the churches, especially larger denominational offices such as the Friends Committee on National Legislation and the Lutheran Office for Governmental Affairs, while harnessing Interfaith's own institutional freedom and visibility to these ends. Conversely, those who favored Interfaith Impact as a membership organization with its own public voice, issue experts, and professional lobbyists saw these features as essential for directly representing their views in Washington, rather than as an effort to usurp the work of the denominations and deny them visibility.[58] These religious agencies and ecumenical groups outside Washington included members of IMPACT who felt it suffered by virtue of its inability to take positions of its own and speak in its own name.

Although these two models of Interfaith Impact as an interdenominational coalition and an advocacy organization in its own right were not mutually exclusive, believed Keys, their divergent aims and emphases stymied development of Interfaith Impact in any single direction. They stood in the way of its growing strong enough to meet the challenge posed by declining dollars coming from the mainline churches for national missions and national interfaith advocacy in particular. "The more Interfaith Impact relies only on agency contributions for support, the more rapid will be its decline," predicted Keys in 1992, attributing its failure to recruit new individual members and contributors mainly to denominational reluctance to make a full-scale commitment to these efforts. Falling financial support led to staff cutbacks, and so to cuts in programs and services, from lobbying and testifying on Capitol Hill to community organizing in the field. This made it harder in turn to recruit members and raise funds. The divisions that surfaced in the process of merger continued to divide Interfaith Impact, concluded Keys, proving that "formal votes on these issues cannot settle the matters because fundamental differences exist in the needs of various member agencies that will not change."[59]

On the other hand, in measuring by the yardstick of best serving the denominations, one director of a church office in Washington, caught in an exasperated moment in 1994, was no less critical of Interfaith Impact than of the churches themselves in relation to it: "Taken one at a time, the various things they are trying to accomplish are estimable," he conceded, referring to Interfaith's efforts to include more women and people of color and to recruit major African American denominations. "But the pieces don't really fit together to make a whole. How are they serving the churches as a whole? Are they coordinating what we do? Making it stronger? They say they're operating as a 'traffic cop' for the churches, but they're not. That's really just part of the same old mistake that hasn't worked for years now, and maybe that we haven't needed to work. For all this time now, Interfaith Impact is a riddle we haven't been able to solve."[60]

A gentler critic among the veteran church lobbyists and policy analysts on Capitol Hill confessed,

> I have stepped away from working with Interfaith the past few years. It seems like other people have, too, people who work on legislation and work the Hill. We don't see them at meetings. We don't see much of their literature on the Hill. Most of it really just reprints stuff from this or that denomination. They don't have any issues staff left in their own shop. Maybe it's hard to see them because they're facing much more toward the churches now. Whatever, it's not the unified voice of the churches in Washington that a lot of people hoped for ten or twenty years ago.

The history that Interfaith Impact has gone through has been so painful, concluded this friendly critic, that "it probably has to die to be reborn, or go into some kind of internal exile in order to make a comeback."[61]

Any such comeback would be fated to fail, in the view of Joan Campbell, general secretary of the National Council of Churches through the 1990s. That is because Interfaith Impact embodied "a faulted idea." It was at odds with the primacy of the churches themselves to interpret the religious meaning of social issues and take specific legislative positions on them, and with the conciliar responsibility of the NCC to bring the churches' views into conversation with one another and back their advocacy. Asked in 1997 to weigh what was most valuable about Interfaith Impact, Campbell replies,

> The strength of IMPACT, before it became part of Interfaith Impact, was a network of committed persons who could respond to social issues on the Hill and help move bills through Congress to make things better in the light of Christian faith. The building of that network was and continues to be of major

importance. Our greatest weakness is not having anything like it. I keep saying to people, for example, do not trash Bill Clinton for signing that welfare
bill, unless you can tell me why were we not out there. Did he get hundreds of
phone calls? No. We did not do our part. We didn't do it.[62]

Campbell faults too many religious advocates for striving to define the
issues for the churches instead of allowing the churches to join together
on common moral ground mapped by their own dialogue, backed by mobilization networks based in the churches but coordinated across them.
"When we were IMPACT alone, we focused on building a network," says
Campbell by way of providing an exemplary precedent. When IMPACT
merged with Interfaith Action, the issues of food, hunger, and the like
entered into their mission, and Interfaith Impact became both an issues
group and a network. "Then they began to compete with their own member bodies, who already had their own policy positions and priorities. The
temptation is always to get into the issues," Campbell explains. "The minute you get into the issues, then you also get into it with the other people
dealing with the issues."

What made Interfaith Impact unique, argues Campbell, was its annual
national briefing for church leaders and activists and its IMPACT communications network to alert, mobilize, and educate them across denominations. "What has lasted?" she asks. "The briefing and the network," she
answers.

> Getting into the issues business was what got Interfaith into difficulty. Yes, some
> people in the churches liked it and funded it. But it was the ultimate liberal issues
> place. It was not tempered by the Orthodox [Christian churches], not tempered
> by the black churches, and to some degree not really tempered by the American
> Jewish community as a whole. It was not, in its depth, truly interfaith.
>
> When mainline Protestants join in any interfaith effort, unless they are very
> clear about its purpose, they give up their birthright. The Catholics don't, the
> Jews don't. They go right on and do their own lobbying, their own work on is-
> sues, and keep their own identity. But our crowd gives it over in the name of
> interfaith relations and inclusiveness. We then lose the edge of saying there is a
> [Presbyterian, Lutheran, Methodist, or common Protestant] Christian position
> on these issues; and eventually the interfaith position breaks up. It doesn't hold.

Acknowledging the activist impetus of Interfaith Impact to select key
issues and back their advocacy by direct mobilization, community orga-

nizing, and voter-registration drives, Campbell notes, "There is usually a kind of messiness to ecumenical work. It goes slow. It's ponderous. Interfaith Impact wanted very much not to deal with that messiness, to just get out there and get things done. I understand that," Campbell grants, but she rejects such zeal as being good cause for marching orders to redirect ecumenical advocacy.

When it comes to ecumenical advocacy in the future, Campbell pledges, "I want the NCC, here in New York and in Washington, to be as active and enterprising as we can be to get the job done. I don't need to have a marriage made in heaven," she allows, in order for the NCC to cooperate with the denominations and their Washington offices. How costly was clashing between Interfaith Impact and the NCC? Could the council have acted to avoid it? "Had we been active and cooperative enough on the Washington front back then," answers Campbell, "I don't think there would have been an opening for the issues part of Interfaith Impact to get out of hand. Costly it was." Can the NCC ever recover the impetus to form a social-justice network to keep the promise once made by IMPACT? "I don't know," responded Joan Campbell in 1997. "Because now you still have people who want to re-create Interfaith Impact. I'm against it, not because I'm against interfaith work, but because it's not really interfaith. It's mainly Protestants from our churches, with just a few Jewish and Catholic groups involved. We'll see what happens," she promised.

The Churches Together and at Odds:
The Case of Health-Care Reform

Both the prospects and problems of ecumenical advocacy among the mainline Protestant churches came to a head in their efforts to support universal access to health care in the 1990s. In many respects, their engagement was a superb example of the role of religion in American public life. In other regards, it can appear sobering, if not discouraging. It began with interreligious recognition of the crisis in medical care in the 1970s, after the War on Poverty stalled and the economy tightened. This recognition gave rise to efforts to open health care to all, especially those left uncovered by private insurance and public programs provided for the poor. Though these efforts led to no such legislation, the churches themselves created formal policy statements and expressions of moral concern over inadequate health care in America that took root and grew over the next two decades into a set of working principles. These principles committed the churches to work together for comprehensive health care for all. It should be financed from "the broadest possible resource base" according to "principles of equity and efficiency." It should be backed by federal leadership and a national budget to foster health by improving standards of living, housing, nutrition, sanitation, and environmental safety.[63]

Led by Lutherans and Presbyterians in 1989, the mainline churches began a series of five interreligious consultations on health-care access. These joined their Washington offices, with backing from the National Council of Churches and National IMPACT before its merger, into a working group that expanded into a larger circle of religious leaders from thirty-three denominations and twenty leaders of nonreligious public-interest and professional groups. They pledged to advance health-care reform by a fivefold strategy featuring (1) a broad campaign to educate the public at large; (2) direct advocacy to Congress, led by the Washington church offices; (3) grassroots education and advocacy within religious congregations; (4) coalition-building with nonreligious advocates and public-interest groups for health-care reform; and (5) use of religious and public media to advance these ends. The churches, in turn, along with the now-merged Interfaith Impact and the NCC, brought together more than a hundred delegates from Protestant, Jewish, and other religious groups to launch the Interreligious Health Care Access Campaign (IHCAC) early in 1991.[64]

At first the campaign stressed broad moral principles and supported no specific legislation. But legislative stalemate over health-care reform between President George H. W. Bush and a Democratic Congress turned into deep division among Democrats. Then the campaign focused its Working Principles to make clear to Congress and the White House—and to congregations and the media nationwide—that only publicly financed plans for health-care reform satisfied these principles. Other plans failed to do so, including the "insurance reform" many Republicans backed and the "employer mandates" Bill Clinton proposed. Insurance reform "offers neither universal coverage nor comprehensive benefits," argued the IHCAC. "It continues and increases unnecessary administrative costs and fails to rationalize health care delivery. Any cost containment features are insignificant." Employer mandates, known as "play or pay," offer little cost control and raise administrative burdens by requiring employers to provide coverage either directly or by paying into a wraparound public system that would also cover the self-employed and the jobless. Only publicly financed "single-payer" approaches, judged the campaign, would "eliminate employer administrative costs and increase workplace flexibility, reduce federal and state bureaucracy, and rationalize health care delivery." Such a system could largely replace private insurance plans with a single, public mode of financing much like Social Security. It would save nearly $74 billion in administrative costs if it were in effect in 1992, the campaign estimated, about "twice as much as would be necessary to pay the difference so that everyone living in the United States could have comprehensive benefits including long-term care."[65]

The IHCAC decided to ask its member organizations if they were willing to endorse a publicly financed approach to health-care reform. With their backing, the campaign lobbied to this end on Capitol Hill, first in behalf of the Universal Health Care Act of 1991 (HR 1300), introduced by Representative Marty Russo (D-Ill.); and, with some reservations, for the Health USA Act of 1991 (S 1446), introduced by Senator Robert Kerrey (D-Neb.). The campaign promoted a mass drive to write "letters to Clinton" upon his election. These letters urged him to weigh the moral imperative of comprehensive health care for all in light of his stated willingness to sign a single-payer bill, if it were passed by Congress, instead of sticking with employer mandates. The campaign conducted press conferences and other public-relations activities. It backed a wide range of public advocacy and educational activities, culminating in two national "lobby days" on Capitol Hill in May of 1993 and June of 1994.

In asking the faithful to join the IHCAC, mainline-church leaders sharpened their calls over the early 1990s. They first quoted Isaiah (57:19) to stress the moral necessity of universal access: " 'It shall be well with the far and the near,' says the Lord, 'and I will heal them.' " Later, they paraphrased Ezekiel (34:2, 4) to underscore the social responsibility all citizens must share for the commonweal: "This is what the Sovereign says: Woe to the shepherds of Israel who only take care of themselves! Should not the shepherds take care of the flock? . . . You have not strengthened the weak or healed the sick or bound up the injured." In a democracy, the campaign urged, all citizens must "share the shepherd's role." They must take responsibility for helping to resolve a crisis of spiraling health-care costs and shrinking coverage. They must act to resolve the striking inequity between rich and poor and to meet the real risks to the middle class, for "the same illness that can cost your job can eliminate your insurance."[66]

In the early days of the Clinton plan for managed competition, the administration reportedly assured church leaders of its commitment to universal coverage and comprehensive care for the neediest, despite the political exigencies that obliged it to back a complex scheme of private insurance over the single-payer public insurance plan that the churches favored. Later, as the Clinton plan gave way to congressional bills that pulled back from mandated employer funding and fell short of universal coverage, the administration wrestled with the prospect of softening its pledge of health care for all. "Early on, with health care," recalled Ruth Flower of the Friends Committee on National Legislation, "we put a lot of effort into getting out analysis and testimony on the issue."

> We put on all-day hearings. White House Healthcare Task Force members showed up. They actually listened, and some of what they heard actually showed up in their plan. We were critical of their plan in many respects. But I was impressed by the degree to which their plan bent, based on stuff I heard church people say to them. They took in critical stuff, they worked it into their plan, things they didn't think up all by themselves, things that made good sense, and not just whatever played well for interest groups.[67]

However, as the congressional debate over health care wore on in the midst of intense lobbying in Congress, the administration, and the mass media to sway political support and public opinion on the issue, mainline-church advocates found the Clinton White House and its congressional allies much less willing to welcome dialogue on the substance of the issues. "They don't want to hear any more about what we think about the issues," remarked one church staffer at the time. "They want us to line up to help them sell the program they've already got, or as much of it as they've got left."[68]

By June 1994, the Senate Labor Committee had voted to require employers to pay most of the cost of their workers' health insurance, as the Clinton administration proposed, and to limit increases in insurance rates. But the bill remained stalled in the Senate Finance Committee. The House Ways and Means Committee, meanwhile, was divided over a bill that required employers to pay 80 percent of their workers' insurance costs and that set up a new branch of Medicare for the poor and those uninsured through their jobs or family. By the end of August 1994, the remnants of Clinton's proposal for health-care reform, incorporated into a compromise bill put together by Senator George Mitchell, had been voted down in the Senate Finance Committee. Polls showed three of four Americans agreeing that "basic healthcare coverage" was a social right for all citizens. But they disagreed on the fiscal and logistical feasibility of proposed plans to realize that right, the fairness of their funding, and the risks they posed to freedom to choose one's own physician and course of treatment.[69] Centrist political critics scolded the administration for failing to make timely compromises on health care. Some assigned striking blame to "the religious left," its congressional allies such as Senator Jay Rockefeller, and "the Democratic National Committee—an Amateur Hour operation, staffed by the religious left," as Joe Klein opined in *Newsweek*. "All or nothing has been the historic position of health-reform enthusiasts on the Hill: 'There is a religious left, and this is its cause,' says a moderate Senate staffer," reported Klein.[70]

Political critics on the left, meanwhile, reported that First Lady Hillary Rodham Clinton summoned leaders of citizens' groups, unions, and religious organizations to the White House in midsummer 1994 to scold them for coming up short in their support. Reported David Corn in *The Nation*: "We're lost on universal coverage, she complained. And who is to blame? You are—advocates of reform too hung up on your own agendas to be able to deliver a unified message to Congress." Hillary Clinton reportedly claimed that legislators had heard little from constituents who favored universal coverage, while their opponents had outspent and out-strategized them in media appeals and mobilizing efforts. She "urged her audience to get its act together," reported Corn, who then criticized the Clinton administration—in terms echoed, more gently, by some advocates in the liberal churches—for losing popular support for its own health-care plan by its very nature. "The First Couple's complex proposal was calculated to win business and inside-the-Beltway backing, not grass-roots support. Now as an ugly denouement approaches, the White House is looking to the left for help and is angry to find it weaker than the business interests assailing reform. No one did more to undermine a popular campaign than Bill and Hillary Clinton. She should be disappointed in herself."[71]

By August 1994, the Clinton administration had come out in support of Senator Mitchell's gradualist bill to push toward universal coverage by 2002 without mandating employer subsidies. The mainline churches protested this compromise, along with the AFL-CIO and some liberal Democrats. Almost alone among the major denominations, the African Methodist Episcopal (AME) Church came out in favor of the Mitchell bill. "Pragmatically speaking, that's about the best we are going to get from the Senate," remarked the head of the AME Church's ecumenical and urban affairs office.[72] "That's crazy," privately countered a mainline-church official. "The administration likely put them up to it. They have been looking for any church group they can find to come out for complete compromise. At this point, the AME is about the only one they've come up with."[73]

During the Reagan-Bush years, the White House had welcomed the absence of unified opposition from the mainline churches, for example, when it was pursuing congressional authorization of the Persian Gulf War. It also tried to counter opposition from liberal Protestants and Jews against outlawing abortion, for example, by appealing to more-conservative Catholics, evangelicals, and Eastern Orthodox Christians. In seeking moral and political allies in the mainline churches, the Clinton administration, by contrast, tried to elicit a unified, supportive voice from the churches. It sought out mainline representatives who could speak for all the churches as a group. But in attempting to shape the churches' univocal moral support to political ends, the Clinton White House, judged many mainline leaders, wound up dividing their voices and setting them at odds.

In the spring of 1994, as formal proposals for health-care reform and then welfare reform finally emerged from the Clinton White House to reach Capitol Hill, mainline-church leaders in Washington found themselves deeply at odds in responding to these overtures from the administration for their univocal support. Said one, "There has been enormous tension between us and Joan Brown Campbell [general secretary of the National Council of Churches] over her getting out in front of us. The churches have staked out a very clear position on health care in particular," in favor of universal coverage guaranteed by government, with employers, medical providers, and private insurers obliged to do their part to make it affordable. "A lot of work has gone into getting that together, and Joan is really a little outside of the consensus on it. The White House keeps going to Joan for our backing, she'll agree to something, and then write her own press release. She'll say to us, 'Let's hold a press conference on Monday.' Then on Friday she's released her own press statement. She is trying to give Clinton the support he needs and make him look good."[74]

Commenting on the same tensions between liberal Protestant church leaders in Washington and the NCC's general secretary, another denominational leader in the capital insisted on the need for collegial and conciliar relations among the churches in seeking to speak with one voice on

key public issues and warned against the dangers of "papal" pronounce-
ment without such relations. "With great respect for the person and the
office of the general secretary of the National Council of Churches," he
emphasized, "it is not possible to fill the role of being the spokesperson
for all the mainline Protestant denominations without consulting with
them. We don't need a majordomo."[75]

By some critical accounts, such problems of conciliar communication
and representation stemmed partly from "estrangement and disconnec-
tion" between the NCC's Washington offices and its larger national organization on one side and the denominations' Washington offices on the
other. "With the NCC, how important am I?" asked one head of a church
office in Washington. "No one ever calls me to ask, where were you today? What are you doing on this bill, who are you talking to? What do
we need to know in order to articulate our collective reflection on this?
It's amazing! And it's sad." He urged, "We have to work with each other
day by day. Pontificating like we have had in the past few weeks [in mid-
1994] works at cross-purposes with what we have been trying to achieve
collectively" in the mainline churches as moral advocates in Washington.
"We've had to apologize for the cross talk, most prominently on health
care, for giving lip service to what appears to be wholesale support of the
Clinton plan. That's not where we are as a denomination, and it's not
where the Interreligious Health Care Campaign is."[76]

Countered Mary Cooper, a longtime NCC staffer in Washington,
"What Joan Campbell has really done is to open doors to the administration to give the churches access to get in there, do their educating, and
make their arguments heard. Don't blame her if the White House keeps
pressing us toward its own position instead of just falling in behind us.
Get in there and do your best to make your case. It's a two-way learning
process." Cooper explained,

We have said to people in the administration, Don't mistake us for a rub-
ber stamp. Yes, we appreciate much of what you're doing, and we agree with
it, like insisting on universal coverage. But we also have the right to object,
and we'll exercise that right where we disagree, like cutting out immigrants
on health-care coverage. Like moving the food-and-shelter program from
FEMA to HUD: we have been mobilizing people around the country to fight
that. Joan [Campbell] has written letters and made phone calls all over the
Hill on that.[77]

After the legislative battle for health care turned against the Clinton
White House as well as the mainline churches, Cooper sharpened her defense of the NCC's role in the struggle:

> Joan Campbell has been leading the fight for the churches on health care with
> the Clinton White House. If people in the churches complain that she is playing
> politics, that is paradoxical. It is true in the sense that she is there in the White
> House, she has the access, and the relationships, and the connections. And they
> are trying to use her. But she is adamant in insisting that it's not good enough
> to come to us when they have a policy end-product.
>
> She could not have been tougher about their failure on health care. They
> didn't come to us early on to shape the moral rationale and filter of it. They
> didn't ask us out front to consult on the why and wherefore of it. They waited
> until after the Christian Coalition got out there in front on their own and
> slammed the Clinton plan as godless big government. Then they came and
> asked for our help. Joan Campbell made it exceedingly clear they had alien-
> ated us.[78]

Tensions between the National Council of Churches and mainline denominational leaders came to a head over health-care reform legislation
late in the summer of 1994, as the Senate began to debate the compromise
bill put together by Democratic Majority Leader George Mitchell from
the shards of the Clinton health plan.

Within days of Senator Mitchell's announcement of his bill, the mainline churches' Interreligious Health Care Access Campaign made public
a letter it had sent to every senator. The prospects for comprehensive
health-care reform "have substantially deteriorated," the letter began. It
criticized the Mitchell bill on three fronts: First, it "fails to create universal
coverage and defers the key elements of an employer mandate for future
consideration." Second, it "fails to create a substantial benefit package
defined in the law." And third, it "fails to create a credible control of
private sector costs which is perhaps the most basic cause of the current
crisis."[79] Despite these failures of coverage, benefits, and cost control, the
campaign's letter acknowledged the bill's positive reforms for those who
can afford to buy insurance and its helpful subsidies for those with low
incomes. But it singled out the Mitchell bill's retreat on mandated support
from employers to help finance universal health-care coverage. It urged
senators to remedy this failure and back a state-level single-payer option
to move back toward universal coverage:

The Mitchell bill proves again that it is impossible to get to universal coverage without employers paying their fair share. Instead of building on the current effort of employers the bill has capitulated to those who would do the least. We fear that the Mitchell bill will accelerate the race to the bottom in terms of coverage by employers and that a key building block for health care in the United States will severely deteriorate. Therefore we urge all Senators to put partisanship aside and move back toward universal coverage by improving the employer mandate provisions in the Senate bill. Because the Mitchell bill has retreated so far from universal coverage, it becomes all the more important to pass a state single payer option without an exemption for multi-state employers.[80]

Members of the IHCAC scheduled a press conference the following week and prepared to pursue there the same lines of pointed criticism and urgent calls for improvement in the Senate bill. "The night before the churches' press conference," reports a well-informed denominational leader, "the White House calls [NCC secretary] Joan Campbell in New York and asks her to come down the next day and come out in favor of the Mitchell bill. And that's exactly what she does, a few hours before the press conference the churches had planned."[81]

Campbell's eloquent, forceful statement emphasized, "Few, if any, other issues unite us as does the issue of health care for every American." Churches and their members "know firsthand from our own experience that our people are hurting; story after painful story documents the tragedies embedded in our present health care system. There is a crisis and change must come." Campbell stressed the primacy of universal coverage in the churches' moral vision of health care: "We have spoken out for universal coverage for all Americans for fifty years. Our position is rooted in the moral mandate. In God's eyes no one deserves or merits health care more than any other. Anything less is morally flawed. We urge the U.S. Senate, as they deliberate in these days, to take seriously the moral challenge before the nation."[82] Campbell upheld the moral principle of universal coverage. But on practical political grounds, she nonetheless endorsed the Mitchell bill in the name of the National Council of Churches.

Soon after being preempted by the NCC's action, a denominational leader in Washington deeply involved in the IHCAC commented on the turn of events: "It was unconscionable, and a lot of us are outraged. There is no point in getting into a public pissing contest with the NCC, but we really are not going to take it anymore. Where does that leave us? If need be, it leaves us headed toward a 'Protestant Policy Council' made up of the major church offices in Washington and their denominations, without the NCC. If it can't work with us like a colleague, if it can't act responsibly as our representative, then it needs to get out of the way."[83]

Looking back on the conflict several years later, Campbell was unapologetic, marking it as a needed, though painful, step in the course of the churches' coming to make their national public advocacy both more representative and more effective in practice. "My own belief is that we were such purists from the beginning that we were politically ineffective," she explains in reference to the IHCAC.

> Their fuss with me in many ways is because I know politics, I have lived in it. I worked with [Mayor] Carl Stokes in Cleveland. I have had to live in the political realm. At this point, I am an ultimately practical person. My bottom line is that we want to affect policy for the good. If you don't merely want to make pronouncements, and you want to affect policy, then you come at it differently. I differed totally with people in the Interreligious Health Care Campaign. I believed that what we should have done was to have entered the political debate, not tried to stand above it and make pronouncements.
>
> It's exactly like when the president defends welfare reform [in 1997] and asks the churches to hire people off welfare to solve the problem. I know our crowd. They will go, "The hell with that," under their breath. But there's another way to go at it, which is to say, "Fine, but that ain't all of it. Now listen to us, we have something else to say besides that about sharing responsibility through government to enable people to find decent work to do."[84]

If the mainline churches want to make a difference in public policy, Campbell judged, "then we had best enter into the political process and find out what is politically possible. I think the churches can do that without selling their soul." Of course, she conceded, "as health care turned out in 1994, none of us got anything—partly, I think, because neither they nor we really did understand how to affect the system, or just how much the powers and principalities were going to come down against us. So that was a bad chapter. It didn't work. It set religious people against one another."

But this episode also marked a turning point in the progress of ecumenical Protestant advocacy in Washington and the NCC's involvement in it, according to Campbell.

> I do believe that this Council of Churches had never, from its New York base, gotten into the issues of social policy in Washington. I think what has happened

is, church people in Washington have accepted the fact that this office and the heads of churches have something to say about policy, and that all of it cannot be left to the Washington people—who are, after all, inside-the-Beltway insiders, who spend a whole lot of time talking to one another. They are not much closer to the people than the members of Congress who have been there forever.

I do feel that I have finally come full circle with the people in the church offices in Washington, and they see me less now as an intruder and more as a player with them. I don't even mind what happened, because I think there was no way to do this nicely. I just had to get into it, and then they had to forgive me.

"To some degree, they have forgiven me," testified Campbell. "If I had asked permission, I'd have never gotten there, never."

"Wrong," retorted one leader of the churches in Washington. "There was no forgiveness, because there was no repentance." In judging relations between the NCC and the mainline denominations in advocacy over health-care reform, he stressed, "we were not complaining that she [Campbell] was playing politics, but betraying her own people" and the positions they had worked out together as a conciliar church heeding the gospel ethic of universal neighbor-love, instead of the political prudence of favoring your friends against their enemies.[85]

What's Next? Prospects for Ecumenical Advocacy

The rise and fall of Interfaith Impact for Justice and Peace over two decades reveals the deep difficulties inherent in the efforts of the Protestant churches in the United States to speak and act as the Church in our public life. But it also shows the growing need for such efforts to go on in our time. It demonstrates the growing capacities and resources available to these efforts, and the growing complexity of their institutional and cultural contexts. Since the demise of Interfaith Impact, mainline Protestant churches and faith groups in Washington have continued to cooperate with one another and their moral allies in advocacy and education efforts across a wide range of public issues. These include reforming health care, welfare, and campaign finance; protecting the environment; making peace in Bosnia and Palestine; and aiding refugees in Rwanda, Zaire, and Darfur. At the same time, many activists and leaders in the mainline Protestant churches say they miss Interfaith Impact, or what it might have become. They remain persuaded that the full potential of interreligious advocacy has not been exhausted or realized by the mainline churches.

Spurred by the challenge of the religious right in particular, some of these predominantly liberal Protestant church leaders joined with others in the NCC, along with Jewish, Catholic, and black Protestant groups, to found the Interfaith Alliance in late 1994. It aims to counter the claims of the Christian Coalition, Focus on the Family, and related groups to speak for all U.S. Christians on public issues, and to expose their partisanship.[86] Like the Christian Coalition itself, in contrast to Interfaith Impact, the Interfaith Alliance is an organization of individual members and contributors, not denominational churches, synagogues, or religious agencies. It speaks in its own name and in the name of its individual members, not in the name of the churches. Some of its leaders initially hoped that the enthusiasm of its growing membership as well as their donations would enable the alliance to move beyond counterpunching against the Christian Coalition to providing the religious mainline with a public forum of its own. This prospect clearly included the kind of analysis, education, advocacy, and mobilization on key public issues to which Interfaith Impact aspired as a membership organization, a prospect now freed from the weight of trying to coordinate or represent the denominations themselves on these fronts.

In 1996 the national Call to Renewal movement was begun by Sojourners, the progressive evangelical religious community and magazine led by Jim Wallis. Organized outside the mainline denominations, much like the Interfaith Alliance, yet drawing support from many of the churches' activist leaders and allies such as Marian Wright Edelman of the Children's Defense Fund, the Call to Renewal opened with a national conference scheduled head-to-head against the Christian Coalition's "Road to Victory" national convention in Washington, and located just blocks away. Organized on short notice on a shoestring budget, this Forum on Faith and Politics nonetheless numbered some thirteen hundred participants, compared to the coalition's five thousand, and it gained side-by-side coverage with the Christian Coalition on the front page of the *New York Times*.[87] The Call to Renewal's forum combined talks by Edelman, Wallis, Jesse Jackson, Bill Bradley, and others with the music, prayers, and dramatic preaching of an urban revival meeting. In the six weeks prior to the 1996 national elections, Wallis brought the Call to Renewal to nearly forty cities across the United States, and afterward promised more to come.[88]

In 1995 the National Council of Churches and the office of its general secretary began to plan and organize a "social policy council" as an advisory committee to its office in Washington.[89] This committee was designed to bring together the heads of the mainline Protestant denominations and their offices in Washington with NCC leaders and advisers. In so doing, ecumenical Protestant leaders aimed to draw together the mainline churches' discussion of public issues and make it more conciliar and more effective. This new body, they hoped, would be more representative of church members and more responsible to the public as a whole than its predecessors. It would better unify the voice of the mainline Protestant churches, they prayed, into the social teaching, moral judgment, and advocacy of the public church.

These developments, probed in the following two chapters, make clear that the impulse to incarnate the public church certainly has not ceased. It persists, even in the aftermath of Interfaith Impact's failure to unify the mainline Protestant denominations in their national advocacy of a full range of moral and social issues, backed by the faithful in local churches and communities. Related organizing efforts have meanwhile continued and even quickened outside the denominations. Some of these efforts take the form of freestanding, member-based parachurch groups that are hard to tell apart in organizational structure or function from nonreligious public-interest political associations or lobbies. Yet their moral dynamics and impulse reach back through a long history of revival, awakening, and reform. This impulse fed the "benevolent empire" of voluntary societies in nineteenth-century evangelical Protestantism, social movements in the Progressive era, and the social-welfare concerns of American government since the New Deal. However dammed or diverted today, it continues to seek new forms and channels.

There are good reasons, in sum, for what went wrong with Interfaith Impact. These reasons underlie the difficulties that the mainline Protestant churches still confront in seeking to speak with one voice on the crucial moral issues that face American society and to join their voice with those of other communities of faith, including Catholics and Jews. These difficulties include the traditional integrity and coherence of diverse church creeds, confessions, and ecclesiologies. They mark real differences in social composition and experience across the membership of these denominations. But the reasons to keep trying are no less compelling. They spring from the all-embracing unity of biblical creation, divine sovereignty, and redemption from sin. They reflect the expansion of the

American state and the pinching of the American middle class. They express its increasing cultural integration, evident even in its moral conflicts, and its loosening denominational loyalties in a society of deepening divides between haves and have-nots, in a world more tightly bound together in progress and peril alike by a global economy, ecology, and violent strife over religious and national identity.

CHAPTER NINE

Members of One Body

The Churches and the National Council of Churches

How can the churches be the Church? That central question remains pressing for the mainline Protestant churches in American public life. It sharpened in the wake of Interfaith Impact's demise, which cleared institutional ground for new ecumenical efforts by the National Council of Churches and others to join the mainline Protestant churches more closely in public advocacy. Specific issues spurred this undertaking. Chief among them was continuing opposition in the churches to tightfisted "welfare reform" and halfhearted health-care coverage in the 1990s, along with growing support for campaign finance reform. These advocacy efforts played out against the backdrop of continuing appeals by the Clinton White House to mainline-church leaders for public involvement and moral unity to help sway voters and members of Congress to its policies. It made pointed requests to the churches to back specific proposals, such as finding jobs for welfare recipients moved to workfare and extending medical coverage to the children of the working poor. Such engagement with the mainline churches offered a striking contrast to the Republican administrations before and after the Clinton years, especially to the silence of President George W. Bush in response to the churches' protests against war in Iraq and deepening poverty and hardship at home.

Religious Advocacy and Political Efficacy

What changing social conditions and cultural ideals have affected the public role of the mainline churches in Washington most decisively over the past generation? Their leaders give several sorts of answers in reply, particularly as a backdrop to the rise and fall of Interfaith Impact and their shifting relations with the National Council of Churches. Who sits in the White House or holds the majority in Congress can make for real differences in how much political access and influence the churches have enjoyed, although these differences are distinct from the moral authority that the churches have exerted and government officials have sometimes heeded. Nonetheless, recounts Jay Lintner, head of the United Church of Christ office in Washington,

> Carter respected us and realized he really needed the religious community on issues like containing hospital costs to protect health care. The administration listened closely to us on the values side of issues like hunger, energy conservation, unemployment. We had amazing access in the Carter years, going to the White House once or twice a week for meetings on hospital-cost containment, going out to Andrews [Air Force Base] to meet the president coming in.
>
> Reagan froze us out. That made us work the Hill harder. It pulled the churches together and pressed us to become much more visible in public during the Reagan years, because we had a clear enemy. The administration and its friends were so ideologically opposed to us they wanted to be our enemies.
>
> [George H. W.] Bush wanted to be polite and keep his distance. He avoided the religious right as much as he could. He was trying to keep things fuzzy, trying to keep away from polarization. When push came to shove, particularly on the Civil Rights Act, Bush wanted a compromise worked out, I think, but others blocked it. Friends came before principles, I want to think, but maybe it was just politics before principles. You couldn't organize against Bush as the enemy. You tried to assume good will, but the good will became badly eroded. The mushiness and lack of principle finally alienated a lot of people.
>
> Clinton welcomed the churches back into the White House, the evangelicals, too. He wanted to do the right thing; he wanted to govern. And he wanted to hold down the political center and keep away from polarization. In that respect, Bush already warmed us up for Clinton.[1]

Thus both "neoliberal" Democrats during the Clinton years and more moderate Republicans during the administration of George H. W. Bush pursued the centrist politics of an overlapping incumbency party attuned to a broad middle-class electorate with weaker party loyalties than an earlier generation of New Deal Democrats and Taft Republicans. They courted a larger proportion of independent voters responsive to single-issue appeals to both their moral convictions and their social interests.

The Republican Revolution flowed from the "Contract with America" to the high point of the 1994 midterm elections, yielding a new Republican majority in the House. Then it ebbed in the election cycles of 1996 and 1998, before resurging to help consolidate Republican House leadership, secure a slim yet significant Senate majority, and win the White House for George W. Bush in 2000. This updated the "Reagan playbook" of playing religious politics directly with white evangelical conservatives on wedge issues such as abortion and gay rights, emphasize some mainline-church leaders, while appealing to more centrist swing voters with charitable good works by volunteers encouraged by the faith-based initiatives of compassionate conservatism. Said one church leader in 2003,

> The Bush team has been pretty successful at holding off the mainline churches, and using or bypassing the middlemen on the right like [Pat] Robertson and [James] Dobson to go directly to evangelicals and Southern Baptists. The president stands up and testifies to his personal faith as a born-again Christian. They're careful with their stands on the cultural issues that really matter to their base. . . . Their faith-based moves show swing voters they care, they have a better answer on social-justice issues that's more loving, costs less, and works without big government.

Though the mainline churches charged the Bush administration with waging an unjust war and pursuing a misconceived crusade in Iraq, "after 9/11 people are still scared, even if they're not sure about invading Iraq or ridding the world of evil. So faith and freedom go together, and God's on our side in the war on terror," as one church leader put it during the 2004 presidential campaign.[2]

Not by access alone, however, do the churches in Washington pursue their advocacy, nor simply by alignment with political allies and opponents do they pick and judge their key issues. After twelve years of Ronald Reagan and George H. W. Bush in the White House, recalls Bob Tiller, head of the Washington office of the American Baptist Church through the 1990s, "it's a week before Clinton's inauguration and I'm already mad at the guy I'm supposed to be excited about," particularly for doing far too little to cut military spending, aid the poor, and help Haitian refugees instead of imprisoning them.[3] Still, says Tiller,

> I'm excited about family medical leaves, the motor-voter bill, the Religious Freedom Restoration Act, important things that had been backed up and

backed over for a long time. I'm looking forward to having more access to the White House and administrative offices. They're more disposed to the mainline churches, and they're working on legislative reform that includes things we're working on, instead of trying to veto everything we're working on.

Some of us actually know people who have gone and taken jobs at the OMB [Office of Management and Budget] or the National Security Council and who will answer our phone calls. That's nice. But the most exciting thing is that for the first time in twelve years, somebody shares our values. That's exciting and interesting, but I don't know how to forecast it.

Why not? Because deeper differences in moral aim and outlook mark off religious advocates from even the most sympathetic politicians. "Folks in political institutions usually operate differently when it comes to how you treat your enemies, those who are different from you, and your upper-middle-class friends," Tiller explains. "Usually you punish your enemies, mistrust those who are different, and reward your friends who are already well-off. So folks from religious institutions who speak to politicians are always trying to convince them to shift their thinking, not just make some incremental policy change. That means we may be disappointed, even when one administration seems more amenable to us than another."

Moral coherence and more or less shared values between the churches in Washington and the administration in the White House do not imply that the churches will line up as political allies to go along with the administration on every issue, or even agree among themselves to coalesce in its support. Says Tiller,

> It depends on what the issue is, what we judge is possible, and how important it is to work for what's possible, or to go for more. I felt concern, for example, about the ease and comfort some of my church colleagues had with support for Clinton's economic package. I gave it maybe one cheer, not three cheers, because it didn't do enough to cut the military or fundamentally restructure the federal budget. Early on I said it's OK for a start, but now let's hold his feet to the fire.

In this process, note mainline-church leaders, they sometimes found more cause for disagreement over hedging their collaboration with the Clinton White House—for example, when its proposals for health-care reform fell short of the single-payer plans the churches favored—than arose from their unity in opposing the Reagan and Bush administrations. There, judges Tiller, "having a strong opposition to the administration helped us to agree, because it shortened our agenda. It cut out a lot of the nuance and complexity." The churches aimed to pass family medical leaves and the Religious Freedom Restoration Act, for example, and they sought to stop aid to the Contras in Nicaragua and reduce military spending. "Those things never got to first base," says Tiller. "So we didn't have to ask how to get to second or third base, how far to go in what direction, and where to stop."

Political Access and Reciprocal Lobbying

How significantly did the changeover from the Reagan-Bush years to the Clinton administration affect the work and outlook of the mainline churches in Washington? How far did it shift their stance from outsider organizing to insider lobbying? The answers depend, judged church leaders, on the nature of the denominational organization in question and the kind of work it was doing. For the United Methodist office in Washington, relatively selective in its day-to-day work of legislative lobbying on Capitol Hill, the arrival of the Clinton administration nonetheless spurred the volume and pace of its work in Washington and slowed its educational work on social issues in the churches. "We've had to tell people in the churches we're a bit behind there just because we've had so much more work to do here in Washington since the new administration came in," reported Thom White Wolf Fassett early in 1993, when he was general secretary of the United Methodist Board of Church and Society. "They are moving more quickly on so many more fronts. They are much more concerned about what we think. They're calling us up wanting to know where we are on health care, the budget, NAFTA, welfare, gun control. It's exciting, but it makes for a bigger workload, too."[4]

Radically improved access to the White House made a big difference in the everyday work of those church leaders most engaged in legislative analysis and collaborative lobbying on Capitol Hill and in Cabinet agencies. "We have a lot more access now," reported Ruth Flower of the Friends Committee on National Legislation in 1993. "That feels surprising, since we learned how to work without access, including information access, under the Reagan-Bush people. They blacked us out. Now you can pick up the phone and call someone in the administration, talk to them and get an answer, get a document, whatever. That's really nice to start with." Gaining entry to policymaking discussion depends not simply on whom you know, but also on knowing what sorts of conversations are going on where in government, involving which questions, evidence, and ideas. Nonetheless, notes Flower,

> Where the real access comes from, say, in the White House, is that now we know some of the folks. They're from groups like ours, and if you don't know the right person to call—just like the other folks used to do with Reagan—you can call up one of your buddies and ask, "Who should I talk to about this? Is it worth doing this or that, are they still listening over there? What really happened over there on this?" Even if you are not walking over to the White House and sitting down at every important meeting, that sort of access to staff actually working on the policies we care about is extremely valuable.[5]

The Reagan years saw the public influence of the liberal churches wane in favor of the religious right, with its access to the White House. This brought the mainline churches closer together in organizing and mobilizing their own members in the pews. It joined them more tightly in lobbying Congress to resist initiatives such as increased defense spending and social-welfare cuts in the original Reagan budget, as the history of Interfaith Impact shows. Conversely, the early days of the Clinton administration reinvigorated the mainline churches' governmental access and insider influence as lobbyists and moral advocates. It also amplified the NCC's voice in Washington.

But some church leaders wondered whether this new access to government would sap the urgency of the churches' efforts to educate, organize, and mobilize their members as morally critical, conscientious citizens. Observed Jay Lintner, "As an organizer, I immediately recognize that Clinton, like Carter, will be a disaster ultimately. We took off like a rocket when Ronald Reagan got elected. Our people were so angry and frightened, and thought the world was going to hell, so they really became a viable force that we could organize. Now, the right wing is experiencing the same thing. So as an organizer, I know that I'm pushing an uphill fight."[6] But, acknowledged Lintner of the access and understanding extended to the mainline churches by the Clinton White House, "I'm having so much fun as a lobbyist that it's hard to worry about it, really. With the access we have, we're in a different phase. It's exciting when the White House calls my boss in Cleveland at eleven o'clock at night and says, 'Hi, can you get to the White House tomorrow morning at 8:30 for the signing of the Family and Medical Leave Act?' "

Staff from the mainline-church offices in Washington found themselves regularly getting into intimate conversations with the Clinton transition team, and then with White House and Cabinet-level staff on issues ranging from social-welfare and environmental policy to religious free exercise. As a consequence, noted Lintner, "we suddenly realize we have an old style of working the issues. We're still talking to Congress first. We're losing it because we didn't get to Clinton early enough." Instead of ignoring or stonewalling the churches, as the Reagan-Bush administrations did, "they are coming to us on issues like the Native American Religious Freedom Act," Lintner reported. "That's an issue we thought was down the road a ways, and we would have to work six months to get the administration's attention on it. We didn't have to work six weeks on it. We held a meeting on it, they found out about it, and they came on their own without any invitation. Amazing!"

Just how eager and effective the new Clinton administration proved in taking the initiative to approach the mainline churches on policy and legislative matters pleasantly surprised many religious leaders. How strategically political these approaches proved also struck them. "They're lobbying us now!" exclaimed the head of the Presbyterian office in Washington, Elenora Giddings Ivory, in 1993.

> It's a pretty incredible turnaround. For years we couldn't get past the White House gate. Now they're lobbying us so hard and fast, some of the stuff they fax us inviting us to meetings, asking us to do things, comes straight in on Democratic National Committee letterhead instead of White House stationery. I keep telling them not to do that. It's embarrassing! We're a church!
>
> They seem to take it for granted that we're their political allies, just like the AFL-CIO or the Sierra Club, or any other Washington political group on the Democratic side. Even if most Presbyterians weren't Republicans, we're officially neutral when it comes to party politics. So it's best not to put things that are supposed to be presidential or bipartisan on DNC letterhead, like we're a party auxiliary.

In fact, she adds, "they want to use us like focus groups, to find out how we feel about issues in order to help them get their message out better." And that, she warns, "still doesn't mean you get a real voice at the table."[7]

What of church-state separation in the course of reciprocal lobbying? "There's no way that any member of the administration would be allowed to appear to be asking us in the churches to do anything partisan," answers Ruth Flower of the Friends Committee, with a smile.[8]

> One nameless official who was trying to tell us which senators to target on the balanced-budget amendment in 1993, for example, was at great pains to say that this was not a message from the White House, and "I am not using any information I gained from the White House legislative liaison to tell you I think these six people are your top priorities. Do you understand that?" We understood, we thanked her, and we went on about our business, secure in the knowledge that they are under orders not to give out any marching orders, at least not officially.

At the same time, reports circulated among religious advocates in Washington that selected church leaders received firsthand requests for help from the highest government officials. A strategic line of political analysis stressed that such appeals reflected the administration's view of the mainline churches as a key avenue of moral persuasion, and a lens to refocus moral perceptions. "We got that message pretty clearly," observed Flower. "It came through loudly in meetings we had with Clinton transition-team members between the election and the inauguration. They were coming to us to see how they could get access and line up allies. All of us kept saying, 'You want allies, you listen to us. It has to be a two-way street.' What we got back was, 'It's a one-way street. We'll let you know.'"

Yet religious lobbyists in Washington were also impressed to find key Clinton administration staffers seriously searching early on for outside opinions on health care and welfare reform. When church groups met with David Ellwood and Mary Jo Bane, welfare experts on leave from Harvard to serve as Health and Human Services officials, reported Flower, "they did not say, 'Line up with us, this is the best deal you can get.' They were listening, to some extent defending, to some extent not defending but simply saying what they were and were not going to be able to do." However, she continued, "when [NCC secretary] Joan Campbell then gets the message from Bill Clinton, 'We want you to stand behind us on health care,' it's more a one-way kind of thing." Likewise, she added, "on the balanced-budget legislation, it was pretty much the same thing. There it wasn't really our aim to work out a policy question so much as our wanting to talk to the administration about reducing military spending further in going after the budget. They certainly didn't want to get into any dialogue on that. It was just, 'Here's the stuff. Sell it for us.'" By 1994, the Clinton administration's plans for reforming health care had hardened and become besieged politically. "The administration and the Democratic Party are just plain selling the plan now," noted Flower. "Discussion time is over, even though there are really a lot of details still to be worked on and decided on in Congress."

The churches in Washington should serve both as moral advocates and moral critics, in this view. On the one hand, reflected Flower, "it's true that sometimes what everyone really needs is for the churches to just plain line up and lead a moral pep rally for good legislation to gather support and go through." That can be a valuable public service for the churches to perform, for example, on health care, "as long as we are honestly convinced the plan is good and fair enough for everyone, especially the neediest and poorest, and we really can't do any better now," says Flower.

> But it's our insistence we really have another kind of role besides leading pep rallies. I don't see that recognized, either on the Hill or by the White House — that we are responsible for introducing a kind of moral commentary on what's going on, and holding to it. We are obliged to make clear what is so critically important, like caring for the poor, that it can't be dealt away. We're just not going to let go of it, and they will not get the troops from us unless they respect that.

But, she admits, "you rarely get the sense that's felt by most politicians, because what's at the top of our agenda is so often slipping off the bottom of theirs. Like, 'Maybe we'll phase in more health coverage for poor people in 2010, if we can.' That slips off so easily, while what affects the insurance companies and the doctors comes up front and center, where government has to negotiate it."

A second line of analysis, akin to the "politics of meaning" promised by the Clintons, stresses the moral common ground that the Clinton administration recognized between itself and the mainline churches on a range of social-welfare issues such as health care, welfare reform, and schooling. Observes David Saperstein, longtime head of Reform Judaism's Religious Action Center in Washington, in the mid-1990s:

> What's happening with Clinton is that, first, there is a lot more access to the White House and the administration than before. Second, they are trying to

lobby us, but no differently than they lobby any other group. That is, "This is
our program, we're lining up supporters. You people play a very important role
in shaping the moral perceptions of Americans. We need your help in further-
ing our agenda."

I think that that approach comes from a kind of confidence on the part of
the administration. Since they come out of much the same kind of moderate,
liberal faith traditions that our coalitions of mainline religious communities
represent, they believe that anything they would choose to do politically would,
of course, be so much better than before that mainline religious groups would
want to be supporting it.[9]

The dilemma for mainline communities of faith, adds Saperstein, stems
from the fact that the politicians are

not really asking for our participation in the shaping of the policy. That is a
major point of frustration for us. To the best of my knowledge, for example,
there was no religious presence in shaping the environmental-justice executive
orders, in shaping the health-care plan. I could go down the list. When the
president invited the religious leaders to breakfast [in early 1994], he spoke
with them on this but didn't ask for any input. There have been some ad hoc
meetings where the president has been very courteous and respectful, and administration officials have listened to church leaders. But there's been nothing
systemic and issue-oriented.

Why not? "They assume they are so much a part of the religious worldview and community we represent that whatever they do reflects those
values, and they don't need to discuss the specifics with us," Saperstein
replies. "Bill Clinton, Hillary, Al Gore, Tipper: they believe this in their
gut." Such confidence in a faithfully shared moral vision joins expert political prudence to seek in the churches moral focus groups, rather than
interlocutors for genuine moral dialogue in the creation of policy. This
problem may also stem from the president's personality, mused Saperstein. "He is a very, very bright man who is an educated intellectual. He
admires intellectual ideas. He has always sought out the best and the
brightest intellectual experts and tried to learn from them to get the best
knowledge available on the substance of social problems and issues. I
think, with some legitimacy, he regards religious leaders and thinkers as
being the quintessential generalists. Therefore he genuinely wants to hear
from religious leaders on religious issues."

But if President Clinton wants answers on health care in particular, says Saperstein, "it doesn't leap to his mind to turn to us. Part of this may be that there's no tradition in his faith community of Baptists of the kind of moral deliberation and debate you find in the Catholic encyclicals and councils or in the Jewish tradition of Talmudic disputation. He respects religious leaders, but he doesn't connect them with the specialists and experts he wants to consult on specific issues." In a world where the play of interests and the authority of experts govern policy, and the dictates of individual conscience override churches as councils of moral delibera-tion, religious leaders become specialists in moral generalization. They are valuable to guide the faithful in the pews to support legislation, but not to debate policy in the moral argument of public life or consult with decision-makers on specific issues.

Public Churches at the Crossroads

An emphasis on grassroots mobilization of pastors and people in the pews to support mainline-church advocacy in Congress mounted and spread during the Reagan years. Then it slowed and floundered during the admin-istrations of George H. W. Bush and Bill Clinton, before resurging against George W. Bush. Over the past generation, however, neither the scale of the mainline-church offices in Washington nor the ecumenical organi-zation of their cooperation, judge denominational leaders, has kept pace with the sheer proliferation and range of policy issues and debate. This proliferation of issues and diversification of public argument over them, church leaders add, has also challenged the coherence of their own moral dialogue and public advocacy. A generation ago, the mainline-church of-fices in Washington numbered little more than a score of staff members, who met often on a relatively small number of central issues, such as civil rights. The limited size of this circle of staffers, their frequent conversation, and the active leadership of a few figures, including the head of the Wash-ington office of the NCC at the time, reportedly gave this group remark-able coherence and made its members fluently familiar with one another's theological and social views, even when they did not fully agree.

Beginning in the mid-1970s, the mainline-church offices in Washington began to grow. "The Presbyterian, UCC, Lutheran, and Methodist offices all became more powerful than any ecumenical structures," recalls one veteran of the era, Jay Lintner.

Then when the denominational money began shrinking, it hurt the ecumenical groups even more severely. Now enough people have been around long enough so there is great trust in this community. We can be ecumenical when it comes to putting together issue coalitions without having any strong ecumenical structure. We know where each other stands, we know what each other's policies are, and we know who we can go to in order to get support on different issues.[10]

At the same time, building ecumenical structures across multiple issues, and setting priorities among them, has proved persistently challenging for the mainline churches in Washington over the past few decades, as the case of Interfaith Impact for Justice and Peace made painfully clear.

As more churches opened Washington offices during the 1960s and then expanded them in the 1970s, their staff members began meeting monthly on an informal, unfunded, and loosely organized basis. These meetings evolved into the Washington Interreligious Staff Council (WISC), which preceded the founding in 1975 of what became Interfaith Impact for Justice and Peace and outlived the demise of Interfaith Impact in 1995.[11] WISC continues to the present. In its range and resilience, it shows the interdenominational virtues of the mainline churches. But it also offers evidence of their limits in organizing ecumenical public advocacy. Across the mainline churches since 1995, observes a sympathetic critic,

we have no program-planning process in place, and we have no policy-development process in place. We have no book on priorities, on what we can say or not say on an issue across the denominations. What we had back when WISC started is what we have now. There are various task forces, and each one has a long list of issues. There are 20–25 issues listed in the task force for civil rights and civil liberties, everything from gun control to affirmative action and domestic violence. Every month we meet and go down the lists. Whoever shows up and decides they want to do an Action Alert can do it, send it out, and put it in the briefing book. There's no process by which we determine real priorities. It's bizarre![12]

The most striking aspect of this problematic situation is the way it reflects the passionate dispersal of single-issue politics in the polity at large, not denominational or doctrinal differences within the mainline churches themselves. It certainly fails to demonstrate their left-wing unity in larger "culture wars" ostensibly waged between religious progressives and liberals on one side and conservative evangelicals and orthodox Bible believers on the other.

The mainline churches face the challenge of cooperating to identify, prioritize, and respond coherently to the most morally urgent social issues their common faith illuminates. Yet they do so, observes Jay Lintner, in "an arena in which most of the players are single-issue people. Their real passion is how to push that single issue—the environment, health care, cutting military spending, whatever it is. They don't want to get bogged down functioning as part of a system or organization with a set of priorities and a core agenda." If the churches are to cooperate more closely in their public advocacy, he urges, "we need to see if we can't agree on an inner circle of issues that becomes our core agenda," for example, environmental justice, health care, race, hunger and poverty. On such a core agenda, the mainline churches need to learn how to speak and act more as a unified conciliar church. "On other issues such as gay rights, where we can't agree or decide it's a priority, we function as a coalition. We're still trying to find out if we can organize ourselves to do this."[13] On this aim, most members of the "maximalist" party among church leaders in Washington agree. But they differ among themselves over how it can be best accomplished—for example, with or without the leadership of the National Council of Churches—or, indeed, whether it can be accomplished at all.

Ecumenical Advocacy and the National Council of Churches

Founded in 1950 at a high-water mark in ecumenical cooperation among American Christians reaching back over a century, the National Council of the Churches of Christ in the USA incorporates more than thirty Protestant, Anglican, and Orthodox denominations with some fifty million people in 140,000 local congregations. It seeks to join them into a "community of Christian communions" in a "covenant with one another to manifest ever more fully the unity of the Church" as the Body of Christ.[14] Almost three hundred representatives of its member communions meet annually as the General Assembly, the NCC's highest policymaking body. A smaller executive board meets several times a year to act in behalf of the General Assembly in many matters. The NCC's general secretary acts as its chief executive, in tandem with a president who serves a two-year term of office and is equivalent to an unpaid chairman of the board. Since

1980, a series of strong, sometimes embattled general secretaries have worked to expand the NCC beyond the mainline Protestant denominations, while continually seeking to cement its leaky finances. The general secretary has served as the NCC's chief public-policy officer with varying success during this period, sometimes coming into conflict with the Washington offices of the mainline churches, particularly after the NCC's own Washington office faded from its key role in collaborating with the churches on Capitol Hill during the civil rights era.

After the eclipse and demise of Interfaith Impact for Justice and Peace, the NCC and its general secretary at the time, Joan Brown Campbell, took the initiative in seeking to reinvigorate the organization's leadership of ecumenical advocacy in Washington. In December 1995, the NCC organized the Washington Consultation on Public Policy Ministries among some two hundred church leaders. This meeting, in turn, proposed calling an annual National Religious Leadership Conference on Public Policy Ministries. The first such NRL Conference met one year later, a month after the 1996 national elections, with seventy participants. They included heads of communions, leaders in social ministries, expert advisers, executives of regional, state, and local councils of churches, and NCC staff members.

The main business of the 1996 NRL Conference, reported the NCC, was "to articulate a moral framework for our public witness" by "identifying and recommending a limited number of public-policy priority issues to be considered by member communions and if appropriate to be held in common and pursued collaboratively through study and strategic advocacy."[15] This concentrated collaboration, in turn, "could allow the churches together to have a significant influence on public life in several clearly identified areas of need," namely, reducing poverty, securing racial justice, preserving religious liberty, and promoting peace, along with reforming campaign financing.

As subsequently proposed by the executive board of the NCC, these priorities in public-policy ministries were formulated as follows:

1) End Poverty As We Know It

This will require attention to welfare issues, both nationally and in state and local areas. It will call us to engage issues of health, jobs, daycare (for both children and the elderly), hunger, housing and all related areas that impact the lives of the poor. The focus of our actions will need to be first on children and families. The biblical mandate to consider the poor informs our commitment to this priority.

2) Secure Racial Justice

The tenacious evil of racism will require us to be attentive specifically to immigration issues, the affirmative action debate and environmental justice matters in the arena of public policy. The list is only a beginning but again this will require attention not only at the federal level but in states and local communities as well.

3) Preserve Religious Liberty

The need is for constant attention to assure and enhance a religiously tolerant and inclusive America. There is a need to carry into public awareness and public decision-making the reality of a religiously pluralistic nation. This will require attention to public school issues, public prayer, religious liberty in the workplace and an engagement with religious liberty internationally.

4) Fewer Weapons, Greater Peace

Since the scope of the issue is so large, specific areas need presently to be identified and pursued: resources for Africa, the elimination of land mines, support for the United Nations (and especially the USA role and financial support), the chemical weapons ban treaty, multinational trading blocks, the role of religious communities both in fueling hostilities and in resolving them.

Additionally, the conference voiced its support for moving quickly in the area of Campaign Finance Reform. The urgency has been created by the legislative agenda of the 105th Congress where reform has a fast time schedule. The Advisory Committee encouraged the Washington Office staff in collaboration with Washington partners to move quickly. As a consequence a campaign has been launched, "An Open Letter to Congress" has been prepared, released at a news conference and sent. Next steps are being developed.[16]

The NCC's executive board urged its member communions to join in commitment, engagement, and collaboration around these priorities. It promised them that collaborative advocacy and public action would accord with their own policy statements as well as the NCC's. It pledged that the NCC's national units and its Washington office—newly reorganized and co-chaired by veteran staffer Mary Cooper and Rev. Dr. Albert Pennybacker, just named as NCC Associate General Secretary for Public Policy—would lead in developing educational programs around these priorities and organizing participation in strategies of public witness and legislative advocacy.

In addition to setting policy priorities and pledging NCC leaders to ecumenical advocacy, the NRL Conference mulled questions of how to build and sustain a larger, more effective network of activists within and across its member churches. "It's hard work to build the kind of network we're talking about," said Rev. Oliver Thomas, NCC counsel on religious and civil liberties. "It's going to take money, energy, time and cooperation among all of us."[17] In contrast to the few thousand members of the old IMPACT network, the NRL Conference goals included tens of thousands of members drawn from each denomination in the NCC, with the potential to combine their ranks into an army of faithful citizens, several hundred thousand strong, in support of selected stands on priorities held in common among the churches.

That prospect would help close a gap that conference participants marked. With its thirty-plus member communions of more than fifty million faithful, the NCC has the potential to exercise great moral leadership in American public life. Yet "the Christian Coalition has often dominated the agenda on public policy issues."[18] The mobilization of the faithful as moral constituents who can also figure in the political judgments of elected officials can make a real difference in shaping the policy agenda, Joan Campbell promised. "One of our shortfalls, as moderate to liberal religious people, is that we don't adequately thank politicians who take up our issues," she observed after the 1996 NRL Conference. "If there had been an outpouring of support when President Clinton first vetoed the welfare reform bill, he might not have signed it later. We intend to build an ecumenical network of grassroots advocates to make sure that doesn't happen again."[19]

"It was a wonderful meeting," Campbell said of the 1996 conference. "I shared those priorities with the general secretary of the Synagogue Council and the general secretary of the Catholic Bishops. For the first time ever, we agreed we will each write to all our people and ask them if we can say, 'These are the top four priorities for all of us.' Now that is real 'interfaith' cooperation," she stressed. The NRL Conference aspired to build a framework for national religious advocacy that echoed Interfaith Impact's official title but fulfilled its promise with unprecedented moral authority and institutional reach. "We have a genuine chance of bringing it together if we stay with it," predicted Campbell. "We agreed to rebuild the networks [first built by IMPACT, of church activists for education and direct mobilization on key issues]. But now the networks would belong to the denominations. They would share them when the issues being addressed

involved one of these four priorities. One message would go out simultaneously through seven networks."

On the recommendation of the 1996 NRL Conference, the NCC established a smaller Advisory Committee on Public Policy Ministries, attached to the NCC office in Washington and chaired by Rev. Paul Sherry,
then president of the United Church of Christ. It was composed mostly of
representatives of the seven mainline Christian churches with Washington
offices, with the head of each communion joining the director of its Washington office. This Advisory Committee reflected Joan Campbell's conviction of the need for a clear-cut institutional body to back ecumenical claims
to speak for the mainline Protestant churches on issues of social policy. "I
think it's a big mistake that the Washington office of the National Council
of Churches has never had an advisory group," she explained. "We have
two hundred committees in the National Council of Churches. Every one
has an advisory group. I am convinced that we need to have a social-policy
advisory group, and that it needs to have both [the national] heads of [de-
nominational] communions and the Washington operatives."

Campbell adamantly opposed making up this NCC Advisory Committee solely of "Washington staff people," as she made clear.

> They were very nervous about that. I said, "No, if we're going to have it, it's got
> to be church qua church. If we're going to speak for the churches, it's got to be
> the head of the Lutherans, the Presbyterians, the Methodists, not just the heads
> of their offices in Washington." Of course, that makes them nervous, because
> the denomination heads and the heads of the Washington offices don't neces-
> sarily talk regularly about social policy.
>
> But if we're going to say, from the National Council of Churches' stand-
> point, "Here is what we agree on," then it's got to be the heads of the churches
> themselves sitting together in Washington. That is the strength of the social-
> policy group.

In principle, more active NCC leadership of ecumenical public advocacy
in Washington could line up support from the NCC's other members behind positions spearheaded by the liberal Protestant churches on selected
issues. It could thereby lend more weight to the work of the Washington offices these churches maintain, which most other churches do not.[20]
NCC leadership of ecumenical advocacy could also give churches without
Washington offices a greater voice in the capital and keep them better
informed and organized on national public issues. "Our goal is to bring in

the churches that do not have Washington offices, so they do not feel so isolated from the situation in Washington," promised Campbell.

Some mainline Protestant leaders hoped that composing an NCC public-policy committee chiefly of representatives from those member churches with offices in Washington would center the committee on the mainline Protestant denominations. This might enable these denominations to pursue their agenda of peace-and-justice issues without having to work through myriad differences across all thirty-plus member bodies of the NCC, including the Orthodox and African American churches, in order to adopt a position or take an action that the NCC Advisory Committee put forward, as long as it fit within the framework of priorities approved by the National Religious Leadership Conference at its annual meetings.

On the other hand, mainline leaders feared, such NCC leadership could also serve to check, control, and dilute the work of the Washington church offices across the mainline denominations. Joan Campbell countered that it would instead make for greater moral accountability within denominations as well as across them. "One problem with the offices of the member churches in Washington is that their staff has less accountability to the people in the churches than I do. I have a lot of accountability. I cannot offend the heads of our churches," she declared. "They are really only responsible to whoever their boss is. And that is really problematic, because they don't stay tuned in" across the broader religious spectrum, charged Campbell. "I have to listen to the Greek Orthodox primate tell me, 'Work on Cyprus!' It may not already be a big issue for me, but it better be an issue we come to understand. They don't have those pressures. They can be purists and get down on the NCC for making all these compromises and dealing with what is politically possible."

The mainline churches need to exercise more ecumenical accountability and political practicality, by this account. They also need to focus more clearly on fewer central issues and speak out on these issues in more disciplined collaboration. "The great failure of the churches in the public policy arena has been the shotgun style we've had," began Rev. Albert Pennybacker in diagnosing the problems to be tackled by the NCC's plans for ecumenical advocacy, soon after he became NCC Associate General Secretary for Public Policy and took the helm of the council's office on Capitol Hill.[21] "The first time an NCC delegation met with President Clinton, for example, at the end he asked us, 'Is there anything you people don't care about?' So we are trying to foster a prioritizing process, in a way that does not prevent any church body from pursuing any issue they want on their own," yet a process that works through the Advisory Committee to draw together the Washington offices of the NCC-related churches with one another and their larger communions, said Penny-backer. However broadly defined they may be as "umbrella areas," the NCC's initial priorities "do begin to give us focus," he promised.

The NCC Advisory Committee would advise the National Council's general secretary as well as its Washington office, specified Pennybacker, since "the general secretary is, in fact, the public-policy officer for the National Council" under its constitution and can therefore speak for the council. "That speaking is always in the context of NCC policy statements," explained Pennybacker. "Under our procedure, part of my job, for instance, is to make sure any policy statement made by anybody in the NCC or in its name conforms to the NCC corporate policy statement on an issue or a document on human rights or the like." Internal to the NCC, then, there is a conciliar ideal of the churches engaged in discussion and argument together. From this council arise its social teachings and advocacy, to be voiced by its officers.

NCC leaders "can't fire from the hip," stressed Pennybacker. To check "hotshot church leaders" tempted to do so in the NCC's name, Penny-backer claimed "the power to call any congressional committee where anybody purports to speak in the NCC's name and say we disavow their testimony and withhold permission to use the NCC's name in relation to it. So we have some capacity to exercise real discipline in how the National Council becomes a voice for this community of religious communities." By contrast, "Interfaith Impact, of which I was a part, collapsed because it was not really rooted in the life of the churches," charged Pennybacker. "It did provide a channel for active legislative education and advocacy. That was its strength," he granted. "We need to recover that, but keep it rooted in the life of the religious community, so when someone speaks out in our name, the reaction in the churches isn't, 'Gee, who's that?' It's, 'Amen! That sounds like us.'"

Fragile Denominations and a Squabbling Council

In weighing the prospects for renewed relations between the NCC and the mainline churches in public advocacy, Joan Campbell voiced the gravest concern about the growing institutional fragility of denominationalism itself. "I worry very much that the NCC is denominationally based, because

I think the day for denominations is essentially over," she revealed.[22] "I believe that the model of the Christian council, which is rooted in the life of congregations, is the model for tomorrow. One of our problems is that many of our boards and committees are made up of people who work for the denominations—in other words, religious bureaucrats. That in no way connects us to the real people in the church. As a matter of fact, it alienates us from them." In a sense, allowed Campbell, "our churches are our competition, and they are not sure they want us to work. When they get most nervous, and sometimes I make them nervous, is when we have come pretty close to making this thing work at points in the last five years," she said. "When the National Council finds its voice in public, it can seem then that the denominations lose theirs, even if in theory that combined voice is more effective. If the point is to affect public policy, that combined voice ought to be a plus. But because we are sinful people," she confessed, "it doesn't exactly work that way."

Because denominations have fallen on hard times, Campbell observed, their allegiance to ecumenical goals has weakened as their sense has grown that ecumenical bodies are competing with them for scarce resources. However, added Campbell, "if we were to call a meeting in this country of everyone interested in the ecumenical idea, we would have a very large group of very enthusiastic people. If we called an ecumenical meeting for people who had to be appointed by their denominations," she smiled, "we would have a much smaller group of very contentious, crabby people. Their very reason for being there would be to protect their denomination. This does not bode well for an ecumenical institution based on denominations," she warned.

The advantage to being a national council of denominational churches, Campbell pointed out, is based on the assumption that it is grounded in the congregational life of its member churches through their highest level of organization. "That worked much better when those churches at that denominational level could 'command' their people," noted Campbell, that is, inspire and teach and shape them. "Now we have more of a shell," she conceded. "Some of our people look at the Catholic bishops, for example, and think they might be better able to do that. They yearn for it. In the past, Protestant churches like the Presbyterians have said to the NCC, 'Hands off. Do not touch our congregations.' Now they are saying, 'Go ahead, deal with our congregations, because we have to.'"

If the NCC is going to make the ecumenical idea a reality, Campbell anticipated, "we have to get involved with congregations, not just denominations." But congregations can be enormously parochial, she cautioned. "They can be very involved with mission on their own doorstep but not have a clue about what it means in its larger sense worldwide." So, she urged, "we need a model for the future that is not entirely based on denominations or congregations, or on individuals. That would give you a special-interest group, however large, which runs directly counter to the diversity that is the essence of any ecumenical community." At once conciliar, congregational, and global in its activism, this ecumenical model for the future, Campbell acknowledged, was still in the making.

On the other hand, denominational leaders in Washington typically supported in principle ecumenical advocacy fostered by NCC initiatives, while they stressed how important in practice are the actual arrangements among religious bodies organized to serve this principle. This pertained in particular to the Advisory Committee to the Washington office of the NCC and its annual National Religious Leadership Conference, which aimed to define key priorities for public policy. "Logically, I am all in favor of the NCC doing its job and taking the ecumenical lead in the churches' social witness," said one Protestant church leader in 1997. "But it has to be more like a real council. The NCC cannot speak for the churches if it does not actually listen to them carefully and confer with them closely on an ongoing basis. In the past, that has not always been done. That's why we have some problems of trust in the present about the NCC coming out more actively and speaking 'for' the churches."[23]

One denominational supporter of NCC initiatives sketched the kind of focused yet flexible collaboration she hoped such initiatives can breed. "The ground has shifted in the last year or two," reported Elenora Giddings Ivory, head of the Presbyterian office in Washington and a former chair of Interfaith Impact, in 1997.[24] "With Interfaith Impact, we were trying to work out one grand ecumenical scheme" for mainline-church advocacy in Washington, grassroots organizing nationwide, and cooperation with nonreligious advocacy groups. "We have given that up," she admitted. "Now we are working more with the divisible parts of that puzzle. I think the NCC Advisory Committee can be a good thing. Those of us in NCC-related denominations have been asking the NCC to get stronger so that they can help us get stronger, not necessarily by directing what we are doing, but by helping coordinate us," distinguished Ivory. "Help us make up a table that works as well together as the National Catholic Conference does for the Catholics or the Religious Action Center does for Reform Jews. At present, honestly, we don't feel we do," she acknowledged.

In particular, the question of who speaks for whom remains unresolved in ecumenical Protestant advocacy, observed Ivory, and it must be addressed. "The one thing we didn't do and still haven't done—and it may still be the downfall of whatever we do ecumenically—is answer the primary question, 'Does the organization speak for itself, for its member churches, or does it coordinate them in speaking on their own behalf?'" she said. That may be less of a question for the NCC, because "they have a long history of speaking in their own name, and Joan Campbell is her own person," Ivory granted. "But that question is still there. She knows that she cannot go beyond where the faith groups are. So do we, when we are speaking ecumenically."

For critics of the NCC, questions of representation, flexibility among denominational members, and accommodating non-Protestant faith groups spurred skepticism over whether the NCC could unify the churches in their ecumenical advocacy without seeking to subordinate them to itself. "The community here is in dire need of coordination," acknowledged the UCC's Jay Lintner in 1997.[25] "Formally, logically, the NCC is the organization best set up to do that," he thought, since it is the biggest, broadest, best-connected ecumenical group in the United States. "The independent 'interfaith' alternative some people in Washington church offices and coalition groups are backing at the moment is just a dream on a piece of paper with no funds," he judged. "In the middle are a lot of people involved in religious advocacy who would like to see some coordination, who think the NCC is ideally the one to do it, and who doubt it will work out, because of all the historical strikes against it—all the conflicts over jurisdiction and authority, over who speaks for whom, over the continuing political relevance of this whole community, or the lack of it," he remarked.

"The NCC is at a crucial moment in its history right now," concluded Lintner. "It's hard to judge which way it will go. They've got potential. At the same time, they've got a huge pile of baggage they lug around," he warned.

Every time they turn around, they're fighting the perception that the emperor has no clothes: no clout, no money, no rock-solid allies in the churches. They're desperately clawing for relevance. Well, sometimes when you desperately claw, you dig something up. They may be able to do that with this Policy Advisory Committee, maybe with the drive for campaign finance reform. It could be a good thing, if they pull it off. If they pull it off halfway, then push it too hard for

MEMBERS OF ONE BODY

their own political advantage, it ends up in squabbles, and we're back where we started.

The NCC needs to strengthen itself by strengthening its member churches in the process of unifying their advocacy efforts, not by subordinating them to NCC direction, insist its critics. By way of example, recalled one, the respected head of a parachurch hunger-relief group stood up at the 1996 National Religious Leadership Conference and suggested that "perhaps some of the money the NCC has been raising to rebuild burned black churches and combat racism be used as seed money to help the African American denominations open up Washington offices and do public advocacy of their own." The immediate NCC response was that "we don't need to do that, because these black churches already work through the National Council. There was palpable murmuring from the African American leaders in the room," reported this critic, and it voiced the widespread impression that the NCC was helping the churches chiefly in order to help itself.[26]

A severe critic of NCC initiatives in ecumenical advocacy assigned it primary responsibility for being at odds with the mainline churches in Washington. "The NCC is out of touch with the denominations on religious advocacy, and it's their own fault," he charged.

> The NCC knows they are out of touch, but they haven't figured out why. It's because the people who can give it access to church activists, and help it reach concerned people in the pews and their pastors, are the second-level denominational leaders like those in the Washington offices. Ecumenical leaders have ignored or spurned us so consistently that we are not particularly eager to help them out, quite frankly. To the extent they respect us at all, they see us as competitors. The NCC has chosen to go for the heads of communions and emphasize its cooperation with them as peers. It assumes that denominational staff in Washington who work full-time on policy pretend to know things but really do not. But since the NCC has no real public-policy staff of its own, it winds up checking with the Children's Defense Fund, for example, if it wants to find out about health-care coverage for poor children.

"People at the NCC trust their own political instincts. They think they understand the issues," this critic concluded wryly. "They have been burned enough times now, though, that you would hope they'd begin to ask themselves a few questions about how to do better."[27]

Yet in detailing this adverse diagnosis, denominational critics of the NCC in the 1990s described its relation to the churches in terms that complemented the views of NCC leaders at key points and pointed up denominational difficulties, too. Said one, "The NCC's organizational strength runs to the heads of communions. That may create a little more space for them to do advocacy. The general secretary pays attention to what they think, and thinks of them as her colleagues. They look to her in the belief that she has policy strengths and [Clinton] White House connections. Some of them want to take advantage of that and pursue those connections to do insider politics." The real problem with this approach, argues this church leader in Washington, stems from the "disconnects," even in some of the most socially active churches, between the denomination's top layer of national leadership and those who work full-time in Washington on policy issues. This varies by person, he explained, not only by denomination.

> The best denominational heads do a good job of staying in touch with the Washington offices and the policy working groups. They take our advice seriously and critically, too. Sometimes they go off on their own, and that's all right, because they have heard us out, and we're able to talk back and forth. But a lot of other denominations lack anybody on staff or in-house doing serious policy work, so they have no way to get to a solid grounding of their own on issues.[28]

Neither does every denominational head actively foster or follow informed conversations about public-policy issues among the ministers and members within the denomination's own districts, dioceses, or conferences, according to this critic. "So you've got a lot of heads of communions just walking around making up their own minds as individuals about issues they know very little about," he charged, "on the basis of what they read in the newspaper or hear from personal acquaintances."[29]

Even the sharpest denominational critics of the NCC acknowledged that the churches themselves share responsibility for faltering in ecumenical advocacy. Collegial models of ecumenical study, education, and advocacy on social issues imply a relative equality of participation that is at odds with actual differences in commitment and investment across many mainline denominations. "Many of the communions in the NCC haven't invested much in policy work, and some of them have," confirmed Jay Lintner. "For example, the Lutherans and the Presbyterians have put a lot of resources into policy development, as opposed to policy advocacy or delivery, maybe ten times more than the UCC." Greater funding and staffing do not of themselves make for greater intelligence and moral insight into public policy, grants Lintner, and "being smart only takes you so far."[30] But the churches nonetheless need a spread of enough "smart people" working on public policy across the full range of denominational doctrines, polities, and memberships. They need to be doing their own work and coming to their own understanding of a given issue, in order to collaborate responsibly and forge a genuine consensus on that issue.

These conditions of collegiality apply to the mainline denominations just as strongly if they take the initiative to subordinate the NCC's role in ecumenical advocacy to something like a Protestant Policy Council of denominations made up of people actually working on policy development and advocacy, as proposed by church leaders critical of the NCC. "Start there and focus on helping those people do it better. That's not the whole answer, but it's a place to start," urged one such church advocate in the late 1990s. "It makes more sense to build coalitions among the denominations than set up a whole new bureaucracy headed by the NCC, if the denominations are willing to play together and share the limelight among their heads," he contended. "Let us talk policy and get more of a sense of where the real convictions lie for different faith groups, and find out what they are now willing to do with one another on this issue or that." If the mainline churches join together ecumenically, by this account, "it will be because the churches themselves agree to cooperate on specific issues and go to our grass roots on those issues. The beauty of that is we can do it right now, an issue at a time, without having the larger structure of the NCC Policy Committee. Then we can decide how this works out over time. We are certainly prepared to do that," vowed this church advocate averse to following the NCC's lead to a more centrally fixed and governed public-policy agenda for the mainline churches.[31]

Church leaders willing to move forward with NCC leadership of new efforts at ecumenical advocacy, despite their doubts and wariness, emphasized the need to approach it as a cooperative experiment in terms of church polity, organizational strategy, and mutual trustworthiness. "It's really a case study in effective differences in polity across the denominations," explained Jay Lintner:

The key question is, "Who makes the decisions?" In some denominations, that's pretty straightforward. In others, that question is almost impossible to answer sensibly. Right now the general secretary of the NCC has decided she is going to make decisions on public advocacy and stand behind them, and she wants to have the heads of denominations and the church offices in Washington discuss them together first.

It's a walk of faith, and I will not agree with every decision that comes out of it, but I have to go along with that in principle, because we have had no work-able alternative to it up to now.[32]

The immediate issue of campaign finance reform, on which the NCC and denominational leaders joined in effective cooperation later in the 1990s with nonreligious advocacy groups such as Common Cause, provided them an opportunity to rebuild trust on both sides.

This was also an opportunity "to begin to invent the next model of mass mobilization for mainline religious advocacy, now that Interfaith Impact is gone," proposed Lintner.

It was actually dead as a model in the eighties. We kept saying it was dead. We kept talking about building a new model, but nobody would really invest in that effort. Instead of trying to reconvene that conversation, it's time now to try out some possibilities and see if they work.

Interfaith Impact was a mixed model. It tried to organize the denominations and to pull in the grass roots with some power and control. The two aims stale-mated each other. That convinces me that denominations can't take the lead in building a model outside the denominations, or try to govern the outcome. The better examples of that, like Bread for the World, will develop their own independent power and maintain good ties with the denominations but keep in control of their own memberships. Single-issue groups can work pretty well like that. I am a lot more doubtful about multi-issue groups. Some of us are following the Interfaith Alliance closely to see if they can figure it out and con-ceptualize what they're doing.

Notwithstanding the arc of the Interfaith Alliance's career, traced in the next chapter, the principle remains, in this view, that "the denomina-tions have got to figure out how to organize the denominations with some power," insisted Lintner. "That cannot be a mixed model. It has to focus on the churches themselves, and try to be more or less ecumenical. The NCC would be a logical place to do it. In fact, it's the only logical place, if there is enough trust between it and the churches for it to happen there," judged Lintner. In creating a new model of public advocacy and mobilization in support of it, however, the churches must be clear about their inherent political limitations, as well as their potential. Likewise looking to the future, Joan Brown Campbell made no apologies for the political realism of the National Council of Churches. She defended its moral integrity while pointing out the ambivalence of its critics who also wished the mainline churches would exert more influence on government. Speaking from NCC headquarters on Morningside Heights in New York City, Campbell observed,

> It's very interesting that people always say, "Oh, if we could just return to the day when Eisenhower laid the cornerstone for this building." But they fuss with me for being a big friend of Bill Clinton. In fact, this is a big myth. I've never talked with Bill Clinton alone, not even on the phone. But if you are the general secretary of the NCC, why isn't it a good thing to have access to the president, not a bad thing? Of course, in their view it is a bad thing, unless you are asking them what to say to the President.[33]

In response to church critics of her leadership in public advocacy, Campbell returned to the touchstone of her ecumenical faith, rather than rehearsing her record of political results. "I couldn't get up in the morning if I didn't believe that embedded in our work are very great convergences of things people in the churches do want to do together, and that we are seeking for them," she testified, "even if we don't always tell each other the truth very much about what we wish the other would do. We tend to triangulate it," she confessed. "In a job like mine, you cannot take personally what gets said about you. I was convinced that it was right for me to take a leadership role in social policy. I believed that we would weather my entry into the system being seen very negatively. If I continued and was faithful to the people I am supposed to be faithful to—all the people in the churches—then we would come to a different place," she vowed.

Looking to the NCC's future, Campbell saw the prospect of a vital biblical synthesis of currents now conventionally set apart as "evangelical" and "liberal" in American religion and politics, to "span much of what divides us" and make "a new center." Both liberal Protestant and conservative evangelical social teachings and political stances have their faults, Campbell pointed out. "The liberal stance is too limited when it just looks at changing laws and policies and doesn't deal with changing the human heart. That is where evangelicals bring religious faith into how people live every day, doing their best to take care of their families and their jobs, even if they too often ignore the responsibility we all have for social justice and the mission of government." Instead, Campbell stressed, "justice has everything to do with love. They are not separate. Too often we think of justice as legalistic. But the Bible's idea of justice and mercy together is far more what we are talking about." In the case of welfare reform, for example, "there is too much sin in the world; there is always going to be some problem with any plan to get everybody off welfare and put them to work. Government can't solve the whole problem, and neither can business and charity. We need justice and mercy together."

The mainline churches and the National Council of Churches need to settle their differences and unify their voice in public. They need to do so clearly and strongly enough, Protestant religious leaders have agreed since the 1990s, to respond to our society's most pressing problems, not only to answer the challenge of those on the religious right in their claim to speak for all Christians concerned about the moral order of American public life. Recognizing the need to unify the mainline churches in American public life spurred the NCC to two organizational efforts aimed in distinct directions over the next decade. First, leaders of the NCC and key mainline Protestant churches joined with liberal Jewish and Catholic leaders to found the Interfaith Alliance, an ecumenical, nondenominational parachurch group designed to speak out in its own voice against the "radical religious right" and counterpunch the Christian Coalition, in particular, within the arena of electoral politics. Second, the NCC turned inward to consolidate its own organization and refocus its own programs more tightly. Then it turned outward again to expand and strengthen its network of allies among the churches and beyond them, among parachurch and nonreligious advocacy groups such as the Children's Defense Fund and Call to Renewal, Bread for the World and Habitat for Humanity, in order to reset the religious mainline in motion.

The Mainline in Motion

Resisting the Right, Remaking the Center

The urgency of efforts by the National Council of Churches to unify the mainline churches as a public church over the past decade stemmed, first, from its mounting concern over the powerfully coalescing political impact of the religious right. Led by the Christian Coalition in its 1990s heyday, followed by Focus on the Family and other organizations, this resurgence drew together as "conservative evangelicals" the Southern Baptist Convention, smaller white Protestant denominations, and independent congregations with diverse parachurch groups, born-again broadcasters, media outlets, Christian schools, and related parallel institutions. Together they formed an increasingly cohesive voting bloc within the Republican Party, with its own distinctive ideology and organizational clout. Second, stronger movement by the NCC to unify the mainline churches as a public church came from within the council itself in response to the growing gap between its demanding aspirations and dwindling resources. It faced the need to clarify its priorities, refocus its programs, and strengthen its alliances in order to advance its overriding aims of witnessing and working for justice and peace in Christ's name. These aims, in turn, shifted the NCC's stance from hopeful cooperation and disappointed compromise with the Clinton White House to sharpening criticism of policies advanced by the administration of George W. Bush.

The Interfaith Alliance versus the Religious Right

In mid-1994, a group of mainline Protestant, Jewish, and Catholic religious leaders joined together to form the Interfaith Alliance (TIA) as "a non-partisan, ecumenical organization" aimed at "promoting the positive role of religion as a healing and constructive force in public life, encouraging the renewal of values within our families and communities, and providing people of faith with an alternative voice to that of the radical religious right."[1] Identifying themselves within the religious "mainstream," the leaders who began this organization included Rev. Joan Brown Campbell, general secretary of the National Council of Churches; Edmond L. Browning, presiding bishop of the Episcopal Church; Rabbi Arthur Hertzberg, former president of the American Jewish Congress; Catholic bishop Thomas J. Gumbleton; and Rev. Gardner Taylor, co-founder with Martin Luther King, Jr., of the Progressive National Baptist Convention.

Neither they nor the score of distinguished others on the alliance board officially represented their denominations or the NCC. For the Interfaith Alliance began as a freestanding, member-based parachurch association, without denominational funding or sponsorship. It was incorporated as a nonpartisan, nonprofit organization under section 501(c) 4 of the tax code. It was nonetheless aided at the outset by a $25,000 grant from the Democratic Congressional Campaign Committee, much like the $64,000 contribution the Republican Congressional Committee allegedly made to the Christian Coalition at its start-up five years earlier.[2]

Affirming "the plurality of religious voices and the strength that diversity brings to our national life," the alliance vowed in its initial mission statement to "challenge any candidate or political organization that explicitly or implicitly claims to speak for all people of faith."[3] Joan Brown Campbell of the NCC explained, "Our concern is that the radical right lays claim to the fact that they uniquely speak for people of faith in this country, in essence that 'God is on our side.' We feel we must come together as an interfaith group and say to this country there is an alternate religious voice."[4] In particular, declared Dr. Herbert D. Valentine, former moderator of the Presbyterian Church (USA) and founding president of the alliance, it stood opposed to the religious right's using either-or "religious litmus tests" on issues such as abortion and homosexuality to practice "spiritual intimidation" in electoral politics and to polarize public life by asserting that "there is absolutely only one way to think and live to be a good Christian. . . . Religious extremism is being used as a weapon to attack politicians, to censor classroom textbooks, to cut back school breakfast programs, to promote discrimination, and to mislead voters."[5]

In seeking to counter the Christian Coalition, the Interfaith Alliance took specific aim at the linkage between the apparently theocratic ideals of its founding president, Rev. Pat Robertson, and his righteous intolerance for ungodly enemies, on the one hand, and, on the other hand, the grassroots organizational strategy of its founding executive director, Ralph Reed, to mobilize enough conservative evangelical Christian activists to win control of the GOP and Congress. Thus alliance literature emphasized Robertson's maxim that "democracy is the next-best government" and his warning that "the time has come now for a godly fumigation" of the feminists, socialists, and other "termites" now destroying America's Christian institutions.[6] The alliance likewise quoted Reed as stating, "What Christians have got to do is take back this country, one precinct at a time, one neighborhood at a time, and one state at a time. I honestly believe that in my lifetime we will see a country once again governed by Christians" and Christian values.[7] Such demonization of all dissenters as "termites to be destroyed," countered Rabbi Arthur Hertzberg, makes the religious right's social agenda and political organizing particularly threatening to all Americans in exercising their right to religious freedom.[8]

The Interfaith Alliance set out to counterpunch the Christian Coalition in the national media and to establish local chapters and statewide affiliates to combat the coalition's grassroots organizing, issues education, and campaigning in behalf of candidates for public office. "We are organizing 'faith monitors' to ensure that state and local meetings of school boards, state legislatures and city councils are not taken over by the right wing agenda," announced Valentine. "We are coordinating forums which focus on issues ranging from family values to prayer in public schools. And we are shining the light on stealth radical right candidates who run for local, state and federal offices."[9] In this mission, why was there no formal involvement on the part of the mainline denominations themselves? "They are too diverse. They are too polite," explained Valentine. "And in some cases, possibly, they are too worried about their own internally dissenting conservative factions to do anything about the Christian Coalition and the attack-style politics it promotes. They keep making up enemies lists without scruple and claiming to speak for all true Christians. Well, some of us finally decided we would not keep letting them do it."[10] Over the next decade, discussion among church leaders in Washington of the Interfaith Alliance's development and destiny reflected, in turn, many of their own larger concerns about the future of social witness among the mainline denominations in relation to the National Council of Churches, parachurch advocacy groups, nonreligious lobbies, and political parties.

A Morality Tale of Two Elections

In the fall of 1994, the Christian Coalition mounted its most ambitious effort to reach voters for a midterm election, and it claimed a decisive role in winning a new Republican majority that ended decades of Democratic control of the House. It distributed some thirty-three million voter guides covering each Senate and gubernatorial race and 350 House races, delivered to congregants in sixty thousand churches on the final Sunday before the election. It phoned two million homes to get out the vote on election day. In the first nationally organized religious opposition to such electoral efforts by the Christian Coalition, the Interfaith Alliance made public a preelection letter it sent to two thousand members of the clergy encouraging them to preach sermons and lead prayers decrying those who "use religion as a vehicle to promote an extreme political agenda."[11] The alliance backed the League of Women Voters in protesting that Christian Coalition voter guides appeared to be more like campaign advertisements than unbiased comparisons of candidates' views. The Interfaith Alliance publicized the Christian Coalition's strategy on using the voter guides, recorded by an alliance member at the coalition's annual convention in September 1994, advising that guides should not be distributed in churches until just before the election, to minimize attacks on their credibility. "You want to hold it until that last Sunday because if they start raising doubts about the voter guides you're going to have a real skittish pastor that's just going to pull them," counseled Chuck Cunningham, director of voter education for the coalition. Ralph Reed denied that the coalition was attempting to avoid scrutiny. The guides were made available to the press, he contended, and the Interfaith Alliance was an "insignificant political group on the radical left" serving as a tool of the Democratic Party.[12]

In 1995 the Interfaith Alliance turned to organizing state and local chapters of clergy, laity, and other concerned citizens as the backbone of a national grassroots movement to offer an "alternative, faith-based voice to that of the radical religious right."[13] Leading up to the 1996 elections, the alliance set out on a "Road to Renewal" project to educate and register voters. It targeted congressional contests and local school-board races in a dozen key states where candidates backed by the Christian Coalition were running on issues such as school prayer, sex education and creationism in the classroom, and public funding for private, religious, and home schooling.

On the eve of the 1996 Republican National Convention, the Interfaith Alliance sponsored an interreligious prayer service and rally nearby in San Diego. There local clergy and moderate Republicans joined with national religious leaders, including the NCC's Joan Brown Campbell, to hear Mary Louise Smith, former chair of the Republican National Committee and a board member of the Interfaith Alliance of Iowa, testify, "I have witnessed with alarm the growing influence of the religious right within the Republican Party. . . . I am a person of faith and a Republican but the Christian Coalition does not speak for me." She challenged Republicans "as people of faith and goodwill to ensure that tolerance, civility, respect and understanding will forever prevail in public life."[14] Denise Davidoff, head of the Unitarian Universalist Association, unveiled the alliance's "Candidate Pledge of Civility." It promised, "We will ask candidates to pledge that they will not use religion as a weapon in their campaign or claim that a vote for them is a vote for God. We will ask candidates to pledge to distance themselves from groups or individuals who appeal to prejudice or intolerance in the political arena."[15]

The Interfaith Alliance also issued its "Call to Faithful Decision Voter Pledge," asking voters to commit themselves to vote for candidates who abided by these principles. By election day, twenty thousand voters had joined in signing this pledge. So did some four hundred candidates for U.S. Senate and House seats, along with President Clinton and his Republican challenger, Bob Dole. Clinton praised the pledge in a personal letter, as did the Dole campaign. In communities such as Des Moines, Iowa, candidates who received wide publicity in local papers for their vociferous opposition to the pledge proved unsuccessful on election day.[16]

The Christian Coalition spent $10 million to print forty-six million voter guides in the 1996 elections and distribute them in some 125,000 churches nationwide, according to Ralph Reed, including 150,000 or more guides in a single congressional district.[17] In an election-eve telephone message to some two million households, Reed warned of liberal groups mobilizing against the faithful. He urged them to get out and vote to defend the conservative congressional majority needed to pass faithful laws on abortion, school prayer, pro-family tax cuts, and school vouchers. At the same time, the Interfaith Alliance distributed five million voter guides of its own in forty-four House and Senate races in eighteen states and led local drives to get out the vote of the twenty thousand people who had signed the alliance's Call to Faithful Decision Voter Pledge.[18]

The Interfaith Alliance challenged the nonpartisan claims of the Christian Coalition's voter guides and its "disrespectful" use of houses of worship to distribute partisan political literature.[19] Local alliance chapters sent letters to fifty thousand pastors to alert them to the bias of the coalition's guides. The alliance called scores of related press conferences, resulting in more than 250 news stories across the country in the months leading up to the November election. In July 1997, the Federal Election Commission filed suit against the Christian Coalition for preparing its voter guides in tandem with the Republican Party, in violation of laws requiring such tax-exempt groups to be nonpartisan. The guides were designed to aid only Republican candidates, the lawsuit charged, and thereby constituted campaign contributions that were illegal for a tax-exempt religious organization to make.[20]

Shortly before the 1996 elections, the Interfaith Alliance revised and enlarged its mission statement, adding to it in broad strokes the outline of a domestic policy agenda to enact "mainstream values" by committing itself to

> SUPPORTING FAMILIES by advocating for a fair living wage that not only keeps working people out of poverty but allows them to spend valuable time together growing and learning; for access to quality child care that protects and nurtures every boy and girl; for safe streets and neighborhoods to keep our children safe; for access to affordable health care which is vital to the well being of families; for a clean environment which protects health and safety; and, for a secure retirement as a reward for a lifetime of hard work by our senior citizens.

> ENSURING OPPORTUNITY by advocating for quality education in public schools where parents can have faith their children are learning about character and respect; for the skill training needed for good paying jobs that will support a family; and, for an accessible college education that will help every generation do better than the last.

> HONORING FREEDOM by encouraging active participation in the political process by people of faith and all people of good will.[21]

Spurred by a meeting between concerned clergy and the governor of Maryland in early December 1996, the Interfaith Alliance quickly organized and released the follow-up "Statement of Concern by the Nation's

Clergy, Religious, and Lay People on the Future of Welfare Reform." It called on the president and Congress to act decisively "to soften the blow of welfare overhaul legislation," much of it a punitive attack on "the victims of poverty, not poverty itself." They should reinstate Supplemental Security Income (SSI) benefits to disabled children, restore food stamps and other aid to legal immigrants, and assure sound job opportunities and adequate child care to former welfare recipients required to work. "As fewer and fewer governmental resources have been allocated to those in need, the nation's churches, synagogues, and mosques have faced massive and increasing pressure to provide frontline services for the poor, the homeless, the unemployed and the underemployed," reported the alliance. "The nation's places of worship and their charitable arms cannot possibly fill the gaping void left by the government's recent actions," it judged. "To do so is impossible."[22] Backed by a petition signed by three thousand religious leaders and activists, the statement on welfare reform paved the way for the alliance's leaders to begin talking with members of Congress and the Clinton White House about its recommendations, all of them backing the president's budget proposals, and to begin planning statewide advocacy efforts that its chapters could carry out.

Initiating this statement on welfare reform and laying these plans for issue-specific advocacy seemed to mark a new step for the Interfaith Alliance beyond its original charter, dedicated as it was to countering the religious right and promoting civility and tolerance in public life. This new step reportedly sparked discussion among members of the national board of the Interfaith Alliance and led them eventually to "agree to disagree," while the alliance pursued its advocacy plans mainly at the local and state levels.

Parachurch Progress and Paradox

After the 1996 elections, Rev. J. Philip Wogaman, the Interfaith Alliance vice president and pastor of the United Methodist church in Washington that the Clintons attended, declared that "the Alliance succeeded in revealing the Christian Coalition's partisan core, lifting their veil of religious authenticity and finally removing its aura of invincibility. No longer will the Christian Coalition have a blank check with which to exploit the faith community in the electoral process." After more than

368

CHAPTER TEN

two years of running at flat-out campaign speed and direly needing to consolidate itself, according to Washington observers, the Interfaith Alliance and its eight-person national staff could claim 109 local chapters in thirty-six states, with a total of thirty to forty thousand members signed up. The Christian Coalition at that time claimed 1.9 million "members and supporters" in twelve hundred chapters in fifty states, led by hundreds of staffers.[23] Critics on the right downplayed the impact of the Interfaith Alliance, seen as consisting chiefly of "leftward-tilted voter guides" and media quotes "blasting the Religious Right." "The bottom line is that the religious conservative organizations have mass support, and they can sway elections," declared the Institute on Religion and Democracy. "The Interfaith Alliance does not."[24]

Nonetheless, observed the IRD, the Interfaith Alliance voter guides were "very cleverly tilted" in behalf of Democratic candidates by favoring such issues as protecting increases in Medicare funding, raising the minimum wage, and restricting assault weapons and tobacco advertising, while ignoring Republican themes such as tax cuts, school vouchers, and a ban on partial-birth abortion. Moreover, alleged the IRD in a charge the alliance neither rebutted nor admitted, distribution of the alliance's voter guides in eight key congressional districts was defrayed by soft-money campaign funds received by the alliance from Project 96, a $4 million fund-raising effort linked to labor unions and the Democratic Party. If this represented the Interfaith Alliance's plans for the future, concluded the IRD, it set a "double standard of partisanship" by bemoaning the politicization of religion on the religious right while itself operating as a "left-wing lobby."[25]

Evaluation of the Interfaith Alliance in relation to the mainline churches and their work in Washington was not so clearly pro or con in discussions among leaders of the church offices in Washington. Some appreciated the capacity of the Interfaith Alliance to counterpunch the Christian Coalition at its zenith with a measure of success in the national media. But others were more reserved about the long-term influence of the alliance in mobilizing people in the pews around key issues and moving them to the polls. Though muted and careful in criticism of the alliance, they saw its ties to the NCC and the Democratic National Committee, however informal, as a troubling reflection of the increasingly partisan politicization of freestanding, member-based religious lobbies on the model of the Christian Coalition. They saw it, too, as a possible sign of their own uncertain place in NCC plans for the future of ecumenical advocacy.

"Insofar as the Interfaith Alliance was set up to counteract the Christian Coalition, I frankly hope it's a temporary thing," attested Jay Lintner of the UCC office in Washington.

> I hope enough people come to see the Christian Coalition for the divisive political-action tool it is. Once it loses steam, the alliance will wind down, too, unless it reinvents itself around the grassroots organizing it's doing now. That could happen, if they find the right way to do it and find the right issues. I've never thought they could steer clear of the issues and just be for tolerance and civility, important as they are, because once you get people together, you have to give them something to do.

Weighing reports that the alliance was out-organizing the mainline churches themselves in the mid-1990s, Lintner averred, "The grass roots of Interfaith Alliance look to be out-organizing their own national operation. And their grass roots are hitting on issues all over the map, since they are reacting to whatever is hot with the Christian Coalition in their town or school district." Unless the Interfaith Alliance could figure out what kind of structures it was building, Lintner warned, it would thrive only as long as "the Christian Coalition keeps riling up people." In the long run, he feared, "the Interfaith Alliance could be more of a distraction than a breakthrough for us in trying to find a good national model for mobilizing the mainline churches."[26]

In spelling out the NCC's strong support for the Interfaith Alliance, Joan Brown Campbell contended that it is vital to appreciate that the National Council of Churches does not deal with political candidates. "I think that is appropriate," she affirmed, "but it has its drawbacks. The attraction of the Christian Coalition is that you can get into the thick and dirty of electoral politics. Politics from a distance isn't much fun. It's only fun when you're in it," she laughed. She elaborated the relationship between the NCC and the Interfaith Alliance in terms of this distinction: "The Interfaith Alliance allows people to say, 'That candidate does not represent our views, so we are backing someone else.' In that sense, they are like the Christian Coalition, but with a different viewpoint and values. They are willing to deal with the down and dirty of politics and indirectly back particular candidates. I think they should do that, and we should not. That's one reason I was very much a founder of the Interfaith Alliance."[27] Concluded Campbell, "If you don't deal with electing people to office, you are not going to be quite so important to politicians who have to run for office. On the other hand, as long as you stand back, you can speak to all politicians in a different way than if you had backed or opposed them for office."

In principle, this division of labor applied to the churches' moral teaching and advocacy on a full range of social issues. The Interfaith Alliance, Campbell argued, should not be defining and staking out its own positions on most such issues. The alliance issued a strong statement on welfare reform, opposing the 1996 Republican bill and its signature by President Clinton and asking religious leaders and activists to sign on with the alliance to remedy welfare cuts by backing Democratic proposals. "But that is not their business," objected Campbell. "That is not why they were created." The denominations and other religious groups that belong to the alliance already have carefully thought out positions on welfare that are not so time-bound or so set against a Republican bill and in favor of positions held by the Democratic Party. "We have always had friends on both sides of the aisle around our welfare policy, even if more of them happen to be Democrats than Republicans for their own reasons. I think the life of the Interfaith Alliance will be very limited if they get involved in policy issues," cautioned Campbell in 1997. "They need to stick to moral issues of politics, and how political life is ordered: what is fair and not fair in the game of politics? Campaign finance reform would be an extremely good problem for them to take on. There we can support them," she promised. "It's something we are going to get into, because it's not partisan. It's a matter of both parties telling the truth instead of corrupting the political process."

Without erasing the principle and the institutional territory at stake, subsequent events eased the practical dilemma between issues advocacy by the churches and electoral activism by the Interfaith Alliance. The alliance's own statement of concern on welfare reform reinforced its criticism of the Christian Coalition's Samaritan Project. Given the concerns of its members in local chapters, the Interfaith Alliance wound up pursuing the causes of both campaign finance reform and welfare reform in 1997 and beyond. But others, including the NCC, took the lead to define these issues on the national religious scene. On campaign finance in particular, the NCC acted through Religious Leaders for Campaign Finance Reform in closer conjunction with committed denominational efforts by key mainline Protestant churches, notably the UCC, and by nonreligious advocacy groups such as Common Cause and Public Citizen.[28]

Meanwhile, larger political events began to shift the stage on which the Interfaith Alliance and the Christian Coalition played out their roles.

Weeks before the 1996 election, Pat Robertson admonished Senator Dole to campaign for the presidency as America's chief moral leader, not its "chief accountant." One day after Dole's defeat, Robertson promised that religious conservatives would begin working in 1997 with sympathetic conservative members of Congress to shape the message of the next Republican presidential campaign around moral issues, such as opposition to abortion, and would settle on a candidate committed to those issues. "I think the conservatives in the Republican Party are going to have to coalesce very early and basically select a candidate," Robertson said, adding that they should "pick someone who's electable." To do so, in light of Senator Dole's defeat in 1996, said Robertson, they must wrest control from "Reagan-era operatives who did not believe that anything but money issues are important." Such inside-the-Beltway Republican operatives would not mislead the next Republican presidential campaign, as they had those in 1996 and 1992, warned Robertson. "I'm not going to participate any longer in a failed effort by these same operatives," he vowed. "I think they're incompetent. I think they missed the mood of the American people."[29]

Republican presidential campaigns to come would not win the rewards of the coalition's grassroots organizing without advancing its issues and heeding its voice. "We're not going to sit by as good soldiers and take whatever is given us," Robertson promised, in contrast to the 1996 campaign. "We were not consulted on this campaign," he said. "We were peripheral."[30] Underscoring Robertson's promise were poll numbers the Christian Coalition released the same day showing that born-again Christians who attend church frequently chose Dole over Clinton by 53 to 36 percent. A larger election-day poll indicated that Dole won 50 percent of the vote of self-identified Protestants to Clinton's 41 percent, while Clinton carried 53 percent of Catholics to 37 percent for Dole.[31]

Comparable voting data would emerge from the presidential elections of 2000 and 2004, with the campaign of George W. Bush holding the Republican lead among white Protestants and increasing its inroads among culturally conservative non-Hispanic Catholics to win a first-ever Catholic majority in 2004.[32] But in the meantime, the very strength of Pat Robertson's postelection promise in 1996 combined with the Christian Coalition's more visible and controversial public profile to lead to unexpected consequences. Popular support narrowed for such aggressive participation in electoral politics by the Christian Coalition, and its membership and contributions ebbed in the later 1990s. Donations dropped from a high of $26.5 million in 1996 to $17 million in 1997 and down to an estimated $3 million in 2000, as the usual dip in revenue in years between presidential elections was deepened by stronger competition from Focus on the Family and other conservative religious-political groups and by dismay at the coalition's inability to deliver victory in the 1998 midterm elections and the drive to impeach President Clinton.[33]

In 2004 the Christian Coalition still proclaimed itself "the largest and most active conservative grassroots political organization in America," with nearly two million members in fifteen hundred local chapters in all fifty U.S. states. But critics estimated its committed members to number only three to four hundred thousand, compared to the 150,000 members the Interfaith Alliance then counted in forty-seven local chapters.[34] Under the guidance of Karl Rove and like-minded political professionals, Republican campaigns grew more astute at seeking the votes of politically and culturally conservative evangelical white Protestants who were beyond the decisive sway of the Christian Coalition. They drew on a wider network of evangelical parachurch groups and religious media, at both the state and national levels. They developed closer relations with independent evangelical churches and denominations themselves, particularly the Southern Baptist Convention.

After Ralph Reed resigned as executive director of the Christian Coalition in 1997, it retrenched by cutting staff and dropping the Samaritan Project and the Catholic Alliance, its programs to reach out to African American churches and recruit conservative Catholics. Faced with an IRS ruling to deny it tax-exempt status under section 501(c)4 of the tax code, for going beyond advocating on issues to work actively to elect conservative Republicans to office, the Christian Coalition withdrew its application for tax-exempt status early in 1999. It then split into two separate legal entities: the for-profit Christian Coalition International to manage its partisan political activities, and the nonprofit Christian Coalition of America to pursue "voter education." This enabled the coalition to continue distributing voter guides and raising funds in evangelical churches without triggering IRS objections and threatening the tax-exempt status of these churches—a danger highlighted in thousands of letters the Interfaith Alliance sent to pastors of conservative churches in successive election cycles.[35]

Organizations across the religious right, meanwhile, continued to grow and enjoy the confidence of conservative Republican leaders in Congress, including Republican House Majority Leader Tom DeLay, and in the administration of George W. Bush. Dr. James C. Dobson's Focus on the Family became by far the largest religious organization on the cultural-political right, with a budget of some $130 million, a staff of thirteen hundred, and a daily listening audience of two hundred million around the world in 2000, on eighty television stations and nearly three thousand radio stations in the United States alone.

In 2004 Focus on the Family established an explicitly political offshoot organization, Focus on the Family Action, to lobby and campaign for conservative causes, such as outlawing same-sex marriage and abortion, without jeopardizing its own tax-exempt status. Now serving as chief executive of both Focus on the Family and its new sister organization was Don Hodel, former president of the Christian Coalition. Without directly endorsing candidates or coordinating with their election campaigns or parties, this new organization could advertise and campaign on issues closely identified with specific candidates, as it did in running advertisements against senators committed to voting against the constitutional ban on same-sex marriage in 2006.[36] It could also complement Dobson's direct political involvement as a private individual in actively endorsing candidates and campaigning for them, as he did in sending out mailings, broadcasting radio commercials, and stumping for anti-abortion representative Patrick J. Toomey in his unsuccessful challenge to moderate Republican senator Arlen Specter in Pennsylvania in April 2004.[37]

The Interfaith Alliance learned from its successes and trials alike in the 1996 elections. It replaced key staff members who were most adept at political organizing with more theologically articulate and judiciously experienced religious leaders, notably Rev. Dr. C. Welton Gaddy, a progressive Southern Baptist pastor from Louisiana who became director of the alliance in 1997. Gaddy directed Christian Citizenship Development for the Christian Life Commission of the Southern Baptist Convention prior to its takeover by fundamentalists. He emerged from this internecine struggle to lead the liberal Alliance of Baptists and head Americans United for Separation of Church and State. He proved an exceptionally apt leader and eloquent spokesman for the Interfaith Alliance over the following years, from the 1998 midterm elections as a referendum on the Republican Revolution and the impeachment of President Clinton to the born-again campaigning and church-state challenges of the election cycles of 2000 and 2004. By then, the alliance had a network of ten thousand activists in forty-seven chapters led by local clergy in thirty-eight states, at the core of a membership of 150,000 drawn from more than seventy different "faith traditions," including Jews, Muslims, Hindus, Buddhists, and Sikhs as well as nonbelievers.[38]

Through its local chapters and a national office in Washington, in coalition with denominational bodies and activist groups, the Interfaith Alliance marshaled support to bring its influence to bear on Capitol Hill, at the White House, and in statehouses on a range of legislative and policy issues. These included, for example, the Houses of Worship Free Speech Restoration Act (HR 235), to enable churches to endorse political candidates without losing their tax-exempt contributions. The alliance weighed in on charitable choice, faith-based initiatives, and "government-funded religion"; state-sponsored school prayer and the Pledge of Allegiance "under God"; the Federal Marriage Amendment, hate crimes, and workplace discrimination against gays; campaign finance reform; school vouchers; and welfare reform. On virtually every such issue, the Interfaith Alliance stood diametrically opposed to the positions of the Christian Coalition, Focus on the Family, and their allies on the religious right, and it argued pointedly against them.

In the public square and the national media, the Interfaith Alliance continued to raise its voice in concert with the National Council of Churches and its mainline Protestant members on major issues at the intersection of religion and politics across faith traditions, and it continued to keep an eye trained on the religious right. For example, the Alliance called on the nation in 2004 to turn on lights or light candles on the eve of Memorial Day until dawn, in response to the atrocities in Iraq revealed at Abu Ghraib prison. "Recent images from Iraq have disclosed horrific and dehumanizing actions," said Gaddy. "These actions, committed by all sides, violate core civic and religious values that are embraced by people of every heritage. We encourage people of faith and good will to reflect prayerfully, to demonstrate compassion to all victims of violence, to acknowledge our anguish and need for self-examination, and to foster reconciliation."[39] While praising many Christian groups for condemning the atrocities in Iraq, alliance board member Dr. Maher Hathout, adviser to the Muslim Public Affairs Council, pointed to "a gaping hole of silence coming from an influential sector of American society: leaders of the Christian right." Naming as examples Pat Robertson, Jerry Falwell, Franklin Graham, and Lt. Gen. William Boykin, Hathout said, "We cannot help but feel that anti-Muslim sentiment and the actions in Iraq are to a large extent fueled by the reckless statements of a small but influential group of religious leaders—in contradiction of American values and intentions."[40]

In the 2004 presidential campaign season, the Interfaith Alliance began tracking and commenting on candidates' statements regarding religion, morality, and politics, posting them on its own Web site and reporting them by e-mail to national, regional, and local media as well as alliance members and allied activists. It exposed and denounced an initiative in mid-2004 from the Bush-Cheney reelection campaign to enlist thousands of religious congregations around the country in directly distributing campaign literature and registering voters in houses of worship.[41] It launched its own Vote 2004 grassroots voter-registration drives through local alliance chapters and via national e-mail and Internet distribution. It also took part in the Faithful Democracy national registration drive co-sponsored by the National Council of Churches. Then it sent to thousands of congregations its "Election Year Guide for Houses of Worship," which offered legal as well as ethical counsel on electoral participation by religious bodies. The alliance coordinated its local chapters in sending clergy-to-clergy letters to thousands of houses of worship. It warned pastors of the fine moral line—and the possible legal sanctions if that line were crossed—that separated thoughtful and prayerful involvement in the electoral process from serving as "distribution centers for partisan political propaganda," such as voter guides from the Christian Coalition.[42]

Over a decade's development, the Interfaith Alliance went a long way in answering questions about its direction that concerned church leaders in Washington. It largely allayed their concern over tensions they saw between "process" and "issues" in the way the alliance worked as a free-standing, member-based parachurch organization with nonetheless close, though informal, ties to the NCC in particular. Commented one such critic of the Interfaith Alliance, "They need to distance themselves from the NCC if they want respect for their integrity on the issues, and if they want to be free to go with their local chapters on the issues that matter to them. They can't have their president and top board members just happening to be the same people at the top of the NCC, not if they're going to be credible."[43]

Added another denominational leader in Washington, more bluntly,

Interfaith Alliance needs to make sure they don't become a mouthpiece for the NCC. Whatever the NCC wants for the alliance, it doesn't want that. Neither do the denominations. And honestly, I don't think anybody wants the Interfaith Alliance to be "interdenominational" in the sense that whenever any problem comes up, everyone is worrying about what their bishop or presbytery

will think. That's not what we need. We need a grassroots coalition group
that really represents what most mainline religious people stand for and want
to work for in their own communities. Let local groups decide on their own
agenda.[44]

Can the Interfaith Alliance develop in this direction? "I was quite skeptical about it when it started, and advised people in our denomination
against joining its board," replied this critic. "It looked like a political creation, staffed by political consultants and designed to fill a political niche.
Now it's being driven more by faith and less by political advantage. That's
evident in some of their recent staff turnover, and the good appointments
they've made," he confirmed. "They should stop worrying about Pat Robertson," he urged. "Concentrate on bringing in new local people, people
we haven't seen before and couldn't get involved through the churches if
you paid them. But now that they're here, they want to work with us for
justice. That's the most valuable thing the alliance has done."[45]

Friends of the Interfaith Alliance within the mainline churches in
Washington pointed up its value in bringing the fresh air of broader
changes into their community. The public-policy people from the national
leadership of the mainline churches and their Washington offices are always going to be important in the business of religious advocacy, said the
UCC's Jay Lintner, but the real question is "how far these new groups
and the new people they bring in will change the way we do our business." Except in moments of national crisis, such as war in the Persian
Gulf or in Iraq, church leaders in Washington are almost always trying
to decide among a multitude of issues—children's health care, welfare
reform, Middle East terrorism, or land mines. "All of those are important issues," granted Lintner. "But grassroots folks want two or three
priorities at most that really come at you and you can organize behind.
The mainline-church policy community has never been able to sit down
and come up with that short list of priorities. This infusion of grassroots
people into the national scene could help church leaders do that, even if
it has to force them to it."[46]

To help mainline religious groups get their message out, as well as raise
funds and mobilize supporters, new allies have come to their aid from the
worlds of political consulting, direct-mail fund-raising, Internet communication, and media production. In a kind of continuum of influence and
migration, many of these allies brought to the churches, via freestanding
parachurch groups and issue coalitions, professional experience gained in

working for nonreligious moral advocacy groups such as the Children's Defense Fund and the Alternative Journalism Center. New sources of funding for such expert help also began to emerge, typically from a younger generation of small foundations, usually located in the liberal political mainstream or on the cultural left. These included the Veatch, HKH, New World, and Ms. foundations. Their support coalesced behind religious and moral advocacy groups such as the Interfaith Alliance in efforts to level the playing field with the Christian Coalition, Focus on the Family, and other such groups. It came in the wake of widening recognition that a handful of ideologically aggressive foundations, such as those directed by Richard Mellon Scaife, have played a large role in sustaining these advocates on the right, as well as others such as the Institute on Religion and Democracy and the Institute on Religion and Public Life. "These new foundations are much more open to funding exactly what groups like Interfaith Alliance want to do," reported one of their beneficiaries. "With the old-line liberal foundations like Rockefeller, you'd have to get a more traditional academic or denominational grant and try to pull it in a more political direction. Not anymore."[47]

Reflecting on such changes, a religious leader in Washington remarked, "The churches are getting the hang of doing direct mail. We send things over to our direct-mail people, just like the Christian Coalition does with 'Infocision.' They cut it down to sound bites, they send it back to us to look over before it goes out. There are people over there who grew up in the Methodist or Episcopal Church. They speak our language, plus they have all the data." Asked whether anything is lost in such targeted-market translation of moral appeals, he replied, "Sure. From time to time it does bother me that we are spending all this money, time, and effort—and we are all doing it, from the Christian Coalition to the mainline—for marketing that would do more real good if it went to feeding needy people or creating jobs for them to earn a decent living, or even spreading the gospel." Is this the way to enter into the kingdom or raise up the Beloved Community? "I doubt it," he admitted. "It bothers me, but it's the world we're living in."[48]

Faced with the challenge of unifying their denominational efforts into the witness of a public church—and the perils of adopting marketing tactics without a moral compass, and political strategies without a soul—mainline-church advocates in Washington agreed strongly on the need for closer, more responsive relationships among denominational boards and offices charged with social witness, church leaders authorized to represent the denomination as a whole, and those who preach and pray in local congregations.

In this view, the greatest good served by the Interfaith Alliance in its first decade in existence lies not in winning seats in school-board contests against the Christian Coalition or helping to save President Clinton from conviction on charges of impeachment. Instead, it lies in keeping the alliance's original promise to speak the gospel truth of the Sermon on the Mount in answer to the claims of sectarian righteousness to map the "road to victory" for all Christians. The real danger in socially narrowed parachurch movements that focus on single-issue politics and bless partisan political ideologies lies in the truncated and corrupted example of religion in public life that they set when they shrink the moral vision and shirk the moral responsibility borne by all real communities of faith—mainline and evangelical, orthodox and progressive. These congregational communities reach across the breadth of religious tradition and revelation to join specific moral positions and social actions to broad teaching and preaching, which they embody in common worship, communal life, and the care of souls. Parachurch groups across the political spectrum threaten both religious awareness and public civility when they forgo the demanding integrity of religious practice and community in their strategic efforts to manage public opinion, mobilize partisan constituencies, and lobby the state along the morally instrumental lines of interest-group politics.

The National Council of Churches Redux

Joan Brown Campbell retired from the helm of the National Council of Churches in 1999, after nine years of serving as its general secretary and as a lightning rod for criticism of its financial and administrative struggles as well as its political conflicts. Through the 1980s and 1990s, the council's fraying finances led to a slow but steady attrition of staff and programming. Its reserves were drawn down from $24 million to less than $3 million to defray deficit program spending, including $12 million in reserves spent from 1994 to 1999. "The Council has never been flush with funds," said Campbell of the NCC's financial crisis in 1999. "The needs of the poor are too great, the expectations of the world are too high, the heart of the church is too empathetic. We say yes because God demands it of us." The NCC's deficit "is not only in dollars," she insisted, "but is in our inability to see in each other promise and potential."[49]

The NCC's African American and Orthodox member churches came in for special thanks from Campbell for having "sheltered and fed and inspired me during my years of ministry." Those churches, she said, play a different role in the lives of their people than do the mainline churches. "They have helped their people survive. They have kept faith alive," she said, and they "have inspired the soul of the Council." She acknowledged the support of the mainline churches, seven of which give more than 90 percent of the NCC's budget. But she also admonished them. "The mainline churches mourn their loss of power and influence in the ecumenical movement," she said. They must realize that "the soul of the ecumenical movement is not in a return to a familiar hegemony but in finding our way forward together." The National Council of Churches is more than the sum of its parts, Campbell concluded. "Our shared witness and our common voice can change the world. We can be the moral force that ends poverty as we know it but first we must forgive and embrace one another."[50]

Taking office as the NCC's new general secretary in 2000 was Rev. Robert W. Edgar, a six-term former Democratic congressman from a heavily Republican district of Pennsylvania, president of a United Methodist seminary for a dozen years, and a self-described optimist, futurist, and coalition builder with a knack for helping institutions re-envision themselves. Accepting the NCC's presidency for 2000–2001 was Rev. Andrew Young, who served on the NCC staff in 1957–61 before going on to become a civil rights leader, U.S. congressman, UN ambassador, and Atlanta mayor. Together the two men led the council in making a series of key changes that were widely welcomed and praised by the NCC's members, contributors, and friends, including the churches in Washington.

Under a radical restructuring plan worked out by the NCC's executive board and approved by its General Assembly in 1999, the council cut its headquarters staff by one-third and streamlined its operations. It separately incorporated Church World Service, the NCC's big-budget, worldwide arm for disaster relief and humanitarian aid, making it semi-autonomous and responsible for its own internal management, finances, and administration. The council merged the self-contained staff for each of its dozen-plus program ministries—including Eco-Justice, Health, Economic Justice/Hunger Concerns, and Public Witness/Legislative Advocacy—into a single "matrix staff" of generalists to work in various configurations depending upon the priorities set by the council's executive board. Cutbacks, streamlining, and increased contributions from member denominations enabled the NCC to begin balancing its operating budgets in 2000 and to begin rebuilding its reserves, with the help of outside grants, by 2003.

Fiscal and administrative necessity was the mother of invention for the NCC's sharply tightened program focus. The fruitful results of these changes for relations between the NCC and the mainline churches in Washington also followed from the top-priority commitment of the council made by Bob Edgar and Andrew Young to the decade-long Mobilization to Overcome Poverty, in closer connection with other partners in "a broadening table of Christian unity." It would mobilize the members of its own "community of communions" more actively yet flexibly, as equals in networks and partners in coalitions with nonreligious groups for moral advocacy and social action. Accordingly, the NCC went on to give staunch support to the 2001 initiative of the Children's Defense Fund, Act to Leave No Child Behind, to combat poverty, neglect, and substandard schooling. The NCC began sharing staff with the Children's Defense Fund to back the CDF's legislative advocacy and carry its campaign into the churches. The council's research and planning director served at the same time as the CDF's Acting Director of Religious Affairs, and the NCC's staff person for its Justice for Children program served as the CDF's Director of Religious Networks. "Organizational structures have changed; the world has changed; we will change. One way we can grow is to form alliances and work through networking, referral and partnering," reported Bob Edgar to the NCC General Assembly in 2000, to explain its new partnerships and shared staff members. "Instead of reinventing the wheel, we are sharing it."[51]

Focusing so strongly on the central issue of ending poverty yet defining the issue so flexibly and broadly enabled the NCC to invite the mainline churches and their Washington offices to join in its Mobilization to Overcome Poverty without asking them to give up their own distinctive policy priorities and programs. It also enabled the NCC to invite its member churches to join with a wider range of nondenominational parachurch groups and nonreligious advocacy groups such as Call to Renewal, the Children's Defense Fund, Bread for the World, Habitat for Humanity, and the United Negro College Fund. Along with such partner organizations and non-NCC Christian churches—especially evangelicals, Pentecostals, and Catholics—the NCC affirmed that it would collaborate closely with the Washington Interreligious Staff Council (WISC). But it would neither press NCC priorities upon the churches in Washington nor cede these churches the lead in the larger initiative's lobbying and organizing.

Thus, in January of 2000, instead of pushing forward with the National Religious Leadership Conference of years earlier, the NCC convened a more issue-specific, organizationally open-ended consultation of some seventy representatives of denominational and ecumenical legislative offices, policy advocates, and interfaith agencies with its own staff. They agreed to work together for passage of the Hunger Relief Act and minimum wage/living wage legislation. They committed to join in opposing violence, addressing AIDS in Africa, and advancing the Jubilee 2000 campaign for debt relief in the third world. A month later, Bob Edgar announced that the NCC's priorities for ecumenical legislative advocacy in Washington would complement the Covenant to Overcome Poverty backed by Call to Renewal, the alliance of faith-based organizations led by Jim Wallis of Sojourners.[52] Edgar joined other national Christian leaders on the east steps of the U.S. Capitol to launch the Covenant's campaign at the conclusion of the four-day annual summit of Call to Renewal, a national meeting now held each year in Washington, like the annual interreligious legislative briefing put on until 1999 by Interfaith Impact for Justice and Peace and the Washington offices of the mainline churches.

To celebrate the NCC's Mobilization to Overcome Poverty, Jim Wallis in turn addressed the NCC General Assembly in November of 2000, along with former congressman William Gray, head of the United Negro College Fund. "We need you now, National Council, more than ever before to stand up and let your light shine brightly," urged Gray, "so that children, the hungry, the needy, the millions without healthcare may know that someone is on the battle-field" in their behalf.[53] Affirmed Wallis,

> I'm very drawn to this Mobilization to Overcome Poverty that the NCC has announced. I believe it is a concrete sign of what I see God doing across this country. When I see the Jubilee 2000 debt reduction campaign, the Call to Renewal, the NCC's Mobilization to Overcome Poverty—I have to believe something new is happening. This is a movement whose time has come.
>
> It's time for a new "network of networks." . . . I hope these new relationships will help fuel greater unity. I see churches dropping their "gang colors," people who've not been together saying, "It's time for us to come together."
>
> We must find a way to take the National Council of Churches, the National Association of Evangelicals, the Roman Catholic Bishops . . . [and] magnify our public voice and lead our nation to a different vision. . . . I'm not sure

I know how to partner and coordinate all this, but we can do it if we think "movement."[54]

Holding up the model of such a movement, mobilization, and network of networks to end poverty offered a clear alternative to pushing for a National Religious Leadership Conference or an NCC Advisory Committee of the heads of the mainline denominations and their Washington offices to set a multi-issue agenda for legislative advocacy. This change of conceptual model and organizational strategy helped settle relations between the NCC and mainline-church offices in Washington, in tandem with a dramatic shift in political circumstances and issues after George W. Bush gained the White House in 2000, al Qaeda attacked the United States on September 11, 2001, and the United States invaded Iraq in 2003.

Underlying structural problems remained between the NCC and the mainline churches in Washington, according to denominational leaders in the capital, but events and people in positions of leadership combined to make a world of difference in the churches and the national polity alike.[55] In 2003, for example, Rev. Dr. Paul H. Sherry, former president of the United Church of Christ and a figure widely admired and trusted by mainline-church leaders on Capitol Hill and across the country, agreed to donate a year of his retirement to leading the NCC's Mobilization to Overcome Poverty. In 2006 he was still at its helm, pressing Congress to raise the minimum wage. "The NCC has found a better way now," sums up a supportive church leader. "Bob Edgar has a sure political touch, he listens, he's good on his feet. He can collaborate, and he can follow through. He's done both on Iraq."[56]

Those virtues also marked NCC initiatives before war in Iraq came to the fore. In the final weeks of the Clinton administration, Edgar declared, "The highlight of this year's legislative process was the successful enactment of the Jubilee 2000 Third World Debt Reduction Legislation, recently signed by the President."[57] Early in the Bush administration, Edgar actively, if cautiously, welcomed the president's faith-based initiative with a careful critique of its limits and problems in light of the charitable-choice provision of the Personal Responsibility and Work Opportunity Reconciliation Act of 1996, which was enacted as part of the "welfare reform" legislation passed by the new Republican majority in Congress and signed into law by President Clinton during his run for reelection.

Bob Edgar represented the NCC on the bipartisan Working Group on Human Needs and Faith-Based and Community Initiatives, led by former senator Harris Wofford. It worked for six months in 2001–2 to wrestle through church-state and charitable-choice issues to agree on "29 recommendations for ways in which President Bush's faith-based social service proposals can be implemented without violating the First Amendment," Edgar reported, "and without putting the financial and spiritual integrity of churches and other faith groups at risk." Now it was Bush's turn to respond to the group's recommendations and realize his own proposals by providing adequate government funding for them, Edgar concluded. "Adequate funding is the President's responsibility," he stressed, underlining the NCC view that charitable churches can complement the essential role of good government to serve justice and sustain public provision, but they cannot replace it.[58]

Meanwhile, the NCC continued to play a key part in the coalition of Religious Leaders for Campaign Finance Reform. This coalition was supported by staff members of the Washington offices of the mainline churches, and it extended beyond them to take in Catholic, Jewish, and Unitarian groups in partnership with Americans for Reform, an umbrella coalition of nonreligious groups such as Common Cause in support of the McCain-Feingold bill for campaign finance reform. These groups applauded the U.S. Senate for finally passing its version of the bill in the spring of 2001. They urged the House and the president to move quickly to "rid government of the buying and selling of votes" and "an electoral process that structurally and systematically favors the wealthiest among us."[59]

At the same time, the NCC formed a new coalition of Protestant churches with Catholic, Jewish, and nondenominational groups such as Bread for the World to oppose the 2001 tax cut proposed by the Bush administration because it was "too inequitable, too large, and threatens the future well being of our nation." Such cuts threaten spending for public education, health care, housing, and international aid that most Americans need and support, argued the Religious Community for Responsible Tax Policy. Government is intended to "serve God's purposes by promoting the common good," so paying taxes to this end is vital to the stewardship citizens share, argued the coalition. The poorest and neediest households deserve to benefit from progressive tax rates and tax credits such as the child tax credit and an expanded earned income tax credit. "As millions of people—parents and children, the elderly, people with disabilities—are driven to seek charity to meet their most basic needs," the coalition declared, "we are appalled that the focus of attention in the

Congress is not on meeting their needs; rather, it is on tax cuts which will mostly benefit the affluent."[60]

Pressing for Peace and Justice

"Out of the ashes and tragedy of September 11, 2001," resolved the NCC General Assembly two months after the attacks, should rise redoubled efforts for peace with justice. They should seek protection of human rights and fundamental freedoms, from Afghanistan to America itself, through shared prayer and repentance to face the future together.[61] The NCC stopped short of calling for an immediate end to the war in Afghanistan. But it stressed the need for the United States to follow the lead of the United Nations in assuring the country's peaceful and sovereign postwar reconstruction. It also urged continuing concern for America's poor in a time of deepening economic difficulty, fewer good jobs, and flattened wages. With time running out on lifetime eligibility under provisions of the 1996 welfare law, the NCC asked local, state, and federal government agencies to "stop the clock" terminating Temporary Assistance for Needy Families (TANF), unemployment insurance, food stamps, and health care. It asked Congress in 2002 to improve and reauthorize these programs, along with the related Child Care and Development Block Grant, in order to eliminate poverty, not just reduce welfare caseloads.

The NCC continued these calls to fight poverty as the drumbeat of the march to war in Iraq quickened over the following months. "Imagine that the kind of time, creativity and money that are being poured into preparations for war against Iraq were being poured instead into the challenge of ending poverty in the United States and around the world," Bob Edgar proposed to three thousand of the faithful who filled Washington's National Cathedral on Martin Luther King Day in January 2003. Then they marched to the White House to protest the war, in an event the NCC co-sponsored with the Children's Defense Fund, Call to Renewal, and Sojourners. "Martin Luther King, Jr., was right—war diverts attention and resources from the needs of impoverished people, especially the children. War is an enemy of the poor," declared Edgar.[62]

As the invasion of Iraq loomed closer, the NCC led religious delegations to meet with European heads of state to counsel against war, and with religious leaders in Iraq to put a human face on the destruction to come. All the while, it pressed urgently, though vainly, for a face-to-face meeting with President Bush. On the eve of the invasion, the NCC joined with religious leaders, churches, and civic groups in the United States and overseas, from Archbishop Tutu to MoveOn.org and the Win Without War coalition, to sponsor a global candlelight vigil for peace on Sunday, March 16, 2003. More than six thousand gatherings around the world lit candles "to rekindle the light of reason—and of hope."[63] After Saddam Hussein's regime fell and President Bush proclaimed the end of major combat in Iraq, the NCC persisted in pressing for peace. In the spring of 2004, it urged nationwide peace vigils to mark the first anniversary of the invasion of Iraq, to mourn the dead, and to pray for all affected. These should include "people living in poverty, veterans whose benefits have been cut, children whose schools have no books, and families with no health insurance. Let us all heed the reminder that in the grim economy of war, the cost of destruction in one place is paid for by deprivation in others."[64]

The NCC, through its coalition of Churches for Middle East Peace and its General Assembly, continued calling for the U.S. government to take the lead in brokering an Israeli-Palestinian ceasefire. It should bring about a two-state peace settlement drawn along the 1967 Green Line, while preserving the City of Jerusalem as an open, shared city with freedom of worship assured for people of all faiths.[65] Upholding this top priority in the Middle East, the NCC protested the building of the Separation Wall by Israel in 2003. It dissented from the Bush administration's endorsement of Israeli prime minister Ariel Sharon's 2004 plan to fortify major Jewish settlements in the West Bank and revoke without compensation the right of Palestinian refugees to return to their former homes in Israel. "The way toward peace is to work for a just resolution of the conflict between Israel and Palestine. That will lead to the end of the terror of suicide bombers and targeted assassinations," declared Jim Winkler of the Methodist General Board of Church and Society in behalf of Churches for Middle East Peace. "Instead of telling Prime Minister Sharon that it's OK now to violate international law and United Nations resolutions, President Bush should be pressuring both sides to stem the violence and start talking again," argued Winkler. "President Bush has effectively told the world that what Israel has taken by force from the Palestinians is now acceptable. This is a road map to war."[66]

As President Bush began his second term in January of 2005, an official NCC Delegation to the Middle East urged him to move to end the Israeli-Palestinian conflict and realize a two-state solution in order to defend the

United States from terrorism as well as free the Palestinian people and assure Israel's security. "Every day the conflict continues, hatred of the United States government is fueled," wrote Bob Edgar and top leaders of Protestant, Evangelical, Orthodox, and Roman Catholic churches and institutions in a public letter featured in a full-page ad in the national edition of the *New York Times*. "With each news report of Palestinian suffering . . . popular support in Arab and Muslim countries for terrorism grows and the threat of attacks directed at the United States increases," along with the suffering and loss of life among Israelis. "A hallmark of your campaign was the commitment to defeat terror and make our country more secure," the letter's fifty-seven signers reminded the newly inaugurated president. "We believe that the promise of peace is the best defense against terrorism," they concluded, and it is attained by answering God's call to "all nations and all people to do justice to one another."[67]

Only a sliver of hope for peace remains, and it must be seized at once, reported the NCC delegation on its return from the Middle East. "Our word is one of alarm and worry. Current policies promise more war, death, and destruction." Countering charges of NCC bias against Israel, as advanced by the Institute on Religion and Democracy and shared by some American Jewish advocates, the NCC delegation reaffirmed its long-standing support of Israel and its right to live in peace and security in accord with justice for the Palestinian people. "We are authentic friends of Israel and we have a vision of peace and security," it testified. "We are not blind in our support and reserve the right to question the actions even of our friends. We believe genuine negotiations and not unilateral action can avoid unimaginable violence in the future." Thus, "while every leader we met—Christian, Jewish, Muslim—condemned violence, it is clear the overriding problem is Israel's continuing occupation of Palestine territory," judged the delegation, citing the crushing burdens of human rights abuses and punishing poverty, intensified by the lethal explosions of violent Palestinian resistance. President Bush must send a credible special envoy to reopen negotiations to end this cycle of violence, demanded the delegation, and American Christians must contact the president and their members of Congress to "insist U.S. policy be balanced toward both Israel and Palestine."[68]

The NCC likewise responded to the escalating hostilities that broke out in Lebanon, Israel, and Gaza in mid-2006. Jesus' lament over Jerusalem (Luke 19:41–42a) echoes over the Middle East and in the hearts of men and women everywhere, it said, in decrying the futile cycle of violent retribution of missile strikes, kidnappings, incursions, shelling, and bombing:

> When will Israeli leaders see that aggression only breeds more aggression, and that security cannot be achieved through the oppression and humiliation of others? When will all Palestinian leaders understand that calls for justice demand the doing of justice, and that suffering injustice does not confer moral license to respond with violence? When will the United States see that being an honest, effective broker for peace requires fairness in our dealings with both the Israelis and the Palestinians, and now the Lebanese, and that doing nothing to end the violence costs us dearly in spirit, blood, treasure and moral integrity?[69]

The NCC called on all parties in the Middle East to end the current hostilities and work toward a just and sustainable settlement of their conflicts. The U.S. government should lead all governments in working through the United Nations to open earnest negotiations and address immediate humanitarian needs. The NCC followed up with a letter to President Bush pressing him to work directly with other world leaders to "secure an immediate cease-fire in the violent conflict now raging between Hezbollah and Israel" and to "launch an intensive diplomatic initiative for the cessation of hostilities" as a necessary first step on the road to peace.[70]

As the American occupation of Iraq foundered in political deadlock and descended into the depths of metastasizing insurgency and sectarian violence, the NCC asked how the United States could expect people of goodwill and nations around the world to help us in fighting terrorism when they see us "betraying our own democratic ideals" in a war no longer epitomized by Iraqis and Americans together tearing down Saddam Hussein's statue, but by U.S. soldiers torturing Iraqi prisoners and Iraqis slaughtering one another. In public statements and an ecumenical pastoral letter, the NCC urged faithful Americans to call on their congressional delegations for a change of course in Iraq. The United States should agree to "turn over the transition of authority and postwar reconstruction to the United Nations—and to recognize U.S. responsibility to contribute to this effort generously through security, economic, and humanitarian support—not only to bring international legitimacy to the effort, but also to foster any chance for lasting peace."[71]

In a 2003 policy paper, "A Vision of Peace in a Time of War," Bob Edgar urged the United States to turn away from the unilateralism of the Bush administration's 2002 National Security Strategy of wars of preemption waged by the United States against any adversary in a growing "axis of evil." Instead, the administration should "adopt a foreign policy based on civil and faith-based respect for multilateral institutions, human rights, and a fair and sustainable global economy." Only thus can we be true to our faith in "the transcending sovereignty and love of God for all creation" and the "dignity and worth of each person as a child of God." This is a vision of foreign policy worthy of America within the community of nations, Edgar concluded, "and we intend to work to make it a reality in our world no matter what the obstacles."[72]

The NCC's continuing efforts to oppose the war in Iraq and fight poverty at home came together in the 2004 election cycle in a national voter-registration drive. It was notable for its overarching civic themes and its range of nonreligious and parachurch partners, much like those sounded and mobilized by Interfaith Impact in the 1980s and by the Interfaith Alliance in the 1990s. "The voice of the poor must be heard, loudly and clearly," proclaimed Bob Edgar at a news conference in January 2004, in which he unveiled a $15 million get-out-the-vote effort aimed at registering more than two million new low-income voters in the coming year. "The ballot box provides that voice."[73] The NCC formed a coalition anchored by the Center for Community Change, a national nonprofit organization that provides technical assistance, training, and policy support to low-income community groups. It promised to work with "organizations with deep roots in the community to help organize voter mobilization" by going door-to-door, working downtown streets, staffing phone banks, and sponsoring local issues forums.[74]

The NCC broadened these efforts to encourage all faithful Americans to engage actively in the democratic process, through a coalition called Faithful Democracy that joined the mainline denominations, Unitarians, and Reform Jews together with the Interfaith Alliance around the themes of religious tolerance and civility long stressed by the alliance.[75] Speaking in behalf of Faithful Democracy, the Interfaith Alliance's Welton Gaddy testified, "What we do not do will speak as powerfully as what we do about our belief in the necessity of keeping separate the institutions of religion and the missions of partisan politicians in order to protect both the vigor of democracy and the integrity of religion in the life of our nation."[76]

After cutting the NCC's staff, focusing its programs, and balancing its operating budget in 2000, Bob Edgar proclaimed, "Like Gideon's army, we are fewer, tougher and more confident."[77] By 2004, the NCC was a smaller army with clearer objectives and a stronger network of allies. The council's Mobilization to Overcome Poverty and its voter-registration drives coupled advocacy in Washington with grassroots organizing across the country. It forged coalitions to join the national leaders of the mainline denominations and the faithful in the pews of local churches together with community groups and nonreligious lobbies. In 2004 the NCC began to strengthen and trumpet these coalitions to link national advocacy and local networks through FaithfulAmerica.org, an "interfaith e-advocacy ministry" numbering a hundred thousand members by late 2005. Located in the NCC's Capitol Hill offices and headed by Vince Isner, a former communications director of the United Methodist General Board of Church and Society, Faithful America aimed to grow tenfold in order to raise "a clear, focused faith-based voice of America, and to help bring about a 'climate change' in Washington that reflects the values of a compassionate, progressive and faithful American people."[78]

In these terms, the National Council offered the mainline churches a prospect for the future built on their sustained aspirations and embattled efforts over the past generation. The NCC's high-profile opposition to war in Iraq proved to be pointed and persistent. It was consensual across the mainline denominations and their leaders in Washington. It was unusually collaborative in reaching beyond the churches themselves to join with a wide range of like-minded parachurch groups, nonreligious advocacy groups, and public-affairs lobbies in the United States and overseas.[79] For example, to mark the "tragic milestone" of the two thousandth U.S. soldier to die in Iraq in October 2005, Bob Edgar asked all Americans to pray for the families of the fallen, and for the war to end. Through Faithful America, the NCC urged all communities of worship to join in a prayerful Remembrance Weekend, immediately following on and linked with 1,354 midweek vigils organized across the nation by MoveOn.org Political Action, TrueMajority, and Democracy for America, political advocacy groups opposed to the Iraq war. In mid-2006, Faithful America likewise joined with nonreligious advocacy groups against the war in the nationwide Ring in Remembrance event. It offered a ringing of bells inside and outside houses of worship to commemorate the twenty-five hundred U.S. military casualties in the Iraq war, as a tribute to the fallen and as a plea to the U.S. government to end the war and bring the troops home.[80]

The NCC continued to have its critics among mainline-church leaders. "Instead of banging the drum against the Iraq war out on the political

left, where he has no base," said one, "Bob Edgar should be right at the
religious center, leading the fight against genocide in Darfur."[81] Added
another, "They're still trying to cover every issue under the sun by churn-
ing out a new e-mail every other day of the week. It's scattershot on the
issues, and it's all preaching to the same choir. They need to concentrate
on a few things, organize more widely, and really carry through."[82] NCC
efforts in 2006 to mobilize voters behind key issues—fighting poverty,
hiking the minimum wage, funding child care, reforming immigration,
rebuilding the Gulf Coast after Katrina, protecting the environment, and
ending the war in Iraq—led astute analysts to likewise echo the debates
involving Interfaith Impact and the Interfaith Alliance over national religious advocacy and grassroots organizing. "The Christian Right has a
ground game," noted one. "Thus far the Christian left mainly has an air
game: they want to throw positions, they want to talk to the media, but
do they have the network in place on the ground to get people out to
vote?"[83]

For some in the mainline churches, structural problems of NCC funding and functioning remained more worrisome in themselves and more
problematic in their implications. The NCC did indeed stabilize itself
financially under Bob Edgar. But support from its member denominations continued to ebb, from $2.9 million in 2000–2001 to $1.75 million in
2004–5, a 40 percent drop, while new income from nonchurch sources
grew nearly fivefold, from $600,000 in 2000–2001 to $2.9 million in 2004– 5.
Foundations contributed $1.76 million in 2004–5, surpassing denomina-
tional support, which declined to only about 30 percent of the revenue
by 2004. The NCC's biggest contributors were still the United Methodist Church ($596,233) and the Presbyterian Church ($410,000), with the
Episcopal Church and the Evangelical Lutheran Church in America placing fifth and eighth, respectively, among the top ten. But the majority of
top-ten, six-figure donors consisted of the National Religious Partnership
for the Environment ($344,514), the Knight Foundation ($300,000), and
the Tides Foundation ($225,000), followed by the Ford and Kellogg
foundations and the Rockefeller Brothers' Fund.[84] With the ranks of the
NCC's own staff thinned from more than a hundred in early 2000 to fewer
than forty in 2006, sharing staff with the Children's Defense Fund and
collaborating more closely with groups such as MoveOn.org certainly
seemed no less a necessity in the nick of time than increased foundation
funding. But would these new resources and partners prove to be virtuous as well as necessary?

From the religious right came an unequivocal answer: long-standing "political alienation between the council and its claimed constituency begot a financial alienation," which was now pushing the NCC past the liberal fringe of mainline denominational headquarters and far beyond the mainstream faithful in the pews, into the deep pockets and demanding arms of the partisan political left. The NCC was reshaping its programs to fit the priorities of its powerful new funders and partners, for example, the pro-abortion and gay-rights Tides Foundation and True Majority.org, the antiwar Internet activist group co-sponsoring the NCC's Faithful America Web site at the behest of Ben Cohen, the populist emperor of upscale ice cream. "With the council's increasing dependency on secular liberal foundations," asked the Institute on Religion and Democracy, "will it ever be able to return to its original purpose?"[85]

For those in the mainline churches, the implications of NCC support shifting from the council's denominational members to foundation grants and large individual donors framed a more difficult and delicate question. "Does non-church funding received by the NCCC [National Council of Churches of Christ] and CWS [Church World Service] unduly impact the agenda of the organization?" asked a report adopted by the 2004 General Assembly of the Presbyterian Church (USA). "There are some examples of influence on the agenda of the NCCC by its partnerships with foundations and other organizations that have their own agendas," notes the Presbyterian report in response. "The NCCC has begun to address this issue and recognizes the potential for conflict with the interests of the member communions." Presbyterian representatives to the National Council, advises the report, "can encourage development of clear policies that ensure accountability to the member churches for the use of funds from non-church sources."[86]

Moreover, member communions should continue to expand their joint planning in setting the agenda and priorities of the National Council of Churches, as they did in restructuring Church World Service. "The NCCC administration often asks the churches to support its agenda rather than assisting the churches in cooperative agenda setting through joint decision-making by their representatives," diagnoses the Presbyterian report. To meet this challenge, it urges that the council's governing board, composed of representatives of its member churches but no foundation officials or private donors, "should take strong leadership that would allow it to set the agenda and direct the priority setting of the NCCC." Accountability to the board's direction, stresses the report, must be "the focus of the development and use of all funds," as foundation support rises as a percentage of council revenues and denominational giving ebbs. More denominational involvement, concludes the Presbyterian report, is likewise needed in the council's various commissions to take an active role in leading it through this time of transition.[87] "NCC accountability to its member churches is an issue we're all working on," sums up one veteran representative to the council from a key mainline denomination. "To some extent, the NCC is doing better than before, but they need to do it more transparently, and we need to keep pushing to help them."[88]

These questions and conclusions remain open enough to justify careful oversight to guard against temptations to shape ecumenical programs to serve the political priorities of outside foundations. They also justify careful inquiry into the subtler isomorphic tug on the NCC and other religious advocates across the cultural-political spectrum to converge toward the organizational forms of the freestanding lobbies, ideological think tanks, and membership-based political-action committees that crowd the American public square today. At the same time, to many in the mainline churches, such questions and criticism of the NCC now sound more constructive and sympathetic than they did in the 1990s, and the NCC seems more attentive in response.

As most Americans came to see the faltering U.S. military occupation of Iraq as too costly in U.S. lives and dollars to continue, however politically polarized they remained over whether President Bush was right or wrong to attack, the NCC broadened its opposition to the war. For example, it rallied behind bipartisan congressional legislation in mid-2005 that urged President Bush to announce by the end of the year a plan for the withdrawal of all U.S. forces from Iraq.[89] The NCC also focused its international attention on Darfur. It joined with leading nongovernmental organizations from the United States, the United Kingdom, and France to press their countries to sponsor a UN Security Council resolution to mandate peace-enforcement operations to stop government-backed genocide and protect civilians in Darfur. The NCC joined with the National Association of Evangelicals, as well as U.S. ecumenical, interfaith, and humanitarian groups such as the Save Darfur Coalition and Africa Action to pray for peace and to spread bipartisan U.S. support for UN peacekeeping intervention. In mid-2006, Senators Bill Frist (R-Tenn.) and Hillary Clinton (D-N.Y.) signed the one millionth postcard from Americans to President Bush through the Save Darfur Coalition, now grown to 167 faith-based advocacy and humanitarian organizations, to press the president to take the lead in creating a multinational force strong enough to protect the people of Darfur.[90]

Instead of trying to reinforce the overarching architecture of fixing priority issues and coordinating advocacy on these issues across all of its member denominations, as promised by the NCC's National Religious Leadership Conference on Public Policy Ministries and its Advisory Committee in the 1990s, the NCC took a more flexibly orchestrated, issue-specific "network of networks" approach under Bob Edgar. For example, the NCC brought together Jewish, Catholic, Orthodox, Protestant, Muslim, and Sikh religious leaders in the United States to meet with leaders of African churches and Bread for the World in the Interfaith Convocation on Hunger at the Washington National Cathedral in mid-2005. It thereby reached back a generation to the single-issue roots of Interfaith Impact in the WISC Taskforce on World Hunger, while it continued to tackle problems of poverty from other angles with other partners.[91]

In opposing the Bush administration's 2006 proposed budget as unjust, for example, the NCC joined in early 2005 with its five major mainline member denominations—the Episcopal Church, the Presbyterian Church (USA), the United Church of Christ, the United Methodist Church, and the Evangelical Lutheran Church in America. It thereby formed an ad hoc kind of Protestant Policy Council, much like that proposed by church leaders in Washington critical of the NCC's role in the failure of their ecumenical campaign for health-care reform in 1994. "For the most part this is a budget that ignores the needs of the poor, children and the elderly," the new conciliar group declared at a news conference on Capitol Hill. It called instead for a budget built around the moral value of caring for society's weakest and most vulnerable members.[92]

Let Justice Roll: Faith and Community Voices Against Poverty, the joint antipoverty campaign led by the UCC's Paul Sherry and backed by the NCC with the Center for Community Change, sponsored a related National Call-In Day on March 8, 2005. It demanded of Congress that the federal budget "should reflect the values of equality, opportunity, and justice that honors the poor, supports families, and builds strong, viable communities." A week later there followed Ecumenical Advocacy Days, on the model of the annual national religious briefing long organized by Interfaith Impact, with much the same mix of sponsors from the mainline denominations, Catholic orders religious, and parachurch social-justice groups. Their advocacy focused on a "more complete moral vision" than abortion and

same-sex marriage to urge lawmakers to take account of the larger biblical mandate that "we act as peacemakers, uplift those who live in poverty
and take care of God's creation," as Bob Edgar put it.[93] This ecumenical
convention in Washington was preceded by a petition drive for a more
just and compassionate budget conducted online by FaithfulAmerica.org,
and it was capped by a Capitol Hill rally co-sponsored by the NCC and
the Interfaith Alliance. This reinvigorated effort brought together national denominational leaders, church offices in Washington, and Catholic orders religious with a wide range of parachurch and moral advocacy
groups to declare, "This budget does NOT reflect our values."

By focusing on the budget as a moral document, as did the 1980s antipoverty campaigns led by the churches in Washington, religious advocates
sought to show the wider implications of a single issue for social concerns
at the heart of biblical faith: caring for the sick and needy, working for
justice, and making peace. They sought, once more, to tie together national advocacy with community organizing and congregational education
by standing against a budget that "eats away at the heart of the American dream" by favoring the wealthy, corporations, and war spending over
families and communities in need of Medicaid, food stamps, good jobs
at living wages, decent public housing, effective education, and reliable
Social Security.[94]

The "middle church" majority of faithful Americans will vote for
America's fundamental moral values, promised Bob Edgar days before
the 2006 midterm elections. "Stem cells and same-sex marriage are taking a back seat to honesty, integrity, truth and justice, the closer we get
to election day."[95] After the election removed Republicans from majorities in Congress, Edgar called for a new season of healing and support
for "a true compassionate government," dedicated to peacemaking, a living wage for all Americans, care for "the least of these," and justice for
God's creation.[96] "This was a moral values election," declared Jim Wallis
of Sojourners. He attributed the narrowing "God gap" in 2006 of frequent
church attenders voting Republican over Democrat to the fact that Iraq
was the top moral issue influencing voters, who had now turned two to one
against the war. Jim Winkler of the United Methodist General Board of
Church and Society testified that "religious-based antiwar activities have
been essential to turning the tide of opinion in the United States against
the stupid and ill-conceived invasion of Iraq." Voters named the war their
top moral concern five to six times more often than they named abortion
or same-sex marriage, according to exit polls, which also reported twice as

many voters seeing poverty/economic injustice and greed/materialism as America's most urgent moral crises compared to abortion and same-sex marriage combined.[97]

On election day in 2006, the NCC's Governing Board (formerly known as the Executive Board) adopted a statement, "Pastoral Message on the War in Iraq," which was affirmed by the General Assembly and made public the following day. In the months before the U.S. invasion, it reminded the faithful, the NCC had opposed the Iraq war as unwarranted in the face of its justification by the U.S. government as part of a global war on terror, a defensive response to the threat of Iraq's weapons of mass destruction and its ties to the 9/11 attacks, and a righteous uprooting of tyranny to plant a new democracy in the Middle East. "All of these justifications have been revealed as false or ill-considered. For this reason, the National Council of Churches USA repeats its call that this war must be brought to an end."[98] The NCC lamented the lapse in U.S. moral leadership and credibility in justifying and conducting the Iraq war through "a pattern of deception." It called for an immediate phased withdrawal of coalition forces linked to benchmarks for rebuilding Iraqi society, provisions for the safety of U.S. troops and benefits to honor their sacrifice, and commitments to restore trust in the multilateral conduct of American foreign policy.

Within weeks of the 2006 election, the NCC welcomed the related recommendations of the Iraq Study Group report to President Bush. The council then urged the faithful to protest his contrary "troop surge" with grassroots petitions and gatherings organized nationwide by the NCC's Faithful America, in partnership with Win Without War and a dozen other progressive political advocacy groups, as well as religious groups such as Sojourners and the United Methodist Board of Church and Society. The president's "act of desperation" only puts more Americans in the "lethal crosshairs of an Iraq civil war," concluded the NCC's "Mandate for Peace" early in 2007. "Moreover, the American people and the new Congress have stated overwhelmingly that they do NOT want to escalate the war. They want to END it!"[99]

Spreading opposition to a failed war, deepening economic inequality and hardship, and an unresponsive White House helped unite mainline-church leaders and core members of the faithful with a revived NCC after 2001. In this light, the future of ecumenical advocacy among the mainline churches looked brighter and clearer than before the NCC's "salvage quadrennium," even as Bob Edgar left the NCC's helm to become president of Common Cause in 2007; and even if underlying structural problems remained to be resolved in bringing together the Church and the churches in Washington, and in the moral argument of American public life.[100]

In the final chapter of this work, we turn to these underlying problems and overarching themes in the self-understanding of the mainline churches and their members as people of faith who are our fellow citizens.

Conclusion

Conclusion:
Public Churches and the Church

Mainline Problems and Prospects

How can the mainline Protestant churches invigorate their social witness and public advocacy in America today? Ask that question of ecumenical and mainline-church leaders engaged in such work, and they commonly respond first that it must be adequately funded and staffed, beginning with moves to reverse denominational cuts that have deepened for decades in some cases. This reply raises from a distinctive angle well-worn issues of less than generous giving in the mainline churches. It justifies renewed concern that they need to deepen their theological understanding of giving itself as a spiritual discipline and moral responsibility inherent in biblical stewardship of a church, and a world, that God entrusts to our common care.[1]

But diagnosis from the angle of the public church also underscores the fact that local giving has increased in the congregations of many mainline churches since the 1980s, often in step with marked increases in their local efforts to feed, clothe, shelter, and otherwise aid the needy, even as denominational giving has ebbed.[2] It flags, too, the multiplication of issue-specific fund-raising appeals, targeted by direct mail at the upper middle class in particular, in an era of mushrooming single-issue lobbies and advocacy groups, religious and secular. A wide array of associational memberships has long accompanied religious participation in the American middle class, in contrast to the more specifically church-centered loyalties of those further down the social ladder. But this more concentrated competition for the charitable dollar of the socially conscientious faithful has already led mainline denominations to tighten controls on how and how often their own social-justice offices and agencies can appeal to the faithful for donations. Unresolved, such intrachurch competition will continue to work to the advantage of freestanding, nondenominational religious advocacy groups and issue-specific coalitions.

Adequate numbers of staff engaged in public advocacy and education by the mainline churches requires adequate funding. Adequate quality of such staff requires more than money. It requires moral fluency and insight that only the best theological education can breed—beginning in Sunday school, not graduate school, and tempered by practical experience in congregational preaching and teaching. Yet it must be coupled with capacities for policy analysis and a grasp of legislation and government comparable to those demonstrated by staff members working for advocacy groups such as the Children's Defense Fund, and indeed for the committees of Congress and the offices of its members. In the gap left between the career trajectories of public-policy specialists or lawyers engaged in such work and the increasingly academic track taken by theologians and religious ethicists, the mainline churches must more intentionally persist in sponsoring specialized training in public policy and law for their most promising clergy, and in drawing their ablest scholars and professionals into serving their communities of faith. University-related divinity schools offer one fitting framework for nationally organized programs to set up internships for students, along with advisory councils and visiting appointments for scholars and professionals to serve the church in Washington and around the country across denominational lines.

A second answer from mainline religious advocates to questions of how to improve their work points to the need for more supportive and responsive relationships between denominational boards, agencies, and offices charged with social witness, on the one hand; and, on the other, those authorized to represent the denomination as a whole, interpret its doctrine, and guide its congregations. In turn, Protestant denominational leaders and officials of the National Council of Churches often stress the need for religious advocates, including those in church offices in Washington, to act more accountably in relation to their denomination's leaders and members by consulting them more closely, following their guidance more carefully, and justifying more doctrinally the public policies and actions they advocate. The National Council of Churches does indeed offer the "logical" institutional site for making ecumenical Protestant advocacy more dialogical and conciliar, as well as more unified and powerful. It behooves the NCC no less than the churches to persist in the efforts needed to overcome the historical sources of political and ecclesiological mistrust among them.

Critics inside and outside the mainline churches point to the spotty success of these denominations in organizing and mobilizing their own members at the grass roots. Here comparisons with the Christian Coalition, Focus on the Family, or the Christian homeschooling movement on the religious right commonly focus on tactical or strategic elements, such as the need for intensified Internet and direct-mail fund-raising or exponentially larger, interlocking networks and phone lists for local activists to get out the vote. But what is most striking about the specifically political aspect of the religious right is the notable exception it offers, along with churchgoing African Americans, to the rule of sharp class-bound declines over the past few decades in political participation and civic voluntarism that deepen as one goes down the social ladder among Americans, with the greatest declines evident in the lower middle class and what was once called the respectable working class. It is precisely such people who fill the pews of evangelical churches, where parachurch groups on the religious right are best organized and draw most of their members nationwide.[3]

By comparison, members of the educated upper middle class are those most involved in the wide range of nonreligious advocacy groups that have come to crowd our polity. Given such engagement, electorally oriented political organizing efforts backed by the mainline churches, the NCC, or affiliated parachurch groups such as the Interfaith Alliance and aimed at better-educated and better-off constituencies within the broader middle class can be expected to generate relatively little political bang for the buck. More importantly, in civic terms, such mainline organizing efforts should aim at engaging, not beating back, the moral attention and commitment of middle Americans hit hardest by flat wages, spreading job insecurity, pinched public provision, and the rising cost of middle-class life. As a vital part of what is now the middle-class majority of the electorate, they are struggling to discern and vote not merely their interests, but what their conscience and faith require of them. High stakes for the entire society rest in the moral balance of their struggle.

Deeper concerns about reaching mainline-church members in the pews point up the need for the churches to better teach and inspire their members week by week in local congregations, through preaching and prayer alike. This moral mandate begins with the formative catechesis of children born into the church and adult converts who reenter it more and more often as denominational switchers or returnees from among the unchurched, many of them raised in mainline churches but still unpracticed in their faith. Here comparison with the religious right might focus less on the Christian Coalition's direct-mail methods or voter guides than on pedagogy in evangelical Bible schools and summer camps. It might shift attention from Focus on the Family to parents in both evangelical and mainline churches trying to transmit their faith by everyday example as well as chapter-and-verse lessons. It might ask how to nurture these efforts of moral formation by creating more social space, stability, and time in families pressed to work longer hours to make ends meet.

Mainline-church offices in Washington and denominational boards of church and society compose and send out tens of thousands of newsletters, journals, and legislative alerts every month. They are paper factories, as one minister put it, raining paper or e-mail on apparently deaf ears that are, in fact, tuned out to appeals too often indistinguishable from sterile policy analyses or eager moralizing in favor of politically packaged programs. Mainline Protestant seminaries devote growing attention to courses and programs in public theology and social ethics. Yet conscientious pastors complain that such programs yield too few graduates who can persuasively preach what they have learned or guide the faithful toward practical action. Church advocates likewise protest how little practical wisdom or inspiration they can find in the academic exercises that pass for much theological scholarship.

On this front, the model of Evangelical Academies in Protestant Europe might help define a network of intermediate institutions to bring together laity and clergy to pursue the theological and social questions that divide them across local congregations, the regional and national leadership of denominations, and church-related institutions for education, charity, and advocacy.[4] Such a network could feed into and democratically inform plenary events such as those convened by the National Council of Churches, the national agencies of the mainline denominations, and the church offices in Washington. It could likewise be linked to year-round seminar programs in Washington and elsewhere at the sites of denominational headquarters and offices, shared by church and parachurch staff members and interns with annual slates of visiting scholars in theology and ethics, as well as specialists in government and public policy.

Mainline Protestant church leaders and activists often rehearse H. Richard Niebuhr's distinctions in calling on the many in their pews to rise up and join the prophetic few in following "Christ transforming culture," instead of resting content in the comfortable embrace of "Christ with culture." Thus leaders of the United Methodist General Board of Church and Society, as we heard in chapter 3, called on the pastors and heads of their denomination for active, articulate support from the pulpit and the Sunday-school classroom of the local church, not only from the policymaking and budgeting bodies of General Conference. Such calls resound in the apt diagnosis of scholars who advise that mainline denominational leaders and pastors can lend greater support to their advocates in Washington and activists everywhere, in the knowledge that most of their members affirm their stands on the issues themselves. Most mainline Protestants favor racial justice, ending poverty, and protecting the environment, for example, although only about one in five know their denomination has an office in Washington, let alone what it does there.[5] In the absence of polarization on the issues themselves, shedding more light on this advocacy promises to spread support for it in the mainline churches, rather than intensify conflict over it.

Given their relatively higher education, their professional or managerial work, and their influential community activities, however, members of mainline churches take part in a wide range of institutions with more social and political efficacy than do their less advantaged counterparts in many other religious communities. This leaves them feeling less in need of distinctively religious advocacy in order to make their voices heard in public. The problem of such efficacious participation in the wider society, observes the sociologist Robert Wuthnow, is that it "also exposes people to cultural messages that instill complacency—messages of material success, comfortable lifestyles, and self-interest." Most of the mainline faithful, like most Americans, do indeed want to work for peace and justice, to end poverty and root out racism. Yet these issues are "not likely to be pursued actively and aggressively unless mainline members and leaders develop a clear oppositional stance toward certain aspects of the wider culture," Wuthnow concludes. "A stance of this kind is likely to be encouraged by a growing appreciation of the church's own gospel message."[6]

Mainline Protestant activists, advocates, and church leaders in Washington sometimes reflect on the distinctive ordering of their churches as it works for or against their efforts to teach and move the people in their pews toward this kind of oppositional moral stance. Such efforts are harder for the mainline churches to advance, says one national leader in Washington, given their stress on "freedom of conscience and freedom of choice," as matters of Protestant principle predicated on the sovereignty of conscience in constitutive relationship to a sovereign God, yet more and more confused with the liberty to do as one wishes. By such accounts, it is not so much that the faithful of the mainline churches are a secure or selfish majority in American society. It is that they make up a middle-class majority whose ordinary experience is more in tune with responsibly doing one's individual best within an existing social order that is relatively fair and livable, for all its inequalities and imperfections, rather than joining together with others to remake this world more truly in the loving and just image of the Kingdom of God.

More strapped than a generation ago by declining public provision, more frayed by longer hours in less secure jobs with lagging wages and benefits, and more adrift amid looser family and neighborhood ties, members of America's expanded middle class are still doing their best for the most part, including doing more charitable and volunteer work and still holding to their voluntarist beliefs in moral perfection and self-help. The moral indignation of the faithful in mainline churches toward partisan politics at play in foiling campaign finance reform, for example—or efforts to make peace in the Middle East, fight poverty, or reverse global warming—mixes with their moral disappointment over public life in general. This yields a predicament marked more by fatigue than complacency, a problem of collective spirit and will that yields little to the intellectual solutions worked out by many recent forms of Protestant public theology.

At the same time, by way of counterexample, mainline-church leaders, activists, and thinkers point to forms of "ecclesial practice," including devotional revival, liturgical renewal, spiritual exercises, and charitable service, which have reinvigorated exemplary congregations and brought their members face-to-face with their neediest neighbors in mutual aid and recognition.[7] Feminist theology and related experiments in worship come in for special mention from some for kindling new forms of women's friendship and "doing church." Others credit environmentalism in particular for bringing to the mainline churches, as to America's schools and communities, a sense of facing problems possessed of a naturally lawful order that can be learned and argued out, agreed on and put into practice, including everyday rites of recycling, by society not as a mass of individuals and interest groups, but as a moral community whose interdependent members will prevail or perish together.

By such varied routes, inquiry into problems of public advocacy and social witness in the mainline Protestant churches today leads back to underlying questions about how the Christian Church in this historical moment and social situation is to preach and practice the truths of its faith—of sin, salvation, and grace—to relatively well-off and well-educated Americans who feel for others, worry about the future, and strive to do better, yet often find it hard to see themselves or the world as fundamentally flawed and in need of redemption. If we are subliminally seeking to be served by our churches no less than by our families, careers, and government, how are we to lose ourselves in order to find ourselves following Christ crucified and serving God within the Body of Christ? To be sure, we need a reformed economy with good work at living wages for all who can care for their own and contribute to the commonweal. We need a more participatory politics to free citizens and their leaders alike from capital-intensive lobbying and electoral advertising campaigns, and enable them to do the democratic handwork of heeding and persuading one another in shared self-government. But our churches are bound to fail in the public advocacy of such reforms if the church cannot revive our spirits by the grace of God and join us in the spirit that embodies our salvation, here and now, in our membership one in another.

The Integrity of the Church in a Divided Society

For the mainline churches to grasp the crisis of social membership and participation Americans now confront requires honestly distinguishing the specific forms, civic as well as economic, that this crisis takes in different social classes in America, and helping them discern the specific responsibilities they face. Communities of faith are crucial in taking on this daunting task, since they are among the least class-divided communities of moral discourse, reflection, and inspiration in our society. Robert Reich described the structure of social class emerging in the United States in the mid-1990s in terms of an "overclass" of educated professionals and bright-collar technical specialists, along with elite owners of investment capital, living in suburban safety; an "underclass quarantined in surroundings that are unspeakably bleak, and often violent"; and a new "anxious class" trapped in "the frenzy of effort it takes to preserve their standing" precariously in the middle.[8]

Systematic economic changes since the 1970s have worked to enrich the best-educated and best-capitalized Americans, while hindering or harming those below the top quintile of earners in ways that conventional social-welfare programs do little to counter. Hardest hit has been a working class once able to afford a middle-class standard of living and now falling further and further away from it. After steady income gains that broadened the middle class for a quarter century following World War II, its members—especially women—have been working longer and harder ever since, taking home relatively flat wages in return and bearing more of the rising costs of middle-class life as public provision ebbs for goods such as housing and higher education. Indignant at this unfairness and angry at government for failing to include them in a growing economy, even as they blame themselves for failing to overcome its obstacles, those caught in the anxious class have had less sympathy to spare for the poor and immigrants, in whose color-coded, undeserving image they identify the "underclass," despite the fact that two of three poor Americans are white, and most of them are children and the elderly.

To meet the rising economic insecurity and ebbing real wages of the anxious class, structural economic solutions must be mounted, and the political willingness to sustain them must be inspired and justified morally. We should continue to ask how religious institutions can persist in contributing to these projects with greater wisdom and courage. But we can see, too, that this economic anxiety has bred anger, cynicism, and fear that tear apart families and erode forms of public participation, from voting to volunteering. For many members of the anxious class, renewed social engagement is likeliest to begin with religious communities whose faithful caring can overcome the isolation and cynicism that beset our society's largest group. Here the mainline churches should attend closely to the mutual care that binds the communities of their evangelical brethren, black and white alike, at their best. They, too, can affirm the value of the family, and heed the best impulses represented by concern for "family values" and the appeal of movements such as Focus on the Family and the Million Man March. They can do so even as they refuse to let larger institutions off the hook of social responsibility in the misplaced hope that all would be well if only individual parents would care for their children, children would obey their parents, and congregations would do more to help the needy.[9]

To take on the structural economic problems of the underclass will require major changes in public policy and investment barely visible on the political horizon. But the poor also wrestle with the imploded sense of personhood and social hardship that have followed on the loss of blue-collar jobs with living wages in the U.S. economy, abetted by the fraying social safety net of public provision and spreading residential segregation by economic class. A recovery of self-respect and a sense of moral agency among the excluded poor can come only through taking part in the shared practices of learning, working, householding, and civic decision-making that enable persons to contribute and belong to the larger society. Not by transfer payments alone, or caseworkers' compassion, will the problems of the poor be solved.[10]

What forms of religious teaching and understanding shed the clearest, most moving light on these social tasks? Mainline-church leaders often point first in response to the 1986 Catholic bishops' letter on the U.S. economy, *Economic Justice for All*. They underscore its policy emphasis on full employment and living wages seen in the moral light of subsidiarity in service to participatory or "contributive" justice. Participatory justice, argues the bishops' letter, asks each individual to give all that is necessary for the common good of society. In turn, it obliges the society to order its institutions so that all persons can work to contribute to the commonweal in ways that respect their dignity and renew their freedom.[11]

The principle of subsidiarity, derived from Catholic social teachings consonant with Protestant and Judaic tenets, directs groups closest to a social problem to respond to it as directly and fully as they can, receiving the help of higher-level social groups wherever needed, but not being re- placed by them wherever possible. This subsidiarity of social membership and cooperation implies, for example, that the modern welfare state as an administrative system of nationalized distribution needs to serve, not supplant, networks and institutions of mutual aid made up of ordinary citizens—amateur helpers as well as professionals—joined in the work of human service. Such communities should be centered locally at the point of giving and receiving, where helping hands actually meet, yet reli- ably seconded by state agencies at the local level. In short, we need more participatory, decentralized, and democratic forms of public provision re- sponsibly supported and framed by government, but neither dominated by the state nor deluded by designs to privatize it. For whole persons can- not accept a social world in which they are helpless to take part even if they are helped.[12]

Once written and made public, how do tenets such as subsidiarity in service to participatory justice actually come to be taught and enacted, and to what practical effect, for example, when it comes to providing good jobs at living wages? The anxious class placed scant confidence in the highly publicized prospect of the 1990s that most U.S. workers could be better educated, trained, and paid to meet the world's growing demand for skilled labor, if only Americans were willing to make the public and private investments needed to underwrite this effort. A decade later, such skepticism appears well justified, in an economy increasingly divided between a top tier of well-rewarded executives, professionals, and technical specialists and a low-wage service sector, separated by a gap gouged out by the rollback of progressive taxation, the drain of domestic manufacturing jobs, and the ebb tide of industrial unions.[13]

Those in the "overclass" who profit most have done so through high gains on substantial investment capital and skyrocketing compensation for top executives, professionals, and high-tech specialists. Median family income doubled in the United States between 1947 and 1973. But it rose by less than 25 percent from 1973 to 2003, while average income doubled for the top 1 percent of Americans and tripled for the top 0.1 percent. Capital gains multiplied as top tax rates tumbled, and American corporations held down wages and benefits to make the most of deregulation and the market dynamics of more mobile capital, increased global competition, and cheaper labor overseas. What business is that of government, let alone of religious communities? It makes a difference how communities of faith answer this question, especially if they do so in practical terms that tell the truth about human injury, responsibility, and integrity in the light of sin and grace and love of neighbor. It makes a difference whether they engage the question at all or wave it aside with the hand of the free market extending from the sleeve of divine providence.

For example, business corporations are creatures of law, in fact, not nature. During the 1990s, their profits and stock prices soared, while pink slips proliferated and paychecks stayed flat below the top quintile of earners. This is because, observed Robert Reich, we allowed corporations to become "the agent of the shareholder alone," freed of responsibilities for their employees and communities. If they should better recognize these responsibilities to their communities and workers as well as to their investors, then we should give them better economic reasons for doing so, for instance, by linking such responsible conduct to the benefits of lawful incorporation, or altering public subsidies and tax exclusions to encourage it. "If we want profitable companies to keep more employees on their payrolls or to place them in new jobs that offer similar wages and benefits, to upgrade their skills, to share more of the profits with them, and to remain in their communities, we have to give them an economic reason to do so," proposed Reich. Such steps are warranted, he concluded, in an era of less liberal government, when middle-class Americans have come to accept its restraint in hopes that a rising tide of private investment will eventually lead to greater opportunities and earnings for all, instead of enabling corporations to maximize shareholder value by holding down wages while increasing productivity and exporting jobs.[14]

Over the past decade, a sustained economic boom gave way to a sharp recession in 2001, a jobless recovery through 2003, and continuing declines in real median wages, even though economic expansion resumed in late 2001 and worker productivity climbed by 14.7 percent through 2005. Inflation-adjusted median household income fell five years in a row, dropping 4 percent from 1999 to 2004. While wages lagged behind inflation and health-care coverage shrank, corporate profits and capital gains rebounded robustly. In comparison to five prior business cycles, the share of corporate income going to compensation during this recovery (41 percent) trailed far behind the historical benchmark (75 percent) from 2001 to mid-2005, while the share going to profits surged ahead (59 percent, compared to the historical 25 percent). Forty-six percent of the growth of total corporate income was distributed as corporate profits, compared to 20 percent previously.[15]

What broke the solid link previously forged between overall economic expansion and productivity growth on one side, and rising wages and living standards of working families on the other? In the absence of effective full-employment job markets, unions with bargaining leverage, and balanced trade, unequal distribution broke the link between workers' producing more per hour and receiving higher wages in return, agreed progressive labor economists and liberal church leaders. A bipartisan political consensus, meanwhile, clung to global competition as good reason not to reconnect productivity and pay through corrective policies of progressive taxation, stronger labor protection, higher minimum wages, and universal health coverage. Such equalizing measures would not interfere with the invisible hand of the market, protested progressives, and without them, working Americans would lose their loyalty to an economy that denied them "a fair share of the growth they themselves are creating."[16]

Issues of social inequality and economic justice since 2000 were spiked by business scandals and controversy over immigrants taking low-wage jobs, to cast doubts on fair play in the marketplace. Health-care and Social Security crises, spiraling energy costs, and New Orleans left in ruin after the flood, together with continuing threats to homeland security after 9/11 and endless violence in Iraq, all modulated the felt meaning of profound questions about the will and responsibility of government to protect Americans and provide for them fairly. Support for the view that "government should help more needy people even if it means going deeper in debt" declined from 64 percent of Democrats in 1992 to 54 percent in 1994 before rising gradually to 62 percent in 2002 and sharply to 72 percent in 2003, according to a series of national polls. Support for government's helping more needy people fell from 43 percent of Republicans in 1992 to 25 percent in 1994 before rising to 33 percent in 2002 and then to 39 percent in 2003. The two trends traced a similar trajectory from the recession of the early 1990s through the Republican Revolution of the 1994 midterm elections, the spreading but still top-heavy economic boom of the late 1990s, and the 2001 recession with its jobless recovery. Their end points, however, left a gap larger by half between Democrats and Republicans—33 percentage points in 2003, compared to 21 points in 1992.[17]

Cynicism and mistrust of big government declined somewhat from their angry peak in the mid-1990s, mainly because Republican hostility toward the federal government dissipated once the GOP won the White House as well as both chambers of Congress. In late 2003, almost 70 percent of Republicans agreed that the government is run for the benefit of all, while only 44 percent of Democrats and 47 percent of independents concurred. African Americans in particular felt much more estranged from government than they did before the advent of the Bush administration, of which they remained overwhelmingly critical. Criticism of business and backing for its closer regulation has grown stronger among Democrats and independents since the 1990s, while pro-business attitudes have rebounded among Republicans since 2002. Republicans were at least as satisfied with their personal financial situation in 2003 as they were four years earlier, while Democrats and independents were significantly less satisfied financially.[18]

If the wealthiest and most powerful Americans belong to any institutions that transcend their own interests, it is to the mainline churches, temples, and synagogues. These communities, in turn, are especially suited to emphasize both the larger responsibilities of established elites and the need to make their responsibilities more inclusive. Biblical ideals of stewardship and covenant have long called on the powerful and wealthy in particular to endow economic institutions to serve everyone—not only to give to the charitable and cultural institutions of their choice—and to do so for the sake of their own souls as well as the good of society. Today, the need to invest capital more intentionally to serve the public good presses most directly on those at the top of the overclass, especially to create decent jobs at wages fair enough to support a family.

Most of those in the overclass do not command the financial capital, head the government, or run the corporations that direct our political economy. Most are members of the educated upper middle class who have studied and worked hard for their rewards in increasingly competitive universities and professional occupations. They typically see themselves contributing through their careers to the society at large, even as they have had to learn to loosen their ties to local communities, churches, and their own extended families in the course of pursuing their careers. They are still religious believers or spiritual seekers, if less often conventional church belongers.[19] Mainline communities of faith should recognize how this occupational elite represents a broader priesthood of all believers in a more educated yet not so secularized society. They stand at its moral and symbolic center, invested with the meritocratic authority of experts, educators, and exemplary professionals. Theirs is the way of life that most middle-class Americans aspire to earn and enjoy. They command the cultural capital and civic skills to illuminate—or obscure—in public the best directions for our society to travel toward liberty and justice for all. They can best justify our efforts at reform or excuse our indifference to it.

Many of the educated have grown away from the major political parties, yet they are among those most involved in the public-interest groups and associations for moral advocacy that have multiplied in our polity over the past generation. Through more critical interactive ties with such groups, with the academy, and with the cultural media, the mainline churches as society-wide communities of moral inquiry and reflection should seek to open out their conciliar conversations to engage the attention of the educated and spur their action. They should also draw further into this conversation more of their own congregational leaders. Here the mainline Protestant churches still have much to learn from their Jewish, Catholic, and African American counterparts, as well as much to share with them in the way of cultural insight and social resources.

It may seem paradoxical, if not perilous, that in seeking to embody the ideal of the church universal, the mainline churches in America must wrestle with the particulars of social class and risk the dangers of economistic idolatry as well as political faction. But the universal community of creation and redemption, which the Church signifies and serves, calls our attention to the particularity of human suffering and need in order to name sin and proclaim grace. To be the Church, not only the denominations of mostly middle-class Americans, the churches must tell the larger truth of human interdependence and shared responsibility. They must keep trying to live out this truth in exemplary ways that can reach into the fearful hearts of the righteous who have earned everything they have, and reach out beyond our economically segregated neighborhoods and national boundaries to embrace those who have so much less of everything except infinite value in the eyes of God.

Only thus can the American churches escape the irony of the American state at the dawn of the twenty-first century and instead engage it critically. For more than a century, the regulatory reach and administrative sway of our state have grown on the moral strength of its almost religious aspiration to do social good, to enlarge human rights and realize human potential among all its citizens as partakers in the good life of the modern middle class. However stunning its failures to achieve these ends fully, the strength of its partial triumph since the New Deal has given us a middle-class majority torn between voting their conscience and voting their interests in the name of the public interest. Unsure how to distinguish the two, they are eager to affirm for everyone their relatively meritocratic experience of schooling and work and to mark off by respectable moral measures those more or less deserving of personal aid.

Especially for middle-class Americans, we cannot forgo the civic promise of religious efforts to enlarge public conscience and cast clearer light on the commonweal. For those who "work hard and play by the rules" still bring to the pews of the mainline churches the burden of both their moral confusions and their faithful convictions. As members of this middle-class majority now question their shifting social rewards and responsibilities amid diverging fortunes and diminished dreams, high societal stakes rest in the moral balance of their counterposed yet interwoven visions of a world worth living in and working for: free, fair, and caring. As the majority in the richest and most powerful nation in the world, they make choices that turn out to entwine the fate of peoples everywhere.

Public Churches and the Public Sphere

Between modern market economies and administrative states lies a social realm as broad as all the rest of society itself, stretching from the family, local churches, and clubs to the political parties and associations that surround official government. Since the early modern era in the West, a public realm between market economies and states has commonly been identified as "civil society," a political community inhabited by democratic citizens.[20] Paying critical attention to civil society makes clear that neither market nor state is an autonomous moral realm of interests and exchanges or rights and duties. Neither is justifiable or even comprehensible in its own terms abstracted from social life as a whole. Neither makes sense apart from expression in terms of the living traditions of moral narrative, dialogue, and argument within communities of discourse, beginning with their dramatic rites and stories of good persons, practices, and relationships within the ways of life that a coherent social order nurtures.

Within this conception of civil society and the polity, religion takes on a very different shape from the authoritarian advocate of absolute principles or divinely revealed commands that modern liberals fear, or the source of legitimation and moral glue for the social order that modern communitarians extol. Instead, religion in public becomes a crucial questioner. It is an interlocutor of states apparently all too certain of their progressive programs and procedural formulas for distributive justice, and of markets all too oblivious to injuries worked by their rationality and efficiency.[21] Precisely because religious faith respects no moral boundaries in facing up to human goodness, evil, and suffering—even when church and state are legally separated institutions—communities of faith are ideally suited to question the state's moral authority to draw the "private-public" boundary lines that separate institutions as different realms of moral understanding and discourse. In a democracy, that is for citizens to decide, again and again, without privileging the moral perspectives of either state or church. That can and should be so because democratic citizens actually do their deciding as different sorts of believers and nonbelievers, workers, students, neighbors, and family members, not as abstracted, unsocialized political beings.[22] They do it through pitching in or pulling away from efforts decided more or less in common. They do it through engaging or following public dialogue about ordering our lives together in practice, not only about making policy, passing laws, or backing candidates and parties.

If public life or the public sphere is defined by such moral argument, dialogue, and "back talk" taking place in it, then we can distinguish the idea of public churches from the paradigmatic forms religion takes within the state, that is, from a state church such as the Church of England or a theocratic state such as the Khomeini regime of Iran. We can also distinguish public churches from the forms religion takes within political society, that is, from specific parties or movements mobilized against other religious or secular parties to work for or against the state itself, like the

Christian Democratic parties of postwar Europe or the Catholic Church in Poland under Communist rule.[23]

In the United States, by contrast, denominational religion has historically been located within civil society, neither established within the state nor institutionalized as a political party, for all the salience of religion in defining political constituencies and inspiring political movements. Nonetheless, denominationally organized religion has long had a voice and a place in the moral argument of public life, both among its own members and others in civil society, and in political society proper. Indeed, the strengthening of Protestant denominations as national institutions through the nineteenth century amplified that voice in relation to increasingly national political parties and movements.[24] The growth of national voluntary societies across and outside the denominations sharpened their voice in political society proper. This was especially true where such societies focused not only on spiritual and moral uplift but on issues of social reform such as education, housing, and clinics for immigrants and the urban poor.

As the "governmentless government" of America in 1800 gradually gave way to an expanding national state after the Civil War, the "benevolent empire" of nineteenth-century evangelical Protestantism found itself more often engaged in persuading and appealing to the state in pursuing its moral aims and social practices. Indeed, many such aims and practices migrated in the Progressive era from the churches to the state itself, via religiously rooted voluntary societies and morally inspired social movements devoted to causes ranging from temperance through child labor to women's wages and suffrage. This process distinctively marked the American welfare state, and transformed the churches in turn.[25] Originally religious ideals of moral and social improvement grew politicized in their cultural formulation as well as their institutional location and social organization. Today denominational offices, interdenominational groups, and freestanding religious associations engaged in public advocacy, education, and political activism interact in the public space of political society proper, even when they do not play electoral or party politics. Like other nonreligious public advocates, educators, and activists, these voices of the public church seek more directly and variously than before to engage the attention of an expanded state and inform its conduct by taking a more persuasive part in the moral argument of public life.

Thinking about democratic self-government in these terms implies the peculiar mix of a relatively weak state and a strong polity in the American case in particular. Here a relatively large and centralized state is nonetheless highly permeable and pluralized. It lacks a dense, formally ideological core of professional bureaucrats that reaches to the top of its administrative and regulatory echelons, in contrast to France, for example.[26] Here the polity in all its diverse, thickly interconnected activity takes on the nature of a forum that embraces the state, and a communicative channel or network that reaches into it. In and through the polity, citizens, associations, and organized social bodies communicate with the state, and through them so do other institutions such as colleges and professions. They communicate quid pro quo interests and exchanges, to be sure, in order to influence the state to serve certain interest groups and constituencies, from automakers and tobacco farmers to senior citizens. But they also communicate ideals and axiomatic convictions in order to persuade the state's legislators, officials, and agencies to make laws and policies in accord with certain truths for certain good reasons, for example, to end hunger and reduce pollution, stimulate business and create jobs, or improve education, health, and housing.

Historically, American political parties have worked along both of these dimensions. Compared to their contemporary European counterparts, however, they have usually appeared more interest-oriented and less profoundly ideological. Their ideals have more clearly reflected their constituents' interests, whether aggregated or counterbalanced, and their platforms have been more strategically organized around key issues embodying these interests.[27] Historically, then, a greater part has been played in the moral argument of American public life by what Tocqueville called "intellectual and moral associations," such as the abolitionist and temperance movements, than by the "political and industrial associations" he saw at work on the strategic model of interest groups.[28]

Seen as processes of progressive democratization, the increased size and diversity of the modern U.S. polity are morally encouraging signs. So are the polity's greater organizational density and its more diverse and inclusive representation of different groups in the larger society. So, too, is the growth of multiple "publics" debating particular issues, norms, and ideals of good. In this view of the polity, such publics are situated like diverse democracies across the varied institutional terrain of modern civil society, reaching from local school boards to national denominational offices on Capitol Hill.[29]

Each such smaller public makes up a circle of cultural conversation distinguished by certain modes of moral discourse, logics of argument, and forms of narration and evaluation. This civic landscape favors the cultural conceptions of some groups over others, not only their social perceptions and interests.[30] Each relatively limited and peculiar public tends to overgeneralize its moral conclusions by more or less uncritically affirming a "false we" as its subject, one projected from too narrow a circle of conversation among socially similar strata to represent the society as a whole. Even where those who are socially or culturally different are not formally excluded from participation or reduced to second-class standing in publics skewed by such cultural bias, they often find themselves interrupted or ignored, or more subtly tongue-tied and unable to define their own deepest needs and concerns in that delimited public's not-so-open cultural idiom and its not-so-universalistic moral dialect.

In response, subordinated social groups in particular tend to form "counterpublics" in seeking to shape and interpret their own ideals, identities, and interests over against centrally established publics, yet in response to them, too.[31] However small the circle of their conversation in fact, insofar as the members of these counterpublics seek to engage a wider public, and in turn to join it and transform the understanding of the public at large, then these counterpublics serve to widen public discourse in stratified and segregated societies like ours. In such societies, moreover, counterpublics can come closer to fulfilling ideals of participatory parity by arguing over the moral order of social life and contesting its definition across distinctive modes of discourse among multiple, conflicting publics than does a single, ostensibly comprehensive, all-inclusive public sphere that actually excludes some persons and groups and disregards others.

How do counterpublics interact, then, with one another and with wider circles of a larger public in societies like ours? What role, if any, do public churches play in this interaction? Languages of human goodness and evil, freedom and dignity, rights and responsibilities do not abruptly begin and break off at the boundaries of class, race, gender, and political party, even if case-specific moral intuitions vary in socially predictable terms. Thus "cultural identities are woven of many different strands, and some of these strands may be common to people whose identities otherwise diverge, even when it is the divergences that are most salient," as the political theorist Nancy Fraser puts it.[32] Religious institutions conserve traditions as continuities of conflict, not consensual blueprints. They reinvigorate moral conflicts as well as cultural commonplaces. In both respects, they help us to communicate coherently in cultural terms even when we disagree morally.

This view contrasts with conventional accounts of a public sphere of open moral argument over social issues that tend to ignore religion or depict it in the adversarial form of a culturally established or claimed moral authority that acts as a "conversation stopper."[33] As such, religion appears instinctively eager to foreclose public argument with absolute moral principles, prescriptions, and axioms authorized in the name of God. These moral absolutes may take the form of revealed religious truth in conservative churches, for example, that human beings are souls from the moment of conception and that abortion is murder. They may also take the form of liberal churches' invocations of the common good to rule out as innately selfish or dangerously shortsighted claims to certain rights and liberties, for example, the right of handgun owners to bear arms or of nations to build nuclear weapons.

Communities of divine worship and faith may indeed tend to speak more readily of ultimate truths and the all-encompassing "we" of humankind than do some social movements and political parties. But compared to many such groups, including those in the ecological, feminist, and "pro-family" movements, the largest U.S. religious communities typically use rhetoric that is no more emphatically moral. They usually feature much greater breadth of social and cultural diversity in their membership and routinely give voice to more diverse perceptions of human needs, interests, and moral goods. Often, if not always, these communities of faith show markedly greater care in moving from stating universal human truths to delivering particular prescriptions on specific social issues.

Significantly, these distinctions between religious and nonreligious participants in public argument have recently been narrowed from both sides. The growth of political associations, advocates, and movements outside the major parties has featured single-issue and public-interest groups of increased ideological appeal, philosophical elaboration, moral vigor, and spiritual inflection. These include "religious special-purpose groups" standing free of both denominational churches and local congregations. But they also include moral advocacy groups that are not explicitly religious. Compared to large denominations, their membership is predictably narrowed along lines that yoke their ideological interests and their social backgrounds.[34] Compared to local congregations, they make up groups whose ideological self-consciousness is not bridged by living, working, and worshipping with faithful neighbors of different political views.

Given the idea of counterpublics whose members aspire to engage in conversation and persuasively transform ever broader circles of a counterfactual yet conceivable "public at large," the institutional reality of public churches in free, self-governing societies does not seem so at odds with other public actors in political and civil society. For the dual character of these counterpublics, as Nancy Fraser notes, is to "function as spaces of withdrawal and regroupment" on the one hand, and on the other as "bases and training grounds for agitational activities directed toward wider publics."[35] Here lies an obvious parallel to passive or aggressive religious sects, seeking refuge from "the world" or seeking to conquer or convert it.

More instructively, though, counterpublics offer analogies to more or less radical movements of religious reform, ranging from monastic orders through Wesleyan preachers to the Southern Christian Leadership Conference of Martin Luther King, Jr. Such movements emerge from the structure of the larger Christian church as "a church within the church," an exemplary *ecclesiola in ecclesia*, seeking to engage the church in dramatically counterpointed conversation and revise its overall articulation as a truly catholic concilium.[36] The Reformation gives rise to the counterpublics of the evangelical and reformed Protestant churches, conceiving themselves as models of civic and political order in the early modern West. In America today, the descendants of both Reformation and Counter-Reformation impulses link denominations organized as voluntary associations within a free society to the historic institution of the Christian Church at large. This genuinely catholic church, organizationally counterfactual yet institutionally conceivable, is itself a concilium of smaller publics and counterpublics (evangelical, liberal, liberationist, fundamentalist, feminist, Pentecostal, traditionalist, Americanist, and more) within and across denominations. Together this conciliar communion of communions, bound by their ongoing argument as well as their worship and fellowship, constitutes a prototypical "superpublic" counterposed to official government yet conversable with it. It is a moral interlocutor of states that citizens can serve well only by being faithful to God before country.[37]

Only by recognizing its own interculturally inclusive "polycentric" nature, conversely, can a truly catholic church embody the Word of God and the spirit of Christ in public dialogue in the world today, in contrast to a monocentric church reinforced against the modern world as a "dictatorship of relativism."[38] For we inhabit a public sphere that is itself indebted to biblical forms of covenantal communal fellowship no less than to the Socratic reciprocity of unforced dialogue between full citizens of a polis. The universalistic, egalitarian moral spirit of modern democracy, human rights, and the sovereignty of individual conscience is "the direct legacy of the Judaic ethic of justice and the Christian ethic of love," as Jürgen Habermas puts it.[39] This legacy remains vital to respecting yet transcending the Eurocentric cultural-political limitations of an Enlightenment universalism whose religious roots are still inseparable from its practical authority to proclaim the dignity of all human beings as true subjects and to protect cultural pluralism from drifting into moral relativism.[40] The Christian Church must sustain this legacy to enable us to meet the challenges of a postnational polity obliged to judge and reform today's economically fragmented, unfairly stratified, and unpacified world of global commerce, communication, and coercion in the direction of a just and peaceful global civilization to come. But the Church must also sustain its reflexive and self-critical awareness by historically conscious dialogue with other world religions, the dialectical thinking of Western philosophy since the Reformation, the skepticism of modern science, and the quasi-scientific pragmatism of modern common sense.[41]

The distinctive stance of churchly engagement toward the larger society in all its diversity gives rise to a recognition that criteria of justice will vary with the kinds of relationships to which persons belong and the kinds of activities—working, parenting, governing—in which they take part in different social institutions. Just recognition and reward of others will vary, for example, according to the relative merit of professional work, the absolute need for parental love, and the equality of democratic votes. But this churchly stance rests on a faith in the moral coherence and integrity of goods distinguished by social spheres such as family, market, and polity yet unified as human virtues in the interdependent lives of persons acting, feeling, and relating together across these spheres in society as a whole. It also rests on a faith that this coherence and integrity can be expressed in exemplary stories of how and why persons so act and feel in relation to God. We can come to know stories of creation, sin, grace, and redemption so truthfully, for example, that no Americans today can witness the suffering of their hungry and homeless neighbors, fail to respond, and go on calling themselves chosen people of God or good citizens of a commonwealth.[42]

Given the wholeness of creation and its human stewardship in biblical terms that ground the church's self-understanding, the church finds itself entrusted by God with the whole of society, not only the whole of its members' social lives. The church carries no ultimate responsibility to or for the state, its policies, or its programs. But it is more ultimately responsible than any other institution for the moral conduct and character of the society as a whole, for its immediate texture and deepest coherence. Raising the matter of such societal responsibility by religious institutions may sound like claims of moral absolutism asserted on highly contested public

ground, and subject to fierce rebuttal in defense of church-state separation and civil liberties. Yet in a curious sense that amounts to little more
than common sense in a differentiated society, such common ground is
more often simply ignored than contested. Communities of faith compose
virtually the only modern American institution that cares to accept such
responsibility, or indeed that can even recognize its form and grasp its
meaning. The welfare state extends rules, rights, and programs into almost every social institution. But its mind is almost always elsewhere, as
it were, divided or distracted by a thousand disparate social issues and
jurisdictional concerns. It is preoccupied by its own bureaucratic career
and political prospects. It is only fitfully aware of its progressive calling,
if not downright doubtful that its programmatic interests really represent
the society's common good.

The church certainly does not claim legal or governmental authority
over the society, nor in any conventional sense over its members' lives in
a denominational society, in which churches, synagogues, temples, and
mosques are voluntary associations. Nor does it conventionally "represent" the society, its politically excluded members, or even the faithful
themselves to the state as if they were its political constituents. Instead,
what the churches and the public church they embody seek to do is to
remain mindful of the society as a whole, of its moral needs and its viewpoints otherwise unmet by the state, especially as such recognition is essential to care for the whole of humankind, human nature, and creation
itself. The church persists in reminding the state that society as a whole
continues to exist and calls for full recognition of its common good, not
only recognition of specific social groups and the goods they affirm to be
essential for their own survival or social membership.[43]

No less significant, the public church seeks to enlarge the public that
underlies and informs the state in a democratic society by helping to
interarticulate the smaller publics, especially those with relatively few
resources of money, power, and influence that would enable them to demand to be heard and heeded by government, the major political parties,
or mass social movements. It seeks to do so in forms that interrelate these
publics dialogically and that offer them more than a foot in the door, a
voicing of demands, or even a vote. Rather, the public church—as one
godparent of a democratic "superpublic," or public at large, outside the
state—seeks to bring publics into conversation and argument with one
another. It seeks to enable their members to exchange good reasons in
mulling over issues and deciding policies. It also seeks to inspire them to

persuade others by the good example of living out their ideals and practicing what they preach. But it seeks, too, to awaken them to grasp and better intuit the differences in experience, social situation, and convictions that shape their reasoning and inspire their action, in order to clarify and open up the terms of their disagreement even when they cannot compromise or as yet find common ground.

If the state is impartial and its justice is blind in the sense of due process, the church is always on the side of the whole of human society and the whole of God's creation. It is always trying to see the big picture, hear the whole story, and discern the justice of the entire social order. It begins and ends with the essence of justice as a virtue incarnated in faithful persons who love and feed their neighbor. It insists on the duty and aim of nation-states of the world to do likewise, even if it is not inherent in their self-defined interests or character to do so.

While the state, then, may see churches as no different in nature from any other voluntary association, nongovernmental organization, public-interest group, political constituency, or lobby, the church sees itself embodying the rest of society and the whole of society. It finds itself insisting on the primacy of the society before the state. Its political reality in a democratic republic thus rests in the polity per se, not in its relationship to the state. There the church is one voice among many. But it is a presence that seeks to set a good example in public by trying to listen more than any of the others to the many in the civic assembly, to weave together their voices, and to center their conversation around the goods that human beings need to live well enough to become good, including public participation and social membership as moral goods in themselves.[44]

The Polity and the Public Church as Moral Communities

In a democratic society such as ours, perhaps the greatest good is participation itself. It is both a right and a responsibility, as embodied, for example, in the right to vote and the right to earn.[45] These are also our shared responsibilities as a people to take part in republican self-government and contribute to the commonweal. Education, work, and economic well-being are not simply the results that individuals achieve or the efforts they undertake. They are themselves constitutive conditions of the public participation that we prize as a moral good essential to our democracy. For such participation endows us with the shared self-knowledge, including the insight that our kingdom is not of this world, that comes from contributing and belonging to a society-wide community of character and practice centered around good work that needs to be done for the common good—that is, for the sake of multiple goods institutionally diverse enough for all of us to share in practice, yet culturally coherent enough for all of us to argue about and pursue in common.

So we should indeed ask which moral ideals best express and justify a good society and inspire us to work for it. But we should also ask which institutional conditions are needed to cultivate these ideals of a good society and nurture the sort of persons who can live them out. What mundane social arrangements, for example, are needed to learn and practice the genuinely dialectical, back-and-forth discourse that a democratic republic calls for? Such moral conversation requires a small enough circle of people possessed of enough shared time and learning to permit an equal and alternative balance of participation in turning a topic round and round. If it is to extend beyond small elites, therefore, thoughtful and decisive civic conversation in a mass society requires sufficiently high economic productivity, bureaucratic efficiency, and broad distribution of their benefits. That is what we need in order to free the time and focus the attention of women and men of every race and economic class for shared reflection, learning, and cultural fluency exercised collegially. For these practical virtues confer the public power to speak in a true commonwealth and the moral authority to be heeded, even when—indeed, especially when—our voice does not carry the day and we do not get our way.

If this sounds like little more than a truism piously invoked at civic and educational rites, we may think for a moment of all the monologues on dialogue we have sat through or, worse, delivered to scores of silent listeners. Think of all the courses we have attended or taught with dozens or hundreds of students, with forty-five minutes of lecture and five minutes left for questions. Think how often these ratios obtain even in the classrooms of elite colleges, where yearly tuition and fees now reach beyond $40,000, as aid ebbs and the median household income of the students whose parents can afford these costs climbs well above $100,000. Think, too, of all those who, however deserving, never reach such college classrooms because they are less advantaged. Finally, think of the demanding institutional changes needed to enable us to put into practice the ideals of democratic dialogue and participation we so fervently preach or routinely rehearse. Once we begin thinking along these lines, which are at once ethical and institutional, we are on the way to becoming radical conservatives marked by a commitment to animating schools, churches, and a full range of public institutions as schools for civic virtue to practice the social goods that our traditions profess.

Because shared public languages and arguments about how to live together are what unite us as a people, not identical interests or univocal values, we need to develop a more educative and civic conception of community itself, instead of the romanticized white-clapboard idea of it that now prevails.[46] We need religious, educational, and communal institutions, not only political institutions, that serve to clarify debate about our moral differences and our confusions about how to live together, instead of striving simply to celebrate our common convictions or broker our opposing interests. Conversely, we need to revive a more educative conception of politics itself, less bound by the utilities of an administrative state and less driven by the group interests of legislative factions and client-citizens. Money and power will talk less loudly in our politics only when citizens are willing and able to participate more equally and speak more clearly in a moral argument of public life that better serves to seek truth for the society as a whole.[47]

This means we also need to revive a more covenantal and catechetical conception of religion rooted in the soul of shared worship and exemplary moral witness yet dedicated to critical, conciliar public dialogue and opposed to theocratic lobbying or special-interest pleading.[48] Even as we safeguard the institutional separation of church and state in America, we should recognize that the synagogue, church, and temple as schools for virtue, like good schools themselves, share with the polity of a good republic an institutional model for civic life that is more like a forum and a collegial assembly—a collegium and concilium—than a marketplace, a bureaucracy, or, for that matter, a bully pulpit. As the community of all God's creatures, the Church offers the larger society no prospect of an orthodox paradise on earth, a sectarian voting bloc, or an ever-cheerful congregational fellowship writ large. Like republican self-government, in fact, it offers us the sometimes uplifting, sometimes tragically troubling, often downright uncomfortable practices of a moral community in which we cannot escape or exclude the strangers who are our true colleagues and biblical neighbors. Let us engage them in argument as well as love.

Appendix

Ecclesiology in Action

Every conception of the Christian church in America today implies a distinctive vision of the surrounding society in relation to the Christian community, and by extension to communities of faith across other religious traditions. Because every ecclesiology embodies an institutionalized answer to the soteriological question of what we must do to be saved, it situates right action in structured social settings. It defines a virtuous way of life in terms of good moral character and well-ordered institutions shaping each other in practice. Comparing such conceptions, each seen as two-sided within the historic Christian typology of church, sect, and mysticism, reveals the varied light they shed from diverse angles on the nature of the public church in action within a social context drawn in distinctive form.

Mysticism in the Not-So-Secular City

A generation ago, the expansion of the American state and the public sphere surrounding it led Talcott Parsons, following Durkheim's lead, to discern in democratic political modernization the society-wide spread of cultural values of human dignity, rights, and progressive social reform from essentially religious roots. As democratic government expanded to integrate the entire society more fully around such values, the not-so-secular city of the society itself, conceived as a moral community, became more and more like a universal, if invisible, church.[1] The process of "Christianizing secular society" institutionalizes the ethical individualism Parsons discerned as Christianity's own taproot, grounded in the idea of God's people in the biblical covenant of Judaic society.[2]

Modern denominational society, in this view, carries moral ideals of the value, dignity, and autonomy of individual humans throughout public life. It spreads individuals' moral responsibility and calling beyond the tutelary authority of a parental church and diffuses them across the social spheres of family life, schooling, and the professions. Modern principles of religious freedom, voluntarism, and toleration combine with the generalization of traditionally religious values of moral obligation, virtue, and responsibility to create "a common matrix of value commitment which is broadly shared between denominations, and which forms the basis of the sense in which the society as a whole forms a religiously based moral community."[3]

Parsons saw a moral upgrading rather than breakdown at work in modern society.[4] A heightened sense of individual autonomy and responsibility arises from values institutionalized in democratic self-government, education, and middle-class family life, cemented by elements of "golden-rule" mutuality inherent in Christian ethics.[5] In ecclesiological terms that reach back a century to Ernst Troeltsch, this prospect represents a peculiarly modern kind of mysticism that recognizes no inherent tensions between an encompassing religious faith, the benign fluidity of modern culture, and the structural arrangement of modern social life within nation-states built around liberal constitutional democratic regimes.[6]

Writing a century ago and thinking chiefly of Christianity in European society, Troeltsch, by contrast, emphasized the uneasy, unstable stance of the religious individualism that modern mysticism assumed in relation to public life and political culture:

> It is neither Church nor sect, and has neither the concrete sanctity of the institution nor the radical connection with the Bible. Combining Christian ideas with a wealth of modern views, deducing social institutions, not from the Fall but from a process of natural development, it has not the fixed limit for concessions and the social power which the Church possesses, but also it does not possess the radicalism and the exclusiveness with which the sect can set aside the State and economics, art and science.[7]

Committed to a directly inward and present religious experience, mysticism is indifferent to outward forms of religious worship, doctrine, and organization and at the same time takes them for granted. It is likewise indifferent to the larger society's political and economic organization through modern administrative, bureaucratic, and market-centered structures. Thus it relies all the more upon such structuring in the absence of its own distinctive institutional arrangement, authority, and social discipline as a community of faith.

In the absence of a gospel ethic or ecclesial tradition of its own, modern mysticism reflects the morally mixed culture surrounding it, especially among the educated and urbanized middle classes, even as it senses itself transcending such bounds to represent the highest ethical ideals of humanity. As it comes to predominate in the modern world, thought Troeltsch, this type of religiosity takes fluid form in a "voluntary association with like-minded people," a purely spiritual fellowship of inner light and love equally remote from the universal Church and perfectionist sects whose interplay shaped Christian tradition.[8]

American society at the dawn of the twenty-first century may prove both Troeltsch and Parsons to be right, each in his own way, regarding the rise of religious individualism across a wide range of carriers and its ambiguous impact on their social ethics and public participation. It extends from new-age religious seekers through many mainline Protestants and Americanist Catholics charting their own spiritual journeys, to softer evangelicals whose voluntarist piety floats free from fundamentalist faith, binding congregational community, and the ethical rigor of prayerful practice.[9] To the ears of some critics, it echoes even in "compassionate conservative" presidential rhetoric that weds faith-based "social entrepreneurs" and market-based economic entrepreneurs as volunteers to solve social ills and help change America, one heart, one soul, one conscience at a time.[10]

At its best, modern religious individualism stresses the need for all doctrinal beliefs to receive personal reinterpretation, and for all religious liberties to lead to both deeper self-understanding and greater social responsibility for the shared fate of humankind. The search for personal meaning and social relevance at the heart of the modern quest for salvation after heaven and beyond belief, especially among the more educated, has led spiritual seekers to explore forms of ritual practice, artistic expression, therapeutic care, and social action well beyond the boundaries of traditional religious institutions. More open and flexible patterns of membership have in turn made for more permeable boundaries and more fluid types of organization in most major denominations. There these changes have spurred conflicts over orthodox belief and faithful discipleship, as well as debates over church growth and decline across generations.[11]

At the same time, mounting evidence points to the unsettling effects of a this-worldly individualism severed from constitutive relationship to God and self-centered in instrumental or expressive cultural terms. From this standpoint comes radical reconstrual of James Madison's deist remonstrance, for example, that the sovereignty of individual conscience and conviction requires free exercise of religion precisely in order to honor its divine Creator and the lawful order of nature and nature's God. For, as Madison reasons, "it is the duty of every man to render to the Creator such homage and such only as he believes to be acceptable to him."[12] Freedom of conscience to worship God and follow reason comes to be contested and recast as freedom of choice to pursue one's own interests and express one's own feelings. Religious individualists often find it difficult to sustain their own sense of moral integrity and responsibility, let alone transmit it to their children, if they do not share its practice in religious communities with some binding sectlike discipline or churchly authority.[13]

Modern forms of instrumental and expressive individualism are attuned respectively to the institutional arrangement of economic and bureaucratic life today and to lifestylish leisure. But they have long coexisted with religious and civic ideals of the dignity, indeed the sacredness, of the individual as defined by moral duties, virtues, and practical relationships within the traditions of biblical religion and civic humanism in American culture. The question its critics pose is whether an individualism centered on the self as a nexus of interests and feelings, and counted as a market actor or client-citizen of the welfare state, can actually sustain a public or a private life coherently.[14] If not, they ask, can civic and religious forms of individualism be critically reworked through communities of shared moral practice and argument? Can we rebalance the moral ecology of private life and public institutions by renewing genuine individuality in relation to a larger social whole and cultural conversation? This challenge invites the Protestant denominations in particular to pursue their own ongoing reformation in ways that balance the religious individualism illuminated by the inward communion of modern mystics and spiritual seekers—and the exemplary moral vigor and prophetic witness inherited from Christian sects as ingathered elects composed of come-outers—with the social realism of the Church as the Pauline Body of Christ, the fundamental sacrament that precedes and nurtures every faithful individual in redemptive relationship to God.[15]

Sects Standing against and Adapted to Liberal Society

If the unity of the modern social world is centered around a state inherently at odds with religious faith and community, in contrast to the moral integrity of the not-so-secular city, then there comes to the fore a very different ecclesiological ideal of a radically reformed church or sect. Church, sect, and mysticism interact over the centuries as the three main types of Christian social development, by Ernst Troeltsch's account, each rooted in the free personal piety of the gospel of Jesus and each stemming in diverse directions from its community of worship. The sect is a voluntary society composed of strict and definite believers bound to each other by the "new birth" of Christian conversion and living in but not of the world to prepare for the coming Kingdom of God. Instead of the sacramental Redeemer of the institutional Church, writes Troeltsch, the "Christ of the Sect is the Lord, the example and lawgiver of Divine authority and dignity, who allows His elect to pass through contempt and misery on their earthly pilgrimage, but who will complete the real work of Redemption at His Return, when He will establish the Kingdom of God."[16]

In contrast to churchly engagement and active compromise with the political and economic institutions of the society at large, the Christian sect from the beginning sharply opposes the world and seeks to realize the ideal of the Sermon on the Mount in all its purity. This impulse takes extreme form in aggressive sects that seek to conquer the society for Christ, particularly when the apocalyptic end of the existing order seems nigh. More often in the history of Christianity, this impulse of opposition takes the form of the passive sect, often persecuted and typically turned inward in small and quiet groups comforted by faith in the coming Kingdom of God, until, says Troeltsch, "through its connection with Ascetic Protestantism, it also found a way of becoming incorporated with the life of this present world."[17] This complex process of incorporation informs the "embattled and thriving" stance of many apparently sectlike yet highly adaptive religious groups in America today. These include, but are hardly limited to, self-described "conservative evangelicals," increasingly integrated into modern social and economic life but mistrustful of government, even as they become politically more active and influential in the very world their own traditions helped create.[18]

Ecclesiastical Protestantism collapsed the corporatist Catholic hierarchy of an ascent from nature to grace into the Lutheran ethic of the calling in the world of everyday work and householding that God gives each individual. Luther separated church and state into "two kingdoms" and ceded authority to princes to maintain order among the wild animals of the political arena. Calvinist Protestantism honed an activist Christian calling in the this-worldly asceticism of a "Protestant Ethic" to order the holy community rationally and restore it within the life of the world. Ascetic Protestantism draws Christian sects away from radical opposition to the world in their efforts to live out the ideal of the Sermon on the Mount, while it resists the antinomianism of modern mysticism in its celebration of individuals as free spirits in a purely inward communion with God and one another. Protestant reformers reemphasize the radical separation between divine and human. Yet they proclaim the world as the theater of God's glory and will, in which selves justified by faith serve God in every walk of life.

By replacing clergy-laity distinctions between two levels of religious perfection with the division between elect and reprobates, Calvinist Anglo-Protestantism in particular helps fuel the historic shift from hereditary kingship and feudal aristocracy to more democratic forms of self-revising, self-governing political order. These depend on more contractual and voluntary modes of association among persons seen as individuals in their roles as both citizens and church members within a priesthood of all believers. Because it so centrally shaped the moral character and convictions of American citizens, Tocqueville concluded that religion should be considered as "the first of their political institutions."[19] But he also discerned the danger of an individualism cut loose from its religious moorings, with every person free to find their beliefs within themselves and to turn their feelings in on themselves. Once democracy breaks the hierarchical chain of reciprocal duties and virtues forged by feudally fixed social stations and frees each link as an equal, then "each man is forever thrown back on himself alone, and there is danger that he may be shut up in the solitude of his own heart," withdrawing into a small circle of family and friends and leaving the larger society to look after itself.[20]

Both the power and the problems of the Christian sect's incorporation into the political and economic order of modern American society inform recent thinking about communities of faith and their place in civil society from Stanley Hauerwas, on the one hand, and from Richard Neuhaus, Peter Berger, and Michael Novak, on the other. The expansion of the modern state and its increased penetration into the affairs and understanding of other institutions—particularly local communities, schools, and families—give greater force and plausibility to sectlike visions of the surrounding social world. Dominated by a regulatory state and a "liberal democratic polity," as Stanley Hauerwas conceives it in theoretical terms drawn from John Rawls, American society and its public life are inherently secular. They invite democratic participation inspired by religious convictions, but they insist that these convictions be expressed and justified in secular terms.

American Christians following in the path of the Social Gospel, which informs key premises of the American sociology that Talcott Parsons reworks, assume that our inherently good democracy enables them to engage in politics to transform our social institutions to aid needy individuals and make our society more nearly just.[21] But such Christian enthusiasm for secular political involvement distracts Christians from the church's first political task as an exemplary witness community of Christian virtue and love, counters Hauerwas. It leads them to acquiesce in "the liberal assumption that a just polity is possible without the people being just." Instead, liberal Christians "simply accepted the assumption that politics is about the distribution of desires, irrespective of the content of those desires, and any consideration of the development of virtuous people as a political issue seems an inexcusable intrusion into our personal liberty."[22]

Rather than incarnating Christian virtue and exemplifying a Christian polity over against a secular one, the mainline churches, by this account, imitate liberal democratic politics in their own social arrangements and moral practices.[23] By so doing, ironically, they fail America's peculiar kind of secular polity, which is predicated on a conscientious, unselfish civic spirit that its own secular nature cannot engender. For the true Christian, Hauerwas declares, "the church is always the primary polity." Its primary task is to make persons holy and genuinely just, not to make the society better or more just, by forming in itself an exemplary "society built on truth rather than fear" bred by the state's coercive power or the market's anxious self-interest.[24]

Let the church be the church, this view exhorts, instead of imitating the social world surrounding it. The church fulfills its first responsibility to society by being itself, less an introverted sect for Hauerwas than a church militant, an apostolic church radically reformed through exemplary *ecclesiolae*, small churches marked by the shared concentration and intimacy of their communal life in worship, work, and witness. As members of such a church militant, Hauerwas comes to stress, Christians can do nothing more significant in America than to become a people formed by the worship of a crucified and resurrected God. For as such, they "might just be complex enough to engage in the hard work of working out agreements and disagreements with others one small step at a time."[25]

Such a church enables its members to recognize what the world is and why its political self-understanding is so limited, for example, by the emptiness of the individual freedom it affirms as an end in itself and the legal procedures it resorts to in the absence of conscientious self-restraint and communally shared responsibility.[26] Crucial to this stance of the church in but not of the world of the larger society, and ready to stand against it, is the premise that American society is now politically unified in institutional fact and in practice in terms of philosophical theories of liberalism. Notwithstanding the richer social and cultural history of the United States, says Hauerwas, "liberalism has become a self-fulfilling prophecy such that now theories of liberalism are not only descriptively powerful but shape our dominant public policies."[27] Social events inexplicable in liberal terms still occur, to be sure, but they denote only "fragments of other political moralities," still legible on the pages of a history barely extant in American life and common sense today.[28] By its very temper as well as its power, liberal democracy, in this view, cannot be deeply influenced by the churches, let alone transformed. Such is the naive, theologically liberal optimism that justifies the churches' selling their Christian birthright to form genuinely just persons for a mess of welfare-state pottage. Such views trace their Protestant lineage to the free churches and sects of the radical Reformation, set against early-modern absolutist states whose coercive social grasp and arrogation of sovereign authority expanded nation-states today seem to rehearse.[29]

By contrast, if the public order of American society today is not seen as a single moral realm but as a constellation of two or more kingdoms—that is, more or less discrete domains each with their own ideals and arrangements whose integrity an expanded welfare state threatens—then religious institutions can best serve as socially adaptive, mildly sectlike "sheltering communities" set within the formal framework of denominations.[30] These sheltering congregational and cultural communities contrast, on the one hand, with radically reformed churches or strong sects set against the world. On the other hand, they contrast with loose, fluid associations of like-minded religious individuals or modern mystics in denominational guise, fully in step with the secular city of the larger society and culture. Instead of rejecting the state and the economy as the world, such sheltering religious institutions conduct their own affairs with measured confidence that truly faithful believers will also be law-abiding and concerned citizens. They can focus on seeking to save souls, shape conscience, and embrace the family, since they trust that conscientious entrepreneurs will be honest in their market dealings and charitable where the market fails to provide for the needy.[31]

On the broad theological ground that surrounds this sheltering, mildly sectlike stance of the church to public life, we find traditionally evangelical Protestant emphases on freedom of worship and conscience protected by "church-state separation." Here, too, stand traditionally Lutheran notions of church and state as two kingdoms, each sovereign in its own realm; and the concern of "Catholic Whigs" for strong boundaries set between economy and government as well as between church and state. Institutionally, we find evangelical support for setting up voluntary associations to help the needy instead of expanding state social-service agencies to do so, Catholic concerns for parochial schools and hospitals, and fundamentalists founding Christian academies to educate their own to keep the faith.

Works by Richard Neuhaus, Peter Berger, and Michael Novak are noteworthy for featuring ecclesiologies of two or more kingdoms that highlight the dangers that an expanding state poses to the denominational equilibrium of a pluralist society.[32] Thus Berger and Neuhaus warned in 1977, "The danger today is not that the churches or any one church will take over the state. The much more real danger is that the state will take over the functions of the church, except for the most narrowly construed definition of religion limited to worship and religious instruction."[33] To counter the state's threat to take over the functions of religious institutions and shrink their authority, Berger and Neuhaus argue for counting religious institutions among the key "players" the public realm should include, and recognizing them as "mediating structures" standing in between individuals and big government. This should lead the welfare state to set policies and programs to support religious institutions, not supplant them, in educating, caregiving, and community-building in their own right and in their intimate involvement with the family. Religious institutions as alternative means of communal provision can help Americans answer the apparent "contradiction between wanting more government services and less government." Moreover, the state should heed "the complex ways essentially religious values infiltrate and influence our public thought."[34]

In relating political and religious institutions, Michael Novak similarly stresses their respective boundaries in the political economy of "democratic capitalism," based on the moral premise of human sin and finitude: "To divide—and to check—social powers is the radical impulse of the form of political economy pioneered in the United States." It divides "the unitary social system of the ancient regime into three spheres: an active political system, a dynamic economic system, and a vital moral and cultural system."[35] Each of the three is to invigorate and restrain the others. The polity may properly do so at times, impelled by "a just solicitude for the common good and a proper respect for law," Novak allows, but to an unprecedented degree the U.S. Constitution limits the state's reach into "moral-cultural" institutions such as religion and the family. "In parallel fashion, and also to an unprecedented degree, the people have restricted the powers of the state over economic institutions (of large businesses and small, of capital and labor)."[36]

Over time, the power of the state has vastly increased, Novak contends, often under the claim of "seeking 'the common good,' although not always achieving that good." To keep these social spheres in balance, religious and moral virtues must inspire citizens and motivate market actors. Yet religion must also encourage the moral habits and practices that "the American political economy has been fertile in promoting." These are "the practice of association, the habits of cooperation, and the habits of the heart guided by self-interest rightly understood—that self-interest which reaches out to embrace the interests of others, near and far."[37] To do more or otherwise in the way of justifying political regulation of the economy on religious grounds, warns Novak in rebuking the 1986 Catholic bishops' letter on the U.S. economy, smacks of "McGovernism," in "secretly smuggling an egalitarian, socialist concept" into Christian ethics and adopting "an un-American concept of justice."[38] By so profoundly misconstruing the moral differences among social institutions in order to free the market and shackle the state, counter Novak's critics, this laissez-faire ethic compartmentalizes Christian love, sacralizes self-interest, and denies human rights to economic necessities. It betrays economic justice for all in favor of economic freedom for an advantaged few.[39]

The ideal of the sect rings true to Americans in standing for the voluntary association of faithful individuals within a Protestant priesthood of all believers joined in God's Word yet free to exercise their own conscience in the light of God's grace and will. The ideal of the sect resonates with our sense of democratic equality and full yet free participation in self-government under the rule of law. Because the sect actively seeks to shape Christian disciples and bind its members into the Body of Christ or the People of God, its nurture and discipline are particularly pertinent to the need of religious individuals and seekers to become members of faithful communities. At the same time, the sect remains fragile, despite or indeed because of all its demands on its individual members to sustain it. This is especially true in a denominational society with growing freedom to switch or leave behind ever more independent congregations if they ask too much or too little of us.

Especially in a society seen as the contractual creation of come-outers who freely form an ingathered elect, strong sects run the risk of ignoring how deeply their elect members are actually involved in the complex moral order of the larger social world they oppose, and how deeply that world enters into their own community. Mild, sheltering sects risk allowing that world to go its own unjust and unconscionable way in return for religious tolerance under the law, freedom of individual conscience, interpersonal support, and psychic solace for the righteous. So the ideal of the Church is a welcome counterbalance to the sect, given its sacramental and liturgical embodiment of the encompassing reality of redemption for the whole of God's people in one organic body of many different members. As Christ's living presence on earth and itself the fundamental sacrament, the Church is not just the offspring of our voluntary association as individuals called out of the world and gathered into an elect. The Church is our Mother, who comes before us as individuals and embraces us.[40]

A Church to Bring Society Back In

Distinguishing between the state and the society conceived as a rich, diverse, yet interwoven whole, rather than a set of discrete political, economic, and moral domains, frames a characteristically "churchlike" ideal of religious institutions. Seen in relation to the state, as the ethicist David Hollenbach observes in behalf of the Catholic bishops' 1986 letter on the economy, society is the more inclusive reality. It is composed of many subcommunities of various institutional kinds: families, neighborhoods, labor unions, small businesses, giant corporations, farm cooperatives, and a host of voluntary associations and religious congregations. Respect for this pluralism of communities across a range of institutions rests on the fact that "justice is not the concern of the political community alone, nor is it to be administered solely by the state. The freedom of these other forms of human community to exist and to operate according to the kinds of communities they are must be protected." Such is the substance of what Catholic social teaching calls the principle of subsidiarity. These other communities are not purely private bodies, Hollenbach stresses. "They are parts of society, ways in which persons come to participate in social life."[41]

This view emphasizes the primary and more inclusive reality of society at large as a diverse set of interdependent communities. They are pluralistic, yet all of them are public in their concerns for the social good. This view marks a typically "church-like" stance of willingness to engage the society as a whole and wrestle with it dialectically, practically, and structurally, in the cautiously hopeful expectation that such engagement can make the world more humane and just. It respects yet seeks to press beyond the stance of the sect as a witness community set against the world or a sheltering community adapted to it. By arguing across multiple moral languages and visions, the church is willing to engage the larger society more intimately and dialectically than the religious kingdom holding itself at arm's length from the political and economic realms. The church, too, seeks to infuse in persons virtues of faith, hope, and charity, first of all, for the sake of salvation and graceful human flourishing. To these ends, it seeks to pacify the play of interests in the marketplace and temper the state's balancing of political power and the representative rule of law. It wishes to engage its institutional neighbors across society in argument as well as love, turning them toward social arrangements restructured to help instead of hinder persons in practicing these virtues.

The Church can engage the larger society in all its mundane diversity and difficulty, thought Troeltsch, because the Christ of the Church is the Redeemer, who in his work of salvation has endowed it as a conciliar institution with the treasures of sacramental grace, forgiveness, and redemption. He has done so, once and for all, not only for an elect who can follow the heroic example of the Lord of the sect, or for the individual who can experience the inner light of the Christ of mysticism. Churchly Protestantism spiritualizes public worship and the sacraments of the Catholic Church, yet sustains through the sermon and the Word in worship the Church's authoritative basis of grace, doctrine, and ministry.[42]

Troeltsch favors the ideal of the Church over the sect and mysticism, because the Church "preserves inviolate the religious elements of grace and redemption; it makes it possible to differentiate between Divine grace and human effort; and it is able to include the most varied degrees of Christian attainment and maturity, and therefore it alone is capable of fostering a popular religion which inevitably involves a great variety in its membership."[43] Yet Troeltsch also sees the characteristic flaws and dangers of the Church-type. It is too ready to compromise with worldly powers and principalities in order to consolidate its own authority. It is too prone to sacrifice both prophetic witness and inner holiness in order to objectify doctrine as dogma and fortify hierarchy as clerical office instead of moral example. It does so, he notes, in forms historically at odds with modern religious pluralism and disestablishment. It also runs counter to the twentieth-century rise of de facto congregationalism in popular churches, movements, and groups tugging away at the denominational principle. So the sect as prophetic witness community is needed to check the churchly tendency to compromise with the powers that be and mute individual conscience. The mystical ideal of a radically loving community is needed to check the Church's tendencies toward self-protective paternalism and dogmatic authority.[44]

Thus, for example, Catholics in the United States over the past generation have entered fully enough into the moral mainstream of American culture, and the educated middle class of American society, to embrace the mutual implications of two ideals: the priesthood of all believers in the Church as the Body of Christ, and the representative participation of all members of the Church as the People of God in its conciliar conversation and decision-making as a self-governing social body. This sea change shaped a new generation of U.S. Catholics, who embraced the church as the People of God in conciliar community instead of genuflecting to an authoritative hierarchy headed by the clergy. It coincided with the Second Vatican Council's call to the church to engage the whole of humankind in addressing their common suffering and aspiration. "The joys and hopes, the griefs and anxieties of the men of this age, especially those who are poor or in any way afflicted," began the Council's *Pastoral Constitution of the Church in the Modern World*, "are the joys and hopes, the griefs and anxieties of the followers of Christ."[45]

This call helped inspire greater collegiality among the American Catholic bishops themselves within a restructured national conference by the 1970s. It led them to speak more cogently and less parochially as moral critics and challengers in national policy debates on issues of economic and social justice, where they questioned both laissez-faire capitalism and state socialism. It led them to take on issues of nuclear disarmament and peacemaking, capital punishment and abortion, which they sought to weave into "a seamless ethic of life." At the same time, from the 1980s to the present, such public participation also involved the American bishops and increasingly vocal Catholic lay groups with political-party leaders and campaigns more intent on building new electoral constituencies around cultural wedge issues such as abortion than on embracing a seamless ethic of life across partisan lines.[46]

Both political parties have vied more actively and evenly for the Catholic vote since it emerged from the breakup of the New Deal coalition in the Democratic Party in the 1960s. In 2004 George W. Bush won the vote of non-Latino Catholics by 53 to 47 percent, a first-ever Republican victory, largely due to increased support from Catholic traditionalists (72 versus 28 percent) and centrists (55 versus 45 percent). But modernist Catholics voted for John Kerry by 69 to 31 percent. Modernist mainline Protestants did likewise, by 78 to 22 percent, creating a 50-50 split between Bush and Kerry among all mainline Protestants, long a strong Republican constituency. This yielded the highest level of Protestant support for a Democratic candidate in recent times, even as evangelical Protestants favored Bush by 78 to 22 percent.[47] Such voting splits and shifts within religious traditions suggest that a growing majority of Catholics, like Protestants, are deliberating their views on a wide range of moral and social issues, not just abortion, in the light of their own consciences. Catholics are voting according to their own convictions and interests, neither commanded by their bishops when they speak with one voice nor confounded by them when they speak with divided voices.[48]

The self-understanding of a new generation of U.S. Catholics reveals them as lay members of a priesthood of all believers mutually responsible for the integrity of the Church as the People of God. It underlies their unmuffled moral outrage and action in response to the wider exposure in recent years of a double failure—by episcopal accessories to crimes of sexual abuse as well as by their pastoral perpetrators—in the exercise of clerical power to protect the safety, health, and moral integrity of children entrusted to the church's care. It also underlies their recognition that arbitrary, caste-bound clerical authority itself endangers the moral integrity of a genuinely catholic church. It impedes its denominational development from the sectlike shell of a self-protective immigrant church and postpones its promise to renew the conciliar truth of Christian tradition as a whole in terms that all faithful Americans can share.

Although the expression of church-type ideals in American Christianity is most familiar in specifically Catholic, Episcopal, and Orthodox Christian idioms, such concern for the institutional integrity of religious faith in relation to the society as a whole is nonetheless grounded in biblical terms that include many in the mainline Protestant denominations, and certainly the American Jewish community as well.[49] In the Reformed tradition of American Protestantism, for example, God's sovereignty over all creation inspires the church's public responsibility to embody universal truth and respect individual conscience in the course of its self-government and social witness. Thus the constitution of the Presbyterian Church (USA) begins its principles of government with the Lordship of Christ as Head of the Church: "All power in heaven and earth is given to Jesus Christ by Almighty God, who raised Christ from the dead and set him above all rule and authority, all power and dominion, and every name that is named, not only in this age, but also in that which is to come. God has put all things under the Lordship of Jesus Christ and has made Christ Head of the Church, which is his Body." Hence, "it belongs to Christ alone to rule, to teach, to call, and to use the Church as he will, exercising his authority by the ministry of women and men for the establishment and extension of his Kingdom."[50]

The great ends of the church are "the proclamation of the gospel for the salvation of human-kind; the shelter, nurture, and spiritual fellowship of the children of God; the maintenance of divine worship; the preservation of the truth; the promotion of social righteousness; the exhibition of the Kingdom of Heaven to the world."[51] In fulfilling these ends, the church must consider "the rights of private judgment" to be universal and unalienable, since "God alone is Lord of the conscience, and has left it free from the doctrine and commands of men which are in anything contrary to his Word, or beside it, in matters of faith or worship," in the words of the Westminster Confession of Faith.[52]

The Reformed tradition stresses an inseparable connection between faith and practice, truth and duty, for "truth is in order to goodness; and the great touchstone of truth, its tendency to produce holiness, according to our Savior's rule, 'By their fruits ye shall know them.'" At the same time, "there are truths and forms with respect to which men of good character and principles may differ. And in all these we think it the duty both of private Christians and societies to exercise mutual forbearance toward each other." It follows that all Church power is only "ministerial and declarative," that is to say, that "the Holy Scriptures are the only rule of faith and manners; that no Church governing body ought to pretend to make laws to bind the conscience in virtue of their own authority; and that all their decisions should be founded upon the revealed will of God."[53]

On this conscientious and scriptural basis, the catholic unity of the Presbyterian Church becomes embodied in its representative self-government. So it is that "the several different congregations of believers, taken collectively, constitute one Church of Christ, called emphatically the Church; that a larger part of the Church, or a representation of it, should govern a smaller, or determine matters of controversy which arise therein; that in like manner, a representation of the whole should govern and determine in regard to every part, and to all parts united: that is, that a majority shall govern." Appeals may be carried from lower to higher governing bodies of the church, "till they be finally decided by the collected wisdom and united voice of the whole Church," on the authoritative "example of the apostles and the practice of the primitive Church."[54]

In more evangelical traditions of American Protestantism, such as Methodism, the unity and authority of the church are no less crucial. They are comparably conceived, though distinctively developed and contested. Thus the United Methodist *Book of Discipline* begins its constitution by affirming, "The church is a community of all true believers under the Lordship of Christ." As part of the church universal, it specifies, "the United Methodist Church believes that the Lord of the church is calling Christians everywhere to strive toward unity." Therefore, it pledges, United Methodism "will see, and work for, unity at all levels of church life," through global relationships with other Methodist churches, through councils of churches, and through plans of union and covenantal relationships with churches of Methodist or other denominational traditions.[55]

In defining Methodism's doctrinal heritage, the *Discipline* sees the Spirit working through the church's communal and revivalist forms of faith, embodied in its connectional ties, to inspire its witness for peace and justice in the world:

> For Wesley there is no religion but social religion, no holiness but social holiness. The communal forms of faith in the Wesleyan tradition not only promote personal growth; they also equip and mobilize us for mission and service to the world.
>
> The outreach of the church springs from the working of the Spirit. As United Methodists we respond to that working through a connectional polity based on mutual responsiveness and accountability. Connectional ties bind us together in faith and service in our global witness, enabling faith to become active in love and intensifying our desire for peace and justice in the world.[56]

John Wesley's "General Rules" to avoid evil, do good, and follow the ordinances of God reveal the spiritual spring of moral action. They point out the path of holy living as a salvific way of Christian discipleship, not a code of church law. "Upon such evangelical premises, Methodists in every age have sought to exercise their responsibility for the moral and spiritual quality of society," the *Discipline* emphasizes. "Our struggles for human dignity and social reform have been a response to God's demand for love, mercy, and justice in the light of the Kingdom."[57]

Thus the "dear uniting love" of the Spirit makes Methodists "one in heart," joined together with one another as members of the Body of Christ, even as they are joined "in one spirit to our Head."[58] Bred by re-vivalist hymns, prayers, preaching, and testimony, this joyful, tearful spirit of the church as a living body of heartfelt grace animates the vast and intricate "machine" of Methodist connectionalism, as Russell Richey ar-gues.[59] It embodies the unity of the Church within the whole family of God as an all-encompassing community of love, bound together in the love of Christ. In its evolving forms of public assembly, federalism, and cor-poratism—from camp meetings through conferences to denominational boards and agencies—Methodist connectionalism in turn has formed and reformed its own peculiar vision of a conciliar, covenantal church, at once profoundly American and Synoptic, riding side-by-side on the road of itinerancy and communing face-to-face at table with Christ.[60]

The catholicity of the church remains a matter of crucial Methodist commitment, ambivalence, and contestation, according to Richey.[61] So Methodists continue to affirm the unity of the "Catholic Spirit" Wesley preached two centuries ago: " 'If thine heart is as mine,' if thou lovest God and all mankind, I ask no more: 'Give me thine hand'. . . . Love me with a very tender affection, as a friend that is closer than a brother; as a brother in Christ, a fellow-citizen of the new Jerusalem."[62] Methodists also con-tinue to contest the meaning of the church's catholicity, as we have seen in the conflict between Good News and the General Board of Church and Society.[63] Amid charges of schismatic moral absolutism in thrall to a false creedalism, for example, Methodists fight to unite their church in terms of scriptural authority, doctrinal certainty, and holy living for all the faithful, not just an orthodox remnant. Amid countercharges of amoral chaplaincy in service to a godless society, they struggle to bring all the faithful, not just the prophetic few, to answer the gospel call to love our neighbor and do God's will for justice and peace on earth as it is done in heaven.

Only through institutional structures consistent with religious free exercise and disestablishment in a denominational society such as ours can we balance the mutual interpenetration of ideals of the Church, sect, and mysticism, united and reconciled as far as possible yet still driven to develop dynamically by their inherent tensions. But precisely because the ideal of the Church is hardest to find or even conceive in a culture where individuals commonsensically come first and freely associate to create sectlike churches, opening up American communities of faith to the spirit of the Church may well be the most valuable step we can take to revive our denominations and inspire them to act as the public church.[64]

Notes

Chapter 1: Faith in Public

1. Religious Leaders for Sensible Priorities, "President Bush: Jesus Changed Your Heart. Now Let Him Change Your Mind," *New York Times*, December 4, 2002, p. A33.

2. Elisabeth Bumiller, "Religious Leaders Ask If Antiwar Call Is Heard," *New York Times*, March 10, 2003, p. A16.

3. Robert W. Edgar, "The Fierce Urgency of Now," Office of the General Secretary, National Council of Churches, undated letter, March–April 2003, here and below; Jim Wallis, quoted in Bumiller, "Religious Leaders Ask If Antiwar Call Is Heard."

4. Bumiller, "Religious Leaders Ask If Antiwar Call Is Heard."

5. White House, "President George Bush Discusses Iraq in National Press Conference," March 6, 2003. The White House transcripts cited here and below are available at http://www.whitehouse.gov/news.

6. Bumiller, "Religious Leaders Ask If Antiwar Call Is Heard."

7. Edgar, "The Fierce Urgency of Now."

8. *San Francisco Chronicle*, February 14, 2003, p. A29; Nanette Asimov, "Protest in San Francisco," *San Francisco Chronicle*, February 17, 2003, p. A14.

9. White House, "President Bush Addresses the Nation," March 19, 2003.

10. "White House Tells Congress Why the Nation Must Go to War," excerpts from a White House report to Congress, *New York Times*, March 20, 2003, p. A18.

11. White House, "Operation Iraqi Freedom: President's Radio Address," April 12, 2003.

12. White House, "President's Remarks in Greeley, Colorado," October 25, 2004.

13. White House, "President Sworn-In to Second Term: Inauguration 2005," January 20, 2005, here and below. See also Bush's remarks on freedom in note 26 below. Cf. presidential speeches after mid-2005 for more stress on winning the Iraq war in order to defend Americans from terror at home, compared to spreading liberty and ending tyranny around the world, and a more muted justification of

preemptive war than that set out by the 2002 National Security Strategy (see note 14 below); see, for example, White House, "President's Radio Address," October 29, 2005; and White House, "President Discusses War on Terror at National Endowment for Democracy," October 6, 2005.

14. "National Security Strategy of the United States of America, and Accompanying Letter by President George W. Bush," September 20, 2002, excerpted in *Historic Documents of 2002* (Congressional Quarterly Press, 2003), online edition, CQ Public Affairs Collection, http://www.library.cqpress.com, pp. 6, 8, 15, 25, drawn from the first, second, and final paragraphs of the president's letter, and sections 5 and 9 of the document.

15. White House, "President Bush Announces Major Combat Operations in Iraq Have Ended: Remarks by the President from the USS Abraham Lincoln at Sea off the Coast of San Diego, California," May 1, 2003, here and below.

16. Jim Winkler, "Publisher's Column," *Christian Social Action*, May–June 2003, p. 2. *Christian Social Action* is the official publication of the General Board of Church and Society of the United Methodist Church, published bimonthly through 2004 and thereafter appearing only online, at http://www.umc gbcs.org.

17. Interview, not for attribution, April 2003.

18. According to 2004 preelection polls, 72 percent of Bush supporters continued to hold to the view that Iraq had actual weapons of mass destruction (47 percent) or a major program for developing them (25 percent) before the war, despite contrary reports by the Senate Intelligence Committee and the Iraq Survey Group. Seventy-five percent of Bush supporters continued to believe that Iraq was providing substantial support to al Qaeda, with 20 percent convinced that Iraq was directly involved in the 9/11 attacks, despite the 9/11 Commission report to the contrary. Sixty-three percent of Bush supporters believed that clear evidence of this support had been found, while 85 percent of Kerry supporters believed the opposite. Majorities of both Bush and Kerry supporters agreed that they continued to hear the Bush administration confirming right up to the election that Iraq possessed weapons of mass destruction (WMDs) and supported al Qaeda. Eighty-five percent of Bush supporters agreed that going to war in Iraq was the right decision, but 58 percent said the United States should not have gone to war if U.S. intelligence services had concluded beforehand that Iraq did not have WMDs and was not providing substantial support to al Qaeda. Sixty-one percent believed that President Bush would not have gone to war in that case. By contrast, 90 percent of Kerry supporters believed going to war was the wrong decision, and 83 percent believed that Bush would have gone to war for other reasons even if he had been given information that Iraq had no WMDs and did not support al Qaeda. Steven Kull, Clay Ramsay, Stefan Subias, Stephen Weber, and Evan Lewis, *The Separate Realities of Bush and Kerry Supporters*, PIPA/Knowledge Networks poll, October 21, 2004, pp. 3–8, http://www.pipa.org. The Program on International Policy Attitudes (PIPA) is a joint program of the Center on Policy

Attitudes and the Center for International and Security Studies at the University of Maryland.

19. Bumiller, "Religious Leaders Ask If Antiwar Call Is Heard."

20. Interview, not for attribution, April 2003.

21. Lynette Clemetson, "Clergy Group to Counter Conservatives," *New York Times*, November 17, 2003, p. A15.

22. Ibid.

23. Interviews, not for attribution, September 2004, October 2004.

24. Religion News Service, "Limping Liberal Clergy Group Redesigns Itself," *Christian Century*, January 25, 2005, p. 14.

25. Interview, not for attribution, September 2004.

26. In addressing the nation on the night of September 11, 2001, President Bush asked Americans to join him to pray for all of those who grieved, that "they will be comforted by a power greater than any of us, spoken through the ages in Psalm 23: 'Even though I walk through the valley of the shadow of death, I fear no evil, for you are with me.'" He invoked a biblical God whose power would comfort the grieving and would bless and protect a nation united in resolve to "go forward to defend freedom and all that is good and just in our world" against "evil, the very worst of human nature." America was targeted for attack because "we're the brightest beacon for freedom and opportunity in the world," Bush judged. He vowed that "no one will keep that light from shining," and he promised to bring to justice those responsible for those evil acts. "Bush's Remarks to the Nation on the Terrorist Attacks," *New York Times*, September 12, 2001, p. A4. At a national prayer service at Washington National Cathedral three days later, Bush prayed to God to comfort and console the grieving, and to watch over the nation in its responsibility to history to "answer these attacks and rid the world of evil." This conflict was "begun on the timing and terms of others. It will end in a way, and at an hour, of our choosing," Bush vowed. Our nation's unhealed wounds lead us to "yield our will to a will greater than our own" through prayer, to realize the Pauline assurance of God's love with which Bush concluded, rewritten from "the love of God in Christ Jesus our Lord" in Romans (8:38–39): "Neither death nor life, nor angels nor principalities, nor powers, nor things present, nor things to come, nor height, nor depth can separate us from God's love. May he bless the souls of the departed, may he comfort our own, and may he always guide our country. God bless America." "Transcript of President's Remarks: 'We Are in the Middle Hour of Our Grief,'" *New York Times*, September 15, 2001, p. A6.

27. President George W. Bush, 2001 inaugural address, transcribed by the *New York Times*, January 21, 2001, pp. A12–13; written by Michael Gerson, a journalist and former theology student at evangelical Wheaton College, who also wrote the 2005 inaugural address.

28. "Bush on the Creation of a White House Office Tied to Religion," remarks by President George W. Bush of January 29, 2001, *New York Times*, January 30,

2001, p. A18. "Charitable-choice" legislation proposed by the Clinton administration and passed by Congress in 1996 allows religious charities to compete equally with nonreligious agencies for grants from HUD.

29. "This is going to be an all-out fight," promised Joseph Conn of Americans United for Separation of Church and State. Liberal and moderate Baptist leaders urged rejection of the initiative on church-state grounds. Executives of Catholic Charities and Lutheran Services in America criticized its public aid to religious agencies that discriminate by hiring the faithful first. Smaller religious groups found equal treatment of diverse faiths cause for concern, fearing that government's picking one faith-based social-service provider over another on "best results" grounds was easy to declare in principle but would be difficult to put into fair practice. See Laurie Goodstein, "Nudging Church-State Line, Bush Invites Religious Groups to Seek Federal Aid," New York Times, January 30, 2001, p. A18; and Goodstein, "For Religious Right, Bush's Charity Plan Is Raising Concerns," New York Times, March 3, 2001, pp. A1, A10. Fears that the initiative could give public funding to "hate groups like the Nation of Islam" were voiced by Jewish leaders, such as Bruce M. Ramer, president of the American Jewish Committee, in a letter to the editor, New York Times, March 12, 2001, p. A18.

30. Laurie Goodstein, "Battle Lines Grow on Plan to Assist Religious Groups," New York Times, April 12, 2001, p. A22.

31. For example, Rev. Raymond Rivera of the Latino Pastoral Action Center, a Bronx-based evangelical social ministry that receives a quarter of its funding through government grants, noted that "historically it's been the Catholics, Lutherans, Episcopalians and Jews that have worked with the government, while evangelicals were locked out of the process. Now we know we have access." Laurie Goodstein, "Bush Aide Tells of Plan to Aid Work by Churches," New York Times, March 8, 2001, p. A10. See also Goodstein, "For Religious Right, Bush's Charity Plan Is Raising Concerns."

32. Goodstein, "For Religious Right, Bush's Charity Plan Is Raising Concerns."

33. Provision by the faith-based initiative to allow religious groups backed by tax dollars to hire only their own faithful adherents spurred opposition from unions in the coalition, including the American Federation of State, County and Municipal Employees, the Service Employees International Union, the National Education Association, and the American Federation of Teachers. Goodstein, "Battle Lines Grow on Plan to Assist Religious Groups."

34. Ibid. The Coalition for Compassion counted thirty-six members, including the National Association of Evangelicals, the American Conservative Union, the Free Congress Foundation, the Eagle Forum (led by Phyllis Schlafly), and American Values. Rev. Pat Robertson and Rev. Jerry Falwell were conspicuously absent from the coalition's ranks.

35. Racial divisions in debates over the Bush plan underlined earlier differences in response to the 1996 charitable-choice legislation, with 64 percent of

predominantly black congregations in a 1998 national survey reporting themselves willing to apply for government funding, compared to only 20 percent of predominantly white congregations. Related research later showed that black congregations in Atlanta were six times more likely than nonblack congregations to pursue public funds, and mainline Protestant congregations were two times likelier than others, with younger clergy who were less worried about strict church-state separation leading the way in congregations that already served the poor through private benevolence, public funding, or both. Only 28 percent of politically conservative congregations surveyed were willing to apply for government funding of charity work, compared to 51 percent of politically moderate or liberal congregations. See Mark Chaves, "Religious Congregations and Welfare Reform: Who Will Take Advantage of 'Charitable Choice'?" *American Sociological Review* 64 (December 1999): 836–46; and Michael Leo Owens, "Which Churches Will Take Advantage of Charitable Choice? Explaining the Pursuit of Public Funding by Congregations" (unpublished paper, Department of Political Science, Emory University, 2004). See also Laurie Goodstein, "A Clerical and Racial Gap over Federal Help," *New York Times*, March 24, 2001, pp. A1, A9.

36. Frank Rich, "The Slumber Party," quoting Prof. John DiIulio to Southern Baptists, *New York Times*, March 17, 2001, p. A23. In August 2001, DiIulio resigned as director of the White House Office of Faith-Based and Community Initiatives, to be succeeded by Jim Towey from 2002 to 2006, and Jay Hein since late 2006.

37. Gustav Niebuhr, "A Point Man for the Bush Church-State Collaboration," *New York Times*, April 7, 2001, p. A7.

38. Town Hall Meeting on the White House Office of Faith-Based and Community Initiatives, Interdenominational Theological Consortium, Atlanta, April 17, 2001. Republican congressional leaders invited an almost all-black audience of four hundred evangelical Christian leaders to a conference on faith-based charities notable for its absence of Democrats and its partisan appeals, according to Elizabeth Becker, "Republicans Hold Forum with Blacks in Clergy," *New York Times*, April 26, 2001, p. A18. Representative Thomas M. Davis III (R-Va.), head of the House Republican campaign organization, afterward announced that he was counting on the faith-based initiative to convince more blacks to vote Republican in the 2002 congressional elections, reported Elizabeth Becker in "Senate Delays Legislation on Aid to Church Charities," *New York Times*, May 24, 2001, p. A16.

39. Eighty-two percent of blacks and Hispanics favored public funding of religious groups to provide social services, compared with 68 percent of whites; and those younger than fifty were more concerned than their elders about keeping church and state separate, according to the Pew Forum on Religion and Public Life, on the basis of polling done by the Pew Research Center for the People and the Press on March 5–18, 2001, and reported on April 10, 2001. See Laurie Goodstein, "Support for Religion-Based Plan Is Hedged," *New York Times*, April 11, 2001, p. A12. Orrin Hatch (R-Utah), the ranking Republican on the Senate

Judiciary Committee, cited the Pew poll to note that 75 percent of Americans support religion-government partnerships to help the needy, while Senator Patrick Leahy (D-Vt.), the committee's chair, noted that 68 percent are concerned over government interference with religious groups and 78 percent opposed such groups' being allowed to hire only persons of the same faith. *Christian Century*, June 20–27, 2001, pp. 8–9. Once specific groups were named, support for public funding of faith-based social services declined from 75 percent generally to 62 percent for Catholic churches, 61 percent for Protestant churches, 58 percent for Jewish synagogues, 52 percent for evangelical Christian churches, 51 percent for Mormon churches, 38 percent for Muslim mosques and Buddhist temples, 29 percent for the Nation of Islam, and 26 percent for the Church of Scientology. The initiative's premise that religious organizations could best provide social services to the needy was shared by only three of eight Americans polled (37 percent), compared to 28 percent favoring federal and state government agencies and 27 percent favoring secular community groups, according to Pew Forum data reported in Goodstein, "Support for Religion-Based Plan Is Hedged."

40. Elizabeth Becker, "House Backs Aid for Charities Operated by Religious Groups," *New York Times*, July 20, 2001, p. A14. The Anti-Defamation League called the faith-based initiative "constitutionally suspect and bad public policy." One Orthodox Jewish group, the Orthodox Union, backed the Bush plan as a good program turned into a "political Rorschach test, with some interest groups projecting their own worst fears upon it," reported the *Christian Century*, June 20–27, 2001, p. 9.

41. Pat Conover, "UCC Justice and Peace Action Network: Update on Welfare Reform," Washington, DC, July 15, 2002, http://www.ucc.org/justice/jpan.htm.

42. White House, "President Discusses Compassionate Conservative Agenda in Dallas: Remarks by the President to the 122nd Knights of Columbus Convention," August 3, 2004.

43. White House, "Fact Sheet: Compassion for Americans in Need," August 3, 2004. In 2004 the Bush administration added $43 million for training and technical aid to faith-based and community service providers under the Compassion Capital Fund, $45 million for mentoring prisoners' children, and competitive access for faith-based providers to some $100 million given to fourteen states and one tribal organization in Access to Recovery grants, to give vouchers to individuals to choose substance abuse treatment programs. The administration proposed to add another $350 million in funding to these programs in 2005.

44. Barry Lynn, executive director of Americans United for Separation of Church and State, quoted in Anne Farris, Richard P. Nathan, and David J. Wright, *The Expanding Administrative Presidency: George W. Bush and the Faith-Based Initiative* (Albany, NY: Roundtable on Religion and Social Welfare Policy, Rockefeller Institute of Government, State University of New York, 2004), p. 18, http://www.religionandsocialpolicy.org.

45. Ibid., executive summary, p. i.

46. Courtney Burke, James Fossett, and Thomas Gais, *Funding Faith-Based Services in a Time of Fiscal Pressures* (Albany, NY: Roundtable on Religion and Social Welfare Policy, Rockefeller Institute of Government, State University of New York, 2004), p. 3, http://www.religionandsocialpolicy.org.

47. Farris, Nathan, and Wright, *The Expanding Administrative Presidency*, p. 18. Congress meanwhile approved more than 400 noncompetitive earmark grants to religious groups in the session including the 2004 presidential election totaling some $190 million, up from $20 million for 60 grants in 1997–99, $30 million in 1999–2001, and $45 million in 2001–3, as religious organizations listed as clients of Washington lobbying firms tripled in number and doubled in fees they paid, according to Diana B. Henriques and Andrew W. Lehren, "Religious Groups Reaping Share of Federal Aid for Pet Projects," *New York Times*, May 13, 2007, pp. 1, 16.

48. White House, "President Discusses Compassionate Conservative Agenda in Dallas."

49. Jodi Wilgoren, "Kerry Invokes the Bible in Appeal for Black Votes," *New York Times*, September 10, 2004, p. A18. Cf. John Kerry, "Speech at the Broward Center for the Performing Arts," October 24, 2004, http://www.johnkerry.com/pressroom/speeches, for its coupling of Calvinist covenant and Catholic corporatism to define the basic compact of a solidary "society of the common good." Kerry echoed the opening lines of the Second Vatican Council's *Gaudium et Spes*, "Solidarity of the Church with the Whole Human Family," in *The Documents of Vatican II*, ed. Walter M. Abbott (New York: Guild Press, 1966), pp. 199–200.

50. "Bush on the Creation of a White House Office Tied to Religion."

51. Marc Lacey with Laurie Goodstein, "Bush Fleshes Out Details of Proposal to Expand Aid to Religious Organizations," *New York Times*, January 31, 2001, p. A15. Cf. Steven Waldman, "Doubts among the Faithful," *New York Times*, March 7, 2001, p. A23.

52. Sheila Suess Kennedy, "Bush's Faith-Based Initiative: Asking the Right Question," *Sightings*, March 22, 2001; Kennedy, "Charitable Choice," ibid., October 29, 2003, both at http://www.marty-center.uchicago.edu/sightings/archive. Kennedy is associate professor of law and public policy at Indiana University–Purdue University at Indianapolis.

53. On January 31, 2001, the United Methodist Church's social-policy agency, the General Board of Church and Society (GBCS), issued an initial response, *Statement on Faith-Based and Community Initiatives* (Washington, DC), approving "the idea that Church and State could work more closely together to curb crime, conquer addiction, strengthen families, and overcome poverty," given the Gospel's call to feed the hungry and clothe the naked in Matthew 25:31–46, but also urging the church to proceed with extreme caution in seeking and receiving public funds. The GBCS criticized faith-based legislation in the House, for reasons like

those it had marshaled against the 1996 "charitable-choice" legislation introduced
into Congress by then–Senator John Ashcroft, since "it would have permitted faith
organizations to discriminate in their hiring practices despite receiving public
money" and would thereby violate the church-state provisions of the First Amendment of the U.S. Constitution. The United Methodist Church's 2000 General
Conference reaffirmed a 1980 denominational resolution that church-sponsored
welfare agencies could, "under certain circumstances, be proper channels for public programs," where churches had founded health, education, and welfare agencies "without regard to religious proselytizing." But governmental provision of
funding for such agencies "inevitably raises important questions of religious establishment," warned Resolution 228. "Extreme caution must be exercised to ensure that religious institutions do not receive any aid directly or indirectly for the
maintenance of their religious expression or the expansion of their institutional
resources." See *The Book of Resolutions of the United Methodist Church*, 2000,
no. 228, "Church-Government Relations," pp. 563–64, 570; and *Christian Social
Action*, July–August 2001, p. 13.

54. General Board of Church and Society, General Board of Global Ministries,
and General Council on Finance and Administration, United Methodist Church,
Community Ministries and Government Funding (Washington, DC, 2001), pp. 4–7,
27–30, http://www.gbgm-umc.org/news/2001/june/faith.htm. The report warned
Methodists to "put faith first" and not just "chase the money," while respecting
"church-state boundaries, which are not always clearly defined."

55. Ibid., pp. 4–7, 10, including par. 163 of the United Methodist Social Principles, quoted from *The Book of Discipline of the United Methodist Church* (Nashville, TN: United Methodist Publishing House, 2000), p. 115.

56. White House, "Remarks by the President in Commencement Address, University of Notre Dame," May 20, 2001, here and below.

57. Interview, not for attribution, May 2001.

58. Interview, not for attribution, May 2001.

59. Call to Renewal, letter to White House, June 9, 2003, http://www.calltorenewal
.com/Pentecost_2003_MR_WHLetter.

60. Elizabeth Bumiller, "Bush 'Compassion' Agenda: An '04 Liability?" *New
York Times*, August 26, 2003, pp. A1, A14.

61. According to Census Bureau data, the national poverty rate rose from
11.3 percent in 2000 to 12.5 percent in 2003 and 12.7 percent in 2004, with child
poverty rising from 16.2 percent in 2000 to 17.8 percent in 2004—when 37 million
people lived below the poverty line of about $19,200 for a family of four, includ-
ing 7.8 percent of whites, 24.7 percent of blacks, and 21.9 percent of Hispanics.
Poverty rates plunged from more than 22 percent in 1960 to 11.1 percent in 1973,
rose in the 1980s, and fell in the 1990s, before reversing course upward since 2001.
Median household income, adjusted for inflation, has increased by almost one-
third since the late 1960s, but income inequality has also increased over the past

three decades and has approached all-time highs in recent years. Median family income fell five years in a row, from $46,129 in 1999 to $44,853 in 2004—a drop of 4 percent—to reach its lowest point since 1997, even as the economy grew before and after the recession in 2000, and even though households worked more hours in 2004 than they did in 2003. Economic productivity rose 14.7 percent between November 2001, when recovery began, and 2004, and it rose 16.6 percent from 2000 to 2006. But average real wages ebbed by 0.1 percent from late 2001 to 2005, as 46 percent of corporate income growth went to corporate profits, compared to 20 percent in previous business cycles. U.S. income gaps between the wealthy and the middle class, and between the wealthy and the poor, reached their widest point on record in 1997, according to 2001 Congressional Budget Office income and tax data, after increasing in the 1980s and 1990s alike. From 1979 to 1997, the share of all pretax income going to the top quintile (the top 20 percent) of households rose from 45.9 to 52.3 percent, while the share for the bottom 60 percent of households fell from 32.2 to 26.9 percent. In 2003, the highest-earning fifth of all U.S. households took home 49.8 percent of the nation's income before taxes, up from 44.7 percent in 1983, though down from the 1997 peak in the wake of the 2000 recession. See Census Bureau, *Income, Poverty, and Health Insurance Coverage in the United States*, 2003, 2004, http://www.census.gov/hhes/www/income/html. For the 2001 Congressional Budget Office analysis of income gaps, see Richard W. Stevenson, "Study Details Income Gap between Rich and Poor," *New York Times*, May 31, 2001, p. C4. For 2001–5 wage and productivity analyses, see Lawrence Mishel and Ross Eisenbrey, *What's Wrong with the Economy?* Economic Policy Institute, June 12, 2006, pp. 1–2, based on data from the Bureau of Labor Statistics, *Current Employment Statistics Survey, 2006*, http://www.bls.gov/ces/home.htm, and Bureau of Economic Analysis, NIPA table 1.14, 2006, http://www.bea.gov/bea/dn/nipaweb/index.asp.

62. Heather Boushey, Chauna Brocht, Bethney Gundersen, and Jared Bernstein, *Hardships in America: The Real Story of Working Families* (Washington, DC: Economic Policy Institute, 2001). In comparison to the number of families below the federal poverty line, 2.5 times more families fall below "basic family budget" levels, the amount a two-parent, two-child family in a given community would need to afford food, housing, child care, health insurance, transportation, and utilities. This amount stood at a national median of $33,511 in 2001—twice the 2001 federal poverty line of $17,463 for a family of that size. On wages well above the legal minimum hourly wage yet effectively below the poverty line, see Tom Waldron, Brandon Roberts, and Andrew Reamer, *Working Hard, Falling Short: America's Working Families and the Pursuit of Economic Security*, a report of the Working Families Project, supported by the Annie E. Casey, Ford, and Rockefeller foundations, October 2004, http://www.aecf.org. This report sets the poverty-level wage for a family of four at $8.84 per hour in 2002. It calculates that one in five workers are in occupations with a lower median wage and that one out

of every four working families earn wages so low they are struggling to survive
financially, even if they are above the official poverty line. Within these 9.2 million families are 20 million children, one out of every three children in the United
States. After the 1996 welfare reform, poverty rates for single-mother families fell
from 42 percent in 1995 to 33 percent in 2000, as a growing demand for labor
met the increased labor supply released by cutting welfare rolls; then these poverty rates rose to 36 percent in 2004, as the job market slackened and the annual
hours of work by single mothers declined, according to Jared Bernstein, *Work,
Poverty, and Single-Mother Families*, Economic Policy Institute, August 9, 2006,
http://www.epinet.org, based on the joint Bureau of Labor Statistics and Census
Bureau Current Population Survey (CPS) data for March 2005.

63. Federal taxes amounted to a comparable 16.2 percent of the U.S. gross
domestic product (GDP) in 1964, their lowest proportion since the early 1950s,
according to data from the Economic Policy Institute reported by Jeff Madrick,
"Economic Scene," *New York Times*, November 25, 2004, p. C2. On poverty rates,
see Lawrence Mishel, Jared Bernstein, and Sylvia Allegretto, *The State of Working America 2004/2005* (Ithaca, NY: Cornell University Press, 2005), pp. 309–27.
By official count of the U.S. Census Bureau, one in eight Americans were living
in poverty in 2005—nearly 37 million Americans making up 12.6 percent of the
population—compared to 11.7 percent at the bottom of the recession in late 2001.
The 2005 poverty rate was 14.1 percent (41.3 million poor Americans, almost one
in seven) by alternative measurement closest to the criteria recommended by the
National Academy of Sciences, which take into account geographical differences
in the cost of living, increased expenses such as out-of-pocket medical costs, and
the value of noncash government benefits like food stamps, which have been erod-
ing since they were last adjusted for inflation in 1996. According to Department
of Agriculture reports for 2005, 35.1 million Americans, including 12.4 million
children, live in the 11 percent of U.S. households that cannot consistently afford enough to eat; 82 percent of eligible children received food stamps in 2004,
including 52 percent of eligible children of immigrant parents. See U.S. Census
Bureau, "Income Climbs, Poverty Stabilizes, Uninsured Rate Increases," press
release (CB06-136), August 29, 2006, http://www.census.gov/archives/income_
wealth/007419.html; U.S. Census Bureau, "Poverty Measurement Studies and
Alternative Measures," http://www.census.gov/hhes/www/povmeas/tables.html;
Mark Nord, Margaret Andrews, and Steven Carlson, *Household Food Security
in the United States, 2005*, U.S. Department of Agriculture Economic Research
Service Report No. ERR-29 (November 2006); "Counting the Poor," *New York
Times*, April 17, 2007, p. A26; and "Hunger and Food Stamps," *New York Times*,
May 13, 2007, p. WK11.

64. Jeff Madrick, "Economic Scene," *New York Times*, June 7, 2001, p. C2, estimates current federal tax expenditures amounting to $700–800 billion a year,
including $100 billion in home-mortgage interest deductions and $70 billion in

health-insurance deductions for business, combined with direct government spending on social programs such as Social Security and Medicare, to add up to true total social spending of 24.5 percent of GDP each year in the United States, as figured by Yale political scientist Jacob Hacker. Cf. Jacob S. Hacker, *The Divided Welfare State: The Battle over Public and Private Social Benefits in the United States* (New York: Cambridge University Press, 2002); and Christopher Howard, *The Hidden Welfare State: Tax Expenditures and Social Policy in the United States* (Princeton, NJ: Princeton University Press, 1997), and Howard, *The Welfare State Nobody Knows: Debunking Myths about U.S. Social Policy* (Princeton, NJ: Princeton University Press, 2006). Using data for 1995, Howard calculates "hidden" federal tax expenditures totaling $346.3 billion in lost tax revenues equivalent to $437.9 billion in actual budget outlays, thereby constituting 38 to 50 percent of the total $896.0 billion in "visible" direct expenditures by the U.S. government for social welfare, including $17.3 billion in federal funds for Aid to Families with Dependent Children and $26.6 billion for food stamps, $294.6 billion for Social Security, $157.3 billion for Medicare, $88.4 billion for Medicaid, and $24.1 billion for housing. *The Hidden Welfare State*, p. 26, table 1.2.

65. Aid to Families with Dependent Children (AFDC) provided about $22 billion total in federal and state dollars to nearly 14 million adults and children, according to the General Accounting Office in October 1996. GAO/HEHS-97-11, p. 2, n. 4, http://www.gao.gov. As of July 1, 1997, AFDC was replaced by the Temporary Assistance for Needy Families (TANF) program. In fiscal year 1997, $27.1 billion went to TANF and related "income security" programs such as Child Support Enforcement. Administration for Children and Families, "Audited Financial Statements," FY 1997, p. 10, http://www.acf.dhhs.gov/programs/acf97aud. htm. By comparison, home-mortgage interest deductions accounted for at least $50 billion and as much as $97 billion in forgone tax revenue in 2000, compared to HUD's entire annual budget of $34 billion, with these deducted benefits varying directly with the beneficiaries' level of income and the marginal tax rate, the market value of the housing a family owns, and the size of the mortgage relative to the value of the housing. Roberta F. Mann, "The (Not So) Little House on the Prairie: The Hidden Costs of the Home Mortgage Interest Deduction," *Arizona State Law Journal* 32 (2000): 1353–65. Mildred Warner, Rosaria Rubeiro, and Amy Erica Smith, "Addressing the Affordability Gap: Framing Child Care as Economic Development," *Journal of Affordable Housing and Community Development Law* 12, no. 3 (Spring 2003): 294–313, calculates the cost of the mortgage-interest deduction at $97 billion in forgone tax revenue in 2000. The Joint Committee on Taxation of the 107th Congress, *Estimates of Federal Tax Expenditures for Fiscal Years 2003–2007*, JCS-5-02, December 19, 2002, p. 20, estimates the deduction as totaling $384.9 billion from 2003 to 2007.

66. U.S. military spending rose 41 percent between 2001 and 2004, compared to the estimated 19 percent rise in social spending for Social Security, Medicare,

and Medicaid; and federal debt ballooned by $1.8 trillion. Annual federal deficits dipped in 2005–6 on the strength of increased tax receipts from corporations and wealthy households, reported the Congressional Budget Office, but it foresaw no fiscal improvement in the next decade, with annual deficits for 2006–15 totaling $2.1 billion—plus $1.3–1.75 trillion more if tax cuts passed since 2001 were made permanent instead of being allowed to expire as scheduled in 2011, and an additional $1 trillion if the government blocked expansion of the alternative minimum tax. See Edmund L. Andrews, "The Meek Shall Inherit the Bill," *New York Times*, January 2, 2005, pp. BU1, 4; and "Brighter '06 Deficit Outlook, but Long Term Looks Grim," *New York Times*, August 18, 2006, p. A12.

67. Jim Wallis, "Will Aid Make Churches Docile?" *New York Times*, February 3, 2001, p. A25.

Chapter 2: Civic Republic and Liberal Democracy

1. This formulation recurs in calls for compassion by President Bush in, for example, his 2004 Christmas Day message: "By volunteering our time and talents where they are needed most, we help heal the sick, comfort those who suffer and bring hope to those who despair, one heart and one soul at a time." White House, "President's Radio Address," December 25, 2004. The White House transcripts cited here and below are available at http://www.whitehouse.gov/news.

2. See Steven M. Tipton, "Republic and Liberal State: The Place of Religion in an Ambiguous Polity," *Emory Law Journal* 39, no. 1 (Winter 1990): 191–202; and Robert N. Bellah, Richard Madsen, William M. Sullivan, Ann Swidler, and Steven M. Tipton, *Habits of the Heart: Individualism and Commitment in American Life* (1985; Berkeley and Los Angeles: University of California Press, 2007), esp. chap. 2, pp. 28–35.

3. John Winthrop, "On Liberty," reprinted in *Old South Leaflets* (Boston, 1896), vol. 3, document no. 66, pp. 8–9.

4. Thomas Jefferson, "A Bill for Establishing Religious Freedom," in *The Papers of Thomas Jefferson*, ed. Julian P. Boyd (Princeton, NJ: Princeton University Press, 1950), 2:545–47; Bellah et al., *Habits of the Heart*, p. 31.

5. Charles Taylor, "Religion in a Free Society," in *Articles of Faith, Articles of Peace*, ed. James Davison Hunter and Os Guinness (Washington, DC: Brookings Institution, 1990), p. 94.

6. Ibid., pp. 101–3.

7. Ibid.

8. Robert Bellah, "Religion and the Legitimation of the American Republic," in *Varieties of Civil Religion*, by Robert Bellah and Phillip E. Hammond (New York: Harper and Row, 1980), pp. 7–10.

9. Ibid., p. 8.

10. Robert N. Bellah, Richard Madsen, William M. Sullivan, Ann Swidler, and Steven M. Tipton, *The Good Society* (New York: Knopf, 1991), chaps. 4, 6; Bellah et al., *Habits of the Heart*, chap. 2.

11. In distinguishing the liberal and republican traditions here and below, I draw on Michael J. Sandel, *Democracy's Discontent: America in Search of a Public Philosophy* (Cambridge, MA: Harvard University Press, 1996), pp. 4–19ff.

12. See, for example, John Rawls, "Kantian Constructivism in Moral Theory," *Journal of Philosophy* 77 (1980): 536, 542; and Rawls, "Justice as Fairness: Political not Metaphysical," *Philosophy and Public Affairs* 14, no. 3 (Summer 1985), pp. 223, 225 n. 5, 226, 230. See also Richard Rorty, "The Priority of Democracy over Philosophy," in *The Virginia Statute for Religious Freedom: Its Evolution and Consequences in American History*, ed. Merrill D. Peterson and Robert C. Vaughan, pp. 257–82 (Cambridge: Cambridge University Press, 1988).

13. Michael J. Perry, *Morality, Politics, and Law: A Bicentennial Essay* (New York: Oxford University Press, 1988), pp. 57–63, 82–90.

14. Ibid., p. 82.

15. Cf. John Rawls, "The Idea of an Overlapping Consensus," *Oxford Journal of Legal Studies* 7, no. 1 (1987): 9–12; Rawls, *A Theory of Justice* (Cambridge, MA: Harvard University Press, 1971), pp. 225–26; and Perry, *Morality, Politics, and Law*, pp. 85–87. See also Richard J. Neuhaus, *The Naked Public Square: Religion and Democracy in America* (Grand Rapids, MI: Eerdmans, 1984).

16. Steven M. Tipton, "Moral Languages and the Good Society," *Soundings* 69, nos. 1–2 (1986): 167–71.

17. Martin E. Marty, "On a Medial Moraine: Religious Dimensions of American Constitutionalism," *Emory Law Journal* 39 (1990): 9–10.

18. Bellah, "Religion and the Legitimation of the American Republic," pp. 11–12; Taylor, "Religion in a Free Society," p. 101.

19. Cf. Bellah, "Civil Religion in America," pp. 168–89 in *Beyond Belief* (Berkeley: University of California Press, 1991). Bellah, "Religion and the Legitimation of the American Republic," pp. 13, 14.

20. Ibid., p. 15.

21. Martin E. Marty, *The Public Church: Mainline, Evangelical, Catholic* (New York: Crossroad, 1981), p. 16.

22. Ibid.; Martin E. Marty, *The One and the Many* (Cambridge, MA: Harvard University Press, 1997).

23. National Conference of Catholic Bishops, *The Challenge of Peace: God's Promise and Our Response: A Pastoral Letter on War and Peace, May 3, 1983* (Washington, DC: U.S. Catholic Conference, 1983); National Conference of Catholic Bishops, *Economic Justice for All: Pastoral Letter on Catholic Social Teaching and the U.S. Economy* (Washington, DC: U.S. Catholic Conference, 1986); David Novak, *Jewish Social Ethics* (New York: Oxford University Press, 1992).

24. Rebecca S. Chopp, *The Praxis of Suffering: An Interpretation of Liberation and Political Theologies* (Maryknoll, NY: Orbis Books, 1986); Ronald Thiemann,

Constructing a Public Theology: The Church in a Pluralistic Culture (Louisville, KY: Westminster John Knox Press, 1991).

25. Marty, *The Public Church*; Marty, *The One and the Many*; Craig Calhoun, ed., *Habermas and the Public Sphere* (Cambridge, MA: MIT Press, 1992); Charles Taylor, "The Politics of Recognition," in *Multiculturalism and "The Politics of Recognition,"* ed. Amy Gutmann, 25–73 (Princeton, NJ: Princeton University Press, 1992).

26. Bellah, "Religion and the Legitimation of the American Republic," pp. 16–17.

27. Alexis de Tocqueville, *Democracy in America* (1848), trans. George Lawrence, ed. J. P. Mayer (Garden City, NY: Doubleday Anchor, 1969), p. 292.

28. Sidney Verba, Kay Lehman Schlozman, and Henry E. Brady, *Voice and Equality: Civic Voluntarism in American Politics* (Cambridge, MA: Harvard University Press, 1995).

29. Evelyn Brooks Higginbotham, *Righteous Discontent: The Women's Movement in the Black Baptist Church, 1880–1920* (Cambridge, MA: Harvard University Press, 1993); N. J. Demerath and Rhys H. Williams, *A Bridging of Faiths: Religion and Politics in a New England City* (Princeton, NJ: Princeton University Press, 1992).

30. Cf. Charles H. Long, "Civil Rights—Civil Religion," in *American Civil Religion*, ed. Russell E. Richey and Donald G. Jones, 211–21 (New York: Harper and Row, 1974); and Sidney E. Mead, "The Nation with the Soul of a Church," ibid., pp. 45–74.

31. Cf. Jürgen Habermas, *The Structural Transformation of the Public Sphere: An Inquiry into a Category of Bourgeois Society* (Cambridge, MA: MIT Press, 1989); Seyla Benhabib, *Situating the Self: Gender, Community, and Postmodernism in Contemporary Ethics* (New York: Routledge, 1992), esp. chap. 3; and Nancy Fraser, "Rethinking the Public Sphere: A Contribution to the Critique of Actually Existing Democracy," in Calhoun, *Habermas and the Public Sphere*, pp. 109–42.

32. Timothy A. Byrnes, *Catholic Bishops in American Politics* (Princeton, NJ: Princeton University Press, 1991); Lester R. Kurtz, *The Nuclear Cage: A Sociology of the Arms Race* (Englewood Cliffs, NJ: Prentice-Hall, 1988).

33. Robert Wuthnow, *The Restructuring of American Religion: Society and Faith since World War II* (Princeton, NJ: Princeton University Press, 1988), pp. 108, 112, 117. By Wuthnow's count, nonreligious, nonprofit national voluntary associations concerned with governmental and public affairs numbered some 1,875 in the mid-1980s, with 1,500 of them started since 1960, compared to 800 nationally organized, nondenominational "special purpose groups in American religion," 300 of them begun since 1960. Assuming that half of such religious special-purpose groups were concerned with public affairs and extending these growth rates since 1960 to the present yields some 640 politically oriented parachurch groups and 7,500 nonreligious political associations in 2005.

34. Named for the section of the tax code that governs them, 527 committees were officially independent of political parties and campaigns but served both, by the design of party financiers, to circumvent limits on the flow of "soft money" intended for party-building activities apart from candidates' campaigns, limits legislated by the McCain-Feingold campaign finance reform bill in 2002. These committees raised $550.6 million for all 2004 election races, including $188 million for Senator Kerry and $62 million for President Bush, according to a report by the Center for Public Integrity, cited in Michael Janofsky, "Advocacy Groups Spent Record Amount on 2004 Election," *New York Times*, December 17, 2004, p. A25. The Democratic National Committee raised $390 million through November 2004, and the Republican National Committee raised $385 million, according to Federal Election Commission reports, with each presidential campaign receiving $75 million in public financing. See Glen Justice, "Both Parties Say Fund-Raising Was Big and Nearly Equal," *New York Times*, December 3, 2004, p. A145.

35. Bellah et al., *The Good Society*, p. 185.

36. Cf. Rawls, *A Theory of Justice*; Rawls, *Political Liberalism* (New York: Columbia University Press, 1993); Michael J. Sandel, *Liberalism and the Limits of Justice* (New York: Cambridge University Press, 1982); Mary Ann Glendon, *Rights Talk* (New York: Free Press, 1991); and Ronald L. Jepperson and John W. Meyer, "The Public Order and the Construction of Formal Organizations," in *The New Institutionalism in Organizational Analysis*, ed. Walter W. Powell and Paul J. DiMaggio, pp. 204–31 (Chicago: University of Chicago Press, 1991), esp. 214–17.

37. Marty, *The Public Church*, pp. 3–22. See also "The Public Church," chap. 6 in Bellah et al., *The Good Society*. On religious lobbies, see Allen D. Hertzke, *Representing God in Washington: The Role of Religious Lobbies in the American Polity* (Knoxville: University of Tennessee Press, 1988), esp. chaps. 3, 4; and Robert Booth Fowler and Allen D. Hertzke, *Religion and Politics in America: Faith, Culture, and Strategic Choices* (Boulder, CO: Westview Press, 1995), chap. 3.

38. Hertzke, *Representing God in Washington*, chap. 3.

39. Wuthnow, *The Restructuring of American Religion*, pp. 130–33, 170–72ff.

40. James Davison Hunter, *Culture Wars: The Struggle to Define America* (New York: Basic Books, 1991); Richard J. Neuhaus, *America against Itself: Moral Vision and the Public Order* (Notre Dame, IN: University of Notre Dame Press, 1992).

41. Paul DiMaggio, John Evans, and Bethany Bryson, "Have Americans' Social Attitudes Become More Polarized?" *American Journal of Sociology* 102, no. 3 (November 1996): 690–755.

42. Bellah et al., *The Good Society*, pp. 202–5; Arthur E. Farnsley, *Southern Baptist Politics: Authority and Power in the Restructuring of an American Denomination* (University Park: Pennsylvania State University Press, 1994).

43. Hunter, *Culture Wars*, p. 128.

44. See Bellah et al., *Habits of the Heart*, pp. 262–67; and Michael Walzer, "Dissatisfaction in the Welfare State," in *Radical Principles: Reflections of an Unreconstructed Democrat*, pp. 23–53 (New York: Basic Books, 1980).

45. Bellah et al., *Habits of the Heart*, updated edition (1996), pp. xxv–xxx.

46. Walzer, "Dissatisfaction in the Welfare State," p. 29.

47. Cf. Jeffrey Stout, *Ethics after Babel: The Languages of Morals and Their Discontents* (Boston: Beacon Press, 1988), chaps. 9, 12; Stout, "Liberal Society and the Languages of Morals," *Soundings* 69, nos. 1–2 (1986): 32–59; and Tipton, "Moral Languages and the Good Society."

48. Philosophical liberals in this debate include John Rawls ("Justice as Fairness") and Richard Rorty ("The Priority of Democracy over Philosophy"). Communitarian critics include Michael J. Perry (*Morality, Politics, and Law*), Stanley Hauerwas (*A Community of Character: Toward a Constructive Christian Social Ethic* [Notre Dame, IN: University of Notre Dame Press, 1981]), and Richard J. Neuhaus (*The Naked Public Square*).

49. Compare Peter L. Berger, "From the Crisis of Religion to the Crisis of Secularity," in *Religion and America: Spiritual Life in a Secular Age*, ed. Mary Douglas and Steven M. Tipton (Boston: Beacon Press, 1983), p. 17, and Wuthnow, *The Restructuring of American Religion*, chaps. 10, 11; to Robert N. Bellah, epilogue to *Meaning and Modernity: Religion, Polity, and Self*, ed. Richard Madsen, William M. Sullivan, Ann Swidler, and Steven M. Tipton, pp. 255–76 (Berkeley and Los Angeles: University of California Press, 2002), and Bellah, introduction (esp. pp. 4–7, 17–18) and introduction to part 2 (pp. 313–17), in *The Robert Bellah Reader*, ed. Robert N. Bellah and Steven M. Tipton (Durham, NC: Duke University Press, 2006).

50. Andrew Delbanco, *The Real American Dream: A Meditation on Hope* (Cambridge, MA: Harvard University Press, 1999).

51. Phillip E. Hammond, *With Liberty for All: Freedom of Religion in the United States* (Louisville, KY: Westminster John Knox Press, 1998).

52. Richard Rorty, *Achieving Our Country: Leftist Thought in Twentieth-Century America* (Cambridge, MA: Harvard University Press, 1999).

53. John Noonan, *The Lustre of Our Country: The American Experience of Religious Freedom* (Berkeley and Los Angeles: University of California Press, 1998).

54. This section draws on Bellah et al., "The House Divided," introduction to the updated edition of *Habits of the Heart* (1996), pp. vii–xxxv.

55. Herbert J. Gans, *Middle American Individualism: The Future of Liberal Democracy* (New York: Free Press, 1988), pp. 23–42; Kevin Phillips, *Boiling Point: Republicans, Democrats, and the Decline of Middle-Class Prosperity* (New York: Random House, 1993); Sandel, *Democracy's Discontent*, pp. 329–33.

56. In 1947–73, U.S. income grew 31 percent more slowly in the top quintile than in the bottom quintile. In 1973–2000, income grew 55 percent more quickly in the top quintile than in the bottom, while real per capita income grew 66 per-

cent. Middle-earning households, with incomes from half to twice the median, shrank from 68.0 percent in 1979 to 60.7 percent in 2002. The official poverty rate stood at 11.1 percent in 1973, 11.3 percent in 2000, 12.1 percent in 2002, 12.5 percent in 2003, and 12.7 percent in 2004. One-third of the growing wage inequality can be explained by labor-market shifts such as de-unionization and the severe drop in the minimum wage, adjusted for inflation, to a fifty-year low in buying power. Another third of the growth in wage inequality can be explained by the increasing globalization of the economy—with immigration, trade, capital mobility, and employment shifts from manufacturing to lower-paying service work, according to a press release from the Economic Policy Institute, "*The State of Working America 2004/2005*: Recovery Yet to Arrive for Working Families," September 2004, pp. 1–6, 10, http://www.epinet.org, based on Lawrence Mishel, Jared Bernstein, and Sylvia Allegretto, *The State of Working America 2004/2005* (Ithaca, NY: Cornell University Press, 2005). See note 74 below regarding increased extreme poverty.

57. Jodie T. Allen and Andrew Kohut, *Pinched Pocketbooks*, Pew Research Center for the People and the Press, March 28, 2006, pp. 1–7, http://pewresearch .org. Most Americans (56 percent) said jobs were hard to find in their communities, including 62 percent of Democrats and 67 percent of independents, but only 38 percent of Republicans. Thirty-two percent of Republicans surveyed by Pew earn annual incomes over $75,000, placing them in or near the top tenth of U.S. incomes, compared to 22 percent of Democrats and 25 percent of independents.

58. Allen and Kohut, *Pinched Pocketbooks*, p. 4, citing Ian Dew-Becker and Robert J. Gordon, "Where Did the Productivity Growth Go? Inflation Dynamics and the Distribution of Income," *Brookings Papers on Economic Activity*, 2005, no. 2. See also Steven Greenhouse and David Leonhardt, "Real Wages Fail to Match Productivity," *New York Times*, August 28, 2006, pp. A1, 13. Cf. Martin Feldstein, *Income Inequality and Poverty*, National Bureau of Economic Research Working Paper No. 6770, October 1998; and Jon E. Hilsenrath and Sholnn Freeman, "Moving Up: Challenges to the American Dream," a four-part series in the *Wall Street Journal*, May–June 2005.

59. Thomas Piketty and Emmanuel Saez, "Income Inequality in the United States, 1913–1998," *Quarterly Journal of Economics* 118, no. 1 (February 2003): 1–39, with tables updated to 2005 in Excel format, March 2007, http://emlab .berkeley.edu/users/saez/; Piketty and Saez, "How Progressive Is the U.S. Federal Tax System? A Historical and International Perspective," *Journal of Economic Perspectives* 21, no. 1 (Winter 2007): 3–24. Cf. David Cay Johnston, "Income Gap Is Widening, Data Shows," *New York Times*, March 29, 2007, pp. C1, C10; Aviva Aron-Dine, "New Data Show Income Concentration Jumped Again in 2005," Center on Budget and Policy Priorities, March 29, 2007, http://www.cbpp.org; and Tyler Cowen, "Why Is Income Inequality in America So Pronounced? Consider Education," *New York Times*, May 17, 2007, p. C3. Greenhouse and Leonhardt,

in "Real Wages Fail to Match Productivity," reported in 2006 that the inflation-adjusted median hourly wage for American workers had declined 2 percent since 2003, as productivity rose. This resulted in a drop in wages and salaries to their lowest share (45.3 percent) of the nation's gross domestic product (GDP) since 1947, when government began measuring these shares—a drop from 50 percent in early 2000 and from a record high of 53.6 percent in 1970, with each percentage point now equaling some $132 billion. Sources cited by Greenhouse and Leonhardt include the U.S. Department of Commerce on shares of GDP, the National Bureau of Economic Research on recessions, the Economic Policy Institute on wages, the Bureau of Labor Statistics on productivity, and analysis of Internal Revenue Service tax data by economists Emmanuel Saez and Thomas Piketty on rising income shares of the top 1 percent of earners. See also Rick Lyman, "Census Reports Slight Increase in '05 Incomes," *New York Times*, August 30, 2006, pp. A1, 12.

60. Greenhouse and Leonhardt, "Real Wages Fail to Match Productivity," quoting UBS investment bank on the current period as a golden age, given corporate profits in 2001–6 that climbed to their highest share (10.3 percent) of the nation's GDP since the 1960s.

61. The median male worker earned about 13 percent less in 1999 than fifteen years earlier, despite being older and better educated, while income doubled in the top 1 percent of households. Worse off were workers without college degrees, who make up three-quarters of the U.S. labor force. For hourly-wage workers with high school educations, such as laborers and machine operators, wages in 1999 remained some 15–20 percent below what they were thirty years earlier—despite 18 million net new jobs generated in the 1990s; some slowing in 1996–2000 of widening income inequality, with a notable uptick in wages for low-skill male workers in particular; and a huge increase since the mid-1970s in hours worked by Americans, especially women. Hardest hit were younger workers, who had less seniority and were less likely to belong to a union. Male high school graduates with five years' work experience lost almost 30 percent in average real wages between 1979 and 1999. See Richard B. Freeman, *The New Inequality: Creating Solutions for Poor America*, ed. Joshua Cohen and Joel Rogers for *Boston Review* (Boston: Beacon Press, 1999), pp. 7–9; and William Julius Wilson, *The Bridge over the Racial Divide: Rising Inequality and Coalition Politics* (Berkeley and Los Angeles: University of California Press, 1999), pp. 25–26.

62. Tom Waldron, Brandon Roberts, and Andrew Reamer, *Working Hard, Falling Short: America's Working Families and the Pursuit of Economic Security*, a report of the Working Families Project, supported by the Annie E. Casey, Ford, and Rockefeller foundations, October 2004, http://www.aecf.org, p. 15, based on Census Bureau data and on Lynn A. Karoly and Constantin W. A. Panis, *The 21st Century at Work: Forces Shaping the Future Workforce and Workplace in the United States* (Santa Barbara, CA: RAND Corporation, 2004).

63. Waldron, Roberts, and Reamer, *Working Hard, Falling Short*, p. 15, based on Jennifer Cheeseman Day and Eric C. Newburger, *The Big Payoff: Educational Attainment and Synthetic Estimates of Work-Life Earnings*, Census Bureau Current Population Reports, July 2002.

64. Waldron, Roberts, and Reamer, *Working Hard, Falling Short*, p. 9. For data on low-wage families, see Katharine Bradbury and Jane Katz, "Are Lifetime Incomes Growing More Unequal? Looking at New Evidence on Family Income Mobility," *Federal Reserve Bank of Boston Regional Review*, 2002, fourth quarter. For data on the working poor, see Harry J. Holzer, *Encouraging Job Advancement among Low-Wage Workers: A New Approach*, Brookings Institution, Policy Brief no. 30, May 2004, http://www.brookings.edu/es/research/projects/wrb/publications/pb/pb30.htm. In the 1990s, 36.3 percent of those who started in the second income quintile stayed there, compared to 27.3 percent in the 1970s and 31.5 percent in the 1980s, according to the Economic Policy Institute, "*The State of Working America 2004/2005*," p. 5. Cf. Wojciech Kopczuk, Emmanuel Saez, and Jae Song, *Uncovering the American Dream: Inequality and Mobility in Social Security Earnings Data since 1937*, National Bureau of Economic Research, March 2007, http://elsa.berkeley.edu/~saez/.

65. Louis Uchitelle, "Expansion Redefines Economy's Limits," *New York Times*, January 30, 2000, pp. BU1, 16.

66. Data from the Census Bureau, Bureau of Economic Analysis, and Bureau of Labor Statistics, ibid.

67. From 1974 to 1996, the wages of those at the top continued to climb (by 7.7 percent in the ninetieth percentile and 4.4 percent in the eightieth), while the wages of those below declined steadily (by 6.6 percent in the fiftieth percentile and 11.8 percent in the tenth percentile). As a result, in 1996, Americans in the top fifth of the distribution commanded 47 percent of the income, eleven times as much as those in the bottom fifth. In the 1990s, the bottom of the wage ladder stopped plunging, largely due to four minimum-wage hikes. But the middle began to sag, as the fiftieth percentile lost 4 percent in 1989–97, and this sagging middle subdued overall wage growth. Not until 1998 did median household income top the 1989 level of $38,837 by rising to $39,744, and to $40,816 in 1999, even as the gaps failed to narrow among the rich, the middle class, and the poor. Wage gaps persisted through the late 1990s, although hourly wages, adjusted for inflation, grew by a respectable 2 percent in 1997–98, and real wage growth was especially impressive for low-wage workers from 1996 to 1998, ranging from 4.7 to 6.4 percent. On widening wage gaps, see Wilson, *The Bridge over the Racial Divide*, pp. 2–3, 23–31, 61–62, citing data from Alan Kreuger, "What's Up with Wages?" (unpublished paper, Industrial Relations Section, Princeton University, 1997). On the 1996 wage differential between the top and bottom quintiles, see Richard B. Freeman, "Unequal Incomes," *Harvard Magazine*, January–February 1998, p. 62.

68. Freeman, *The New Inequality*, p. 7.

69. Adding capital-gains earnings to income widens measures of the economic gap between the most affluent and other Americans. Earnings from capital gains rose from 1993 to 1998 by a factor of 2.6 (from $163 billion to $427 billion), with the great bulk of these earnings going to those with incomes over $200,000. The value of equity investments jumped fourfold in the Dow Jones industrial average (DJIA) from 1992 to 2000. From 1994 to 2000, Standard and Poor's 500-stock index more than tripled, and the value of U.S. stocks rose by more than $10 trillion, to $16 trillion. Stocks overall underwent a 50 percent decline in 2000–2002, based on the peak-to-trough performance of the S&P 500 and with a 75 percent decline in the NASDAQ index, before rebounding in 2003–4 to approach their previous highs. The DJIA peaked at 11,723 in January 2000, fell to a low of 7,286 in October 2002, and rebounded to 10,783 by the end of 2004—92 percent of its previous high. Ownership of stocks spread to nearly half of all U.S. households in the 1990s, but 90 percent of their total value remained concentrated among the wealthiest 10 percent of all households, with 60 percent held by the wealthiest 1 percent. See Arthur B. Kennickell, *An Examination of Changes in the Distribution of Wealth from 1989 to 1998: Evidence from the Survey of Consumer Finances*, Federal Reserve Board, Survey of Consumer Finances, June 2000; and Arthur B. Kennickell, Martha Starr-McCluer, and Brian J. Surette, "Recent Changes in U.S. Family Finances," *Federal Reserve Bulletin*, January 2000, pp. 1–29.

70. Bureau of Labor Statistics, news release, August 5, 2005, http://www.bls .gov/ces; reported in Eduardo Porter, "Employers in U.S. Add 207,000 Jobs to July Payrolls," *New York Times*, August 6, 2005, pp. A1, B4. See also David Leonhardt, "U.S. Poverty Rate Was Up Last Year," *New York Times*, August 31, 2005, pp. A1, A14. In August 2005, unemployment stood at 4.3 percent for whites, 9.5 percent for blacks, and 5.5 percent for Hispanics, totaling 7.5 million people, plus 9.4 million more "hidden jobless"—either "marginally attached" workers or those working part-time but wanting full-time work.

71. Median household income fell from $49,133 in 1999 to $46,242 in 2005, according to analysis of Census Bureau data reported in Lyman, "Census Reports Slight Increase in '05 Incomes," and an accompanying editorial, "Downward Mobility," *New York Times*, August 30, 2006, p. A20. Median household income ticked up 1.1 percent from 2004 to 2005, despite declining wages, on the strength of more family members taking jobs to make ends meet, as well as gains from investment income and Social Security. Twenty-three million households headed by someone over sixty-five accounted for the entire 2005 increase in median household income, while the median income fell by half a percent, or $275, for the 91 million households headed by those under sixty-five, as wages and salaries among men working full-time fell for the second year in a row and for the third straight year among women working full-time. Overall median income for those under sixty-five was $2,000 lower in 2005 than in 2001, at the bottom of the recession.

Annual productivity growth rose to 3.8 percent between 2000 and 2003, from
2.4 percent growth in the late 1990s and 1.4 percent growth from 1973 to 1995. But
real wages fell in 2003 by 1.2 percent for blue-collar workers and by 0.9 percent
for all men at the fiftieth percentile of earnings, after the recession and subsequent jobless recovery cut real family median income by 2.4 percent in 2000–2002.
From the first quarter of 2001 to mid-2005, virtually all (98.5 percent) of the real
income growth in the corporate sector accrued to capital income (profits, interest,
and dividend payments), in contrast to capital income's 16.3 percent share of total
corporate income when the recession started in early 2001. From November 2001,
when recovery from the recession began, to mid-2005, 59 percent of corporate income growth accrued to corporate profits alone and 41 percent to compensation,
compared to 25 percent to corporate profits and 75 percent to compensation on
average during the recovery stage of five prior business cycles. Tax cuts in 2001–3
shifted 0.8 percent of all after-tax income from the bottom 99 percent to the top
1 percent of households by saving the top 1 percent $67,000 on average, middle-
income families $600 on average, and bottom-quintile families $61 on average.
See Economic Policy Institute, "*The State of Working America 2004/2005*,"
pp. 1–3; Sylvia Allegretto and Jared Bernstein, *The Wage Squeeze and Higher
Health Care Costs*, Economic Policy Institute, Issue Brief no. 218, January 27,
2006, p. 4, fig. D.

72. Louis Uchitelle, "Labor's Lost: For Blacks, a Dream in Decline," *New
York Times*, October 23, 2005, pp. WK1, WK3, based on analysis of data from
the Bureau of Labor Statistics. The fall in median wages for African Americans is
linked to their disproportionate loss of union membership, down by 14.4 percent
in 2000–2005, compared to a 5.4 percent drop among whites. This loss accounted
for 55 percent of the 304,000 union jobs lost in 2004, although whites outnumbered
blacks in unions by six to one (12.4 million to 2.1 million). As a result, just one in
seven African American workers were union members in 2005, compared to one
of every four in the 1980s.

73. The median net worth of U.S. Hispanic households in 2002 was $7,900,
9 percent of the $88,651 net worth of white households. The net worth of black
households was $5,988, less than 7 percent of median net worth among whites.
Inflation-adjusted net worth increased 17 percent for white households from 1996
to 2002 and 14 percent for Hispanic households, but it fell by 16 percent for black
households. Both Hispanics and blacks lost nearly 27 percent of their net worth
from 1999 to 2001 in the economic recession, but Hispanics recovered almost all
(26 percent) of their losses by 2002, while blacks recovered almost none (5 percent). Hispanics made job gains in lower-paid, lower-skilled areas such as service
and construction work, while "last hired, first fired" blacks lost manufacturing and
professional jobs that went unreplaced. Rakesh Kochhar, *The Wealth of Hispanic
Households: 1996 to 2002* (Washington, DC: Pew Hispanic Center, 2004), pp. 1–2,
5–8, 11–13ff., http://www.pewhispanic.org.

74. The share of the U.S. population living in poverty in 2005—12.6 percent—held steady from 12.7 percent in 2004, the first year without a rise since 2000, but it remained above the 11.7 percent recorded at the trough of the 2001 recession. The 43 percent of the poor living below half the poverty line in 2005—$7,800 for a family of three—marked the highest percentage of people in "extreme poverty" or "deep poverty" since the government started tracking those numbers in 1975, according to Census Bureau data cited in "Downward Mobility." See also Census Bureau, *Income, Poverty, and Health Insurance Coverage in the United States: 2003*, August 26, 2004, http://www.census.gov/hhes/www/income.html.

75. Census Bureau, *Income, Poverty, and Health Insurance Coverage in the United States: 2003*. Increases in the nation's child-poverty rates from 1979 to 2000 were concentrated among Hispanic children; their rate was up 6.4 percent (from 28 to 34.4 percent), while the rate for white non-Hispanic children was up 0.5 percent and the rate for African American children was 4.5 percent lower, according to Census Bureau data reported in Don Terry, "U.S. Child Poverty Rate Fell as Economy Grew, but Is above 1979 Level," *New York Times*, August 11, 2000, p. A10.

76. Wilson, *The Bridge over the Racial Divide*, pp. 35–37.

77. Fox Butterfield, "Number in Prison Grows despite Crime Reduction," *New York Times*, August 10, 2000, p. A10.

78. See the National Urban League annual report for 2000, summarized in the *New York Times*, July 26, 2000, p. A19.

79. Wilson, *The Bridge over the Racial Divide*, pp. 41–42; Heidi Hartmann, "Through a Gendered Lens," in Freeman, *The New Inequality*, p. 34.

80. Mishel, Bernstein, and Allegretto, *The State of Working America 2004/2005*; and Economic Policy Institute, "*The State of Working America 2004/2005*."

81. Robert Reich, foreword to Freeman, *The New Inequality*, pp. vii–ix; Freeman, "Unequal Incomes," p. 62.

82. The percentage difference in earnings by college-educated workers compared to high school–educated workers rose steadily, from 123 percent in 1979 to 145 percent in 2000, before leveling off as income inequality continued to grow, according to Bureau of Labor Statistics data analyzed by the Economic Policy Institute and reported in Louis Uchitelle, "College Degree Still Pays, but It's Leveling Off," *New York Times*, January 13, 2005. Cf. Day and Newburger, *The Big Payoff*; Freeman, *The New Inequality*, pp. 8–9; and Freeman, "Unequal Incomes," p. 62. Despite the dramatically rising economic return on higher education during the 1980s in particular, college enrollment by children from lower-income families barely rose between 1980 and 2000. Enrollments grew largely from rising numbers of children from better-off families choosing to go to college and on to careers, and the proportion of the population with bachelor's degrees rose only slightly, to about 30 percent. From 2001 to 2005, entry-level wages for male college graduates fell 7.3 percent, to $19.72 an hour, and wages for female

graduates fell 3.5 percent, to $17.08; entry-level pay for high school graduates de-
clined 3.3 percent for men, to $10.93 per hour, and 4.9 percent for women, to $9.08
per hour, according to the Economic Policy Institute; see Steven Greenhouse,
"Many Entry-Level Workers Feel Pinch of Rough Market," *New York Times*,
September 4, 2006, p. A10.

83. Freeman, *The New Inequality*, pp. 8–9.

84. Uwe E. Reinhardt, Peter S. Hussey, and Gerard F. Anderson, "U.S. Health
Care Spending in an International Context," *Health Affairs* 23, no. 3 (2004): 10;
Reinhardt, "The Swiss Health System: Regulated Competition without Managed
Care," *Journal of the American Medical Association* 292, no. 10 (September 8,
2004): 1227–31. U.S. national health spending, at $1.7 trillion, topped 15 percent of
the U.S. gross domestic product for the first time in 2003, according to the federal
Centers for Medicare and Medicaid Services. See Robert Pear, "Nation's Health
Spending Slows, but It Still Hits a Record," *New York Times*, January 11, 2005,
p. A14. The United States ranked forty-second among nations in infant mortality
rates, with 6.8 deaths for each thousand live births in 2001 and 7.0 deaths in 2002,
according to data from the Centers for Disease Control and Prevention, reported
in Nicholas D. Kristof, "Health Care? Ask Cuba," *New York Times*, January 12,
2005, p. A23. The number of uninsured Americans increased by 1.3 million from
2004 to 2005, to a record 15.9 percent; and the number of uninsured children under
eighteen rose for the first time since 1998, from 10.8 percent in 2004 to 11.2 percent in 2005. These highs, exceeding levels at the bottom of the 2001 recession,
reflected the shortfall of public aid to help families or companies bear the surging
costs of health care. See "Downward Mobility."

85. Frank Levy, *The New Dollars and Dreams: American Incomes and Economic Change* (New York: Russell Sage Foundation, 1998), pp. 3–4, quoted in
Wilson, *The Bridge over the Racial Divide*, pp. 2–3.

86. Bureau of Labor Statistics, "Union Members Survey," January 27, 2005, p. 1,
http://www.bls.gov/cps.

87. The poverty rate among working families rose nearly 50 percent between
1980 and 2000, with 70 percent of poor families with children in 2000 including
a person who worked, usually in retail or service trades. Thirty-nine percent of
households receiving emergency food assistance in 2000 included at least one
working adult, half of them working at least forty hours per week. These households numbered twenty-one million needy persons, more than eight million of
them children. The poverty rate of children under the age of eighteen rose to
18.7 percent in 1998 from 16.2 percent in 1979, then declined in 2000 to just
above its 1979 level. But it jumped almost 39 percent from 1979 to 1993, then fell
17 percent from 1993 to 1998, before rebounding to 17.8 percent in 2004. See
Terry, "U.S. Child Poverty Rate Fell as Economy Grew." Data on emergency food
assistance to the working poor, compiled by America's Second Harvest, are cited
in Anne Adams Lang, "Behind the Prosperity, Working People in Trouble," *New*

York Times, November 20, 2000, p. A21. For evidence of poverty among one-third of working families in the United States as members of the "new poor" working hard for low wages, see Heather Boushey, Chauna Brocht, Bethney Gundersen, and Jared Bernstein, *Hardships in America: The Real Story of Working Families* (Washington, DC: Economic Policy Institute, 2001).

88. Deborah Leff, president of America's Second Harvest, quoted in Lang, "Behind the Prosperity, Working People in Trouble."

89. Reich, foreword to Freeman, *The New Inequality*, pp. viii–x.

90. Delbanco, *The Real American Dream*, p. 67.

91. Reich, foreword to Freeman, *The New Inequality*, p. xii; see also Robert D. Putnam, *Bowling Alone: The Collapse and Revival of American Community* (New York: Simon and Schuster, 2000), esp. chaps. 2–5, 11–15.

92. Verba, Schlozman, and Brady, *Voice and Equality*, esp. chaps. 7–12.

93. Betty Breene and Fred Grandy, quoted in Lang, "Behind the Prosperity, Working People in Trouble."

94. Freeman, *The New Inequality*, p. 9.

95. U.S. Conference of Catholic Bishops, Office of Social Development and World Peace, "Senate Vote Needed on Minimum Wage," July 2002, http://www.nccbuscc.org. The purchasing power of the minimum wage, adjusted for inflation, eroded from $7.50 in 1970 to $6.10 in 1980 and from $5.10 in 1986 to $4.46 in 2002, leaving a single mother working full-time to raise two children living just above the poverty line in 1997 with the help of the earned income tax credit, and below it in 2003. In 1968 the annual earnings of a full-time worker in a minimum-wage job equaled 120 percent of the poverty threshold for a family of three, the highest ratio ever, and in 2003 such earnings came to 74 percent of the poverty threshold, according to Waldron, Roberts, and Reamer, *Working Hard, Falling Short*, p. 14, based on data from the Census Bureau and Department of Labor.

96. Freeman, *The New Inequality*, pp. 10–11; Freeman, "Unequal Incomes," pp. 63–64.

97. The following examples are drawn from proposals by Richard Freeman, Heidi Hartmann, and Paul Krugman in Freeman, *The New Inequality*, pp. 12–28, 35–37, 40–43.

98. Reich, foreword to Freeman, *The New Inequality*, pp. xi–xii.

99. Wilson, *The Bridge over the Racial Divide*, pp. 40–41; Paul Krugman, "Safe as Houses," *New York Times*, August 12, 2005, p. A19. For analysis of the 1996 welfare-to-workfare reforms, see Lawrence Mishel, Jared Bernstein, and Sylvia Allegretto, *The State of Working America 2006/2007* (Ithaca, NY: Cornell University Press, 2007).

100. In 1994 Newt Gingrich (R-Ga.) led the Republican Revolution to win the first GOP majority in the House in forty years, on the strength of the party's "Contract with America" promising smaller government through deep tax cuts, balanced budgets, defeat of universal health care, the end of Aid to Families with

NOTES TO PAGES 59-60

Dependent Children (AFDC), and a stress on personal morality instead of social entitlements. In 1996 the Clinton administration won reelection after acceding to welfare reform to end decades of AFDC for the poor, while resisting Republican budgetary threats to "shut down the government" that raised the specter of endangering Social Security, Medicare, and related benefit programs crucial to the middle-class majority of the electorate. By protecting these benefits and cutting budget deficits and the national debt, Clinton revised the image of Democrats as the party of tax-and-spend profligacy, while aiming to pin fiscal irresponsibility on his Republican predecessors for a $290 billion deficit and a national debt quadrupled by the tax cuts and increased military spending of the 1980s. In 1992–2000, overall federal spending fell from 22 to 19 percent of GDP, largely due to defense cuts after the Cold War. In 1993–2000, spending rose 59 percent for education, 129 percent for child support, 23 percent for the environment, and 53 percent for Native Americans. See Robert J. Samuelson, "Who Governs?" *Newsweek*, February 21, 2000, p. 33; and Paul Light, *The True Size of Government* (Washington, DC: Brookings Institution, 1999).

101. George W. Bush's Republican National Convention acceptance speech, *New York Times*, August 4, 2000, p. A20.

102. Richard W. Stevenson, "News on Budgets, Homeownership and Jobs Is Wonderful, but It Isn't Helping Gore Yet," *New York Times*, August 12, 2000, p. A10; Al Gore's speech accepting the Democratic nomination, *New York Times*, August 18, 2000, p. A19.

103. Mainline Protestant congregations have sustained relatively high rates of civic engagement and social service compared to other Protestants and, to a lesser extent, Catholics—with the significant exception of specifically political activity, according to Mark Chaves, Helen M. Giesel, and William Tsitsos, "Religious Variations in Public Presence: Evidence from the National Congregations Study," in *The Quiet Hand of God: Faith-Based Activism and the Public Role of Mainline Protestantism*, ed. Robert Wuthnow and John H. Evans, pp. 108–28 (Berkeley and Los Angeles: University of California Press, 2002). See also, for example, Robert Wuthnow, *Acts of Compassion: Caring for Others and Helping Ourselves* (Princeton, NJ: Princeton University Press, 1991); and Wuthnow, *Learning to Care: Elementary Kindness in an Age of Indifference* (New York: Oxford University Press, 1995).

104. Alberto Alesina and Edward L. Glaeser, *Fighting Poverty in the US and Europe: A World of Difference* (New York: Oxford University Press, 2004), pp. 4–12, 45–46, 183–216; Jina Moore, "Upwardly Immobile," *Harvard Magazine*, January–February 2005, pp. 14–16.

105. Alesina and Glaeser, *Fighting Poverty in the US and Europe*, pp. 15–54. Since 1964, the United States has defined poverty by adjusting the cost of a standard diet against the consumer price index and multiplying by three—since Americans on average spend one-third of their after-tax income on food—to draw a

poverty line (of roughly $18,700 for a family of four in 2003 and $19,200 in 2004) across the country, from Manhattan to Mississippi. See Boushey et al., *Hardships in America*, for variable standards of poverty in relation to median income and the actual cost of living in specific areas. These standards typically double the official U.S. poverty line, upping it by three to four times in costly metropolitan areas such as Boston and San Francisco. See Waldron, Roberts, and Reamer, *Working Hard, Falling Short*, p. 30.

106. Bellah et al., *Habits of the Heart*, pp. 20, 242, 334.

107. Alesina and Glaeser, *Fighting Poverty in the US and Europe*, chaps. 4–6, attributes half the difference between U.S. and European redistribution policies to racial diversity and half to deliberately constructed differences in their political systems, including majoritarian instead of proportional representation, federalism, and governmental checks and balances. The greater the racial diversity of individual U.S. states, the less those states spend on welfare. The greater the racial, ethnic, linguistic, and religious homogeneity within European nations, the more generous their welfare policies and the stronger the socialist political parties that support them. Among Americans, opposition to redistribution correlates more strongly with Caucasian racial identity than with income, gender, place of residence, or any other social factor. See Moore, "Upwardly Immobile," pp. 15–16.

108. Here and below, I draw on Bellah et al., "The House Divided."

109. John W. Meyer, "Self and Life Course: Institutionalization and Its Effects," in *Institutional Structure: Constituting State, Society, and the Individual*, by George M. Thomas, John W. Meyer, Francisco O. Ramirez, and John Boli, pp. 242–60 (Newbury Park, CA: Sage Publications, 1987); John Boli, "Human Rights or State Expansion?" ibid., pp. 133–49.

110. On increased religious voluntarism and switching, see Wade Clark Roof and William McKinney, *American Mainline Religion: Its Changing Shape and Future* (New Brunswick, NJ: Rutgers University Press, 1987), pp. 40–71, 162–85; and Wade Clark Roof, *A Generation of Seekers: The Spiritual Journey of the Baby Boom Generation* (San Francisco: HarperCollins, 1993), pp. 151–81. On declining religious participation, see Putnam, *Bowling Alone*, pp. 65–79; Robert Wuthnow, "Mobilizing Civic Engagement: The Changing Impact of Religious Involvement," in *Civic Engagement in American Democracy*, ed. Theda Skocpol and Morris P. Fiorina, pp. 331–66 (Washington, DC: Brookings Institution Press; New York: Russell Sage Foundation, 1999); and Wuthnow, *Loose Connections: Joining Together in America's Fragmented Communities* (Cambridge, MA: Harvard University Press, 1998).

111. Theda Skocpol, "Civic Engagement in American Democracy," testimony prepared for the National Commission on Civic Renewal, Washington, DC, January 25, 1997, p. 1; Skocpol, "Advocates without Members: The Recent Transformation of Civic Life," in Skocpol and Fiorina, *Civic Engagement in American Democracy*, pp. 461–510.

112. Verba, Schlozman, and Brady, *Voice and Equality*, p. 509.

113. Michael Hout, Andrew Greeley, and Melissa J. Wilde, "The Demographic Imperative in Religious Change in the United States," *American Journal of Sociology* 107, no. 2 (2001): 468–500.

114. Verba, Schlozman, and Brady, *Voice and Equality*, pp. 18, 19, 518–21.

115. See Richard L. Wood, *Faith in Action: Religion, Race, and Democratic Organizing in America* (Chicago: University of Chicago Press, 2002); and Robert Wuthnow, "Beyond Quiet Influence? Possibilities for the Protestant Mainline," in Wuthnow and Evans, *The Quiet Hand of God*, pp. 381–403.

Chapter 3: United Methodism in Crisis: Prophetic Witness

1. Thom White Wolf Fassett, interview, Washington, DC, March 1997.

2. Thom White Wolf Fassett, "United Methodists on Capitol Hill," Directory of Board Members and Staff of the General Board of Church and Society (Washington, DC, 1989), p. 4.

3. *The Book of Discipline of the United Methodist Church* (Nashville, TN: United Methodist Publishing House, 2000), pars. 1002–4. The General Board of Discipleship, the General Board of Global Ministries, and the General Board of Higher Education and Ministry are the three counterparts to the GBCS. All citations are to the 2000 edition of the *Book of Discipline* unless otherwise noted.

4. George Ogle, interview, Atlanta, GA, May 2003.

5. John C. Green and James L. Guth, "United Methodists and American Culture: A Statistical Portrait," in *The People(s) Called Methodist: Forms and Reforms of Their Life*, ed. William B. Lawrence, Dennis M. Campbell, and Russell E. Richey, pp. 27–53 (Nashville, TN: Abingdon Press, 1998), esp. p. 29. Here and below, I draw in detail on this masterpiece in miniature. I am indebted to John Green for elaborating its data on political partisanship by personal communication.

6. Ibid., pp. 38–39, 45–48.

7. Ibid., pp. 30–37.

8. Ibid., p. 35.

9. Michael Novak, *Choosing Our King: Powerful Symbols in Presidential Politics* (London: Macmillan, 1974), p. 132.

10. Fifty-nine percent of all United Methodists reside in major metropolitan areas—38 percent in suburbs and 21 percent in cities, according to Green and Guth, "United Methodists and American Culture," p. 36. Cf. Tex Sample, *U.S. Lifestyles and Mainline Churches: A Key to Reaching People in the 90s* (Louisville, KY: Westminster/John Knox Press, 1990); Michael Hout, Andrew Greeley, and Melissa J. Wilde, "The Demographic Imperative in Religious Change in the United States," *American Journal of Sociology* 107, no. 2 (2001): 468– 500; and Robert Wuthnow, *The Restructuring of American Religion: Society and Faith since World War II*

(Princeton, NJ: Princeton University Press, 1988) on the changing demographics of U.S. Protestant churches.

11. Green and Guth, "United Methodists and American Culture," p. 39.

12. Ibid., pp. 39–43.

13. Ibid., p. 30.

14. Ibid., pp. 45–48.

15. James L. Guth, John C. Green, Corwin E. Smidt, Lyman A. Kellstedt, and Margaret M. Poloma, *The Bully Pulpit: The Politics of Protestant Clergy* (Lawrence: University Press of Kansas, 1997), pp. 186–92. A survey of United Methodist clergy classified in terms of this typology found 29 percent of them to be "conventional liberals," flanked by 16 percent "quiescent liberals" toward the middle and 13 percent "New Breed" activists on the left. On the other side, "conventional conservatives" made up 21 percent of the 1989 sample, flanked by 16 percent "old breed" conservatives toward the middle and 7 percent "Christian Right" activists on the right. Since 1989, Methodist activists on the right have grown in size and influence, given their younger age cohort, continuing mobilization, and the growing membership and proportional representation in General Conference of the more conservative Southeastern and South Central jurisdictions. But the extent and implications of a larger shift to the right in United Methodism remain uncertain and intensely debated. By comparison, the Presbyterian Church (USA) included 5 percent Christian Right, 12 percent conventional conservatives, 10 percent old breed, 18 percent quiescent liberals, 33 percent conventional liberals, and 22 percent New Breed. The Southern Baptist Convention included 14 percent Christian right, 42 percent conventional conservatives, 29 percent old breed, 7 percent quiescent liberals, 7 percent conventional liberals, and 1 percent New Breed.

16. Ibid., p. 190.

17. Martin E. Marty, personal communication, 2006.

18. Jim Winkler, "Publisher's Column," *Christian Social Action*, January–February 2004, p. 2.

19. H. Richard Niebuhr, *The Social Sources of Denominationalism* (New York: Henry Holt, 1929), pp. 11–16, 59–89.

20. *Book of Discipline*, pp. 9–20, 41–86; Robert N. Bellah, Richard Madsen, William M. Sullivan, Ann Swidler, and Steven M. Tipton, *The Good Society* (New York: Knopf, 1991), pp. 182–83, 204–6.

21. Jacob Riis, quoted in Charles W. Keysor, *Our Methodist Heritage* (Elgin, IL: D. C. Cook, 1973), p. 25.

22. *Book of Discipline*, par. 705.2j; Thomas Edward Frank, *Polity, Practice, and the Mission of the United Methodist Church* (Nashville, TN: Abingdon Press, 1997), p. 249.

23. *Book of Discipline*, 1972, par. 68, esp. pp. 49–52; cf. *Book of Discipline*, 2000, par. 102, esp. pp. 59, 101–3; and par. 69, esp. pp. 80–81, on Methodist doctrinal "standards," discipline, traditions, and history regarding "theological pluralism."

24. *Book of Discipline*, 1988, par. 69, sec. 4, pp. 80–81.

25. *Book of Discipline*, pars. 130, 7–52, here and below. See also Frank, *Polity, Practice, and the Mission of the United Methodist Church*, pp. 218–20; and Bishop Oliver Eugene Slater, "Episcopal Greetings," in *Book of Discipline*, 1972, p. v. Regarding United Methodist polity as discussed here and below, I am indebted to Russell E. Richey and Thomas E. Frank for their comments as well as their cited works.

26. *Book of Discipline*, pars. 7–42. Annual conferences also send delegates to five regional jurisdictional conferences in the United States, marked off by state boundaries into the Northeastern, Southeastern, North Central, South Central, and Western jurisdictions. These delegates elect bishops to preside over annual conferences within the bounds of that jurisdiction. But United Methodism does not have a diocesan episcopacy. Bishops are not the executives of the annual conferences over which they preside, even though thirty-three of fifty bishops serving in the United States in 2000 were each presiding over a single annual conference. Rather, by virtue of their election to the episcopacy in jurisdictional conferences, United Methodist bishops are bishops of the whole church, with their church membership and episcopal authority residing in a churchwide Council of Bishops. Local charge conferences make up districts within annual conferences, and ordained district superintendents are appointed by bishops to compose a cabinet for each annual conference. Just as the Council of Bishops is "the collegial expression of episcopal leadership in the Church and through the Church into the world," so "the cabinet under the leadership of the bishop is the expression of superintending leadership in and through the annual conference," according to the *Book of Discipline*, pars. 427–28. Assigned to each district of the annual conference, the district superintendent (DS) presides at the meetings of charge conferences, interprets the views and needs of local church pastors and lay officers to the bishop and cabinet, and communicates with the local church in behalf of the annual conference, general church agencies, and the bishop. Harking back to the early-nineteenth-century role of the presiding elder who traveled circuits to administer the Lord's Supper and hold quarterly conferences, the office of district superintendent embodies the church's connectional reality most immediately for many Methodists today and likely represents "the key office in making the connection work," according to Frank, *Polity, Practice, and the Mission of the United Methodist Church*, p. 220. See *Book of Discipline*, pars. 7–59 (elaborated in pars. 501–666), for constitutional provision of the chain of United Methodist conferences—general, jurisdictional, central, annual, district, and charge—in relation to the episcopacy and judiciary.

27. *Book of Discipline*, pars. 15, 45. See also Russell E. Richey and Thomas Edward Frank, *Episcopacy in the Methodist Tradition: Perspectives and Proposals* (Nashville, TN: Abingdon Press, 2004).

28. *Book of Discipline*, pars. 54, 906.

29. United Methodism 101, http://www.umc.org, under "Structure and Organization," p. 1.

30. Ibid.

31. Thomas Frank, personal communication, 2005. See William J. Everett and Thomas E. Frank, "Constitutional Order in United Methodism and American Culture," in *Connectionalism: Ecclesiology, Mission, and Identity*, ed. Russell E. Richey, Dennis M. Campbell, and William B. Lawrence, pp. 41–73 (Nashville, TN: Abingdon Press, 1997).

32. *Book of Discipline*, par. 130. Connectionalism takes form in many shifting institutional arrangements and social settings over the history of American Methodism, not only in the national boards and agencies that have served as its chief connecting structures in the twentieth century. From the late eighteenth century, Francis Asbury led an itinerant general superintendency and episcopacy, backed by an itinerant general ministry and presiding elders deployed nationwide across local and regional conference lines. In the nineteenth century, Methodists continued to hear a common Arminian gospel, increasingly communicated across the nation by national papers, tracts, hymnals, books of discipline, and editions of the Bible. It was spread by missions and Sunday schools with standardized lesson plans; and was later carried by freestanding benevolent societies, such as the Missionary Society, the Tract Society, the Church Extension Society, the Board of Education, and the Sunday-School Union. See Russell E. Richey, "Is Division a New Threat to the Denomination?" and "Connectionalism: End or New Beginning?" both in *Questions for the Twenty-first Century Church*, ed. Russell E. Richey, William B. Lawrence, and Dennis M. Campbell (Nashville, TN: Abingdon Press, 1999), pp. 109–11, 316–17.

33. Richey, "Is Division a New Threat to the Denomination?" pp. 111–16. See also Richard P. Heitzenrater, *Wesley and the People Called Methodists* (Nashville, TN: Abingdon Press, 1995), pp. 207ff.

34. Richey, "Is Division a New Threat to the Denomination?" pp. 114–15.

35. Richey, "Connectionalism," pp. 317–18.

36. Russell E. Richey, "Are the Local Church and Denominational Bureaucracy 'Twins'?" in *Questions for the Twenty-first Century Church*, pp. 234–35.

37. *Book of Discipline*, par. 1004.

38. *Christian Social Action*, the flagship publication of the GBCS, reached every local United Methodist congregation in the United States, as well as bishops, district superintendents, and other key church leaders, with a net press run of 28,000 copies bimonthly in 2004. The print edition of the magazine gave way to the e-newsletter on the GBCS Web site, http://www.umc-gbcs.org, in 2005.

39. *Book of Discipline*, par. 1006. GBCS members and staff also compose various administrative committees: Biblical/Theological Interpretation, By-Laws/Legislation, CRASH (Confronting Racism, Ageism, Sexism, Handicappism), Ethnic Local Church Grants, Evaluation and Review, Nominations, Personnel, Finance, and Trustees. Forty-one GBCS board members are elected from the Methodist

jurisdictional conferences upon nomination from their annual conference. They are joined by six bishops named by the Council of Bishops, seven representatives from missionary conferences and overseas churches, and nine additional members elected by the jurisdictions to ensure inclusivity and expertise.

40. Ibid., par. 1005.

41. "The Doctrines and Disciplines of the Methodist Episcopal Church, 1908," *Christian Social Action*, March–April 1988, p. 7.

42. Martin E. Marty, *Modern American Religion* (Chicago: University of Chicago Press, 1986), 1:296.

43. *Book of Discipline*, pars. 160–65.

44. Ibid., par. 166.

45. Herman Will, interview, Louisville, KY, April 1992, here and below.

46. See Robert T. Handy, *Undermined Establishment: Church-State Relations in America, 1880–1920* (Princeton, NJ: Princeton University Press, 1991).

47. Erik J. Alsgaard, "Editorial: Well-Done," *Christian Social Action*, September–October 2000, p. 2. Upon his retirement in 2000, Thom White Wolf Fassett had served as GBCS general secretary for twelve years, the maximum permitted by denominational rules.

48. Jim Winkler, "Publisher's Column," *Christian Social Action*, March–April 2003, p. 3; Winkler, "Publisher's Column," *Christian Social Action*, July–August 2003, p. 2.

49. Thom Fassett, "Called to Be a Special People Witnessing Our Faith," *Christian Social Action*, May–June 1992, p. 45, here and below.

50. Thom Fassett, "Between 'Guns and Oranges,'" *Christian Social Action*, January–February 1993, pp. 7–10, here and below.

51. Green and Guth, "United Methodists and American Culture," pp. 40–43.

52. Ibid.

53. *Book of Discipline*, 1972, par. 72D.

54. *Book of Discipline*, 1988, par. 71G.

55. *Book of Discipline*, 2000, par. 161J, reads in full: "The beginning of life and the ending of life are the God-given boundaries of human existence. While individuals have always had some degree of control over when they would die, they now have the awesome power to determine when and even whether new individuals will be born. Our belief in the sanctity of unborn human life makes us reluctant to approve abortion. But we are equally bound to respect the sacredness of the life and well-being of the mother, for whom devastating damage may result from an unacceptable pregnancy. In continuity with past Christian teaching, we recognize tragic conflicts of life with life that may justify abortion, and in such cases we support the legal option of abortion under proper medical procedures. We cannot affirm abortion as an acceptable means of birth control, and we unconditionally reject it as a means of gender selection. We oppose the use of late-term abortion known as dilation and extraction (partial-birth abortion) and call for the end of

this practice except when the physical life of the mother is in danger and no other medical procedure is available, or in the case of severe fetal anomalies incompatible with life. We call all Christians to a searching and prayerful inquiry into the sorts of conditions that may warrant abortion. We commit our Church to continue to provide nurturing ministries to those who terminate a pregnancy, to those in the midst of a crisis pregnancy, and to those who give birth. Government laws and regulations do not provide all the guidance required by the informed Christian conscience. Therefore, a decision concerning abortion should be made only after thoughtful and prayerful consideration by the parties involved, with medical, pastoral, and other appropriate counsel."

56. Fassett, "Between 'Guns and Oranges,'" pp. 8–10, here and below unless otherwise cited.

57. Thom White Wolf Fassett, interview, Washington, DC, February 1993.

58. The United Methodist Council of Bishops decided in the 1990s to alternate its meetings between major U.S. cities and the rural retreats of either St. Simons Island or Lake Junaluska.

59. Gretchen Hakola, "Who Do You Say That I Am?" *Christian Social Action*, May–June 2002, p. i; and see Green and Guth, "United Methodists and American Culture," pp. 30–38 and tables 1–6, regarding "nominal" Methodists and Methodist "alumni." Cf. Dean R. Hoge, Benton Johnson, and Donald A. Luidens, *Vanishing Boundaries: The Religion of Mainline Protestant Baby Boomers* (Louisville, KY: Westminster/John Knox Press, 1994); Wade Clark Roof, *Spiritual Marketplace: Baby Boomers and the Remaking of American Religion* (Princeton, NJ: Princeton University Press, 1999); and Roof, *A Generation of Seekers: The Spiritual Journey of the Baby Boom Generation* (San Francisco: HarperCollins, 1993). Does more radical, leftist, or liberal "peace and justice" advocacy in mainline churches such as United Methodism since the 1960s play a part in membership losses in these denominations? Heightened moral conflict within these denominations has often focused on contesting church stands on issues such as abortion, gay ordination, ending the Vietnam War, or defending AFDC welfare spending on the poor, although most mainline Protestants agree on the good of ending poverty, gender discrimination, and war, according to Wuthnow, *The Restructuring of American Religion*; and Wuthnow, "Beyond Quiet Influence? Possibilities for the Protestant Mainline," in *The Quiet Hand of God: Faith-Based Activism and the Public Role of Mainline Protestantism*, ed. Robert Wuthnow and John H. Evans, pp. 381–403 (Berkeley and Los Angeles: University of California Press, 2002). In fact, however, membership losses in mainline denominations stem mostly from declining fertility rates among mainliners compared to rates among more conservative Protestant church members before and after the postwar baby boom, with some contribution from the slowing crossover to mainline churches of upwardly mobile converts from more conservative Protestant churches since 1970, and a small but significant increase in mainline defections to the ranks of the

unchurched, but no evidence of increased switching from mainline to conservative denominations. Hout, Greeley, and Wilde, "The Demographic Imperative in Religious Change."

60. Fassett, interview, February 1993.

61. Jim Winkler, "Publisher's Column," *Christian Social Action*, July–August 2001, p. 2.

62. Interview, not for attribution, May 2003.

63. George Ogle, interview, Washington, DC, May 1991, here and below.

64. Will, interview, April 1992.

65. See Leon Howell, *United Methodism @ Risk: A Wake-Up Call* (Kingston, NY: Information Project for United Methodists, 2003), chaps. 1, 4, for cognate criticism of the Board of Church and Society and the Women's Division mounted by the Good News movement and RENEW: A Network for Christian Women. See chapter 7 of this volume for Capitol Hill criticism of the GBCS; and see the elaboration of H. Richard Niebuhr's fivefold typology of Christ and culture later in this chapter.

66. Fassett, interview, February 1993, here and below. The *Book of Discipline*, 2000, pars. 101–2 (1988, pars. 66–67; 1996, pars. 60–61), describes the "consensual process" of defining the common heritage of Christians grounded in the apostolic witness to Jesus Christ as Savior and Lord, and consistent with Wesley's approach: "In essentials, unity; in non-essentials, liberty; and in all things, charity."

67. Jim Winkler, "Publisher's Column," *Christian Social Action*, January–February 2002, p. 2.

68. Jim Winkler, "Publisher's Column," *Christian Social Action*, May–June 2003, p. 2.

69. Winkler, "Publisher's Column," January–February 2002.

70. H. Richard Niebuhr, *Christ and Culture* (New York: Harper and Row, 1951), pp. 39–43.

71. Thom White Wolf Fassett, interview, Washington, DC, March 1996. Cf. H. Richard Niebuhr, *The Kingdom of God in America* (1937; Middletown, CT: Wesleyan University Press, 1988), esp. chap. 5.

72. Bishop Melvin Talbert, interview, Washington, DC, March 1996.

73. Fassett, interview, March 1996, here and below.

74. Thom White Wolf Fassett, interview, Atlanta, GA, November 1998, here and below.

75. Jim Winkler, "Publisher's Column," *Christian Social Action*, November–December 2002, p. 2, here and below.

76. More than two of three Americans say they are at least fairly interested in helping the poor, protecting the environment, and overcoming gender discrimination and racial inequality. Most likewise support religious groups' engaging in such civic activities, especially at the local level. But only 48 percent of 5,603 Americans surveyed in 2000 favored mainline Protestant churches' becoming more active in "bringing religious values to bear on public policy," while 38 percent

wanted them to become less active. Only 33 percent of mainline congregants (compared to 48 percent of evangelicals) wanted to see their own denomination "doing more to influence public policy in Washington," with more educated, older males the likeliest to disapprove. But only about one in five church members are aware that their denomination has a Washington office, as do all the mainline churches. Those who do know are much likelier to favor such public advocacy, although they do oppose church leaders' running for office or heading partisan political movements. Members of congregations engaged in social action or civic discussion are likelier than others to express interest in peace-and-justice issues, to know of their denomination's national advocacy, and to support it. See Wuthnow, "Beyond Quiet Influence?"

Chapter 4. United Methodism in Crisis: Scriptural Renewal

1. Jay Lintner, interview, Washington, DC, March 1996. See the *United Methodist Newscope*, October 10, 1980, pp. 2–3, for Outen's plans to restructure the GBCS into five departments administered more directly by a smaller secretarial council and to increase the proportion of ethnic minorities in the professional staff to one-third and the proportion of women to one-half by 1984. For news of subsequent staff dismissals, appointments, and protests, see *United Methodist Newscope*, January 2, 1981, p. 1; January 9, 1981, p. 4; January 23, 1981, p. 4; and February 27, 1981, pp. 2–3.

2. See, for example, Robert N. Bellah, Richard Madsen, William M. Sullivan, Ann Swidler, and Steven M. Tipton, *The Good Society* (New York: Knopf, 1991; Vintage Books, 1992), pp. 202–6.

3. Charles W. Keysor, "Methodism's Silent Minority," *New Christian Advocate*, July 14, 1966, pp. 9–10, here and below. A graduate of Northwestern University's Medill School of Journalism, Keysor worked as managing editor of *Kiwanis* magazine and as a public-relations account executive with J. Walter Thompson Company, then the world's largest advertising agency, before his conversion at age thirty-five during a Billy Graham crusade. After graduating from Garrett Theological Seminary and being ordained as an elder of the Methodist Church, he was serving as pastor of the 320-member Grace Methodist Church in Elgin, Illinois, west of Chicago, when James Wall, then editor of the Methodist ministers' magazine, *New Christian Advocate* (and later the longtime editor of *Christian Century*), invited Keysor to write an article describing the central beliefs and convictions of Methodism's evangelical wing, to which Wall knew Keysor belonged. See Charles W. Keysor, "The Story of Good News," *Good News*, March–April 1981, pp. 8–19, 22–25, 50, esp. pp. 9–10.

4. John A. Lovelace, "Grading Good News," *Good News*, March–April 1987, pp. 24–26.

5. Charles W. Keysor, "Reaching Those the Church Often Forgets," *Good News*, September–October 2002, pp. 12–13, adapted from Keysor, *Our Methodist Heritage* (Elgin, IL: D. C. Cook, 1973). See also, here and below, Sara L. Anderson and James V. Heidinger II, "20 Years at a Glance," *Good News*, March–April 1987, pp. 13–18; and Heidinger, "25 Years of Vision," *Good News*, March–April 1992, pp. 15–19.

6. Keysor, "The Story of Good News," pp. 16–18, here and below.

7. *The Book of Discipline of the United Methodist Church* (Nashville, TN: United Methodist Publishing House, 1972), par. 72C, p. 86.

8. Edmund W. Robb, Jr., interview, Louisville, KY, April 1992. Robb died in 2004. See James V. Heidinger II, "Remembering Ed Robb: United Methodism's Revivalist and Reformer," *Good News*, March–April 2005, pp. 18–21; and Edmund W. Robb, Jr., *Contending for the Faith: The Ed Robb Story* (Anderson, IN: Bristol Books, 2002).

9. James V. Heidinger II, interview, Louisville, KY, April 1992, here and below. Charles Keysor died of cancer in 1985.

10. Robb, interview, April 1992, here and below.

11. See Andy Langford and William H. Willimon, "Why We Support Voluntary Apportionment$," *Good News*, July–August 1998, pp. 18–22; and Langford and Willimon, *A New Connection: Reforming the United Methodist Church* (Nashville, TN: Abingdon Press, 1995).

12. James V. Heidinger II, "The Vision of Good News," *Good News*, January–February 1983, p. 35.

13. Heidinger, interview, April 1992. Cf. John C. Green and James L. Guth, "United Methodists and American Culture: A Statistical Portrait," in *The People(s) Called Methodist: Forms and Reforms of Their Life*, ed. William B. Lawrence, Dennis M. Campbell, and Russell E. Richey (Nashville, TN: Abingdon Press, 1998), p. 39.

14. Cf. Green and Guth, "United Methodists and American Culture," pp. 45–48, for evidence that lay Methodists as a whole are nearly twice as likely to identify themselves as "conservative" as the clergy, but the two groups are quite similar in their partisan leanings. Traditionalist clergy perceive fewer and generally smaller moral-political differences with their congregations than do more liberal and moderate pastors. Sixty percent of traditionalist clergy report feeling discouraged by their denominational superiors against engagement on social and political matters, while 54 percent of clergy with more liberal views report sensing denominational encouragement for such involvement.

15. "Abortion Rights Group Moves out of Methodist Building," *Good News*, March–April 1994, p. 39.

16. Heidinger, interview, April 1992, here and below.

17. Established by General Conference in 1972 to coordinate and evaluate the denomination's general boards and agencies, the 64-member General Council on Ministries (GCOM) was dissolved by the 2004 General Conference and replaced

by the 47-member Connectional Table, with promises of more proportional representation across jurisdictions and more holistic collaboration, after rejection of an alternative proposal for a 131-member superagency. Long-standing debate over GCOM featured charges that its arrogation of executive authority violated articles of the church's constitution and infringed bishops' rightful responsibility for the entire church; these charges were countered by claims that GCOM had only assumed oversight responsibilities assigned to it by General Conference for good reason and by due legislative process. See Russell E. Richey, "Do General Agencies Still Have a Place in the Church?" *Quarterly Review* 24, no. 4 (Winter 2004): 411–16.

18. James V. Heidinger II, "A Different Kind of General Conference: Beginning the Return to 'Classical Christianity,'" *Christian Social Action*, July–August 2000, pp.13–14; Heidinger, "Cleveland Brings Reason for Hope," *Good News*, July–August 2000, p. 5.

19. Regarding homosexuality, the 2000 *Book of Discipline* (par. 161G, "Human Sexuality," p. 101) states in its Social Principles: "Homosexual persons no less than heterosexual persons are individuals of sacred worth. All persons need the ministry and guidance of the church in their struggles for human fulfillment, as well as the spiritual and emotional care of a fellowship that enables reconciling relations with God, with others, and with self. Although we do not condone the practice of homosexuality and consider this practice incompatible with Christian teaching, we affirm that God's grace is available to all. We implore families and churches not to reject or condemn their lesbian and gay members and friends. We commit ourselves to be in ministry for and with all persons." The penultimate sentence was added by the 2000 General Conference, which also voted to mandate the General Commission on Christian Unity and Interreligious Concerns to engage the church in a continued dialogue about homosexuality. In 1996, paragraph 65C of the Social Principles regarding marriage stated: "Ceremonies that celebrate homosexual unions shall not be conducted by our ministers and shall not be conducted in our churches." In 2000 it was excised from paragraph 161C of the Social Principles but was added as paragraph 332.6 to proscriptions of "unauthorized conduct" by "the ministry of the ordained." Paragraph 806.9 requires the General Council on Finance and Administration to ensure that "no board, agency, committee, commission, or council shall give United Methodist funds to any gay caucus or group, or otherwise use such funds to promote the acceptance of homosexuality." At the same time, paragraph 162H of the 2000 *Book of Discipline* affirms: "Certain basic human rights and civil liberties are due all persons. We are committed to supporting those rights and liberties for homosexual persons." Paragraph 162H also affirms church support of "efforts to stop violence and other forms of coercion against gays and lesbians."

20. Heidinger, "Cleveland Brings Reason for Hope."

21. "2000 General Conference," *Good News*, July–August 2000, p. 7.

22. Heidinger, "Cleveland Brings Reason for Hope."

23. Harry C. Kiely, "Judgment and Grace at General Conference," *Christian Social Action*, July–August 2000, pp. 8–10, here and below.

24. Heidinger, "Cleveland Brings Reason for Hope."

25. James M. Wall, "A Simple Solution," *Christian Century*, July 19–26, 2000, p. 739.

26. Interview, not for attribution, March 2004.

27. James V. Heidinger II, "A Bittersweet 2004 General Conference," *Good News*, May–June 2004, p. 3, here and below.

28. The United Methodist Judicial Council, by a 6-3 vote, ruled in Decision No. 984 of April 29, 2004, that "Paragraph 304.3 of the 2000 Discipline is a declaration of the General Conference of the United Methodist Church that 'the practice of homosexuality is incompatible with Christian teaching.' The practice of homosexuality is a chargeable offense under Par. 2702.1b of the 2000 Discipline." Paragraph 304.3 prescribes, "Since the practice of homosexuality is incompatible with Christian teaching, self-avowed practicing homosexuals are not to be accepted as candidates, ordained as ministers, or appointed to serve in The United Methodist Church." It notes that "'self-avowed practicing homosexual' is understood to mean that a person openly acknowledges to a bishop, district superintendent, district committee of ordained ministry, board of ordained ministry, or clergy session that the person is a practicing homosexual. See Judicial Council Decisions 702, 708, 722, 725, 764, 844." *Book of Discipline*, 2000, p. 305. See also Neil Caldwell, "Judicial Council Clarifies Church Standards," *Good News*, May–June 2004, pp. 19–21. The 2004 General Conference delegates voted against accepting openly gay ministers or gay marriage by consistent margins of 2 to 1 or more. But votes against more moderate initiatives to soften opposition to gays in the church approached 55 to 45 percent, offering liberal church leaders hope for future progress. The Judicial Council's more conservative membership after 2004 and its stiffer stance against "self-avowed practicing homosexuals" in ordained ministry informed its rulings of October 31, 2005. In Decision No. 1027 it voted 6-2, with one judge absent, to defrock Rev. Irene Stroud, an openly lesbian minister in Philadelphia living in a "covenanted relationship" with a partner, thereby reaffirming a conference jury's verdict that had been overturned by a regional appeals panel citing legal errors and the ambiguity of the church's constitutional pledge of no discrimination on the basis of "status." The council also ruled that church laws superseded two resolutions against anti-gay bias, one passed by the church's California-Nevada Regional Conference holding sexual orientation to be innate rather than sinful, and the other passed by the Pacific Northwest Conference affirming tolerance for a plurality of views on sexuality. As "an historical statement without prescriptive force," neither resolution had bearing on church laws, held the council. More controversially, in Decision No. 1032 the Judicial Council voted 5-3 to reinstate Rev. Edward Johnson, a Virginia pastor suspended by the Virginia

Conference for denying membership in his congregation to a gay man unrepentantly involved in a same-sex relationship. The council cited church laws that give local pastors the discretion "to make the determination of a person's readiness to affirm the vows of membership," including, "Do you renounce the spiritual forces of wickedness, reject the evil powers of this world and repent of your sin?" This decision touched off alarm across the denomination, not just among liberals, and prompted the United Methodist Council of Bishops to issue a unanimous letter of rebuttal on November 2, 2005. The letter stressed that "homosexuality is not a barrier" to church membership and that "pastors are accountable to the bishop, superintendent, and the clergy in matters of ministry and membership" in light of General Conference's constitutional call for "inclusiveness and justice for all as it relates to church membership," based on the sacred worth of all persons without regard to "race, color, national origin, status or economic condition." See Alan Cooperman, "Methodist Court Rules against Homosexuals," *Washington Post*, October 31, 2005.

29. Heidinger, "A Bittersweet 2004 General Conference."

30. Ibid.

31. Ibid.

32. James V. Heidinger II, "Speech Heard around the World," *Good News*, May–June 2004, p. 16; Maxie Dunnam, "Truth Getting Distorted about 'Amicable Separation,'" *Good News*, July–August 2004, p. 27.

33. Heidinger, "Speech Heard around the World." See also, for example, Laurie Goodstein, "Conservative Methodists Propose Schism over Gay Rights," *New York Times*, May 7, 2004, p. A20; and Goodstein, "Methodists Vote Overwhelmingly against Call to Split the Church," *New York Times*, May 8, 2004, p. A18.

34. Bill Hinson, "Is It Time for an Amicable and Just Separation?" *Good News*, May–June 2004, pp. 17–18, here and below.

35. Troy Plummer, quoted in Goodstein, "Conservative Methodists Propose Schism."

36. Troy Plummer, quoted in Heidinger, "Speech Heard around the World."

37. C. Dale White, quoted in Heidinger, "Speech Heard around the World."

38. Cf. Heidinger, "Speech Heard around the World"; "UMC Works through Differences, Approves Statement of Unity," *United Methodist Newscope*, May 14, 2004, p. 1; and Alice M. Smith, "Delegates Pledge Unity amid Rumors of Schism," *Wesleyan Christian Advocate*, May 21, 2004, pp. 1, 10.

39. "UMC Works through Differences," p. 1.

40. Heidinger, "A Bittersweet 2004 General Conference."

41. Good News Board of Directors, "Good News Board Responds to Unity Statement," *Good News*, May–June 2004, p. 44. In 1980, University of North Carolina professor Frederick P. Brooks, a former board member of Good News, told eight hundred people at its Lake Junalaska Convocation, "It is time now to take the next step and work out in love a way to divide the church into two independent

bodies, each unified by its own theological integrity." Brooks reasoned that the 1972 General Conference's doctrinal statement in favor of theological pluralism marked a first "step forward toward theological honesty and open recognition of a fact long dodged—that much of the UMC no longer believes our ancient doctrine." Brooks proposed that "a loving division" could be prepared by a twenty-member task force appointed by the bishops. "Some will deduce that Good News wants to start a new church," responded Charles Keysor, to make clear the official position of Good News on the issue. "People have laid that upon us since we began, but it's 14 years later, and we're still around." James Heidinger, then chair of the Good News board of directors, attested, "Separation is not even an agenda item with us." "UM Professor Proposes UMC Be Divided into Two Independent Parts," *United Methodist Newscope*, August 8, 1980, p. 3.

42. Goodstein, "Methodists Vote Overwhelmingly against Call to Split the Church."

43. Ibid.

44. See Green and Guth, "United Methodists and American Culture," pp. 28–35, 38–48; and James L. Guth, John C. Green, Corwin E. Smidt, Lyman A. Kellstedt, and Margaret M. Poloma, *The Bully Pulpit: The Politics of Protestant Clergy* (Lawrence: University Press of Kansas, 1997), pp. 188–91.

45. Smith, "Delegates Pledge Unity," p. 10.

46. Ibid.; and see Goodstein, "Conservative Methodists Propose Schism," quoting Professor James R. Wood.

47. Jim Winkler, "Publisher's Column," *Christian Social Action*, July–August 2004, p. 2.

48. Ibid.

49. Good News editors, "General Conference 2004 Issues: Marriage, Bio-ethics, and Iraq," *Good News*, May–June 2004, p. 28.

50. Winkler, "Publisher's Column," July–August 2004. For example, in October 2005, the GBCS issued a statement, "A Call to End the U.S. Military Presence in Iraq," urging Congress to speed withdrawal of U.S. troops by adopting legislation such as the bipartisan Homeward Bound Act (H.J. Res. 55) and to investigate and "hold accountable those responsible for the misleading 'intelligence' and disastrous decisions that fueled this war." The board cited facts established by the Kean-Hamilton commission on 9/11 that no weapons of mass destruction were stored in Iraq, no attempts to purchase Niger uranium were made by Saddam Hussein's government, and no ties were found between it and al Qaeda or the 9/11 attacks. Thus, argued the GBCS, "thousands of lives have been lost and hundreds of billions of dollars wasted in a war that the United States initiated and never should have fought. The United States is now morally obligated to provide the vast economic resources needed to aid in the post-war reconstruction of Iraq. The ongoing cost of the war continues to drain public resources that are desperately needed in Iraq as well as in the United States. We grieve for all those whose

lives have been lost in this needless and avoidable tragedy. Military families have suffered undue hardship from prolonged troop rotations in Iraq and loss of loved ones. It is time to bring them home," and time to cooperate with the United Nations to bring peace to Iraq and rebuild the country. United Methodist General Board of Church and Society, Fall 2005 Board Meeting statement, October 16, 2005, http://www.umc-gbcs.org.

51. Philip Amerson, interview, Louisville, KY, April 1992, here and below.

52. Herman Will, interview, Louisville, KY, April 1992, here and below.

53. Bishop Dale White, interview, Louisville, KY, April 1992, here and below.

54. Bishop William Dew, interview, Louisville, KY, April 1992, here and below.

55. George McLain, interview, Louisville, KY, April 1992, here and below.

56. James Lawson, quoted in Heidinger, "Cleveland Brings Reason for Hope." Good News supports and works with the Institute on Religion and Democracy (IRD), the Mission Society for United Methodists, and the Confessing Movement within the United Methodist Church, a "renewal movement" launched in 1994 out of concern that the church is "in danger of abandoning the gospel" and composed of more than 1,300 churches representing 600,000 Methodists. See *Good News,* November–December 1999, p. 31.

57. Heidinger, "Cleveland Brings Reason for Hope."

58. James Lawson, interview, Louisville, KY, April 1992, here and below.

59. Theodore Runyon, quoted pseudonymously as Gene Sansom in Bellah et al., *The Good Society,* pp. 204–5.

60. Bishop Bruce Blake, interview, Louisville, KY, April 1992, here and below.

61. Bishop Joseph Yeakel, GBCS opening address, as tape-recorded and transcribed by the author, Washington, DC, March 1993, here and below.

62. *Book of Discipline,* 2000, par. 130. See pars. 7–59, 501–666; and chap. 3, n. 26, on the chain of United Methodist conferences in relation to the episcopacy and judiciary.

63. Bishop Yeakel, GBCS opening address, 1993, here and below.

64. Bishop Yeakel, interview, March 1993, here and below.

65. See Robert Wuthnow, *Acts of Compassion: Caring for Others and Helping Ourselves* (Princeton, NJ: Princeton University Press, 1991); and Wuthnow, *Loose Connections: Joining Together in America's Fragmented Communities* (Cambridge, MA: Harvard University Press, 1998).

66. Cf. Wade Clark Roof, *A Generation of Seekers: The Spiritual Journey of the Baby Boom Generation* (San Francisco: HarperCollins, 1993); and Wade Clark Roof, Jackson W. Carroll, and David A. Roozen, *The Post-war Generation and Establishment Religion* (Boulder, CO: Westview Press, 1995).

67. Jim Winkler, "Publisher's Column," *Christian Social Action,* January–February 2002, p. 2.

68. Jim Winkler, "Publisher's Column," *Christian Social Action,* July–August 2002, p. 2.

69. Jim Winkler, "Publisher's Column," *Christian Social Action*, September–October 2003, p. 2.

70. Ibid.

71. Winkler, "Publisher's Column," July–August 2002.

72. Jim Winkler, "Publisher's Column," *Christian Social Action*, May–June 2003, p. 2.

73. Russell E. Richey, "Connectionalism: End or New Beginning?" in *Questions for the Twenty-first Century Church*, ed. Russell E. Richey, William B. Lawrence, and Dennis M. Campbell (Nashville, TN: Abingdon Press, 1999), pp. 313–15.

74. Charles P. Minnick and Thomas Edward Frank, *Vital Congregations, Faithful Disciples: Vision for the Church*, foundation document, Council of Bishops of the United Methodist Church (Nashville, TN: Graded Press, 1990), p. 21, quoted in Richey, "Connectionalism," pp. 314–15.

75. Richey, "Connectionalism," pp. 314–15.

76. Ibid., pp. 318–19.

77. Jim Winkler, "Publisher's Column," *Christian Social Action*, July–August 2003, p. 2.

Chapter 5: Faith and Freedom

1. David Jessup, *Preliminary Inquiry regarding Financial Contributions to Outside Political Groups by Boards and Agencies of the United Methodist Church, 1977–1979* (photocopied document, Washington, DC, April 7, 1980), p. 1; adapted as David Jessup with Cindy D. Vetters, "How United Methodist Dollars Are Given to Marxist Causes," *Good News*, September–October 1980, pp. 26–34. See also David Jessup, "A Response from Mr. Jessup," *Good News*, January–February 1981, pp. 54–57, in reply to criticism of the original Jessup Report from Bishop Roy C. Nichols of New York, president of the Council of Bishops and president of the World Division of the Board of Global Ministries of the United Methodist Church. Nichols's reply was incorporated into a six-page denominational "white paper" answering Jessup's charges, prepared as a special bulletin of United Methodist Communications (with the cooperation of the Board of Global Ministries and the Board of Church and Society) by Edwin H. Maynard, "The Use of Money in Mission—an Opportunity for Understanding," issued October 17, 1980. It sets out biblical bases for mission as humanitarian aid to bring justice and mercy to "the widow and orphan, the poor and the powerless." It describes related criteria used by church agencies in making grants and discusses twenty-one specific grants cited by Jessup, noting that the grants Jessup challenged totaled one-third of 1 percent of the $120 million granted only by the Board of Global Ministries in the 1977– 79 period that Jessup probed. See Charles W. Keysor, "Touching a Tender Nerve," *Good News*, January–February 1981, pp. 48–54, for criticism of

"The Use of Money in Mission" as defending denominational policies unjustified by the Word of God and requiring counter-mobilization in order to wrest control of the denomination's political process from the political left, identified with the McGovern wing of the Democratic Party. For an overview of early exchanges between Methodist leaders and David Jessup in the wake of his report, see *United Methodist Reporter*, September 26, 1980; and the denomination's official newsletter, *United Methodist Newscope*, vol. 8, nos. 40–43, 45, 50 (September 19, 26; October 3, 10, 24; December 12, 1980).

2. Jessup, *Preliminary Inquiry*, pp. 1, 3, here and below.

3. David Jessup, interview, Washington, DC, March 1992, here and below.

4. Maynard, "The Use of Money in Mission," p. 2.

5. Jessup, *Preliminary Inquiry*, pp. 2, 26.

6. James M. Wall, "A Simple Solution," *Christian Century*, July 19–26, 2000, p. 739.

7. Bishop C. Dale White et al., "Wake, Awake!" preface to Leon Howell, *United Methodism @ Risk: A Wake-Up Call* (Kingston, NY: Information Project for United Methodists, 2003), p. 4. See also Leon Howell, *Funding the War of Ideas* (Cleveland, OH: United Church Board for Homeland Ministries, 1995), pp. 1–86, esp. chap. 5; Howell, "Old Wine, New Bottles: The Institute on Religion and Democracy," *Christianity and Crisis*, March 21, 1983, pp. 74, 89–94; and Howell, "Religion, Politics, Money and Power" (Interfaith Alliance Foundation, 2001). Mainline-church leaders in Washington generally appreciate and agree with Howell's long-standing, detailed criticism of the IRD. For recent elaboration of such criticism, see Andrew J. Weaver and Nicole Seibert, "Follow the Money: Documenting the Right's Well-Heeled Assault on the UMC," *Zion's Herald*, January–February 2004, http://www.zionsherald.org, including the transcription of a telephone interview conducted with Mark Tooley on December 16, 2003; and Andrew J. Weaver, "Neocon Catholics Target Mainline Protestants," Media Transparency, August 11, 2006, http://www.mediatransparency.com.

8. Jessup, *Preliminary Inquiry*, pp. 1, 3–5, 15–18, 20–21, 24. For Jessup's view of the military implications of food aid to Vietnam, see "*Newscope* Asked Wrong Questions, Charges Jessup," *United Methodist Newscope*, September 26, 1980, p. 3.

9. J. Harry Haines, "UMCOR Chief Blasts Jessup Report, Notes World Crises," *United Methodist Newscope*, October 3, 1980, p. 3.

10. Herman Will, "Memo re. David Jessup," July 7, 1980, to Bill Cobun, George Outen, and Carolyn McIntyre, Board of Church and Society, United Methodist Church, Washington, DC.

11. Roy C. Nichols, "From the President of the Council of Bishops," a public letter of October 3, 1980, in response to the Jessup Report, incorporated into Maynard, "The Use of Money in Mission," p. 6.

12. Peggy Billings, Assistant General Secretary, Section of Christian Social Relations of the Women's Division of the Board of Global Ministries, quoted in

Cindy D. Vetters, "Some Reactions to the Jessup Report," *Good News*, September–October 1980, p. 39. Jessup and Methodist Church leaders disagreed over few facts regarding how much money denominational boards and agencies granted to which nondenominational organizations. They disagreed fiercely over the moral and theological justification of these grants and over the factual characterization of their recipients. Each side in the controversy commonly depicted the other as driven by political ideology at odds with Christian faith, moral responsibility, and respect for the factual truth; and each responded with indignation to the moral arrogance it found in the other.

13. Maynard, "The Use of Money in Mission," p. 5.

14. Jessup, *Preliminary Inquiry*, p. 2.

15. Joseph A. Harriss, "What Master Is the World Council of Churches Serving . . . Karl Marx or Jesus Christ?" *Reader's Digest*, August 1982, pp. 130–34; Rael Jean Isaac, "Do You Know Where Your Church Offerings Go?" *Reader's Digest*, January 1983, pp. 120–25; Charles Austin, "New Church Group Assails Support of Left," *New York Times*, November 15, 1981, p. 46; Austin, "Protestant Leaders Debate the Role of Religion in Public Affairs," *New York Times*, March 25, 1982, p. A16; Austin, "National Church Council Faces New Type of Critic," *New York Times*, November 3, 1982, p. A19; Austin, "New Clergy Group Assails Church Aid to Leftists," *New York Times*, February 16, 1983, p. B9. See also Howell, "Old Wine, New Bottles," p. 92; and Howell, *United Methodism @ Risk*, pp. 41–42.

16. Richard John Neuhaus and Edmund Robb, Jr., in "The Gospel according to Whom?" *60 Minutes*, CBS, January 23, 1983, CBS transcript, pp. 1, 5–7.

17. See, for example, National Council of Churches of Christ (NCCC), Office of Information, "The Gospel according to '60 Minutes,'" 1983; NCCC, "Response to *Reader's Digest* Article, "Do You Know Where Your Church Offerings Go?" December 17, 1982; and World Council of Churches, Communications Department, "Response to *Reader's Digest* Article, 'Karl Marx or Jesus Christ?' August 1982," July 24, 1982. Each is a six- to twelve-page photocopied typescript mailed to mainline-church leaders.

18. David Jessup elaborates: "I went to these summer mission studies programs, where they use these texts from the NCC Friendship Press that Methodists help write. Here are these incredible mass-education projects, seventy-five or a hundred of them every summer for a week all over the country, with two to three hundred people in each one of them. That's bigger than what the AFL-CIO does. It reaches a lot of people, and what it reaches them with is so off the wall it was astonishing to me they would try to put this forward, and that the people receiving it didn't get more upset by it. . . . The people who tend to go to these summer institutes center around a core of insiders who come from the regional bureaucracies. They are already plugged into the national bureaucracy. In political terms on the left, we would call them cadres. They are people who may look like the audience, but in actuality they are part of the apparatus who put on the show and make the whole

thing work by riding herd on the audience. Other people did walk in as innocents and were outraged. They thought this was terrible. Many of them joined renewal groups, or they formed small dissident communities. . . . Those people weren't political like I am, but they were treated by the church hierarchy like they were absolute pariahs instead of being theological dissidents." Interview, March 1992.

19. Ibid.

20. Richard Penn Kemble, interview, Washington, DC, March 1992, here and below.

21. Eric Hochstein with Ronald O'Rourke, *A Report on the Institute on Religion and Democracy*, a photocopied document of 55 pages with an additional 6 preliminary and 9 appended pages, commissioned by the United Methodist General Board of Church and Society and the Board of Global Ministries and the United Church of Christ Board for Homeland Ministries, October 1981, reprinted as "An American Dream: Neo-conservatism and the New Religious Right in the USA," pp. 17–32 in *IDOC International Bulletin*, nos. 8–9 (1982): 20.

22. Edmund W. Robb, Jr., interview, Louisville, KY, April 1992.

23. Kemble, interview, March 1992, here and below.

24. Richard J. Neuhaus, *Christianity and Democracy: A Statement of the Institute on Religion and Democracy* (Washington, DC: IRD, 1991). Originally issued for circulation at a press conference at Freedom House in New York City on November 10, 1981, this statement was first published by the IRD as a twelve-page pamphlet in 1982. In 1991 George Weigel slightly revised the text, notably by softening "pervasive" to "evident" on page 10 to yield, "Arguments for oppression are evident in our several churches, in some churches more than others."

25. Ibid., pp. 1–2.

26. Peter Steinfels, "'Christianity and Democracy': Baptizing Reaganism," *Christianity and Crisis*, March 29, 1983, pp. 80–85. See also Steinfels, *The Neoconservatives* (New York: Simon and Schuster, 1980); and Richard Neuhaus and Peter Steinfels, "Continuing the Discussion: 'Christianity and Democracy,'" *Christianity and Crisis*, May 10, 1982, pp. 135–36.

27. Steinfels, "'Christianity and Democracy': Baptizing Reaganism," p. 81; Neuhaus, *Christianity and Democracy*, pp. 2–3.

28. Neuhaus, *Christianity and Democracy*, pp. 4–5.

29. Steinfels, "'Christianity and Democracy': Baptizing Reaganism," p. 81.

30. Neuhaus, *Christianity and Democracy*, pp. 4–5.

31. Steinfels, "'Christianity and Democracy': Baptizing Reaganism," pp. 81–83.

32. Neuhaus, *Christianity and Democracy*, pp. 5–6; Steinfels, "'Christianity and Democracy': Baptizing Reaganism," pp. 81–82.

33. Neuhaus, *Christianity and Democracy*, pp. 8–9; Steinfels, "'Christianity and Democracy': Baptizing Reaganism," p. 82.

34. Steinfels, "'Christianity and Democracy': Baptizing Reaganism," pp. 82–83.

35. Ibid.

36. Ibid., p. 83.

37. Neuhaus, *Christianity and Democracy*, pp. 9–11. Note George Weigel's 1991 revision of the document to soften this indictment (see note 24 above).

38. Neuhaus, *Christianity and Democracy*, p. 7.

39. Steinfels, "'Christianity and Democracy': Baptizing Reaganism," pp. 83–84.

40. Ibid.

41. Ibid., p. 84.

42. Kemble, interview, March 1992, here and below. See also Gunnar Myrdal, *An American Dilemma* (Harper and Brothers, 1944), chap. 1.

43. See note 55 below regarding the Young Socialist League.

44. Richard N. Ostling, "Warring over Where Donations Go," and "The Little Institute Facing Goliath," *Time*, March 28, 1983, pp. 58–59; Ben Wattenberg, "Protestants Protest," *Ben Wattenberg at Large*, PBS, November 1981. For the reports on *60 Minutes* and in *Reader's Digest* and the *New York Times*, see notes 15 and 16 above. For earlier anticommunist criticism of the NCC and mainline churches, see Clarence W. Hall, "Must Our Churches Finance Revolution?" *Reader's Digest*, October 1971, pp. 1–6; and Stanley High, "Methodism's Pink Fringe," *Reader's Digest*, February 1950, pp. 134–38. For polarized follow-up coverage in the religious and political press, see criticism of the NCC in, for example, Isaac C. Rottenberg, "Why Did the NCC Get Such Bad Press?" *Christianity Today*, May 20, 1983, pp. 25–26; Herman Nickel, "The Corporation Haters," *Fortune*, June 16, 1980, pp. 126–33; Rael Jean Isaac and Erich Isaac, "Sanctifying Revolution: Protestantism's New Social Gospel," *American Spectator*, May 1981, pp. 7–11, 37–40; Joshua Muravchik, "Pliant Protestants," *New Republic*, June 13, 1983, pp. 15–18; and Rael Jean Isaac, "Mainline Church Activism," *Midstream*, March 1984, pp. 12–19. For criticism of the IRD, see, for example, Cynthia Brown, "The Right's Religious Red Alert," *The Nation*, March 12, 1983, pp. 293–306; and Wayne H. Cowan et al., "I Am Not Making These Charges," *Christianity and Crisis*, March 21, 1983, pp. 75–79. Some religion writers in key mainstream national media outlets were friendly to the IRD and presented it as politically centrist or moderate— for example, Charles Austin in articles in the *New York Times*, cited in note 15 above. Other such writers were more critical and questioning; see, for example, Kenneth L. Woodward, "Ideology under the Alms," *Newsweek*, February 7, 1983, pp. 61–62.

45. Cf. Robert McAfee Brown, "IRD: One-Sided Terms for Dialogue," *Christian Century*, May 25, 1983, pp. 530–31; and Richard John Neuhaus, "The IRD and Church Dialogue," *Christian Century*, April 6, 1983, pp. 317–20, for contrary views of the *60 Minutes* program.

46. Hochstein and O'Rourke, *Report on the Institute on Religion and Democracy*, p. 17. See Michael Novak, "The Snoop Report," *National Review*, December 11, 1981, p. 148, for a rejoinder; and James M. Wall, "Neoconservatives Aim at Liberals," *Christian Century*, November 4, 1981, pp. 1115–17, for a reflection.

47. Hochstein and O'Rourke, *Report on the Institute on Religion and Democracy*, p. 17.

48. Ibid., pp. 17, 19–20.

49. Roy Howard Beck, "UM Agencies Investigate Critics: Unprecedented Action Alleges 'Institute' Political Link," *United Methodist Reporter*, November 13, 1981, p. 3; Melinda Gipson, "Public TV Show Critical of Methodist Leadership Creates Stormy Reaction," Religion News Service, November 13, 1982, p. 7.

50. Hochstein and O'Rourke, *Report on the Institute on Religion and Democracy*, pp. 19–21, here and below; see also Institute on Religion and Democracy, "Religion and Politics: Is There a Problem in Your Denomination?" (Washington, DC, 1981), sides 4–6 of a single-page brochure folded into six sides. In this brochure, the IRD invites contributors to check a box indicating "Please enroll me as a member of the Institute on Religion and Democracy, a project of the Foundation for Democratic Education, Inc. My $25 tax-deductible donation is enclosed (please make checks payable to FDE-IRD)." Among the IRD's board of advisors, this brochure also identifies Penn Kemble as "President, The Foundation for Democratic Education Incorporated." In its press release of November 10, 1981, for the issuing of "Christianity and Democracy," the IRD also describes itself as "a tax-exempt educational organization established a year ago to strengthen democratic values in American religious organizations." See Howell, "Old Wine, New Bottles," p. 89.

51. Hochstein and O'Rourke, *Report on the Institute on Religion and Democracy*, pp. 19–26. See also Leon Howell, "The Uses of Religious Liberty—Some News for You: Elliott Abrams Has an Agenda," *Christianity and Crisis*, May 27, 1985, pp. 209–11. For mainline-church leaders, Elliott Abrams exemplifies the deep roots and long branches intertwining the IRD and CDM in the hawkish anticommunism of the Cold War, stretching from his work in the 1970s for Senator Henry "Scoop" Jackson (D-Wash.) to fortify U.S. foreign policy against the cautionary effects of the Vietnam War, through his collaboration in waging the Nicaraguan Contra war with John Negroponte on point as U.S. ambassador to Honduras in the Reagan administration in tandem with Abrams as Assistant Secretary of State for Latin America, to the vital roles of Abrams and Negroponte in executing the Middle East foreign policy of President George W. Bush. Negroponte served Bush as U.S. ambassador to the UN and then to Iraq before becoming the first U.S. director of national intelligence in 2005, then deputy secretary of state in 2007. Abrams directed Middle East affairs on the National Security Council. He helped negotiate the U.S. endorsement in 2004 of Israeli prime minister Ariel Sharon's unilateral plan to evacuate the Gaza Strip of its 7,500 Jewish settlers and fortify Israel's hold on major Jewish settlement blocs in the West Bank with more than 225,000 settlers—a plan at odds with a two-state solution to the conflict, according to its critics in the churches. In coordinating and defending Iran-Contra policy, Abrams clashed often and angrily with mainline-church groups and human rights

advocates such as Amnesty International, who charged him with covering up horrendous abuses committed in Nicaragua, El Salvador, Honduras, and Guatemala by governments backed by the United States. In 1991 Abrams pled guilty to two counts of withholding Iran-Contra information from Congress and was granted a Christmas Eve pardon a year later by President George H. W. Bush, weeks before he left office. Abrams spent much of the ensuing Democratic interregnum at the Ethics and Public Policy Center, arguing for the forceful Palestinian agenda of Likud and its allies in Israel and the United States, and bolstering ties between conservative evangelical Christians and Jews to support a strong Israel. In a chapter on Israel in *Present Dangers: Crisis and Opportunity in America's Foreign and Defense Policy*, edited by Robert Kagan and William Kristol (New York: Encounter Books, 2000), Abrams spelled out a new U.S. Middle East policy based on willingness to use U.S. military strength to effect regime change in Iraq and to back Israel in cracking down on the Palestinian Authority. See Michael Dobbs, "Back in Political Forefront," *Washington Post*, May 27, 2003, p. A1. Before large-scale hostilities broke out between Israel and Hezbollah in Lebanon in 2006, Abrams allegedly joined Vice President Dick Cheney's office in vetting and supporting Israeli plans for the extensive air war, as reported by Seymour M. Hersh in "Watching Lebanon," *New Yorker*, August 21, 2006, pp. 28-33, and denied by a spokesman for the National Security Council.

52. Hochstein and O'Rourke, *Report on the Institute on Religion and Democracy*, pp. 18, 28.

53. Ibid., pp. 19-20, 31 n. 16.

54. Ibid., pp. 17-18, 19, 23. See, for example, Paul Seabury, "Trendier than Thou," *Harper's Magazine*, October 1978, pp. 1-7, reprinted by the Ethics and Public Policy Center; and Ed Robb, "Chairman's Corner," *Good News*, November-December 1976, p. 65, both cited by Hochstein and O'Rourke. Writes Seabury, a political scientist, Episcopal layman, and member of the IRD board and of the Social Democrats, USA: "By the late 1960s, national [Episcopal] church authorities were dispensing millions of dollars of missionary funds collected from parishes and dioceses to radical political movements across the land . . . and Third World liberation movements. . . . In 1970, the national church leadership reached its peak of politicization, demanding immediate withdrawal of American forces in Vietnam; drastic dismantling of U.S. strategic forces in other parts of the world; support for Black Panther militants; and church funding for political strikes." Prays Ed Robb, "I want a revolution in our [United Methodist] Board of Global Ministries. I want liberation from any misguided leaders who use their positions of influence to support Marxism instead of sharing the Good News of Jesus."

55. Hochstein and O'Rourke, *Report on the Institute on Religion and Democracy*, pp. 21-22, 31 nn. 36-39. See also George Vickers, "What's Left? A Guide to the Sectarian Left," *The Nation*, May 17, 1980, pp. 591-96. Gus Tyler, an official of ILGWU (International Ladies' Garment Workers' Union),

describes the sectarian progress of Max Shachtman as a true Trotskyist's trek from left to right within a complex genealogy of esoteric labor parties in search of a mass following: "Finally, the 'Trots': the Communist League of America (Opposition), begat by the Trotskyists out of the Communist Party . . . [begat] the American Workers Party that lay with the Socialist Party briefly to depart for the Fourth International and beget the Socialist Workers Party, from which Schachtman [an alternative spelling] separated to beget the Workers Party that changed its name to the Independent Socialist League that begat a youth move-ment—the Young Socialist League—that mated with the Young People's So-cialist League to beget the Socialist Youth League with a national membership of 83. These and others passionately shared the same vision of a world blessed with 'peace, plenty and freedom' while engaging in endless internecine warfare waged in institutional poverty amid enthralling dogma." The "others" included the left-leaning Socialist Party, the right-leaning Social-Democrat Federation, and the Student League for Industrial Democracy, from which sprang "the hell raising, heaven-bent Students for a Democratic Society." Gus Tyler, "Comrades in Arms," review of *If I Had a Hammer: The Death of the Old Left and the Birth of the New Left*, by Maurice Isserman, *New York Times Book Review*, Septem-ber 14, 1987, p. 31.

56. For an inspired vision of the Social Democratic movement today, woven into a tribute to Tom Kahn as a "guiding spirit of America's Social Democratic com-munity for over 30 years," see Penn Kemble, "Let the Circle Be Unbroken," *Notes-online*, March 2005, pp. 1-8, http://www.socialdemocrats.org/Notesonline3-9-05.html; and the National Committee of Social Democrats, USA, "The New Social Demo-crats," 2003, pp. 1-5, http://www.socialdemocrats.org/newsocialdemocrats.html.

57. Hochstein and O'Rourke, *Report on the Institute on Religion and Democ-racy*, p. 22.

58. Institute on Religion and Democracy, *Christianity, Democracy, and the Churches Today*, 1982, p. 2.

59. Ibid., p. 21.

60. Hochstein and O'Rourke, *Report on the Institute on Religion and Democ-racy*, pp. 20-21, 31 nn. 25-29. According to Hochstein and O'Rourke, the Smith Richardson Foundation reportedly had ties to the CIA through the foundation's Center for Creative Leadership, which trained CIA staff personnel in a course later transferred to the intelligence agency for in-house use. Scaife was linked to the CIA through his ownership of Forum World Features, a British-based news service closed in 1975 after it was widely identified in the press as a CIA front to counter communist propaganda, according to Karen Rothmyer, "Citizen Scaife," *Columbia Journalism Review*, July–August 1981, p. 44.

61. Hochstein and O'Rourke, *Report on the Institute on Religion and Democ-racy*, pp. 20-21; cf. Steve Askin, "IRD 89% Funded by Right," *National Catholic Reporter*, February 4, 1983, p. 7; Paula Herbut, "Church Council Policies 'Leftist,'

Institute Charges in New Booklet," *Washington Post*, March 19, 1983, p. B6; Leon Howell, "Who Funds IRD?" *Christianity and Crisis*, March 21, 1983, pp. 90–91. Hochstein and O'Rourke (*Report on the Institute on Religion and Democracy*, p. 20) reported that the Smith Richardson Foundation, along with Richard Mellon Scaife, provided at least $25,000 in seed money to the Committee for the Free World—also backed by Penn Kemble's Coalition for a Democratic Majority—at the same time that it funded the IRD's start-up. Subsequent reports focused on Scaife as a major contributor to the IRD. See Public Eye, "Group Watch: Institute on Religion and Democracy," 1989, http://www.publiceye.org/magazine/v15n1/GroupWatch/entries-76.htm. Scaife reportedly contributed some $620 million (in 1999 dollars) to conservative political causes and institutions from 1965 to 1998, gaining notoriety in the 1990s for funding efforts to investigate and impeach President Clinton, according to R. G. Kaiser and I. Chinoy, "The Right's Funding Father: Fighting a War of Ideas," *Washington Post*, May 2, 1999, pp. A1, A23–25. In 1984 the United Methodist Board of Church and Society criticized the IRD for taking funds from a foundation controlled by Scaife. The IRD countered that the GBCS had itself accepted more than $1 million from the Scaife foundation between 1970 and 1976. These Methodist grants for education on population and birth-control issues predated Richard Scaife's takeover of the foundation from a cousin and his redirection of its giving to right-wing political causes, countered the GBCS. See "News of the Church: Methodists Botch Attack on IRD," *National Catholic Reporter*, March 23, 1984. In the 1970s, Smith Richardson likewise redirected its giving to conservative political causes from general social welfare, to which it reverted at the end of the 1990s. See Howell, *United Methodism @ Risk*, p. 104; and Howell, "Religion, Politics, Money and Power," p. 36.

62. Penn Kemble, quoted in Steve Askin, "IRD: Institute Says It Reveals Threat—Others Say It Is Threat—to U.S. Church," *National Catholic Reporter*, February 4, 1983, p. 19.

63. See, for example, the Web site of the Social Democrats, USA, http://www.socialdemocrats.org. Cf. Gary Dorrien, "Michael Harrington: Socialist to the End," *Christian Century*, October 11, 2000, pp. 1002–9.

64. Jack Clark, quoted in Askin, "IRD: Institute Says It Reveals Threat," p. 19. Clark was president of the New York City local of the Democratic Socialist Organizing Committee.

65. Robert McClean, interview, New York City, February 1992, here and below. See, for example, *New America* 18, no. 6 (November–December 1981), a publication of the Social Democrats, USA, for an outline of their distinctive positions on the evil of Soviet communism and the value of Israel as the West's only outpost in the Middle East; their opposition to the "New Politics" of the DSA and to the "new class," held in common with neoconservatives; and their pro-labor stands on domestic policy that mark off the SD/USA from neoconservatives and the Reagan administration.

66. Executive Council of the Industrial Union Department (AFL-CIO), "Resolution on Relationships between Organized Labor and the Church," adopted June 21–22, 1984. See John Herling, "IUD Condemns NLRB and IRD," *John Herling's Labor Letter*, July 14, 1984, pp. 1–2; Jean Caffey Lyles, "Liberal Church Aides Drive Wedge between Unions and Capitol Lobby," Religion News Service, July 10, 1984, p. 3; and Religion News Service, "Labor Denounces IRD," *Christian Century*, August 15–22, 1984, p. 769.

67. Religion News Service, "Labor Denounces IRD," p. 769.

68. Kemble, interview, March 1992.

69. Jessup, interview, March 1992, here and below. Jessup remained at the AFL-CIO until 1998, four years after John J. Sweeney swept Lane Kirkland from the union's presidency. Jessup left to become executive director of the New Economy Information Service (NEIS), a project of the Foundation for Democratic Education—as was the IRD originally under Kemble, then the foundation's president. NEIS "provides information and reviews debate on the impact globalization and technological change has on democracy at home and abroad," in conjunction with the Social Democrats, USA, which Jessup led as president in 2005. See http://www.newecon.org and http://www.socialdemocrats.org.

70. David E. Anderson, "Labor-Church Alliance Imperiled," *Washington Post*, July 16, 1983, p. C10; Russ Schroeder, "Minutes of the Special Board Meeting, Religion and Labor Conference, June 23, 1983," United Labor Agency, Cleveland, OH; Steve Askin, "Church Groups Urge Union 'Distance' Itself from IRD Connection," *National Catholic Reporter*, July 29, 1983, p. 7; Askin, "Churches Question IRD Connection," *In These Times*, August 10–23, 1983, p. 11; David Moberg, "Social Democrats' Christian Crusade," *In These Times*, April 7, 1982, p. 2.

71. Institute on Religion and Democracy, "The Church Left on Workers' Rights: Activists Press Labor on Jessup Role," *Religion and Democracy*, August–September 1983; Lyles, "Liberal Church Aides," p. 3.

72. Jack Sheinkman, ACTWU Secretary-Treasurer, to Thomas R. Donahue, AFL-CIO Secretary-Treasurer, May 23, 1983.

73. Lane Kirkland and his spokesman Murray Seeger, quoted in Robert S. Greenberger, "Divided Unions," *Wall Street Journal*, October 25, 1983, pp. 1, 22.

74. Lane Kirkland to Claire Randall, August 3, 1983, pp. 1–2.

75. Penn Kemble, quoted in Askin, "Church Groups Urge Union."

76. Ibid. See also Askin, "Churches Question IRD Connection," pp. 6, 11.

77. Greenberger, "Divided Unions," pp. 1, 22.

78. Social Democrats, USA, "The Global Vision of Social Democracy," resolution adopted by the national convention of SD/USA, *New America* 18, no. 1 (January–February 1981): 1, 10–11.

79. Social Democrats, USA, "Resolutions: On the 1980 Elections," *The Social Democrat*, Spring 1981, pp. 9–10; and SD/USA, "On Foreign Policy," ibid., pp. 10–13.

80. Robert S. Greenberger, "Divided Unions," p. 22.

81. Kathy Sawyer, "AFL-CIO Toils in Foreign Vineyards," *Washington Post*, November 19, 1983, p. A2. See Douglas Fraser, Jack Sheinkman, and William Winpisinger, Labor Committee in Support of Democracy and Human Rights in El Salvador, "Labor, Terror, and Peace," July 18, 1983, in dissent from AFL-CIO headquarters in rejecting the democratic legitimacy of the El Salvador government and indicting it for wholesale violation of human rights and trade-union freedom, including persecution of nongovernment unions by means of kidnapping, imprisonment, torture, and assassination. Liberal union leaders successfully pressed the AFL- CIO to go on record against further U.S. military aid to the government of El Salvador until it improved human rights conditions. But AFL-CIO headquarters put little of its considerable lobbying power behind anti-intervention efforts—in part, charged its liberal labor critics, because its Latin America arm, the AIFLD, received 90 percent of its funds from the U.S. government and was slated in 1983 to receive from the Reagan administration $2 million in "economic support" funding (defined by law as an adjunct to U.S. military aid), in addition to $10 million yearly in U.S. "development aid" for projects including land-reform programs. Instrumental in this funding was Senator Orrin G. Hatch (R-Utah)—chair of the Senate Labor Committee and otherwise seen as a nemesis of organized labor—because, said a Hatch aide, the AFL-CIO worldwide "has tremendous leverage for political activity compared to, say, CIA covert operations," which often fail; and, the aide added, "the AFL-CIO in general takes foreign policy positions to the right of Ronald Reagan." Quoted in Sawyer, "AFL-CIO Toils in Foreign Vineyards." In a 1981 study, Oxfam-America charged that the land-reform program backed by USAID and AIFLD in El Salvador "excludes the majority of the country's impoverished peasants and has left an estimated 150,000 others with plots of land insufficient to support a single family." It found no evidence that the first $50 million spent by USAID had resulted in any land-ownership titles being transferred, and it compared the program to the "peasant pacification" Phoenix plan in Vietnam. AIFLD executive director William C. Doherty, Jr., countered that 210,000 peasant families had received land, amounting to some two-thirds of all formerly landless peasants, with another 25,000–75,000 families to be helped if the program received additional funding of $425 million proposed for 1981–85, according to "Land Reform a Fraud?" *Christian Century*, February 25, 1981, p. 193.

82. Celia Weisin, president, Local 285 of the Service Employees International Union, quoted in Greenberger, "Divided Unions," p. 22.

83. Cf. Penn Kemble, "The New Anti-union Crusade," *New Republic*, September 19 and 26, 1983, pp. 18–20; and Bob Kuttner, "Can Labor Lead?" *New Republic*, March 12, 1984, pp. 19–25.

84. John J. Sweeney, president of the Service Employees International Union, AFL-CIO, "1983 Labor Day Address," Catholic Labor Institute Breakfast, Los

Angeles, September 5, 1983, pp. 4–5 of speech text. This speech incorporates much of the draft of the AFL-CIO Religion and Labor Conference's "Resolution regarding Attacks on Religious Institutions," which in turn incorporates Sweeney's last sentence quoted here into its final version of October 26, 1983.

85. Institute on Religion and Democracy, "Prospectus for a Church Economic Programs Information Service (CEPIS)," 1984, p. 1; Jean Caffey Lyles, "Capital Gadfly Offers to Help Business Watch Church and Economics," Religion News Service, May 25, 1984, pp. 6–7.

86. Gerda Ray, "Legitimating the Right: The Neoconservatives Build a Base," *Crime and Social Justice* 19 (Summer 1983): 83.

87. Philip R. Newell, Jr., interview, Louisville, KY, June 1992.

88. Don Hewitt, interview with Larry King, *Larry King Live*, CNN 2, December 2, 2002, cited in Howell, *United Methodism @ Risk*, p. 41.

Chapter 6: From Cold War to Culture Wars

1. Diane Knippers, interview, Washington, DC, March 1994, here and below.

2. Coined by Jim Wallis, editor of *Sojourners*, the phrase is cited by James M. Wall in "Anticommunism Binds IRD to White House," an editorial in the *Christian Century* (November 28, 1984, p. 1115) charging that the IRD worked closely with Reagan administration officials to orchestrate campaigns to discredit foreign and domestic opponents of its policies—for example, the Evangelical Committee for Aid and Development in Nicaragua (CEPAD), Nicaragua's Protestant relief agency, along with its supporters in the U.S. mainline churches.

3. Knippers, interview, March 1994.

4. Institute on Religion and Democracy, "Statement for Freedom in El Salvador," 1981, accompanied by a sign-on letter from Edmund Robb of August 5, 1981. Cf. Terry J. Allen, "Public Serpent," *In These Times*, August 6, 2001, p. 4.

5. Institute on Religion and Democracy, "IRD Report: Church Support for Pro-Sandinista Network," 1984, p. 2, accompanied by a petition campaign for "religious freedom in Nicaragua" and announced by an IRD public letter of August 8, 1984.

6. Amy L. Sherman, "Other Voices: Economic Alternatives for Latin America," IRD Economic Studies Program Briefing Paper, 1990, p. 1.

7. Kent R. Hill, interview, Washington, DC, March 1991.

8. Kent R. Hill, letter of August 1, 1986, Washington, DC.

9. Kent R. Hill, preface to Richard J. Neuhaus, *Christianity and Democracy: A Statement of the Institute on Religion and Democracy* (Washington, DC: IRD, 1991).

10. Hill, interview, March 1991, here and below.

11. Robert McClean, interview, New York City, February 1992.

12. Hill, interview, March 1991.

13. *Religion and Democracy*, June 1992, pp. 4–5. The IRD published *Religion and Democracy* some ten times per year until 1993, when it gave way to a quarterly newsletter, *Faith & Freedom*.

14. Hill, interview, March 1991, here and below.

15. Theodore Runyon, interview, Atlanta, GA, March 1994.

16. The IRD circulated a reader survey in its *Religion and Democracy* newsletter of November 1992, with a letter of November 4, 1992, from Kent Hill announcing his resignation as IRD president. He served as president of Eastern Nazarene College in Quincy, Massachusetts, from 1992 to 2001, when he became Sub-Administrator for Europe and Eurasia for the U.S. Agency for International Development under President George W. Bush.

17. Kent R. Hill, *The Soviet Union on the Brink: An Inside Look at Christianity and Glasnost* (Portland, OR: Multnomah Press, 1991); Matthew F. Murphy, *Sowing Confusion among the Flock: Church Leaders and Anti–Gulf War Reasoning* (Washington, DC: IRD, 1991); Frederick P. Jones, ed., *Reading the World: An Integrated Reference Guide to International Affairs* (Washington, DC: IRD, 1992), pp. 7–15; Roy Howard Beck, *Prophets and Politics* (Washington, DC: IRD, 1995), quoting back cover copy.

18. Diane L. Knippers, "Installation Address," October 3, 1993; Institute on Religion and Democracy, "Diane L. Knippers Elected President of IRD," news release, July 14, 1993.

19. Hill, interview, March 1991.

20. Richard Penn Kemble, interview, Washington, DC, March 1992, here and below.

21. Cf. "new economy" themes shared by the Social Democrats, USA (http://www.socialdemocrats.org/newsocialdemocrats.html), David Jessup's New Economy Information Service (NEIS; http://www.newecon.org), and the Democratic Leadership Council, which praised NEIS as created by labor-oriented intellectuals associated with the Social Democrats, USA, to replace "old, class-warfare militancy against capitalism" with "a new, Information Age collaborative strategy" to join unionists and their political allies; see "NDOL.org: New Democrats Online," http://www.ndol.org/ndol_ci.cfm?kaid=170&subsid=297&contentid=3519.

22. Penn Kemble, "Candidates: What Kind of President?" *Religion and Democracy*, June 1992, p. 8.

23. Kemble, interview, March 1992, here and below.

24. Kemble served on the U.S. Board of International Broadcasting under President George H. W. Bush, before President Clinton in 1993 appointed him deputy director of USIA. He later headed USIA as acting director during its merger into the State Department, where he then served as a special representative of the secretary of state, Madeleine Albright, to a new international organization dedicated to bolstering democracies. After eight years in government service at the subcabinet level under Clinton, Kemble returned to Freedom House as

a Senior Scholar, directed the Project on Democracy and the Global Economy, and continued to lead the Social Democrats, USA, as a member of its executive committee. In 2002 Secretary of State Colin Powell named Kemble chair of the International Eminent Persons Group on Slavery, Abduction and Forced Servitude in Sudan. At Freedom House, Kemble subsequently established and led the Transatlantic Democracy Network to bind Europe and North America in promoting democratic institutions, especially in the Middle East, until his death from cancer in 2005.

25. David Corn, "Beltway Bandits," *The Nation*, December 21, 1992, p. 764.

26. Diane Knippers, IRD membership letter, April 1993.

27. Institute on Religion and Democracy, "Is Your Church Abdicating Its Social Responsibility?" 1995.

28. Diane Knippers, "What Is the IRD's Purpose?" membership letter, April 28, 1995.

29. Institute on Religion and Democracy, "Is Your Church Abdicating Its Social Responsibility?"

30. Ibid.

31. Knippers, "What Is the IRD's Purpose?"

32. Ibid.

33. Ibid.

34. Ibid.

35. Leon Howell, "The IRD's New Face(s): Low-Intensity Conflict in the Churches," *Christianity and Crisis*, August 14, 1989, pp. 234–35; Diane Knippers, "We Are Praising God!" IRD fund-raising letter, December 4, 1995.

36. The IRD founded Presbyterians for Democracy and Religious Freedom as a subsidiary group based in Nashville, Tennessee, before merging with it and relocating it to Washington, D.C., in 1985. The IRD established the United Methodist Committee for Faith and Freedom in 1994 and published the first issue of its quarterly newsletter, *United Methodist Action*, in the spring of that year.

37. See the Confessing Movement Web site, http://www.confessingumc.org/information.html; and Leon Howell, *United Methodism @ Risk: A Wake-Up Call* (Kingston, NY: Information Project for United Methodists, 2003), pp. 27–31.

38. James V. Heidinger II, "A Brief History," on the IRD Web site, http://www.ird-renew.org/Issues/IssuesList/cfm?c=20#acr-purpose; Howell, *United Methodism @ Risk*, p. 32.

39. Mark Tooley, *UMAction: The United Methodist Church Is in Crisis!* a brochure and accompanying letter, February 20, 1996.

40. Mark Tooley, "Should We Send More Money to the Board of Church and Society?" *Good News*, January–February 1997, p. 43.

41. Ibid.

42. Jaydee Hanson, interview, Atlanta, GA, November 1998.

43. "Good News Announces New Leadership Initiatives," *Good News* November–December 1999, p. 36.

44. Mark Tooley, UMAction Briefing, September 2001, quoted in Howell, *United Methodism @ Risk*, pp. 68–69.

45. Ibid.

46. Clifton Ives, *Christian Social Action*, July–August 2001, p. 33.

47. Institute on Religion and Democracy, "Reforming America's Churches Project, 2001–2004: Executive Summary," appended to Howell, *United Methodism @ Risk*, pp. 167–70.

48. Ibid., p. 167.

49. Ibid., p. 168.

50. Ibid., pp. 168–69.

51. Ibid., p. 169.

52. Thomas C. Oden, *The Trust Clause Governing Use of Property in the United Methodist Church*, pp. 1–24, http://www.goodnewsmag.org/news/122902TrustClause_FULL.pdf.

53. William Hinson, quoted in Laurie Goodstein, "Conservative Methodists Propose Schism over Gay Rights," *New York Times*, May 7, 2004, p. A20. For further details of the controversy over schism at the 2004 United Methodist General Conference, see chapter 4.

54. Goodstein, "Conservative Methodists Propose Schism."

55. Interview, not for attribution, Atlanta, GA, June 2004.

56. Guidestar, "Institute on Religion and Democracy," 2002, http://www.guidestarbasicinformation.htm.

57. Media Transparency, "The Money behind the Media: Institute on Religion and Democracy, Inc.," 2003, http://www.mediatransparency.org.

58. Ibid.; National Committee for Responsive Philanthropy, "Conservative Foundations Prevail in Shaping Public Policies: New Report Documents Public Policy Impact of 12 Core Foundations," 1997, http://www.ncrp.org/reports, cited by Andrew J. Weaver and Nicole Seibert, "Follow the Money: Documenting the Right's Well-Heeled Assault on the UMC," *Zion's Herald*, January–February 2004, p. 2; available at http://www.zionsherald.com. See also Leon Howell, *Funding the War of Ideas* (Cleveland, OH: United Church Board for Homeland Ministries, 1995); and Howell, *United Methodism @ Risk*.

59. Mark Tooley, interview, December 2003, transcribed in Weaver and Seibert, "Follow the Money," pp. 12–13.

60. Weaver and Seibert, "Follow the Money," p. 8.

61. Ibid., p. 5.

62. C. McMullen, "Beliefs: Cries of the Hawk Not Silenced," *Lakeland (FL) Ledger*, September 2002, cited in Weaver and Seibert, "Follow the Money," p. 5.

63. Tooley, interview, in Weaver and Seibert, "Follow the Money," p. 11.

64. Ibid., p. 12.

65. David Berg, "Commentary: Anti-war Protestants," May 9, 2003, IRD Web site, http://ird-renew.org/news/news.cfm. Self-identified as a television producer, Berg was neither an IRD employee nor a United Methodist.

66. Mark Tooley, "A Methodist President and His Bishops," *Good News*, March 14, 2001, http://www.goodnewsmag.org/news/bushbish_03_14_01.html; Weaver and Seibert, "Follow the Money," p. 3.

67. Mark Tooley, "Flogging the President," *Weekly Standard*, December 6, 2005; and Institute on Religion and Democracy, "A Special Message from Mark Tooley," December 22, 2005, http://www.ird-renew.org, both cited in Andrew J. Weaver, "Neocon Catholics Target Mainline Protestants," Media Transparency, August 11, 2006, p. 5, http://www.mediatransparency.com.

68. Coalition for United Methodist Accountability, "Coalition Planning," press release, September 8, 2000; and "Renewal Groups Established," press release, February 16, 2000, cited in Howell, *United Methodism @ Risk*, p. 34.

69. Institute on Religion and Democracy, "Reforming America's Churches," http://www.ird-renew.org/About/About.cfm, quoted in Weaver and Seibert, "Follow the Money," p. 2.

70. In November 2000, for example, the IRD joined Good News and the Confessing Movement to file a complaint against the Methodist Board of Church and Society and its official periodical, *Christian Social Action*, for violating a church prohibition on pro-homosexuality advocacy by publishing in its issue of November–December 2000 at least ten articles that affirmed the practice of homosexuality. The GBCS was exonerated by a review panel of the Methodist General Council on Finance and Administration, which is charged with responsibility for enforcing paragraph 806.3 of the *Book of Discipline* forbidding any church agency to "give United Methodist funds to any gay caucus or group, or otherwise use such funds to promote the acceptance of homosexuality." The review panel found that *Christian Social Action* had not violated church law but instead had "focused on the life stories and experiences of homosexual persons and their families," to yield valuable insight to a church called to be in ministry with homosexuals, and that the periodical had declined to publish an article that openly called for disobedience to the church's stance. Mark Tooley, "Finance Agency Declines to Act against UM Magazine," *Good News*, May–June 2001, pp. 39–40. The ruling is available at http://umns.umc.org, release no. 122, 2001.

71. Laurie Goodstein, "Methodists Put Pastor on Trial for Declaring Herself a Lesbian," *New York Times*, March 18, 2004, pp. A1, A21; Matthew Preusch and Laurie Goodstein, "Jury of Methodists Clears Gay Minister over a Relationship," *New York Times*, March 21, 2004, p. 14; Preusch, "Verdict for Lesbian Minister Looms over Religious Meeting," *New York Times*, March 22, 2004, p. A16. Twice in the previous four years, clergy panels in the Pacific Northwest region of the United Methodist Church dismissed the charges against Rev. Dammann, but the

national denomination's Judicial Council insisted that the trial go ahead. A jury of thirteen of her fellow ministers decided by a vote of 11-0, with two undecided, that Rev. Dammann had not violated church law. They found that the *Book of Discipline* stated that homosexuality was "incompatible with Christian teaching," but it did not rule on whether homosexual men or women could join the clergy and practice ministry, and it did encourage inclusiveness in the church.

72. Laurie Goodstein, "Lesbian Remains a Methodist Cleric, for Now," *New York Times*, May 5, 2004, p. A18. Cf. Laurie Goodstein and David D. Kirkpatrick, "Conservative Group Amplifies Voice of Protestant Orthodoxy," *New York Times*, May 22, 2004, pp. A1, A12, for a sketch of the IRD's controversial character as drawn by its critics and defenders. In keeping with 2004 General Conference votes against allowing openly gay ministers, and with the appointment of three more-conservative members to its panel of nine, the Judicial Council ruled in October 2005 to defrock a lesbian minister in Philadelphia and to void gay-inclusive resolutions by the Pacific Northwest and California-Nevada conferences as superseded by church laws. The council also voted to reinstate a Virginia pastor suspended for denying membership in his congregation to a gay man, prompting denomination-wide alarm and a unanimous letter of rebuttal from the Methodist Council of Bishops. See chapter 4, note 33.

73. Mark Tooley, "United Methodists Fight over Sex and Much Else," *Faith & Freedom*, Summer–Fall 2004, pp. 7, 9.

74. Jim Winkler, "Publisher's Column," *Christian Social Action*, July–August 2004, p. 2. See also Gretchen Hakola, "General Conference and Justice," *Christian Social Action*, July–August 2004, p. 7.

75. Mark Tooley, quoted in Goodstein, "Methodists Put Pastor on Trial," p. A21.

76. Mark Tooley, ed., UMAction Briefing, Spring 2004, pp. 1–5, here and below.

77. Ibid. See also Mark Tooley, "Who Profits from the Methodist Building?" *Faith & Freedom*, Summer–Fall 2004, p. 6.

78. John Lomperis and Alan Wisdom, "NCC Finds a New Base," *Faith & Freedom*, Spring 2006, pp. 9–10.

79. Ibid.

80. Ed Robb, quoted in Steve Askin, "IRD: Institute Says It Reveals Threat—Others Say It Is Threat—to U.S. Church," *National Catholic Reporter*, February 4, 1983, p. 19.

81. Gerda Ray, "Legitimating the Right: The Neoconservatives Build a Base," *Crime and Social Justice* 19 (Summer 1983): 82.

82. Erik R. Nelson and Alan F. H. Wisdom, *Human Rights Advocacy in the Mainline Protestant Churches (2000–2003): A Critical Analysis* (Washington, DC: Institute on Religion and Democracy, 2004).

83. Institute on Religion and Democracy, "IRD President Knippers' Opening Remarks at Human Rights Report Press Conference," September 27, 2004, p. 1, http://www.ird-renew.org.

84. Institute on Religion and Democracy, "IRD to Release Report Document-ing Imbalance in Mainline Church Human Rights Advocacy," September 23, 2004, http://www.ird-renew.org.

85. National Council of Churches, "NCC General Secretary Responds to IRD Report on Human Rights Advocacy," September 27, 2004, http://www.ncccusa .org/news/04usnews.html.

86. Institute on Religion and Democracy, "IRD Responds to NCC Criticism of Human Rights Report," September 28, 2004, pp. 1–2, http://www.ird-renew.org.

87. Alan Cooperman, "Israel Divestiture Spurs Clash," *Washington Post*, September 29, 2004, p. A8; Keith Peters, "Mainline Churches Selective about Human Rights Abusers," *Family News in Focus*, September 28, 2004, http://www.family .org/cforum/fnif/news.

88. John Leo, "When Churches Head Left," *U.S. News & World Report*, October 18, 2004, p. 81, here and below.

89. National Council of Churches, "NCC's Edgar Blasts U.S. News & World Report for 'Smear' of Protestant Churches' Activism," October 14, 2004, p. 1, http://www.ncccusa.org/news/04usnews.html.

90. The IRD pronounced the cause of divesting from Israel to be "puttering out" across the mainline denominations by mid-2006, but it predicted that the "Religious Left, including Presbyterians and mainline church officials, will certainly look for new avenues to express their hostility towards Israel," according to Mark D. Tooley, "Anti-Israel Divestment Campaign Stalls," *FrontPageMagazine. com*, June 16, 2006. By then, Episcopalians and Lutherans had declined to endorse divestment initiatives. United Methodists had not brought divestment before their General Conference, although their largest regional conference had endorsed it. The United Church of Christ had not implemented the divestment resolution passed by its 2005 General Synod. Presbyterians continued to debate the divest-ment decision passed by their 2004 General Assembly to begin a phased selective divestment in multinational corporations operating in Israel, such as Caterpillar and Motorola, in order to press for an end to the Israeli occupation of Palestine. The IRD tracked the controversy closely, highlighting American Jewish protests calling such resolutions "unconscionable" and "functionally anti-Semitic" for sin-gling out Israel as a human rights abuser while "turning a blind eye to actual abuse in tyrannical regimes around the world," as Rabbi Abraham Cooper of the Simon Wiesenthal Center stated. See Alan Wisdom, "Divesting Presbyterians Raise a Ruckus," *Faith & Freedom*, Winter 2005, p. 12. Critics of the IRD saw it fanning the controversy's flames across the churches and coordinating dissent across de-nominational "renewal groups" joined in the Association for Church Renewal, in-cluding the Biblical Witness Fellowship (BWF) in the UCC. Targeting the UCC's endorsement of divestment and same-sex marriage, the IRD attacked it as "the Church of SpongeBob," as Mark Tooley termed it (*Faith & Freedom*, Summer 2005, pp. 16–17). UCC president John Thomas, in turn, denounced the BWF and

the Evangelical Association of Reformed, Christian and Congregational Churches as "intent on disrupting and destroying our life together" with the "no longer deniable" backing of the IRD as part of its "long term agenda of silencing a progressive religious voice while enlisting the churches in an unholy alliance with right wing politics." See John Lomperis, "UCC President Lashes Out at IRD and Other Renewal Groups," *Faith & Freedom*, Fall 2005, p. 19. Cf. David Runnion-Bareford, "Biblical Witness Fellowship: An Apology to our Jewish Friends and Neighbors for the Action of the United Church of Christ," July 7, 2005, http://www.ird-renew.org, for its charge of UCC anti-Semitism; and Donald Shriver et al., "Presbyterians Concerned for Jewish and Christian Relations: Toward a Just and Lasting Peace in the Middle East," June 2005, http://www.pcjcr.org, for its conciliatory concern in petitioning to reverse the Presbyterian divestment decision—which the 2006 General Assembly voted to do—since it is wrong to single out Israel when "other states and parties in the region are also guilty of serious human rights violations that can and must be addressed." Cf. Anti-Defamation League, "ADL Denounces Presbyterians' Actions on Jews and Israel," July 13, 2004, http://www.adl.org; and the Central Committee of the World Council of Churches, "WCC Central Committee Encourages Consideration of Economic Measures for Peace in Israel/Palestine," February 21, 2005, http://www2.wcc-coe.org.

91. John Leo, "Social Issues Shock Dems," United Press Syndicate, November 8, 2004, http://www.townhall.com/columnists/johnleo.

92. Robert Edgar, quoted in Associated Press, "Liberal Dismayed by 'Moral Values' Claims," November 8, 2004, http://www.pflag-madison.org.

93. Knippers, "What Is the IRD's Purpose?"

94. Alan Wisdom, "IRD Becomes Foil for NCC Fundraising," *Faith & Freedom*, Summer 2005, p. 9, quoting the *New York Times*, May 22, 2005.

95. Alan Wisdom, "IRD Becomes Foil for NCC Fundraising," quoting the NCC's fund-raising letter of June 2005, signed by Bob Edgar. The letter featured the IRD's 2001 pledge to "push for the final dismantling of the National Council of Churches" and its assurance that the IRD, in the institute's own words, "monitors most major gatherings of the National Council of Churches, and when possible the World Council of Churches. We work to discredit these bodies' radical political advocacy and to weaken support for the councils."

96. Weaver, "Neocon Catholics Target Mainline Protestants," p. 1, quoting a story on President Bush's religious views in *Time* magazine, February 7, 2005.

97. Leon Howell, telephone interview, July 1995.

98. Ibid. For related criticism of IRD political organizing in the guise of church reform, see Janice Love, *United Methodism in a World Context: Navigating the Local and the Global*, Occasional Papers, no. 100, United Methodist General Board of Higher Education and Ministry, December 2006, pp. 10–12.

99. The IRD's core staff and board include Diane Knippers, who came to the IRD in 1982 after seven years at Good News and served as IRD's president from

1993 until her death in 2005; and Vice President Alan F. H. Wisdom, a twenty-year IRD veteran who became acting head of staff at that time. Long-standing IRD board members include Richard Neuhaus, Michael Novak, and George Weigel, "Catholic Hawks" with key ties to, respectively, the Institute for Religion and Public Life, the American Enterprise Institute, and the Ethics and Public Policy Center. Methodist evangelicals and Good News activists Edmund Robb, Jr., and then Helen Rhea Stumbo chaired the IRD board through the 1980s and 1990s before turning over the chair to Professor Thomas C. Oden, long active in Good News and a director of the Confessing Movement. Sharing Oden's involvement in the Confessing Movement and his advocacy of schism in the United Methodist Church is Riley Case, a member of the IRD's UMAction advisory board, a leader of the Confessing Movement, and a board member of Good News and contributing editor of *Good News* magazine. Others serving on the IRD board for decades are Ira Gallaway, also a leader of the Confessing Movement and longtime Good News activist; and Rev. Edmund Robb III (son of Edmund Robb, Jr.), a former IRD and Good News staff member and a director of A Foundation for Theological Education, founded by his father with the backing of Good News. See Howell, *United Methodism @ Risk*, pp. 42-44.

100. IRD Board of Directors, "Dr. James Tonkowich Named New IRD President," *Faith & Freedom*, Winter 2006, p. 6.

101. James Tonkowich, "About IRD," 2006, http://www.ird-renew.org.

102. Mark Tooley, "What Is the Fight Really About?" July 30, 2003, http://www.ird-renew.org/About/About.cfm; Tooley, "Report to UM Action Board of Directors," UM Action News, October 7, 2003, http://www.ird-renew.org. See also Weaver and Seibert, "Follow the Money," pp. 7, 10. In 1995 Diane Knippers estimated that the IRD had 1,000-1,100 "partners" who contributed $25 or more per year, including 400 members of the United Methodist Committee for Faith and Freedom, 200 members of the Episcopal Committee on Religion and Freedom, and 350 members of Presbyterians for Democracy and Religious Freedom, according to Leon Howell, "Notes on IRD" (unpublished paper, Washington, DC, 1995), pp. 3-4, based on interviews with Diane Knippers and Alan Wisdom, January 26, 1995. For an estimate that individual donations reduced the IRD's reliance on foundations to about 30 percent in 2001, see Uwe Simeon-Netto, "Faith and Power Profiles: Diane Knippers," United Press International, March 22, 2001, cited in Howell, *United Methodism @ Risk*, p. 43.

103. Howell, *United Methodism @ Risk*, p. 43, based on the IRD's IRS data; Howell, "Notes on IRD," pp. 2-3; Howell, *Funding the War of Ideas*, chap. 5, based on audited financial statements and estimates provided by the IRD. For 2005 data, see Wisdom, "IRD Becomes Foil for NCC Fundraising," p. 9.

104. Howell, *United Methodism @ Risk*, pp. 46-47; Institute on Religion and Democracy, "Reforming America's Churches," p. 168.

105. Weaver and Seibert, "Follow the Money," p. 7.

106. Howell, *United Methodism @ Risk*, pp. 43, 45, 103–5. The Smith Richardson Foundation reoriented its funding policies, and by 2001 it was no longer continuing its pattern of grants to conservative political groups.

107. Ibid., pp. 46–47.

108. Institute on Religion and Democracy, "News: IRD in the Media," http://www.ird-renew.org, searched August 23, 2006.

109. David Horowitz Freedom Center, "Center for the Study of Popular Culture to Become the David Horowitz Freedom Center," July 7, 2006, http://www.frontpagemag.com and http://www.horowitzfreedomcenter.org.

110. Howell, *United Methodism @ Risk*, pp. 43, 45; Howell, *Funding the War of Ideas*, chap. 5.

111. Peter Steinfels, "'Christianity and Democracy': Baptizing Reaganism," *Christianity and Crisis*, March 29, 1983, pp. 84–85, here and below.

112. See Irving Kristol, *On the Democratic Idea in America* (New York: Harper and Row, 1972); Peter Berger, "Ethics and the Present Class Struggle," *Worldview*, April 1978, pp. 6–11; Berger, "The Class Struggle in American Religion," *Christian Century*, February 25, 1981, pp. 194–99; Berger, "The Worldview of the New Class: Secularity and Its Discontents," in *The New Class?* ed. B. Bruce-Briggs, pp. 49–55 (New York: McGraw-Hill, 1981); and related essays by Norman Podhoretz, Jeane J. Kirkpatrick, and others in *The New Class?*

113. See, for example, Steven G. Brint, *In an Age of Experts: The Changing Role of Professionals in Politics and Public Life* (Princeton, NJ: Princeton University Press, 1994); and Daniel Bell, "The New Class: A Muddled Concept," in Bruce-Briggs, *The New Class?* pp. 169–90.

114. Steinfels, "'Christianity and Democracy': Baptizing Reaganism," p. 85.

115. Ibid. In the 1970s, the American Enterprise Institute began sponsoring seminars on economics for church leaders. By 1982, Michael Novak and Robert Benne, both IRD advisers, had published books—Novak's *The Spirit of Democratic Capitalism* (New York: Simon and Schuster, 1982) and Benne's *The Ethic of Democratic Capitalism* (Philadelphia: Fortress Press, 1981)—that offered detailed religious arguments for America's corporate economy. By the later 1980s, a wider range of related conferences and publications on religion, morality, law, and economic issues were being sponsored by the IRD, the Institute on Religion and Public Life under the leadership of Richard Neuhaus, and the Ethics and Public Policy Center under George Weigel, both IRD board members and advisers.

116. Steinfels, "'Christianity and Democracy': Baptizing Reaganism," p. 85.

Chapter 7: Religious Lobbies and Public Churches

1. On United Methodist ecclesiology, see chapter 4, esp. "The Covenant of a Conciliar Church," and the appendix, esp. "A Church to Bring Society Back In."

2. On church, sect, and modern mysticism as forms of ecclesiology grounded in Christology, see Ernst Troeltsch, *The Social Teaching of the Christian Churches* (1911; New York: Harper and Row, 1960), esp. pp. 993–1013; and the appendix to this volume.

3. Interview, not for attribution, March 1997.

4. Thom White Wolf Fassett, interview, March 1992, here and below. All interviews cited in this chapter were conducted in Washington, DC, unless otherwise noted.

5. See Allen D. Hertzke, *Representing God in Washington: The Role of Religious Lobbies in the American Polity* (Knoxville: University of Tennessee Press, 1988); and Robert Booth Fowler and Allen D. Hertzke, *Religion and Politics in America: Faith, Culture, and Strategic Choices* (Boulder, CO: Westview Press, 1995), esp. chap. 3. Cf. Matthew C. Moen, *The Christian Right and Congress* (Tuscaloosa: University of Alabama Press, 1989); and Moen, *The Transformation of the Christian Right* (Tuscaloosa: University of Alabama Press, 1992).

6. Fassett, interview, March 1992.

7. Jay Lintner, interview, March 1997, here and below.

8. John C. Green, "Religion and Politics in the 1990s: Confrontations and Coalitions," in *Religion and American Politics: The 2000 Election in Context*, ed. Mark Silk, pp. 19–40 (Hartford, CT: Pew Program on Religion and the News Media / Center for the Study of Religion in Public Life, Trinity College, 2000).

9. Jaydee Hanson, interview, Atlanta, GA, November 1998, here and below.

10. Interview, not for attribution, March 1996.

11. Ruth Flower, interview, March 1996, here and below.

12. Mark A. Chaves, "Secularization as Declining Religious Authority," *Social Forces* 72, no. 3 (March 1994): 749–75.

13. Lintner, interview, March 1997, here and below.

14. Gretchen Eick, interview, June 1991, here and below.

15. Bob Tiller, interview, January 1992.

16. Lintner, interview, March 1997, here and below. Note the debated disjunction between increased conflict within mainline denominations such as United Methodism and the UCC over church stands on "peace-and-justice" issues such as abortion, gay ordination, and welfare spending; and membership losses in mainline denominations due mostly to declining fertility rates, not moral controversy or political partisanship. See chapter 3, note 59.

17. Section 501(c)3 of the IRS tax code defines the tax-exempt status of the denominational boards and agencies maintaining offices in Washington for religious advocacy to prohibit their participation in electoral politics in behalf of candidates for office and to delimit their participation on related issues to 20 percent of their annual budget.

18. Interfaith Impact Alliance Foundation, *Briefing Guide* (Washington, DC, 1996), pp. 17–20.

19. Eick, interview, June 1991.

20. Cf. Paul DiMaggio, John Evans, and Bethany Bryson, "Have Americans' Social Attitudes Become More Polarized?" *American Journal of Sociology* 102, no. 3 (November 1996): 690–755; and Pew Research Center for the People and the Press, *Evenly Divided and Increasingly Polarized: 2004 Political Landscape* (Washington, DC: Pew Research Center, 2003).

21. Ruth Flower, interview, October 1996, here and below.

22. Interfaith Action for Economic Justice, "The Poor Have Suffered Enough" (Washington, DC, 1982).

23. Interfaith Action for Economic Justice, "Statement on Poverty" (Washington, DC, 1982).

24. See the appendix for contrasting conceptions of justice set in ecclesiological context.

25. Cf. Joan Huber and William Form, *Income and Ideology: An Analysis of the American Political Formula* (New York: Free Press, 1977); and Robert E. Lane, "Fear of Equality," in *Political Ideology: Why the American Common Man Believes What He Does*, pp. 57–81 (New York: Free Press, 1962).

26. See Jim Winkler, "Publisher's Column," *Christian Social Action*, March–April 2003; and Winkler, "Publisher's Column," *Christian Social Action*, July–August 2003, p. 2.

27. Elenora Giddings Ivory, interview, March 1993, here and below.

28. Lintner, interview, March 1997.

29. Cf. United Methodist General Board of Church and Society, *Faithful Witness on Today's Issues: Human Rights* (Washington, DC: GBCS, 1990), for its grounding of human rights in biblical ideals of creation in the image of God and a covenantal community that shares responsibility for human needs through living in interdependent relationship with God and neighbor; and National Conference of Catholic Bishops, *Economic Justice for All: Pastoral Letter on Catholic Social Teaching and the U.S. Economy* (Washington, DC: U.S. Catholic Conference, 1986), esp. chap. II.B.2, for its formulation of human rights as prerequisites for a dignified life in a just community that enables all persons to flourish through sharing participation in the common good and responsibility for it.

30. Interview, not for attribution, March 1996, here and below.

31. Flower, interview, October 1996, here and below.

32. See Jennifer Hochschild, *What's Fair? American Beliefs about Distributive Justice* (Cambridge, MA: Harvard University Press, 1981), on difficulty in interrelating ethics of rights, needs, and earning. See also Robert N. Bellah, Richard Madsen, William M. Sullivan, Ann Swidler, and Steven M. Tipton, *The Good Society* (New York: Knopf, 1991), esp. chap. 4; Michael J. Sandel, *Democracy's Discontent: America in Search of a Public Philosophy* (Cambridge, MA: Harvard University Press, 1996), on related forms of cultural and ethical contrariety between liberal and republican public philosophies; and John W. Meyer, "Self

and Life Course: Institutionalization and Its Effects," in *Institutional Structure: Constituting State, Society, and the Individual*, by George M. Thomas, John W. Meyer, Francisco O. Ramirez, and John Boli, pp. 242–60 (Newbury Park, CA: Sage Publications, 1987), regarding the social multiplication and diversification of rights.

33. See, for example, Ken Home, "Hungry for Food and Economic Justice," *Christian Social Action*, January–February 2000, pp. 14–16, for related arguments for the social good of legislation to raise the minimum wage.

34. Eick, interview, June 1991, here and below.

35. Hanson, interview, November 1998.

36. Interfaith Action for Economic Justice, "The Poor Have Suffered Enough."

37. Flower, interview, March 1996.

38. See Green, "Religion and Politics in the 1990s," regarding moral and religious differences on key social issues.

39. Lintner, interview, March 1997, here and below.

40. Douglas C. Meeks, *God the Economist* (Philadelphia: Fortress Press, 1989), marks one promising effort to rethink Christian economic theology in terms true to Anglo-Protestant tradition and to contemporary American society. So does Jon P. Gunnemann, "Capital Ideas," *Religion and Values in Public Life, Harvard Divinity School Bulletin*, Winter 1999, reprinted in *Religion and Values in Public Life: Anthology/2000*, pp. 97–109 (Cambridge, MA: Center for the Study of Values in Public Life, Harvard Divinity School, 2000).

41. Robert H. Frank, "Do We Need More, Bigger Cars or Better Schools?" *New York Times*, July 31, 1999, p. A27; Richard B. Freeman, *The New Inequality: Creating Solutions for Poor America*, ed. Joshua Cohen and Joel Rogers for *Boston Review* (Boston: Beacon Press, 1999).

42. See, for example, Christian Smith, *Resisting Reagan: The U.S. Central America Peace Movement* (Chicago: University of Chicago Press, 1996), regarding religious efforts to resist the Contra war and related Latin American policies of the Reagan administration; and Sharon Delgado, "On the Front Lines at the Battle in Seattle," *Christian Social Action*, January–February 2000, pp. 4–9, regarding participation by religious groups in 1999 protests against the World Trade Organization in Seattle.

43. Arthur Keys, Jr., interview, December 1997.

44. Ruth Flower, interview, March 1992.

45. Philip R. Newell, Jr., interview, Louisville, KY, June 1992, here and below.

46. Lintner, interview, March 1997, here and below.

47. Eick, interview, June 1991, here and below.

48. Paulo Freire, *Pedagogy of the Oppressed* (New York: Herder and Herder, 1970), defines conscientization as a liberating process of mutual learning among democratic equals to enable persons to "name the world" as social and historical

subjects. Liberation theologies conceive this as a process of becoming human in solidarity with God and with the poor that typically takes place in small "basic communities."

49. Interview, not for attribution, March 1997.

50. Jay Lintner, interview, March 1996.

51. Eick, interview, June 1991.

52. See Hertzke, *Representing God in Washington*; and Moen, *The Transformation of the Christian Right*.

53. Lintner, interview, March 1996.

54. Jay Lintner, interview, March 1994.

55. Timothy L. Smith, *Revivalism and Social Reform in Mid-Nineteenth Century America* (Nashville, TN: Abingdon Press, 1957).

56. See, for example, the Children's Defense Fund Web site, http://www .childrensdefense.org, for this registered logo.

57. Lintner, interview, March 1997.

58. Ibid.

59. Flower, interview, March 1997.

60. See Bellah et al., *The Good Society*, chap. 6; Hertzke, *Representing God in Washington*; and Robert Wuthnow, *The Restructuring of American Religion: Society and Faith since World War II* (Princeton, NJ: Princeton University Press, 1988), chap. 6.

61. Flower, interview, March 1997.

62. Interview, not for attribution, March 1994.

63. Flower, interview, March 1997.

64. See Arthur R. Simon, *Bread for the World* (New York: Paulist Press, 1975), and http://www.bread.org. Simon, a Lutheran pastor and brother of former senator Paul Simon (D- Ill.), led BFW until 1991, when its presidency passed to David Beckmann, a clergyman, economist, and former World Bank official.

65. Flower, interview, March 1997.

66. Ibid.

67. David Saperstein, interview, March 1994, here and below.

68. See chapter 8 on the origins of Interfaith Action for Economic Justice in the Presbyterian Taskforce on Hunger and Food Policy.

69. Eick, interview, June 1991.

Chapter 8: The Challenge of Ecumenical Advocacy

1. See chaps. 2 and 7; and Robert N. Bellah, Richard Madsen, William M. Sullivan, Ann Swidler, and Steven M. Tipton, *The Good Society* (New York: Knopf, 1991), chap. 6, "The Public Church," pp. 185ff. Cf. Mary Ann Glendon, *Rights Talk* (New York: Free Press, 1991).

2. Mary Cooper, "National IMPACT: A Summary," in *Advocates for Justice* (Washington, DC: Interfaith Action for Economic Justice, 1991), pt. 1, p. 3.

3. Martin McLaughlin, *Advocates for Justice*. This thirty-eight-page history of Interfaith Action for Economic Justice was published under the organization's auspices in loose-leaf form. Mary Cooper and Christie L. Goodman contributed separately authored, titled, and paginated sections to this history, as cited above and below in notes 2 and 29, respectively.

4. A month before forming the Taskforce on World Hunger, many of its founders and supporters took part in the Aspen Consultation on Global Justice and subscribed to the "Statement of Conscience by Christians and Jews" that it issued, which pointed out the central role of U.S. policies, institutions, and ways of living in the "ongoing and global catastrophe of famine, hunger, and malnutrition." It stressed that "it is the ethical responsibility of all persons, but in a very special way of the American people, not only to seek immediate remedies and deploy massive resources to halt the present catastrophe, but also to halt and then reverse the present process, which is continuing to aggravate the injustice prevalent on our globe." McLaughlin, *Advocates for Justice*, pp. 7–8.

5. The Washington Interreligious Staff Council itself originated and developed in response to the expanded social-welfare role of the federal government during the 1960s within a polity already growing more crowded with denominational and religiously related issue groups. Thus WISC aimed to "maximize the resources and impact of the religious community in the federal legislative process" by helping its members "avoid duplications of efforts and by providing a forum in which strategy could be developed by specialists who could call on colleagues in other fields for assistance," coordinate their testimony before congressional committees, and "reach larger groups of constituents at the grassroots." Cooper, "National IMPACT," p. 3.

6. McLaughlin, *Advocates for Justice*, pp. 9–10.

7. Ibid.

8. Jay Lintner, interview, March 1991. All interviews cited in this chapter were conducted in Washington, DC, unless otherwise noted.

9. WISC, by comparison, was a looser, broader, unincorporated umbrella body for moderate-to-liberal religious groups with Washington offices working on Capitol Hill, and so it remains. Its members included representatives of national denominations, regional religious organizations, and various religiously funded single-issue groups such as the Churches' Center for Theology and Public Policy and the Washington Office on Africa. Its aims embraced "connectedness, problem solving, information sharing and community building" among staff members of Washington offices of religious communities and committees. Unlike IMPACT and Interfaith Action, "WISC has no staff, no board, no budget, no priority issues, no strategies, no policies, no lobbying, no mailing lists, no media work," in the words of its 1990 chair, Robert Tiller of the American Baptist Church, in a March 1993 interview. It

did not speak to or for anyone in its own name. IMPACT, likewise, did not lobby, define policy positions, or speak in its own name. But it had a staff, board, and budget of its own, created to serve the denominational offices and religious agencies who made up its members. IMPACT was supported primarily by the mainline Protestant denominations and secondarily by individual members who subscribed to its literature and contributed to its organization at $25 annually as Christian citizens and grassroots moral constituents, to be mobilized in behalf of legislation on the model of those mobilized during the battles for civil rights legislation in the 1960s. In 1975 IMPACT began to organize its individual members into state-by-state affiliates, known as state IMPACTs.

10. McLaughlin, *Advocates for Justice*, p. 10.

11. Ibid.

12. George Chauncey, June 5, 1975, quoted in McLaughlin, *Advocates for Justice*, p. 21.

13. Ibid., p. 11.

14. McLaughlin, *Advocates for Justice*, p. 11.

15. The lion's share of U.S. food aid should shift from the government-to-government program of Title I to the food-donation program of Title II, insisted the Taskforce, with allocation criteria tightened in favor of the poorest countries and the law's self-help provisions bolstered in practice. By the end of 1976, the Taskforce had drafted major policy statements on its four lead issues and recommended related action to the Carter-Mondale transition team. It prepared a voting record on the Ninety-fourth Congress on a full range of hunger issues for IMPACT, met requests for thirty thousand additional copies, fielded hundreds of calls on its own toll-free phone line, and published its own series of Food Policy Notes (six in 1976, thirty-five in 1978), distributed directly to regional and local hunger groups nationwide. By 1980, Taskforce representatives had testified before the Presidential Commission on World Hunger and six congressional committees, written formal letters to members of Congress on thirty-four occasions, and engaged them directly in hundreds of office visits. Internationally, the Taskforce took part in the 1979 UN Conference on Trade and Development (UNCTAD-V) in Manila, the World Food Council, and the World Conference on Agrarian Reform and Rural Development. In the churches, the Taskforce supported and distributed through IMPACT some fifty thousand copies of three major publications on world hunger by 1980, and led sessions in the national briefings that IMPACT and WISC put on for religious leaders and activists each spring in Washington, D.C.

16. McLaughlin, *Advocates for Justice*, p. 12.

17. Ibid., p. 13.

18. Ibid., p. 14.

19. See Ruth Flower, *Will Poor Americans Go Hungry in the 1980s?* (Washington, DC, 1982), a study of six federal food programs, including Food Stamps, National School Lunch, Elderly Nutrition, and the Special Supplemental Food

Program for Women, Infants, and Children (WIC). It judged that all six programs had succeeded strongly in reducing U.S. hunger yet now faced critical funding cuts from the Reagan administration in the face of congressional inaction. See McLaughlin, *Advocates for Justice*, pp. 15–16.

20. McLaughlin, *Advocates for Justice*, pp. 17, 27.

21. Quoted in McLaughlin, *Advocates for Justice*, p. 26. To address food policy and international affairs, for example, Interfaith Action co-sponsored a briefing titled "The Crisis in Foreign Aid" just prior to 1985 Senate action on foreign aid appropriations. The briefing was followed up by a congregational workbook on the global debt crisis, *Putting People First* (November 1987), and an emergency meeting of religious leaders on the "crisis of money and influence" between the United States and the UN.

22. McLaughlin, *Advocates for Justice*, pp. 18–19, 27.

23. Chauncey, 1985, quoted in McLaughlin, *Advocates for Justice*, p. 16.

24. Arthur Keys became executive director of Interfaith Action in March 1985, and Gretchen Eick became national director of IMPACT in October 1987.

25. McLaughlin, *Advocates for Justice*, p. 28.

26. Under Gretchen Eick's direction in 1988, IMPACT began the Leadership Network, a pilot program in grassroots organizing by congressional district to train local religious activists nationwide in advocacy skills, create a book and related video (*Concern into Action: An Advocacy Guide for People of Faith*), and assist in forming local interreligious community-development coordinating committees, linked by networks with local councils of churches and other advocacy groups. This program overlapped with work already being done by Interfaith Action's work groups on "domestic human needs" and "women in poverty," according to Interfaith Impact leaders. Interfaith Action was meanwhile seeking to develop local constituencies by working more directly with local voter-registration groups, with local and regional councils of churches, and with local advocacy groups via consultations and "grassroots lobby days" on farm policy, international development, and the third-world debt crisis. Interfaith Action developed a new strategy for publications in 1988 to serve each of its work groups, including economic-justice issues on which it then had a contract to provide information and literature for IMPACT publications. This move seemed to place it in competition with IM-PACT in reaching individual subscribers and thereby recruiting individual members. See Interfaith Action for Economic Justice, "Contract between IMPACT and Interfaith Action," June 27, 1988; IMPACT, "Programs of National IMPACT and the IMPACT Education Fund," 1989; Interfaith Action, minutes of board meetings, May 15–16, 1986, and November 1988; and Interfaith Action, "IMPACT and Interfaith Action Dynamics and Interests," memo, May 7, 1988. See also McLaughlin, *Advocates for Justice*, p. 17; and Arthur Boyd Keys, Jr., "Crisis in Religious Advocacy" (D.Min. thesis, Candler School of Theology, Emory University, 1992), pp. 119–21.

27. National Association of Ecumenical Staff formed a working group on public-policy advocacy in 1986, which counted some sixty-six national groups they worked with during 1988 on projects of public advocacy and education.

28. See Walter L. Owensby, "Toward a More Integrated Washington Public Policy Program," Presbyterian Church in the USA (Washington, DC, May 14, 1986); and Keys, "Crisis in Religious Advocacy," p. 123.

29. Christie L. Goodman, "Interfaith IMPACT," in *Advocates for Justice*, p. 36.

30. "Interfaith Impact for Justice and Peace: Program," draft document, September 7, 1990.

31. Arthur B. Keys, Jr., "The Significance of Interfaith Impact" (D.Min. thesis proposal, Candler School of Theology, Emory University, January 15, 1992).

32. Arthur Boyd Keys, "Ecumenical Advocacy: What Future?" *Christianity and Crisis*, August 14, 1989, pp. 339–42, esp. 341.

33. Keys, "Crisis in Religious Advocacy," p. 121.

34. Ibid.

35. Keys, "Ecumenical Advocacy."

36. Ibid.

37. Interfaith Impact, "Draft for October 9, 1990 Vote," goals 3F, 3G, and 5B. Board members also discussed recommendations from a professional planning and marketing consultant for a development plan to sharpen Interfaith Impact's program and image. It should pare down its publications and market more of them for profit, especially to nonmember congregations and other nonprofit organizations. It should explore the profit-making possibilities of its annual briefing and likewise consider plans for a weekly television show on public issues. Senior staff positions should be created to focus on membership and fund-raising, backed by direct-mail campaigns and fund-raising events aimed at "high dollar donations." Program staff should be actively involved in fund-raising, including project grants from foundations, unions, and denominations, in order to raise most of their own salaries. See Judith R. Mark, "Preliminary Recommendations for Interfaith Impact Development Plan," October 5, 1990.

38. Such development promised in the longer term to strengthen the mainline denominations themselves, anticipated Keys. In 1990–91, Interfaith Impact under his leadership proposed a project to study fifty to a hundred mainline congregations highly active on social issues. It would analyze the quality of their activism in relation to their social composition and the growth, decline, or stability of their membership in light of then-current academic research into declines in the membership of "liberal" and "moderate" churches while their "conservative" counterparts grew, coincident with cleavage between cultural liberals and conservatives within the large mainline denominations. The Interfaith project intended to test the hypothesis of "captive congregations" in the liberal churches, deserted by baby boomers in particular because "they do not see the churches doing anything of real value," according to James Davidson, "Captive Congregations," in *The Political*

Role of Religion in the United States, ed. Stephen D. Johnson and Joseph B. Tamney (Boulder, CO: Westview Press, 1986), p. 252, quoted in Arthur Keys, "Concept Paper: Research on Effectiveness of Mainline Religious Institutions in Influencing U.S. Public Policy" (Interfaith Impact, 1990), p. 2. By focusing on cases of growing congregations responding to the social concerns of their community, the project sought to discover how advocacy groups such as Interfaith Impact could join with denominational agencies in "helping mainline religion to 'capture' both the affluent and not-so-well-off baby boomers," especially religious dropouts raised in mainline churches, by testing three ways of moving congregations to engage in social concerns and influence public policy: by stressing biblical motivations for public advocacy, stressing denominational loyalty and teaching, and stressing specific social issues such as international peace, domestic poverty, civil rights, and the environment. Keys, "Concept Paper," pp. 2–5.

39. Jay Lintner, "The Future of Interfaith Impact," Interfaith Impact board memo, July 1991, here and below.

40. A third perspective on the future of Interfaith Impact came from a self-described group of "marginal but creative" staff members of the church offices in Washington appointed to a "dream team" to envision what the new organization should look like. Their perspective enjoyed less organized backing than other positions from the boards of directors of Interfaith Action and IMPACT, but its stress on collegial "work groups" appealed to many of their fellow staff members. The dream team's report looked forward to a community of religious lobbyists and activists, drawn from the church offices based in Washington, taking part in work groups focused on issues that their offices asked them to cover, for example, civil and religious liberties. Hemmed in by "fewer boards, less confusion and simpler processes," yet better facilitated by new forms of central administrative support, these work groups would prepare and publish "action alerts" to mobilize church activists, direct phone banks, commission educational videos, and execute media strategies. A central entity would support but not govern their communication with state-level IMPACT groups and other local organizers and activists in order to "empower local people in religious or interfaith organizations to affect public policy." See Ruth Flower, Faith Evans, Larry Hollar, Lynn Landsberger, Sally Timmel, Andrea Young, Karen Woodall, Ralph Paige, Kent Ward, and elmira nazombe, "Report of the Dream Team," October 9, 1990, pp. 1–4.

41. Interview, not for attribution, March 1992.

42. Jay Lintner, interview, March 1992.

43. Ibid.

44. James Bell, interview, March 1993, here and below.

45. See Dean R. Hoge and David A. Roozen, eds., *Understanding Church Growth and Decline: 1950–1978* (New York: Pilgrim Press, 1979); and Michael Hout, Andrew Greeley, and Melissa J. Wilde, "The Demographic Imperative in

Religious Change in the United States," *American Journal of Sociology* 107, no. 2 (2001): 468–500.

46. Thom White Wolf Fassett, interview, March 1994.

47. Kay Dowhower, interview, March 1994, here and below.

48. Mary Cooper, interview, March 1994.

49. Mary Cooper, interview, March 1995, here and below.

50. Interview, not for attribution, March 1994.

51. Jay Lintner, interview, March 1994.

52. Arthur Keys, personal communication, December 1996; see also Keys, "Crisis in Religious Advocacy," pp. 126–27.

53. Keys, personal communication, December 1996; and Keys, "Crisis in Religious Advocacy," pp. 126–27.

54. Interview, not for attribution, March 1994.

55. Kim Bobo, interview, Atlanta, GA, November 1998.

56. Keys, "Crisis in Religious Advocacy," pp. 126–37.

57. elmira nazombe, interview, March 1993.

58. Keys, "Crisis in Religious Advocacy," p. 137.

59. Ibid., p. 167.

60. Interview, not for attribution, March 1994.

61. Interview, not for attribution, March 1994.

62. Joan Brown Campbell, interview, New York City, January 1997, here and below.

63. Interreligious Health Care Access Campaign (IHCAC), "Working Principles," Washington, DC, 1991; and "Talking Points," Washington, DC, 1992.

64. IHCAC, "History," Washington, DC, 1993, here and below.

65. IHCAC, "Universal Health Care Advocacy," Washington, DC, 1993.

66. Ibid.

67. Ruth Flower, interview, March 1994.

68. Interview, not for attribution, March 1996.

69. See Michael Wines and Robert Pear, "The Clinton Record: Health Care," *New York Times*, July 30, 1996, pp. A1, A8; and Theda Skocpol, *Clinton's Health Security Plan* (New York: W. W. Norton, 1996).

70. Joe Klein, "The Religious Left," *Newsweek*, July 25, 1994, p. 23; Klein, "Chafee at the Bit," *Newsweek*, August 1, 1994, p. 23.

71. David Corn, "Capitol Dunciad," *The Nation*, July 18, 1994, p. 78.

72. AME Bishop H. H. Brookings, quoted in Adam Clymer, "The Health Care Debate," *New York Times*, August 5, 1994, p. A8.

73. Interview, not for attribution, August 1994.

74. Ibid.

75. Interview, not for attribution, August 1994.

76. Interview, not for attribution, August 1994.

77. Cooper, interview, March 1994.

78. Cooper, interview, March 1995.

79. IHCAC, letter to U.S. Senate, August 1994.

80. Ibid.

81. Interview, not for attribution, March 1995.

82. Joan Brown Campbell, NCC statement on healthcare reform, Washington, DC, August 1994.

83. Interview, not for attribution, August 1994.

84. Campbell, interview, January 1997, here and below.

85. Interview, not for attribution, March 1997.

86. See chapter 10.

87. Francis X. Clines, "A Religious Tilt toward the Left," *New York Times*, September 16, 1996, pp. A1, A8.

88. Jim Wallis, "Hearts and Minds: No Ways Tired," *Sojourners Magazine*, November–December 1996, 7–8.

89. See chapter 9.

Chapter 9: Members of One Body

1. Jay Lintner, interview, March 1997. All interviews cited in this chapter were conducted in Washington, DC, unless otherwise noted.

2. Interview, not for attribution, May 2003.

3. Bob Tiller, interview, March 1993, here and below.

4. Thom White Wolf Fassett, interview, March 1993.

5. Ruth Flower, interview, March 1993.

6. Jay Lintner, interview, March 1993, here and below.

7. Elenora Giddings Ivory, interview, March 1993.

8. Ruth Flower, interview, March 1994, here and below.

9. David Saperstein, interview, March 1994, here and below.

10. Jay Lintner, interview, October 1996.

11. See chapter 8 on Interfaith Impact for Justice and Peace.

12. Lintner, interview, March 1997.

13. Ibid.

14. National Council of Churches, "Statement of Faith," from the preamble to the NCC constitution, http://www.ncccusa.org/about/about_ncc.htm.

15. National Council of Churches, "Statement on Public Policy Priorities," New York, December 17, 1996.

16. Ibid.

17. National Council of Churches, "Churches Plan Policy Initiatives," press release, New York, December 17, 1996.

18. Ibid.

19. Joan Brown Campbell, interview, New York City, January 1997, here and below.

20. Mainline Protestant denominations with offices in Washington include the United Methodist Church, the Presbyterian Church (USA), the United Church of Christ, the Episcopal Church, the American Baptist Church, Church of the Brethren, and the Society of Friends. The NCC's Advisory Committee on Public Policy Ministries included members from all of these denominations. It had additional members from several churches without Washington offices: the Reformed Church in America, the Greek Orthodox Church, the African Methodist Episcopal Church, and the Progressive National Baptist Convention. Some "peace churches," such as the Mennonites, and some more evangelical Protestant denominations, such as the Southern Baptist Convention, maintain Washington offices but do not belong to the National Council of Churches. The Unitarian Universalist Association, confessionally precluded from membership in the National Council of the Churches of Christ, also has a Washington office.

21. Albert L. Pennybacker, interview, February 1996, here and below.

22. Campbell, interview, January 1997, here and below.

23. Interview, not for attribution, April 1997.

24. Elenora Giddings Ivory, interview, April 1997, here and below.

25. Jay Lintner, interview, April 1997, here and below.

26. Interview, not for attribution, April 1997.

27. Interview, not for attribution, April 1997.

28. Interview, not for attribution, April 1997.

29. Ibid.

30. Lintner, interview, April 1997.

31. Interview, not for attribution, April 1997.

32. Lintner, interview, April 1997, here and below.

33. Campbell, interview, January 1997, here and below.

Chapter 10: The Mainline in Motion

1. Interfaith Alliance, "The Interfaith Alliance," July 1994.

2. See Mark Tooley, "A PAC in 'Mainline' Robes," *Faith & Freedom*, Spring 1997, pp. 10–11.

3. Interfaith Alliance, "Mission Statement," July 1994.

4. Richard L. Berke, "Mainline Religion Forms Lobby for 'Alternate' View," *New York Times*, July 14, 1994, p. A12.

5. Interfaith Alliance, "Statement by Dr. Herbert D. Valentine," July 14, 1994.

6. Interfaith Alliance, undated letter (TIA6091C08), 1994.

7. Ibid.

8. Interfaith Alliance, "Statement of Rabbi Arthur Hertzberg," July 14, 1994.

9. Interfaith Alliance, "Statement by Dr. Herbert D. Valentine."

10. Herbert D. Valentine, telephone interview, August 1994.

11. Laurie Goodstein, "Christian Coalition Has Big Plans for Sunday: Clergy Group Sets Counteroffensive," *Washington Post*, November 3, 1994, p. A1.

12. Ibid.

13. Interfaith Alliance, mailing, May 1995.

14. Interfaith Alliance, *The Light*, Autumn 1996, pp. 1-2.

15. Interfaith Alliance, "Candidate Pledge of Civility," September 1996.

16. Larry Witham, "Clerics Push Civility in Politics," *Washington Times*, September 22, 1996, p. A4.

17. Interfaith Alliance, *The Light*, Autumn 1996, p. 4.

18. Interfaith Alliance, *The Light*, Spring 1997, pp. 3-4.

19. David S. Broder, "Christian Coalition Guides Challenged," *Washington Post*, July 21, 1996, p. A22.

20. Ibid.

21. Interfaith Alliance, "Mission Statement," Autumn 1996.

22. Interfaith Alliance, *The Light*, Spring 1997, pp. 1-2.

23. Ibid.

24. Quoted in Tooley, "A PAC in 'Mainline' Robes."

25. Ibid.

26. Jay Lintner, interview, Washington, DC, March 1997.

27. Joan Brown Campbell, interview, New York City, January 1997, here and below.

28. Jay Lintner, then head of the UCC's Washington office, and the NCC's Albert Pennybacker co-chaired the interfaith working group Religious Leaders for Campaign Finance Reform, housed in the Washington office of the NCC. Sparked by 1997 coverage in Capitol Hill's *Roll Call* and endorsement by former senator Bill Bradley on *Meet the Press*, the churches' campaign attracted collaboration and funding from public-interest groups such as Common Cause and Public Citizen. The passage of campaign finance legislation in 2001-2 demonstrated to mainline-church leaders in Washington the efficacy of such flexible, tenacious ecumenical advocacy in sustained partnership with a larger network of public-interest and civic groups.

29. Pat Robertson, quoted in Gustav Niebuhr, "Christian Group Vows to Exert More Influence on the GOP," *New York Times*, November 7, 1996, p. B10.

30. Ibid.

31. Christian Coalition voting data, from a Wirthlin Worldwide Poll ($n = 1030$) compared to a Voter News Service poll ($n = 16,359$), cited in Gustav Niebuhr, "Religion Journal," *New York Times*, November 9, 1996, p. 13.

32. See, for example, John C. Green, Corwin E. Smidt, James L. Guth, and Lyman A. Kellstedt, *The American Religious Landscape and the 2004 Presidential*

Vote: Increased Polarization (Washington, DC: Pew Forum on Religion and Public Life, 2005); and John C. Green, *The Fifty Percent Solution: The 2000 Election and the New Religious Order* (Akron, OH: Bliss Institute of Applied Politics, University of Akron, 2001).

33. Cf. Christian Coalition of America, "About Us," http://www.christiancoalition .com/about.cfm; Hoover's Online Business Information Authority, "Christian Coalition of America Fact Sheet," http://www.hoovers.com/factsheet.xhtml; People for the American Way, "Right Wing Watch: Christian Coalition," 1999–2003, http://www.pfaw.org/pfaw/general; and Interfaith Alliance, "About Us," http:// www.interfaithalliance.org/About.

34. People for the American Way, "Right Wing Watch."

35. The Interfaith Alliance sent out more than thirty-five thousand such letters in 2002, according to Interfaith Alliance, "Clergy Ask Houses of Worship Not to Distribute Partisan Voter Guides," October 31, 2002, http://www.interfaithalliance .org/News/News.cfm?ID=4445&c=37. See also People for the American Way, "Right Wing Watch." Former congressman Randy Tate gave up his role replacing Ralph Reed as executive director of the Christian Coalition in order to become its chief lobbyist in Washington in 1999. Departing at the same time was Chuck Cunningham, the coalition's longtime national director of field operations and architect of its voter guides and grassroots mobilization efforts, along with the coalition's chief operating officer and several key state directors.

36. Jim Rutenberg, "With Marriage Ban in Senate, Conservatives Keep Score," *New York Times*, June 6, 2006, p. A15.

37. David D. Kirkpatrick, "Warily, a Religious Leader Lifts His Voice in Politics," *New York Times*, May 13, 2004, p. A21.

38. Interfaith Alliance, "About Us."

39. Interfaith Alliance, "Multifaith Nation Turns on Lights Memorial Day Eve," May 26, 2004, http://www.interfaithalliance.org.

40. Interfaith Alliance, "Interfaith Leaders Call for More than Apologies to Iraqis," May 7, 2004.

41. David D. Kirkpatrick, "G.O.P. Seeking Congregations for Bush Effort," *New York Times*, June 3, 2004, pp. A1, A18; Interfaith Alliance, "Bush-Cheney '04 Commits 'an Astonishing Abuse of Religion,'" June 2, 2004.

42. Interfaith Alliance, "One Nation, Many Faiths. Vote 2004."

43. Interview, not for attribution, March 1997.

44. Interview, not for attribution, March 1997.

45. Ibid.

46. Lintner, interview, March 1997.

47. Interview, not for attribution, March 1997.

48. Interview, not for attribution, March 1997.

49. National Council of Churches, "Struggles 'Not a Sign of Weakness,' Departing General Secretary Tells NCC," press release, November 13, 1999.

50. Ibid.

51. National Council of Churches, "A Protocol for a Mobilization to Overcome Poverty," draft of October 24, 2000, pp. 1–3; National Council of Churches, "Partnerships with Habitat for Humanity, Others," June 1, 2001, p. 2; Robert W. Edgar, "General Secretary's Annual Report to the NCC General Assembly," November 14, 2000. See also Bob Edgar, *Middle Church: Reclaiming the Moral Values of the Faithful Majority from the Religious Right* (New York: Simon and Schuster, 2006).

52. National Council of Churches, "Ecumenical Community's Legislative Priorities Complement Call to Renewal's 'Covenant to Overcome Poverty,'" February 2000.

53. National Council of Churches, "NCC Assembly Takes Up Mobilization to Overcome Poverty," November 15, 2000, p. 2.

54. Ibid.

55. In late 2000, for example, the NCC appointed as director of its Public Policy Office in Washington Brenda Girton-Mitchell, a lawyer and former legislative assistant to Senator Birch Bayh (D-Ind.). Named NCC Associate General Secretary for Public Policy, Girton-Mitchell became head of the Justice and Advocacy Commission the NCC established in 2003 to coordinate its legislative advocacy. Rev. Albert Pennybacker directed the NCC's Washington office from 1996 until retiring in March 1999. See National Council of Churches, "Girton-Mitchell to Head NCC Program for Public Policy Witness," September 5, 2000, p. 1.

56. Interview, not for attribution, February 2004.

57. Robert Edgar, "General Secretary's Annual Report," National Council of Churches, November 2000, p. 2.

58. National Council of Churches, "NCC's Edgar, at White House, Welcomes New Director," February 1, 2002, p. 1. See also Eileen W. Lindner, "Considering Charitable Choice," in *2001 Yearbook of American and Canadian Churches*, ed. Eileen W. Lindner (New York: National Council of Churches, 2001), http://www.ncccusa.org/news/01news10a.html.

59. Religious Leaders for Campaign Finance Reform, letter, March 16, 2001, and statement, April 2, 2001.

60. National Council of Churches, "'Religious Community for Responsible Tax Policy' Is Launched," April 5, 2001.

61. NCC General Assembly, "Out of the Ashes and Tragedy of September 11, 2001," November 15, 2001, pp. 2–3. Cf. NCC General Assembly, "After September 11, 2001: Public Policy Considerations for the United States of America," November 16, 2002.

62. National Council of Churches, "'We Can Still Stop This War'—MLK Day Service Draws 3,200 to Washington National Cathedral; Peace March Follows," January 20, 2003.

63. MoveOn.org, "Global Candlelight Vigil for Peace," March 16, 2003.

64. National Council of Churches, "Call to a Time to Reflect . . . NCC Urges Peace Vigils Nationwide during March to Mark First Anniversary of the Invasion of Iraq," March 2004, p. 1.

65. NCC General Assembly, "Resolution on the Conflict in the Middle East," November 6, 2003, p. 1; Churches for Middle East Peace, "Letter to President George W. Bush," September 12, 2002; National Council of Churches, "51 Protestant, Orthodox, Catholic, Evangelical Leaders Petition President Bush to Reconsider Iraq Invasion," September 12, 2002.

66. National Council of Churches, "U.S. Church Leaders, Citing Risks, Fault President Bush for Concessions to Israel's Prime Minister Sharon," April 15, 2004, pp. 1–2.

67. National Council of Churches, "Letter to Bush Says Israeli-Palestinian Conflict Threatens U.S.," January 21, 2005.

68. NCC Delegation to the Middle East, "Barriers Do Not Bring Freedom," February 6, 2005, pp. 2–4.

69. National Council of Churches, "A Statement of the National Council of Churches USA and Church World Service on the Current Violence in the Middle East," July 14, 2006.

70. National Council of Churches, "NCC Joins Call for US Brokered Cease-Fire in Mideast," with text of letter from Churches for Middle East Peace to President George W. Bush, July 21, 2006.

71. National Council of Churches, "NCC Releases Ecumenical Pastoral Letter on Iraq," May 11, 2004, p. 2; National Council of Churches, "NCC Issues Statement on Devolution of the Iraq Crisis," May 5, 2004, pp. 1–2.

72. Robert W. Edgar, "A Vision of Peace in a Time of War: The Need for a Peace-Centered Foreign Policy," paper prepared in conjunction with an address delivered at the University of San Diego, April 2003, pp. 1–8.

73. National Council of Churches, "NCC Part of Drive to Activate Two Million New Low-Income Voters," January 14, 2004, p. 1.

74. Ibid.

75. National Council of Churches, "Interfaith Coalition Promotes Voting as a Matter of Faith," April 2, 2004, pp. 1–2.

76. Ibid.

77. Edgar, "General Secretary's Annual Report," November 2000, p. 1.

78. See http://www.faithfulamerica.org/about.php.

79. The Religious Newswriters Association ranked as a top religion news story of 2003 the split between the mainline churches and conservative evangelicals over the war in Iraq, with the NCC leading opposition to the war.

80. National Council of Churches, "Edgar: 2000th Death in Iraq Is a 'Tragic Milestone' That 'Didn't Have to Happen,'" October 25, 2005; Faithful America, "2000th U.S. Soldier Dies in Iraq—Religious Leaders Urge Remembrance Weekend," October 25, 2005; MoveOn.org Political Action, "Attend a Vigil Tonight—

Media Misses 2,000 Killed in Iraq," October 26, 2005; MoveOn.org Political Action, "The Next Step after the Vigils. New TV Ad," October 27, 2005; National Council of Churches, "Bells Toll a Mournful Milestone: 2500 Dead in Iraq," June 15, 2006.

81. Interview, not for attribution, June 2004.

82. Interview, not for attribution, November 2004.

83. Mark Silk, as reported by CBS News, "Religion Taking a Left Turn?" July 10, 2006.

84. John Lomperis and Alan Wisdom, "NCC Finds a New Base," *Faith & Freedom*, Spring 2006, pp. 8–10, summarizing Lomperis and Wisdom, "Strange Yokefellows: The National Council of Churches and Its Growing Non-church Constituency," Institute on Religion and Democracy, 2006.

85. Ibid.

86. Edward Chan, Oscar McCloud, Donald Shriver, Peggy Shriver, Kenneth Thomas, Kristin Thompson, Wayne Wilson, and Belle Miller-McMaster, "Report on the Review of the National Council of Churches of Christ in the U.S.A.," pp. 1–10, esp. 6, 9. Item 06-07, General Assembly Committee on Ecumenical and Interfaith Religions (GACER), 2004 General Assembly of the Presbyterian Church (USA).

87. Ibid.

88. Interview, not for attribution, April 2007.

89. National Council of Churches, "National Council of Churches Urges Grassroots Campaign to Call on Congress to Pass Bipartisan 'End the War' Resolution," June 16, 2005, in support of legislation introduced by Reps. Walter Jones (R-N.C.) and Neil Abercrombie (D-Hawaii). See also Bob Edgar, General Secretary, National Council of Churches; Joe Volk, Executive Director, Friends Committee on National Legislation; and Jim Winkler, Board of Church and Society, United Methodist Church, "Religious Leaders Urge Congress to Declare That War in Iraq Is Not Open-Ended," an op-ed overview of mainline-church opposition to the Iraq war since 2002 that calls on Congress to pledge, without a timetable, not to keep U.S. forces in Iraq indefinitely or establish permanent military bases there. On July 4, 2005, the NCC sent to the White House a related petition signed by more than six hundred national religious leaders and fifteen thousand church members. A survey in May 2005 by the Pew Research Center for the People and the Press found that 57 percent of respondents approved of how President Bush was handling the war on terror, down from 62 percent in January 2005; on Iraq, only 37 percent approved, down from 45 percent in January. See Sheryl Gay Stolberg, "No Surprise, New Terror Attack Quickly Is Grist of Politics," *New York Times*, July 10, 2005, p. WK 4. In mid-2006, a New York Times/CBS News poll found 63 percent (versus 30 percent) of Americans judging the Iraq war not worth the U.S. lives and dollars lost, with only 25 percent convinced its continuation would make the United States safer from terrorism. But three of four Republicans said the United States did the right thing in attacking Iraq, while only 24 percent

of Democrats did, with independents split down the middle. See Jim Rutenberg and Megan C. Thee, "Poll Shows Growing Skepticism in U.S. over Peace in the Middle East," *New York Times*, July 27, 2006, p. A20; and Robin Toner and Jim Rutenberg, "Partisan Divide on Iraq Exceeds Split on Vietnam," *New York Times*, July 29, 2006, pp. A1, A20.

90. National Council of Churches, "NCC and NGO's from U.S., U.K., and France, Call for Security Council Action on Darfur," July 27, 2005; National Council of Churches, "Frist, Clinton, Sign the Millionth Postcard Urging President to Act on Darfur," June 29, 2006.

91. National Council of Churches, "Persons of Faith Promise to Advocate the End of Hunger," June 7, 2005. In his keynote address at the convocation, Njongonkulu W. H. Ndungane, Anglican Archbishop of Cape Town, South Africa, pointed to the simultaneous growth of the world economy and global hunger to attribute the problem to a lack of political will rather than a lack of economic resources.

92. National Council of Churches, "Five Denominations, NCC Join to Declare FY2006 Proposed Budget 'Unjust,'" March 8, 2005.

93. Ibid.; National Council of Churches, "March 11–14 Ecumenical Advocacy Days Focus on a 'More Complete Moral Vision,'" January 24, 2005; "Let Justice Roll: Faith and Community Voices against Poverty," http://www.ncccusa.org/povertymarch2005/LJRBudgetVision.html.

94. National Council of Churches, "Five Denominations, NCC Join to Declare FY2006 Proposed Budget 'Unjust'"; National Council of Churches, "Preserving and Protecting Social Security—an NCC Curriculum for Congregations," July 27, 2005.

95. National Council of Churches, "NCC's Edgar Sees Americans Voting for 'Honesty, Integrity, Truth and Justice,'" November 3, 2006; Robert Edgar, "The Faithful Will Vote for American Values," *San Francisco Chronicle*, November 3, 2006.

96. National Council of Churches, "NCC's Edgar Calls for 'Season of Healing' after Election," November 8, 2006.

97. Jim Wallis, "This Was a Moral Values Election," *Sojourners Magazine*, November 15, 2006; Jim Winkler, quoted in Ed Stoddard, "U.S. Churches Sharply Divided on Iraq War," Reuters, November 4, 2006; Katie Bargie, "Exit Poll Shows Shift in Religious Vote Driven by 'Kitchen Table' Moral Issues," Faith in Public Life, November 15, 2006. Cf. Greg Smith, Scott Keeter, and John Green, "Religion and the 2006 Elections," Pew Forum on Religion and Public Life, 2006, http://pewforum.org, for evidence showing Democratic gains in 2006 concentrated among voters who attended worship less often, widening the "God gap." By late August 2006, major polls from CNN, the Associated Press, Princeton Survey Research Associates International, and CBS News/New York Times reported some two-thirds of Americans saying they opposed the war. The CBS/

New York Times poll of August 17–21, for example, showed 65 percent of Americans disapproving of the way President Bush was dealing with Iraq, including 67 percent of self-identified political independents. See Tom Regan, "Polls Show Opposition to Iraq War at All-Time High," *Christian Science Monitor*, September 1, 2006, http://www.truthout.org. Among white evangelical Protestants, those convinced that the United States was right in deciding to invade Iraq to oust Saddam Hussein fell from 71 percent in September 2006 to 58 percent one week prior to the November election, according to Pew Research Center polls reported in Stoddard, "U.S. Churches Sharply Divided." Support among Americans for the increased troop levels announced by President Bush on January 10, 2006, plunged to less than 20 percent. Sheryl Gay Stolberg, "Bush's New Strategy for Iraq Risks Confrontations on Many Fronts," *New York Times*, January 11, 2007, p. A19.

98. Governing Board and General Assembly of the National Council of Churches USA, "Pastoral Message on the War in Iraq," November 8, 2006.

99. National Council of Churches, "NCC welcomes Iraq Study Group Report and Agrees with Many of Its Recommendations," December 6, 2006; Faithful America, "Mandate for Peace," January 9, 2007. Cf. Jim Winkler, "Out Now!" January 2, 2007, http://www.umc-gbcs.org; and Jim Wallis, "A Criminal Escalation of an Unjust War," *Sojourners Magazine*, January 11, 2007.

100. National Council of Churches, "NCC Board Celebrates Council's Continuing Fiscal Recovery," October 1, 2003.

Chapter 11: Conclusion: Public Churches and the Church

1. See Dean R. Hoge, Michael J. Donahue, and Charles E. Zech, *Money Matters: Personal Giving in American Churches* (Louisville, KY: Westminster John Knox Press, 1996); Robert Wuthnow, *The Crisis in the Churches: Spiritual Malaise, Fiscal Woe* (New York: Oxford University Press, 1997); and John L. Ronsvalle and Sylvia Ronsvalle, *The State of Church Giving, 2000* (Champaign, IL: Empty Tomb, 2002).

2. Cf. Mark Chaves, *Congregations in America* (Cambridge, MA: Harvard University Press, 2004), chaps. 2, 3, esp. pp. 36–39, 46–54; and Mark Chaves, Helen M. Giesel, and William Tsitsos, "Religious Variations in Public Presence: Evidence from the National Congregations Study," in *The Quiet Hand of God: Faith-Based Activism and the Public Role of Mainline Protestantism*, ed. Robert Wuthnow and John H. Evans, pp. 108–28 (Berkeley and Los Angeles: University of California Press, 2002).

3. By the Christian Coalition's own count, fewer than one-third of its 1.7 million members in late 1995 had graduated from college; more than one-half were high school or vocational-school graduates; more than half were older than fifty-five;

and the average household income was $27,000. Only 3 to 5 percent were African Americans, who make up at least a third of all religiously conservative evangelicals in the United States. See Richard Berke, "Christian Coalition Is United on Morality, but Not Politics," *New York Times*, September 8, 1995, p. A12.

4. Robert N. Bellah, Richard Madsen, William M. Sullivan, Ann Swidler, and Steven M. Tipton, *The Good Society* (New York: Knopf, 1991), p. 218.

5. Robert Wuthnow, "Beyond Quiet Influence? Possibilities for the Protestant Mainline," in Wuthnow and Evans, *The Quiet Hand of God*, pp. 381–403, esp. 399–401. Cf. critiques of cultural Christianity a generation ago, including Peter Berger, *The Noise of Solemn Assemblies: Christian Commitment and the Religious Establishment in America* (Garden City, NY: Doubleday, 1961); and Pierre Berton, *The Comfortable Pew: A Critical Look at Christianity and the Religious Establishment in the New Age* (Philadelphia: Lippincott, 1965).

6. Wuthnow, "Beyond Quiet Influence?" p. 401.

7. See, for example, Rebecca S. Chopp, *Saving Work: Feminist Practices of Theological Education* (Louisville, KY: Westminster John Knox Press, 1995); Chopp, "Bearing Witness: Traditional Faith in Contemporary Expression" (unpublished paper, Emory University, 1996); Craig Dykstra, "Reconceiving Practice," in *Shifting Boundaries: Contextual Approaches to the Structure of Theological Education*, ed. Barbara G. Wheeler and Edward Farley, pp. 35–66 (Louisville, KY: Westminster John Knox Press, 1991); and Russell E. Richey with Dennis M. Campbell and William B. Lawrence, *Marks of Methodism: Theology in Ecclesial Practice* (Nashville, TN: Abingdon Press, 2005).

8. See Robert B. Reich, *The Work of Nations: Preparing Ourselves for 21st-Century Capitalism* (New York: Knopf, 1991). Here and below, this section draws on Robert N. Bellah, Richard Madsen, William M. Sullivan, Ann Swidler, and Steven M. Tipton, "The House Divided," introduction to the updated edition of *Habits of the Heart: Individualism and Commitment in American Life* (Berkeley and Los Angeles: University of California Press, 1996), esp. pp. xi–xvi, xxxi–xxxiii.

9. Bellah et al., "The House Divided," pp. xxxii–xxxiii.

10. Ibid.

11. National Conference of Catholic Bishops, *Economic Justice for All: Pastoral Letter on Catholic Social Teaching and the U.S. Economy* (Washington, DC: U.S. Catholic Conference, 1986), pars. 70–77.

12. Michael Walzer, "Socializing the Welfare State," in *Democracy and the Welfare State*, ed. Amy Gutmann, pp. 13–26 (Princeton, NJ: Princeton University Press, 1988).

13. Here and below, see Bureau of Labor Statistics, "The Employment Situation: July 2005," news release, August 5, 2005, http://www.bls.gov/ces; and Economic Policy Institute, "*The State of Working America 2004/2005*: Recovery Yet to Arrive for Working Families," September 2004, http://www.epinet.org. U.S. manufacturing jobs declined by 17 percent—a loss of three million jobs—in 2001–

5, according to Bureau of Labor Statistics data, and union membership fell to 7.9 percent of all private-sector workers by 2005.

14. Robert Reich, quoted in the *New York Times*, January 4, 1996, p. A13.

15. Jared Bernstein, "What's Wedged between Productivity, Living Standards?" Economic Policy Institute, March 2, 2006. See also Sylvia Allegretto and Jared Bernstein, *The Wage Squeeze and Higher Health Care Costs*, Economic Policy Institute, Issue Brief no. 218, January 27, 2006, for comparison of shares of corporate income growth going to profits and compensation across business cycles, based on data from the Bureau of Economic Analysis, National Income and Product Accounts (NIPA) through the second quarter of 2005. See Lawrence Mishel and Ross Eisenbrey, *What's Wrong with the Economy?* Economic Policy Institute, June 12, 2006, for comparison of corporate profits since 2001 and earlier, based on the Bureau of Economic Analysis, NIPA table 1.14, http://www.bea.gov/bea/dn/nipaweb/index.asp. Employers' health-care costs rose 8 to 12 percent annually in 2000–2, then fell below 8 percent after mid-2004, in part due to shrinking coverage in the face of higher costs and weaker labor markets; meanwhile, family health costs rose 43–45 percent for couples with children, single mothers, and young singles in 2000–2003, according to Lawrence Mishel, Michael Ettlinger, and Elise Gould, *Less Cash in Their Pockets*, Economic Policy Institute, Briefing Paper no. 154, 2004. Only 53 percent of all workers in private industry participate in health-care benefits, including only 39 percent of workers earning average wages under $15 per hour, according to 2000–2005 data from the Bureau of Labor Statistics, Employment Cost Index, and National Compensation Survey, cited in the Economic Policy Institute studies above, at http://www.epinet.org.

16. Bernstein, "What's Wedged between Productivity, Living Standards?" p. 2.

17. Pew Research Center for the People and the Press, *Evenly Divided and Increasingly Polarized: 2004 Political Landscape*, released November 5, 2003, esp. pp. 1–2, 6–9 of "Overview," at http://people-press/reports.

18. Ibid.

19. Bellah et al., "The House Divided," pp. xxxii–xxxiii.

20. See Michael Walzer, "The Idea of Civil Society," *Dissent*, Spring 1991, pp. 293–304; Charles Taylor, "Modes of Civil Society," *Public Culture* 3, no. 1 (Fall 1990): 95–118; and Adam Seligman, *The Idea of Civil Society* (New York: Free Press, 1992). This section is indebted throughout to the excellent overview by Jeff Weintraub, "The Theory and Politics of the Public/Private Distinction," in *Public and Private in Thought and Practice*, ed. Jeff Weintraub and Krishan Kumar, pp. 1–42 (Chicago: University of Chicago Press, 1997); and to José Casanova, *Public Religions in the Modern World* (Chicago: University of Chicago Press, 1994), esp. chap. 2.

21. Weintraub, "Theory and Politics," pp. 7–13, 34–38; Casanova, *Public Religions*, pp. 57–58.

22. See Steven M. Tipton, "Moral Languages and the Good Society," *Soundings* 69, nos. 1–2 (1986): 167–71; and Michael J. Perry, *Morality, Politics, and Law: A Bicentennial Essay* (New York: Oxford University Press, 1988), pp. 82–90.

23. Casanova, *Public Religions*, pp. 61–62, 70ff.

24. See Jon Butler, *Awash in a Sea of Faith: Christianizing the American People* (Cambridge, MA: Harvard University Press, 1990); and Timothy L. Smith, *Revivalism and Social Reform in Mid-Nineteenth Century America* (Nashville, TN: Abingdon Press, 1957).

25. Cf. Theda Skocpol, *Protecting Soldiers and Mothers: The Political Origins of Social Policy in the United States* (Cambridge, MA: Harvard University Press, 1992); Paula Baker, *The Moral Frameworks of Public Life* (New York: Oxford University Press, 1991); and Constance H. Buchanan, *Choosing to Lead: Women and the Crisis of American Values* (Boston: Beacon Press, 1996), chaps. 5–6.

26. See Ronald L. Jepperson and John W. Meyer, "The Public Order and the Construction of Formal Organizations," in *The New Institutionalism in Organizational Analysis*, ed. Walter W. Powell and Paul J. DiMaggio, pp. 204–31 (Chicago: University of Chicago Press, 1991), esp. pp. 214–17 for a comparison of individualist, statist, corporatist, and segmented forms of the modern polity. See also Ronald L. Jepperson and David Kamens, "The Expanding State and the U.S. 'Civic Culture': The Changing Character of Political Participation and Legitimation in the Post-war U.S. Polity" (paper presented at the annual meeting of the American Political Science Association, New Orleans, 1985).

27. Bellah et al., *The Good Society*, chap. 4.

28. Alexis de Tocqueville, *Democracy in America* (1848), trans. George Lawrence, ed. J. P. Mayer (Garden City, NY: Doubleday Anchor, 1969), pp. 516–17.

29. Seyla Benhabib, "Models of Public Space," in *Habermas and the Public Sphere*, ed. Craig Calhoun (Cambridge, MA: MIT Press, 1992), p. 87; Jean Cohen, "Discourse Ethics and Civil Society," *Philosophy and Social Criticism* 14, nos. 3–4 (1988): 328.

30. Nancy Fraser, "Rethinking the Public Sphere: A Contribution to the Critique of Actually Existing Democracy," in Calhoun, *Habermas and the Public Sphere*, pp. 119–20. Cf. Seyla Benhabib, "The Generalized and the Concrete Other," in *Situating the Self: Gender, Community, and Postmodernism in Contemporary Ethics*, pp. 148–77 (New York: Routledge, 1992).

31. Fraser, "Rethinking the Public Sphere," p. 123.

32. Ibid., p. 124.

33. Here and below, see Geoff Eley, "Nations, Publics, and Political Culture," in Calhoun, *Habermas and the Public Sphere*, pp. 289–339; and Fraser, "Rethinking the Public Sphere," pp. 125–30. Cf. Richard Rorty, "Religion as Conversation Stopper," *Common Knowledge* 3 (Spring 1994): 1–6, reprinted as chap. 11 in his *Philosophy and Social Hope* (New York: Penguin, 1999); and Rorty, "The Priority

of Democracy over Philosophy," in *The Virginia Statute for Religious Freedom: Its Evolution and Consequences in American History*, ed. Merrill D. Peterson and Robert C. Vaughan, pp. 257–82 (Cambridge: Cambridge University Press, 1988), for its Rawlsian defense of a liberal-democratic polity against religion. Note Fraser's related critique of Rorty in her *Unruly Practices: Power, Discourse, and Gender in Contemporary Social Theory* (Minneapolis: University of Minnesota Press, 1989), and its incorporation by Stanley Hauerwas into "The Politics of Justice: Why Justice Is a Bad Idea for Christians," in *After Christendom? How the Church Is to Behave If Freedom, Justice, and a Christian Nation Are Bad Ideas* (Nashville, TN: Abingdon Press, 1991), pp. 48, 172 nn. 2, 7.

34. Bellah et al., *The Good Society*, chap. 6; Robert Wuthnow, *The Restructuring of American Religion: Society and Faith since World War II* (Princeton, NJ: Princeton University Press, 1988).

35. Fraser, "Rethinking the Public Sphere," p. 124.

36. H. Richard Niebuhr, *The Social Sources of Denominationalism* (New York: Henry Holt, 1929), p. 282; Ernst Troeltsch, *The Social Teaching of the Christian Churches* (1911; New York: Harper and Row, 1960).

37. Cf. Martin E. Marty, *The Public Church: Mainline, Evangelical, Catholic* (New York: Crossroad, 1981), pp. 16–22.

38. Jürgen Habermas, "Israel or Athens: Where Does Anamnestic Reason Belong? Johannes Baptist Metz on Unity amidst Multi-cultural Plurality," in *Religion and Rationality: Essays on Reason, God, and Modernity*, ed. Eduardo Mendieta, pp.129–38 (Cambridge, MA: MIT Press, 2002), esp. pp. 135–87 on "the polycentric world Church." See also Johannes Baptist Metz, "Im Aufbruch zu einer kulturell polyzentrischen Weltkirche," in *Zukunftsfähigkeit*, edited by F. X. Kaufmann and J. B. Metz, pp. 93–115 (Freiburg: Herder, 1987). Cf. Cardinal Joseph Ratzinger, "Homily at the Mass for the Election of the Roman Pontiff," Vatican City, April 18, 2005, http://www.insidethevatican.com/newsflash-apr18-05.htm, for its defense of having "a clear faith, based on the Creed of the Church," to withstand the modern multiplication of ideological and sectarian "error" and the modern establishment of egoistic relativism.

39. Jürgen Habermas, "A Conversation about God and the World," in *Religion and Rationality*, p. 149.

40. Ibid., pp. 136, 149–50.

41. Ibid., pp. 149–50.

42. See, for example, Albert Vorspan and David Saperstein, *Tough Choices: Jewish Perspectives on Social Justice* (New York: Union of American Hebrew Congregations, 1992), chaps. 1, 15. Cf. John Boli, "Human Rights or State Expansion?" in *Institutional Structure: Constituting State, Society, and the Individual*, by George M. Thomas, John W. Meyer, Francisco O. Ramirez, and John Boli (Newbury Park, CA: Sage Publications, 1987), pp. 143–44.

43. Charles Taylor, "The Politics of Recognition," in *Multiculturalism and "The Politics of Recognition,"* ed. Amy Gutmann, pp. 25–73 (Princeton, NJ: Princeton University Press, 1992).

44. David Hollenbach, "Justice as Participation: Public Moral Discourse and the U.S. Economy," in *Justice, Peace, and Human Rights: American Catholic Social Ethics in a Pluralistic World* (New York: Crossroad, 1988), pp. 82–83.

45. Judith Shklar, *American Citizenship: The Quest for Inclusion* (Cambridge, MA: Harvard University Press, 1991), pp. 63–101.

46. Christopher Lasch, "The Communitarian Critique of Liberalism," *Soundings* 69, nos. 1–2 (1986): 60–76.

47. Sidney Verba, Kay Lehman Schlozman, and Henry E. Brady, *Voice and Equality: Civic Voluntarism in American Politics* (Cambridge, MA: Harvard University Press, 1995), pp. 509–33.

48. Bellah et al., *The Good Society*, chap. 6; Parker J. Palmer, *The Company of Strangers* (New York: Crossroad, 1981).

Appendix: Ecclesiology in Action

1. See Talcott Parsons, "Christianity and Modern Industrial Society," in *Religion, Culture and Society: A Reader in the Sociology of Religion*, ed. Louis Schneider, pp. 273–98 (New York: Wiley, 1964), reprinted from *Sociological Theory, Values, and Sociocultural Change*, ed. Edward Tiryakian (New York: Free Press, 1963). See also the derivative formulation of Harvey Cox, *The Secular City: Secularization and Urbanization in Theological Perspective* (New York: Macmillan, 1965).

2. Parsons, "Christianity and Modern Industrial Society," p. 278.

3. Ibid., p. 295.

4. Ibid., p. 284.

5. Ibid., pp. 296–98.

6. Ernst Troeltsch, *The Social Teaching of the Christian Churches* (1911; Harper and Row, 1960), 1:378–82.

7. Ibid., 1:381.

8. Ibid., 1:381–82.

9. Cf., for example, Robert N. Bellah, Richard Madsen, William M. Sullivan, Ann Swidler, and Steven M. Tipton, *Habits of the Heart: Individualism and Commitment in American Life* (1985; Berkeley and Los Angeles: University of California Press, 2007), pp. 232–48; Alan Wolfe, *The Transformation of American Religion: How We Actually Live Our Faith* (New York: Free Press, 2003); Wade Clark Roof, *Spiritual Marketplace: Baby Boomers and the Remaking of American Religion* (Princeton, NJ: Princeton University Press, 1999); and Christian

Smith, *American Evangelicalism: Embattled and Thriving* (Chicago: University of Chicago Press, 1998).

10. White House, "President Discusses Compassionate Conservative Agenda in Dallas: Remarks by the President to the 122nd Knights of Columbus Convention," August 3, 2004, http://www.whitehouse.gov/news

11. Cf. Robert N. Bellah, "Religious Evolution," in *Beyond Belief* (1970; Berkeley and Los Angeles: University of California Press, 1991), pp. 39–44, on the "modern" stage of religious evolution; and Robert Wuthnow, *After Heaven: Spirituality in America since the 1950s* (Berkeley and Los Angeles: University of California Press, 1998), esp. chaps. 1, 7.

12. James Madison, "Memorial and Remonstrance" (1785), in *The Papers of James Madison*, vol. 8, ed. William T. Hutchinson and William M. E. Rachal (Chicago: University of Chicago Press, 1971), p. 299.

13. Bellah et al., *Habits of the Heart*, p. 246.

14. Ibid., pp. 143, 243.

15. Ibid., p. 243.

16. Troeltsch, *Social Teachings*, 2:729–802, 991 94.

17. Ibid., 2:1000.

18. See Smith, *American Evangelicalism*. Better educated and better off, self-identified "evangelicals" in this study hold conversionist-revivalist views, in contrast to separatist-rejectionist views characteristic of less educated and occupationally successful self-identified "fundamentalists." This distinction amplifies the degree to which increased cultural assimilation and upward social mobility have led such "traditional" Protestants into the suburban middle-class mainstream over the past generation, moving them to further inflect but not surrender a sectlike sense of standing in but not of the modern world that their own early-modern voluntarist soteriology has helped to form. Cf. George Marsden, *Fundamentalism and American Culture: The Shaping of Twentieth Century Evangelicalism, 1870–1925* (New York: Oxford University Press, 1980), for a more comprehensive historical account of these revivalist-rejectionist dynamics.

19. Alexis de Tocqueville, *Democracy in America* (1848), trans. George Lawrence, ed. J. P. Mayer (Garden City, NY: Doubleday Anchor, 1969), p. 292.

20. Ibid., p. 508.

21. Stanley Hauerwas, "The Church and Liberal Democracy: The Moral Limits of a Secular Polity," in *A Community of Character: Toward a Constructive Christian Social Ethic* (Notre Dame, IN: University of Notre Dame Press, 1981), p. 73.

22. Ibid., pp. 73, 247 n. 8.

23. Ibid., p. 247 n. 5. Cf. H. Richard Niebuhr, *Christ and Culture* (New York: Harper and Row, 1951).

24. Hauerwas, "The Church and Liberal Democracy," pp. 74, 78.

25. Stanley Hauerwas, "On Being a Christian and an American," in *Meaning and Modernity: Religion, Polity, and Self*, ed. Richard Madsen, William M. Sul-

livan, Ann Swidler, and Steven M. Tipton (Berkeley and Los Angeles: University of California Press, 2002), p. 235, as revised from its previous publication in Hauerwas, *A Better Hope: Resources for a Church Confronting Capitalism, Democracy, and Postmodernity* (Grand Rapids, MI: Brazos Press, 2002), pp. 23–34.

26. Hauerwas, "The Church and Liberal Democracy," p. 75.

27. Ibid., p. 249 n. 19.

28. Ibid., pp. 247 n. 9 and 246 n. 4, comparing John Courtney Murray and Reinhold Niebuhr on church-state relations.

29. Cf. John W. Meyer, John Boli, and George M. Thomas, "Ontology and Rationalization in the Western Cultural Account," in *Institutional Structure: Constituting State, Society, and the Individual*, by George M. Thomas, John W. Meyer, Francisco O. Ramirez, and John Boli (Newbury Park, CA: Sage Publications, 1987), pp. 27–28, for a contrasting account of the religious dimensions of modern nation-states indebted to Perry Anderson, *Lineages of the Absolutist State* (London: Schocken, 1974).

30. Peter L. Berger, "From the Crisis of Religion to the Crisis of Secularity," in *Religion and America: Spiritual Life in a Secular Age*, ed. Mary Douglas and Steven M. Tipton (Boston: Beacon Press, 1983), pp. 20–22. Cf. Smith, *American Evangelicalism*, pp. 150ff., for its "subcultural identity theory" that evangelicalism "maintains both high tension with and high integration into mainstream American society simultaneously."

31. Michael Novak, *Toward the Future: Catholic Social Thought and the U.S. Economy* (New York: Lay Commission on Catholic Social Teaching and the U.S. Economy, 1984), p. 11.

32. See, for example, Peter L. Berger and Richard John Neuhaus, *To Empower People: The Role of Mediating Structures in Public Policy* (Washington, DC: American Enterprise Institute, 1977); Berger, "From the Crisis of Religion to the Crisis of Secularity"; Richard J. Neuhaus, *The Naked Public Square: Religion and Democracy in America* (Grand Rapids, MI: Eerdmans, 1984); Neuhaus, *The Catholic Moment: The Paradox of the Church in the Postmodern World* (New York: Harper and Row, 1987); Novak, *Toward the Future*; Novak, *Free Persons and the Common Good* (Lanham, MD: Madison Books, 1989); Novak, *The Catholic Ethic and the Spirit of Capitalism* (New York: Free Press, 1993) and Novak, *The Spirit of Democratic Capitalism* (New York: Simon and Schuster, 1982).

33. Berger and Neuhaus, *To Empower People*, p. 30.

34. Ibid., p. 1.

35. Novak, *Toward the Future*, p. 10. See Novak, *The Spirit of Democratic Capitalism*, pp. 171–86, for its elaboration of "the division of the political system from the moral-cultural system, and of the economic system from both," by reference to Daniel Bell. Cf. Daniel Bell, *The Cultural Contradictions of Capitalism* (New York: Basic Books, 1976), esp. pp. 10–15, for its model of contemporary society's three distinct realms—techno-economic, political, and cultural—"each of

which is obedient to a different axial principle" and set of norms legitimating different types of behavior. In the economy, functional rationality balances costs and benefits to calculate utility and maximize efficiency. In the polity, justice regulates conflicts under the rule of law and democratic principles of equal rights and representation. Expressive symbolism holds sway in the cultural realm of modern arts, religious rites and liturgy, and lifestylish leisure to enhance self-realization and fulfill the "whole" person. Bell's formulation makes clear that each institutional sphere has its own inherently moral dimension of principles, norms, and practical conduct. There is no separate "moral and cultural" sphere, contrary to Novak's construal, and neither the economy nor the polity is nonmoral.

36. Novak, *Toward the Future*, p. 11.

37. Ibid., pp. 11, 24. Cf. Novak, *Free Persons and the Common Good*; and Michael Walzer, *Spheres of Justice: A Defense of Pluralism and Equality* (New York: Basic Books, 1984), pp. 243–48, on religion.

38. Michael Novak, "McGovernism among the Bishops," *Washington Times*, October 25, 1985, quoted in David Hollenbach, "Justice as Participation: Public Moral Discourse and the U.S. Economy," in *Justice, Peace, and Human Rights: American Catholic Social Ethics in a Pluralistic World* (New York: Crossroad, 1988), p. 72.

39. See, for example, Hollenbach, "Justice as Participation," pp. 72–73; Hollenbach, "Religious Freedom and Economic Rights," in *Justice, Peace, and Human Rights*, pp. 101–7; and Robert Wuthnow, *The Restructuring of American Religion: Society and Faith since World War II* (Princeton, NJ: Princeton University Press, 1988), pp. 257–58.

40. Bellah et al., *Habits of the Heart*, p. 244.

41. Hollenbach, "Justice as Participation," pp. 72, 81.

42. Troeltsch, *Social Teaching*, 2:994–96.

43. Ibid., 2:993–96, 1007.

44. Ibid., 2:1009–10.

45. *Pastoral Constitution*, in *The Documents of Vatican II*, ed. Walter M. Abbott (New York: Guild Press, 1966), p. 291. Here and below, see Timothy A. Byrnes, *Catholic Bishops in American Politics* (Princeton, NJ: Princeton University Press, 1991), esp. pp. 39–44, 50–53, 127–46.

46. Byrnes, *Catholic Bishops in American Politics*.

47. John C. Green, Corwin E. Smidt, James L. Guth, and Lyman A. Kellstedt, *The American Religious Landscape and the 2004 Presidential Vote: Increased Polarization* (Washington, DC: Pew Forum on Religion and Public Life, 2005), pp. 1–2.

48. The issue of abortion figured only slightly larger in 2004 voting decisions of white Catholics than in decisions of mainline Protestants (40 versus 34 percent), well below its high importance for 61 percent of white evangelical Protestants. Banning gay marriage was very important for 49 percent of white evangelicals,

but for only 23 percent of mainline Protestants and 21 percent of white Catholics. Stem-cell research was important for some 40 percent of all major religious groups, including seculars, according to the Pew Research Center, "Race Tightens Again, Kerry's Image Improves," pp. 2–6, 13, released October 20, 2004, http://www.people-press.org. Catholic voters seemed to be wrestling with a broad range of moral issues, consonant with the central "tasks and questions for believers" set out in late 2003 by the U.S. Catholic Conference in its election-year guide, *Faithful Citizenship: A Catholic Call to Political Responsibility*. This guide contrasted with the short list of "non-negotiable" issues, including abortion and the use of embryonic stem cells for research, advanced by a handful of hard-line bishops and lay leaders at odds with others who were urging parishioners to vote their conscience. Vatican officials stressed that Catholics should vote on issues in accord with church doctrine, including opposition to capital punishment and criticism of injustice in the war against Iraq, but that American Catholic bishops should refrain from involvement in the "concrete aspects" of elections and should avoid speaking with divided voices that confuse the faithful. See U.S. Conference of Catholic Bishops, *Faithful Citizenship: A Catholic Call to Political Responsibility*, October 2003; U.S. Conference of Catholic Bishops, "Catholics in Political Life," July 2004, http://www.nccbuscc.org; Peter Steinfels, "Beliefs: Religion, Politics and the Good—or Harm—That May Result from the 2004 Campaign," *New York Times*, October 23, 2004, p. A15; and Ian Fisher, "In Vatican, Unease with Bush Vies with Qualms on Kerry," *New York Times*, October 24, 2004, p. 22.

49. Hollenbach, "Justice as Participation," pp. 82–83.

50. Presbyterian Church (USA), *Book of Order* (Louisville, KY: Westminster John Knox Press, 2004), "Form of Government," pt. 2, G-1.0100.

51. Ibid., G-1.0200.

52. Ibid., G-1.0301.

53. Ibid., G-1.0304, 1.0305, 1.0307.

54. Ibid., G-1.0400.

55. *The Book of Discipline of the United Methodist Church* (Nashville, TN: United Methodist Publishing House, 2004), pt. 1, "The Constitution," Preamble, Articles IV, VI, pp. 21–23.

56. *Book of Discipline*, 2004, par. 101, p. 48.

57. Ibid., pp. 48–49.

58. John Wesley, *The Bicentennial Edition of the Works of John Wesley* (Nashville, TN: Abingdon Press, 1984–), vol. 7, *Hymns*, pp. 712–13, no. 520, quoted in Russell E. Richey with Dennis M. Campbell and William B. Lawrence, *Marks of Methodism: Theology in Ecclesial Practice* (Nashville, TN: Abingdon Press, 2005), p. 17.

59. Richey, *Marks of Methodism*, pp. 17–19, 23–24.

60. Ibid., pp. 26–40. See also William Johnson Everett and Thomas Edward Frank, "Constitutional Order in United Methodism and American Culture," in

Connectionalism: Ecclesiology, Mission, and Identity, ed. Russell E. Richey, Dennis M. Campbell, and William B. Lawrence (Nashville, TN: Abingdon Press, 1997), pp. 41–73.

61. Richey, *Marks of Methodism*, pp. 91–112.

62. John Wesley, "Catholic Spirit," in *Works*, 2:90–92, quoted in Richey, *Marks of Methodism*, p. 92.

63. Cf. Richey, *Marks of Methodism*, pp. 110–12; and chaps. 3 and 4 of this volume.

64. Troeltsch, *Social Teaching*, 2:1009; Bellah et al., *Habits of the Heart*, p. 244.

Bibliography

Abbott, Walter M., ed. *The Documents of Vatican II*. New York: Guild Press, 1966.

Alesina, Alberto, and Edward L. Glaeser. *Fighting Poverty in the US and Europe: A World of Difference*. New York: Oxford University Press, 2004.

Allegretto, Sylvia, and Jared Bernstein. *The Wage Squeeze and Higher Health Care Costs*. Economic Policy Institute, Issue Brief no. 218, January 27, 2006.

Anderson, Perry. *Lineages of the Absolutist State*. London: Schocken, 1974.

Baker, Paula. *The Moral Frameworks of Public Life*. New York: Oxford University Press, 1991.

Bell, Daniel. *The Cultural Contradictions of Capitalism*. New York: Basic Books, 1976.

———. "The New Class: A Muddled Concept." In *The New Class?* edited by B. Bruce-Briggs, pp. 169–90. New York: McGraw-Hill, 1981.

Bellah, Robert N. Epilogue to Madsen et al., *Meaning and Modernity*, pp. 255–76.

———. "Religion and the Legitimation of the American Republic." In *Varieties of Civil Religion*, by Robert N. Bellah and Phillip E. Hammond, pp. 3–23. New York: Harper and Row, 1980.

———. "Religious Evolution." In *Beyond Belief*, pp. 20–50. Berkeley and Los Angeles: University of California Press, 1991.

———. "Civil Religion in America." In *Beyond Belief*, pp. 168–89.

Bellah, Robert N., Richard Madsen, William M. Sullivan, Ann Swidler, and Steven M. Tipton. *Habits of the Heart: Individualism and Commitment in American Life*. 1985. Berkeley and Los Angeles: University of California Press, 2007.

———. *The Good Society*. New York: Knopf, 1991.

———. "The House Divided." Introduction to the updated edition of *Habits of the Heart*, pp. vii–xxxv. Berkeley and Los Angeles: University of California Press, 1996.

Bellah, Robert N., and Steven M. Tipton, eds. *The Robert Bellah Reader*. Durham, NC: Duke University Press, 2006.

Benhabib, Seyla. "The Generalized and the Concrete Other." In *Situating the Self*, pp. 148–77.

———. "Models of Public Space." In Calhoun, *Habermas and the Public Sphere*, pp. 73–98.

Benhabib, Seyla. *Situating the Self: Gender, Community, and Postmodernism in Contemporary Ethics*. New York: Routledge, 1992.

Benne, Robert. *The Ethic of Democratic Capitalism*. Philadelphia: Fortress Press, 1981.

Berger, Peter L. "From the Crisis of Religion to the Crisis of Secularity." In *Religion and America: Spiritual Life in a Secular Age*, edited by Mary Douglas and Steven M. Tipton, pp. 14–24. Boston: Beacon Press, 1983.

———. *The Noise of Solemn Assemblies: Christian Commitment and the Religious Establishment in America*. Garden City, NY: Doubleday, 1961.

———. "The Worldview of the New Class: Secularity and Its Discontents." In *The New Class?* edited by B. Bruce-Briggs, pp. 49–55. New York: McGraw-Hill, 1981.

Berger, Peter L., and Richard John Neuhaus. *The Role of Mediating Structures in Public Policy*. Washington, DC: American Enterprise Institute, 1977.

Berton, Pierre. *The Comfortable Pew: A Critical Look at Christianity and the Religious Establishment in the New Age*. Philadelphia: Lippincott, 1965.

Boli, John. "Human Rights or State Expansion?" In Thomas et al., *Institutional Structure*, pp. 133–49.

Boushey, Heather, Chauna Brocht, Bethney Gundersen, and Jared Bernstein. *Hardships in America: The Real Story of Working Families*. Washington, DC: Economic Policy Institute, 2001.

Brint, Steven G. *In an Age of Experts: The Changing Role of Professionals in Politics and Public Life*. Princeton, NJ: Princeton University Press, 1994.

Brooks Higginbotham, Evelyn. *Righteous Discontent: The Women's Movement in the Black Baptist Church, 1880–1920*. Cambridge, MA: Harvard University Press, 1993.

Buchanan, Constance H. *Choosing to Lead: Women and the Crisis of American Values*. Boston: Beacon Press, 1996.

Burke, Courtney, James Fossett, and Thomas Gais. *Funding Faith-Based Services in a Time of Fiscal Pressures*. Albany, NY: Roundtable on Religion and Social Welfare Policy, Rockefeller Institute of Government, State University of New York, 2004.

Butler, Jon. *Awash in a Sea of Faith: Christianizing the American People*. Cambridge, MA: Harvard University Press, 1990.

Byrnes, Timothy A. *Catholic Bishops in American Politics*. Princeton, NJ: Princeton University Press, 1991.

Calhoun, Craig, ed. *Habermas and the Public Sphere*. Cambridge, MA: MIT Press, 1992.

Casanova, José. *Public Religions in the Modern World*. Chicago: University of Chicago Press, 1994.

Chaves, Mark. *Congregations in America*. Cambridge, MA: Harvard University Press, 2004.

———. "Religious Congregations and Welfare Reform: Who Will Take Advantage of 'Charitable Choice'?" *American Sociological Review* 64 (December 1999): 836–46.

———. "Secularization as Declining Religious Authority." *Social Forces* 72, no. 3 (March 1994): 749–75.

Chaves, Mark, Helen M. Giesel, and William Tsitsos. "Religious Variations in Public Presence: Evidence from the National Congregations Study." In Wuthnow and Evans, *The Quiet Hand of God*, pp. 108–28.

Chopp, Rebecca S. *The Power to Speak: Feminism, Language, God.* New York: Crossroad, 1989.

———. *The Praxis of Suffering: An Interpretation of Liberation and Political Theologies.* Maryknoll, NY: Orbis Books, 1986.

———. *Saving Work: Feminist Practices of Theological Education.* Louisville, KY: Westminster John Knox Press, 1995.

Cohen, Jean. "Discourse Ethics and Civil Society." *Philosophy and Social Criticism* 14, nos. 3–4 (1988): 315–37.

Cooper, Mary. "National IMPACT: A Summary." In *Advocates for Justice.* Washington, DC: Interfaith Action for Economic Justice, 1991, pp. 3–4.

Corn, David. "Beltway Bandits." *The Nation*, December 21, 1992, p. 764.

———. "Capitol Dunciad." *The Nation*, July 18, 1994, pp. 77–78.

Cox, Harvey. *The Secular City: Secularization and Urbanization in Theological Perspective.* New York: Macmillan, 1965.

Delbanco, Andrew. *The Real American Dream: A Meditation on Hope.* Cambridge, MA: Harvard University Press, 1999.

Demerath, N. J., and Rhys H. Williams. *A Bridging of Faiths: Religion and Politics in a New England City.* Princeton, NJ: Princeton University Press, 1992.

DiMaggio, Paul, John Evans, and Bethany Bryson. "Have Americans' Social Attitudes Become More Polarized?" *American Journal of Sociology* 102, no. 3 (November 1996): 690–755.

Dykstra, Craig. "Reconceiving Practice." In *Shifting Boundaries: Contextual Approaches to the Structure of Theological Education*, edited by Barbara G. Wheeler and Edward Farley, pp. 35–66. Louisville, KY: Westminster John Knox Press, 1991.

Edgar, Robert W. "The Fierce Urgency of Now." Office of the General Secretary, National Council of Churches, undated letter, March–April 2003.

———. *Middle Church: Reclaiming the Moral Values of the Faithful Majority from the Religious Right.* New York: Simon and Schuster, 2006.

———. "A Vision of Peace in a Time of War: The Need for a Peace-Centered Foreign Policy." Paper prepared in conjunction with an address delivered at the University of San Diego, April 2003.

Eley, Geoff. "Nations, Publics, and Political Culture." In Calhoun, *Habermas and the Public Sphere*, pp. 289–339.

Everett, William J., and Thomas E. Frank. "Constitutional Order in United Methodism and American Culture." In Richey, Campbell, and Lawrence, *Connectionalism*, pp. 41–73.

Farnsley, Arthur E. *Southern Baptist Politics: Authority and Power in the Restructuring of an American Denomination.* University Park: Pennsylvania State University Press, 1994.

Farris, Anne, Richard P. Nathan, and David J. Wright. *The Expanding Adminis-trative Presidency: George W. Bush and the Faith-Based Initiative.* Albany, NY: Roundtable on Religion and Social Welfare Policy, Rockefeller Institute of Government, State University of New York, 2004.

Fowler, Robert Booth, and Allen D. Hertzke. *Religion and Politics in America: Faith, Culture, and Strategic Choices.* Boulder, CO: Westview Press, 1995.

Frank, Thomas Edward. *Polity, Practice, and the Mission of the United Methodist Church.* Nashville, TN: Abingdon Press, 1997.

Fraser, Nancy. "Rethinking the Public Sphere: A Contribution to the Critique of Actually Existing Democracy." In Calhoun, *Habermas and the Public Sphere,* pp. 109–42.

———. *Unruly Practices: Power, Discourse, and Gender in Contemporary Social Theory.* Minneapolis: University of Minnesota Press, 1989.

Freeman, Richard B. *The New Inequality: Creating Solutions for Poor America.* Edited by Joshua Cohen and Joel Rogers for *Boston Review.* Boston: Beacon Press, 1999.

Freire, Paulo. *Pedagogy of the Oppressed.* New York: Herder and Herder, 1970.

Gans, Herbert J. *Middle American Individualism: The Future of Liberal Democracy.* New York: Free Press, 1988.

General Board of Church and Society, United Methodist Church. *Statement on Faith-Based and Community Initiatives.* Washington, DC, 2001.

General Board of Church and Society, General Board of Global Ministries, and General Council on Finance and Administration, United Methodist Church. *Community Ministries and Government Funding.* Washington, DC, 2001.

Glendon, Mary Ann. *Rights Talk.* New York: Free Press, 1991.

Green, John C. *The Fifty Percent Solution: The 2000 Election and the New Religious Order.* Akron, OH: Bliss Institute of Applied Politics, University of Akron, 2001.

Green, John C., and James L. Guth. "United Methodists and American Culture: A Statistical Portrait." In *The People(s) Called Methodist: Forms and Reforms of Their Life,* edited by William B. Lawrence, Dennis M. Campbell, and Russell E. Richey, pp. 27–53. Nashville, TN: Abingdon Press, 1998.

Green, John C., Corwin E. Smidt, James L. Guth, and Lyman A. Kellstedt. *The American Religious Landscape and the 2004 Presidential Vote: Increased Polar-ization.* Washington, DC: Pew Forum on Religion and Public Life, 2005.

Gunnemann, Jon P. "Capital Ideas." In *Religion and Values in Public Life: Anthol-ogy/2000,* pp. 97–109. Cambridge, MA: Center for the Study of Values in Public Life, Harvard Divinity School, 2000.

Guth, James L., John C. Green, Corwin E. Smidt, Lyman A. Kellstedt, and Mar-garet M. Poloma. *The Bully Pulpit: The Politics of Protestant Clergy.* Lawrence: University Press of Kansas, 1997.

Habermas, Jürgen. *Religion and Rationality: Essays on Reason, God, and Modernity.* Edited by Eduardo Mendieta. Cambridge, MA: MIT Press, 2002.

———. *The Structural Transformation of the Public Sphere: An Inquiry into a Category of Bourgeois Society.* Cambridge, MA: MIT Press, 1989.

Hacker, Jacob S. *The Divided Welfare State: The Battle over Public and Private So-cial Benefits in the United States*. New York: Cambridge University Press, 2002.

Hammond, Phillip E. *With Liberty for All: Freedom of Religion in the United States*. Louisville, KY: Westminster John Knox Press, 1998.

Handy, Robert T. *Undermined Establishment: Church-State Relations in America, 1880–1920*. Princeton, NJ: Princeton University Press, 1991.

Hartmann, Heidi. "Through a Gendered Lens." In Freeman, *The New Inequality*, pp. 33–38.

Hauerwas, Stanley. "The Church and Liberal Democracy: The Moral Limits of a Secular Polity." In *A Community of Character*, pp. 72–86.

———. *A Community of Character: Toward a Constructive Christian Social Ethic*. Notre Dame, IN: University of Notre Dame Press, 1981.

———. "On Being a Christian and an American." In Madsen et al., *Meaning and Modernity*, pp. 224–36, 303–6.

———. "The Politics of Justice: Why Justice Is a Bad Idea for Christians." In *After Christendom? How the Church Is to Behave If Freedom, Justice, and a Christian Nation Are Bad Ideas*, pp. 45–68. Nashville, TN: Abingdon Press, 1991.

Heitzenrater, Richard P. *Wesley and the People Called Methodists*. Nashville, TN: Abingdon Press, 1995.

Hertzke, Allen D. *Representing God in Washington: The Role of Religious Lobbies in the American Polity*. Knoxville: University of Tennessee Press, 1988.

Hill, Kent R. *The Soviet Union on the Brink: An Inside Look at Christianity and Glasnost*. Portland, OR: Multnomah Press, 1991.

Hochschild, Jennifer. *What's Fair? American Beliefs about Distributive Justice*. Cambridge, MA: Harvard University Press, 1981.

Hochstein, Eric, with Ronald O'Rourke. *A Report on the Institute on Religion and Democracy*. 1981. Reprinted as "An American Dream: Neo-conservatism and the New Religious Right in the USA." *IDOC International Bulletin*, nos. 8–9 (1982): 17–32.

Hoge, Dean R., Michael J. Donahue, and Charles E. Zech. *Money Matters: Personal Giving in American Churches*. Louisville, KY: Westminster John Knox Press, 1996.

Hoge, Dean R., Benton Johnson, and Donald A. Luidens. *Vanishing Boundaries: The Religion of Mainline Protestant Baby Boomers*. Louisville, KY: Westminster John Knox Press, 1994.

Hoge, Dean R., and David A. Roozen. *Understanding Church Growth and De-cline: 1950–1978*. New York: Pilgrim Press, 1979.

Hollenbach, David. "Justice as Participation: Public Moral Discourse and the U.S. Economy." In *Justice, Peace, and Human Rights: American Catholic Social Eth-ics in a Pluralistic World*, pp. 71–84. New York: Crossroad, 1988.

———. "Religious Freedom and Economic Rights." In *Justice, Peace, and Human Rights: American Catholic Social Ethics in a Pluralistic World*, pp. 101–7. New York: Crossroad, 1988.

Hout, Michael, Andrew Greeley, and Melissa J. Wilde. "The Demographic Imper-ative in Religious Change in the United States." *American Journal of Sociology* 107, no. 2 (2001): 468–500.

Howard, Christopher. *The Hidden Welfare State: Tax Expenditures and Social Policy in the United States.* Princeton, NJ: Princeton University Press, 1997.

———. *The Welfare State Nobody Knows: Debunking Myths about U.S. Social Policy.* Princeton, NJ: Princeton University Press, 2006.

Howell, Leon. *Funding the War of Ideas.* Cleveland, OH: United Church Board for Homeland Ministries, 1995.

———. "Old Wine, New Bottles: The Institute on Religion and Democracy." *Christianity and Crisis*, March 21, 1983, pp. 79, 89–94.

———. *United Methodism @ Risk: A Wake-Up Call.* Kingston, NY: Information Project for United Methodists, 2003.

Huber, Joan, and William Form. *Income and Ideology: An Analysis of the American Political Formula.* New York: Free Press, 1977.

Hunter, James Davison. *Culture Wars: The Struggle to Define America.* New York: Basic Books, 1991.

Jefferson, Thomas. "A Bill for Establishing Religious Freedom." In *The Papers of Thomas Jefferson*, edited by Julian P. Boyd, 2:545–47. Princeton, NJ: Princeton University Press, 1950.

Jepperson, Ronald L., and David Kamens. "The Expanding State and the U.S. 'Civic Culture': The Changing Character of Political Participation and Legitimation in the Post-war U.S. Polity." Paper presented at the annual meeting of the American Political Science Association, New Orleans, 1985.

Jepperson, Ronald L., and John W. Meyer. "The Public Order and the Construction of Formal Organizations." In *The New Institutionalism in Organizational Analysis*, edited by Walter W. Powell and Paul J. DiMaggio, pp. 204–31. Chicago: University of Chicago Press, 1991.

Jessup, David. *Preliminary Inquiry regarding Financial Contributions to Outside Political Groups by Boards and Agencies of the United Methodist Church, 1977–79.* Photocopied document, Washington, DC, April 7, 1980.

Kagan, Robert, and William Kristol. *Present Dangers: Crisis and Opportunity in America's Foreign and Defense Policy.* New York: Encounter Books, 2000.

Karoly, Lynn A., and Constantin W. A. Panis. *The 21st Century at Work: Forces Shaping the Future Workforce and Workplace in the United States.* Santa Barbara, CA: RAND Corporation, 2004.

Kennickell, Arthur B. *An Examination of Changes in the Distribution of Wealth from 1989 to 1998: Evidence from the Survey of Consumer Finances.* Federal Reserve Board, Survey of Consumer Finances, 2000.

Kennickell, Arthur B., Martha Starr-McCluer, and Brian J. Surette. "Recent Changes in U.S. Family Finances." *Federal Reserve Bulletin*, January 2000, pp. 1–29.

Keys, Arthur Boyd. "Ecumenical Advocacy: What Future?" *Christianity and Crisis*, August 14, 1989, pp. 339–42.

Keysor, Charles W. "Methodism's Silent Minority." *New Christian Advocate*, July 14, 1966, pp. 9–10.

———. *Our Methodist Heritage.* Elgin, IL: D. C. Cook, 1973.

———. "The Story of Good News." *Good News*, March–April 1981, pp. 8–19, 22–25, 50.

Kochhar, Rakesh. *The Wealth of Hispanic Households: 1996 to 2002*. Washington, DC: Pew Hispanic Center, 2004.

Kopczuk, Wojciech, Emmanuel Saez, and Jae Song. *Uncovering the American Dream: Inequality and Mobility in Social Security Earnings Data since 1937*. National Bureau of Economic Research, March 2007. http://elsa.berkeley.edu/~saez/.

Kristol, Irving. *On the Democratic Idea in America*. New York: Harper and Row, 1972.

Kull, Steven, Clay Ramsay, Stefan Subias, Stephen Weber, and Evan Lewis. *The Separate Realities of Bush and Kerry Supporters*. PIPA/Knowledge Networks poll (Program on International Policy Attitudes, University of Maryland), October 21, 2004.

Kurtz, Lester R. *The Nuclear Cage: A Sociology of the Arms Race*. Englewood Cliffs, NJ: Prentice-Hall, 1988.

Lane, Robert E. "Fear of Equality." In *Political Ideology: Why the American Common Man Believes What He Does*, pp. 57–81. New York: Free Press, 1962.

Langford, Andy, and William H. Willimon. *A New Connection: Reforming the United Methodist Church*. Nashville, TN: Abingdon Press, 1995.

Lasch, Christopher. "The Communitarian Critique of Liberalism." *Soundings* 69, nos. 1–2 (1986): 60–76.

Levy, Frank. *The New Dollars and Dreams: American Incomes and Economic Change*. New York: Russell Sage Foundation, 1998.

Light, Paul. *The True Size of Government*. Washington, DC: Brookings Institution, 1999.

Long, Charles H. "Civil Rights—Civil Religion." In *American Civil Religion*, edited by Russell E. Richey and Donald G. Jones, pp. 211–21. New York: Harper and Row, 1974.

Madison, James. "Memorial and Remonstrance." 1785. In *The Papers of James Madison*, vol. 8, edited by William T. Hutchinson and William M. E. Rachal, pp. 298–304. Chicago: University of Chicago Press, 1971.

Madsen, Richard, William M. Sullivan, Ann Swidler, and Steven M. Tipton, eds. *Meaning and Modernity: Religion, Polity, and Self*. Berkeley and Los Angeles: University of California Press, 2002.

Mann, Roberta F. "The (Not So) Little House on the Prairie: The Hidden Costs of the Home Mortgage Interest Deduction." *Arizona State Law Journal* 32 (2000): 1347–97.

Marsden, George. *Fundamentalism and American Culture: The Shaping of Twentieth Century Evangelicalism, 1870–1925*. New York: Oxford University Press, 1980.

Marty, Martin E. *Modern American Religion*, vol. 1. Chicago: University of Chicago Press, 1986.

———. "On a Medial Moraine: Religious Dimensions of American Constitutionalism." *Emory Law Journal* 39 (1990): 9–20.

———. *The One and the Many*. Cambridge, MA: Harvard University Press, 1997.

———. *The Public Church: Mainline, Evangelical, Catholic*. New York: Crossroad, 1981.

McLaughlin, Martin. *Advocates for Justice*. Washington, DC: Interfaith Action for Economic Justice, 1991.

Mead, Sidney E. "The Nation with the Soul of a Church." In *American Civil Religion*, edited by Russell E. Richey and Donald G. Jones, pp. 45–74. New York: Harper and Row, 1974.

Meeks, Douglas C. *God the Economist*. Philadelphia: Fortress Press, 1989.

Metz, Johannes Baptist. "Im Aufbruch zu einer kulturell polyzentrischen Weltkirche." In *Zukunftsfahigkeit*, edited by F. X. Kaufmann and J. B. Metz, pp. 93–115. Freiburg: Herder, 1987.

Meyer, John W. "Self and Life Course: Institutionalization and Its Effects." In Thomas et al., *Institutional Structure*, pp. 242–60.

Meyer, John W., John Boli, and George M. Thomas. "Ontology and Rationalization in the Western Cultural Account." In Thomas et al., *Institutional Structure*, pp. 12–37.

Minnick, Charles P., and Thomas Edward Frank. *Vital Congregations, Faithful Disciples: Vision for the Church*. Foundation document, Council of Bishops of the United Methodist Church. Nashville, TN: Graded Press, 1990.

Mishel, Lawrence, Jared Bernstein, and Sylvia Allegretto. *The State of Working America 2004/2005*. Ithaca, NY: Cornell University Press, 2005.

———. *The State of Working America 2006/2007*. Ithaca, NY: Cornell University Press, 2007.

Moen, Matthew C. *The Christian Right and Congress*. Tuscaloosa: University of Alabama Press, 1989.

———. *The Transformation of the Christian Right*. Tuscaloosa: University of Alabama Press, 1992.

Myrdal, Gunnar. *An American Dilemma*. New York: Harper and Brothers, 1944.

National Conference of Catholic Bishops. *The Challenge of Peace: God's Promise and Our Response: A Pastoral Letter on War and Peace, May 3, 1983*. Washington, DC: U.S. Catholic Conference, 1983.

———. *Economic Justice for All: Pastoral Letter on Catholic Social Teaching and the U.S. Economy*. Washington, DC: U.S. Catholic Conference, 1986.

Neuhaus, Richard J. *America against Itself: Moral Vision and the Public Order*. Notre Dame, IN: University of Notre Dame Press, 1992.

———. *The Catholic Moment: The Paradox of the Church in the Postmodern World*. San Francisco: Harper and Row, 1987.

———. *Christianity and Democracy: A Statement of the Institute on Religion and Democracy*. Washington, DC: IRD, 1991. First published 1981.

———. *The Naked Public Square: Religion and Democracy in America*. Grand Rapids, MI: Eerdmans, 1984.

Niebuhr, H. Richard. *Christ and Culture*. New York: Harper and Row, 1951.

———. *The Kingdom of God in America*. 1937. Middletown, CT: Wesleyan University Press, 1988.

———. *The Social Sources of Denominationalism*. New York: Henry Holt, 1929.

Noonan, John. *The Lustre of Our Country: The American Experience of Religious Freedom*. Berkeley and Los Angeles: University of California Press, 1998.

Novak, David. *Jewish Social Ethics*. New York: Oxford University Press, 1992.

Novak, Michael. *The Catholic Ethic and the Spirit of Capitalism*. New York: Free Press, 1993.

———. *Choosing Our King: Powerful Symbols in Presidential Politics*. London: Macmillan, 1974.

———. *Free Persons and the Common Good*. Lanham, MD: Madison Books, 1989.

———. *The Spirit of Democratic Capitalism*. New York: Simon and Schuster, 1982.

———. *Toward the Future: Catholic Social Thought and the U.S. Economy*. New York: Lay Commission on Catholic Social Teaching and the U.S. Economy, 1984.

Owens, Michael Leo. "Which Churches Will Take Advantage of Charitable Choice? Explaining the Pursuit of Public Funding by Congregations." Unpublished paper, Department of Political Science, Emory University, 2004.

Palmer, Parker J. *The Company of Strangers*. New York: Crossroad, 1981.

Parsons, Talcott. "Christianity and Modern Industrial Society." In *Religion, Culture, and Society: A Reader in the Sociology of Religion*, edited by Louis Schneider, pp. 273–98. Reprinted from *Sociological Theory, Values, and Sociocultural Change*, edited by Edward Tiryakian. New York: Free Press, 1963.

Perry, Michael J. *Morality, Politics, and Law: A Bicentennial Essay*. New York: Oxford University Press, 1988.

Pew Research Center for the People and the Press. *Evenly Divided and Increasingly Polarized: 2004 Political Landscape*. Washington, DC: Pew Research Center, 2003.

Phillips, Kevin. *Boiling Point: Republicans, Democrats, and the Decline of Middle-Class Prosperity*. New York: Random House, 1993.

Piketty, Thomas, and Emmanuel Saez. "How Progressive Is the U.S. Federal Tax System? A Historical and International Perspective." *Journal of Economic Perspectives* 21, no. 1 (Winter 2007): 3–24.

———. "Income Inequality in the United States, 1913–1998." *Quarterly Journal of Economics* 118, no. 1 (February 2003): 1–39.

Presbyterian Church (USA). *Book of Order*. Louisville, KY: Westminster John Knox Press, 2004.

Putnam, Robert. *Bowling Alone: The Collapse and Revival of American Community*. New York: Simon and Schuster, 2000.

Ratzinger, Cardinal Joseph. "Homily at the Mass for the Election of the Roman Pontiff." Vatican City, April 18, 2005. http://www.insidethevatican.com/newsflash-apr18-05.htm.

Rawls, John. "The Idea of an Overlapping Consensus." *Oxford Journal of Legal Studies* 7, no. 1 (1987): 1–25.

———. "Justice as Fairness: Political Not Metaphysical." *Philosophy and Public Affairs* 14, no. 3 (Summer 1985): 223–51.

———. "Kantian Constructivism in Moral Theory." *Journal of Philosophy* 77 (1980): 515–72.

Rawls, John. *Political Liberalism*. New York: Columbia University Press, 1993.

————. *A Theory of Justice*. Cambridge, MA: Harvard University Press, 1971.

Ray, Gerda. "Legitimating the Right: The Neoconservatives Build a Base." *Crime and Social Justice* 19 (Summer 1983): 75–86.

Reich, Robert B. *The Work of Nations: Preparing Ourselves for 21st-Century Capitalism*. New York: Knopf, 1991.

Reinhardt, Uwe E. "The Swiss Health System: Regulated Competition without Managed Care." *Journal of the American Medical Association* 292, no. 10 (September 8, 2004): 1227–31.

Reinhardt, Uwe E., Peter S. Hussey, and Gerard F. Anderson. "U.S. Health Care Spending in an International Context." *Health Affairs* 23, no. 3 (2004): 10–25.

Religious Leaders for Sensible Priorities. "President Bush: Jesus Changed Your Heart. Now Let Him Change Your Mind." *New York Times*, December 4, 2002, p. A33.

Richey, Russell E. "Are the Local Church and Denominational Bureaucracy 'Twins'?" In Richey, Lawrence, and Campbell, *Questions for the Twenty-first Century Church*, 232–41, 338.

————. "Connectionalism: End or New Beginning?" In Richey, Lawrence, and Campbell, *Questions for the Twenty-first Century Church*, 313–19, 342–43.

————. "Do General Agencies Still Have a Place in the Church?" *Quarterly Review* 24, no. 4 (Winter 2004): 411–16.

————. "Is Division a New Threat to the Denomination?" In Richey, Lawrence, and Campbell, *Questions for the Twenty-first Century Church*, pp. 105–16, 329–31.

Richey, Russell E., with Dennis M. Campbell and William B. Lawrence. *Marks of Methodism: Theology in Ecclesial Practice*. Nashville, TN: Abingdon Press, 2005.

Richey, Russell E., Dennis M. Campbell, and William B. Lawrence, eds. *Connectionalism: Ecclesiology, Mission, and Identity*. Nashville, TN: Abingdon Press, 1997.

Richey, Russell E., and Thomas Edward Frank. *Episcopacy in the Methodist Tradition: Perspectives and Proposals*. Nashville, TN: Abingdon Press, 2004.

Richey, Russell E., William B. Lawrence, and Dennis M. Campbell, eds. *Questions for the Twenty-first Century Church*. Nashville, TN: Abingdon Press, 1999.

Robb, Edmund W. Jr. *Contending for the Faith: The Ed Robb Story*. Anderson, IN: Bristol Books, 2002.

Ronsvalle, John L., and Sylvia Ronsvalle. *The State of Church Giving, 2000*. Champaign, IL: Empty Tomb, 2002.

Roof, Wade Clark. *A Generation of Seekers: The Spiritual Journey of the Baby Boom Generation*. San Francisco: HarperCollins, 1993.

————. *Spiritual Marketplace: Baby Boomers and the Remaking of American Religion*. Princeton, NJ: Princeton University Press, 1999.

Roof, Wade Clark, Jackson W. Carroll, and David A. Roozen. *The Post-war Generation and Establishment Religion*. Boulder, CO: Westview Press, 1995.

Roof, Wade Clark, and William McKinney. *American Mainline Religion: Its Changing Shape and Future*. New Brunswick, NJ: Rutgers University Press, 1987.

Rorty, Richard. *Achieving Our Country: Leftist Thought in Twentieth-Century America*. Cambridge, MA: Harvard University Press, 1999.

———. "The Priority of Democracy over Philosophy." In *The Virginia Statute for Religious Freedom: Its Evolution and Consequences in American History*, edited by Merrill D. Peterson and Robert C. Vaughan, pp. 257–82. Cambridge: Cambridge University Press, 1988.

———. "Religion as Conversation Stopper." *Common Knowledge* 3 (Spring 1994): 1–6.

Sample, Tex. *U.S. Lifestyles and Mainline Churches: A Key to Reaching People in the 90s*. Louisville, KY: Westminster John Knox Press, 1990.

Sandel, Michael J. *Democracy's Discontent: America in Search of a Public Philosophy*. Cambridge, MA: Harvard University Press, 1996.

———. *Liberalism and the Limits of Justice*. New York: Cambridge University Press, 1982.

Seabury, Paul. "Trendier than Thou." *Harper's Magazine*, October 1978, pp. 1–7.

Seligman, Adam. *The Idea of Civil Society*. New York: Free Press, 1992.

Shklar, Judith. *American Citizenship: The Quest for Inclusion*. Cambridge, MA: Harvard University Press, 1991.

Simon, Arthur R. *Bread for the World*. New York: Paulist Press, 1975.

Skocpol, Theda. "Advocates without Members: The Recent Transformation of Civic Life." In *Civic Engagement in American Democracy*, edited by Theda Skocpol and Morris P. Fiorina, 461–510. Washington, DC: Brookings Institution Press; New York: Russell Sage Foundation, 1999.

———. *Clinton's Health Security Plan*. New York: W. W. Norton, 1996.

———. *Protecting Soldiers and Mothers: The Political Origins of Social Policy in the United States*. Cambridge, MA: Harvard University Press, 1992.

Smith, Greg, Scott Keeter, and John Green. "Religion and the 2006 Elections." Pew Forum on Religion and Public Life, 2006. http://www.pewforum.org.

Smith, Christian. *American Evangelicalism: Embattled and Thriving*. Chicago: University of Chicago Press, 1998.

———. *Resisting Reagan: The U.S. Central America Peace Movement*. Chicago: University of Chicago Press, 1996.

Smith, Timothy L. *Revivalism and Social Reform in Mid-Nineteenth-Century America*. Nashville, TN: Abingdon Press, 1957.

Steinfels, Peter. " 'Christianity and Democracy': Baptizing Reaganism." *Christianity and Crisis*, March 29, 1983, pp. 80–85.

———. *The Neoconservatives*. New York: Simon and Schuster, 1980.

Stout, Jeffrey. *Ethics after Babel: The Languages of Morals and Their Discontents*. Boston: Beacon Press, 1988.

———. "Liberal Society and the Languages of Morals." *Soundings* 69, nos. 1–2 (1986): 32–59.

Taylor, Charles. "Modes of Civil Society." *Public Culture* 3, no. 1 (Fall 1990): 95–118.

———. "The Politics of Recognition." In *Multiculturalism and "The Politics of Recognition,"* edited by Amy Gutmann, pp. 25–73. Princeton, NJ: Princeton University Press, 1992.

———. "Religion in a Free Society." In *Articles of Faith, Articles of Peace,* edited by James Davison Hunter and Os Guinness, pp. 93–113. Washington, DC: Brookings Institution, 1990.

Thiemann, Ronald. *Constructing a Public Theology: The Church in a Pluralistic Culture.* Louisville, KY: Westminster John Knox Press, 1991.

Thomas, George M., John W. Meyer, Francisco O. Ramirez, and John Boli. *Institutional Structure: Constituting State, Society, and the Individual.* Newbury Park, CA: Sage Publications, 1987.

Tipton, Steven M. "Moral Languages and the Good Society." *Soundings* 69, nos. 1–2 (1986): 165–80.

———. "Republic and Liberal State: The Place of Religion in an Ambiguous Polity." *Emory Law Journal* 39, no. 1 (Winter 1990): 191–202.

———. "Social Differentiation and Moral Pluralism." In Madsen et al., *Meaning and Modernity,* pp. 15–40.

Tocqueville, Alexis de. *Democracy in America.* 1848. Translated by George Lawrence. Edited by J. P. Mayer. Garden City, NY: Doubleday Anchor, 1969.

Troeltsch, Ernst. *The Social Teaching of the Christian Churches.* 1911. New York: Harper and Row, 1960.

Tyler, Gus. "Comrades in Arms." Review of *If I Had a Hammer: The Death of the Old Left and the Birth of the New Left,* by Maurice Isserman. *New York Times Book Review,* September 14, 1987, p. 31.

United Methodist Church. *The Book of Discipline of the United Methodist Church.* Nashville, TN: United Methodist Publishing House, various years.

Verba, Sidney, Kay Lehman Schlozman, and Henry E. Brady. *Voice and Equality: Civic Voluntarism in American Politics.* Cambridge, MA: Harvard University Press, 1995.

Vorspan, Albert, and David Saperstein. *Tough Choices: Jewish Perspectives on Social Justice.* New York: Union of American Hebrew Congregations, 1992.

Waldron, Tom, Brandon Roberts, and Andrew Reamer. *Working Hard, Falling Short: America's Working Families and the Pursuit of Economic Security.* A report of the Working Families Project, supported by the Annie E. Casey, Ford, and Rockefeller foundations, October 2004. http://www.aecf.org.

Wallis, Jim. "Hearts and Minds: No Ways Tired." *Sojourners Magazine* 25, no. 6 (November–December 1996): 7–8.

———. "Will Aid Make Churches Docile?" *New York Times,* February 3, 2001, p. A25.

Walzer, Michael. "Dissatisfaction in the Welfare State." In *Radical Principles: Reflections of an Unreconstructed Democrat,* pp. 23–53. New York: Basic Books, 1980.

———. "The Idea of Civil Society." *Dissent,* Spring 1991, pp. 293–304.

————. "Socializing the Welfare State." In *Democracy and the Welfare State*, edited by Amy Gutmann, pp. 13–26. Princeton, NJ: Princeton University Press, 1988.

————. *Spheres of Justice: A Defense of Pluralism and Equality*. New York: Basic Books, 1984.

Warner, Mildred, Rosaria Rubeiro, and Amy Erica Smith. "Addressing the Affordability Gap: Framing Child Care as Economic Development." *Journal of Affordable Housing and Community Development Law* 12, no. 3 (Spring 2003): 294–313.

Weintraub, Jeff. "The Theory and Politics of the Public/Private Distinction." In *Public and Private in Thought and Practice*, edited by Jeff Weintraub and Krishan Kumar, pp. 1–42. Chicago: University of Chicago Press, 1997.

Wilson, William Julius. *The Bridge over the Racial Divide: Rising Inequality and Coalition Politics*. Berkeley and Los Angeles: University of California Press, 1999.

Witte, John Jr., ed. *Christianity and Democracy in Global Context*. Boulder, CO: Westview Press, 1993.

Wolfe, Alan. *The Transformation of American Religion: How We Actually Live Our Faith*. New York: Free Press, 2003.

Wolff, Edward N. *Top Heavy: A Study of the Increasing Inequality of Wealth in America*. New York: New Press, 1996.

Wood, Richard L. *Faith in Action: Religion, Race, and Democratic Organizing in America*. Chicago: University of Chicago Press, 2002.

Wuthnow, Robert. *Acts of Compassion: Caring for Others and Helping Ourselves*. Princeton, NJ: Princeton University Press, 1991.

————. *After Heaven: Spirituality in America since the 1950s*. Berkeley and Los Angeles: University of California Press, 1998.

————. "Beyond Quiet Influence? Possibilities for the Protestant Mainline." In Wuthnow and Evans, *The Quiet Hand of God*, pp. 381–403.

————. *The Crisis in the Churches: Spiritual Malaise, Fiscal Woe*. New York: Oxford University Press, 1997.

————. *Learning to Care: Elementary Kindness in an Age of Indifference*. New York: Oxford University Press, 1995.

————. *Loose Connections: Joining Together in America's Fragmented Communities*. Cambridge, MA: Harvard University Press, 1998.

————. "Mobilizing Civic Engagement: The Changing Impact of Religious Involvement." In *Civic Engagement in American Democracy*, edited by Theda Skocpol and Morris P. Fiorina, pp. 331–66. Washington, DC: Brookings Institution Press; New York: Russell Sage Foundation, 1999.

————. *The Restructuring of American Religion: Society and Faith since World War II*. Princeton, NJ: Princeton University Press, 1988.

Wuthnow, Robert, and John H. Evans, eds. *The Quiet Hand of God: Faith-Based Activism and the Public Role of Mainline Protestantism*. Berkeley and Los Angeles: University of California Press, 2002.

Index

abortion, vii–ix, 110, 133, 530n48; and
United Methodist Church, 119–20,
473n55
Abrams, Elliott, 187, 488n51
Affirmation, 123, 204. *See also* United
Methodist Church: and homosexuality
Afghanistan, 13
AFL-CIO, 190, 493n81; Committee on
Political Education (COPE) of, 64,
146–47, 171, 178; and communism, 174,
181–83; and Institute on Religion and
Democracy, xi, 177–79; and Protestant
mainline churches, 180, 183. *See also*
Kirkland, Lane
African Americans, 42, 53–54; socio-
economic status of, 463nn72–73. *See also*
African Methodist Episcopal Church
(AME); black churches
African Methodist Episcopal Church (AME),
323–24
African National Congress, 152–53
Ahmanson, Howard Fieldstead, 210
American Creed, 166–67
American Enterprise Institute, 64, 158, 171,
221. *See also* neoconservatism
American Institute for Free Labor Develop-
ment, 178, 182
Americans for Reform. *See* campaign
finance reform
Americans United for Separation of Church
and State, 23, 373. *See also* church-state
separation; faith-based initiatives
Amerson, Philip, 128–29
Anabaptists, 241. *See also* Friends Committee
on National Legislation (FCNL);
Quakers

antipoverty campaigns, 380, 382, 393
Anti-Saloon League, 85
Association for Church Renewal, 203, 206–7

Balanced Budget Act of 1997, 58
Bauer, Gary, 21
Bell, Daniel, 529n35
Bell, James, 303–7
Bellah, Robert, 40–41, 454–58, 468n16,
468n18, 527n9, 528n11
Berger, Peter, 430, 433; and Institute on
Religion and Democracy, 155–58
Berlin Wall, fall of, 188
Billings, Rev. Peggy, 152
black churches: and civil rights movement,
167; and faith-based initiatives, 446n35,
447n38; and National Council of
Churches, 355; and Republican Party, 21
Blake, Bruce (Bishop), 135
Bobo, Kim, 314
Boli, John, 468n109
Book of Discipline, United Methodist
Church, 78, 81, 83, 93, 119, 121, 136, 214,
440–41
Bread for the World, 44, 273, 278, 287
Brouwer, Arie, 175
Browning, Edmond L. (Bishop), 362
budget, U.S. federal, 293, 394, 453nn65–66
Bush, George H. W., 195
Bush, George W.: compassionate conserva-
tism of, ix, 16–18, 23, 27–31, 195; elec-
tion and administration of, vii–viii, x, 59;
and faith-based initiatives, 383, 448n43;
and federal budget, 393; and Iraq War,
4–11, 395, 444n18; and Middle East
peace, 386; National Security Strategy